SPORTS
THE COMPLETE VISUAL REFERENCE

SPORTS
THE COMPLETE VISUAL REFERENCE

François Fortin

FIREFLY BOOKS

A FIREFLY BOOK

Published by Firefly Books Ltd. 2000

First Printing

U.S. Cataloging-in-Publication Data
Fortin, François
Sports : the complete visual reference. –1st ed.
[384]p. : col. ill. ; cm.
Includes index.
Summary : illustrated guide to the history, rules and strategies of more than 125 sports.
ISBN 1-55209-540-1
1. Sports – Miscellanea. 2. Sports – Rules. I. Title.
796   21   2000   CIP

Canadian Cataloguing in Publication Data

Sports : the complete visual reference
Includes index.

ISBN 1-55209-540-1
1. Sports.   I. Fortin, François.

GV704.S663 2000   796   C00-930875-X

Published in Canada in 2000 by
Firefly Books Ltd.
3680 Victoria Park Avenue
Willowdale, Ontario   M2H 3K1

Published in the United States in 2000 by
Firefly Books (U.S.) Inc.
P.O. Box 1338, Ellicott Station
Buffalo, New York 14205

Firefly Associate Publisher: Michael Worek
Cover design: Jacqueline Hope Raynor

Printed and bound in Canada by Friesens, Altona, Manitoba

The Publisher acknowledges the financial support of the Government of Canada through the Book Publishing Industry Development Program for its publishing activities.

Sports: The Complete Visual Reference was created and produced by:

QA International
329, rue de la Commune Ouest, 3e étage
Montréal (Québec) H2Y 2E1 Canada
T 514.499.3000 **F** 514.499.3010
www.qa-international.com

Publisher	Jacques Fortin
General editor	François Fortin
Editor-in-chief	Karine Delobel
Writers	Denis Fourny, Benoit Fradette, Jean Gounelle, Francis Magnenot, Anne-Marie Villeneuve, Jessie Daigle, Jean-François Lacoste
Art director	Jean-Yves Ahern
Assistant art director	Claude Thivierge
Computer-graphics supervisors	Jocelyn Gardner, Rielle Lévesque, Michel Rouleau
Illustrators	Yan Bohler, Mélanie Boivin, Charles Campeau, Mivil Deschênes, Martin Desrosiers, Jonathan Jacques, Danièle Lemay, Alain Lemire, Martin Lortie, Raymond Martin, Annie Maurice, Nicolas Oroc, Frédérick Simard, Yan Tremblay, Mathieu Blouin, Sébastien Dallaire, Hoang Khanh Le, Anne-Marie Ouellette, Pierre Savoie, Mamadou Togola
Graphic designer	Anne Tremblay
Layout	Véronique Boisvert, Pascal Goyette, Lucie Mc Brearty, Josée Noiseux, Yan Bohler, Mario Bergeron
Researchers	Jessie Daigle, Nancy Lepage, Sophie Pellerin, Sylvain Robichaud, François Vézina, Gilles Vézina, Kathleen Wynd, Daniel Provost, Isabelle Lafrance
Photograph retouching	Hélène Coulombe
Translators	Argos interprètes et traducteurs inc. Käthe Roth
Proofreaders	Veronica Schami, Denis Fourny
Computer programmer	Daniel Beaulieu
Production coordinator	Guylaine Houle
Preprint technician	Tony O'Riley
Consultants	Paul Ohl, Guy Thibault

editor's note

Sport plays an ever-growing role in our daily lives. Sports and games are found in a wide variety of forms and on every continent. Major international and national sports events are broadcast to ever-increasing audiences the world over.

Although there is a large amount of information available on individual sports, it tends to be scattered. It is often easier to find material on the most popular sport in one's hometown than on events such as world cups or seasonal championships.

Sports: The Complete Visual Reference brings together more than 120 sports, described and explained in concise, clear texts with an abundance of spectacular illustrations. It is an essential and comprehensive guide to the sports world in the context of international competitions. To give readers a real understanding of what athletes do and how each sport works, the designers of this unique book have provided up-to-date and complete facts, drawing on the knowledge of recognized experts in their fields: federation directors, elite athletic trainers, and the athletes themselves.

Readers will discover the history of each sport and its evolution into its current form. Athlete profiles provide information about the training techniques for each discipline and offer a glimpse of the daily challenges faced by athletes aiming for the elite level. Amateur athletes can compare their own skills and training regimens with those of the champions in their sports.

The physical environment for competitions, the roles of the players and officials, and the dynamics of each sport are presented, along with specific terms and expressions. Thanks to clear and lively illustrations and descriptions, readers can discover new sports and games or quickly find visual guidelines and information about a discipline with which they are familiar.

Key movements are broken down into series of illustrations with clear descriptions to explain how athletes perform these movements. Finally, the equipment used in each sport is shown and explained.

In short, *Sports: The Complete Visual Reference* is an ideal guide to exploring the world of contemporary sport. Readers can use this attractive resource in any number of ways as they seek out specific information or simply allow their curiosity to discover the wonderful world of sport!

François Fortin

introduction

Pushing the limits of one's abilities is both a personal undertaking and an experience common to all sporting endeavors. There could therefore be as many definitions of "sport" as there are athletes. All sports, however, share one need: rules that establish a fair framework within which to place performances. This basic principle is the only connection between the Olympiads of Antiquity, which had an essentially religious nature, and the "physical culture" of the 19th century, considered a form of training and education. The notion of pleasure, without which today's athletes—including professionals—could not reach the highest levels, gradually came to the fore over the course of the 20th century.

A number of factors led to the emergence of modern sports. The British were largely responsible for setting structures; the modernization of performance measurement led to the creation and keeping of records; and the birth of the Olympic movement was a key event in popularizing sports and games. In more recent times, the social and economic impact of sport has grown considerably thanks to an explosion in media coverage. A massive infusion of money has encouraged the circulation of funds from organizations to team owners, and finally to the athletes themselves. In the current sports environment, the interests of athletes, sponsors, and broadcasters are tightly linked and dependent on viewer ratings.

* * *

In the late 19th century, Baron Pierre de Coubertin, an active proponent of the benefits of physical exercise, decided to bring the modern Olympics to life. The Games were to be founded on a democratic search for perfection—a concept inherited from the ancient games. De Coubertin was responsible for the creation of the International Olympic Committee (IOC) by the Congrès de Paris in June 1894, and the first Games of the modern era were played in 1896 in Athens, Greece. Although special stamps were issued along with government funding, it took the assistance of a Russian millionaire (George Avenarius) for the stadium to be finished on time. The opening ceremonies took place before an audience of 70,000—public enthusiasm was spectacular—and 311 athletes from 14 countries competed in nine events.

De Coubertin played a major role in the Olympic organization. He chaired the IOC until 1925, writing the Olympic Charter and Protocol, the athletes' oath, and the protocol for the opening and closing ceremonies. He took part in all decisions and devoted all his energy to developing the spirit of the modern Olympics according to his ideals. For him, the athletes' commitment to convey, through competition, "their concept of honor and impartiality regarding sport to the same degree as their physical training" provided an example of the kind of harmony that would transcend narrow nationalism and individual glory.

The Olympic symbols and ceremony protocols that de Coubertin created include:

• The Olympic motto: *Citius* (swifter), *altius* (higher), *fortius* (stronger). Borrowed from a French cleric, the words refer to the struggle to outdo oneself, the desire and courage needed in competition, and the three basic activities in track and field: running, jumping, and throwing.

• The Olympic emblem, which appears on the Olympic flag. There are five interlacing rings, which symbolize the five continents and the friendship that unites all people on Earth. Each nation has at least one of the colors of the Olympic flag on its own flag.

* * *

Today, sport is an international cultural phenomenon, conveying the social values of fame and success. Many commercial brands try to take advantage of the Olympics' prestigious image. Sports, broadcast live throughout the world, have gone beyond national borders by transforming their financing from gate receipts to revenues from television and sponsors. This globalization has resulted in a consolidation of structures to form a complex network linking sports institutions, athletes' agents, commercial partners (usually manufacturers), and broadcasters. The two major currents of modern sport, amateurism (exemplified by the Olympics) and professionalism, have merged. Seeking larger audiences, and thus a source of greater revenues, many sports are changing to make broadcasting easier. The choices of sites and dates and competition

introduction

formats are being changed to adapt to laws of the marketplace, and the Olympic movement has not escaped this transformation.

The 1960 Olympics marked a turning point, with the sale of television rights. Since then, the number of competitions has grown steadily, audiences have expanded considerably, and private sponsors seeking greater visibility have been increasingly attracted to the Games. The ever-growing popularity of professional sports has meant record-setting in the professional arena where, in many cases, the athletes are the best. The Olympics officially abandoned amateurism in 1981, and commercial exploitation of the Olympic symbols was authorized in 1986. These two decisions by the IOC led to an explosion in revenues, and other events of global interest (World Cup soccer, Formula 1 racing, and tennis and golf tournaments, to name a few) followed suit. The biggest sports events are now retransmitted to more than 200 countries, have viewers numbering in the billions, and generate revenues in the many hundreds of millions of dollars.

* * *

This full-scale entry of sport into the world of showbiz and high performance has not been without its problems. The use of doping substances to improve performances is just one example. The public's identification with athletes is based on the principle of transparency: exploits are achieved in front of a huge number of spectators. For viewers, this corresponds, legitimately, to a guarantee of truth and reality, but it places athletes in a contradictory position. Their income is based on the marketability of their results: as long as they are a profitable investment, the sky's the limit. The objective of the athlete's employers or sponsors is to reduce the uncertainty associated with athletic endeavor so that they can predict the economic returns. Athletes must therefore provide reliable performances, even though the constant increase in effort required pushes them ever closer to the natural limits of the human body.

Forced to stake out a clear position, international authorities count on anti-doping controls to settle questions of contested performances. Beyond this official and dominant current of thought, however, there have been a few notable initiatives in different directions. The International Powerlifting Federation, for instance, keeps sets of records in two categories: with drug testing, and without drug testing.

Nevertheless, a new type of elite athlete seems to have sprung up precisely to defy the constraints of contemporary sport; these athletes can both meet the obligation to produce results and handle media pressure. Alain Prost in Formula 1, Michael Jordan in basketball, Wayne Gretzky in ice hockey, and Greg Norman in golf, for example, in spite of the enormous expectations placed upon them, became legendary for their ability to stay at the top of their game over exceptionally long careers. By accumulating the most prestigious titles in their sports, they became models whose influence extends beyond sport.

Meanwhile, there has been spectacular growth in the popularity of "extreme" sports. The highly acrobatic aspect of these newcomers is indicative of a desire for discovery of new forms of self-expression and independence from the established models. Even at the elite level, the new events are performed in a spontaneous and risk-taking style. The objective is less to guarantee a result than to provide entertainment. To a great extent, the oldest disciplines—including track and field—have profited from this iconoclastic movement. They have thus managed to attract new viewers who appreciate the pure beauty of motion and the showmanship—a better reflection of the athletes' personal accomplishments.

And this is what we invite you to discover in the pages of *Sports: The Complete Visual Reference*. This contemporary portrait of top-level sport will introduce you to the athletes themselves. From the 110-meter hurdles to snowboarding to equestrian sports, we offer you the great diversity of international competition and the achievement of excellence.

Many international sports and Olympic events use the metric system. The following table will help readers unfamiliar with the metric system to convert imperial measures.

METRIC CONVERSION CHART			
LENGTH		**WEIGHT**	
1 inch	2.540 centimeter (cm)	1 once	28.35 grams (g)
1 foot	0.305 meter (m)	1 pound	453.592 grams (g)
1 yard	0.914 meter (m)		
1 mile	1.609 kilometer (km)		
1 millimeter (mm)	0,039 in.	1 gram	0,035 ounces (oz)
1 centimeter (cm)	0.394 in.	1 kilogram (kg)	2.205 pounds (lbs)
1 meter (m)	3.281 ft.		
1 kilometer (km)	0.621 mile		

contents

Track and Field

🏃 track and field

The stadium in Athens hosted the first Olympic Games of the modern era in 1896; the Olympics had last been held in this very stadium 1,502 years before. In front of a crowd of 70,000, 311 athletes from 14 countries competed in 9 events.

Track and field is primarily an individual sport grouping together approximately 30 different events, which were formerly divided into track events (sprints, middle and long distance races) and field events (jumping and throwing). A primitive form was practiced in Egypt more than 4,000 years ago, and the Cretans became the first to engage in it systematically, around 1500 B.C., followed by the Achaean Greeks. The word athlete comes from the Greek word athlos, which means competition, and the word stadium comes from stadion, an ancient Greek measure of length equivalent to about 180 m. Modern track and field began in England, where it evolved around the end of the 17th century and the beginning of the 18th century, mostly in the form of running and walking races. The early 19th century saw the first professional meets and wagering. Oxford and Cambridge Universities entered the scene around 1860, and the first official British Championships were held in 1866. The sport then spread to the United States and continental Europe. The first modern Olympic Games, in 1896, consisted mainly of track and field events.

GENERAL RULES FOR A MEET

The order of competition is determined by random draw. Athletes who miss their turn in an event are not allowed to make it up. An athlete who is late without a valid reason may be disqualified from the contest. Athletes who are late a second time are disqualified from further turns, and only their performance prior to the disqualification counts. Judges may let an athlete take a turn over in the event of interference. Competitors wear shorts and a jersey, or a skintight suit.

In either case, the attire must be clean and not transparent. They must also wear a bib bearing their entry number.

Athletes may wear one shoe, two shoes, or no shoes. With the exception of the marathon and walking races on public roads, footwear is light and sturdy, with a maximum of 11 cleats on each shoe to provide better traction.

STADIUM

To host an official competition, a stadium must have a 400 m track divided into 6 or 8 lanes, areas for the jumping and throwing events, and a water jump for the steeplechase. Races are always run counterclockwise, with the runners' left arms toward the inside of the track.

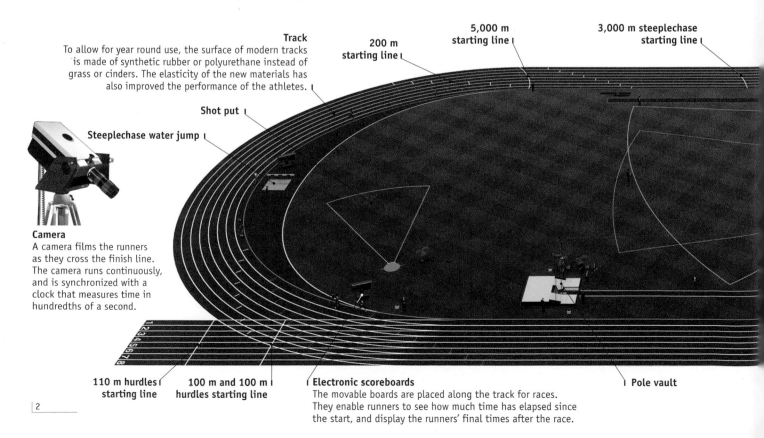

Track
To allow for year round use, the surface of modern tracks is made of synthetic rubber or polyurethane instead of grass or cinders. The elasticity of the new materials has also improved the performance of the athletes.

Shot put

Steeplechase water jump

200 m starting line

5,000 m starting line

3,000 m steeplechase starting line

Camera
A camera films the runners as they cross the finish line. The camera runs continuously, and is synchronized with a clock that measures time in hundredths of a second.

110 m hurdles starting line

100 m and 100 m hurdles starting line

Electronic scoreboards
The movable boards are placed along the track for races. They enable runners to see how much time has elapsed since the start, and display the runners' final times after the race.

Pole vault

MEASUREMENTS

Because Great Britain was the birthplace of modern track and field, Imperial measurements dominated. One yard is 0.914 m, and one pound is 0.454 kg. Although most stadium tracks around the world today are 400 m long, some English-speaking countries still have tracks measuring 440 yards (402.34 m). The distance was derived from the original basic unit, the mile (1,760 yards or 1,609.35 m). Sprint races were 1/16 of a mile, or 110 yards. The growing popularity of track and field, and its expansion into continental Europe, led officials to adopt the metric system. For throwing events, three judges measure the distance with a certified steel measuring tape. Measurements are taken from the center of the circle or the arc of the circle where the athlete was at the time of the throw to the point where the projectile hit the ground. The official registered distance is 1 or 2 cm (depending on the event) less than the actual throw. A similar system is used for measuring the long jump and the triple jump.

Starting blocks

Originally just a depression in the ground dug out by the athlete, and later made from wood, today's starting block is a portable metal device. Since 1928, starting blocks have been used in races of up to 400 m to give runners a firmer push-off, and to prevent runners from slipping during the start. In international meets, they are connected to a device that detects false starts.

Timing

A race starts when the starter fires his pistol. An electronic timer that is activated by the pistol or an approved start device determines the official result. Moreover, three officials near the finish line time races manually with stopwatches. The results are compared if a record is set. Races up to 10,000 m are timed in hundredths of a second. Longer races are timed to the tenth of a second, or even to the second.

FIRST YEAR FOR TRACK AND FIELD EVENTS AT THE OLYMPIC GAMES		
Event	Men	Women
100 m	1896	1928
200 m	1900	1948
400 m	1896	1964
100 m hurdles	—	1972
110 m hurdles	1896	—
400 m hurdles	1900	1984
4 x 100-m relay	1912	1928
4 x 400-m relay	1912	1972
800 m	1896	1928
1,500 m	1896	1972
3,000 m	—	1984–1992*
3,000 m steeplechase	1920	—
5,000 m	1912	1996
10,000 m	1912	1988
Decathlon	1912	—
Heptathlon	—	1984
Discus	1896	1928
Javelin	1908	1932
Hammer throw	1900	2000
Shot put	1896	1948
Marathon	1896	1984
10-km walk	1912–1952*	1992–1996*
20-km walk	1956	2000
50-km walk	1932	—
Pole vault	1896	2000
High jump	1896	1928
Long jump	1896	1948
Triple jump	1896	1996

* Last appearance as an Olympic event.

Relay races

Three baton passing zones are located along the track.

Long jump and triple jump

1,500 m starting line

Hammer throw and discus

Javelin

High jump

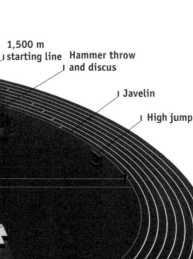

Anemometer

This device measures and records the wind speed for races under 200 m, as well as for the long jump and triple jump. For a record to be approved, a tailwind must be less than 2 m per second.

Finish line for all races

10,000 m and 4 x 400 m relay starting line

800 m starting line

400 m, 400 m hurdles, and 4 x 100 m relay starting line

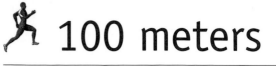

100 meters

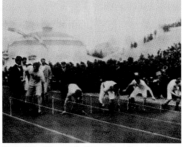

The he 100 meter, a test of pure speed over a straight distance, was first run at the first Olympics of the modern era, in Athens in 1896. It quickly became the star event of the Games, with the winner of the race recognized as the fastest human being in the world. The first Olympic track events for women were held at the Amsterdam Games in 1928.

Start of the 100 m at the first modern Olympics in Athens, 1896

THE COMPETITION

The 100 m event involves several series of qualifying heats. The 8 runners with the best times in the heats run in the final. The lanes are assigned according to the best times obtained in the heats, with the fastest runners in the center lanes.

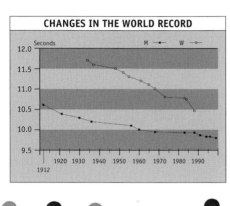

CHANGES IN THE WORLD RECORD

TECHNIQUE

1. Set

The runner concentrates deeply and holds his breath so that he can propel his body forward at the start. The interval between the start signal and the instant when the athlete pushes off the blocks is called the reaction time. A quick reaction time is not an absolute requirement for setting a record, since many of the athletes with the best times have had the slowest starts.

2. Start

When the starter's pistol fires, the runner lets out his breath and he moves his arms and legs in an explosive action that propels his body forward at a 45° angle until the back leg is fully extended. If a runner has two false starts, he is automatically disqualified.

3. Acceleration

The sprinter reaches his running position between the fifth and eighth stride. He runs on his toes; his heels never touch the track.

4. Maximum speed

Acceleration continues with an increase in stride frequency until maximum speed is reached, generally around the 60th meter. Among elite sprinters, the number of strides may reach 5 per second, for a speed of 12 meters per second or 40 km/h.

Starting line

Width: 1.22 m

EQUIPMENT

Shirt

Athlete number

Shoes with cleats

Shoes
They have neither a heel nor arch support. The 11 cleats must not be more than 9 mm long. Only the athlete's toes touch the ground during the race.

Florence Griffith-Joyner (USA)
Gold medalist in the 1988 Seoul Olympics and Olympic record holder. She ran the 100 m in 10.54 seconds.

Carl Lewis (USA)
He won 19 Olympic and world championship medals, including 17 gold medals in the 17 years of his international career.

A complete stride may be 2.40 m long

5. Maintaining speed

At the 60th meter, stride amplitude is at its maximum.

6. Decline in speed

From 80 m to the finish line, the athlete tries to keep his strides fluid and maintains a very high stride rate to mitigate the inevitable loss of speed; it is physically impossible to maintain the maximum speed.

7. Finish line

The timer is stopped when the athlete's chest crosses the finish line (rule that came into effect in 1932). A record cannot be registered if there is a following wind of more than 2 m/s.

NOTABLE MALE ATHLETES IN THE 100 M

There were 103 years between Burke's race, in 1896, and Greene's, in 1999. The difference of 2.21 seconds would have left Burke 12.25 m behind Greene.

	1999	9.79	Maurice Greene (USA)
	1991	9.86	Carl Lewis (USA)
3	1983	9.93	Calvin Smith (USA)
4	1968	9.95	Jim Hines (USA)
5	1960	10.0	Armin Hary (FRG)
6	1936	10.2	Jesse Owens (USA)
7	1930	10.3	Percy Williams (CAN)
8	1896	12.0	Thomas Burke (USA)

Finish line |

🏃 200 meters

I n this race, classified as a long sprint, athletes run 200 meters as fast as possible. The ancestor of this competition, a race one-stadium (an ancient Greek measure) in length, was an event in the ancient Olympics. In 1896, at the first modern Olympic Games in Athens, the distance was officially set at 200 meters, although the race was not held. It was not until the Olympics in Paris, 4 years later, that the event was included in the men's track and field program. The women's 200 meter made its debut in the London Games in 1948.

Jesse Owens (USA) won the gold medal with a time of 20.7 seconds in the 200 m at the Berlin Olympics in 1936.

THE RACE

1. The start

The race has a staggered start to make up for the tighter curve in the inside lanes. As in the 100 m, the athletes break out of the blocks explosively.

2. The curve

To counter centrifugal force, athletes lean toward the inside of the curve. The transition from the curve to the straightaway is the hardest part of the race. It is where runners achieve maximum speed, about 40 km/h among elite athletes, and the risk of slipping sideways due to the centrifugal force is high. Simulations show that the tighter curves have a slowing effect corresponding to 0.012 seconds, which means that the runner in the outside lane has an advantage of about 0.08 seconds over the runner in the inside lane.

3. The straightaway

It is impossible for athletes to maintain their maximum speed all the way to the finish line. However, the second 100 m is run faster than the first because the runner does not have to overcome the inertia of the start.

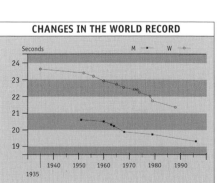

ATHLETE PROFILE

- The best male 200 m runners are on average about 5'9" tall and weigh 165½ lbs. For women, average height is about 5'5¾"; average weight, about 132½ lbs.

- This sprint requires more strength and agility than the 100 m. Because of the start on the curve and the effort produced in a leaning position, the risk of injury is higher.

- In training, starts on the curve from all lanes are practiced repeatedly. Athletes run many sprints, increase their speed over short distances (30–60 m), and work on strength on longer runs (80–200 m).

CHANGES IN THE WORLD RECORD

Seconds   M ●—●   W ○—○

Michael Johnson (USA)
Double gold medal in the 1996 Olympics in Atlanta, with a world record of 19.32 seconds for the 200 m and a first place in the 400 m, in 43.49 seconds.

Marie-José Perec (FRA)
She achieved an Olympic double, winning gold in the 400 m in Barcelona in 1992 and in Atlanta in 1996. In the latter Games, she also won gold in the 200 m.

400 meters

Athletes who compete in this long sprint run 400 meters as fast as possible. In 1850, the first track and field competition held at Exeter College, Oxford, Great Britain, included a quarter-mile race (402 m). This distance was dropped to 400 meters and included in the first modern Olympics in 1896. At first, the 400 meters was not run in lanes; it was a very tactical race with frequent incidents and much jostling. In 1908, the rules were changed and it became the longest race run in lanes. The women's 400 meters made its Olympic debut in Tokyo in 1964. Men's and women's 400 meter races were featured in the first world championships in 1983.

Start of the 400 m at the Amsterdam Olympics in 1928

THE RACE

1. The start

The stagger at the start is greater than for the 200 m, as the race involves 2 curves. Athletes start fast and use a long stride, but they must never surpass 90% of their maximum speed; if they go out too fast, they will run out of energy before the end of the race.

2. First straightaway

Athletes reach their maximum speed in the second half of the first straightaway. If they begin to feel tired entering the second curve, they will be even more uncomfortable leaving it. They must concentrate on keeping their speed constant and not stiffening up, which causes a loss of energy.

3. The second curve

As in the 200 m, the athlete must fight against centrifugal force by leaning toward the inside of the curve. The runner in the outside lane has an advantage of about 0.16 seconds over the runner in the inside lane.

4. Last straightaway

Athletes inevitably slow down in the last straightaway because of the effort expended in the first 300 m. They run each 100 m section in a time very similar to their best performance over that distance, 10–12 seconds.

EQUIPMENT

Shoes
Identical for the 200 m and 400 m, they have no heel and a maximum of 11 9-mm cleats.

CHANGES IN THE WORLD RECORD

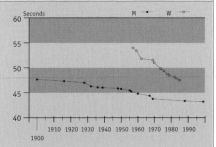

Seconds — M · W

60
55
50
45
40
1900 1910 1920 1930 1940 1950 1960 1970 1980 1990

ATHLETE PROFILE

- Athletes must be very strong, have a high pain threshold, and be able to spread their exertion very effectively, as it is physiologically impossible to run at maximum speed for more than 7 seconds.

- The morphological profile of the 400 m racer is very similar to that of the 200 m racer, and training is also similar. For increased strength, they more frequently run distances of between 200 m and 600 m at a fast pace.

relays: 4 x 100 and 4 x 400 meter

The 1932 Olympics at the Coliseum Stadium in Los Angeles

These races are run in teams of 4 athletes, who must carry the baton one after another from the start to the finish as quickly as possible. Although in ancient times very fast runners with great stamina transmitted messages from city to city, relay races were not in the ancient Olympics. They were invented in the late 19th century, when American firefighters organized races in which teams passed a red pennant every 300 yards. The idea was taken up by two professors in Pennsylvania, who organized the first official relay in 1893. Americans loved these races, and relays over various distances were added to international track and field competitions, leading to the inclusion of the men's 4 x 100 and 4 x 400 meter relays in the Olympic Games in Stockholm in 1912. The first Olympic women's 4 x 100 meter relay was held at the Amsterdam Games in 1928, and the women's 4 x 400 meter relay made its Olympic debut in Munich in 1972.

THE RACE

Eight 4-person teams compete in the final. In the 4 x 100 m, the baton must be exchanged quickly, and dropped batons and awkward exchanges can spell disaster for the best teams. Racers pass the baton in a passing zone measured from 10 m before to 10 m after the 100 m, 200 m, and 300 m lines. Each 20 m zone is preceded by a 10 m run-up zone. Team members must remain in their lane so that they do not impede the other competitors. In the 4 x 400 m, the speed is slower and passing the baton is less risky, but tactical considerations are more important. There is no run-up zone. Only the first lap and the first turn of the second lap are run in lanes. After the first 100 m of the second lap, the second runners break for the inside.

4 X 100 M RELAY

1. Run-up

The receiver takes 6 to 8 strides in the run-up zone. If he starts too early, the passer won't catch up to him; if he starts too late, he will be too close to the passer and time will be lost. To increase coordination, athletes often place a marker 6 to 9 m before the run-up zone. When the passer crosses the marker, the receiver begins to run.

2. Passing

The passer shouts to the receiver indicating that he should stretch his arm behind him. When he is within reach of his teammate, he puts the baton in the palm of his hand. The receiver's hand automatically closes around the baton and holds it firmly. In a good pass, the baton is moved at a constant speed.

3. Finish of the relay

The receiver continues the sprint he started during the pass. The passer stays in his lane and does not leave the track until he is no longer in danger of impeding the other competitors.

TACTICS

In both relays, the first runner is usually known for a quick start, while the athlete with a strong finish is the last runner. In the 4 x 100 m, the first and third runners must know how to run the curves.

4 x 100 m relay

4 x 400 m relay

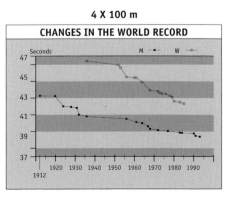

4 X 100 m

CHANGES IN THE WORLD RECORD

FACILITIES

Track and run-up and passing zones for
the 4 x 100 m and the 4 x 400 m.

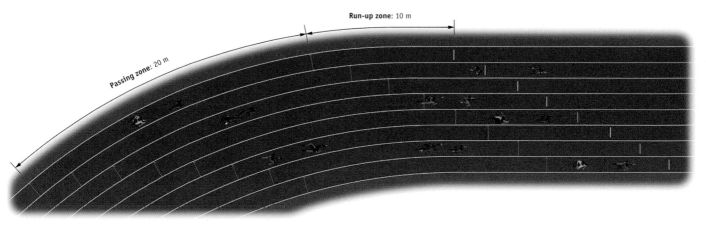

Run-up zone: 10 m

Passing zone: 20 m

4 X 400 M RELAY

In the 4 x 400 m relay, there is visual contact between the
runners rather than a blind pass. Because the passer's fatigue
may affect his speed, an automatic pass is too risky.

PASSING THE BATON

American grip
When the runners are almost side
by side, the baton is passed in a
downward motion. This grip is
popular in the 4 x 400 m.

French grip
In an upward motion, the passer
places the baton in the very open
hand of the receiver. Used mainly
in the 4 x 100 m, this method
reduces the distance covered by
the baton to a minimum, but it is
riskier than the American grip,
because the two runners must be
perfectly coordinated.

3.8–4.0 cm

28–30 cm

Baton
The baton is a rigid, smooth tube made of a single piece of wood or metal,
weighing at least 50 g. It is the baton that is timed and not the athlete.
If a runner drops a baton, he or she must pick it up.

EQUIPMENT

Shoes
Designed for sprinting, they have a maximum of
11 cleats and no heel or arch support. They are
made of very light nylon.

In the 4 x 100 m, the United
States men's team set a world
record of 37.40 seconds at the
1992 Olympics in Barcelona.

In the 4 x 400 m, the Soviet
women's team set a world
record of 3:15:18 at the 1988
Olympics in Seoul.

ATHLETE PROFILE

- The 4 x 100 m uses sprinters who can
  maintain a high speed for more than 100 m,
  while the 4 x 400 m features specialists in
  the 400 m and 800 m with a very high level
  of stamina. In both races, the runners are
  psychologically strong and technically
  precise.

- Training is intense and frequent: speed heats,
  baton passing (for automatic, well-timed
  passes), side-by-side sprints (comparing
  strides to the adversary's).

4 X 400 m
CHANGES IN THE WORLD RECORD

Minutes: seconds   M ● W ○

3:45
3:30
3:15
3:00
2:45

1911 1920 1930 1940 1950 1960 1970 1980 1990

100 and 110 meter hurdles

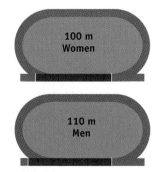

110 m hurdles at the Amsterdam Olympics in 1928

Both races are sprints with evenly spaced obstacles. The first competitions took place in Great Britain in the early 19th century, and the 120 yard hurdles was an official event in the Cambridge-Oxford track and field meet in 1864. At the end of the century, the French added a few centimeters to the race, converting it to a metric distance, and the 110 meter hurdles was part of the first modern Olympics in 1896. The 100 meter women's hurdles race, introduced in the Munich Olympics in 1972, was 100 instead of 110 meters to allow for the fact that women's strides are about 1 meter shorter than men's. Female athletes quickly developed strength and speed, however, so the distances between the hurdles were adjusted and the height of the hurdles was raised.

THE COMPETITION

The 100 m and 110 m hurdles are run in lanes, and there are 10 hurdles in each lane. In these very technical races, athletes constantly alternate between sprinting and jumping obstacles.

Runners can touch or knock down any number of hurdles without penalty, but are disqualified if they deliberately knock a hurdle over or place their leg or foot outside a hurdle.

TECHNIQUE

1. Start and takeoff

The runner starts like a sprinter, but aims for stride speed rather than length. He accelerates as much as possible in his first 4 strides, then prepares to jump the hurdle by straightening his torso during the following 4 strides. He sees the hurdle without focusing on it, and takes off between 1.9 m and 2.35 m before the hurdle.

2. Flight

The athlete tips his body forward and looks toward the next hurdle.

3. Landing

The hurdler lands about 1 m after the obstacle and immediately regains impetus for the next stride. The ankle plays a major part in this forward movement.

4. Run between hurdles

The athlete accelerates for 3 strides. The last stride before the next takeoff is shorter and higher. Speed is at its maximum between the hurdles and stride rhythm must never be interrupted.

5. Last hurdle and final sprint

The landing after jumping the last hurdle must be powerful to permit maximum speed to be attained. In general, it takes 6 to 7 strides of acceleration to cross the finish line in the final sprint.

100 m Women

110 m Men

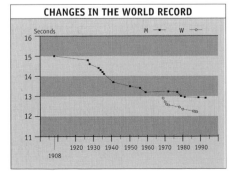

CHANGES IN THE WORLD RECORD

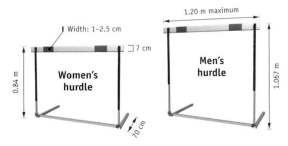

Width: 1–2.5 cm

7 cm

Women's hurdle

0.84 m

70 cm

1.20 m maximum

Men's hurdle

1.067 m

400 meter hurdles

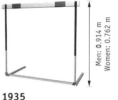

R aces with obstacles, unknown to the ancient Greeks, were inspired by horse races. Like the 120 yard hurdles, the 440 yard hurdles was officially introduced to men's track and field during the Cambridge-Oxford meet of 1864. Also converted to a metric distance by the French in the late 19th century, this event became a men's Olympic event in the Paris Games of 1900. Some 84 years later, in Los Angeles, the women's 400 meter hurdles became an Olympic event.

Robert Tisdall (IRL) at the last hurdle of the 400 m hurdles at the Los Angeles Olympics in 1932

THE COMPETITION

The 400 m hurdles is run in lanes and has 10 hurdles. As in the 100 and 110 m, runners can touch or knock down any number of hurdles without penalty, but are disqualified if they deliberately knock a hurdle over or place their leg or foot outside a hurdle.

TECHNIQUE

1. Impetus

Athletes run an odd number of strides (usually 23) before reaching the first hurdle, so that they jump off the left leg and avoid being carried outward in the curve by centrifugal force. Because the hurdle is lower than in the 100 m and 110 m hurdles, the takeoff point, about 2.4 m, is a few centimeters farther away.

CHANGES TO THE FACILITIES

Men: 0.914 m
Women: 0.762 m

1864
Gates resting on 2 fixed supports.

1895
Lighter structures on upside-down T supports. Athletes are eliminated if they knock down 3 hurdles.

1935
Introduction of the L-shaped, metal-and-wood hurdle. A counter-weight keeps the hurdle from falling.

EQUIPMENT

Shoes
They resemble sprinters' shoes, but the cleats in the front are shorter so that they don't get caught in the hurdle. The heels are reinforced to absorb the shock of landing.

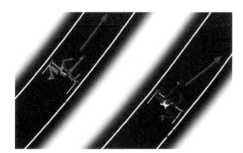

2. Flight

Because they jump a barrier every 35 m, runners must adjust their strides carefully and spread their exertion effectively. The hurdles are lower than in the 110 m, so the runners don't touch them when they jump, and their torsos lean forward less.

3. Running between hurdles

Racers land about 1.2 m after the barrier and run between 13 and 17 strides between each hurdle.

ATHLETE PROFILE

- Runners train as for 100 m and 400 m sprints, with an emphasis on flexibility, technique, joint mobility (particularly the hips), impulsion, sense of rhythm, and coordination. It is essential to strengthen the abdominal and back muscles, the lumbar region, and all leg muscles.

- Women are about 5'5" and weigh 125 lbs. Men are about 6'1" and weigh 172 lbs.

- A good racer takes about 3 seconds longer to run a hurdles course than to run the same distance without obstacles.

Edwin Moses (USA)
The all-time best hurdler, he set a number of Olympic and world records between 1972 and 1984.

Yordanka Donkova (BUL)
Olympic champion in the 100 m hurdles at the Seoul Games in 1988, and world record holder (12.21 seconds).

CHANGES IN THE WORLD RECORD

Seconds   M ●—●   W ○—○

56
54
52
50
48
46

1908 1920 1930 1940 1950 1960 1970 1980 1990

800 meter and 1,500 meter

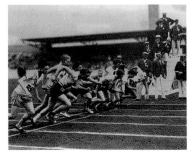

The start of the women's 800 m at the Amsterdam Olympics in 1928

D uring these middle distance races, the athlete must run the prescribed distance in the shortest possible time. The predecessor of the 800 meter race that we know today, first run in 1896, was the half-mile (805 meters), introduced to men's track and field championships in England in 1871. Although the women's 800 meter was first run at the Amsterdam Olympics in 1928, it was not until 1960, in Rome, that the event was officially included in Olympic track and field. The 1,500 meter race is the metric equivalent of the mile (1,609 meters), which was first run in Great Britain in the second half of the 19th century. Men have competed in this event, in which attacks, finishing kicks, and jostling are common features, since the Athens Olympics of 1896. The women's 1,500 meter has been an Olympic event since 1972.

THE COMPETITIONS

The athletes begin both races without starting blocks. In the 800 m final, the 8 racers run the first curve in lanes assigned by drawing lots, then break to the inside of the track. In the 1,500 m final, a maximum of 12 racers line up on a starting line that is curved so that the athletes on the outside of the track run the same distance as those placed closer to the inside.

Start of the 1,500 m

TACTICS

There are two main race tactics: some athletes try to front-run the entire race, while others depend on their finishing kick. In races where it is important to place well, tactics often involve changes of pace, and the times suffer. Whatever the strategy used, all racers must know how to use their elbows and keep an eye out to avoid falling. Since these races are not run in lanes, athletes must keep track of their position in the pack. By following another runner very closely, a racer can benefit from a major reduction in wind resistance, which can add up to a potential improvement of several seconds and an important savings of energy that can be used at the end of the race. In some races, "rabbits" are used; these runners set a very fast early pace, providing other racers with an opportunity to break records. As in the fable, the rabbit, who starts out too fast, cannot finish the race.

The rabbit in the 1,500m

BREAKING TO THE INSIDE

A rule adopted in 1959 requires the athletes to run the first curve of the 800 m in lanes to avoid jostling at the beginning of the race. Runners can then break to the inside—the lane on the left-hand side of the track.

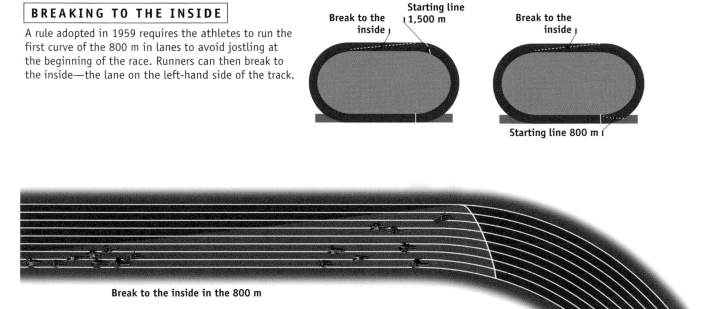

Break to the inside in the 800 m

Sebastian Coe (GBR)
Holder of the 800 m world record from 1979 to 1997, he is the only athlete to have won the 1,500 m in two consecutive Olympics (1980, 1984).

Tatiana Kazankina (USSR)
Her time of 3:52:47 in the 1,500 m final in Zurich in 1980 was a world record for 13 years.

EQUIPMENT

Shoes
Shoes for the 800 m usually have no heels; for the 1,500 m, they do have heels. In both cases, the front of the sole has a maximum of 11 9-mm cleats.

800 m

1 500 m

800 m

CHANGES IN THE WORLD RECORD

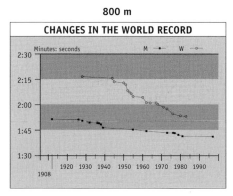

1,500 m

CHANGES IN THE WORLD RECORD

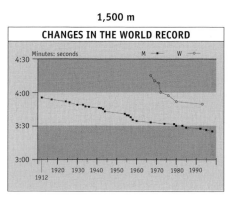

ATHLETE PROFILE

- Elite 800 m and 1,500 m male racers on average weigh 150 lbs. and are 5'9" tall. For women, average weight is 121 lbs; average height, 5'4".

- Athletes develop endurance by running long distances over varied terrain at a moderate speed. To increase aerobic power—level of energy produced through oxygenation of cells—they run fast over short distances on the track.

- A large part of training on the track is devoted to changes of pace, which must be performed easily so that athletes can improve their position in the pack without too much effort.

3,000 meter steeplechase

The Los Angeles Olympics in 1932

Originally, the steeplechase was a horse race with obstacles, fashioned after 18th century Irish fox hunting, in which the hunt ended near a church with a steeple. This equestrian discipline inspired the 3,000 meter steeplechase, invented by Oxford University students in 1850. The first competitions took place in the open countryside: the runners raced over a 2 mile (3,218 meters) course with obstacles including hurdles and streams. In 1879, the steeplechase was included in men's track and field championships in England. In 1882, the Paris Racing Club organized steeplechase races. The 1900 Olympic Games in Paris featured steeplechases over 2,500 and 4,000 meters. The rules were standardized in 1954, and the first world records were registered. Today, the steeplechase is still for men only.

RUNNING THE RACE

The 3,000 m steeplechase takes place on the stadium track, outside the lanes. In the final, 8 to 12 runners line up on a curved starting line. There are no obstacles in the first 200 m; the third and fourth hurdles are set up during the race.

During the following 7 laps, runners face 5 jumps per lap, with the fourth being the water jump. The race includes a total of 28 efforts over hurdles and 7 efforts through water jumps, which provide the most spectacular and risky moments in the race. Racers are not penalized if they use their hands to help them over the obstacles, step on the hurdles, or put a foot in the water.

FIRST LAP — Starting line · Second hurdle · First hurdle

FOLLOWING LAPS — Water jump · Third hurdle · Fourth hurdle · Finish line

JUMPING STEEPLECHASE HURDLES

1. Approaching the hurdles

Racers use a technique similar to that for the 400 m hurdles: a fluid, relaxed running style. Since they must run in a group at a fast pace, they keep a flowing, rhythmic stride throughout the race to avoid falls and maintain their cadence and speed over the hurdles. They try not to take a half-step before jumping the obstacles; they also try to keep a distance from other runners to avoid bumping and to keep their pace as they go through the hurdles.

2. Jumping the hurdles

So that they don't break their rhythm, runners try to take the hurdles in stride, whether the right or left leg leads. They lean forward to avoid raising their center of gravity, and they use their arms for balance. After the jump, they keep their stride flowing forward. Among the best racers, jumping the hurdle represents a time loss of 0.4–0.7 seconds.

- The steeplechase specialist combines the talents of a middle distance runner (quick and strong) and a hurdler (agile and energetic). Muscle tone, flexibility, a sense of rhythm, and coordination are essential.

- To develop muscle and joint strength, runners do specific weight-lifting exercises, practice over obstacles, and perform various jumps.

- Races over short and long distances, changes in speed, and workouts at different speeds and over varied terrain are essential for runners to maintain cardiovascular fitness. Maximum oxygen consumption is almost double that for a sedentary person of the same age, and this translates into great endurance.

CHANGES TO THE WORLD RECORD

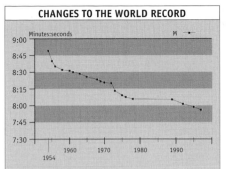

Since the early 1970s, the Kenyans have dominated the 3,000 m steeplechase.

Moses Kiptanui (KEN)
Three-time world champion (1991, 1993, 1995). In 1995, at age 24, he was the first to run the 3,000 m steeplechase in under 8 min.

JUMPING THE WATER JUMP

Steeplechase hurdle

Depth: 0.7 m

Water jump
length and width: 3.66 m

RUNNER EQUIPMENT

Shoes
Made of nylon, stable and comfortable even when wet, with a maximum of 11 cleats.

1. Approaching the water jump

The runner begins his jump about 2 m from the hurdle. As he leaps up, he plants one foot flat on the hurdle for a moment. The supporting leg bends without resistance, enabling him to push his hips forward in as horizontal a motion as possible.

2. Jumping the water jump

The runner usually lands about 30 cm from the end of the ditch, runs out of the water with short, quick steps, and regains his race stride. Some top steeplechasers do not touch the water at all, but for most athletes this requires a very powerful push-off that takes too much energy.

FACILITIES

Steeplechase hurdle

3.96 m

0.911–0.917 m

race walking

Ugo Frigerio (ITA) won the gold medal at the Paris Olympics in 1924, walking 10 km in 47 min and 49 sec.

Race walking involves a very difficult technique, which the athlete uses to move forward as quickly as possible without running. Inspired by English servants in the 12th and 13th centuries, who followed their masters' coaches by alternately walking and running, it became a sports event in the 18th century. In 1866, a 7 mile walk was included in the English championships. In the London Olympics in 1908, the men's walk was featured in two races: 3,500 meters and 10 miles. The 10 and 20 km races were introduced respectively at the 1912 Stockholm and 1956 Melbourne Olympics; the 50 km walk was on the Olympic program for the first time in Los Angeles in 1932. The first women's Olympic walk was held over 10 km at the Barcelona Olympics in 1992, and the women's 20 km was introduced at the Sydney Games in 2000. Today, the women's 10 km is not an Olympic event, although it is run in some international competitions. At the Olympics and world championships, the 50 km, a race lasting almost 4 hours, is still for men only, while the 20 km is raced by both men and women.

THE COMPETITION

Races take place on a track or road. Judges observe the walkers very closely, for a competitor will be disqualified if he does not step onto a straight leg or loses contact with the ground more than twice. If a judge sees an infraction, he issues a first warning. If there is a second infraction, a disqualification warning is posted on a board visible to all competitors on course. If three judges charge an athlete with an infraction, he is disqualified.

TECHNIQUE

The technique is slightly different for uphill and downhill walking. When climbing, walkers tilt their bodies forward, shorten their stride, and bend their arms a little more and swing them less to save energy and speed. When going downhill, they lean back, lengthen their stride, and lower their forearms and swing them more, in order to keep contact with the ground.

1. Relaxation

The very straight position of the upper body gives a false impression of stiffness. On the contrary, athletes try to remain as relaxed as possible and maintain this position for general balance while walking.

2. Propulsion

The athlete pushes off his back leg and stretches the other leg forward, with a swing of the hip that causes the hip rotation characteristic of race walking. Energetic arm movements give the stride maximum amplitude, because they aid with balance as the weight is transferred.

3. Both feet on the ground

Before the back foot leaves the ground, the athlete puts his other foot on the ground. The feet are placed one in front of the other in a straight line.

4. Pull

By using his upper leg muscles and transferring his center of gravity, the athlete moves his body forward. Elite walkers may walk faster than 15 km/h.

Starting line

Finish line

Feeding station
Athletes may take water, with or without glucose added, and sponges at two or three feeding stations.

Judges
Six to 9 judges are posted along the route.

Chief judge
She makes sure that the competition runs smoothly, supervises the judges, and receives their requests.

Feeding station

Course
Walkers make two or three circuits of the track before leaving the stadium. The course is a loop that the athletes walk until they have reached the required kilometers. Races of 10 km are run on loops of up to 1.5 km, while loops for 20 and 50 km races may be a maximum of 2.5 km in length. The athletes cross the finish line after one circuit of the stadium track.

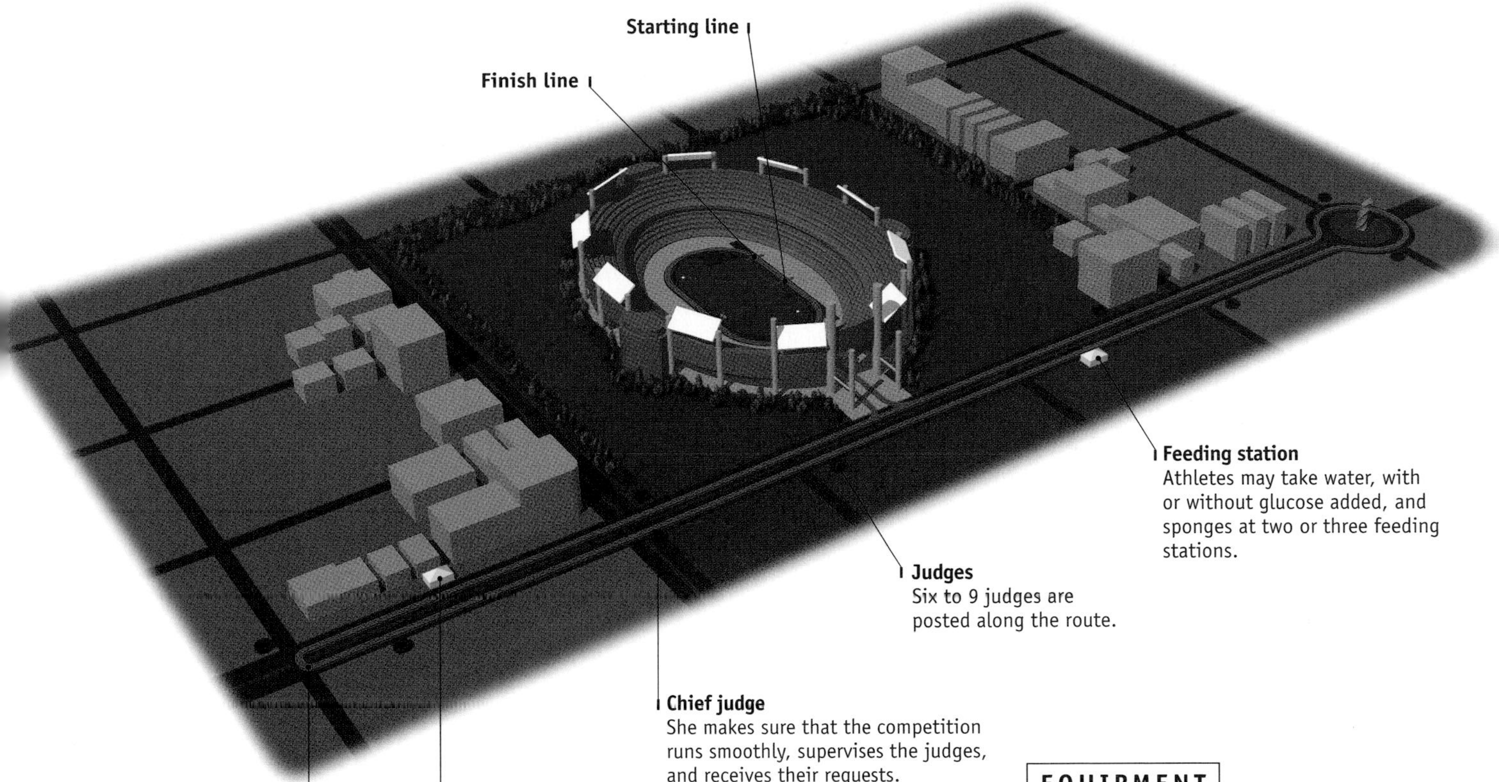

EQUIPMENT

Shoes
Race walking shoes are light, and the soles are thin to reduce friction with the ground.

ATHLETE PROFILE
• Athletes are light and slender. They must master a technique that is more complex than it looks, be flexible, and have endurance. Training includes walks of 2,000 to 5,000 m, sprints, and development of the thigh, abdominal, and back muscles.

20 km on track

CHANGES TO THE WORLD RECORD

Hours, minutes   M

1:50
1:40
1:30
1:20
1:10
1:00

1930 1940 1950 1960 1970 1980 1990
1918

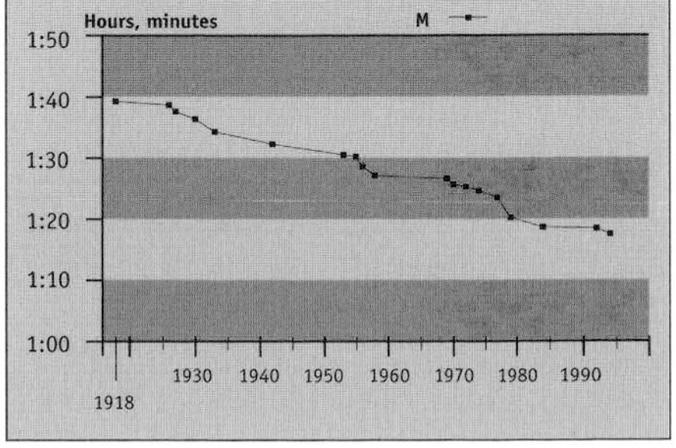

10 km on track

CHANGES TO THE WORLD RECORD

Hours, minutes   W

0:50
0:48
0:46
0:44
0:42
0:40
0:38

1990
1981

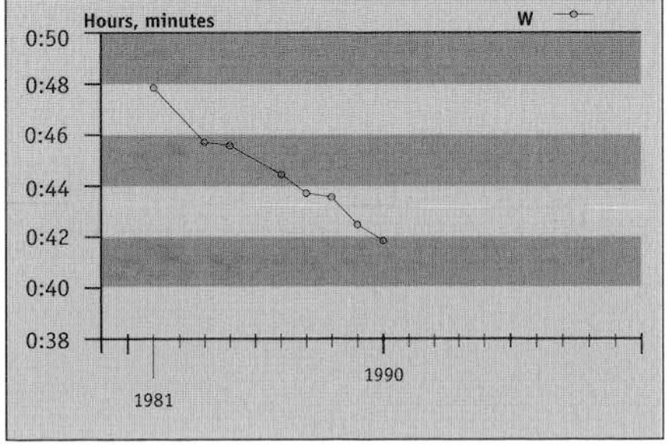

Maurizio Damilano (ITA),
World champion over 20 km in 1987 and 1991, and gold medalist at the Moscow Olympics in 1980.

5,000 meter and 10,000 meter

Start of the 5,000 m at the Amsterdam Olympics in 1928

In antiquity, the Olympic program included a long distance race, the dolichos, in which athletes had to run a distance of almost 5,000 meters as quickly as possible. From the 3 mile (4,828 meters) and 6 mile (9,656 meters) races run in England in the 19th century came the metric adaptations: the 5,000 and 10,000 meter races. In 1912, both races were included in the men's events at the Olympics in Stockholm. The women's 10,000 meter made its Olympic debut only in 1988, in Seoul, one year after it was included in the world championships in Rome. The women's Olympic 5,000 meter was run for the first time in Atlanta in 1996, replacing the women's 3,000 meter of the three previous Olympic Games.

THE COMPETITION

In the 5,000 m final, the 12 competitors run 200 m and then 12 laps of the track. In the 10,000 m, a maximum of 20 competitors complete each of the 25 laps of the race at a pace of between 63 and 68 seconds, although the last lap may be run in under 60 seconds.

Start 5,000 m

Start 10,000 m

TACTICS

Athletes avoid running the curves outside of the second lane so that they don't run a longer distance than their adversaries. Over a 5,000 m race, running just 0.5 m farther outside than necessary on each curve adds up to running 50 extra m.

Champions in the 5,000 m and 10,000 m cannot be just extremely fast starters or finishers. They must be able to call on their speed at different times, depending on the circumstances, their condition, and how the race unfolds. A winning racer knows how to force adversaries to break their rhythm and tire themselves out early.

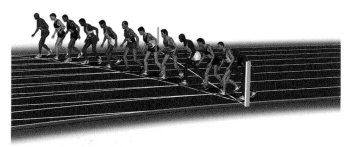

ATHLETE PROFILE

- At the international level, the male distance runner is about 5'6" and weighs 132 lbs.; women are 5'4" tall and weigh 110 lbs. They have the mental capacity for sustained, prolonged exertion.

- Training aims mainly to develop endurance by slow runs of between 1,000 and 10,000 m on varied terrain. To increase aerobic power – the level of energy produced through oxygenation of cells – they also run fast over distances of 400 to 1,000 m on the track.

- Specialists in the 5,000 m and 10,000 m generally run 10 to 30 km per day, in some cases at an average speed of more than 17 km/h.

5,000 m

CHANGES IN THE WORLD RECORD

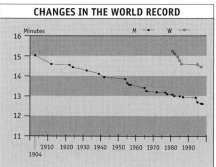

Minutes — M · W ○

16
15
14
13
12
11

1904 1910 1920 1930 1940 1950 1960 1970 1980 1990

10,000 m

CHANGES IN THE WORLD RECORD

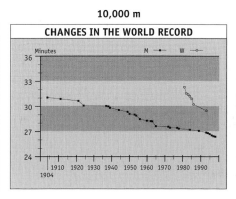

Minutes — M · W ○

36
33
30
27
24

1904 1910 1920 1930 1940 1950 1960 1970 1980 1990

Wang Junxia (CHN)
In 1993, she was world champion in the 10,000 m and the first woman to run the distance in under 30 min.

Emil Zátopek (CZE)
Nicknamed "the Czech locomotive," he was unbeaten from 1948 to 1954 over 10,000 m, was 4 times Olympic champion, and broke 18 world records.

cross-country

Cross-country is a long distance race run over rough terrain. The first cross-country championship, held in 1876, was a failure, since all of the runners got lost in the English countryside. International competition, between France and England, first took place in 1898; the Cross des Nations, predecessor of today's world championships, was inaugurated in 1903. Although they are no longer Olympic events, cross-country races were run in individual and team competitions from 1912 to 1924; women's international championships were held for the first time in 1967. In 1998, a short 4 km race (men and women) was added to the longer 12 km (men) and 8 km (women) races in the world championships. There are many variations of these very popular races. Competitions over difficult terrain, particularly on mountains, are held all over the world; they are most popular in Europe.

Vladimir Kuts (USSR), winner of the international cross-country race in Vincennes in 1957

THE COMPETITION

The number of competitors varies between 100 and more than 35,000. When the race is over, 2 finishing orders are established: individual and team. In the latter case, the placings of the teammates, usually 4, are added, and the lowest total determines the winning team.

CHANGES TO THE FACILITIES

The race course is generally 3 to 12 km. The start and finish lines are usually in the same place, and the course is a loop. For financial and practical reasons, official cross-country organizations are abandoning the countryside for stadiums; the courses are easier and the distance is about 12 km, run in almost 40 minutes.

Running on hilly terrain sprinkled with natural obstacles, athletes often also do battle with the weather.

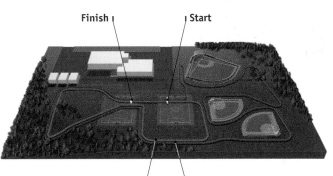

Finish   Start

1 km loop   2 km loop

EQUIPMENT

Shoes
Usually made of nylon, they have a maximum of 11 rubber cleats.

Kenya has won most cross-country world championships for men and women since 1986. Here is the 1998 winning men's team.

ATHLETE PROFILE

- Athletes' bodies are submitted to a tough test during the many climbs and descents and constant changes of rhythm. They must therefore be strong and enjoy extreme exertion.

- A natural extension of middle distance training, cross-country enables racers to strengthen joints and muscles, work on their balance, improve their respiration, and develop their endurance.

marathon

Athletes leave the Berlin Olympic Stadium for the marathon of the 1936 Olympics.

The marathon is the ultimate endurance test. In 490 B.C., the Athenian soldier Philippides died of exhaustion after running the 40 km from Marathon to Athens with news of the Greek victory over the Persians. To commemorate this feat, a race of about 40 km was included in the first Olympics of the modern era, in Athens in 1896. The distance of 42.195 km (26 miles, 385 yards) was run for the first time in 1908 at the London Olympics and officially adopted at the Paris Olympics of 1924. In the 1960s, a number of women, mainly Americans, repeatedly tried to take part in marathons, which had been the exclusive preserve of men. It was not until the following decade that women were officially allowed to enter such events as the New York and Boston marathons; in 1984, the first Olympic women's marathon was run in Los Angeles. Today, this test of pure endurance is one of the few in which men and women often run together.

THE COMPETITION

Some marathons draw more than 30,000 racers. Amateur runners and elite athletes all run together; the same rules apply to everyone.

The competitors in the Olympics and world championships usually start and finish on the 400 m track in the stadium. They run most of the race on roads and must deal with environmental factors such as heat, wind, pollution, and hills of various slopes.

TACTICS

To optimize their effort and avoid the two principal pitfalls, dehydration and exhaustion of their energy reserves, marathon runners constantly check that their pace is neither too fast nor too slow. Well-trained athletes monitor their pace during the first half of the race to ensure that they have the energy to run the second half of the race and a reserve for a finishing kick. Often, groups of runners formed at the beginning of the marathon dissolve as competitors attack and fatigue levels increase. Champions know how to conserve their energy and overcome their physical and mental exhaustion.

BOSTON MARATHON

Inaugurated on April 19, 1897, the Boston Marathon became an international sports event after the First World War. It has become one of the most prestigious marathons.

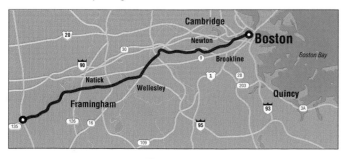

Marathon runner

Sprinter

During this test of endurance, short strides are most efficient. Unlike the sprinter, the marathon runner seeks stride frequency, not amplitude.

EQUIPMENT

Shoes

Lightweight (often less than 280 g per pair), they provide foot stability and absorb some of the shock caused by each stride.

CHANGES IN THE WORLD RECORD

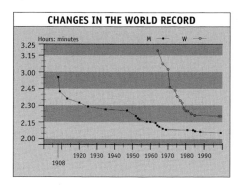

Hours: minutes   M ● ─■─   W ─○─

3.25
3.15
3.00
2.45
2.30
2.15
2.00

1908   1920 1930 1940 1950 1960 1970 1980 1990

MARATHON RUNNER PROFILE

- A light skeleton and a strong heart are two indispensable assets for the athlete. The main leg muscles used are the gemellus, quadriceps, and anterior tibial.

- The muscles cannot store enough energy reserves to run at great speed for the full distance, so many marathon runners follow a special diet in the days leading to a competition. They make a last intensive run to lower their muscular energy reserves, then reduce their consumption of carbohydrates (sugar in all forms) for one to three days by avoiding foods such as pasta, cereals, bread, and potatoes. Three days before the race, they increase their carbohydrate intake to the maximum. Eating and drinking during the race, by using the feeding stations set up along the route, is an important element in the athlete's success.

- Marathon runners' training aims at developing endurance and increasing aerobic power—the level of energy produced through oxygenation of cells. Training plans vary widely and may combine many repetitions of short distances (400–1,000 m) at a high speed, repetitions of middle distances (1,000–5,000 m), and runs of 10–40 km.

Competition number

Joan Benoit (USA)
Best world performance in the Boston Marathon in 1983; she won the first women's Olympic marathon in 1984 with a time of 2:24:52.

Abèbè Bikila (ETH)
A surprise at the 1960 Olympics in Rome, he won the gold medal running barefoot (2:15:16.2), eclipsing Emil Zátopec's Olympic record (2:23:03.2).

	First race session	Second race session
Monday	10–12 km in 40–50 min	• 1:30 h in forest, on hills, and on the flat at a comfortable pace, with speed sprints of 10–15 seconds
Tuesday	10–12 km in 40–50 min	• 20 min warm-up • In 1:04 h, three series of 5-6 laps of a 400 m track with a recovery lap between efforts and 2-3 recovery laps between the series. • 15 min cool-down
Wednesday	10–12 km in 40–50 min	• 2–2:15 h on the road at a comfortable pace, ending with 5 accelerations over 50–80 m
Thursday	10–12 km in 40–50 min	• 20 min warm-up • At the target pace for the next marathon, 8 periods of effort (3 x 2 km; 2 x 3 km; 1 x 4 km; 1 x 3 km; 1 x 2 km), separated by recovery periods of about 2 min • 15 min cool-down
Friday	10–12 km in 40–50 min	• 1:45–2 h on hills with several 1–2 min accelerations
Saturday	10–12 km in 40–50 min	• 1:30 h at a comfortable pace
Sunday	35–40 km at a pace of 3:10–3:20 min per km for the last hour	

TYPICAL WEEKLY TRAINING PLAN FOR AN ELITE INTERNATIONAL MARATHON RUNNER IN INTENSIVE PHASE

Feeding station
In hot weather, some marathon runners can lose up to 3 liters of water per hour through sweating. Feeding stations provide them with water and drinks containing carbohydrates, but they are still at risk of dehydration, as the body can absorb only 1 liter per hour, even under the best conditions.

javelin

A postcard portraying an ancient Greek javelin thrower, issued in 1920 to encourage Swiss participation in the Olympics in Anvers, Belgium

In this event, athletes throw the javelin as far as possible. Originally used in hunting and war, the javelin has been part of athletics since 708 B.C., when an olive wood javelin was thrown in two events: with a sling and at a target. In the 19th century, the Scandinavians developed the modern sport of javelin throwing. It was included for the first time in the track and field championships in England in 1906. In the modern era, it made its Olympic debut at the London Games in 1908, and the women's javelin was included in the Los Angeles Games in 1932.

THE COMPETITION

If there are 8 or fewer competitors, each gets 6 attempts. If there are more, each athlete throws the javelin 3 times, and the 8 with the longest throws make 3 more attempts. A throw is valid when the javelin touches the ground with the tip first, whether or not it sticks in the ground. Competitors are disqualified if they take more than 1.5 minutes to complete their attempt or leave the throwing area before the javelin lands.

Starting marker
Before he begins his attempt, the athlete places a marker to indicate where to start his run.

Midway marker
This marker, placed before the athlete starts the attempt, indicates where he should begin his run to plant.

Javelin grips
There are three main grips. In all of them, two fingers are placed behind the cord grip to hold the apparatus firmly.

TECHNIQUE

1. Start

The athlete visualizes the series of movements he will make. His throwing shoulder and arm are relaxed and his chest muscles are stretched.

2. Run-up

The thrower runs 10 to 12 very quick strides, accelerating to reach a speed of about 7 meters per second. He concentrates his energy and looks straight ahead, running to gain momentum.

3. Run to plant

The first step is stressed, and in the following strides, at least 5, the athlete turns to the side and his legs cross to provide maximum amplitude for the throw.

EQUIPMENT

Javelin

In the 1950s, Franck Held developed a new type of javelin with a bigger diameter. It flies more efficiently (and has increased distances by 3 to 6 m).

The javelin may be made of metal or wood, but it must have no moving parts that would change its center of gravity and make it easier to throw.

Shaft		Cord grip	Tip
	Men: 2.60–2.70 m/800 g		
	Women: 2.20–2.30 m/600 g		

CHANGES IN THE WORLD RECORD

Meters — M ● — W ○

110
100
90
80
70
60
50
40

1912 1920 1930 1940 1950 1960 1970 1980 1990

ATHLETE PROFILE

- Thinner than other throwers (men: height 6'2", weight 209 lbs; women: height 5'7", weight 154 lbs), international caliber athletes are good runners and have explosive muscular power.

- Throwing balls and weighted balls and exercises using elastic resistance are needed to develop coordination, flexibility, and balance.

- Throwers devote many hours to flexibility exercises for the throwing elbow, groin, throwing shoulder, ischium, adductors, and lumbars. Muscle building exercises and jumps complete the training program.

Jan Zelezny (CZE)
His throws of 89.66 m in Barcelona in 1992 and 88.16 m in Atlanta in 1996 made him a double Olympic gold medalist. He set a world record of 98.48 m in 1996.

FACILITIES

The run-up track ends at a curved white wood or metal strip. The throw is measured from the point of impact to the front of the stopboard.

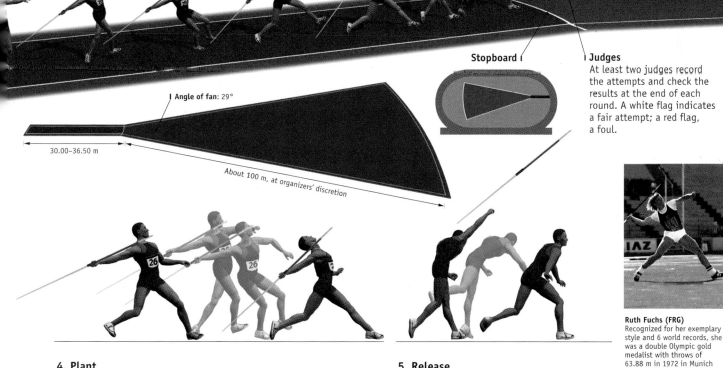

Angle of fan: 29°

30.00–36.50 m

About 100 m, at organizers' discretion

Stopboard

Judges
At least two judges record the attempts and check the results at the end of each round. A white flag indicates a fair attempt; a red flag, a foul.

Ruth Fuchs (FRG)
Recognized for her exemplary style and 6 world records, she was a double Olympic gold medalist with throws of 63.88 m in 1972 in Munich and 65.94 m in 1976 in Montreal.

4. Plant

In the last two strides, the feet touch the ground almost at the same time. The athlete keeps the javelin behind his shoulder as long as possible. His body is extremely tense for 0.04–0.06 seconds. He concentrates on relaxing his muscles and making as energetic a throw as possible.

5. Release

The athlete suddenly stops running and the javelin is thrown powerfully, in an explosive movement of the shoulder and arm muscles. Because of the extreme accuracy required for throwing the javelin, the thrower's arm must be very flexible. The optimal throwing angle for the javelin is between 25° and 40°. It flies almost 100 m at a speed of up to 31 meters per second, or 112 km/h.

Shoes
Made of light leather or nylon, they have a maximum of 11 cleats 4 mm in diameter and 12 mm long.

✶ discus

The winner of the discus competition is the athlete who throws the discus the farthest. The oldest of the throwing events, discus draws its inspiration from ancient warriors who threw their shields to shed weight before crossing a river. It was part of the pentathlon in the ancient Olympic Games in 708 B.C., and in *The Odyssey* Homer glowingly described Ulysses throwing the discus. Over the centuries, the Celts, Saxons, Scots, and English included the event in their traditional competitions, and athletes threw a wooden discus in the early 19th century in some Swiss cantons. The first Olympic medals for men's discus were awarded in the 1896 Olympics in Athens, and those for women's discus 32 years later, in Amsterdam in 1928. The discipline became part of the world track and field championships for men and women in 1983.

Roman copy of Discobolus, by Myron, dating from the second century B.C. (Museo Nazionale Romano, Italy)

THE COMPETITION

Athletes have 1.5 minutes to make a throw. Each competitor has 3 attempts, and the 8 with the best throws then make 3 more attempts. When the competition has 8 or fewer competitors, each makes 6 throws. The winner is the one who has made the longest throw without stepping outside of the throwing circle before the discus touches the ground.

Gripping the discus
The hand is placed flat on the discus, which is held at the end of slightly spread fingers, with the thumb used for balance. During the throw, the speed of rotation keeps the discus under the hand.

ı Protective cage

TECHNIQUE

1. Swing

In a swinging, rhythmic action, the athlete moves the discus back and forth in a movement that follows the arc of the rotation to come. His arms and shoulders are relaxed and he concentrates intensely.

2. Spin

During a one-and-a-half-turn rotation, the athlete's body accumulates as much energy as possible. A right-handed thrower pushes powerfully off his left leg, while his left arm acts as a counterweight along the axis of the shoulders. His feet leave the ground momentarily.

3. Drive

Up to the last moment, the trunk and arms are behind the movement of the feet, legs, and hips. To maintain his balance during this short but complex movement, the thrower spots a fixed visual reference.

4. Release

Using his right leg as a lever, the athlete quickly straightens his body. The discus is released in an explosive motion as the arm is whipped around.

CHANGES IN THE WORLD RECORD

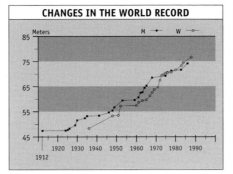

Meters — M — W

85 75 65 55 45

1912 1920 1930 1940 1950 1960 1970 1980 1990

Alfred Oerter (USA)
Dominated the world scene for four Olympics, winning gold each time: 1956, 1960, 1964, and 1968.

Martina Hellmann (GDR)
World champion in 1983 and 1987, she won gold at the 1988 Olympics in Seoul, with a 72.30 m throw.

Discus fan

80–100 m, at organizers' discretion

THROWING AREA

The throwing circle is partly enclosed in a protective cage made of panels of natural-fiber cord, synthetic-fiber cord, or metal wire. In 1958, to limit the danger posed by increasingly powerful throws, the angle of the discus fan was reduced from 90° to 60°. In 1970, the angle was reduced to 40°, requiring even greater technical mastery by athletes.

Throwing circle

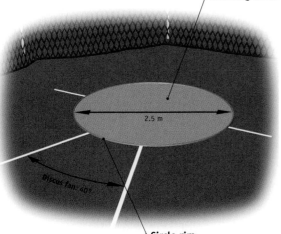

2.5 m

Discus fan: 40°

Circle rim

Judges
During international competitions, at least two judges record the attempts and verify the results at the end of each round. One official indicates whether the attempt is valid, raising a white flag for a successful attempt, red for a foul. An attempt is unsuccessful if the thrower leaves the circle before the discus touches the ground, if his foot touches the circle rim, or if the throw lands outside the discus fan.

EQUIPMENT

Shoes
Made of suede or leather, they have flexible soles and no cleats, to allow maximum adherence to the cement surface of the throwing circle.

Discus
Made of wood or another suitable material, rimmed with iron, with inlaid circular metal plates in the center of both sides. During major international competitions, only discuses supplied by the organizers are used.

Men
Weight: 2 kg

Women
Weight: 1 kg

219–221 mm
Thickness: 44–46 mm

180–182 mm
Thickness: 37–39 mm

hammer

Matthew McGrath (USA), gold medalist in the hammer throw at the Stockholm Olympics in 1912

In this event, the thrower propels the hammer as far as possible. The Tailteann Games, held in ancient Ireland, included throwing the roth cleas, a cartwheel with a handle on its axle. The wheel was soon replaced by a stone attached to a stick, then in the 14th century by a blacksmith's sledgehammer. The event was included in the meets at Oxford and Cambridge in 1866, and the English track and field championships added the hammer throw in 1875. The first Olympic medals were awarded in Paris in 1900, when the blacksmith's hammer was replaced by the ball-shaped hammer we know today. It was not until 1999, in Seville, that women's hammer throw was an official event in the world championships, and it made its Olympic debut in Sydney in 2000.

THE COMPETITION

Competitors have 1.5 min to make each of their 3 attempts. The athletes with the 8 best attempts make 3 more throws. The winner is the athlete with the longest throw. If there is a tie, placings are decided according to the second best throw.

TECHNIQUE

Gripping the hammer
The athlete uses a leather glove with thick fingers to ensure a solid grip.

1. Swing

His back to the hammer fan, the athlete swings the hammer in a pendulum movement. He concentrates intently and makes sure his muscles are relaxed.

2. Windmill sequence

The thrower swings the hammer in 2 or 3 rotations, using his arms and upper body. His shoulder muscles remain very relaxed. These swings bring the hammer up to 55% to 65% of its speed at release and enable the athlete to find his balance.

3. Spin

The athlete begins his first spin using his legs. The following 2 to 3 rotations accelerate the thrower and hammer. With the high speed of rotation, centrifugal force on the athlete can exceed 3 times his body weight. Between the beginning of the windmill motion and the throw, the hammer travels more than 80 m.

4. Release

After the third or fourth rotation, the athlete's legs straighten, his spine stretches, and his arms violently shoot upward. The fingers release their grip and the hammer is thrown at an angle of almost 45° at a speed of up to 30 meters per second (112 km/h).

John Flanagan (USA)
Gold medalist in 1900, 1904, and 1908, he is the only hammer thrower to win triple Olympic gold.

Yuriy Sedykh (USSR)
Holder of the world record a number of times since 1980, he was a double Olympic gold medalist in 1976 and 1980.

ATHLETE PROFILE

- Athletes must have concentration, relaxation, and flexibility as well as strength, quickness, excellent coordination, and a superb sense of balance.

- In addition to hundreds of throws every week, athletes devote many hours to muscle building (weights and barbells), races, hurdles, jumps, and flexibility exercises.

- The best male hammer throwers are on average 6'1" tall and weigh 243 lbs. Women generally are 5'7" tall and weigh 176 lbs. They are the most powerful athletes in the throwing events.

CHANGES IN THE WORLD RECORD

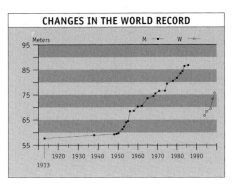

Hammer fan

Judges
In international competitions, at least two judges record all attempts and verify the results at the end of each round. A white flag is raised if the attempt is fair; a red flag, if it is a foul. An attempt is a foul if the thrower leaves the throwing circle before the hammer touches the ground, if his foot touches the circle rim, or if the throw lands outside the hammer fan.

80–100 m, at organizers' discretion

THROWING AREA

The concrete throwing circle is partly enclosed in a protective cage made of panels of cord, or metal wire, which protects officials and spectators from these spectacular and dangerous throws. Because throws have increased in distance, the angle of the hammer fan was reduced for safety reasons from 90° to 60° in 1958, to 45° in 1965, and finally to 40° in 1970. This reduced angle requires even greater technical mastery on the part of the athlete.

EQUIPMENT

Hammer
The head, linked to a handle by a steel wire, is made of brass or of another solid, dense material and covered with a thin layer of metal.

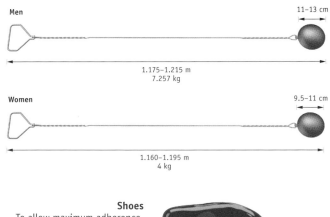

Men

11–13 cm

1.175–1.215 m
7.257 kg

Women

9.5–11 cm

1.160–1.195 m
4 kg

Throwing circle

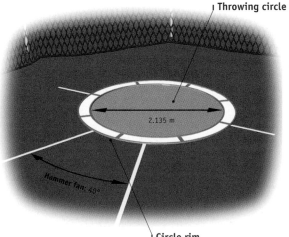

2.135 m

Hammer fan: 40°

Circle rim

Shoes
To allow maximum adherence, the soles have no cleats. The rounded edge of the sole makes rotation easier.

shot put

Through the ages, throwers have always had the same goal: to propel an object as far as possible. The shot put competition is directly descended from throwing a heavy stone, a war technique used in antiquity. After cannons were invented in the 14th century, cast iron balls replaced the stones, and it was this type of ball that was used in track and field in British colleges around 1850. The men's shot put was an event in the 1896 Olympics in Athens; women's shot put was first included in the Olympics in London in 1948.

Ralph Rose (USA), shot put champion at the London Olympics in 1908

THE COMPETITION

To qualify, competitors make 3 throws. Those who have made the best 8 throws make 3 more attempts. When the competition has 8 competitors or fewer, they are all allowed 6 throws each. In international competition, at least 2 judges record the attempts and verify the results at the end of each round. A white flag indicates that the throw is good, while a red flag means that it was a foul (if the throw is out of the landing area, if the athlete leaves the throwing circle before the shot lands, or if the athlete's foot touches the top of the stopboard).

SHOT PUT FAN

Landing area
In 1969, its angle was reduced from 45° to 40°.

About 30 m, at organizers' discretion

O'BRIEN TECHNIQUE

In 1952, American Parry O'Brien began his throws with his back to the shot put fan. Because this gave him an extra quarter-turn, it increased his propulsion and improved his performances by about 1 m.

Gripping the Shot
The shot is held in an open hand, resting at the base of the fingers, which are bent and slightly spread. During the putting phase, the shot must never be taken behind the line of the shoulder. The optimal putting angle is slightly more than 40°.

1. Starting position

The athlete is relaxed and concentrates intensely. All of his weight is on his supporting leg and his starting position is as stable as possible. He has 1.5 minutes to complete his throw.

2. Crouch

The athlete coils his body like a spring. The ankle remains flexible in anticipation of the energetic movement that will follow.

3. Shift

The free leg stretches out behind as the supporting leg pushes off. The athlete accelerates horizontally, moving as straight as possible, then rotates his hips and trunk. He continues to face the back of the circle as long as possible.

4. Thrust

The athlete locks his legs and pushes powerfully, energetically engaging the shoulder and chest muscles. A sudden extension of his putting arm propels the shot; the best shot putters throw at a speed of up to 14 meters per second (50 km/h).

CHANGES IN THE WORLD RECORD

Meters — M ● W ○

26
24
22
20
18
16
14

1909 1920 1930 1940 1950 1960 1970 1980 1990

ATHLETE PROFILE

- The best male shot putters have an average height of 6'2" and weigh 277 lbs; for women, the average height is 5'9" and average weight is 198 lbs. Shot putters have very strong abdominal, lumbar, and back muscles.

- Shot putters must be strong, quick, and flexible and have excellent coordination, sense of balance, and technique.

- In training, athletes put shots and throw balls of various weights hundreds of times a week. Many hours are devoted to muscular development: weights and barbells, jumps, running.

EQUIPMENT

Shot
It has a smooth surface and is made of bronze, copper, or a similar metal. It may also be made of another material and covered with a thin layer of metal.

Minimum legal weight

Men 7.3 kg	Women 4 kg
11–13 cm	9.5–11 cm

Shoes
They are made of leather or suede and offer maximum support to a stocky athlete. They do not have cleats, since the surface of the throwing circle is cement. The flat sole offers maximum stability.

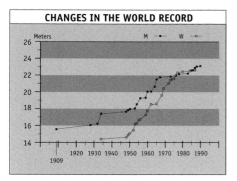

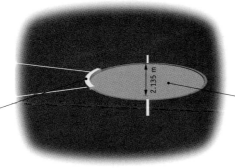

Stopboard
Length: 1.21–1.23 m
Width: 11.2–30 cm
Height: 10 cm higher than the inside of the circle.

2.135 m

Throwing circle
In 1908, the throwing area was changed from a square to a circle. The following year, a stopboard was added to give shot putters a point of support for their foot.

BARYSHNIKOV TECHNIQUE

In 1972, Russian Alexsandr Baryshnikov developed a technique involving a spin similar to that used by discus throwers. The rotation provides energy that enables the athlete to propel the shot at greater speed when it is concentrated at the moment of release. It is the most popular technique today.

Parry O'Brien (USA)
Olympic double gold medalist in shot put, in 1952 in Helsinki and 1956 in Melbourne.

1. Push-off

The upper body is positioned similarly to the O'Brien technique and the shot is held the same way, but the legs are placed as if for the discus throw.

2. Spin

In an explosive spinning push, the athlete coordinates with extreme precision the twisting of his body and the optimal muscle tension in his legs, arms, and putting hand.

3. Thrust

Poorly channeled, the energy resulting from the spin can carry the athlete outside the circle or send the shot off trajectory. The attempt is a foul if the athlete touches the top of the stopboard or leaves the circle before the shot has touched the ground.

Tamara Press (USSR)
She set 12 world records and was a double medalist at the 1964 Olympics in Tokyo.

29

high jump

The high jump facilities at the Los Angeles Olympics in 1932

The high jump consists of clearing a horizontal bar without knocking it down, using only the strength of one's body. The Celts held high jump competitions hundreds of years ago, and it became an official event in 1840, in Great Britain. After the rules were written, in 1865, the high jump became part of the Olympics in 1896 in Athens. The first women's competition took place in 1895 in the United States, and women competed in the Olympics for the first time in 1928 in Amsterdam.

THE COMPETITION

A draw determines the order in which athletes will jump. Officials raise the bar by 5 cm at a time, then reduce the difference in height to a minimum of 2 cm. The event organizers set a minimum qualifying height, which must be jumped successfully in a maximum of 3 attempts; athletes have 1.5 minutes for each attempt. For strategic reasons, a competitor may choose not to jump the qualifying height and begin to make attempts once the bar is raised. Once the first height has been successfully cleared, the athlete may jump any of the ensuing heights at will. The jump must be made off one foot only. An athlete is eliminated from competition after 3 successive failures.

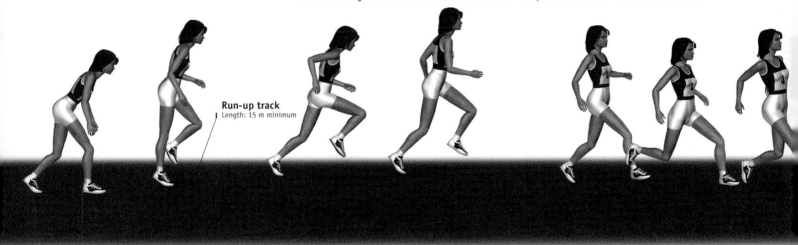

Run-up track
Length: 15 m minimum

1. Start

Before starting, the athlete spots on the ground the exact place where she will begin her run, make her curve, and take off as a function of how many strides she will take. High jumpers run an average of 12 m between the start and the bar.

2. Approach

The athlete accelerates for about 7 long strides, during which her speed might reach 8 meters per second. In the next 3 to 5 strides, she resists the force of the curve so that she does not slow down. She begins to increase the frequency of her strides.

3. Link between approach and takeoff

In the second-to-last stride, the leg on the outside of the turn is bent, while the other leg, which will become the takeoff leg, is fully extended.

EQUIPMENT

Shoes
The sole must be no more than 13 mm thick; it has cleats under the ball of the foot and the heel. The athlete may wear a normal running shoe on the other foot.

Crossbar
3.98 m; 2 kg

3 m

5 m

Javier Sotomayor (CUB)
World record holder in 1993 (2.45 m). This athlete, 1.96 m tall, has jumped higher than his own height by 49 cm.

Stefka Kostadinova (BUL)
World champion in 1995 and world record holder since 1987 (2.09 m).

CHANGES IN PERFORMANCE

Since the Mexico City Olympics in 1968, the high jump has been revolutionized thanks to a new jumping technique developed by American champion Dick Fosbury. Jumping with the back to the bar, was made possible by the introduction of the mattress that year.

1874
Marshall Brooks (GBR)
1.80 m
Standing jump, feet first

1895
Michael Sweeney (USA)
1.97 m
Scissors

1912
George Horine (USA)
2 m
Western roll

1968
Dick Fosbury (USA)
2.24 m
Fosbury Flop

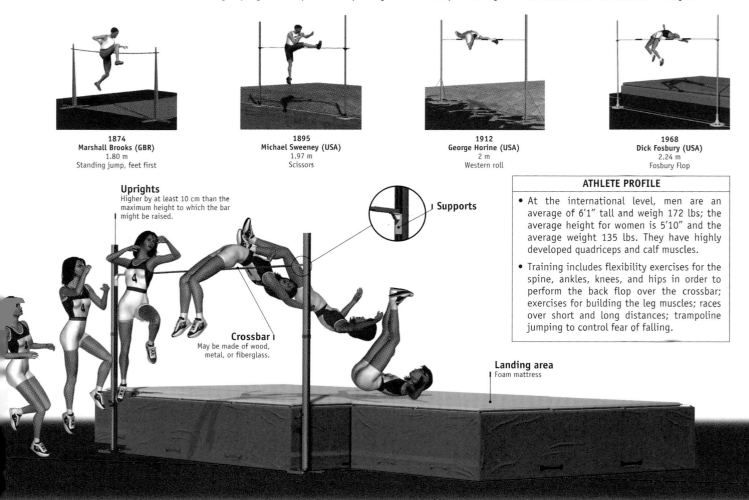

Uprights
Higher by at least 10 cm than the maximum height to which the bar might be raised.

Supports

Crossbar
May be made of wood, metal, or fiberglass.

Landing area
Foam mattress

ATHLETE PROFILE

- At the international level, men are an average of 6'1" tall and weigh 172 lbs; the average height for women is 5'10" and the average weight 135 lbs. They have highly developed quadriceps and calf muscles.

- Training includes flexibility exercises for the spine, ankles, knees, and hips in order to perform the back flop over the crossbar; exercises for building the leg muscles; races over short and long distances; trampoline jumping to control fear of falling.

4. Takeoff

The athlete pushes strongly off the takeoff leg. This push enables her to prepare for the rotation that she will make with her legs, hips, and shoulders.

5. Drive

This is the extension of the takeoff. The athlete relaxes her body to concentrate on position and continues her rotation by raising her free leg to the level of her takeoff leg to prepare for achieving a horizontal position with her back to the crossbar.

6. Arch

By tipping her shoulders back and bringing her heels under her thighs, the athlete arches her body, enabling her hips to rise over the crossbar. The athlete's center of gravity is sometimes underneath the bar.

7. Landing

When her hips have passed the bar, the athlete strongly flexes her hips, which raises her chest and legs very rapidly. Forming this angle with her body enables her to avoid contact with the crossbar and prepare for landing on her shoulders.

pole vault

In Anvers in 1920, Frank Foss (USA) jumped 4.09 m.

This event involves using a flexible pole to clear a bar set as high as possible. The pole vault is the only jumping event that involves using a tool to achieve height. According to historians, the origins of the pole vault may go back to antiquity. It became an official event in 1812 during the first track and field meets in England, and was in the Cambridge University championships in 1857. Although the women's pole vault was introduced just a few years later, the women's competition did not become an Olympic event until Sydney in 2000. Women do, however, compete in the pole vault in the world championships, the Commonwealth Games, and the World University Championships.

THE COMPETITION

Event organizers decide on and announce the initial height of the bar and the increases in each round. The order of competition is decided by draw. Pole vaulters can begin to jump at any height they choose and attempt any subsequent height at will. Athletes are eliminated after 3 consecutive failed attempts at any height (except in the case of a tie for first place).

CHANGES IN PERFORMANCE

Of all track and field events, pole vault is the one in which performance improvements have been most directly related to the material used.

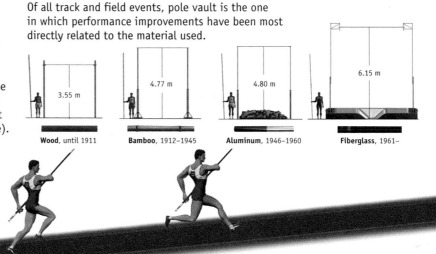

Wood, until 1911 — 3.55 m
Bamboo, 1912–1945 — 4.77 m
Aluminum, 1946–1960 — 4.80 m
Fiberglass, 1961– — 6.15 m

RUN-UP AND FLIGHT

1. Start
The athlete grips the pole between 4.9 m and 5.1 m from the end. He begins his run balancing the pole at an angle.

2. Seeking speed
The pole vaulter accelerates, increasing stride speed and length to reach maximum speed (32–34 km/h). The faster the run-up, the higher the jump.

3. Seeking impulsive energy
He gradually lowers the pole and prepares it for the plant. Once the pole is in a horizontal position, it causes the athlete to lose balance, and he slows to a speed of about 28 km/h.

POLE

The pole can be made of any material as long as its surface is smooth. There are no length or diameter restrictions. Although they are heavier than aluminum poles, carbon-fiber and fiberglass poles are preferred because they spring back and absorb vibration better, offering better propulsion. Athletes' size, weight, height, and speed are aspects considered when they select a pole. Athletes generally bring 3 poles to competitions in case one or two break.

Maximum of two layers of adhesive tape

Length : athlete's choice

The crossbar rests on pegs.

Brackets

Crossbar
4.48–4.52 m

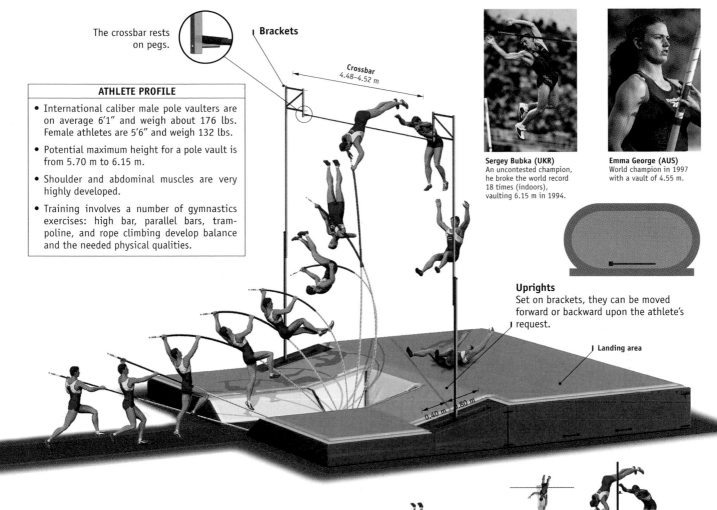

Sergey Bubka (UKR)
An uncontested champion, he broke the world record 18 times (indoors), vaulting 6.15 m in 1994.

Emma George (AUS)
World champion in 1997 with a vault of 4.55 m.

Uprights
Set on brackets, they can be moved forward or backward upon the athlete's request.

Landing area

0.40 m 0.80 m

4. Takeoff

As the jump starts, the pole vaulter rises off the ground at a 20° angle. At the same time, the pole bends under his weight.

5. Flight

The flexibility of the pole, combined with the athlete's energy, thrusts him into a handstand position. He increases his upward motion by extending his hips and legs.

6. Clearing the bar

The athlete pivots so that he is facing the bar as he clears it, giving a powerful push on the pole with his arms before letting it go.

JUMPING AREA

Competitors may place markers beside the run-up track, as long as they are not on the track itself.

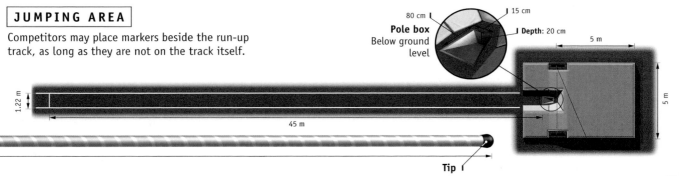

80 cm   15 cm
Pole box
Below ground level
Depth: 20 cm
5 m

1.22 m

45 m

5 m

Tip

🏃 long jump

Bob Beamon (USA) established a world record in 1968 that remained unbeaten for almost 23 years: 8.90 m, 55 cm longer than the preceding record.

The long jump consists of covering the greatest distance possible by making an energetic jump at the end of a high speed sprint. As long ago as 2000 B.C., the event was part of some Celtic games; the first record, 6.92 meters, was established by Chionis, a Spartan athlete, at the Olympics in 656 B.C. The long jump was included in the first track and field competitions at Exeter College at Oxford in 1850 and has been an Olympic event since the first modern Games, in Athens in 1896. The women's long jump has been part of the Olympics since the 1948 Games in London.

THE COMPETITION

Each qualified competitor makes 3 jumps in an order determined by a draw. Athletes have 1.5 minutes to make each jump. The jumpers with the 8 best attempts go on to make 3 more jumps. The ranking is established according to each competitor's best jump.

Takeoff board
A band of Plasticine is placed after the takeoff board, and officials check to make sure that the jumper did not leave a mark on it.

TECHNIQUE

1. Approach

The athlete accelerates. His body is relaxed and he takes long strides.

2. Link between approach and takeoff

As the athlete's strides quicken, his knees get higher and his body is upright. Maximum speed is reached in the 2 strides before takeoff.

3. Takeoff

The athlete lengthens his second-to-last stride to begin his final propulsion. He pushes off from one foot, placed flat on the takeoff board, while his shoulders rise to help him attain height and his arms remain in a running position. The horizontal speed of some champions can reach 10.7 meters per second.

- Athletes are excellent sprinters at both the 100 m and 200 m distances. At the international level, men's average height is 6'1" and average weight is 172 lbs; for women, these figures are 5'8" and 130 lbs.

- Training includes sprints over 20 to 40 m and longer distances on the track, with changes in stride frequency and length. Jumping, skipping, throwing the medicine ball, and stretching and muscle building sessions targeting the legs are essential.

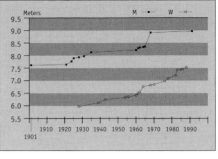

CHANGES IN THE WORLD RECORD

FACILITIES

Run-up track: 40 m minimum   1 m

1.22 m   2.75 m

Takeoff board

Landing area
9 m minimum

EQUIPMENT

Shoes
Athletes may exert up to 360 kg of pressure on the takeoff board. The shoes must therefore be designed to hold the foot very firmly and discourage twisting, while cleats ensure traction and stability.

Landing area
Its surface is raked after each jump, so that it is at the same level as the runway. The distance jumped is measured from the front edge of the takeoff board to the closest imprint to the board left by the athlete in the sand.

Marion Jones (USA)
On the professional track and field circuit created in 1997, she was the first American woman to win three different events (100 m, 200 m, and long jump) at the prestigious Jesse Owens International Trophy Award.

Carl Lewis (USA)
He won 4 consecutive Olympic gold medals in 1984, 1988, 1992, and 1996.

4. Flight
The movements the athlete makes when he is in the air do not change his trajectory but keep him from tipping forward. The hitch kick (shown above) or extension styles help him keep his balance and prepare for the best possible landing so that the jump is not unnecessarily shortened.

5. Landing
The athlete throws his legs and arms forward to land as far as possible from the takeoff board. The best athletes land almost 9 m from the takeoff board.

Judges
During international competitions, at least two judges record all attempts and verify the results at the end of each round. After each attempt, a judge raises a white flag if the jump was successful or a red flag if there was a foul. The jump is a foul if the athlete places his foot beyond or beside the takeoff board, steps back in the landing area after the jump, or somersaults during the jump.

triple jump

The triple jump, a long jump preceded by a hop and a step, is probably the result of a poor interpretation of ancient athletics. The Greeks added the results of the three best performances in the long jump competition, which may have led to the belief that athletes performed a triple jump. In the 19th century, the Irish competed in a triple jump, from a standing or running start, consisting of a hop, a step, and a jump landed on both feet. In 1860, the English and Americans codified the triple jump, performed from a running start, and the competition was part of the English athletics championships in 1875. It was on the program at the first modern Olympics in 1896. The first women's triple jump competition in the track and field world championships took place in 1993; at the Olympics, in 1996.

Chuhei Nambu (JAP), gold medalist in the triple jump (15.72 m) at the Los Angeles Olympics in 1932

THE COMPETITION

In qualifying, athletes have 3 attempts. Those with the 8 best jumps go to the final, where they are allowed 3 attempts. A successful jump is signaled with a white flag; a foul, with a red flag. Before an attempt, the athlete is allowed to place two markers on the side of the runway. The attempt, which must take place within 1.5 minutes, is a foul if the athlete begins the attempt after having passed the takeoff board or does not reach the landing area at the end of the attempt. An attempt is measured from the front edge of the takeoff board to the closest imprint to the board left by the athlete in the landing area, and the ranking is established according to each competitor's best attempt.

TECHNIQUE

The effort must be well distributed between the 3 jumps, since each phase affects the next one and thus the final result. On average, the distance covered by each jump is in the following proportions: 37%, 30%, 33%.

Takeoff board
A band of Plasticine is placed after the takeoff board so that officials can check to make sure that the jumper did not leave a mark on it.

20 cm

I **Plasticine band:** 10 cm

1. Approach

The length of the approach sprint is not limited, but athletes generally choose to run about 40 m. They run for 6 or 7 strides, then take another dozen to perform a controlled acceleration. If they have too much speed, they will lose their balance when they start the jump.

2. Hop

The athlete places his foot on the takeoff board without looking at it, which would slow him down. His impetus is more horizontal than vertical. While he is in the air, he uses his arms to keep his balance as the takeoff leg goes from behind him to in front of him.

3. Step

Almost as soon as his landing leg pushes off, the knee of the jumper's free leg moves forward as he stretches to jump as far as possible.

ATHLETE PROFILE

- Athletes should have speed, power, coordination, relaxation, and flexibility. For men, average height is 6' and average weight is 165 lbs, for women, average height is 5'8" and average weight is 135 lbs.

- Because the triple jump involves both sprinting and long jumping, athletes follow part of the training program for the 100 m sprint, do flexibility and balance exercises, and throw balls. Muscle building is aimed at strengthening the legs.

Adhemar Ferreira da Silva (BRA)
Olympic champion at the Olympic Games in Helsinki in 1952 and Melbourne in 1956.

Viktor Saneyev (USSR)
He won gold at the Olympics in Mexico City in 1968, Munich in 1972, and Montreal in 1976, and established a world record in 1972.

CHANGES IN THE WORLD RECORD

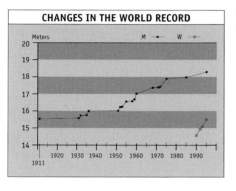

EQUIPMENT

Shoes
With a maximum of 11 9-mm cleats, they firmly support the feet on landing.

Landing area
Its surface is raked after each jump, so that it is at the same level as the runway. The distance jumped is measured from the front edge of the takeoff board to the closest imprint to the board left by the athlete in the sand.

FACILITIES

Takeoff board

1.22–1.25 m

2.75 m

Minimum 40 m

Minimum 13 m (men), 11 m (women)

10 m

Runway

Officials
During international competitions, at least 2 officials record the attempts and verify the results at the end of each round.

4. Jump

The athlete jumps off one foot. He uses a long jumping technique, but at a lower speed.

5. Landing

After extending or hitch-kicking, the jumper brings his legs forward. The best triple jumpers cover a distance of up to 18 m between the takeoff board and the landing area.

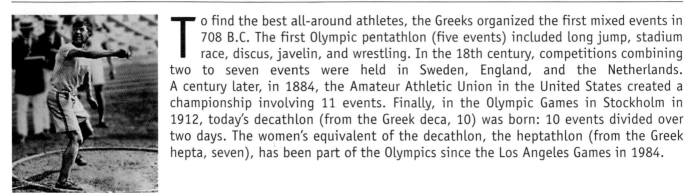

heptathlon and decathlon

To find the best all-around athletes, the Greeks organized the first mixed events in 708 B.C. The first Olympic pentathlon (five events) included long jump, stadium race, discus, javelin, and wrestling. In the 18th century, competitions combining two to seven events were held in Sweden, England, and the Netherlands. A century later, in 1884, the Amateur Athletic Union in the United States created a championship involving 11 events. Finally, in the Olympic Games in Stockholm in 1912, today's decathlon (from the Greek deca, 10) was born: 10 events divided over two days. The women's equivalent of the decathlon, the heptathlon (from the Greek hepta, seven), has been part of the Olympics since the Los Angeles Games in 1984.

Jim Thorpe (USA), decathlon gold medalist at the 1912 Stockholm Olympics

THE COMPETITION

The rules for each individual event apply to the events in the decathlon and heptathlon, except that each competitor gets 3 attempts rather than 6 in the throwing events and the long jump, and it takes 3 false starts for an athlete to be eliminated from the races. The events and the order in which they are run were decided in 1912. Because track and field events alternate, athletes can recover between events. The long races take place at the end of the day for two reasons: they are the most exhausting, and they are more exciting than the short races, providing extra motivation for the athletes. A day of competition takes, on average, 8 to 10 hours.

Athletes win points in each event according to a points table set by the International Amateur Athletics Federation. A heptathlete can accumulate a maximum of 9,971 points; a decathlete, 13,471 points. The winner is the athlete with the most points.

THE EVENTS

HEPTATHLON

Day 1

1. 100 m hurdles
Maximum 1,361 points

2. High jump
Maximum 1,498 points

3. Shot put
Maximum 1,500 points

4. 200 m
Maximum 1,342 points

Day 2

5. Long jump
Maximum 1,520 points

6. Javelin
Maximum 1,500 points

7. 800 m
Maximum 1,250 points

DECATHLON

Day 1

1. 100 m
Maximum 1,223 points

2. Long jump
Maximum 1,461 points

3. Shot put
Maximum 1,350 points

4. High jump
Maximum 1,392 points

5. 400 m
Maximum 1,250 points

Day 2

6. 100 m hurdles
Maximum 1,249 points

7. Discus
Maximum 1,500 points

8. Pole vault
Maximum 1,396 points

9. Javelin
Maximum 1,400 points

10. 1,500 m
Maximum 1,250 points

RECORDS

Since the 1970s, performances by decathletes and heptathletes have become closer and closer to those of event specialists. There is still a gap of about 15%, however, since overspecialization in one event would contradict the mixed-event athlete's goal, which is to obtain all-round development in order to garner the maximum possible points.

The largest gaps are in the throwing events, in which results are lower by about 30%. For example, the best world performance in javelin in the decathlon was 69.98 m in 1993, while the world record set in 1992 was 91.46 m.

Jackie Joyner-Kersee (USA)
Silver medalist at the Los Angeles Olympics in 1984, 4 years later she set a world record with a total of 7,291 points. In Barcelona in 1992, she won the gold medal.

ATHLETE PROFILE

- Athletes combine speed and endurance, energy and stability, brute strength and lightness, power and relaxation.

- It takes years of training to excel in one discipline, and even longer to excel in several. Athletes with the best performances are generally 25–28 years old.

- The morphological profile is comparative: larger and heavier than a sprinter, shorter than a jumper, heavier than a middle distance runner, lighter than a thrower. The result is an average height of 6'1" and weight of 187 lbs for decathletes; height of 5'7" and weight of 150 lbs for heptathletes.

- The training program has four main sections: running, muscle building, jumping, and throwing.

- Running training uses a variety of distances (30–400 m) and intensities, with recovery times. Types of runs include building speed, speed heats, and long distance.

- The muscles targeted for strengthening are the extensors of the legs, in particular around the ankle joint, and the extensor and flexor muscles of the arms, especially those of the hand, which are needed in four of the events.

Dan O'Brien (USA)
Best decathlete of the 1990s, he was world champion in 1991, 1993, and 1995, and set a world record in 1992 with 8,891 points. He was gold medalist at the Atlanta Olympics in 1996.

Cycling

road racing

Individual 320-km race around Lake Mälaren at the Olympics in Stockholm in 1912.

The first sketch of a bicycle with two spoked wheels, pedals and a chain transmission would have been drawn in Italy by Leonardo da Vinci in the late 15th century. The technology of the time, however, did not allow its inventor to go beyond the paper stage. In 1817, Karl Von Drais invented an apparatus which used a pivot on the front wheel so that it could be powered by the feet; his innovation was called the draisienne. The first pedal bicycle was built in 1839. In 1861, a crank was added to the front wheel, and after that various technical improvements were made: wheels with metal spokes, solid rubber tires, brakes, and dérailleur gears. In 1885, propulsion was moved to the back wheel, and three years later the Irishman J.B. Dunlop developed the hollow tire with an inner tube. The first road race took place in France between Paris and Rouen, in 1869. The Union vélocipède de France was founded in February 1881; in 1895, the first speed racing world championships were held. As for road racing, world championships did not start before 1927. In 1896, six cycling races were included in the first modern Olympics, including three road races, all for men only: 10 km, 100 km, and a 12 hour race. Women's world championships were first held in 1958, and women's cycling became an Olympic event in Los Angeles in 1984.

THE RACE

Racers ride bicycles over a given distance as quickly as possible. The main objective is to cross the finish line ahead of the other competitors. Even though the results are recorded for individuals, racers form teams of 6 to 10 cyclists. Teamwork is essential: racers on a team must often help their best racer or put him in an ideal position to win a race, for example by controlling breakaways by opponents.

Team car
Each team has several cars for its coach, mechanics, and trainers. This way, the coach can stay close enough to his team during the race to supply them with food and give them instructions.

Peloton
Depending on the race, it may contain more than 150 racers. If there is a breakaway, cyclists on opposing teams try to draw the peloton in pursuit.

CUPS AND CHAMPIONSHIPS

Road races are divided into four types, depending on duration and format. The Men's World Cup (created in 1989) is an annual ranking according to points earned in a 10 race season. These races are all "classics" (tour races and world championships are not included). Racers score from 1 to 100 points depending on their final placing in each race. The Women's World Cup (created in 1998) is an annual ranking according to points earned in 9 classic races; racers earn from 1 to 75 points depending on their final placings in these races.

1. Circuit races

Racers ride a defined number of laps on a predetermined road course. The circuit may have various challenges (hills). The race, with a group start, is held in a single day. The main circuit race for men is the world championship, which has been run since 1927 on a different circuit every year. Unlike other races, world championships are run in national teams. The women's world championship has been an annual event since 1958.

2. Classics

These are usually races linking two cities on a predetermined course. Classics have a group start and are held in a single day. They have been very popular since the beginning of the 20th century and are held once a year. Each has specific features (cobblestones, difficult hills). The major classics are Paris–Roubaix (since 1896, over approximately 270 km, including 50 km on cobblestones, making it one of the most spectacular races of its type in the world), Milan–San Remo (since 1907, 294 km), the Tour des Flandres (since 1913, approximately 270 km and 15 hills), the Flèche-Wallonne (since 1936, 200 km, 10 hills, including the "Huy Wall," where the finish line is), and Liège–Bastogne–Liège (since 1892, approximately 265 km).

3. Time trials

Racers leave individually at set intervals (every minute or two) and must ride a course (open or circuit) as quickly as possible; the length of courses varies. The most demanding of all race formats, the time trial demands constant individual effort with no time to relax. Average speed sometimes surpasses 50 km/h. Time trials have led to major innovations in bicycle aerodynamics. The most important time trial is the Grand Prix des Nations, held every year since 1932. Most stage races have one or several individual or team time trials; the latter are held only during tour races. Teams of 4 to 9 racers generally leave every 4 minutes, and the finish time is counted from the finish of the third team member.

4. Stage races

They are held over a number of days (2 to 22) on a predetermined course. Each stage is a one-day race over a distance not exceeding 260 km. The racers are ranked cumulatively from one stage to the next. The winner is the racer who covers the entire distance in the least time (general ranking). Various rankings (hill climbing, points) within the race enable various racers to shine in their areas of expertise. These races involve different types of stages (flat, climbing, individual and team time trials). The most famous stage race is the Tour de France, held every year since 1903 (22 stages, maximum distance 4,000 km). The other major tours are the Tour of Italy (the "Giro," since 1909, 22 stages, 4,000 km maximum) and the Tour of Spain (the "Vuelta," since 1935, 4,000 km maximum).

Sprint finish
It usually takes place in races or tour stages in which no racer was able to break away definitively from the peloton. Specialists from each team try to place themselves at the head of the pack for the last 5 km. The pace and strategic moves intensify until the final sprint on the last straightaway.

Race director
He is responsible for organization of the event and rides in a car so that he can follow the race closely and supervise events.

Motorcycle
A number of motorcycles with camera operators on board film the race for broadcast.

Lead motorcycle
It precedes the lead racer to announce that the racers will soon be passing through and to make sure that the course is clear.

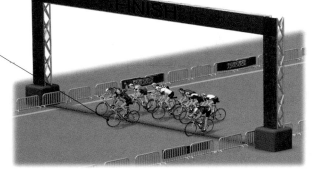

RACING TECHNIQUES

Breakaway

It occurs when one or several racers suddenly accelerate to try to put a distance between themselves and the peloton. If a single racer breaks away, it takes extraordinary sustained effort; if several racers break away, they must work together.

Fan (or column) formation

This is the technique most frequently used by groups of racers. They ride one behind the other to minimize wind resistance. The lead rider makes the most effort because he is not protected. When he is tired, he lets the other racers pass him and takes a place at the back of the formation. The following racer does the same thing. The fan formation also provides a better view of the road.

Climbing

Depending on the degree of the slope, the racer climbs in a sitting position or by standing on the pedals, shifting the bicycle to the right and left as he pushes with his legs as hard as he can.

Descent

The racer holds his body horizontal and as low as possible. His hands are in the hollow of the handlebars, his upper legs are close to his body, and the cranks are parallel to the ground. In a descent, racers can sometimes reach speeds of over 90 km/h.

Francesco Moser (ITA)
First cyclist to cover more than 50 km in one hour, he was world champion in road racing in 1977 and world champion in pursuit in 1976. He won the Tour of Italy in 1984 and many classics, among which the Milan–San Remo in 1978 and the Paris–Roubaix in 1978, 1979 and 1980. He was also champion of Italy three times between 1973 and 1988.

Fausto Coppi (ITA)
Winner of the Tour of Italy in 1940, 1947, 1949, 1952, and 1953. He also won the Tour de France in 1949 and 1952, the Milan–San Remo in 1946, 1948, and 1949, the Grand Prix des Nations in 1946 and 1947, the Paris–Roubaix in 1950, and the Tour of Lombardy five times. Professional road-racing world champion in 1953, he was also world champion in pursuit in 1947 and 1949.

CYCLIST PROFILE
• Cycling is one of the most physically demanding sports. Races are long and very intense, requiring great effort from the respiratory and cardiovascular systems.
• Nutrition is particularly important. Foods rich in carbohydrates (pasta, cereals, fruits) are essential components of the cyclist's diet.
• The muscles of the thighs are constantly in use. The quadriceps and ischium work to keep the pedals in circular motion: the quadriceps push the pedal down and the ischium contracts to pull the leg up.

EQUIPMENT

TIME-TRIAL BICYCLE

The importance of this type of race (many Tours de France have been won in the time trials) has led to research on and development of high-performance aerodynamic systems.

Seat tube
It is inclined backward to make pedaling more efficient and allow a more aerodynamic position.

Back wheel
It is a disk for better aerodynamics. Generally, only the back wheel is a disk, since it is protected from the wind by the racer's legs and the bicycle frame. A disk front wheel would be too likely to be pushed by a side wind.

Sprockets

Chain rings

Crank

Gear ratio
This is the ratio between the number of teeth on the chain wheel and those on the sprockets. It determines the distance the bicycle goes on each turn of the pedals. With the front and rear dérailleur gears, the racer chooses a gear ratio depending on the difficulties on course and the speed.

Tubeless tires
They are narrower and lighter than those on a classic racing bike, offering less wind and ground resistance. Some racers inflate them with helium, the lightest gas. Tire pressure may reach 9 bars (opposed to 7 bars in other races).

Clipless pedals
More streamlined than regular pedals (the pedal and are a single piece, which fits into a safety binding under the shoe).

Eddy Merckx (BEL)
Winner of more than 500 races, he was professional world champion in 1967, 1971, and 1974, winner of five Tours de France (1969, 1970, 1971, 1972, and 1974) and of five Tours of Italy (1968, 1970, 1972, 1973, and 1974). He also beat the world record for one hour in 1972 (49.431 km).

ROAD-RACING BICYCLE

The road-racing bicycle is designed and built for speed. Its geometry must enable the racer to adopt an aerodynamic position, with elbows bent to absorb bumps and chest relaxed to facilitate breathing. A typical bicycle has 2 chain wheels and 9 sprockets, for a total of 18 possible gears.

Jersey
It is made of Lycra to absorb perspiration and let the skin breathe. It must cling to the body without flapping (a flapping shirt can cost several tenths of seconds in time trials and track races).

Helmet
Helmets are light and designed to offer a minimum of wind resistance; they are narrower at the back for optimal aerodynamics. Wearing a helmet is required for competition in some countries.

Shorts
Long and tight-fitting, they protect the thighs from irritation due to rubbing against the saddle. They are made of aerodynamically efficient fabrics such as nylon or Lycra and are elasticized so that they do not ride up the thighs.

Leather gloves
They protect against bumps and reduce vibrations. They can help the racer avoid injury in falls.

Brake and dérailleur gear levers

Brakes

Forks
They are attached to the head tube. They are very strong and absorb bumps to the front wheel on roads.

Tires
Clincher tires are replacing the traditional tubeless tires. They are 20 to 22 mm wide.

Dérailleur gears

Frame
It must support the cyclist's weight and transform his pushing on the pedals into horizontal movement of the bicycle. Aluminum and carbon-fiber frames, which are more rigid, lighter, and stronger, have replaced steel frames.

Jeannie Longo (FRA)
With more than 20 medals in various championships (road racing, track) between 1978 and 1998, she has the most titles of any cyclist. Olympic champion in road racing in 1996, she was world champion 13 times. She also won three women's Tours de France (1987, 1988, and 1989) and holds 11 world track records.

Rim

Shoes
They must be rigid enough to hold the racer's foot flat. They have cleats on the sole that attach to a toe-clip that keeps the foot on the pedal.

Pedals
The widest part of the foot must be placed exactly over the axis of the pedal to transmit maximum energy and create the most efficient driving force.

Chain rings

Wheels
They are very important to performance, and their weight and shape play a role in the cyclist's performance. Spoked wheels are lighter but have greater wind resistance. "Mag" wheels (with 3 to 5 wide spokes elliptical in cross-section, made of carbon fiber) are heavier and require greater effort to accelerate, but they have less wind resistance. Deep-rimmed wheels are more aerodynamic.

track cycling

In 1937, cyclists finish the international Six-Day race held on the Wembley track in England.

The technological development and popularity of the bicycle at the end of the 19th century was quickly embraced by show organizers intent on bringing the action closer to the spectators. The idea of bringing racers together and having all the action take place on a closed circuit is applied for the first time in 1868, when the first race is organised in Saint-Cloud (France). The first wooden tracks appeared in Paris, France, Cologne, Germany, and in the United States. Races were initially 1, 5, and 10 km long, but were soon joined by endurance races, lasting 12 or 24 hours without interruption. In 1878, a new challenge was introduced in England: the Six Days, during which racers pedalled for six consecutive days, stopping only briefly to rest. Around the same time, track cycling developed its own sprint and endurance events, some of which have been featured in the Olympic Games since 1896: the sprint and the kilometer time trial. New events, such as points races and pursuits, have been added to the traditional events. The track experienced incredible popularity in Japan, where there is extensive wagering on the Keirin, which is their speciality. Women's track cycling events have been part of the Olympic Games since 1988.

CHALLENGE

While the objectives of the race vary depending on the event— catching up to an opponent or scoring the most points—the racer's goal remains the same: to pedal faster than his opponents over a specific distance. Depending on the event, the racer will rely on pure sprinting ability (attaining the fastest speed as quickly as possible and maintaining it for as long as possible) or endurance (maintaining a sustained rhythm over a certain distance). Track races often pit two racers against each other, and tactics and technique are of the utmost importance. During timed races, the clock is stopped once the front of the bicycle crosses the finish line.

TRACK

Since January 2000, three track lengths have been standardized: 250 m (short track), and 333.33 m and 400 m (long tracks). Tracks are between 7 and 9 m wide.

Photoelectric cell
Placed along the finish line, this cell records the arrival of racers, and allows the finish order to be verified.

Racers' area
This is the area where racers rest and receive care between races. The racers' entourage (coaches, mechanics, and trainers) are stationed here.

Finish line
Events other than pursuits use this finish line.

Jury platform
Ten judges control the race and broadcast the results. They rule on the first place finish and the rankings, are in charge of the timing device and finish times, and keep track of the laps.

Pursuit lines
Located in the middle of each straightaway, these are the start and finish lines for pursuit events.

Straightaways
Depending on the length of the track, straightaways measure between 37 and 100 m, and have a slope of between 4° and 13°.

200 m line
In sprint events, the clock starts when a racer reaches this line.

HOW OLYMPIC COMPETITIONS ARE ORGANIZED

Track races are classified into two types of events: sprint and endurance. The sprint events take place over distances ranging from 500 m to 2 km. For endurance events, the distance varies from 3 to 60 km. In addition to the Olympic events, the other main track races have been integrated into the world championships.

ENDURANCE EVENTS

Individual pursuit

Two racers compete against each other, starting from the middle of each straightaway and racing either 4 km (men) or 3 km (women). The goal is to catch up to the opponent. The racer who covers the entire distance in the shortest time wins the race. The race plan relies on timing, fluid and regular pedalling, and extreme concentration on the pedalling rhythm. This event has been included in the men's world championships since 1939 and the women's world championships since 1958.

Team pursuit

This exclusively male discipline adheres to the same rules as individual pursuit, except that the competitors are two teams of four racers. The team that covers the 4 km distance in the shortest time wins. The final time is taken once the third racer crosses the finish line. Team pursuit has been a world championship event since 1962.

Olympic sprint

This recent and spectacular event features two teams of three riders racing over three laps. The teams take their starting positions at each of the pursuit lines. Each rider must lead his team for one complete lap. The clock stops once the third racer crosses the line at the end of the third lap. The first leader is generally a sprinter, who must reach his maximum speed quickly, without necessarily maintaining it over a long distance. The leader in the final lap must be a good kilometer racer: fast and with good endurance, so he can keep up the pace during the final lap.

Points race

This individual event has been included in the world championships since 1980, and covers 40 km for men and 24 km for women. Several racers compete at the same time. Points are awarded during sprints that take place every 2 km on a 250 m track, or every 10 laps on longer tracks. The final sprint counts for double points. The racer who completes the most laps wins. If the laps are tied at the end of the race, the racers are ranked based on the number of points accumulated.

Madison (paired) race

This event is called the Madison because it was first held at Madison Square Garden in New York. It features several teams of two racers who take turns riding during the race. The races take place over distances of 20 to 60 km. A maximum of 18 teams may race on tracks measuring 333 m or less, and a maximum of 20 teams are permitted on the longer tracks. One team member races while the other pedals slower and warms down. Each rider's turn lasts as long as it takes him to catch up to his teammate—usually one and a half laps. Once a rider completes his leg, his teammate takes over the race on the lower part of the track. The objective is to complete the most laps during the allocated time. Points are earned during the intermediate sprints at specific times during the race, and are used as a tie-breaker if two teams finish with the same number of laps. The final sprint counts for double points. The Madison race has been a world championship event since 1995.

Pole line
The official distance that the racers must cover is measured on this line, which is located at the base of the track.

Sprinter's line
During a sprint, the two racers must be positioned on either side of this line.

Banking of turns
The longer the track, the less steep the banking: from 22° on a long track to 42° on a short track.

Blue band (Côte d'Azur)
This is a lane located at the base of the track that is used by racers as a transition zone before riding back up the bank. It is also used during the first lap of a sprint, and for warming down during Madison races.

SPRINT EVENTS

Time trials

The racer, who is the only one on the track, waits behind the start line. When the starting signal is given, he starts to pedal, and attempts to cover the distance as quickly as possible. This is a pure sprint event, and leaves no room for strategy. The men's time trial covers a distance of 1,000 m, while the women race over 500 m. This individual race has been a world championship event since 1966 (the 500 m women's event has been included since 1995).

Match sprint

The match sprint is a short, three-lap race, during which only the final 200 m are timed. A line is drawn 200 m from the finish line, and is used as a guide for the clock. The race features two racers who start from the same line. The racer who loses the coin toss must lead the race for the first lap. During the second lap, the racers generally attempt to force each other to take the lead by riding slowly or stopping and balancing. When the sprint starts, the trailing rider can take advantage of his opponent's slipstream. The leading rider is at a disadvantage because he cannot see his opponent until he is even with him. A race between two riders is decided on the basis of winning two of three heats. The sprint has been a world championship event since 1895 (original event) and a women's world championship event since 1958.

Keirin

This exclusively male event was created in Japan in 1948. It features nine racers competing over a distance of 2 km. Each racer starts in his own lane. At the starting signal, the racers struggle to catch up to a lightweight motorcycle that is already running. The motorcycle sets the pace of the race, which lasts 3 to 5 laps. When the motorcycle leaves the track at the start of the second last lap, the racers sprint to the finish. These sprints require strength, courage, and aggressiveness, and the racers do not hesitate to elbow their opponents. The race conditions and speeds (over 60 km/h) often result in serious accidents. A more regulated form of Keirin (no elbowing or cutting off opponents) has been a world championship event since 1980.

RELAY TECHNIQUE

During the Six Days or the Madison races, racers on the same team take turns riding. The switching method is spectacular, and requires a great deal of practice before it is perfected. The racer coming into the race accelerates as his teammate gets close to him. When they are side by side, the outgoing rider literally throws his teammate into the race using a handline. To complete the switch, the outgoing racer grabs a part affixed to his partner's bicycle and, using his own momentum, pushes his partner forward. He may instead choose to grab his partner's hand to throw him forward, again propelled by his own momentum.

DRAFTING

On the track or on the road, one of the main racing tactics is drafting, or using the slipstream effect one racer creates for the racer behind him. The drafting racer gets into position in behind the leading racer, settling a few centimeters from the rear wheel. The pulling rider creates a path of lower wind resistance behind him, thereby allowing the drafting rider to go faster. Using this method, several cyclists riding together form a paceline. Each rider takes his turn in the lead, which requires greater effort, and tows the others for a short distance, thereby allowing them to rest. The paceline technique can allow a small number of racers to maintain their lead over a larger pack.

EQUIPMENT

Compared to its counterpart, which is designed for the road, the track bike is very basic, with no brakes or shifting mechanism (only one gear). Depending on the race, equipment varies.

Track bike
This bike does not have a rear disk wheel. It is used in relay races.

Koichi Nakano (JPN)
The most successful sprinter of all time, he was World Sprint Champion from 1977 to 1986.

PURSUIT BIKE

Saddle

Seat tube
The angle is more pronounced on the track bike, because it must reach faster speeds on a flat, smooth track.

Rear hub
This is a fixed gear hub with no freewheel device. Pedalling is continuous until the bike stops.

Helmet
The helmet, which is mandatory, is streamlined for an aerodynamic effect during sprints.

Glove
Can be used to brush debris from tires to prevent punctures.

Aerobars
Extended toward the front, they allow the racer to establish an aerodynamic position.

Bullhorns
These are placed low, and allow the cyclist to "dance" off the starting line.

Rear disk wheel
The aerodynamic shape of the wheel allows for faster speeds with the same effort.

Erika Salumiaee (EST)
She was the Olympic Sprint Champion in 1988 and 1992, and the World Sprint Champion in 1987 and 1989. She broke the 200 m world record six times, and the 500 m record once.

bmx

C reated as an alternative to motocross, BMX now involves a number of events whose common point is that they combine the physical skills of the cyclist and the mastery of increasingly difficult acrobatic techniques. Invented in the late 1960s in the United States, BMX (bicycle motocross) quickly gained popularity. Since 1979, three federations (NBA, NBL, ABA) have governed the American competition circuit, which involves professional cyclists, and the sport is being exported to Europe—mainly France, Belgium, and Holland. The International BMX Federation (IBMXF) was created in 1981, and it organized the first world championships for track races in Pontiac, Michigan. This type of competition was adopted at the worldwide level by the Union cycliste internationale (UCI) in 1993. Freestyle, or acrobatic BMX was an event at the first European championships, in 1983, and it has grown in popularity with spectators since 1995 thanks mainly to demonstration competitions such as the X-Games in the United States.

Matt Hoffman (USA), called "the Condor," was world champion in BMX from 1987 to 1994 and gold medalist at the X-Games in 1995 and 1996.

THE TRACK RACE

Cyclists race on a clay track 300 to 400 m long and dotted with obstacles. Qualification heats involve 8 participants; the slowest 4 in each heat are eliminated, and the final involves the 8 cyclists who were fastest in the heats. In international competitions, competitors aged 19 years and over are in the Elite category. The Junior category is for competitors aged 17 and 18. In other types of competition, there is a Challenge category for boys and girls aged 5 to 16.

TACTICS

The race takes 30 to 45 seconds. The racer who reaches the first curve in first place can take the most favorable path and control the pace of the race. The fastest cyclists never stop pedaling and try to stay on the ground as much as possible when they go over obstacles so that they do not lose speed.

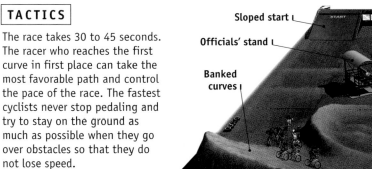

Sloped start

Officials' stand

Banked curves

Finish line

Double bumps

Tabletop

Staircase

DIRT COMPETITION

In both qualifications and finals, competitors have 3 jumps. The competition area is made of clay with one or several bumps. The cyclist gains speed up the side of a bump then jumps and does tricks in the air. There are more than two dozen different tricks. Four judges mark the jumps for their difficulty and execution, and give an overall mark out of 100 points. The winner of the event is the one with the most points after 3 jumps in the finals.

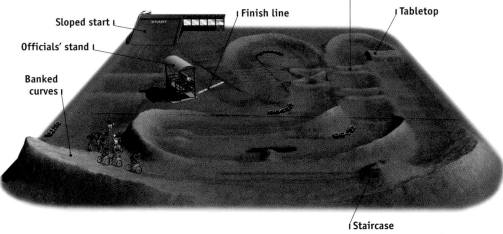

Tailwhip

1. The cyclist gains enough speed to make a big jump. **2.** With his right foot, he pushes on the back wheel to spin the frame 360°. When the rotation is finished, the left foot contacts the pedal. **3.** The right foot stabilizes the bike. **4.** Throughout the trick, the cyclist looks ahead to anticipate the landing.

ACROBATIC OR FREESTYLE BMX

Freestyle involves 3 disciplines: flatland, street, and half pipe.

FLATLAND

This is a very demanding specialty that requires constant training. On a flat area, cyclists perform a number of tricks on their bicycles with musical accompaniment. They are penalized every time one of their feet touches the ground. A pass usually lasts 2:30 min. Each competitor makes 2 qualifying passes. The 20 highest ranked competitors after the qualifications reach the final. Four judges evaluate the performances and give an overall mark out of 100 points. Technical difficulty, choreography, and the originality of the links between tricks are taken into account.

Decade

1. With his feet on the back footpegs, the athlete brakes hard on the back brake and lifts his front wheel. **2.** He puts his right foot on the frame of the bicycle to start his rotation around the handlebars. **3.** His body weight resting completely on the handlebars, he makes a complete rotation (360°) in a tuck position. **4.** At the end of the rotation, he puts his left foot on the frame and lets the front wheel descend. **5.** The figure is complete when the cyclist puts his right foot on the pedal.

STREET

The principle of street, which had its origins, in fact, on the street, is to use any obstacles encountered (staircases, benches, walls) to execute tricks. In competition, the event consists of performing a series of tricks on a variety of different modules within a time limit. Each competitor has 2 qualifying passes, at the end of which the 20 top ranked cyclists reach the finals. They then have 3 passes, usually lasting 1:30 min. Four judges give an overall mark out of 100, and technical difficulty and originality of the tricks are most important. There are 2 categories of tricks: jumps and grinds, which consist of sliding the bicycle on its footpegs on the coping of an obstacle or on a staircase.

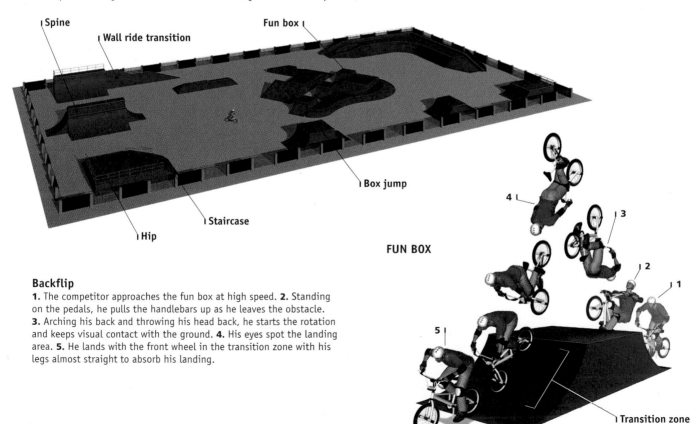

Spine

Wall ride transition

Fun box

Box jump

Staircase

Hip

FUN BOX

Transition zone

Backflip

1. The competitor approaches the fun box at high speed. **2.** Standing on the pedals, he pulls the handlebars up as he leaves the obstacle. **3.** Arching his back and throwing his head back, he starts the rotation and keeps visual contact with the ground. **4.** His eyes spot the landing area. **5.** He lands with the front wheel in the transition zone with his legs almost straight to absorb his landing.

HALF PIPE

Athletes have 1:30 min to perform aerial tricks with musical accompaniment on a half pipe with vertical extensions. Lip tricks are executed on the coping of the half pipe, and aerials are jumps above the half pipe. Each competitor has 2 chances to be among the 20 qualifiers for the final. The final consists of 3 passes, also lasting 1:30 min, and the winner is the one with the highest cumulative score over the 3 passes. Four judges give an overall mark out of 100 for height, technical difficulty, and fluidity of execution of tricks.

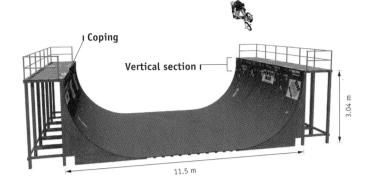

Coping

Vertical section

3.04 m

11.5 m

EQUIPMENT

Helmet with chin guard
Required for racing, widely used in dirt and half pipe.

Kneepads

Elbow pads

Shin guards

CYCLIST PROFILE

- Training for all BMX events involves stretching and gaining overall muscle strength while preserving flexibility.

- In racing, work on concentration and visualization is important. Competitors develop the ability to keep pedaling at a high speed by running and cycling on hills.

- Athletes practice their freestyle tricks over a foam landing area or a swimming pool before attempting them over hard ground.

Stem

Tires
They are smooth and very sticky for freestyle, and knobby for racing and dirt.

Front brake

Footpeg

Wheels
They have a diameter of 508 mm and have 48 spikes for maximum strength.

Pedals
They are wide so that the feet stay on them.

Single chain wheel

Helmet

Handlebars
A ring system that pivots around the axis of the handlebars lets the brake cables follow the handlebar's movements so that it is completely free to spin 360°.

Gloves

Rear brake

Footpegs
They are used only in freestyle; as footpegs in flatland; to perform grinds on staircases; and for lip tricks in street and half pipe.

Single sprocket
Gear changes are not needed in BMX.

Jay Miron (CAN)
Nicknamed "the Canadian Beast," he was champion at the 1995 X-Games in the dirt category and twice silver medalist in street (1996 and 1998).

mountain biking

The Atlanta Olympics in 1996: first Olympic podium in mountain biking history. Dutch racer Bart Jan Brentjens won the gold medal.

Specialists in mountain biking combine endurance and the skill to negotiate natural or artificial obstacles at high speed in order to cross the finish line first. The event was born in the mountains of California during the 1970s; many attribute its invention to Joe Breeze or Gary Fisher, but various other pioneers claim the idea. Because it links technical advances and a return to nature, mountain biking has been one of the quickest commercial successes of the 20th century. The first race took place on Mount Tamalpais, California, in 1976, and was won by Bob Burrowes. Following the first World Championships in Villard-de-Lans (France), in 1987, the Union cycliste internationale (UCI) recognized the sport by sanctioning the 1990 edition, in Purgatory, Colorado. The World Cup series started in 1989 in Europe, and cross-country made its Olympic debut at the Atlanta Games in 1996. The descent event appeared on the international circuit in 1993.

CROSS-COUNTRY COMPETITION

This test of endurance takes place on natural terrain in a single day. The race begins with a group start, and cyclists try to be the first across the finish line. The length of the course, varying between 25 and 40 km, is determined in relation to an optimal race duration (about 2 h 15 min for men and 2 h for women). Some races, such as the World Cup, take place on a 6 to 8 km closed course. Racers are not allowed any outside assistance; they must finish the course on their own regardless of mechanical breakdown, weather conditions, or flat tires. Stations are set up along the course to offer drinks and food to the racers.

TECHNIQUES

A good sense of anticipation is needed to make the appropriate technical moves on trails with natural or artificial obstacles.

Crossing obstacles

The cyclist approaches the obstacle in a sitting position and pedals to maintain speed. Just before the front wheel contacts the obstacle, he pulls the handlebars up and pedals harder. When the front wheel has crossed the obstacle, he brings his weight forward to help the back wheel over.

CATEGORIES AT WORLD CHAMPIONSHIPS AND WORLD CUP
Masters men and women (30 years and over)
Elite men (23 years and over)
Elite women (19 years and over)
Hopefuls (men 19 to 22 years)
Junior men (17 and 18 years)
Junior women (17 and 18 years)
(In descent, the Hopefuls category is replaced by the Elite men category, which starts at 18 years.)

OLYMPIC CATEGORIES
Elite men (19 years and over)
Elite women (19 years and over)

Power climbing

This is a technique for climbing short hills without losing speed. As he approaches the hill, the cyclist checks that the terrain offers good adherence, since his standing position brings his weight forward and increases the risk of the back wheel skidding. The cyclist chooses a path in advance so that he can climb the hill without losing his momentum. On longer or steeper hills, the cyclist stays sitting in order to ensure maximum traction on the back wheel. Leaning forward on the seat, with his forearms parallel to the ground and his nose over the stem, he brings his center of gravity forward to obtain good control of the front wheel.

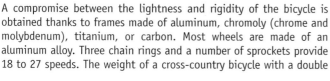

EQUIPMENT

A compromise between the lightness and rigidity of the bicycle is obtained thanks to frames made of aluminum, chromoly (chrome and molybdenum), titanium, or carbon. Most wheels are made of an aluminum alloy. Three chain rings and a number of sprockets provide 18 to 27 speeds. The weight of a cross-country bicycle with a double suspension system is generally between 9.5 and 10.8 kg. Racers carry, under the seat or in their jersey, a repair kit composed of a set of wrenches, an innertube and "spoons" to take the tire off the rim, and a container of CO_2 under pressure to reinflate the repaired tire.

Helmet
It is required.

Goggles
They protect the eyes from mud, pebbles, and insects.

Short-sleeved jersey

Shifter
For changing gears.

Gloves

Front fork
Its suspension, with an air-oil or elastomer system, allows for accurate riding over rough terrain.

Front brake
It is attached to the moving part of the fork.

Shorts

Back brake

Shoes
They have a rigid knobby sole. Removable spikes are screwed in when the terrain is very muddy.

Chain rings

Back suspension
It greatly increases adherence to the ground and the bicycle's stability.

Tires
Cyclists choose them according to the conditions of the terrain. Many models are available. They are 48 to 53 mm wide and inflated to a pressure of 2 to 3 bars.

Rear derailleur

Clipless pedals
They are equipped with a safety system that allows the foot to be attached and freed quickly.

DOWNHILL COMPETITION

The event, open to men and women, takes place on a steep natural slope dotted with obstacles. It is a two-round race against the clock, and the winner is the one who finishes both rounds in the shortest time. Competitors start at intervals of between 30 sec and 3 min. The course has a vertical drop of at least 400 m over a length of between 2 and 5 km. A qualifying race takes place if there are more than 140 competitors. The top 50 men and 25 women in the world rankings are automatically qualified for their respective semi-finals. During the semi-finals, competitors start in an order determined by their ranking in previous races. The 70 quickest men and 25 quickest women take part in their respective finals. The slowest competitor in the semi-finals is the first to start in the finals, and the fastest competitor starts last.

High-speed turn

To stay on the path that he has chosen, the cyclist leans his bicycle and moves the leg on the inside of the turn to lower his center of gravity and increase his stability. If he skids, his foot can act as an extra point of support.

TECHNIQUES

Downhill is a speed event that depends on the athlete's ability to anticipate difficulties. In a race that lasts about 4 min, athletes might ride at an average of 40 to 50 km/h, and up to 90 km/h at certain points. To absorb shocks, particularly in steep sections, cyclists keep their legs bent and their pedal cranks parallel to the ground. Their fingers are touching the brake levers so that they can control their speed whenever necessary. Their arms are slightly bent and most of their weight is shifted backward to avoid somersaulting. Before the event, cyclists inspect the course with their coaches.

EQUIPMENT

Because of the risk of falling, cyclists are required to wear back, shoulder, and chest protection, knee and elbow protections, a helmet with chin guard, gloves, and long-sleeved shirts. The weight of the bicycle (11 to 13 kg) is less important than its strength, a powerful braking system, and a high-clearance suspension system to absorb shocks from jumps and large obstacles. These bicycles generally have 8 speeds.

Protective goggles

Raised handlebars

Front fork

Pedal with wide platform

Single chain ring with chain guide

Hydraulic disk brakes

Pedal cranks

Tires
Between 63 and 76 mm wide, they are inflated to a pressure of 1 to 3 bars, depending on the terrain.

Missy Giove (USA)
A specialist in downhill, she was world champion in 1994, 1995, and 1996, she also won the World Cup in 1996 and 1997.

Alison Sydor (CAN)
World champion in 1994, 1995, and 1996, she also won the World Cup in 1996.

Nicolas Vouilloz (FRA)
World champion in downhill from 1995 to 1999, he also won the World Cup in 1995 and 1996.

CYCLIST PROFILE

- In cross-country, it takes years of intensive practice to reach the top level, at an average age of 25 to 28 years. The technical skills for downhill are acquired more rapidly, and the best athletes are 19 to 25 years old.

- Cross-country events are physically very taxing and require high-level cardiovascular training. Athletes work on their organic and muscular endurance for up to 3 or 4 hours daily in season.

- In cross-country, racers avoid dehydration by drinking water every 15 minutes during a race.

- Cyclists must learn to fall properly to reduce the risk of serious injury. Shaving the legs makes massages easier and reduces the risk of infection if there are open wounds.

Gymnastics

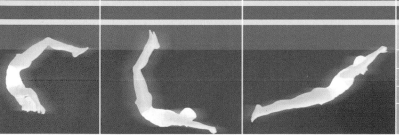

artistic gymnastics

Women take part in Olympic-level artistic gymnastics, a demonstration event at the Stockholm Olympics (Sweden) in 1912.

Every move a gymnast makes, no matter how difficult, must be performed with confidence, ease, and flawless technique. In ancient Greece and Rome, gymnastics was as much a part of a child's education as the arts. The Germans rediscovered the discipline in the 18th century, and invented most of the apparatus. The revival, which began as simple calisthenics as part of the fitness training of firefighters and soldiers, ultimately led to the creation of the International Gymnastics Federation (FIG) in 1881. The first competition was held in Germany in 1894, and gymnastics appeared on the program at the Athens Olympics two years later. Women had to wait until the 1928 Amsterdam Games to compete. A gymnastics competition in those days still included events such as the 60 meter dash, the long jump, and the javelin throw. The format of today's meets first appeared in 1954, at the world championships in Rome.

HOW A MEET IS ORGANIZED

Men compete in 6 events, in Olympic order as follows: floor exercise, pommel horse, rings, vault, parallel bars, and horizontal bar. Women perform 4 events in the following order: vault, uneven parallel bars, balance beam, and floor exercise (performed to music). Men and women usually compete simultaneously. The apparatus and floor mat are installed on a raised surface, known as "the podium." To avoid distracting a competing gymnast, other athletes, coaches, and officials stay off the podium.

PODIUM

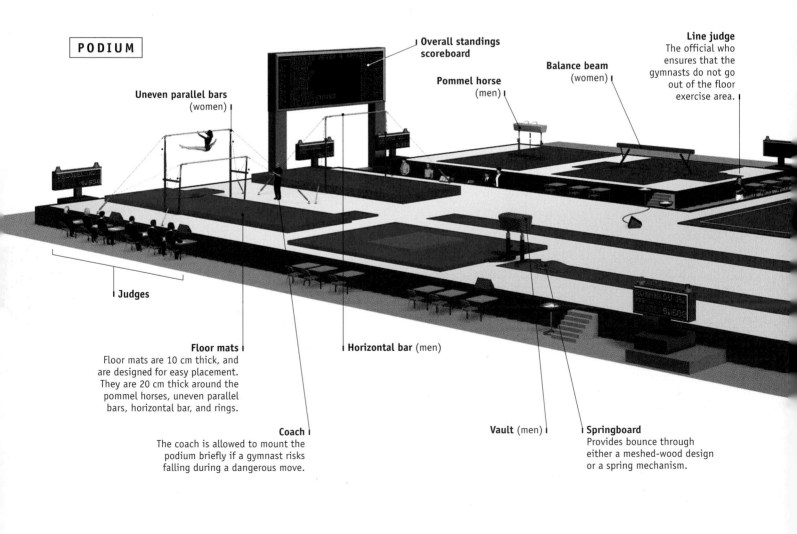

Overall standings scoreboard

Line judge
The official who ensures that the gymnasts do not go out of the floor exercise area.

Balance beam (women)

Pommel horse (men)

Uneven parallel bars (women)

Judges

Floor mats
Floor mats are 10 cm thick, and are designed for easy placement. They are 20 cm thick around the pommel horses, uneven parallel bars, horizontal bar, and rings.

Horizontal bar (men)

Coach
The coach is allowed to mount the podium briefly if a gymnast risks falling during a dangerous move.

Vault (men)

Springboard
Provides bounce through either a meshed-wood design or a spring mechanism.

EVENTS

In team competitions, the winning team (4 to 7 gymnasts) is determined by totaling the best scores obtained in each event. At the end of the competition:

• The top 36 gymnasts qualify for the multiple individual competition, in which the top athletes are determined by their individual total scores in each event.

• The 8 gymnasts with the highest scores for an event in the team competition qualify for the individual finals to determine the best in each event.

Gymnasts compete in freestyle events. The men's floor exercise is timed. Their routine must last at least 50 but no more than 70 seconds. Similarly, the women's floor and balance beam exercises must last at least 70 but no more than 90 seconds.

SCORING

Scoring is based on the level of difficulty of the moves attempted by the gymnast. Before competing, gymnasts give the judges a list of the elements in their program. Two of the 6 international judges then determine the starting score, which is the top score that can be earned for a particular routine. For every mistake the gymnast makes, the other 4 judges deduct points from the starting score. Under the international Code of Points, which is reviewed by the FIG every 4 years, the highest possible starting score is currently set at 10 points.

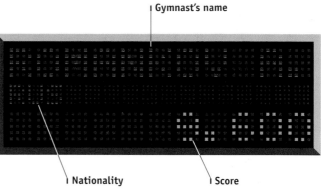

Gymnast's name

Nationality   Score

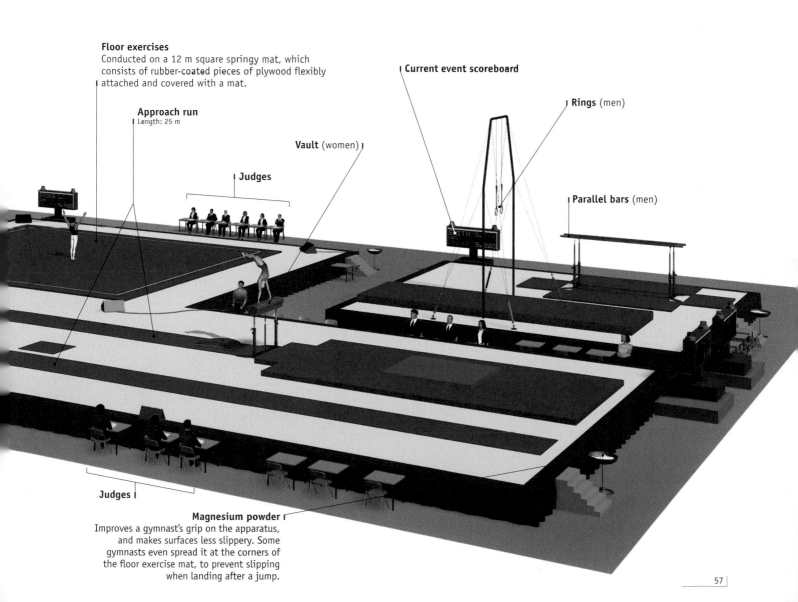

Floor exercises
Conducted on a 12 m square springy mat, which consists of rubber-coated pieces of plywood flexibly attached and covered with a mat.

Approach run
Length: 25 m

Vault (women)

Judges

Current event scoreboard

Rings (men)

Parallel bars (men)

Judges

Magnesium powder
Improves a gymnast's grip on the apparatus, and makes surfaces less slippery. Some gymnasts even spread it at the corners of the floor exercise mat, to prevent slipping when landing after a jump.

TECHNIQUE

For every event, the FIG Code of Points recommends that a routine consist of a minimum of 10 elements. Gymnasts are free to attempt more, but each additional element increases the risk of losing points. There are specific techniques for each event.

Some allow for acrobatic dismounts, which are usually very complex, spectacular moves designed to impress and to end the performance on a strong note.

MEN'S FLOOR EXERCISE

This event is expected to exhibit the gymnast's artistry, coordination, agility, and fitness. The program must cover the entire area of the mat. Tumbling lines with twists have a high value.

Reverse double salto in the tuck position

A reverse handspring provides the momentum for the double salto. Just before taking off, the gymnast focuses on a distant spot and must not lose sight of the floor while in the air.

WOMEN'S FLOOR EXERCISE

This event is expected to exhibit the gymnast's artistry, coordination, agility, and fitness. The program must consist of a combination of jumps and flips demonstrating originality.

Reverse double salto in the pike position

The pike position is more commonly used by female gymnasts.

Double Schuschunova

Usually performed as the finale for a series of moves, it provides the artistic component that is compulsory for female gymnasts.

BALANCE BEAM

The program consists of a combination of jumps and gymnastic and acrobatic elements. Gymnasts are expected to use the entire length of the beam, and display elegance, flexibility, balance, and self-control. This exercise generally culminates in a series of moves that provide the momentum for an acrobatic dismount of a high degree of difficulty.

Rulfova

Obtaining proper momentum for the backspring is a major problem. The gymnast must regain sight of the beam as early as possible.

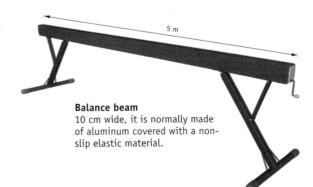

Balance beam
10 cm wide, it is normally made of aluminum covered with a non-slip elastic material.

5 m

VAULT (MEN)

Power, speed, and acrobatic skill are essential. The jump must be long enough and high enough to allow for multiple turns. A fully controlled landing is also an integral requirement of the exercise. The gymnast is penalized for any loss of balance, regardless of the difficulty of the jump.

Full-twisting layout Tsukahara

The amplitude necessary for this move requires a strong approach run. Horizontal speed is essential, but makes the landing harder to control.

Vault

Springs are built into the frame of the vault to reduce the risk of injury from the force of contact. It is covered in leather or a synthetic material. Men use it lengthwise.

1.35 m

VAULT (WOMEN)

The jump must have sufficient amplitude for each movement in the series—a combination of rotations—to be distinct. Gymnasts are expected to display acrobatic skill and speed. The landing must also be fully controlled.

Yurchenko

In doing the cartwheel before the springboard takeoff, the gymnast loses sight of the horse, but achieves the momentum required for the subsequent double backflip.

Vault

Except for its size, it is exactly the same as the men's vault. In contrast with men, women use it widthwise.

1.25 m

POMMEL HORSE

Continuous, swinging movements are expected. The gymnast must display coordination, agility, and strength. The program should consist of circular swings, leg scissors, and leg circles performed over the length of the horse, as well as a routine on one pommel.

Thomas flair

The gymnast can only see the pommels when his legs are behind the horse. He must spread his legs as far apart as possible.

Pommel horse

Made of wood or steel, it is covered in leather or a synthetic material. The handles are made of wood or plastic.

1.60 m

40–45 cm

1.05 m

UNEVEN PARALLEL BARS

Acrobatic skill and athletic power are expected in a routine that must consist of a series of continuous, balanced movements performed above or below the bar, involving body rotation as well as changes in grip. The acrobatic dismounts are usually very complex, swift, and spectacular.

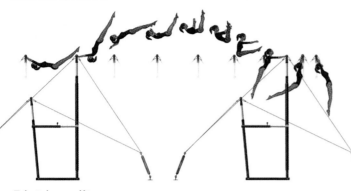

Tchatchev splits

The gymnast must be in perfect position to properly grasp the high bar; any imbalance in weight may result in a faulty grip.

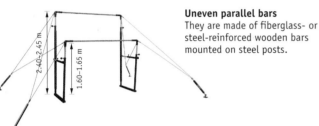

Uneven parallel bars
They are made of fiberglass- or steel-reinforced wooden bars mounted on steel posts.

PARALLEL BARS

In a routine that must span the full length of the bars, the gymnast is required to display acrobatic skill and athletic power. Saltos between the bars, leaps, and still positions on one or both bars are especially important. The program ends with an acrobatic dismount.

Diamidov

Balance must be fully regained after a complete turn on one arm. As the gymnast's arms are fully extended, momentum is derived from shoulder and bar flexibility.

Parallel bars
They are made of fiberglass-reinforced wood, mounted on steel posts.

HORIZONTAL BAR

The gymnast's movements around the bar must be continuous and smooth, including changes in grip, releasing and regrasping the bar, and forward or backward rotations. Elements involving flight and combinations of turns and supports on the bar are essential. The acrobatic dismount is usually very spectacular.

Horizontal bar
The bar is made of stainless steel, and is supported by adjustable steel posts.

Dislocation

The gymnast moves his straight legs between his arms and stretches his body, pivoting around his shoulders. He finishes the move with an inverted swing.

RINGS

At the start of this event, the coach helps the gymnast to reach the rings. The gymnast is expected to display muscular strength and balance through a series of demanding still positions attained with or without swinging movements. The program ends with an acrobatic dismount.

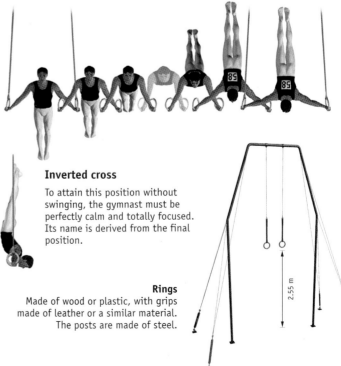

Inverted cross

To attain this position without swinging, the gymnast must be perfectly calm and totally focused. Its name is derived from the final position.

Rings
Made of wood or plastic, with grips made of leather or a similar material. The posts are made of steel.

EQUIPMENT

With the use of new materials, gymnastic equipment has changed considerably. Bouncier springboards, more flexible apparatus, and improved shock absorption upon landing are improving athletic performance.

Leotards
Worn only by female gymnasts.

On the apparatus, men wear Sokol-style pants with footstraps and socks. For the vault and floor exercise, they may wear shorts and perform barefoot.

Hand protectors
Improve a gymnast's hold on the apparatus. The fold enables the gymnast to achieve a stronger grip with less effort.

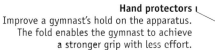

Shorts
Worn by men, primarily in the floor exercise and vault.

Shoes
Gymnasts are free to decide whether or not to wear shoes in performing their routines.

GYMNAST PROFILE

- Physically, gymnasts are generally small and light, and have a balanced physique as the result of a very thorough training program. Flexibility, agility, and muscle power are essential qualities, achieved by at least 4 hours of practice every day and thousands of repetitions.

- Mentally, gymnasts require strong powers of concentration and must be virtually immune to stress. These qualities are indispensable because, after countless hours of training, the gymnasts only have seconds to give an optimum performance in front of the judges. Despite all this, gymnasts often enter their first international competition at a very young age. A good coach-gymnast relationship and complete mutual trust are key factors for success.

Mitsuo Tsukahara (JPN)
World champion in horse vault in 1970 and team world champion from 1966 to 1974, he was gold medalist in horizontal bar at the Olympics in 1972 and 1976, and team Olympic champion from 1968 to 1976.

Lilia Podkopayeva (UKR)
Overall and floor exercise Olympic champion in 1996, she also won the overall and vault competitions at the 1995 world championships, as well as a silver medal in the beam and uneven bars in 1995.

Vitali Scherbo (BLR)
Ten-time world champion and 6-time European champion, he won 6 gold medals at the 1992 Olympics before becoming 1993 world champion in the overall competition.

Nadia Comaneci (ROM)
She became legendary by earning the first perfect score in the history of women's gymnastics, which she followed with 6 more perfect scores at the 1976 Olympics in Montreal. Her record remains unequaled.

rhythmic gymnastics

Rhythmic gymnastics, a combination of gymnastics and dance, is for women only. The result of a search for natural, fluid movement, it was invented in the early 20th century in Germany and Sweden. Although the first competition took place in the USSR in 1948, the sport remained in the shadow of artistic gymnastics until 1956. Its artistic aspect made it very popular throughout Eastern Europe, and the International Gymnastics Federation (FIG) recognized it as an independent sport in 1962. The first world championship took place in Budapest in 1963, but it was not until 1970 that the FIG published the first "points code for modern gymnastics." Dubbed "sports rhythmic gymnastics" in 1975, it has now returned to its original name: rhythmic gymnastics. It has been an Olympic event since 1984.

Australian Lorraine Whitecombe, finalist at the 9th rhythmic gymnastics world championship in the Wembley Arena (GBR) in 1979.

THE COMPETITION

Rhythmic gymnastics is performed with 5 apparatuses—rope, ball, hoop, ribbon, and clubs—but international competitions use only 4, chosen every 2 years by the FIG. (The clubs are not yet in the Olympic program.) In individual and team competitions, gymnasts perform before the judges in turn; in group competitions, 5 gymnasts perform together. In team competition, the winning team's athletes have accumulated the best marks. Only the 30 best gymnasts take part in the individual competition, where the athlete with the most points wins. The 8 best gymnasts on each apparatus qualify for the apparatus finals, which rewards the most accomplished athletes. In the group competition, each group performs with 5 identical apparatuses and then with 2 different apparatuses. The winner of the general competition is the group with the best overall score, while the finals competition involves the 8 best groups on each exercise.

The gymnast's performance lasts between 75 and 90 seconds; she uses her choice of instrumental music. During the program, the apparatus must be kept in constant motion, used by both hands, and involve movements specific to that apparatus; the program must use the entire area of the platform.

PLATFORM

The ceiling must be at least 8 m high so that the apparatuses can be thrown to their full height.

OFFICIALS

Technical judges (2–4) They evaluate the difficulty of the program out of 5 points: movements and specific use of the apparatus.

Judge coordinator She oversees the judges. The total of points awarded is divided by 2 to give a mark out of 10.

Chief judge She supervises the entire competition.

Execution judges (3–5) They evaluate execution quality out of 10: technical errors, expressiveness, and virtuosity.

Artistic value judges (2–5) They evaluate composition of the performance out of 5 points: rhythm, continuity, and harmony with the music.

Safety zone: 1 m
12 m
12 m

Hair Always tied up so as not to impede the gymnast's movement.

Leotard Does not impede movement.

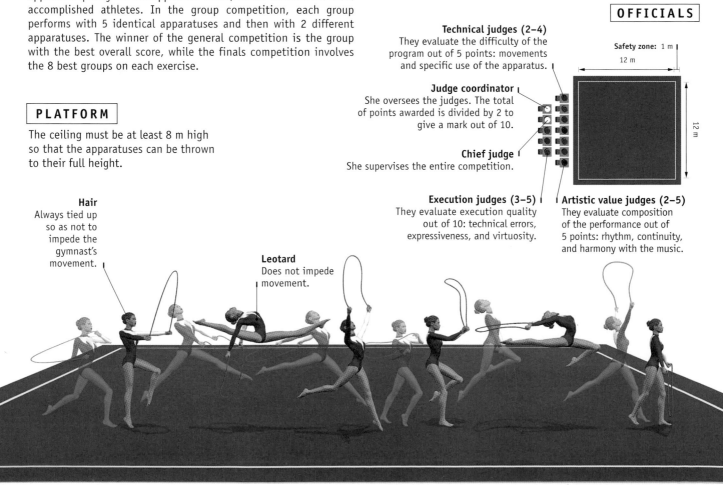

FIGURES

With all apparatuses, choreography must include basic body movements.

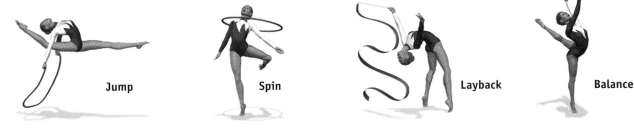

Jump

Spin

Layback

Balance

EQUIPMENT

Expressiveness is an integral part of rhythmic gymnastics. On the marking scale, all apparatuses are equal: it is up to gymnasts to exploit the possibilities offered by each one. Once made of natural materials (wood, rubber, hemp), the apparatuses are now made mostly of synthetic materials.

Width: 4–6 cm
Maximum length : 6 m
Handle: 50–60 cm long;
maximum diameter: 1 cm

40–50 cm
150 g

Clubs
With the clubs, rhythm and choreography are emphasized with twirls, throws and asymmetrical movements.

400 g
18–20 cm

Ball
It highlights flexibility and body expression, fluidity of rolls, contrasts between the strength of throws and the softness of catches.

Ribbon
It must always be in movement and stay in the air in very specific pre-established patterns.

The length of the rope is proportional to the gymnast's height.

Knots make the rope easier to hold.

80–90 cm
300 g

Hoop
It can be handled many ways: rotations, throws, rolls, athlete passing through.

Slippers
They have no heel and increase the effectiveness of spins and jump landings.

Rope
This is the most physically demanding apparatus. The main movements are jumps and skipping.

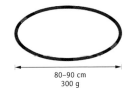

Ekaterina Serebrianskaya (UKR)
Gold medalist in overall individual competition at the Atlanta Olympics in 1996, she also won many gold medals at the world and European championships.

Maria Petrova (BUL)
European champion in Stuttgart, Germany, in 1992, and in Thessalonia, Greece, in 1994. World champion at Alicante, Spain, in 1993, Paris, France, in 1994 and Vienna, Austria, in 1995.

GYMNAST PROFILE

- It takes at least 7 years for an athlete to reach championship level.

- The gymnast is flexible, well versed in ballet and modern dance, and has balanced musculature. Excellent muscle control is needed to eliminate any tension that reduces the range and fluidity of movements.

- Each aspect of the sport (handling the apparatus, harmony with the music, and body technique) can be worked on separately, but many hours of practice are needed to acquire overall expressiveness.

competitive aerobics

Aerobic training for the women's army auxiliary, Kent County, England, in 1940.

The fifth official discipline of the International Gymnastics Federation (FIG), competitive aerobics is an event performed as a routine accompanied by music. It is drawn from an exercise regime that oxygenates the tissues and models the body. The inventor of aerobic exercise, Kenneth Cooper, was an American army physician who wanted his troops to emphasize cardiovascular fitness rather than muscle building. In 1968, Cooper's principles began to gain a higher profile, but it was not until the late 1980s that aerobics became an international competitive sport for both men and women. The event is very popular in Europe and in Brazil, whose athletes excel in the individual, pair, and team (three-person) disciplines. The Romanians and Bulgarians are known for their technical ability. The first world championships under the aegis of the FIG was held in Paris in 1995, and 34 countries participated. Since then, world championships and international competitions have taken place regularly.

THE COMPETITION

To energetic music that they have chosen, athletes perform a 1 minute 45 second choreography that requires power, endurance, flexibility, and coordination. The competitors must perform 12 elements, including one from each family. The choreography and music must start and end at the same time. Athletes must move rhythmically and cover the entire competition area. The expression, originality, and intensity of the performances make the event exciting for spectators. Competitors must be at least 18 years old, and categories are individuals (men and women), pairs, and teams of 3. Teams of 6 will be added later. There are 2 competition juries: group A marks individual competitors, and group B marks pairs and teams of 3.

PODIUM

Lines
They mark the limits of the competition area.

The curtain helps athletes concentrate and gives them a spatial reference point.

A wooden surface is placed on a special flooring that provides bounce and shock absorption.

OFFICIALS

INDIVIDUAL COMPETITION
The artistic, execution, and difficulty judges each give the competitors a mark. These 3 marks are combined in a formula to give the official mark.

Control jury and appeal jury
Each jury has two members and a chairperson, appointed by the Commission of Aerobic Sports; they supervise the competition.

Referees (2)
They are responsible for point deductions.

Time judges (2)
They time the duration of the performance.

Artistic judges (4)
They analyze the performance and the originality of the choreography. The music is very important to the artistic marks.

Execution judges (4)
They mark coordination, technical skill, synchronization, and intensity of the choreography.

Line judges (2)
They make sure that the competitor stays in bounds.

Difficulty judges (4)
They evaluate the level of difficulty and the correctness of elements executed.

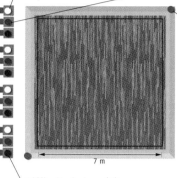

7 m

Yuriko Ito (JPN)
She won first place in the national championships in 1994 and 1997. Also in the individual category, she won the gold medal at the world championships in Catania, Italy, in 1998 and in Hanover, Germany, in 1999.

ATHLETE PROFILE
Usually long-limbed, athletes are strong and flexible and have endurance, an excellent sense of rhythm, and great coordination. Cardiovascular workouts form the basis of typical training, and muscle building is added since all muscles are constantly used.

TECHNIQUE

The routine must contain basic aerobic steps including whip kicks, lunges, walking, running, knee lifts, high kicks, and jumping jacks, as well as elements with set difficulty levels. The elements are grouped into families:

Dynamic strength
Includes push-ups, free falls, circles, the A form, and the Wenson.

Static strength
Composed mainly of lifts on the hands.

Balance
Involves positions that must be held.

Jumps
Includes straddle jumps, scissor jumps, split jumps, and somersaults.

Flexibility
Includes splits and elements of great amplitude.

EQUIPMENT

Costume
Strictly regulated, it is a one-piece stretchy costume and skin-colored tights for women, and a 1- or 2-piece stretchy costume for men.

Shoes
They must be flexible and offer support and shock absorption. White is the most common color but is not required by the rules.

trampoline

The Jumpsville outdoor trampoline center in East Meadow, New York, in 1955

Invented in 1936 by George Nissen, an American physical education teacher, the trampoline is named after two Italian trapeze artists, the Due Trampoline, who bounced on the safety net after their performance. Used as a training tool by American soldiers during the Second World War, trampolining became a sport in 1948, when the first American championship was held. The Fédération internationale de trampoline (FIT) was created in 1964, and that year the first world championships were held in London for men and women (individual and synchronized). Tumbling and double mini-trampoline competitions were added in 1976. The spectacular nature of competition makes these events very popular with spectators. Under the authority of the International Gymnastics Federation (FIG) since 1999, trampolining made its debut in the Olympics in Sydney in 2000.

THE COMPETITION

Athletes execute aerial routines while maintaining complete control of their rebounds. In both individual and synchronized trampoline, the competitors perform 3 routines of 10 tricks. In the synchronized competition, 2 trampolinists execute the same tricks at the same time, attempting unison. It is forbidden to execute the same tricks twice in a routine. The 10 best competitors go on to the finals. In all disciplines (trampoline, tumbling, double mini-trampoline), 7 judges and 1 referee mark the athletes out of 10 points, according to quality of execution and level of difficulty. Athletes often specialize in a single discipline.

The Rudolph
This trick has 1 somersault and 1½ twists. Complex tricks require "flight plans," which competitors must memorize.

CHANGES IN PERFORMANCES

Recently, new techniques have caused major changes in performances. Video and biomechanical research have improved the understanding of how the body moves in space. Neurology has determined that visual reference points and reflexes come into play during a bounce. Thanks to such advances, trampolinists are presenting more difficult tricks in competition.

Front somersault pike

TRAMPOLINE

Bed

Frame protector

Spotters (4)
If the trampolinist loses control, the spotters limit the risk of injury by breaking his fall. They must not talk to the competitor during the performance under pain of penalty.

Frame

1.155 m

Springs
The bed is held taut by 120 springs.

Trainer
He is allowed to bring a landing mat to the trampoline if he feels that it is necessary.

DOUBLE MINI-TRAMPOLINE

Developed from the mini-trampoline, used by gymnasts in training, the double mini-trampoline is an event in international competition alongside trampoline and tumbling. After a run-up, jumpers perform 2 aerial tricks, bouncing off the 2 mini-trampoline impulsion zones, and finish on the ground in a still position.

Ten finalists, selected after 2 series of 2 tricks, present 2 new routines in the finals.

Rudolph

Double back somersault pike

All equipment is surrounded by many landing and protective mats.

Penalty zone
Athletes must not touch this zone.

TUMBLING

Tumbling involves aspects of the gymnastics floor exercise and trampolining. The event consists of performing a series of acrobatic movements very quickly on a springy track. Competitions were organized in the 1930s, but the first international competition took place only in 1976. In 1999, tumbling came under the authority of FIG.

Chief judge

Landing area
3.6 m x 1.8 m

Run-up track
20 m

5 m

Referee

Execution judges | **Difficulty judges**

Rudolph

Back somersault layout

Double back somersault pike

Any steps out of the landing area is penalized.

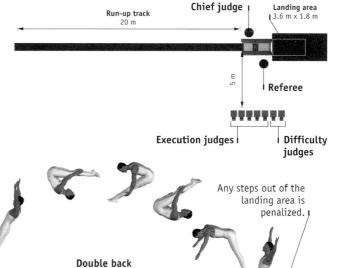

Execution judges | **Difficulty judges**

The figures must be executed inside the jump zone.

Chief judge

The judges are placed on a platform raised by 1 m.

5 m

Referee

2.14 m

4.28 m

Tumbling track
The surface is springier than previously, which has enabled difficulty levels to be raised. Champions execute their tumbling runs at a speed of 20 km/h.

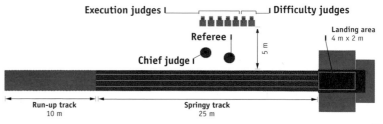

Execution judges | **Difficulty judges**

Referee

Chief judge

5 m

Landing area
4 m x 2 m

Run-up track
10 m

Springy track
25 m

67

TRICKS

Tricks are combinations of somersaults (front-to-back rotations) and twists. Somersaults are started from an impetus provided by a change in the athlete's center of gravity. Twists can be started in the air or in contact with the floor or bed. In the air, bending or stretching an arm creates enough change in balance to produce transversal rotation. One of the most difficult tricks currently performed is the "full full full": a triple somersault with a twist in each somersault.

Each trick can be executed in 3 different positions: layout, pike, and tuck. The arms must be held against the body. Pike and layout tricks are more difficult and earn more points.

Layout

The gymnast holds his legs straight in the axis of the hips.

Pike

The body and head stay straight, as do the legs and feet.

Tuck

Feet and toes are pointed; the body must stay compact.

At takeoff and landing, both feet must touch the bed at the same time.

Back somersault layout

As he rises and descends, the trampolinist keeps his eyes on the trampoline frame so that he can correct his trajectory.

JUDGES

In all 3 events, competitors' performances are judged on 2 complementary aspects: accomplishment of the difficulty level announced and perfection in execution of the tricks.

Chief judge
He supervises the entire competition (general operations and calculation of marks) and settles any disputes.

Referee
He makes sure that the athlete remains within bounds.

Execution judges
These 5 judges mark the athlete's staying in the center of the bed, uniformity of bounce heights, and general style.

Difficulty judges
These 2 judges count the somersaults and twists and make sure that they are presented in the position announced (tuck, pike, layout).

- In somersaults, 90 degrees of rotation is worth $1/10$ of a point.
- In twists, 180 degrees of rotation is worth $1/10$ of a point.
- $1/10$ of a point per somersault is added to the total if the figure is executed in pike or layout position.

CHANGES IN MATERIALS

In both trampoline and tumbling, the advent of synthetic fibers for the bed and of metal alloys for the springs and frames has helped to increase the height of tricks. Trampolinists are bouncing up to 8 m, and tumblers up to 2.5 m, which gives them time to execute more complicated tricks than previously.

TRAMPOLINIST PROFILE
• Quick execution, memorization of acrobatic tricks, and an extraordinary sense of spatial orientation are essential.
• The most-used training method is the part method, in which complex movements are learned in small sequences. Athletes gradually find the reference points they need to execute multiple combinations of twists and somersaults.
• Tumbling specialists are often former gymnasts, whose training is based on muscular strength. They must have strong impulsion to attain great horizontal speed.

Strength
Sports

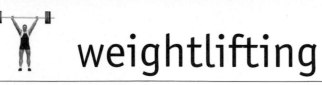

weightlifting

One-armed lift, an event until 1928

I n weightlifting, strength and speed are combined to lift as heavy a weight as possible above the head onto straight arms. Although weightlifting was included in the first Olympic Games of the modern era, in Athens in 1896, it became an official Olympic sport only at the Anvers Games in 1920. Regulated by an international federation, the sport comprised 5 different lifts, and athletes competed in 5 body-weight categories. The number of lifts was dropped to 3 in 1928, and to 2 in 1972, when the press was dropped. The body-weight categories have undergone a number of changes since 1920, and today there are 8 for men and 7 for women. The first women's world championships took place in 1987, and women's weightlifting was included in the Olympics for the first time in 2000. The Chinese hold most of the women's weightlifting records.

THE COMPETITION

Weightlifting involves 2 lifts: the snatch and the clean and jerk. Athletes compete in categories based on their body weight. They announce their starting weight and have 3 attempts per weight. They choose and announce the weight for each attempt; weights must be increased by at least 2.5 kg after a successful lift (or a minimum of 0.5 kg for a world-record attempt). Weightlifters have 1 minute between the time their name is called and when they must begin their lift. The winner of the competition is the weightlifter who has lifted the highest total weight in the 2 lifts.

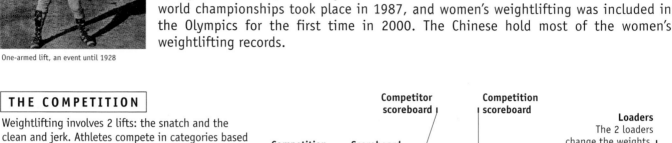

Competitor scoreboard

Competition scoreboard

Loaders
The 2 loaders change the weights.

Competition secretary

Scoreboard operators

Timer

Announcer

Jury
The jury members supervise the referees.

Platform

Entrance to platform

Light system
Each referee controls 2 lights: a white one, indicating a successful lift, and a red one, indicating a failed lift. A minimum of 2 lights of the same color determines the outcome of an attempt. The apparatus located in front of the weightlifter gives a visual and audio signal to inform him that he can put down the weight.

Magnesium-powder bowl

Referees
Three referees decide whether the lift was successful. Technical faults, ranging from touching the floor with the knee to an incorrect final position, lead to a failed lift.

TECHNIQUES

Although the techniques differ for the snatch and the clean and jerk, the weightlifter's muscular actions are almost the same for both lifts. The snatch is the more difficult, since the weightlifter must raise the weight to its maximum height in one movement.

SNATCH

1. Start of the lift

The weightlifter applies maximum strength to begin the weight's upward movement.

2. Clean

The weight is pulled upward so that the weightlifter can slide under the bar.

3. Transfer under the bar

This raises the barbell to maximum height over the weightlifter's head.

4. Final push

The weightlifter locks his arm joints to control the weight over his head.

EQUIPMENT

Lead weights
They range in weight from 0.25 to 25 kg.
Each weight has a specific color.

0.25 kg
0.5 kg
1.25 kg
2.5 kg
5.0 kg

10 kg
15 kg
20 kg
25 kg

Barbells
men: 2.2 m women: 2.01 m

Collars
2.5 kg

Wrist bandages
They must not be
more than
100 mm wide.

Steel bar
Diameter : 28 mm for men,
25 mm for women; 20 kg
for men and 15 kg for women.

Costume
Must be one-piece and
leave knees and elbows
uncovered.

Vasili Alexeev (USSR)
Called "the strongest man in
the world" in any category,
he raised the Olympic record to
640 kg in three lifts in 1972.

**Abdominal and lumbar
support belt**
Must be visible and less
than 120 mm wide.

WEIGHTLIFTER PROFILE

- The most-used, and therefore most-developed, muscles are the quadriceps, trapezoids, and muscles in the lumbar region. The thighs are massive, but the calves are not. Some muscles, including the biceps and pectorals, are not developed in training because they are not used in lifts.

- The phenomenal exertion made by a weight-lifter can cause the heart rate to increase to more than 190 beats per minute.

- Elite international weightlifters may lift a total of more than 25 tons in a single training session.

Naim Suleymanoglu (TUR)
Nicknamed the "Pocket
Hercules," he lifted double
his weight in the snatch and
triple his weight in the
clean and jerk. In 1996, he
held 46 world records.

Knee bandages
Must not be more than
300 mm wide.

Shoes
Raised to provide the stability
needed to accomplish lifts.

CLEAN AND JERK

1. Start of the lift

The weightlifter's effort is the same as for the snatch, but the grip on the bar is not as wide.

2. Clean

The upward motion is performed mainly by the thigh and back muscles.

3. Transfer under the bar

The athlete brings the barbell under control to stabilize the weight before the jerk.

4. Jerk

As he pushes with his legs, the athlete straightens his body and propels the weight to a straight-arm position. He stabilizes the weight by locking his shoulders and balances himself by bringing his feet together.

71

powerlifting

This test of pure strength, open to both men and women, consists of lifting and controlling the most weight possible, in 3 different lifts. Powerlifting, invented in the early 1960s in the United States, takes its 3 lifts from exercises performed by bodybuilders in gyms. When the International Powerlifting Federation (IPF) organized its first world championships in the United States in 1970, only a few nations were represented. In the 1980s, strong delegations of athletes from the USSR and the creation of an over-40 age class helped to popularize the sport. Today, powerlifting is part of the World Games, held every 4 years for non-Olympic sports. In 1999, more than 76 national federations belonged to the IPF.

Ed Coan (USA), national champion in 1983 and world champion in 1984

THE COMPETITION

Competitors make 3 attempts at the squat, bench press, and deadlift, recorded by 3 judges. Only the best lift is retained, and any loss of control of the weight disallows the lift. An attempt must be validated by 2 judges, and 3 failed attempts mean elimination. Competitors determine the weight that they attempt to lift, with the first being the one attempting the lightest weight. In case of a tie in a lift category, the winner is the athlete who weighed less at the official weigh-in. If the lifters' weights are the same, an extra weigh-in at the end of regular competition determines the winner.

Bandages
Total width of wrist bandages must not exceed 10 cm.

Costume
Supports the thighs and back through strong compression. For bench press, the athlete must also wear an undershirt.

Weightlifter's shoes

Squat

The competitor takes the weight off the rack, backs up, and stands still. When the judge signals "Squat," he squats with the weight on his shoulders. His hips must descend below the level of his knees. He then returns to the starting position in a continuous movement and waits for the judge's "Rack" signal before placing the weight on the rack. There is no time limit.

Bench shirt
Made of synthetic fabric, it strongly compresses the chest and shoulders, helping to provide impulsion.

Protective belt

Bench press

When the judge signals "Start," the competitor, his arms tense and shoulders locked in position, lowers the bar until it contacts his chest. He pauses, then lifts the weight to the original position before placing it on the rack upon the judge's signal. His head, shoulders, and thighs must remain in constant contact with the bench, and his feet must not leave the ground. Two side judges check the athlete's contact with the bench and the spotters see to his safety during the attempt and may help him place the weight back on the rack.

Standing position

Classic starting position

Bandages
Total width of knee bandages must not exceed 30 cm.

Shoes
Athlete's choice

Deadlift

The powerlifter must lift the weight until he is standing upright, then place it back on the ground. The movement can be executed in "sumo" position (legs apart) or classic position (legs together). At the top of the lift, the competitor's knees are straight and locked, and his shoulders are behind his hips. When the judge signals "Down," the weight is returned to the floor without loss of control. The hands are in opposing grips to provide a more secure grasp of the bar.

POWERLIFTER PROFILE

- There are 11 weight categories for men (from 52 kg to 125+ kg) and 10 for women (from 44 kg to 90+ kg), and 4 age classes, from 14 years to 50+ years. A shorter athlete has an advantage because he has to lift the weights to a lower height.

- Eight to 10 weeks before a competition, muscle-building exercises gradually move toward shorter series with heavier weights, to increase power without drawing too much on energy reserves. The thighs, pectorals, deltoids, triceps, and back muscles are highly developed.

Aquatic
Sports

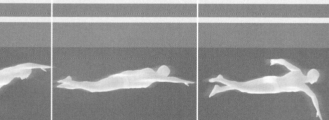

swimming

Site of the swimming competitions at the 1920 Olympics in Anvers, Belgium

There are many references to swimming competitions in Greek and Roman history; in Japan, the first races were organized in 1603. It was not until 1837, in London, that swim meets were organized by a sports association; in Sydney, a championship over 440 yards was held in 1846. The Association Metropolitan Swimming Club was founded in London in 1869, and that year it codified the rules for competing. Swimming, for men only, was included in the first modern Olympic Games over three distances: 100, 500, and 1200 meters. The races took place in the sea; only in 1924 did they move to pools. In 1908, the Fédération internationale de natation amateur (FINA) was created with 10 member nations, and at that year's Olympics, the first races in different strokes (backstroke, breaststroke, and freestyle) were held. The first women's races took place in 1912. Today, the biggest competitions are the Olympics and the world championships, inaugurated in 1973, which take place every two years, in odd-numbered years. The 25 meter world championships have been held every two years since 1993, now taking place in even-numbered years.

THE COMPETITION

Competitors must swim a defined distance. Races take place in a 25 m or 50 m pool. Men and women compete in 4 strokes: breaststroke, backstroke, butterfly, and freestyle. Some races combine all 4 strokes (medleys). The goal of competition is a race against the other swimmers and the clock. At the starter's first signal, the competitors take their position on the starting blocks (or backstroke grips) in their respective lanes. At the second signal (gun or electronic tone), they dive into the pool. If a swimmer has a false start he or she is disqualified. During the race, the swimmers must stay in their lanes.

OLYMPIC POOL

Referee
He is responsible for running the meet. He confirms the decisions made by the other judges and makes the final decision if there is an appeal.

Starter
He has full control of the swimmers from the time the referee turns the swimmers over to him until the race has commenced.

Stroke judges (4)
They check that each swimmer is performing the stroke legally.

Stroke judge
He makes sure that the swimmers' heads are above the surface of the water when they pass the 15 m line.

False start recall rope
It is placed 15 m from the start wall. When a false start is called, a signal identical to that for the start indicates to swimmers that they must return to the blocks. At the same time, the rope falls into the water.

Timers

Chief timer
He verifies the electronically recorded times, after checking with the timers.

Finish judge
He decides and reports the placing of the swimmers.

Stroke judge

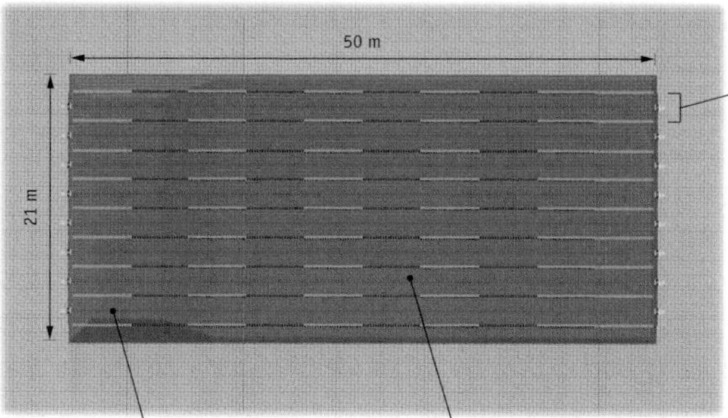

SCOREBOARD

Lane lines
Painted on the bottom of the pool, in the center of each lane.

Pool depth
It must be uniform for the Olympic Games (1.8 m), but can vary for world championships. The water must remain at one level and at a constant temperature (24°C).

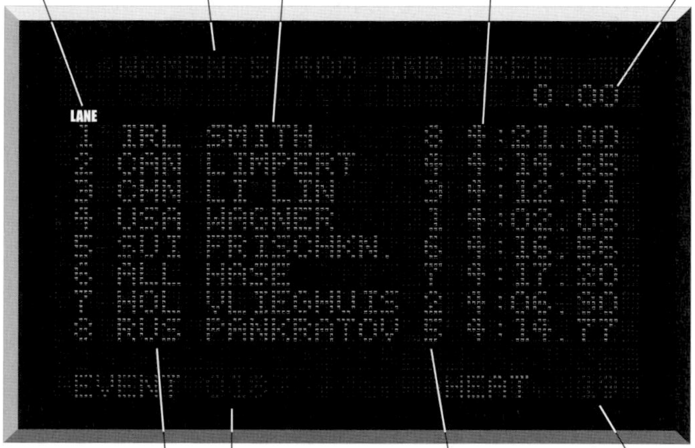

Type of race

Lanes

Swimmers' names

Swim times

Timer

Swimmers' countries

Competition number

Order of finish

Competition stage
Race identification (heat, quarter-final, semi-final, final).

Electronic touch pads
Set at the end of each lane, they measure 2.4 m x 0.9 m, and their upper edge must be 30 cm above the surface of the water. They are linked to a timing system programmed to stop the clock when the swimmer touches them, and they must be sensitive enough that light pressure activates the signal for the timing system.

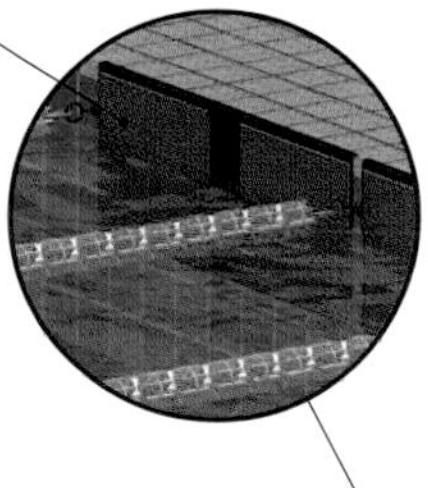

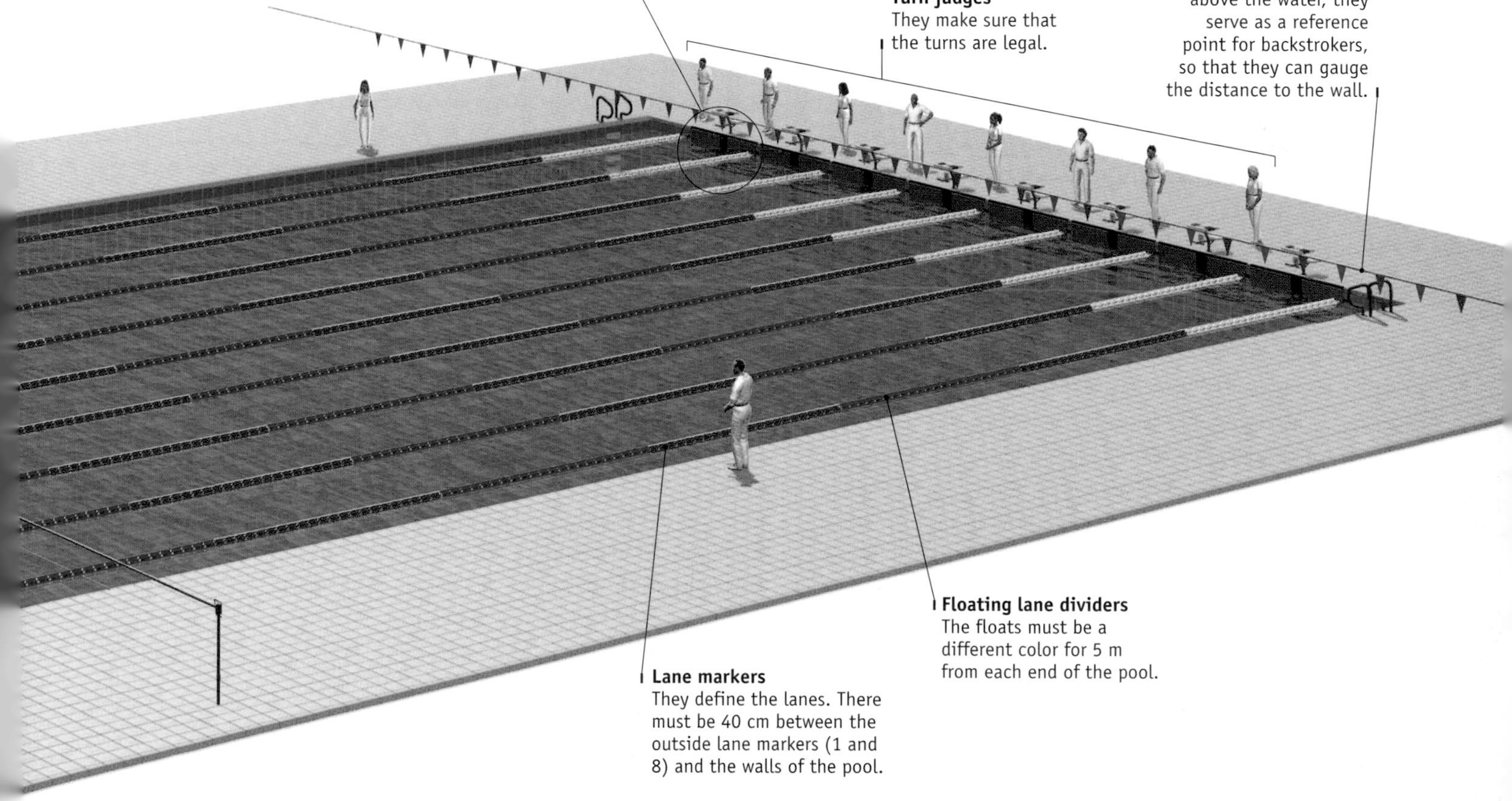

Turn judges
They make sure that the turns are legal.

Backstroke flags
Placed 5 m from the end of the lane and 1.8 m above the water, they serve as a reference point for backstrokers, so that they can gauge the distance to the wall.

Lane markers
They define the lanes. There must be 40 cm between the outside lane markers (1 and 8) and the walls of the pool.

Floating lane dividers
The floats must be a different color for 5 m from each end of the pool.

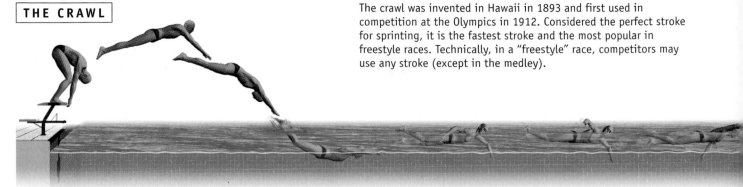

THE CRAWL

The crawl was invented in Hawaii in 1893 and first used in competition at the Olympics in 1912. Considered the perfect stroke for sprinting, it is the fastest stroke and the most popular in freestyle races. Technically, in a "freestyle" race, competitors may use any stroke (except in the medley).

Forward start

The swimmer holds his breath and concentrates until the start signal is given. He then pushes off strongly with his legs, stretching his body fully.

Starting to swim

Once under water, the swimmer returns to the surface with powerful flutter kicks.

THE BACKSTROKE

An Olympic event since 1900, the backstroke was invented in the late 19th century as a variant of the crawl, which was also being developed at the time. It is one of the least popular strokes, as many swimmers like to face the direction in which they are going. The biggest change in style took place in the mid 20th century, when swimmers realized that they could gain speed by bending their arms when they were submerged (previously, the arm was held straight throughout the cycle).

Backward start

The hands are placed on the starting grips, and the feet, braced against the wall, must be entirely under water. At the signal, the swimmer lets go of the grips and uses his legs to push off.

Starting to swim

While submerged, the swimmer does dolphin kicks (an undulating motion) or flutter kicks. He must not remain submerged for more than 15 m.

THE BREASTSTROKE

An Olympic event since 1908, the breaststroke is a complicated stroke. It demands the highest energy expenditure and perfect synchronization of simultaneous arm and leg movements. If the swimmer loses this synchronization, she is considered to be swimming freestyle and is disqualified.

Forward start

As for the crawl, the swimmer holds her breath until the start signal; she then pushes off with her legs and her body is fully stretched.

Starting to swim

The body must remain fully stretched and in a stomach-down position. The swimmer performs one complete pull of the arms before kicking with her legs. She can perform only one complete stroke under water after the start and the turns.

COMPETITIONS

Recognized distances at the Olympic Games and world championships:
- Men: 50, 100, 200, 400, and 1,500 m individual, 4 x 100 m, 4 x 200 m relays
- Women: 50, 100, 200, 400, and 800 m individual, 4 x 100 m, 4 x 200 m relays

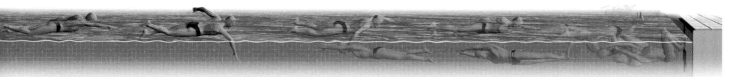

Stroke technique

The legs are submerged and perform flutter kicks, while the arms are alternately lifted forward then pulled through the water. The swimmer breathes out when his head is submerged.

Flip turn

The swimmer bends his body, dives slightly toward the bottom of the pool, and somersaults. He can touch the wall with any part of his body, but he in fact uses his feet, pushing off with them to gain impetus as he stretches his body.

COMPETITIONS

Recognized distances at the Olympic Games and world championships:
- Men: 100 and 200 m individual
- Women: 100 and 200 m individual

Other meets have added the 50 m individual (men and women)

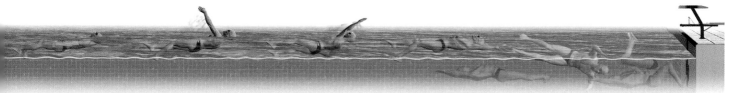

Stroke technique

The arms are lifted forward alternately, then pulled through the water between 45 and 60 cm below the surface. At the same time, the legs flutter kick to propel the swimmer.

Flip turn

The swimmer flips onto his stomach and then makes the somersault. As in the crawl, swimmers may touch the wall with any part of their body, but they generally use their feet to push off. The swimmer must have returned to the back-down position before his feet leave the wall.

COMPETITIONS

Recognized distances at the Olympic Games and world championships:
- Men: 100 and 200 m individual
- Women: 100 and 200 m individual

Other meets have added the 50 m individual (men and women)

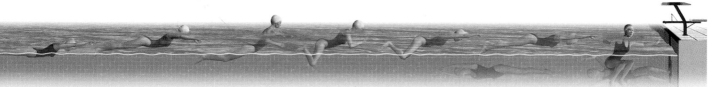

Stroke technique

The arms make three lateral movements in order: an "outward pull" (away from the body), then a "downward pull" (toward the bottom of the pool), and finally an "inward pull" (toward the body). In the kick, the legs bend to propel the swimmer and return to their initial position. The breaststroke kick provides more propulsion (about 70%) than do kicks in the other strokes (5–10%).

Open turn

The swimmer must touch the wall with both hands, above or below the water line; she then turns and puts her feet against the wall to push off. She must be in a horizontal position before her feet lose contact with the wall.

THE BUTTERFLY

Long known as the breast-butterfly, it became a style on its own at the Olympic Games in Helsinki in 1952.

Forward start

The swimmer holds his breath until the start signal, then pushes off strongly with his legs, his body fully stretched.

Starting to swim

The swimmer may make his first kicks while submerged; he may remain under water to a maximum distance of 15 m.

THE MEDLEY

Athletes swim each stroke for at least 50 m (one length of the pool). This race combines technique, speed, and endurance. The 4 strokes are the breaststroke, the backstroke, the butterfly, and the freestyle, which can be any stroke but the first three. (Swimmers in fact use the crawl.)

THE MEDLEY RELAY

The medley relay involves teams composed of specialists in each stroke. All freestyle specialists use the crawl.

The order of the strokes is set and is different for individuals and relays.

Individual: 1. Butterfly – 2. Backstroke – 3. Breaststroke – 4. Freestyle.

Medley relay: 1. Backstroke – 2. Breaststroke – 3. Butterfly – 4. Freestyle.

The first swimmers start from the backstroke position, and the other team members use the starting blocks.

COMPETITIONS

Recognized distances at the Olympic Games and world championships:
• Men: 200 and 400 m individual; 4 x 100 m relay
• Women: 200 and 400 m individual; 4 x 100 m relay

SWIMMER PROFILE

• Swimmers must have strength and endurance, and they undergo intense physical training.

• Training involves many high intensity splits (repetitions of short distances); some athletes also develop their strength (both arms and legs) with sessions in the weight room (weights, muscle building). Before any competition, athletes gradually reduce the amount of training, while continuing high intensity splits. The reduction in fatigue level that follows is more important than the reduction in fitness level.

• Deltoids, trapezoids, and back thigh muscles are generally most developed; the hips are narrow (less resistance). Taller athletes have better reach (both arms and legs).

Alexandre "Sasha" Popov (RUS)
Best swimmer in the world since 1991. Quadruple Olympic champion and world champion over 50 m (1994).

Mark Spitz (USA)
Olympic champion in 1968 and star of the 1972 Olympics, he broke 26 individual world records and 35 American records between 1967 and 1972.

Jingye Le (CHN)
First female swimmer in history to swim 50 m in under 25 seconds. Olympic champion, she is also 4-time world champion.

Krisztina Egerszegi (HUN)
The greatest woman backstroker ever. An Olympic and world champion, she holds the world record for the 200 m backstroke.

COMPETITIONS

Recognized distances at the Olympic Games and world championships:
• Men: 100 and 200 m individual
• Women: 100 and 200 m individual
Other meets recently added the 50 m individual (men and women).

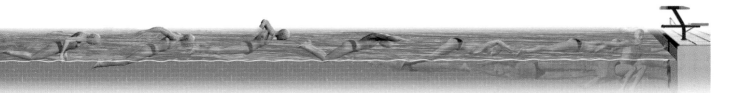

Stroke technique

Both arms are lifted forward and pulled backward symmetrically for propulsion. The shoulders must stay horizontal and parallel to the water surface. The legs also move in unison in the dolphin kick, completing the undulating movement begun by the arms. The swimmer breathes in at the end of the stroke, as the arms return over his head.

Open turn

The swimmer must touch the wall with both hands before turning and pushing off the wall with his feet. The athlete may dolphin-kick several times before returning to the surface, but must be in a stomach-down position before his feet lose contact with the wall.

CHANGES IN THE WORLD RECORD

Since 1991, records have been kept for races in the 25 m pool (before that, only in the 50 m pool).

100 M BACKSTROKE

4 X 100 MEDLEY

100 M BREASTSTROKE

100 M BUTTERFLY

100 M FREESTYLE

EQUIPMENT

The only authorized equipment is the swimsuit, swim cap, and goggles. Competitors are not allowed to use or wear anything that may increase their speed, ability to float, or endurance.

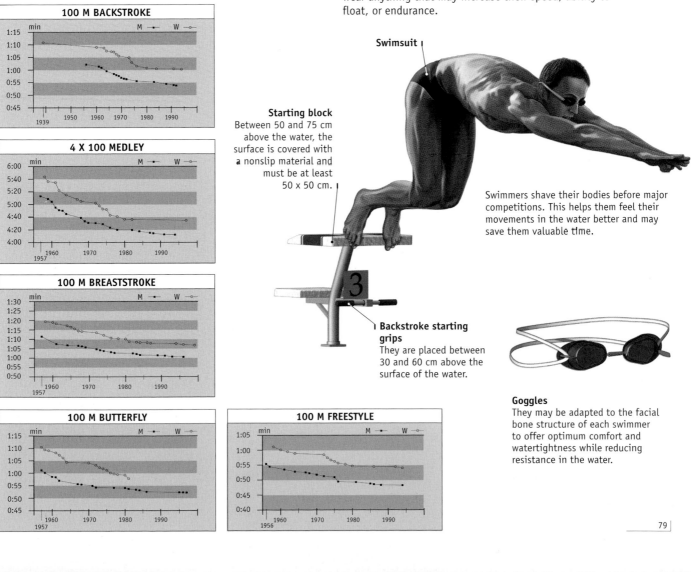

Swimsuit

Starting block
Between 50 and 75 cm above the water, the surface is covered with a nonslip material and must be at least 50 x 50 cm.

Swimmers shave their bodies before major competitions. This helps them feel their movements in the water better and may save them valuable time.

Backstroke starting grips
They are placed between 30 and 60 cm above the surface of the water.

Goggles
They may be adapted to the facial bone structure of each swimmer to offer optimum comfort and watertightness while reducing resistance in the water.

synchronized swimming

Jersey Swimming Club Dolphins team practice in the Havre des Pas (GBR) pool in 1935

Developed in the early 1900s by Canadian swimmers, according to some historians, or Australian swimmers according to others, synchronized swimming is a sport performed exclusively by women; it combines swimming, dance, and gymnastics. It got its current official name in 1934, but it was not until the Olympic Games in Helsinki in 1952 that the sport was first demonstrated. The same year, the Fédération internationale de natation amateur (FINA) recognized synchronized swimming and integrated it into its official program. The technical aspect quickly took over from the artistic side with the first world championships. Synchronized swimming became an official Olympic event in Los Angeles in 1984, with solo and duet competitions. In 1996, team competition was the only synchronized swimming event, with duets once again on the roster in 2000. Aside from the Olympics, the world championships are a major competition. Since 1973, they have been taking place every three or four years, with three types of competition: solo, duet, and team.

THE COMPETITION

In competition, swimmers perform two routines for the judges: the first technical, the second free. The technical routine involves required elements executed in a defined order (6 figures in solo, 7 in duet, 8 in team), while the free routine allows swimmers to present an artistic composition including technical elements of their choosing, combined in a choreography. For each routine, swimmers receive 2 marks, one for technical merit and one for artistic impression; the marks are out of 10, in increments of $1/10$ of a point.

Swimmers combine various figures in the water to musical accompaniment, in 3 events: solo, duet, and teams of 8. For the latter 2 events, the synchronization must be perfect, both with the music and between the swimmers.

Competitors are judged on their technical and physical abilities (quality, accuracy, difficulty) and their artistic performance (presentation, transitions, interpretation, creativity).

POOL

Judges (10)
They mark each program: 5 give a technical mark and 5 give an artistic mark. They are placed 2 by 2 (one artistic and one technical). They enter their marks on a computer keyboard and a central unit makes the final calculation.

Assistant referee
She checks the placement of the swimmers and signals the start of their programs.

Meet referee
She makes sure that the competition runs smoothly and that FINA rules are respected, and she imposes penalties.

AWARDING MARKS

Technical routine

Solo swimmers have 2 min, duets have 2:20 min, and teams have 2:50 min. The technical mark is worth 60% of the total; the artistic mark 40%.

Free routine

Solo swimmers have 3:30 min, duets have 4 min, and teams have 5 min. A maximum of 10 seconds of "deck work" (movements on the edge of the pool) is allowed. The artistic mark is worth 60% of the total; the technical mark 40%.

The marks for the two routines are combined: the technical routine is worth 35% of the total; the free routine 65%. The total mark determines the final rankings. Swimmers are penalized 2 points if they do not perform the figures in the proper order in the technical routine or if they support themselves on the edge or the bottom of the pool in any routine.

EQUIPMENT

The hair is tied or held back with gelatin so that it does not get in the swimmer's way.

Swimsuit
It must not have any decorations.

Nose clip
Made of plastic covered metal, this keeps water from reaching the sinuses. Many swimmers now prefer gelatin "plugs" inserted in the nostrils that take the shape of the sinuses.

20 m

30 m
Depth: 3 m

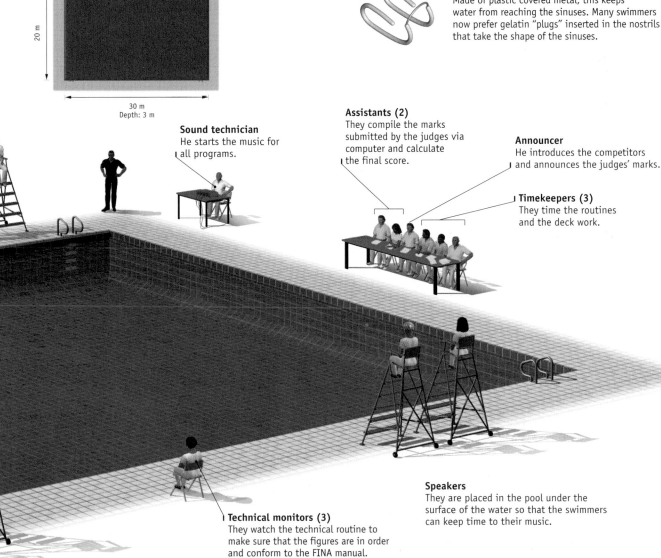

Sound technician
He starts the music for all programs.

Assistants (2)
They compile the marks submitted by the judges via computer and calculate the final score.

Announcer
He introduces the competitors and announces the judges' marks.

Timekeepers (3)
They time the routines and the deck work.

Technical monitors (3)
They watch the technical routine to make sure that the figures are in order and conform to the FINA manual.

Speakers
They are placed in the pool under the surface of the water so that the swimmers can keep time to their music.

BASIC POSITIONS AND FIGURES

The actions and figures that form a routine are built around some 20 basic positions. A routine is a series of figures joined by transitions that let the swimmer cover the pool and breathe, while presenting a specific choreographic number.

Barracuda

Vertical position
The body is stretched perpendicular to the surface. The legs are together, the head down. The head, hips, and ankles must be aligned.

Front walkover

Castle position
The swimmer is in a vertical floating position, the body stretched. The small of the back is arched, with the hips, shoulders, and head aligned vertically. One leg stretches backward as close as possible to horizontal, with the foot on the surface.

Back walkover

Split position
The legs are horizontally open toward the front and back of the swimmer's body. The feet and legs remain on the surface and the body is perpendicular.

Forward pike position
The body bends 90°. The legs and hips remain horizontal on the surface; the body (trunk straight, back flat, head aligned) is perpendicular to the surface.

ROUTINE

The routine presented by the swimmer involves various basic positions that are connected to form figures. In the technical program, swimmers must execute exactly the figures described in the FINA manual. In the free routine, they present variations (hybrids) of these figures, without reproducing them exactly.

The swimmer executes a figure inspired by the barracuda: from a back layout position, she lifts her legs to vertical; the body sinks to take a back pike position, followed by a boost that puts her in a vertical position.

She then tucks and transitions to the surface.

The transition, accompanied by an arm movement, lets her incorporate creative choreographic elements. She also uses the transition to cover the pool.

TEAM COMPETITION

The synchronization between the swimmers and with the music must be perfect. In the free routine, the swimmers do not have to perform the same figures at the same time. Difficult figures and transitions are the elements practiced most in training.

PROFILE OF SWIMMERS

- Training takes 7 to 9 hours per day, 6 days a week, divided among different activities.
- Preparation is physical, technical, artistic, and psychological:

  Physical: muscle building (abdominals, neck, trapezius, and back, arm, and leg muscles), cardiovascular exercise (running, swimming lengths with weights), and flexibility.

  Technical: mastery of figures, routines, body movement, aquatic sessions, and work on "high-risk" elements (platform, carries).

  Artistic: dance training (jazz and ballet), gymnastics, and choreography. Swimmers must also develop a musical sense so that they can follow their music.

  Psychological: visualization, relaxation, motivation, and land drills (rehearsals outside of the pool).

- A swimmer reaches the elite level at the age of 15 to 16 and rarely maintains this level after 28 to 29 years of age.

Sylvie Fréchette (CAN)
She won the World Cup in solo in 1991 and was Olympic champion in solo in 1992.

Platform

Without touching the bottom of the pool, the swimmers group themselves under water to make the "platform." The shorter the preparation time, the higher the mark. At the end of the figure, the platform may sink, or the swimmer on top may dive. The platform is a very spectacular figure.

Olga Sedakova (RUS)
World champion in 1998 in solo, duet, and team. European champion in solo and pairs in 1991; in solo, duet, and team in 1993; in solo and team in 1995 and 1997.

DUET

The duet event requires excellent coordination between the two swimmers and with the music. In the free routine, the two swimmers are not required to perform the same figures at the same time, as long as the program is homogeneous and artistic.

At the end of this movement, she moves into an Eiffel walk.

During this movement, she includes a hybrid, a variation on the original figure (for example, bending a leg before entering the split position).

She continues the routine with a front walkout and may perform another transition.

water polo

The Hungarian team, gold medalists at the Berlin Olympics in 1936. Since then, Hungary has won a number of Olympic titles and world championships

Water polo is a ball sport played in the water between 2 teams; it combines speed, endurance, accuracy, and team spirit. The first ball game in water was played around 1840: players astride barrels pushed a ball toward a goal with paddles. This game's resemblance to polo on horseback gave rise to the name water polo. The first rules were written around 1870. Between 1880 and 1888, water polo took more or less the form it has today; the rules were unified in 1908, when the Fédération internationale de natation amateur (FINA) was formed, then changed in 1950. Water polo has become a more technical than physical game, calling upon speed, good swimming skills, and team spirit. A 2 referee system was introduced at the Montreal Olympics (1976). In parallel to the Olympic Games, FINA organizes world championships every four years and a World Cup every two years, including women's water polo (since 1979 in the World Cup, since 1986 in the world championships). The longest standing team sport in Olympic history, men's water polo was introduced in Paris in 1900, while women's water polo becomes an official Olympic sport in Sydney in 2000.

THE GAME

Each team has 13 players: 7 in the pool and 6 reserves. Among the 7 active players, one is the goalkeeper. The aim is to score more goals than the opposing team in a defined time (4 7-minute periods in real time). Players must stay in the water without touching the bottom (except the goalkeeper) or supporting themselves in any way. At the beginning of the game and each period, the players line up on their respective goal lines. The referee throws the ball into the middle of the pool and the players race to take possession. After each goal, players go to their side of the pool, and the team against which the goal was scored puts the ball into play. With the exception of the goalkeeper, players may not hold the ball with both hands or hit it with their fists. The team in possession of the ball must throw at the opposing goal within 35 seconds after it takes possession. If a game that requires a winner ends in a tie, extra time (2 3-minute periods) is played.

Secretaries (2)
The first keeps track of goals scored, fouls, and exclusions (temporary and permanent). The second tells temporarily excluded players when they can return to the play.

Timekeepers (2)
The first keeps track of playing time and exclusions. The second keeps track of possession time by the attacking team (35 seconds).

THE POOL

Referee

Goal judge

Goal line

PLAYER POSITIONS

Men: 30 m (25 minimum) Women: 25 m
Minimum depth: 1.8 m

Men: 20 m (10 minimum) Women: 17 m

Right winger
He passes the ball to the player best placed to throw at the goal (center forward or guard) or throws the ball himself. In defense, he blocks the other team's left guard.

Right guard
Blocks the other team's left winger and helps with offense.

Goalkeeper
Keeps the ball from entering the goal and starts the attack.

Center guard
Blocks the other team's center forward and directs offensive moves.

Left winger
He passes accurately (to the center forward) and is a fast swimmer. He often throws at the goal. In defense, he blocks the other team's right guard.

Center forward
In front of the opposing goal, he either throws at the goal or draws an opposing player to free up space for his teammates. In defense, he blocks the other team's center guard.

Left guard
Blocks the other team's right winger and helps with offense.

Goal judges (2)
They signal valid goals (the ball must be completely across the goal line) and balls out of bounds behind the goal line (goal or corner throws).

Goals
Made of fiberglass or plastic, they are held in the water by cables attached to the side of the pool or attached to the wall (in smaller pools). There must be at least 30 cm between the goal lines and the pool wall.

3 m

0.90 m

Reserves

Coach

Penalty zone

2 meter line

4 meter line

7 meter line
Markers in distinct colors are placed on both sides of the pool to indicate the various play zones.

Half distance line

Referees (2)
A referee on either side of the pool watches the half of the pool to his right. If a foul is committed, he whistles the play dead. With one arm, he indicates where the ball must be put back into play. With the other, he points in the direction of offense. He indicates when excluded players can return to the play, using blue and white flags (according to the team color).

TECHNIQUES AND TACTICS

Free throw

The ball is put into play by the team against which a foul was committed. All players must be able to see the ball leave the thrower's hand. A free throw may be aimed directly at the goal from outside of the 7 meter zone. Inside this zone, 2 players must touch the ball before a throw at the goal is made. A player can make a free throw to himself by dribbling the ball.

Numerical advantage

During a numerical advantage following an exclusion, the attacking team places 4 players across the 2-m line: 2 in front of the goal and 1 on each wing. The 2 remaining players are placed 5 m from the goal. The wingers are usually the best passers, while the drawn-back players are the best throwers. The defending team places 3 players between the 4 attackers on the 2-m line. The 2 remaining players face the 2 drawn-back players to try to block their throws.

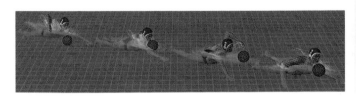

Dribbling

The player opens his arms and pushes the ball forward, protecting it from opposing players. The player in possession of the ball may also use his body as a screen between the ball and the opposing player, as long as he does not make any deliberate move to push the other player away.

Penalty shot

This takes place after a major foul by a defending player in his 4 m zone. It can be made by any player on the attacking team except the goalkeeper. Upon the referee's signal, the player immediately throws the ball toward the net in an uninterrupted motion. If the ball rebounds off the goalkeeper or a goalpost, it is in play and the game continues.

GOALKEEPER TECHNIQUE

His playing position is leaning forward near the surface of the water so that he can straighten and make a rapid thrust with his arms to stretch out and catch the ball. His leg and abdominal muscles are used constantly. When a shot is directed toward him, he tries to stop or slow it by putting his arms forward. When the ball falls in front of him, he can grab it and start his team's attack.

EQUIPMENT

Cap
One team wears dark blue caps; the other, white caps, except for the goalkeepers, who wear red caps so that they are clearly identified. The caps are numbered on both sides. The goalkeeper wears the number 1; the other players take numbers 2 to 13. The ear protectors are soft.

Ball
It is waterpoof and must not be covered with any oily substance.

Men: 68–71 cm
Women: 65–67 cm
Weight: 400–450 g

FOULS

Water polo has 2 types of fouls, ordinary and major, that entail various penalties.

Ordinary foul
This is any action against the rules: not respecting the zone lines, keeping the ball longer than permitted, and so on. For these infractions, a free throw is whistled against the offending team. The throw is made at the spot where the foul took place (except within the 2 m zone, when it is made on the line at the place closest to the foul).

Major foul
Any deliberate physical action made against an opposing player or official and any misconduct or unsportsmanlike conduct are considered major fouls. A major foul results in a free throw or penalty shot, depending on where it was committed. Major fouls are counted against a player as personal fouls and entail a 20 second penalty. If he commits 3 personal fouls, a player is permanently excluded from the game and can be replaced only after 20 seconds, unless a goal is scored against his team during that time.

PLAYER

He is always in motion in the water. If he isn't swimming, he treads water (performs leg movements that keep him on the surface). When he is in possession of the ball, his arm is extended backward to protect it from opposing players, and his trunk and shoulders are turned. When the player throws the ball, he uses his entire torso.

PLAYER PROFILE

- Water polo players must be excellent swimmers with high endurance and have an excellent cardiorespiratory system. The most developed muscles are those of the torso (trunk, abdominals, and shoulders) for ball handling, and the legs (players must constantly be treading water).

- Training has 3 aspects: muscle warm up (calves, thighs, trunk, abdominals, arms, shoulders) outside of the pool, swimming work (lengths in crawl and backstroke, with and without the ball), and ball plays (passes, throws). Athletes also develop endurance and muscle strength with gym exercises, running, and exercises with the medicine ball.

Manuel Estiarte (SPA)
Olympic champion in 1996, silver medalist in 1992, and world champion in 1998, he is one of the greatest players in the history of water polo.

Francesco Attolico (ITA)
Olympic champion goalkeeper in 1992 and bronze medalist in 1996. He was world champion in 1994 and European champion in 1993 and 1995.

apnea freediving

pnea is defined as temporarily stopping respiration, or holding one's breath. The amount of time that divers can hold their breath depends on their respiratory pulmonary volume. The origins of apnea freediving go back to prehistoric times. Shells found in archaeological excavations and at certain water depths reveal that people were diving tens of thousands years ago. Writing in the 9th century B.C., Homer mentioned diving, and military historians in Antiquity related the exploits of "divers over the side" who held their breath under water to attack enemy ships. The use of divers for military purposes continued into modern times. In peacetime, apnea freediving was used for fishing and gathering pearls, sponges, or coral in three different parts of the world: the eastern Mediterranean, the Persian Gulf, and the Yellow Sea. Today, apnea freediving is practiced by both men and women. The Association internationale pour le développement de l'apnée (AIDA), formed in the 1992, has organized world championships. The World Underwater Federation (CMAS) limits itself to keeping a register of records.

The legendary Jacques Mayol (FRA) began to apnea freedive at age 30; at age 49, he was the first man to dive below 100 m. He beat his own record 7 years later, in 1983, reaching a depth of 105 m. In 1988, his lifelong love became the subject of a movie, *Le Grand Bleu*.

TYPES AND RISKS OF DIVING

Prior to diving, the apnea freediver does respiratory exercises before breathing in as much air as possible; this is called moderate hyperventilation. The dangers of apnea are real. It can lead to loss of consciousness (fainting) or barotrauma. Resurfacing requires a state of maximum relaxation. AIDA recognizes 5 disciplines: constant ballast, variable ballast, static apnea, dynamic apnea (horizontal dives), and free immersion. Men's and women's records have been established in each category. There are also 3 demonstration disciplines to which AIDA sends observers: no limits, apnea freediving in the ocean, and successive apnea freedives in one hour.

CONSTANT BALLAST

The diver descends headfirst along a cable using only fins. He cannot use the cable to resurface and must keep the ballast (lead belt) that he started with. This is a physically demanding event.

Judges
They make sure that the freediver has attained the targeted depth and resurfaces without touching the cable.

Surface freediver
He is responsible for watching the freediver in the final meters before resurfacing.

Buoy
It holds the cable at the surface.

Divers
Placed along the descent, they make sure that the freediver is safe.

Tightener
Made of cement or lead, it weighs between 30 and 80 kg, depending on the type of dive. On its top is a metal platter with tags on it that the diver must bring back to the surface.

NO LIMITS DIVING

This consists of diving as deep as possible using a weight (sled) and resurfacing using a balloon or inflatable apparatus. Frenchman Jacques Mayol used the no limits technique when he was the first to freedive past 100 m in depth. This type of diving, done in a vertical position, is considered more a form of applied experimentation on the human body than true competition. The race to break depth records and the resulting proliferation of accidents have forced the CMAS to stop recording these feats, and it only acts as an observer at such events.

STATIC AND DYNAMIC DIVING

In static apnea freediving, the diver submerges to a shallow depth and stays under water as long as possible. In dynamic apnea freediving, with or without flippers, the diver submerges to a shallow depth and swims as far as he can without resurfacing.

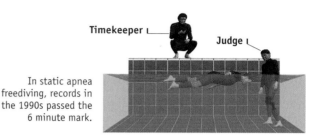

Timekeeper

Judge

In static apnea freediving, records in the 1990s passed the 6 minute mark.

RECORDS

The first record in apnea freediving was made in 1949, when Italian Raimundo Bucher reached a depth of 30 m with a sled. At the time, it was thought that the ribcage would be crushed by water pressure below a depth of 50 m. In November 1976, Frenchman Jacques Mayol reached the symbolic depth of 100 m thanks to training based on relaxation and yoga. In October 1992, Cuban Francisco "Pipin" Ferreras Rodriguez dived to a depth of 120 m. Then, in November 1996, Pipin reached 133 m before being beaten by Italian Umberto Pelizzari at 150 m. Among women, Cuban Deborah Andollo holds the variable ballast record (90 m) and French Audrey Mestre the no limits record (115 m).

EQUIPMENT

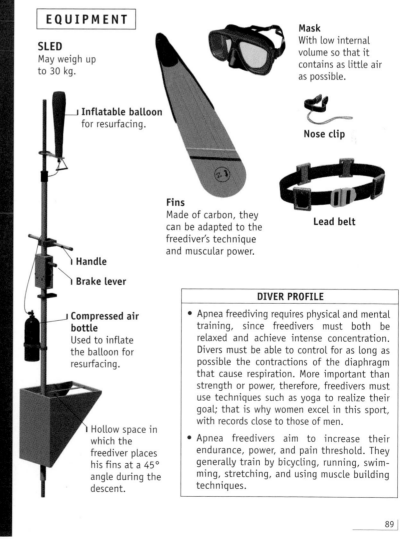

Physician

Judge

Winch

SLED
May weigh up to 30 kg.

Inflatable balloon
for resurfacing.

Handle

Brake lever

Compressed air bottle
Used to inflate the balloon for resurfacing.

Hollow space in which the freediver places his fins at a 45° angle during the descent.

Mask
With low internal volume so that it contains as little air as possible.

Nose clip

Lead belt

Fins
Made of carbon, they can be adapted to the freediver's technique and muscular power.

DIVER PROFILE

- Apnea freediving requires physical and mental training, since freedivers must both be relaxed and achieve intense concentration. Divers must be able to control for as long as possible the contractions of the diaphragm that cause respiration. More important than strength or power, therefore, freedivers must use techniques such as yoga to realize their goal; that is why women excel in this sport, with records close to those of men.

- Apnea freedivers aim to increase their endurance, power, and pain threshold. They generally train by bicycling, running, swimming, stretching, and using muscle building techniques.

diving

Diving board in Highgate, north of London, used for the King's Cup competition in 1903

Diving, which involves plunging into water from a platform, dates back to the 4th century B.C. The Vikings practiced it 12 centuries later, and we know that the Mexican Indians were diving in the 18th century. Between 1800 and 1840, gymnastics programs were developed in Germany and Sweden that included diving off platforms. The first attempts to standardize and regulate the discipline date back to the end of the 19th century. Diving evolved as a sport first in England and Australia, and then spread to the United States and continental Europe. In 1904, diving made its official appearance on the St. Louis Olympic Games program, with one men's event on the 10 meter platform. Three meter springboard diving was introduced in 1908, and also in that year, a table of dives together with a rating of their degree of difficulty was introduced. Women's events first appeared in the Olympic Games in 1912 (plain high diving), and then in 1920 (springboard), with the first world championships being held in 1973. Since 1991, in addition to the usual Olympic events, the world championships have also included the 1 meter springboard for men and women. Synchronized diving (3 meter and 10 meter) was added in 1995, making its Olympic debut at the 2000 Games. Diving is regulated by the Fédération internationale de natation amateur (FINA).

HOW A COMPETITION IS ORGANIZED

Diving involves physical and technical skills. Divers jump from a platform or diving board and perform a figure as perfectly as possible before touching the surface of the water. Judges award marks for the mastery and ease with which divers perform the figure. Divers must enter the water with as little splash as possible. The order and details of each dive are indicated on a score sheet and given to the officials several hours before the start of the event. The dives begin at the referee's signal.

Olympic Games (men and women): individual and synchronized high diving (10 m platform), and individual and synchronized 3 m springboard diving.

World championships: individual events on the 1 m springboard, in addition to usual Olympic events. The 5 m and 7.5 m diving boards are used in other meets. All divers must perform a specific number of dives:

• high dive: 10 (men), 9 (women)

• springboard: 11 (men), 10 (women)

Olympic competitions consist of 3 phases:

• Preliminaries (involves all divers). From the 10 m platform, men perform 6 dives, and women do 5. The same applies to the 3 m springboard. For all of these dives, there is no limit to the degree of difficulty. The top 18 divers advance to the next round.

• Semi-finals. Men and women perform 4 dives from the 10 m platform and 5 from the 3 m springboard. A maximum degree of difficulty is imposed on the entire series of dives. The scores are added to the results from the preliminaries. The 12 best divers move on to the finals.

• Finals. In the finals, the results from the preliminaries are eliminated. The divers perform the same number of dives as in the preliminaries, and the degree of difficulty is open. The points earned are added to those from the semi-finals to obtain the final score. For each series, divers must select one dive from each dive category.

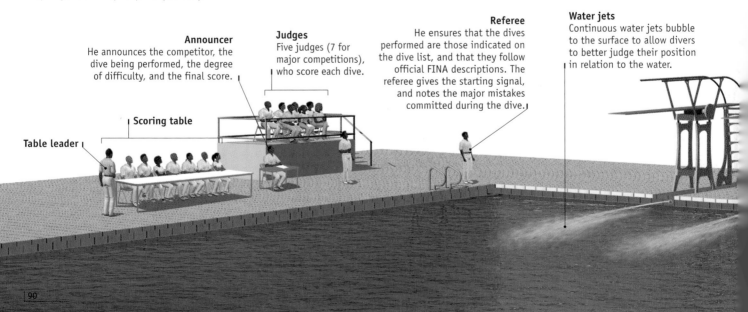

Announcer
He announces the competitor, the dive being performed, the degree of difficulty, and the final score.

Judges
Five judges (7 for major competitions), who score each dive.

Referee
He ensures that the dives performed are those indicated on the dive list, and that they follow official FINA descriptions. The referee gives the starting signal, and notes the major mistakes committed during the dive.

Water jets
Continuous water jets bubble to the surface to allow divers to better judge their position in relation to the water.

Scoring table

Table leader

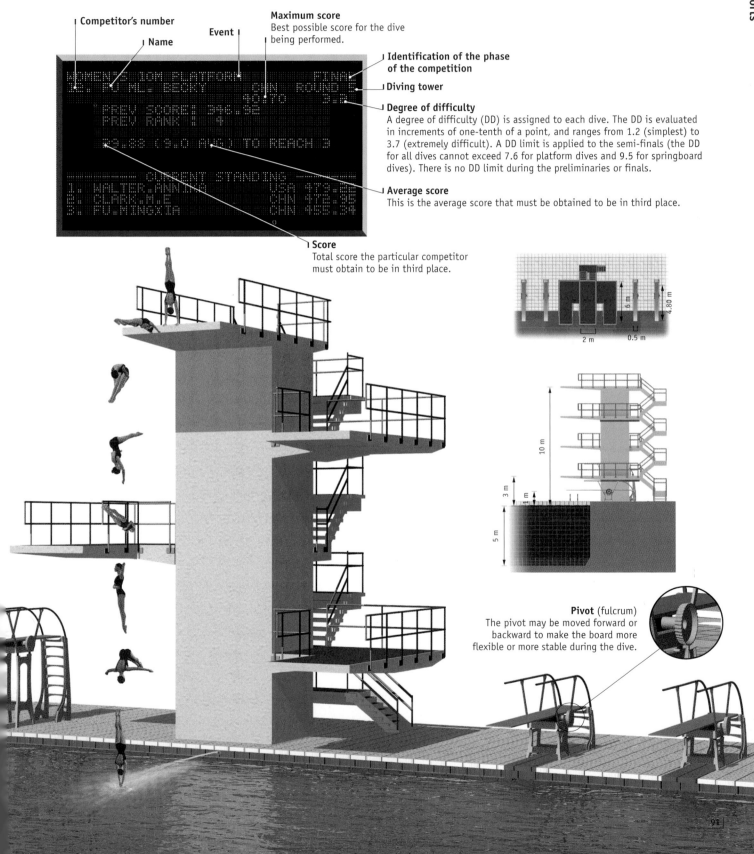

SCORING

Once the points are awarded, the highest and lowest scores are eliminated. The remaining scores are totalled and multiplied by the difficulty factor. If there are 7 judges, the total of the remaining scores is divided by 5, then multiplied by 3, to obtain results comparable to events judged by 5 judges. The calculations are done by computer. If there is a problem, the officials at the scoring table do a manual recalculation.

Competitor's number

Name

Event

Maximum score
Best possible score for the dive being performed.

Identification of the phase of the competition

Diving tower

Degree of difficulty
A degree of difficulty (DD) is assigned to each dive. The DD is evaluated in increments of one-tenth of a point, and ranges from 1.2 (simplest) to 3.7 (extremely difficult). A DD limit is applied to the semi-finals (the DD for all dives cannot exceed 7.6 for platform dives and 9.5 for springboard dives). There is no DD limit during the preliminaries or finals.

Average score
This is the average score that must be obtained to be in third place.

Score
Total score the particular competitor must obtain to be in third place.

Pivot (fulcrum)
The pivot may be moved forward or backward to make the board more flexible or more stable during the dive.

TECHNIQUE

The FINA manual lists 91 platform dives and 70 3-m springboard dives. Competitors must select the series of dives they will perform during a competition from this list. The dives are divided into 5 groups for both platform and springboard dives. A sixth group of arm stand dives is allowed only in platform diving.

In each of these groups, the dives are distinguished by form (straight, pike, tuck, or free), by the movements presented (the number of somersaults, etc.), and by type of entry into the water (head first or feet first).

Some dives include somersaults (360° rotations of the body), and half-turns (180° rotations). They are differentiated by the number of half-turns completed (one, one-and-a-half, two, two-and-a-half) and by the number of half-twists.

DIVE GROUPS

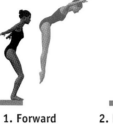    

| 1. Forward | 2. Backward | 3. Reverse | 4. Inward | 5. Twist | 6. Arm stand |

The arm stand position position must be held for five seconds.

BODY POSITION

Regardless of the type of dive selected, body position must be graceful, supple, and fluid. The diver must have mastery of each movement. Body position must be one of the 3 authorized by FINA regulations. A fourth (free) position allows the diver to perform a movement of his choice, but the free position must correspond to an existing position.

Approach

An approach is used for forward and reverse dives. Both of the diver's feet must be in contact with the springboard (3 m and 1 m boards) at takeoff, specifically when the diver pushes down on the board to lift off. For platform competitions, divers are allowed to take off on one foot.

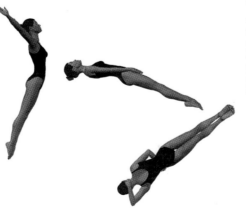

Pike

The body must be bent at the hips. The legs must be straight, without any flexion in the knees. The feet must be together, with the toes pointed. The arms may be stretched toward the toes, or held out at the diver's side or under the thighs or calves.

Straight

Arm position is optional (either stretched above the head or held alongside the body). There must be no flexion at the knees or the hips. The feet must be together, with the legs straight and the toes pointed.

Tuck

The body must be in a tuck position; both hips and knees are flexed, with the knees tucked tightly under the body and in line with the feet. The hands must be on the legs, and the toes must be pointed.

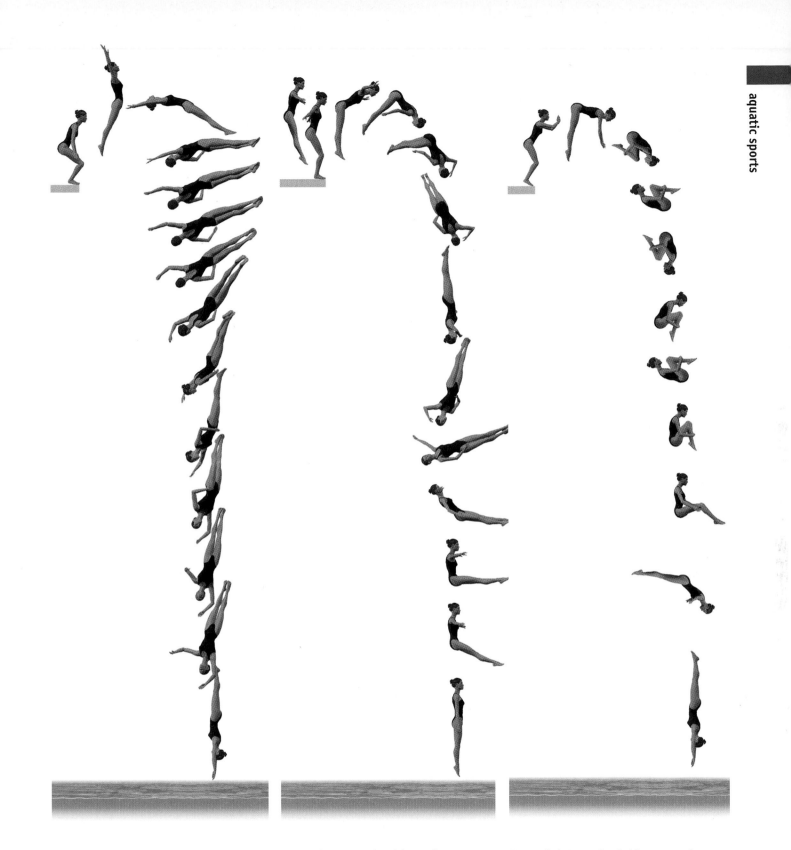

Reverse dive with a twist

This dive is performed in a series with a limit being placed on the degree of difficulty. The dive must appear effortless. At the beginning of the rotation, the diver lowers one arm to set the body into a spin.

Forward somersault with a twist

This dive requires perfect control over the sequence of movements, beginning with the approach. After springing up, the diver momentarily brakes and then slowly guides the body into a rotation.

Forward three-and-a-half somersault in the tuck position

The takeoff from the platform must be high enough to ensure the complete progression of all movements. The diver must guide her body properly in the air in order to straighten out before entering the water.

WATER ENTRY

Feet first

The body must be perfectly extended. The diver must pay special attention that there is no flexion at the ankles, knees, hips, or shoulders.

Head first

The hands must be crossed and pressed tightly together. At the point of entry into the water, the diver executes a quick movement of the hands, wrists, and arms, as if opening a space to allow the rest of the body to pass through. This movement helps reduce splashing.

PROFILE OF A DIVER

- Technical impression (grace, expertise, and effortlessness) counts for a large portion of the points awarded. It is essential that the diver present the most aesthetically pleasing and elegant silhouette possible.

- Muscle building activities focus on stretching and power. Divers must also develop flexibility and propulsion capabilities by practicing gymnastics. These activities include working the legs, arms, back, and more generally, joint movements (ankles, knees, shoulders, wrists). Training is rounded out with trampoline and dry board sessions (the diver wears a harness), during which the athlete learns to guide his body in the air, and becomes familiar with new movements.

- During training sessions, the coach operates a compressor, which creates a cushion of air bubbles at the bottom of the pool. This cushion of air rises when the diver enters the water, thus allowing the diver to dive with complete confidence.

- A top level career normally begins between the ages of 14 and 16, with performance peaking around the age of 21 or 22, and dropping off after the age of 26 (1 or 2 years later for women).

Fu Mingxia (CHI)
Three time Olympic champion: twice on the platform and on the springboard in 1996.

Greg Louganis (USA)
Double Olympic champion, in the platform and springboard events, in 1984 and 1988. World platform champion in 1978, 1982, and 1986, and world springboard champion in 1982 and 1986. He was the first diver to receive a perfect score of 7 10-point marks in the platform events.

SYNCHRONIZED DIVING

Two synchronized diving events are currently recognized, specifically the 10 m platform dive and the 3 m springboard dive. Two divers team up to perform simultaneous dives. The movements must be executed gracefully and at the same time. It is rare for the movements of both divers to be identical, as it is extremely difficult to synchronize the movements, which are the same as those performed during individual competition. In platform diving, both divers take off from the same platform, and must be at least 1 m apart at the start of the dive. For synchronized springboard, the divers use springboards that are side by side. The scores are awarded by 9 judges assigned to either the execution or synchronization aspects of the dive. The first set of judges observe only one of the divers. The second set of judges only consider the synchronization of the divers.

Nautical Sports

rowing

The famous race between Oxford and Cambridge in 1870

I n rowing, one or more rowers in a specially designed shell try to row as quickly as possible across a body of water. In ancient times, the Phoenicians, Greeks, and Egyptians raced galleys on natural waterways, or even on artificial lakes in giant Roman coliseums that were converted for the occasion. The first modern rowing regattas appeared in England in the 18th century but an Oxford-Cambridge student boat race organized in 1829 inaugurated the competitive sport of rowing. The first of England's now famous Henley Royal Regattas was held in 1839, and the sport's popularity spread to France around the same time. In the United States, Harvard and Yale held their first boat race, similar to the one between the two British universities, in 1852. Meanwhile, the sport continued to expand throughout Europe, and the International Rowing Federation (FISA) was founded in 1892. Three years later, in 1896, rowing made its debut at the modern Olympic Games. In 1976, women's rowing was included, but female competitors are still excluded from coxed pairs and coxless fours. The first men's world championship competition was held in 1962, and the first women's championship followed in 1974. FISA oversees the sport of rowing, and organizes international championships.

HOW A RACE IS ORGANIZED

The course runs in a straight line, and is divided into 6 to 8 lanes. Races also take place on rivers, and cover distances of 4 to 6 km. Depending on the number of competitors, the qualifying rounds consist of trials, quarterfinals, and semifinals. Those with the best time in the semifinals are given the privilege of starting in the center lane in the finals, giving them a better view of their opponents' progress. In the Olympic Games, there are 8 events for men and 6 events for women.

Aligners (6)
Stretched out on the starting docks, they keep the shells held in place.

Alignment judge
He makes sure that all the shells are lined up properly.

Starting zone (100 m)
A race may be stopped because of technical problems, such as a broken oar, only within this zone.

Umpire
He follows the racers in a boat. When he waves a red flag, it means that a crew has veered out of its lane and they have been disqualified. He uses a white flag to indicate that the race is running normally.

Safety officials
Stationed along the course, they ensure the safety of the competitors. They have at the ready a boat and diving equipment to help crews in need of assistance.

Starter
He calls the competitors and gives the starting signal. He also rules on false starts.

Starting zone buoys
They are yellow or orange for the first 250 m.

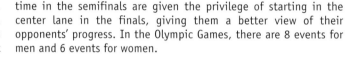

Starting docks (6)

Course buoys
They are white, and are used to mark the course between the first and last 250 m.

SCULLING TECHNIQUE

1. Catch

As the rower leans forward with knees bent and arms stretched out, the oar blade enters (catches) the water and propels the shell forward.

2. Drive

At the beginning of the stroke, the upper body remains in place, and the legs do all the work. Once the legs start pushing against the foot stretchers, the rower slides backward, keeping the arms and back straight. Then, once the hands pass the knees, the arms are quickly pulled in toward the trunk to give the shell its speed.

3. Feathering

The oar handle is lowered, raising the blade out of the water. Once the blade clears the water, the rower turns the handle to position the blade parallel to the water.

4. Recovery

With the blade out of the water, the rower begins the recovery by stretching the hands forward beyond the knees. As the body follows the hands, the seat slides forward and the rower is ready to start a new stroke. In a 2,000 m race, rowers complete an average 32 to 40 strokes a minute. During training, the pace is generally 18 to 20 strokes per minute.

THE BASIN

Ideally, it should be sheltered from wind and have no current. As waves can interfere with a race, the sides should be able to absorb rather than reflect them.

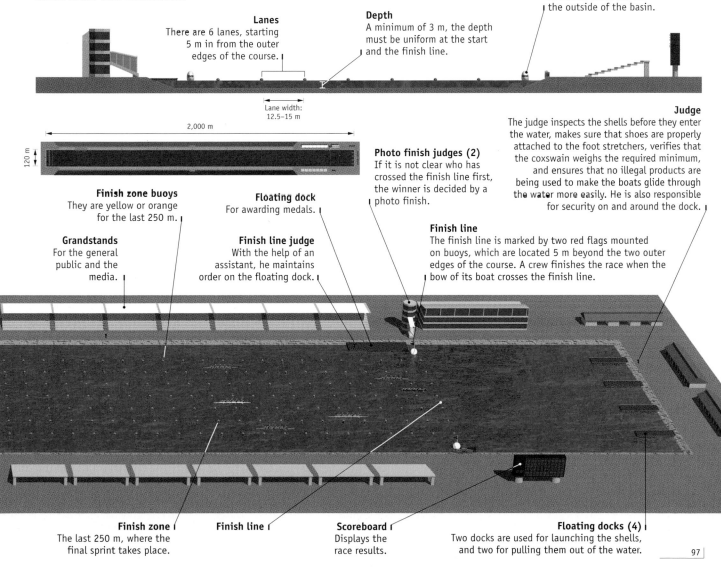

Lanes
There are 6 lanes, starting 5 m in from the outer edges of the course.

Depth
A minimum of 3 m, the depth must be uniform at the start and the finish line.

Markers
White markers are placed at 500 m intervals, on the outside of the basin.

Lane width: 12.5–15 m

2,000 m

120 m

Photo finish judges (2)
If it is not clear who has crossed the finish line first, the winner is decided by a photo finish.

Judge
The judge inspects the shells before they enter the water, makes sure that shoes are properly attached to the foot stretchers, verifies that the coxswain weighs the required minimum, and ensures that no illegal products are being used to make the boats glide through the water more easily. He is also responsible for security on and around the dock.

Finish zone buoys
They are yellow or orange for the last 250 m.

Floating dock
For awarding medals.

Finish line
The finish line is marked by two red flags mounted on buoys, which are located 5 m beyond the two outer edges of the course. A crew finishes the race when the bow of its boat crosses the finish line.

Grandstands
For the general public and the media.

Finish line judge
With the help of an assistant, he maintains order on the floating dock.

Finish zone
The last 250 m, where the final sprint takes place.

Finish line

Scoreboard
Displays the race results.

Floating docks (4)
Two docks are used for launching the shells, and two for pulling them out of the water.

TYPES OF SHELLS

In sweep boats, each rower has only one oar; in sculls, each rower has two oars. Except for skiffs, which are rowed by a single person, shells have between 2 and 8 rowers, with or without a coxswain. They may be made of wood, but are usually made of carbon fiber.

SCULLING BOATS

Name	Crew	Length	Weight
Skiff	1	8.2 m	14 kg Men-Women
Coxless Double	2	10.4 m	27 kg Men-Women
Coxless Quadruple	4	13.4 m	52 kg Men-Women
Coxed Quadruple	4	13.7 m	51 kg Men-Women
Coxed Octuple	8	19.9 m	96 kg Men-Women

SWEEP BOATS

Name	Crew	Length	Weight
Coxless Pair	2	10.4 m	27 kg Men-Women
Coxed Pair	2	10.4 m	32 kg Men
Coxless Four	4	13.4 m	50 kg Men
Straight Four	4	13.7 m	51 kg Men-Women
Coxed Eight	8	19.9 m	96 kg Men-Women

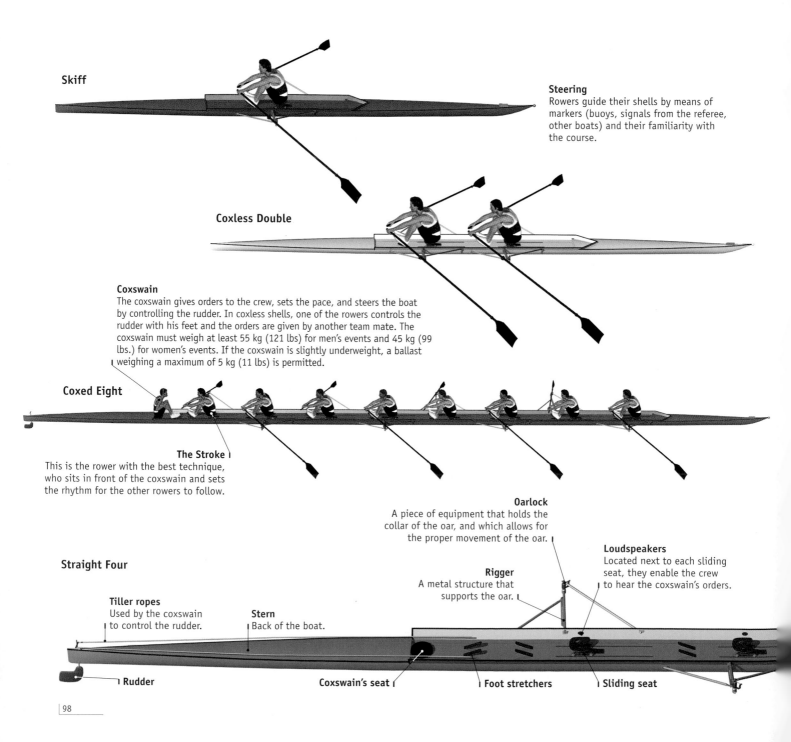

Skiff

Steering
Rowers guide their shells by means of markers (buoys, signals from the referee, other boats) and their familiarity with the course.

Coxless Double

Coxswain
The coxswain gives orders to the crew, sets the pace, and steers the boat by controlling the rudder. In coxless shells, one of the rowers controls the rudder with his feet and the orders are given by another team mate. The coxswain must weigh at least 55 kg (121 lbs) for men's events and 45 kg (99 lbs.) for women's events. If the coxswain is slightly underweight, a ballast weighing a maximum of 5 kg (11 lbs) is permitted.

Coxed Eight

The Stroke
This is the rower with the best technique, who sits in front of the coxswain and sets the rhythm for the other rowers to follow.

Oarlock
A piece of equipment that holds the collar of the oar, and which allows for the proper movement of the oar.

Loudspeakers
Located next to each sliding seat, they enable the crew to hear the coxswain's orders.

Rigger
A metal structure that supports the oar.

Straight Four

Tiller ropes
Used by the coxswain to control the rudder.

Stern
Back of the boat.

Rudder

Coxswain's seat

Foot stretchers

Sliding seat

EQUIPMENT

Seat
The seat slides on two rails to facilitate the rower's movements, and to increase the length and power of the strokes.

Foot stretchers
Attached to the bottom of the shell, they hold the rower's feet in place. Normally, the rower's shoes are bolted to the foot stretchers.

Jersey
In the rower's national, federation, or club colors.

Shorts

OARS

Originally made of wood with a symmetrical blade, oars are now made of carbon fiber and have asymmetrical blades to improve their catch in the water. Sweep oars are longer and have a wider blade, as the force comes from the rower's arms.

1996

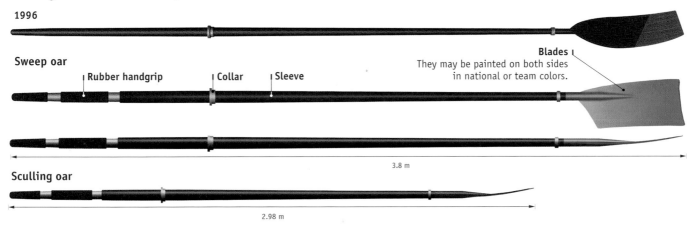

Blades
They may be painted on both sides in national or team colors.

Sweep oar

Rubber handgrip **Collar** **Sleeve**

3.8 m

Sculling oar

2.98 m

PROFILE OF A ROWER

- The physical exertion involved in rowing is equivalent to that required for cross country skiing or long track speedskating. The ability to row 2,000 m in approximately 6 minutes requires tremendous aerobic capacity.

- Leg, back, and shoulder muscles do most of the work.

- Since rowing is predominantly a team sport, characteristics such as good timing, balance, skill, strength, and physical fitness are essential, both individually and collectively.

- Rowing also demands concentration, motivation, and aggressiveness.

Marnie McBean (CAN)
She won 3 Olympic medals with team mate Kathleen Heddle (left); the coxless pairs in 1992, the double scull in 1996, and the eight in 1992. She also won the bronze medal for the quadruple scull in 1996, along with several world championships.

Steve Redgrave (GBR)
The only rower in history to win 4 gold medals at 4 consecutive Olympics (1984 to 1996). Also world champion 7 times (1986, 1987, 1991, 1993, 1994, 1995, and 1997).

Bow ball
Made of white plastic or rubber, it is used in judging photo finishes, and provides protection in case of ramming.

Splashguard
Keeps waves from entering the shell. Its tip is made of wood or carbon fiber.

Bow
Front of the boat.

99

canoe kayak: flatwater racing

C anoes and kayaks were invented more than 6,000 years ago by indigenous peoples in Canada and Greenland, who used them as a means of transportation on the rivers, lakes, and polar waters of these vast lands. In the 19th century, they began to be used in different sports, including flatwater racing, a test of speed in a canoe or kayak on still water. The first canoe club was established in London in 1865; in 1924, the International Repraëtantschaft für Kanuspart (IRK) was set up in Copenhagen. In the same year, flatwater racing was a demonstration sport on the Seine at the Olympic Games in Paris; in 1936, at the Olympics in Berlin, it became an official Olympic event. Flatwater racing is the oldest form of canoe kayak competition. In 1946, the International Canoe Federation (ICF) was created in Stockholm to replace the IRK. Both men and women compete.

Pair Sergei Chukhrai and Vladimir Parfenovich (USSR) were double Olympic champions, winning the 1000 m K2 and 500 m K2 in Moscow in 1980

THE COMPETITION

Flatwater racing in a canoe or kayak is a test of speed against the clock. In the Olympics, races are over distances of 500 and 1,000 m for men and 500 m for women. At the world championships, the 200 m distance for men and women is added. The boats must be immobile at the starting jetty, and all forestems must be aligned on the start line. If a competitor breaks her paddle within the 25 m start zone, the race is recalled. A draw determines the starting positions.

TACTICS

In 500 and 1,000 m races, quick starts are important, as is maintaining a rhythm and sprinting capacity. Traveling in a straight line is fastest.

BASIN

It is used for all race distances—200, 500, and 1,000 m— depending on the host country's facilities. There are 9 lanes marked by buoys that are white for the beginning of the course and red for the last 200 meters. The race ends when the boats reach the end of the red buoys.

PROFILE OF CANOE AND KAYAK RACER

- Flatwater racing in a canoe or kayak requires excellent aerobic capacity and muscular endurance.

- The arm, shoulder, and back muscles are the most used.

- The sport also requires power, agility, coordination, motivation, and competitive spirit.

- Training over at least 10 years is needed to become competitive internationally.

Caroline Brunet (CAN)
Silver medalist at Atlanta in 1996, she won gold medals in K1 at the 200, 500, and 1,000 m distances at the world championships in 1997. At the 1998 world championships, she won gold and silver; in 1999, 3 gold and 1 silver.

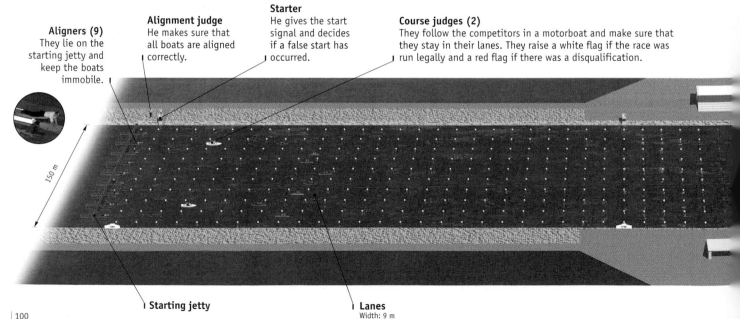

Aligners (9)
They lie on the starting jetty and keep the boats immobile.

Alignment judge
He makes sure that all boats are aligned correctly.

Starter
He gives the start signal and decides if a false start has occurred.

Course judges (2)
They follow the competitors in a motorboat and make sure that they stay in their lanes. They raise a white flag if the race was run legally and a red flag if there was a disqualification.

150 m

Starting jetty

Lanes
Width: 9 m

EQUIPMENT

In competition, the different types of canoes and kayaks are usually designated by their first letter followed by a number indicating the number of passengers. Thus, K2 designates a pairs kayak, C1 a singles canoe, and so on.

C1 CANOE

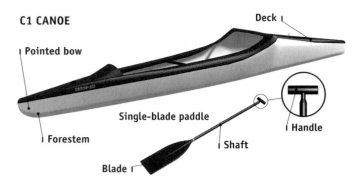

Pointed bow · Deck · Single-blade paddle · Handle · Forestem · Shaft · Blade

K1 KAYAK

Cockpit · Seat · Rudder · Double-blade paddle · Spoon · Tapered bow · Handle · Back

SIZE OF FLATWATER RACING CANOES			
Class	Maximum length	Minimum width	Minimum weight
C1	5.2 m	75 cm	16 kg
C2	6.5 m	75 cm	20 kg

SIZE OF FLATWATER RACING KAYAKS			
Class	Maximum length	Minimum width	Minimum weight
K1	5.2 m	51 cm	12 kg
K2	6.5 m	55 cm	18 kg
K4	11 m	60 cm	30 kg

CANOE PADDLING TECHNIQUE

1. Catch
With both arms stretched and the paddle out of the water, the paddler prepares to start the stroke.

2. Brace
The blade is completely immersed and vertical in the water and the paddler pulls it toward himself.

3. Recovery
When the pulling phase is over, the paddler straightens his back and lifts the paddle out of the water.

4. Return to catch
The paddler is ready to begin the next stroke.

Spectator stands (2)
Located on either side of the basin for the public.

Announcer
In the control tower, she introduces the participating countries, announces the order of finish, and relays messages from the chief official.

Chief official
From the control tower, he supervises the race and makes final decisions with regard to disqualifications.

Finish line judges (9)
They use timers to verify the time of each boat. Manual timing is used in case the electronic system—electronic timing, video cameras, and photo finish apparatus—fails.

Finish jetty

Scoreboard
Lists the 9 competitors' names, lane numbers, countries, times, and positions.

canoe kayak: whitewater

Canadian aboriginal peoples, who used canoes for transportation, were shooting river rapids hundreds of years ago. Today's whitewater slalom race is a test of both speed and accuracy in which paddlers must negotiate a series of gates, some of them in an upstream direction. Slalom races are quite new; after being included in the Olympics in Munich in 1972, they were absent from the Games for 20 years, until Barcelona in 1992. Whitewater slalom was an Olympic event in both Atlanta in 1996 and Sydney in 2000, where whitewater canoe kayak competition was open to men in C1 and C2 and to men and women in K1.

Scott Strausbaugh and Joe Jacobi (USA) whitewater canoe kayak gold medalists in the Barcelona Games.

THE COMPETITION

Whitewater slalom competitions are held in individual and team categories in K1, C1, and C2 for men and in K1 for women. Competitors must negotiate a series of gates in numerical order and in the proper direction, without touching them with their paddle blade, boat, or body. Gates are negotiated downstream or upstream. Generally, a competition involves 2 races, and the cumulative result determines the final rankings. Athletes who touch a gate receive a 2 second penalty; for passing through a gate in the wrong direction or missing it completely, a 50 second penalty is incurred. The start order is determined by draw, and athletes start at intervals of about 1 minute.

WATER COURSE

The course may be natural or artificial and has 20 to 25 suspended, numbered gates, including at least 6 that must be negotiated upstream.

Safety personnel
This team of 7 or 8 people see to the athletes' safety. They are equipped with cables, harnesses, and flotation devices so that they can respond to any emergency. Some are on the ground and others are in kayaks.

Gate judges
One judge at each gate makes sure that it is passed legally.

The course
300–600 m

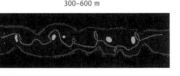

Safety official

Upstream gate
It has red poles.

Chief official
His decisions are final and he coordinates the other officials.

Course gates
They are held over the water by wires across the course. The bottom of a gate is 15 cm above the water surface.

Downstream gate
It has green poles.

Gate number
It is yellow or white and indicates to competitors the order and direction in which the gates must be negotiated. A diagonal red bar indicates the wrong direction.

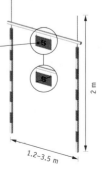

2 m

1.2–3.5 m

Other officials
The starter makes sure that the athlete is ready and gives the start signal with an electronic device. Boat controllers are stationed near the start line to make sure that the boats are legal and safe. They check weight, length, and life jackets, and place a sticker on the boat to show that it has been inspected. Timekeepers check the time of each racer.

TECHNIQUES AND TACTICS

Athletes must become familiar with the course before the race by studying it from the shore, and they plan tactics for each gate. It can be useful to observe the techniques used by other competitors. Finally, all maneuvers should increase or maintain speed.

PADDLING A KAYAK

1. Catch

The kayaker prepares to put her paddle in the water.

2. Brace

The quality of the brace determines the quality of the stroke.

3. Stroke

The paddle is almost vertical and the boat is propelled forward.

4. Transition

The blade is quickly lifted out of the water and the catch on the other side begins.

EQUIPMENT

The canoe is paddled with a single blade paddle from a kneeling position, while the kayak is paddled with a double blade paddle from a sitting position.

SIZES OF SLALOM BOATS			
Boat	Maximum length	Minimum width	Maximum weight
K1	4 m	60 cm	9 kg
C1	4 m	70 cm	10 kg
C2	4.58 m	80 cm	15 kg

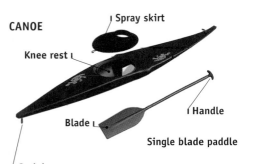

CANOE

Spray skirt

Knee rest

Blade

Handle

Single blade paddle

Grab loop

Safety straps attached to each end of the boat so that the boat can be caught if there are problems.

KAYAK

Spray skirt

Seat

Cockpit or wide washboard

Handle

Double blade paddle

Richard Fox (GBR)
This slalom specialist was K1 world champion five times: 1981, 1983, 1985, 1989, and 1993.

PROFILE OF CANOEISTS AND KAYAKERS

- Aside from indispensable technical knowledge, athletes must have strength, power, and agility.

- Training away from the water consists of running and weightlifting to maintain cardiovascular endurance and muscular power. On the water, long distance training builds muscular endurance, middle distance training improves speed and paddling cadence, and short distance training develops intensity at maximum cadence.

Helmet
It is required equipment. Made of plastic, fiberglass, or carbon, it keeps the competitor's head protected from impact against rocks or gates. Water must drain out of it quickly.

Life jacket
It must not impede the athlete's movements.

Spray skirt
It fits around the paddler's waist and is attached to the boat. Indispensable in whitewater, it keeps water from getting into the boat. Spray skirts are usually made of neoprene and are waterproof, resistant, and adjustable. Canoe spray skirts are round; kayak spray skirts are oval.

sailing

Éric Tabarly (FRA), a sailing legend. Among other races, he won the Transat in 1964 and 1976 and the Fastnet in 1967; in 1980, he established a new world record for crossing the Atlantic: 10 d, 5 h, 14 min, 20 s. He won the Coffee Route in 1997; in 1998, he perished in the Irish Sea.

There are many kinds of sailing competition involving different classes of boats, on every ocean, and under all weather conditions. In the 4th century B.C., the Egyptians used the power of the wind to push their papyrus rafts on the Nile, and the Polynesians used outriggers to make their dugout canoes with sails—the ancestors of today's multihull boats—go faster. In Antiquity, the Romans, Phoenicians, Greeks and Chinese all improved the capabilities of sailboats; later, the Spanish, Portuguese, French, and English did the same. In 1660, the first regatta took place in England between boats belonging to the Duke of York and Charles II. In 1749, the Prince of Wales created a trophy for a race between sailboats in the estuary of the Thames. The Hundred Guineas Cup was raced in 1851; an American boat won, and the renowned America's Cup race was born. In the early 20th century the exploits of navigators such as Slocum, Chichester, Moitessier, and Tabarly kept the popularity of sailing alive. Today, sailing is both a recreational activity and a high level sport; it has been an Olympic event since 1896. Competitions are run and governed by the International Sailing Federation (ISAF).

THE COMPETITION

There are 3 general categories of sailing competition: regattas on Olympic-type courses, ocean races, and match, or head-to-head, races. Although the boats and courses differ, the objective is the same in all races: to finish ahead of the competition. Races are open to men and women except for certain specific categories in the Olympics. In ocean racing, the international rules for preventing collisions are in force in addition to the competition rules. There are 9 classes of boats in the Olympics, and the races take place on a triangular Olympic course, the length of which is determined by the stretch of water used, the prevailing wind direction, weather conditions and the number of sailboats racing. The course is marked by buoys that must be passed in a specific order so that the team, usually composed of a helmsman who steers the boat and a crew, sail close hauled, in a reach, and in a run. The distance between the buoys varies according to the type of boat in the competition.

The Soling

This keelboat is the largest of the Olympic sailboats and has been in the Olympics since 1972.

Length: 8.2 m
Mainsail area: 13.6 m²
Jib: 8.1 m²
Crew: 3 men, 3 women, or mixed
Helmsman: 75–100 kg
Crew: 85–110 kg

The Star

This keelboat has been in the Olympics since 1932.

Length: 6.92 m
Mainsail area: 22.35 m²
Jib: 6.5 m²
Crew: 2 men, 2 women, or mixed
Helmsman: 75–100 kg
Crew: 95–135 kg

The Tornado

This catamaran, the fastest of the Olympic sailboats, has been in the Olympics since 1976.

Length: 6.09 m
Mainsail area: 16.87 m²
Jib: 5.2 m²
Crew: 2 men, 2 women, or mixed
Helmsman: 60–70 kg
Crew: 60–70 kg

The 49er

This centerboard boat was included in the Olympics for the first time in 2000.

Length: 4.99 m
Mainsail area: 15 m²
Jib: 6 m²
Crew: 2 men, 2 women, or mixed
Helmsman: 63–75 kg
Crew: 63–75 kg

The Finn

This centerboard boat has been in the Olympics since 1952.

Length: 4.5 m
Mainsail area: 10 m²
Crew: 1 man
Competitor: 70–100 kg

The Laser

A fast centerboard boat, it is among the most popular in the world and has been in the Olympics since 1996.

Length: 4.23 m
Mainsail area: 7.06 m²
Crew: 1 man
Competitor: 70–90 kg

Mistral class sailboard

A sport for both men and women, sailboarding has been in the Olympics since 1984.

Length: 3.7 m
Mainsail area: 7.4 m²
Crew: 1 man or 1 woman
Competitor: 50–70 kg

The Europe

Light and fast, this small centerboard boat is sailed by women and has been in the Olympics since 1992.

Length: 3.35 m
Mainsail area: 7 m²
Crew: 1 woman
Competitor: 45–63 kg

Full batten
Used to hold the shape of the upper part of the sail.

Leech
Outside edge of the sail.

Halyard
Rope or cable used to hoist the sails; it is named for the sail it hoists, for example, the jib halyard.

Mast
Spar made of metal or composite material that supports the sails.

Mast rigging
Keeps the stays and shrouds attached to the mast.

Luff
The edge of the sail attached to the mast.

Standing rigging
Stays and shrouds which support the mast.

Mainsail
The main sail of the boat stretched along the mast.

Spreaders
Attached to the mast, they keep the shrouds spread.

Shroud
Cable supporting the mast from the side.

Stay
Cable supporting the mast from the front.

Foot
The bottom edge of the sail stretched along the boom.

Jib
Triangular front sail.

Boom
Metal spar supporting the foot of the sail.

Trapeze
Enables a crew member to lean completely outside the cockpit.

Port
Left side of the boat looking toward the front.

Window
Allows the crew to see.

Bow
Front of the boat.

Running rigging
Sheets and tackle used to adjust the sail.

Sheet car
A pulley that slides on a rail to guide the sheets.

Centerboard control
Raises and lowers the centerboard.

Stern
Back of the sailboat.

Centerboard
Keeps the boat from moving sideways while sailing.

Starboard
Right side of the boat looking toward the front.

Rudder
Used to steer the boat.

The 470

This centerboard boat owes its name to its length, 4.70 m. It opened up Olympic competition to women at the 1988 Olympic Games.

Length: 4.7 m
Mainsail area: 9.88 m²
Jib: 3.76 m²
Crew: 2 men or 2 women
Helmsman: 50–70 kg
Crew: 50–70 kg

OLYMPIC COURSE

This is the course most frequently used in regattas for sailboats of all classes. The distance between the buoys varies according to the class. The length of the course depends on the class and number of sailboats, the stretch of water, and the weather conditions. The course is marked by buoys, which must be rounded in a precise order so that the boat sails close hauled, in a reach and in a run. Races last between 45 min and 1.5 hours.

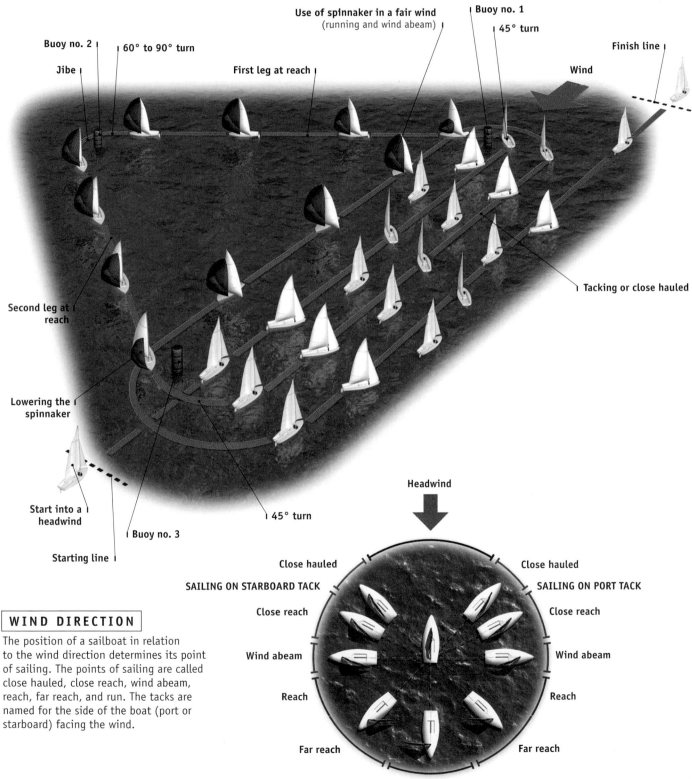

Use of spinnaker in a fair wind
(running and wind abeam)

Buoy no. 1

45° turn

Finish line

Buoy no. 2

60° to 90° turn

Jibe

First leg at reach

Wind

Tacking or close hauled

Second leg at reach

Lowering the spinnaker

Start into a headwind

Buoy no. 3

45° turn

Starting line

Headwind

WIND DIRECTION

The position of a sailboat in relation to the wind direction determines its point of sailing. The points of sailing are called close hauled, close reach, wind abeam, reach, far reach, and run. The tacks are named for the side of the boat (port or starboard) facing the wind.

Close hauled

SAILING ON STARBOARD TACK

Close reach

Wind abeam

Reach

Far reach

Close hauled

SAILING ON PORT TACK

Close reach

Wind abeam

Reach

Far reach

Running downwind

HULL TYPES

Multihull boats—catamarans and trimarans—are faster than monohull boats. However, they are harder to handle, capsize more easily, and are more difficult to right.

Mono-hull   **Catamaran**   **Trimaran**

CENTERBOARD AND KEEL

Both keep the boat from moving sideways. The keel is fixed and ballasted, while the centerboard is movable. On a centerboard boat, the crew's weight acts as the ballast.

Keel boat   **Centerboard boat**

SAILING TECHNIQUES

Sailing requires mastery of techniques such as tacking, jibing, and hiking out. Tacking consists of navigating in a zig zag, switching the sails from one side of the boat to the other, when the wind is coming from in front of the boat, while jibing consists of coming about when the wind is coming from in back of the boat. Jibing requires good skills; the sail swings about 160° from one side of the boat to the other.

TACKING

JIBING

1. The sailboat sails close hauled on the port tack and the crew, sitting facing the mainsail, is ready to come about. **2.** The helmsman pushes the tiller to leeward and the bow of the boat heads into the wind. **3.** The crew frees the sheet to leeward on the starboard side. The mainsail begins to luff and the jib flutters. **4.** The boat bears off the wind and the boom swings over. **5.** The tiller is brought back to center; the jib and mainsail are trimmed. The boat now sails close hauled on the starboard tack.

1. The boat is sailing on the port tack downwind. The crew, facing the mainsail, is ready to jibe. **2.** The helmsman moves to the center, keeping control of the mainsail sheet and trimming it quickly. The boat comes into the wind. **3.** The helmsman prepares for the boom to swing over and the crew moves to the center of the boat. The jib flutters and the mainsail moves quickly to the other side of the boat. **4.** The crew balances the boat as the boom swings over and the helmsman centers the tiller. **5.** The helmsman and crew sit on the windward side of the boat. The jibe is completed and the boat is now on the starboard tack.

HIKING OUT

The crew leans outside the boat to keep it from heeling (tipping) over too far in a strong wind. There are two positions: hiking and trapeze; in the latter, the sailor is hooked to a harness.

Hiking out

The sailor is hiking out when he is sitting partway outside the boat.

Trapeze

1. Starting from a hiking out position and leaning back, the sailor places one foot on the gunwale and leans outward, keeping his body straight.

2. When both feet are on the gunwale, the sailor lets go of the grip and leans out as far as he can in the trapeze position.

OCEAN RACES

SOLO

The Europe 1-Star

Once called OSTAR (Observer Singlehanded Transatlantic Race), it is the oldest solo transoceanic race. The race starts at Plymouth, Great Britain, and ends at Newport, Rhode Island, USA. This race of 3,000 nautical miles (5,555 km) has been held every four years since 1960.

The Rum Route

The race starts at Saint-Malo, France, and finishes at Pointe-à-Pitre, Guadeloupe. It is open to monohull and multihull boats and is 3,700 nautical miles (6,852 km) long and has been held every four years since 1978.

Rum Route

WITH CREW

The Mini-Transat

A race with stopovers that has taken place every 2 years since 1977. Its route goes from Concarneau, France, to Tenerife, Spain, a distance of 1,370 nautical miles (2,537 km), then from Tenerife to Fort-de-France, Martinique, a distance of 2,700 nautical miles (5,000 km). It is unique in that the sailboats must be the same size: 6.5 m long and 3 m wide; the mast must be 14 m high and the boat must draw 2 m. This race requires audacity and great technical skill.

The Quebec–Saint-Malo Transat

Created in 1984, this race takes place every 4 years, from Quebec City, Canada, to Saint-Malo, France. During this race of 2,900 nautical miles (5,370 km), the boats must sail down the St. Lawrence River and through the Gulf of St. Lawrence before crossing the Atlantic. This race, the only one to cross the ocean from west to east, is open to sailboats of different sizes, monohull or multihull.

The Jacques Vabre Transat

Once known as the Coffee Route because it ends in Columbia, this race has taken place every 4 years since 1993. It goes from Le Havre, France, to Cartagena, Colombia, and is open to monohulls and multihulls between 13.72 and 18.29 m long. The distance is 4,420 nautical miles (8,185 km) for monohulls and 5,520 nautical miles (10,222 km) for multihulls.

REGATTAS

They generally take place close to the coast, on a course marked by three buoys. The starts are always spectacular: the first sailboat to pass the start buoy has an advantage in the race.

America's Cup

The most famous regatta is an event in which each sailboat has a crew of 16. The competition starts with elimination rounds between participating countries to determine a challenger for the title holder. The challenger and the title holder compete in a series of at least 7 races, the winner being the boat that wins 4 races. The regatta takes place in the country of the title holder.

Starting line

Course of the America's Cup

The course of 18.55 nautical miles (34 km) includes 3 tacking legs and 3 running legs. The longest distance in a straight line is 3 nautical miles.

This regatta gave rise to a new class of boats: the International America's Cup Class, or Class America, sloops about 22 m long.

AROUND THE WORLD RACES

The Volvo Race or Whitbread

Created in 1973, it is the oldest crewed around the world race. The boats sail about 31,600 nautical miles (58,523 km) in 9 stages. The boats are in the W60 class, specially designed for this race; they are minimum 18.3 m long and 5.25 m wide, and can support 500 m² of sail in a fair wind. The race starts in Southampton, England, and ends in La Rochelle, France.

The Vendée-Globe

A solo race that starts and ends at Sables d'Olonne, France. The participants must go around Antarctica and pass Cape Horn. In this race of about 25,000 nautical miles (46,300 km), competitors must sail without assistance or stopovers in mono-hulled boats with a maximum length of 18.29 m.

Florence Arthaud (FRA)
One of the first outstanding women in sailing, she established a new record for a solo crossing of the Atlantic in 1990, with a time of 9 d 21 h 42 min; the same year, she won the Rum Route.

ADMIRAL'S CUP

It consists of 6 races in the Irish Sea, the English Channel, and off southwest England: 2 Olympic races, 2 coastal races, and 2 races in the open sea. The most difficult event is the Fastnet, off the tip of Ireland, because of the weather conditions there. These races have been run every 2 years since 1957, organized by the Royal Ocean Racing Club (RORC); teams from many countries compete.

SAILOR PROFILE
• Sailors are brave and adventurous, intuitive, and used to dealing with the elements.
• They must be in excellent physical shape and good health to confront temperature changes, difficult maneuvers, short periods of sleep in transatlantic crossings, and frequent contact with cold water, sun, and wind.

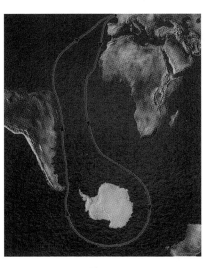

Vendée-Globe

Dennis Conner (USA)
This winner of the America's Cup in 1980, 1987, and 1988 was also a bronze medalist in the 1976 Olympics.

EQUIPMENT

Safety

All boats must have safety equipment. Among other things, there are flares of different colors, distress beacons that emit a signal that can be picked up by satellite, buoys, life jackets, and, in some cases, an inflatable life raft.

Life jacket

Safety harness

Gloves

Trapeze

Waterproof, isothermal pants

No slip boots

GPS (Global Positioning System)
This system enables a ship to establish its position, in latitude and longitude, by linking to a satellite from anywhere in the world.

sailboarding

California Robby Naish won his first world championships in 1976 at age 13.

A combination of sailing and surfing, sailboarding uses a variety of speed and acrobatic techniques. Because their sport depends on the weather, sailboarders must learn to identify different kinds of wind and wave movements. A number of people claim to have invented this relatively new sport, but two Americans, Hoyle Schweitzer and James Drake, patented it in 1968. In the 1980s, changes to the equipment gave rise to a shorter and more controllable board, the funboard, making sailboarding more accessible. The first competitions took place in the 1970s, and the first funboard world championships were organized in 1986. More than 15 million people throughout the world sailboard; the sport became an Olympic event in Los Angeles in 1984 for men, and in Barcelona in 1992 for women.

THE COMPETITION

There are three main types of competition: races with buoys—long distance, slalom, and other courses—open to all types of sailboards; wave and freestyle competitions; and Olympic races, in which the equipment is strictly regulated. Speed races are less common.

Long distance buoy races

Race courses may be point-to-point or out-and-back; they last 2 to 4 hours. Ideally, wind speed is above 15 knots. The winner is the first across the finish line.

Slaloms and other courses with buoys

The start takes place on the beach or in the water. Competitors race in elimination rounds to reach the final, where the winner is the first one across the finish line. Racers round the buoys as quickly as possible using jibes for the slalom; for other courses, racers round the buoys either jibing or coming about. In the slalom, competitors sail only in a broad reach; the other courses also involve sailing closer to the wind. The number of legs and buoys varies from one competition to another. A slalom race lasts 5 to 10 minutes, while races on other courses last 20 to 30 minutes.

Waves and freestyle

Wave competitions take place exclusively on the ocean—where there are breakers—and last 10 to 15 minutes. Ideally, the waves are 2 or more meters high and the winds are at 14 knots. Competitors try to execute the highest number of surfing maneuvers, changes of sail with figures (transitions), and jumps. Freestyle competitions take place on lakes, the ocean, or artificial stretches of water. Sailboarders must make as many transitions, maneuvers, and figures as they can without stopping for 10 to 15 minutes. A panel of 3 to 5 judges gives marks from 0 to 10 for the artistic and technical value of the figures.

Olympic course

Each end of the course is marked with 2 to 4 buoys. There is a group start, and the winner is the one who has had the best finishes in the heats, the number of which may vary from 3 to 12. All racers use the same type of sailboard, the Mistral One Design. A minimum wind of 6 knots is required for a race. Each heat lasts from 20 to 60 minutes, depending on wind velocity. Racers may use the "pumping" technique (moving the sail), which increases board speed in low wind.

Speed

There is no start signal: the average speed is measured over 500 meters. The winner is the one with the fastest average time.

MANEUVERS

The jibe

This is a quick move designed to change direction without losing speed. The sailboarder's body leans into the turn. He bends his knees and presses on the rail with his back leg. As the sail crosses over, the sailboarder catches it as quickly as possible to preserve speed. At the same time, he switches the position of his feet, moving the back one forward and the front one back.

Speed loop (freestyle)

The sailboarder reaches maximum speed. To begin the rotation of the sail, the athlete pulls hard on the wishbone boom. At the same time, he moves his weight forward and, using his back leg, solidly anchored in the foot strap, he suddenly lifts the board up to his hips. His body is crouched to make the rotation smoother. To complete the circular motion, he looks over his back shoulder to finish the rotation.

TYPES OF SAILBOARDS

2.65–3 m

55–75 cm

6–9 m²

Slalom

The slalom board is made for speed and capability of planing.

3.72 m

63.5 cm

7.4 m²

Olympic

The board is long and thick. It is made to be used in widely varying wind conditions.

2.40–2.75 m

55–65 cm

3.5–6 m²

Wave

The board is strong, light, short, and easy to handle. This type of sailboard is particularly maneuverable and can be controlled in high winds.

Masthead

Battens

Mast

Sail

Wishbone boom
It controls the sail and helps the sailboarder balance.

Uphaul
Rope attaching the wishbone boom to the rig; the sailboarder uses it to lift the rig when it falls in the water.

Foot strap

Rails

Skeg

Mast foot

Board

SAILBOARDER PROFILE

- Although it does not require great muscular strength, sailboarding requires strong arms and legs. As well, athletes who are light and tall find it easier to lean away from and control the sail.

- A solid program of muscle building and stretching for the arms and legs is essential.

Björn Dunkerbeck (DEN)
An extraordinary champion who had 12 world championship titles in 1999.

ocean surfing

Hawaiian Duke Kahanamoku, gold medalist in the 100-m freestyle swim at the 1912 and 1920 Olympics, was also the ambassador of surfing to the world. He made the sport popular in Hawaii in 1910 and in Australia, starting in 1915.

In his account of his trip to Hawaii in 1778, Captain Cook mentioned swimmers who went out into the ocean and returned to shore riding the waves on planks of wood. An ancient practice, surfing was banned in the 19th century by Christian missionaries, who saw it as a pagan rite that was incompatible with their teachings. It reappeared on Hawaiian beaches at the beginning of the 20th century. In 1907, the Outrigger Canoe Club, responsible for the revival of surfing, was founded in Waikiki, on Hawaii Island. In the 1950s and 1960s, with the invention of light boards made of new materials, surfing was exported to California, where modern surfing was born. The International Surfing Federation (ISF) was founded during the first world championships in Australia, in 1964, followed by the first professional world championships in 1970. In 1976, the ISF changed its name to International Surfing Association (ISA). The World Surfing Games, held every other year since 1980 and organized by the ISA, along with the World Qualifying Series and the World Championship Tour, organized by the Association of Surfing Professionals (ASP), attract the world's best surfers, both men and women.

CUPS AND CHAMPIONSHIPS

The ISA's World Surfing Games, open to professionals since 1998, has competitions for national teams and individuals. There are 4 events: longboard, shortboard, bodyboard, and kneeboard. The Big Waves World Championship takes place on waves between 9 and 18 m high in the shortboard category only. The professional surfing circuit, under the aegis of the ASP, comprises the World Competitive Tour (WCT) and the World Qualifying Series (WQS), which are individual championships on shortboard only.

The 16 best surfers after the WQS replace the last 16 in the WCT ranking, which lists the 44 best surfers for that year. The circuit includes some 50 events on 5 continents; events are ranked on a scale of 1 to 5 stars, which are converted to between 500 and 2,500 points in the annual ranking. The ranking is determined at the end of the year based on the competitors' 8 best results: a victory in a 5-star event can thus be decisive in the general ranking.

COMPETITION

The competitors try to stay on the waves as long as possible and exploit their potential by performing maneuvers. During the WQS, 4 surfers compete at the same time (2 at a time in the WCT) in 20-minute direct elimination heats, during which they are judged on their best 3 or 5 waves by the competition director and 4 or 5 judges. They are evaluated on 4 criteria: quality of maneuver, placement on the wave, level of difficulty of the wave chosen, and duration of position on the wave. Five minutes before the heat ends, a yellow flag is raised to warn the competitors. The top 2 surfers in each heat go to the next round, while the last 2 are eliminated. The finals last 20 to 30 minutes, depending on wave conditions.

Take-off

The surfer lies on the board, his hands holding on at shoulder level. He uses his arms to bring his legs up under his body along the axis of the board. Then, he lets go of the board and stands up, legs slightly bent and knees turned outward. After starting, he generally executes a bottom-turn (turn at the foot of the wave) that enables him to pick up the speed he needs to execute his maneuvers.

Floater

After riding quickly up the wave, the surfer leans back. The front of the board turns rapidly. When the change of direction is made, the surfer transfers his weight to the back foot to let the wave slide under the board.

Cut-back

At the top of the wave, the surfer transfers his weight to his heels and leans back, while his upper body anticipates the turn slightly. At the end of the turn, he hits the foam to get back on the wave. Cut-backs can be performed facing or with the back to the wave.

EQUIPMENT

BOARD

In the early 20th century, boards were made of wood and weighed 50 to 70 kg. Synthetic materials (polystyrene, fiberglass, and epoxy fibres) invented in the 1960s led to boards that weighed less than 1 kg and were much more controllable. The board's profile (cut), which determines how it behaves on the wave, can be closely adapted to the types of waves encountered and the surfer's style.

Longboard

Much longer and heavier than the shortboard, the longboard is very stable and hard to turn. Today it is used by beginners, but it is still a category in the ISA world championships.

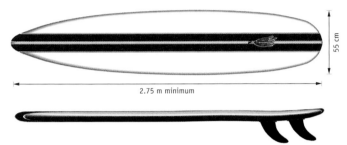

55 cm

2.75 m minimum

Shortboard

This board is used by international-level surfers. It is light and streamlined to allow very rapid maneuvers and direction changes. A longer board, the "gun," is used on very big waves for better stability at high speeds, especially during bottom-turns.

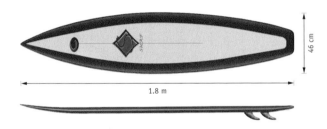

46 cm

1.8 m

Wetsuit

It is isothermal, generally made of neoprene, and lets a thin film of water penetrate to insulate the body. It can be one piece; the summer suit is usually tight-fitting shorts and a top with or without sleeves. Neoprene boots are sometimes used in very cold water or to protect the feet from coral and sharp rocks.

Leash

This cord is attached to the surfer's ankle with a Velcro strap; the other end is attached to the board so the surfer will not lose it if he falls. The length of the strap can be adjusted to the types of waves encountered.

Boots

Wax

Spread on the top of the board, it provides good adherence for the surfer's feet. It is changed regularly. Some surfers prefer nonslip pads glued to the board.

Approximately 1.15 m

Approximately 46 cm

Bodyboard

It was first used to learn surfing. But bodyboarders have developed their own techniques and are now included in international competitions within the ISA and their own organization (Global Organization of Bodyboarders). Bodyboarders ride waves lying on their boards, which are made of rigid foam, and wear diving fins.

Summer suit

There is no typical summer suit. Shorts and a light Lycra top protect the skin from the sun and from irritation caused by contact with the board.

SURFER PROFILE

- Surfers must have excellent knowledge of the ocean and waves to get the best rides in competition. These athletes are in top physical condition and are exceptional swimmers: they may sometimes find themselves far from shore, and falls in big waves can be very dangerous.

- Their skills include the ability to observe conditions at the competition site very carefully, a solid technique for clearing waves that are not surfable, and sharp reflexes in emergency situations.

Kelly Slater (USA)
This native of Cocoa Beach, Florida, was world champion in 1992 and from 1994 to 1998. At 20, he dethroned Australian Mark Richards and became the youngest world champion in the history of surfing.

water skiing

Alfredo Mendoza (MEX) won the world championships five times in the 1950s: twice in jumping and combined, and once in slalom.

W ater skiing is a sport during which skiers, pulled by a boat, plane across the water on a monoski or on two skis. Spectator sport, recreational activity, and high level sporting event, water skiing is a cross between surfing and skiing, and requires coordination, foresight, and balance. American Fred Waller filed the first patent on water skis in 1925, and the first European Championships were organized by the Fédération française de ski nautique in 1947. In 1949, the first World Championship competition took place in Juan-les-Pins, France. The International Water Ski Federation (IWSF) is seeking official participation for the sport in the 2004 Olympic Games in Athens, Greece. In the men's and women's categories, four international competition events are currently held: jumping, slalom, figures, and wakeboard. The World Championships are held every second year.

HOW A COMPETITION IS ORGANIZED

During water ski competitions, elimination heats are organized according to the number of registered contestants. Generally speaking, and weather permitting, a meet begins with the slalom competition. This is followed by figures, with the jump event closing the meet. The order in which contestants compete is decided on the basis of the skiers' previous performances, with the top ranking contestants competing last. The course is generally standard from one competition to the next, and requires little studying by the skiers. Wakeboard events are organized separately.

JUMPING

After being towed up a jump ramp, competitors attempt to jump over the greatest distance possible. Skiers are entitled to 3 qualifying jumps. The maximum speed of the towboat is 51 km/h for women and 57 km/h for men. Besides the length of the jump, the performance criteria are: speed at the time of reaching the jump ramp, body position in the air, and landing. The jump is confirmed once the athlete skis 100 m after landing. Men may achieve jumps that exceed 65 m, and women, 45 m.

500 m

70 m

BASIN
The water must be calm, waveless, and sheltered from the wind.

Ramp
The jump ramp is a rectangular, inclined plane on a floating dock.

1.50–1.80 m

6.4–6.8 m

Officials
The event is supervised by one chief judge, and by 2 judges positioned at the edge of the water. The landing point is measured by computer and filmed on video.

Before mounting the jump ramp, the skier maximizes his acceleration speed by turning his shoulders away from the boat. The skier bends the knees so as to minimize the pressure caused by the slope of the ramp. At the time of the jump, the skier tilts his hips toward the ski tips. The skier holds the line taut with the handle, focuses above the horizon, and keeps the hands held toward the water to maintain balance and stability. The skier lands with his knees bent, and his body and skis leaning backward.

SLALOM

Performed in the same basin as the jumping event, slalom is a race that is characterized by a succession of high speed sinuous turns performed on a single ski, and during which the skier negotiates around 6 buoys. After completing the course successfully in one direction, the skier repeats the course in the opposite direction, with the boat speed increased by 3 km/h. After reaching maximum speed, 55 km/h for women and 58 km/h for men, the tow line is shortened, which increases the technical difficulty of the course by giving the skier less leeway and requiring a faster reaction. The skier can choose the starting speed, but the starting line length must be 18.25 m. From the preliminaries to the finals, contestants are awarded points according to the number of buoys they ski around. The winner is the skier who rounds the most buoys with the shortest line at each of the different speeds.

Officials

Four judges positioned in a tower 3 m above the water, and a chief judge oversee the smooth operation of the event. Another judge rides in the boat.

Making the turns

With the body leaning into the turn, the skier pulls against the boat's momentum to accelerate. After crossing the wake of the boat, the skier must shift his weight to negotiate the turn. After completing the turn, the skier's body is perpendicular to the desired trajectory.

Buoys (6)

Round and flexible, these must be fluorescent.

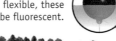

FIGURES

During each of 2 20-second passes, the skier must perform as many figures and combinations as possible. In competition, contestants cannot perform any maneuver more than once. Before the start, skiers must submit a "routines sheet" to the jury, indicating figures they intend to perform and the order in which they will be executed. Skiers can select boat speed and line length. Skiers are rated on the execution of figures rather than esthetics.

Officials

Five judges positioned in a tower 3 m above the water, as well as a chief judge, are in charge of supervising the figures event.

WAKEBOARD

During two passes lasting 25 seconds each, the skier must execute a combination of 5 figures. In competition, basic jumps are rolls, with or without twists. At the end of the course, the skier may perform an additional figure. If he fails to complete this figure, he will not be penalized, but if successful, it may influence the judges. The winner is the skier with the best combination of esthetics, style, fluidity, and technical difficulty of the maneuvers executed.

Backroll

The skier initiates a turn at a good distance from the wake of the boat so as to ensure maximum speed. Once on the wave crest the competitor throws her body and board upward and begins the rotation. Upon landing, the skier must look toward the boat to stop the rotation and control her balance.

EQUIPMENT

Line
Usually made from polypropylene, the line measures 6 mm in diameter. Its maximum length depends on the type of event: 18.25 m for slalom, 23 m for jumps, 15 m for figures, and 18 m for wakeboard.

Boat
The boat must be between 5 and 6.4 m in length and between 1.85 and 2.5 m wide. It is equipped with large rear-view mirrors and speedometers, and must also have a mast between 65 cm and 1.20 m above the water, to which the tow line is attached.

Judge
The judge is accompanied by a timekeeper, and may ask for a reride if the boat speed or path do not conform to regulations.

Boat driver
Chosen by the competition organizer or director, he drives the boat for all contestants, with whom he has no ties. The precision of the boat's trajectory and the regulation of boat speed are the driver's responsibility. The driving style varies according to the event.

TYPES OF SKIS

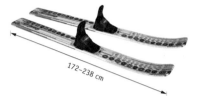

172–238 cm

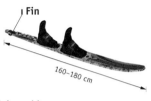

Fin

160–180 cm

102–112 cm

127–147.32 cm

Jump skis
These are made from fiberglass, carbon, Kevlar, and dimpled aluminum.

Slalom skis
These have sharp edges and are equipped with a shaped fin, and are tapered and rounded at the rear.

Figure skis
These have bevelled edges and a smooth underside.

Wakeboard
The tapered edges and grooves under the board improve how the board handles in the water. One or more fins may be installed under the two ends of the board to help stabilize the board in the water.

TYPES OF HANDLES

Jump helmet

Depending on the event, the shape of the handle may differ. The handle is made with a rubberized nonslip surface.

Gloves
These ensure a better grip on the handle.

Slalom handle

Figure-skiing handle

Life jacket

Neoprene suit

Bindings
These are made from rubber and keep the foot in place, yet allow for easy release in the event of a fall.

Edge
Angle of the ski base.

SKIER PROFILE

- Training for a high level career begins at age 5 and focuses primarily on coordination of movements, development of strength, and muscle power. Skiers practice jumps on the trampoline and do weight training exercises. The muscles worked most are biceps, pectorals, dorsal muscles, trapezius muscles, and quadriceps.

Jarret Llewellyn (CAN)
World champion in jumping in 1997 (65.4 m) and 1999 (66.6 m).

Patrice Martin (FRA)
At age 14, in 1978, he was European figure skiing champion. He holds ten individual world skiing championship titles: for figures in 1979, 1985, 1987 and 1991, and for combined in 1989, 1991, 1993, 1995, 1997 and 1999. He set a world record by becoming a five-time American Masters champion.

Equestrian
Sports

equestrian sports

Xenophon wrote the first text on equitation, "On the Equestrian Art," in 400 B.C. Most of his principles are still applied today.

The first people to ride horses were likely the nomads of the Asian steppes between 3,500 and 4,000 B.C. Use of the horse in the fundamental activities of humankind—war, transportation, and hunting—developed over centuries, and changes to the equipment used—saddles and bridles, bits, horseshoes—gradually gave rise, in Europe and Asia, to very elaborate battle techniques based on the horse. In the 14th century, Europeans began to become interested in the academic and military aspects of the equestrian art, while the English turned toward more sporting uses of the horse, especially racing and hunting. Horses were imported to the New World by the Spanish conquistadors in 1500, and they quickly became the partners of both colonists and indigenous peoples from Argentina to the United States. In the 19th century, when mechanical engines began to replace horses in both work and transportation, the sports aspects of equitation, many of them derived from military traditions, came to the fore. Today, the popularity of horse racing and equestrian competitions provides the means to finance breeding and preserve the diversity of horse breeds.

HORSES

To produce horses that are well suited to the use to which they will be put, the best stallions and mares are selected for breeding from their results in competition. This practice was born in the 17th century, when King Charles II of England founded the Thoroughbred breed for racing. Since then, about 200 breeds have been created and registered in studbooks (genealogical records) for their aptitudes and physical characteristics. The Selle Français, English Hunter, and German Hanoverian, recognized for their exceptional talents at jumping and dressage, result from the crossbreeding of Arabians, Thoroughbreds, and local breeds. The French Trotteur, the American Standardbred, and the Orlov Trotter, used in harness racing, are from Thoroughbred and Arabian lines.

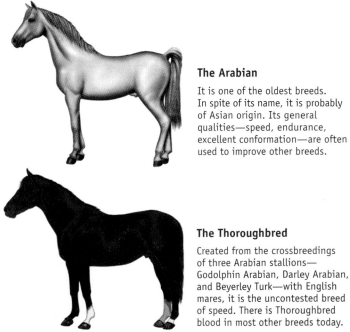

The Arabian

It is one of the oldest breeds. In spite of its name, it is probably of Asian origin. Its general qualities—speed, endurance, excellent conformation—are often used to improve other breeds.

The Thoroughbred

Created from the crossbreedings of three Arabian stallions—Godolphin Arabian, Darley Arabian, and Beyerley Turk—with English mares, it is the uncontested breed of speed. There is Thoroughbred blood in most other breeds today.

GAITS

The natural gaits are instinctive to all horses; walk, trot, and canter are the 3 natural gaits used most often in competition. Certain gaits, including the pace, are learned through training.

The walk

This is a slow, 4-beat gait: each of the horse's hooves touches the ground in turn.

The trot

This is a medium-speed symmetrical gait, with 2 beats separated by a moment of suspension. The hooves touch the ground 2 by 2: front right and left hind; left front and right hind. In the racing trot, the strides are much longer than in the normal trot.

The canter

This is a fast, asymmetrical gait, with 3 beats and a moment of suspension, during which the horse's hooves do not touch the ground. It wasn't until photography was invented that its component parts were observed.

SPEED IN RACES	
Gait	Average speed
Canter	60 km/h
Pace	52 km/h
Trot	50 km/h

TECHNIQUES AND EQUIPMENT

In addition to the voice, riders have 2 types of "aids" to control and direct their horse: the legs press on the horse's sides to ask for forward movement, and the hands, linked to the horse's mouth by the reins and bit, slow and turn the horse.

THE TACK

This is the equipment used to ride the horse; the 2 essential pieces of tack are the bridle (headstall, reins, and bit) and the saddle. Competition has produced very different styles of equitation, and the tack has been adapted to each style. Each type of saddle has a corresponding type of bridle.

HORSESHOES

Horseshoes, which became widespread in the Middle Ages, now come in a wide variety of types for different terrain and activities. In equestrian sports, good shoeing can be decisive and the farrier plays a very important role.

Racing saddle

It is flat and very light, with a cutback pommel. With its short stirrups and the jockey's perched position, it gives the horse great freedom of movement. The reins are held short to give the rider direct, strong control.

Flap

Pommel

Jumping saddle

It is designed for efforts over obstacles. The seat is slightly curved in, the wide flaps provide support for the knees, and the rider stays in balance in the stirrups. The reins are held long to allow the horse's neck to stretch when it jumps.

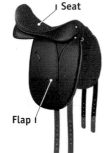

Seat

Dressage saddle

It has a deep seat, and its long, straight flaps are flexible so that the slightest movement of the legs is transmitted to the horse. The bridle uses the combined action of the curb reins and bridoon bits to allow a wide variety of nuances.

Flap

Jumping shoe

This shoe can be equipped with caulks or removable rubber pads, depending on the terrain.

Racing shoe

This shoe is light, usually made of aluminum, and grooved.

DRESSAGE BRIDLE

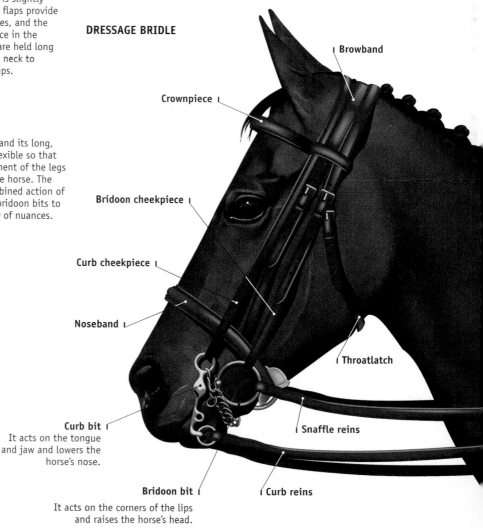

Browband

Crownpiece

Bridoon cheekpiece

Curb cheekpiece

Noseband

Throatlatch

Curb bit
It acts on the tongue and jaw and lowers the horse's nose.

Snaffle reins

Bridoon bit
It acts on the corners of the lips and raises the horse's head.

Curb reins

The roots of **vaulting** lie with the acrobatics of Cossack horsemen and, more recently, equestrian acts in the circus. Athletes must perform a series of tricks with the horse in all three gaits, alone or in pairs. The main objectives are balance and harmony with the horse's movements.

Endurance consists of going distances of between 20 and 160 km on a single horse at an imposed speed of between 12 and 17 km/h. Veterinary checks ensure that the horses remain in perfect physical condition from beginning to end of the event. Riders dismount and run beside their horses in difficult parts.

dressage

The "Father of French Equitation," François Robichon de La Guérinière (1688–1751), revolutionized the art of riding.
The principles of this riding instructor of Louis XV are still practiced at the Spanish Riding School in Vienna.

Dressage competition is judged according to the horse's willing obedience to the rider's smallest commands (aids) and purity of execution of movements. It was with these objectives in mind that Xenophon wrote the first known equitation manual in 400 B.C. He was writing for Greek horsemen, whose lives depended on how quickly their mounts reacted in battle. In the Middle Ages, the subtleties of dressage disappeared under the weight of the knights' armor. With the advent of firearms, mounted combat once again became rapid and acrobatic; the equestrian art, now indispensable, reached its peak in the 18th century. Dressage was separated from its military origins relatively recently, when horses were replaced by motorized vehicles. It became an Olympic event in 1912 and has continued to evolve. The International Equestrian Federation (FEI) sanctions many international competitions, which attract crowds of connoisseurs all over the world.

THE COMPETITION

Men and women compete against each other. In team competition, the order of nations and of the 4 riders in each team is drawn by lot. Each rider rides a grand prix test for the judges, and the 3 best results from each team are used to determine the winner. In individual competition, the order of ride is drawn by lot. The winner of the competition is the rider with the best score calculated on the results from 3 tests presented in the following order: grand prix, grand prix special, and freestyle (kür).

AWARDING OF POINTS

Five judges, including a president of the jury, evaluate the performances of the competitors by marking each movement out of 10. The movements are performed in the horse's 3 natural gaits: walk, trot, and canter. The horse must be so sensitive to the rider's aids that the rider appears to be sitting perfectly still. Regularity of gaits and accuracy of execution are important elements.

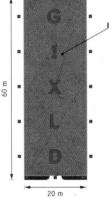

60 m

20 m

Show ring footing
It must be very flat. Shredded rubber is sometimes added to a sand footing to make it softer.

Letters
They are spaced at specific distances as reference points for the movements to be performed. The letters down the center of the arena are not marked. The meaning of the placement of the letters has been lost.

SHOW RING

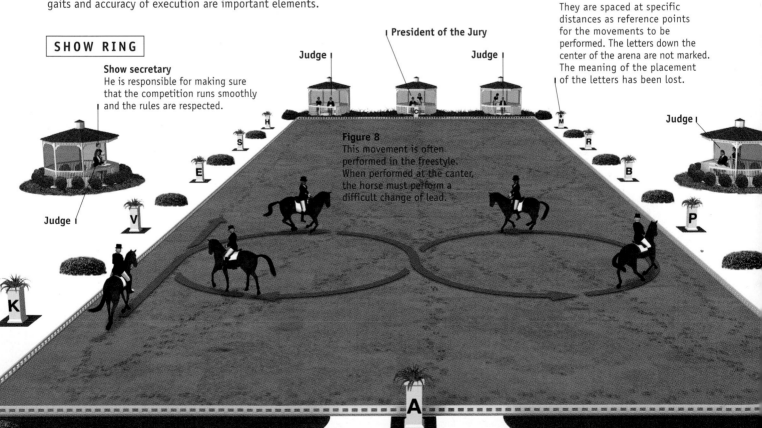

Show secretary
He is responsible for making sure that the competition runs smoothly and the rules are respected.

President of the Jury

Judge

Judge

Judge

Judge

Figure 8
This movement is often performed in the freestyle. When performed at the canter, the horse must perform a difficult change of lead.

TECHNIQUE

COLLECTION

Collection is the result of the search for an ideal position. The horse must bring its hind legs closer to its front legs to shorten its base of support. The basis for attaining the mobility and lightness needed in competition, collection is also the ideal position for carrying the rider in any form of equitation.

Horse not collected

The hind legs are behind the horse and most of the weight is carried on the front legs.

Horse collected

The ideal balance is attained when the hind legs "engage" under the horse's body.

THE ADVANCED MOVEMENTS

Piaffe

The horse seems to trot on the spot. The movement has a very slow cadence and the front legs are lifted high.

Half-pass

The horse moves forward and sideways, crossing its legs.

Passage

In this elevated trot, the horse spends less time on the ground and the moments of suspension are longer. The passage must be executed in perfect collection, with the legs lifted high.

TESTS

The FEI recognizes 20 high-level tests, containing up to 35 movements that must be executed by memory in a time of between 5 and 7½ min. The tests, written by the FEI, are changed periodically. The movements in a test (half-pass, piaffe, passage, pirouettes, canter change of lead every second stride and every stride) follow each other in a particular order, have a prescribed size, and are performed at specified places in the arena.

Test	Movements	Music
Grand Prix	imposed	no
Grand Prix special	imposed, with a higher level of difficulty than Grand Prix	no
Freestyle	free, with compulsory figures	yes

INTERNATIONAL LEVEL MOVEMENTS

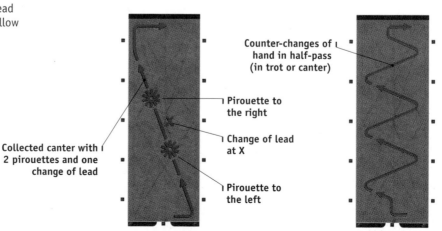

Counter-changes of hand in half-pass (in trot or canter)

Collected canter with 2 pirouettes and one change of lead

Pirouette to the right

Change of lead at X

Pirouette to the left

THE SCHOOLS

Cavalry officers were trained in the equestrian arts at special schools. Some, run by exceptional masters such as Pignatelli in Naples in the 16th century and La Guérinière in Versailles in 1730, were greatly influential and received students from all over Europe. Until 1920, military prestige was closely associated with equestrian schools. Some schools are still active today, among them the Spanish Riding School in Vienna and the Cadre Noir in Saumur; they perpetuate the tradition of academic equitation and perform all over the world.

EQUIPMENT

The rider's clothing and horse's tack are strictly prescribed. Use of a dressage whip and any protective boots or wraps on the horse's legs is forbidden.

Top hat or military cap

White shirt and stock tie

Gloves

Dark jacket or military jacket

Dressage saddle
Encourages contact between the rider's legs and the horse's sides.

Black boots or uniform boots

Bridoon bit
It lifts the horse's head.

Curb bit
It lowers the horse's nose.

Bridoon rein

Curb rein
With the combined action of the bridoon and curb reins, the rider can give a wide variety of precise, subtle commands to her horse.

PROFILE OF RIDER AND HORSE

- The rider must be able to convince his horse, not force it to do his will. Patience, authority, concentration, and the ability to listen to the horse are very important. Most riders make their own training plan. A coach on the ground, who has a different view, helps to direct execution of movements. Experience, acquired with age, is an asset.

- The highest levels can be reached only with a horse that is physically capable and psychologically stable. Advanced training begins around 5 years of age, when the basic training is completed. Daily suppling exercises and gymnastics lead gradually to collection and execution of the movements.

- Thoroughbreds crossed with the less temperamental German warmbloods are very suitable for dressage. In general, sport horses bred in Europe dominate the event.

Reiner Klimke (GER)
He had a very long career, from 1964 to the 1980's at the Olympic Games and has been twice individual world champion (1974 and 1982).

Nicole Uphoff (GER)
Quadruple Olympic champion in dressage (individual and team) in 1988 and 1992. World champion in 1990 (individual and team) and 1994 (team). Four times European champion between 1989 and 1995. All won with the same horse, Rembrandt.

jumping

I n jumping competitions, the aim is to jump obstacles as quickly as possible without knocking them down, and the rider's skill is a complement to the horse's muscular strength. This form of equestrian sport was created in the mid 19th century during mounted hunts in the English countryside, where natural obstacles—brush fences, ditches, and walls—abounded. The officers of the British Cavalry considered jumping a good training exercise, and other European cavalries followed their example. The first international jumping competition took place in Paris in 1900, where it was first included in the Olympics. Until after 1945, jumping was strongly influenced by the military: some competitions were open only to military riders. Since the first world championships, in 1953, at which competitors had to exchange horses, the International Equestrian Federation (FEI) has been the sport's governing body; in 1974, men and women were allowed to compete together. The Olympic Grand Prix is among the Games' most anticipated events. National Grand Prix circuits determine the qualifiers for other prestigious competitions, such as the World Cup, World Championships, and Nations' Cups.

Alberto Valdes, member of the Mexican team that won the famous Nations Cup at the Wembley Stadium (GBR) in 1948.

THE COMPETITION

There is a minimum speed of 350 to 400 m/min. Today's courses, created by specialized course designers, are between 700 and 1,000 m in length. A course is composed of 12 to 15 obstacles, including at least 3 combinations. Riders may inspect the course on foot once before the competition. International events are judged according to Tables A and C.

• **Table A**: The course must be completed within a set time. Faults (knockdowns, refusals or runouts, fall of horse or rider) are converted into penalty points. Going over the time allowed incurs ¼ point per second over the limit.

• **Table C**: It is often used for speed classes. The competitor's round is timed, and there is no time limit. Penalty faults are converted into seconds and added to the total running time.

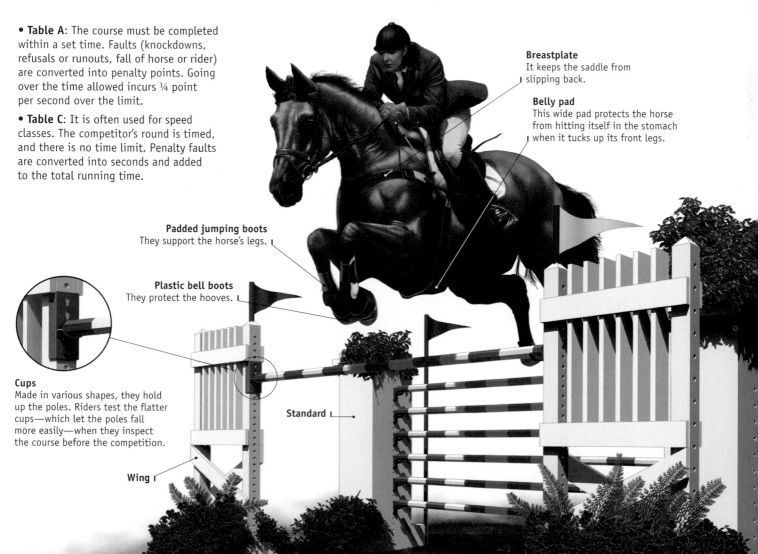

Breastplate
It keeps the saddle from slipping back.

Belly pad
This wide pad protects the horse from hitting itself in the stomach when it tucks up its front legs.

Padded jumping boots
They support the horse's legs.

Plastic bell boots
They protect the hooves.

Cups
Made in various shapes, they hold up the poles. Riders test the flatter cups—which let the poles fall more easily—when they inspect the course before the competition.

Standard

Wing

JUMPING TECHNIQUE

In the past, riders stayed sitting in the back of the saddle and leaned backward. Not only was this position difficult for the rider, it greatly inhibited the horse's movement. In 1904, an Italian soldier, Federico Caprilli, developed "natural equitation," in which the rider supports himself in the stirrups and leans forward over the horse's neck so that he can actively affect the horse's balance in the different phases of its jumping effort. This novel method was in complete contradiction to all principles of classical equitation at the time, but it was so effective that it was ultimately adopted by all riders, and it is still used in competition today.

1. Controlling the approach

To exploit his horse's capacities to the fullest, the rider lengthens or shortens the horse's stride to arrive at an accurate takeoff point.

2. Controlling balance

The weight of the rider's body is essential to the horse's balance. By varying his position, he tries not to disturb his mount's impulsion and jumping curve (bascule).

3. Landing calmly

The course is jumped in the canter, which can make horses excited. To ensure that the horse doesn't rush at the jumps, the rider must never lose control of it.

THE COURSE

The start and finish lines and the jumps are marked by red and white flags. White flags are always on the left; red ones, on the right. They indicate where the horse must go and the edges of the obstacles. The obstacles are numbered in the order in which they must be jumped and can be composed of 1 to 3 elements.

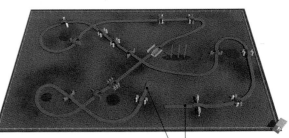

Finishing line | **Starting line**

Planks
They are less stable than poles. They lie on flat cups and can fall more easily.

Combination
Group of 2 or 3 elements placed close together that count as a single obstacle.

Wall
It is made of wooden blocks that fall easily.

Jump crew
Under the supervision of the course steward, they rebuild obstacles that have been knocked down. The members of the 10-person crew stay hidden behind elements on course so that they do not distract the competitors.

Triple bar
Obstacle with three vertical elements of increasing heights.

Veterinarians (2 or 3)
On the evening before or morning of the competition, they verify the horses' identities from their official passports and make sure that they are not lame. During the competition, they are ready to intervene, especially if a horse is lame before entering the arena.

PROFILE OF RIDER AND HORSE

- Although some credit the horse with up to 70% of the result, jumping owes a lot to the rider's influence. The horse must be confident and understand very clearly what the rider wants so that it can give its best effort. This subtle partnership is never permanently established; it must be confirmed and maintained daily by various exercises over all kinds of obstacles.

- Horses jump naturally, but competition requires solid experience acquired over 4 years of training. They are in top condition between 9 and 15 years of age. In early training, an experienced horse often goes first to convince more timid horses to jump. Before the competition season begins, their pulmonary and muscular capacities, used to the maximum on course, are built up by galloping sessions (for respiration) and long trots (for the propulsive muscles).

Gail Greenough (CAN)
She was the first woman to win the world championships, in 1986, with her horse Mister T.

Hans Gunther Winkler (GER)
He won five Olympic gold medals from 1956 to 1976 with his horses Halla and Trophy (he rode in 6 successive Games, a record for longevity).

Pierre Jonquères d'Oriola (FRA)
He was the first civilian to win an individual Olympic title, with Ali Baba (Helsinki, 1952). To date, the only rider to win a second Olympic title (in Tokyo in 1964), with Lutteur B.

Course steward
He makes sure that the general rules are respected and applied in terms of the course (height and number of obstacles, distances between obstacles). During the competition, he controls competitors' entrances to and exits from the course and makes sure that obstacles knocked down are properly rebuilt.

Obstacle profile
The vertical element of an obstacle that the horse sees. It must be supported on wings or standards only. The highest pole is always a single pole or a plank.

Water jump
A jump judge watches the horse's takeoff and landing: it is a fault if the horse splashes in the water or touches the lathe on the landing side. Knocking over the small brush before the water is not a fault.

Width: 4.15–4.75 m

Water jump judge

Jury
It is composed of 4 jump judges, including a chairperson, appointed or approved by the IOC or the FEI, depending on the competition. Judges calculate the competitors' faults on course according to the standard of the class.

Oxers
They are made of 2 vertical elements of equal height (square oxer) or different heights (ascending oxer). They must not be wider than they are high.

Medical team
They are ready to intervene if a rider is injured.

Vertical
Composed of several poles in a single vertical plane.

combined eventing

Combined eventing is the most complete test of horse and rider: each horse-rider combination must compete in three phases: dressage, endurance, and stadium jumping. In a three-day event, each phase is held on a different day. The first combined event was held in 1902 by the French army at the Championnat du Cheval d'Armes to test its cavalry. The three-day event was included in the Stockholm Olympics in 1912; it took its current form at the Paris Games in 1924. It was called the "militaire" until 1949, when the Duke of Beaufort founded the Badminton Horse Trials, which is open to civilians. Other prestigious three-day events are held every year in Burghley, England; Punchestown, Ireland; Boekelo, Holland; Luhmülen, Germany; and Lexington, Kentucky. Competitions in this very technical and spectacular sport also take place at the annual European championships, and at the world championships and the Olympics, which alternate every two years; these events draw large numbers of spectators.

Brigadier Bolton and Greylag at the famous Badminton Horse Trials in 1952.

THE COMPETITION

Men and women compete against each other. Each phase is judged individually and has a different coefficient. Out of a total of 16 coefficient points, dressage is worth 3, endurance 12, and stadium jumping 1. Penalty points are assigned to the competitor's dressage score and to jumping and time faults in the endurance and stadium-jumping phases. Rankings are determined by adding up the penalty points accumulated in all three phases; the winner is the competitor with the lowest number of points over the entire competition. Individual and team competitions are run at the same time: 4 riders are designated by their country to form a team in advance, and the team result is the total of the 3 best individual results.

Day 1: dressage

The first phase, dressage, is intended to demonstrate the horse's obedience and the communication between horse and rider. There are 18 set movements in a test that takes about 8 min; the test is not as difficult as a top-level dressage test, as there are no series of lead changes, canter pirouettes, piaffe, or passage.

Day 2: endurance

This is the most physically and psychologically challenging day for horse and rider. Technique and courage on the cross-country course are paramount: the slightest error can be very costly. Horse and rider are in complete partnership, and sometimes the horse makes up for rider mistakes. The endurance test has 4 separate phases (A, B, C, D), each of which must be completed in a designated time depending on its length. After phase C, there is a compulsory 10-min halt during which a veterinarian checks the horse's heart rate and legs to make sure that it is fit for the effort of the cross-country course.

Day 3: stadium jumping

This is the last phase. After a very thorough veterinary check, horses go in reverse order of ranking (the horses with the best results in the first 2 days go last). The course is of medium difficulty (about 12 obstacles with a maximum height of 1.2 m) and is designed to test the horse's power of recuperation and concentration after the major effort made on day 2.

ENDURANCE: CROSS-COUNTRY COURSE

PHASES OF THE ENDURANCE TEST			
Phase	Gait	Features	Duration
A: Road and tracks	Canter or trot speed 220 m/min (13.2 km/h)	4,400–5,500 m long	20–25 min
B: Steeplechase	Gallop speed 690 m/min (41.4 km/h)	8–10 obstacles 1.40 m high 4 m wide, over 3,105 m	4.5 min
C: Road and tracks	Canter or trot speed 220 m/min (13.2 km/h)	7,700–9,900 m long	35–45 min
D: Cross-country	Gallop speed 570 m/min (34.2 km/h)	7,410–7,980 m long 45 obstacles	13–14 min

TACTICS

Eventing emphasizes the horse's soundness and endurance. During the endurance test, a lead acquired at the end of one phase can be used as extra recovery time. Today's cross-country courses often offer 2 options at certain obstacles: one path that is fast but risky, and another that is less risky but takes much longer. As the current level of competition is very high, a poor performance in one of the 3 phases can greatly affect the final score. A good dressage score is very important, but the endurance test is usually the decisive phase.

PROFILE OF HORSE AND RIDER

- It is not unusual for riders to stay at the elite level for 20 years (from age 20 to 40). Among the most enduring riders have been Italian Mauro Checcoli (Olympic champion in 1964, Olympic competitor in 1984) and American Mike Plumb (8-time Olympic competitor).

- Riders train their own horses to develop their confidence, which is essential to successful competition. Only after 2 to 3 years can it be determined whether a horse has the talent to master all 3 phases, which require different skills and abilities.

- Aside from daily work devoted to each phase, the horse's physical condition is maintained with a program similar to that for human athletes: muscular strength and respiration, more than pure speed, are developed by regular gallops and slow hill work.

- Experience has shown that champion horses may be of very different builds and breeds. The events are too grueling for horses to compete in more than 3 per year. Therefore, most top international riders have two elite horses and others at various stages of development.

Obstacles
They are fixed and marked with numbered flags. The horse does not see them before it must jump them, and so it must have great confidence in its rider. Outside of the penalty zone (10 m on the sides, 20 m after) around each obstacle, falls, refusals, and run-outs are not counted. It must be possible to take closed and semi-closed obstacles apart so that an injured horse can be evacuated quickly.

Jump judges
They determine whether the horses have gone over each obstacle, and they are in contact by walkie-talkie with the officials responsible for scoring.

Protective gear
During the endurance phase, a helmet with chinstrap is required for riders. Most riders also wear back protectors, as falls can be very dangerous. Often, the horse's legs are covered with grease to keep them from being injured if they hit an obstacle.

Mark Todd (NZL)
Twice Olympic champion (1984, 1988) with the same horse, Charisma, he also won Badminton in 1980, 1984, and 1996. His performances have helped to put New Zealand in the forefront of equestrian sports.

Mary King (GBR)
Member of the world-champion team in 1994 and the European champion team in 1995, she has won the open championships of England and Scotland several times, as well as Badminton in 1992 and Chantilly in 1997.

racing: turf

I n turf racing, the fastest equestrian sport, jockeys and their horses gallop full out to beat competitors to the finish line. This exceptional partnership between horses and humans was forged long ago: ritual races took place in China in prehistoric times, and the Olympic Games in ancient Greece had both chariot races and mounted races. The first racetrack was built at Newmarket, England, in the early 17th century. As the Thoroughbred breed was developed, galloping races were on the rise: the Jockey Club, formed in 1750, sets the rules for many big and very popular races, such as the Epsom Derby and the Ascot Gold Cup. Today, these are two of the most prestigious races, along with the Arc de Triomphe in Paris and the Kentucky Derby in the United States.

The legendary American jockey Tod Sloan (d. 1933) invented a new way of riding, the "monkey crouch," with very short stirrups.

THE RACE

The horses are loaded into the starting gate in an order chosen by draw. The start judge starts the race whenever he wants, without waiting for a difficult or badly placed horse. So that all horses have an equal chance to win, the best horses must carry extra weight of up to 5 kg. The handicap is determined by experts who estimate and compare the performances of each horse in the previous races. Race judges confirm the order in which horses pass the finish line. If the pack is tightly bunched, a photograph is used to determine the order of finish. If the apparatus doesn't work, the race judges' decision is final and cannot be appealed.

Starting gate
Used mainly for races at the gallop. The gates open simultaneously so that all horses start at the same time.

BETTING

Money from betting allows breeders to produce race horses. Bets determine the odds of a horse winning before the start of a race. The more money bet on a horse, the lower its odds; the less chance that a horse will win, the higher its odds. A horse winning at odds of 2 to 1 will pay off twice the amount bet.

RACETRACK

Judges' stand
It holds 4 or 5 race judges and the technicians responsible for the photo-finish apparatus.

Tote board

Length post

Finish line

Grandstand

Paddock
Before each race, the horses in the race and their jockeys are shown to the spectators.

Paddock turn

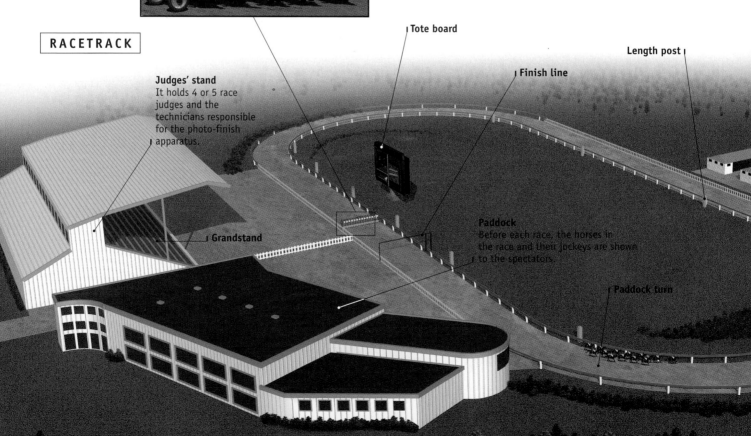

TYPE OF RACE	HORSE'S AGE	DISTANCE	NUMBER OF OBSTACLES	EXAMPLE
flat gallop	2 years	1,200–1,600 m	none	Grand-Critérium de Longchamp (France)
flat gallop	3 years	2,000 m	none	Kentucky Derby (United States)
hurdles	3–4 years	2,500–5,000 m	8–15	Auteuil (France)
steeplechase	4 years	about 7,200 m	30	Liverpool Grand National (Great Britain)

TACTICS

During the race, the jockey makes all the decisions and must adapt his tactics to how his mount is running. Taking advantage of the horse's gait, placing it well in the pack, and closing (giving the most effort) at the right moment are the keys to victory. If he is not boxed in, the jockey can choose where on the track to run the homestretch. On turns, the inside of the track (the rail) is the best place to be.

EQUIPMENT

JOCKEY'S POSITION

The current riding style (short reins and stirrups, body bent forward on the horse's neck) was invented by an American jockey, Tod Sloan, in the late 19th century. At first criticized, even ridiculed, it was adopted quickly by most jockeys because it obtained excellent results on the racetrack.

Shadow roll
It limits the horse's ability to see the ground, so that it does not jump over shadows, thinking that they are obstacles.

Helmet

Silks

Goggles

Whip

Handicap weights
They are distributed in pockets sewn into the saddle pad.

Saddlecloth number

Stables

Turf
The word turf designates the surface (grass) on which the horses race. In the United States, tracks are usually flat and have a soft surface made with a mixture of wood shavings, earth and sand.

Lester Piggot (GBR)
The most famous jockey in England, he won the national championships 11 times. Between 1954 and 1983, he won the prestigious National Derby 9 times. He retired from professional equestrian competition in 1995.

Pat Day (USA)
Winner of the Eclipse award in 1984, 1986, 1987, and 1991, he has also won 10 races in the famous Breeders Cup, including the turf race in 1987 on Theatrical (IRE).

PROFILE OF JOCKEY AND HORSE

- Jockeys' ideal weight is about 110 pounds, so they must have a small frame. Most begin as stablehands, taking care of the horses and riding them in training, then start riding in small races. The best get their professional license in about 40 races.

- For yearlings (horses 1 year old), daily training is essentially composed of short, very fast gallops. Horses are at their fastest at the age of 3 or 4 and training includes endurance, generally with a view to converting them from flat racers to steeplechasers.

- The career of a champion is shorter (15 to 20 races, often winning all of them) than is that of an average horse (50 to 70 races).

harness racing: trot and pace

Trotting race at the 1935 Richmond Horse Show.

Harness races take place on a track. A sulky (light two-wheeled cart) is used, and the winner is the horse that crosses the finish line first without changing gaits. The first trotting races were informal affairs organized by farmers, and the horses often trotted or paced. Trotting developed simultaneously in the United States and Europe in the 19th century, but the United States soon began its own racing system on different tracks; pacing became more popular than trotting. The Société du Cheval in France, founded in 1864, and the United States Trotting Association gave harness racing its professional structures. With the advent of pari-mutuel wagering, the popularity of harness racing took off: races such as the Roosevelt International in the United States and the Prix d'Amérique in France now draw tens of thousands of spectators, and many more watch on television. Champion horses become legendary and make their owners a fortune.

THE RACE

Starting positions are determined by the horses' results in preceding races. So that each horse has the same chance, the best horses are handicapped: in running starts behind the mobile gate, they are placed on the outside of the track. In standing starts, they must run an extra distance of up to 100 m. A race is usually one lap around the track. On some short racetracks, races might be 2 laps. To see whether a horse breaks gait, the race is filmed and followed by the gait judge in a car, sometimes assisted by several stewards. If the finish is very close, a photograph helps the judges determine which horse crossed the finish line first.

FAULTS

The faults penalized involve the horse's gait (trot or pace) and behavior during the race. In Europe, breaking gait causes disqualification. In North America, the horse's finish placing is moved below the horse that finished behind it; it is allowed to finish the race if it goes to the outside of the track and resumes the proper gait. A horse that bumps another horse is disqualified in Europe; in North America, it is placed behind the horse it bumped.

TACTICS

The essential tactic is to preserve the horse's energy so that it will give its best effort at the right moment in the race. The driver has to be able to let the horse extend its stride to the maximum without losing its balance or breaking gait.

Racetrack
In North America, a flat oval with a surface usually composed of stone dust. Length varies from ½ mile to 1 mile. European tracks are grass-covered and can range from 1 mile to 1⅜ miles in length.

RACETRACK

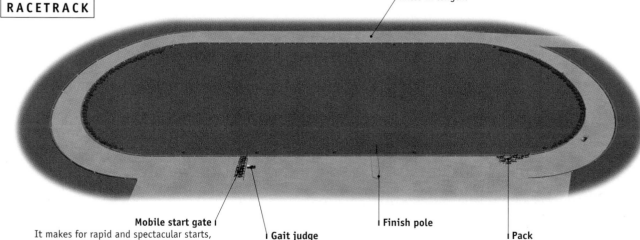

Mobile start gate
It makes for rapid and spectacular starts, for races with between 8 and 12 horses. Standing starts are used in Europe and can accommodate up to 20 horses.

Gait judge
He watches the race from start to finish.

Finish pole

Pack
At both the first and last turns, it is important not to get boxed in by the pack.

Moving wing

Mobile start gate
Once the horses are moving at speed, the 2 moving wings of the gate fold forward as the gate passes the start line, leaving the horses free to race.

GAITS

While races in Europe feature trotting, either mounted or in harness, North American races feature both trot and pace in harness. Both are rapid two-beat gaits. Proper weight distribution of the horseshoes extends the horse's strides and can gain precious seconds. Pacers are easier to train than trotters: pacing hobbles, invented in the United States around 1885, make it almost impossible for the horse to break gait.

Trot

The diagonal legs (left front and right hind, for example) touch the ground at the same time. The strides are much longer in the racing trot than in a normal trot.

Pace

The horse moves both legs on the same side of the body at the same time. The pace is faster than the trot.

Greyhound (USA)
A gelding that raced in the 1930s, he was possibly the best trotter of all time. Thanks to his 6 m stride, he established 25 world records between 1934 and 1940, some of which still stand.

Bret Hanover (USA)
A standardbred that raced in the 1960s, he won 62 of his 68 races and established 9 world records for pacing. Elected Horse of the Year 3 times (1964 to 1966), he also won the Triple Crown in 1965.

MAJOR RACES

The Roosevelt International in New York, the Prix d'Amérique in Vincennes, France, and the Trot Mondial, in Montreal, Canada, are major races open to horses of all ages and from all countries, and the purses are very big. The strong competition between French and American trotters is a highlight. The ultimate prize for American horses is the Triple Crown, awarded to the horse that wins three prestigious races: for trotters, the Yonkers Trot, the Hambletonian, and the Kentucky Futurity; for pacers, the Messenger Stakes, the Cane Futurity, and the Little Brown Jug.

EQUIPMENT

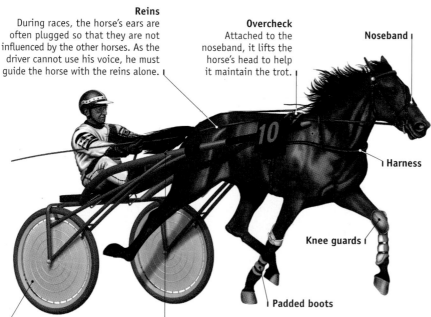

Reins
During races, the horse's ears are often plugged so that they are not influenced by the other horses. As the driver cannot use his voice, he must guide the horse with the reins alone.

Overcheck
Attached to the noseband, it lifts the horse's head to help it maintain the trot.

Noseband

Harness

Knee guards

Padded boots

Wheels
Their diameter is standardized. The spokes are covered with plastic disks for the safety of the horses and better aerodynamics.

Sulky
Invented around 1892 in the United States, it remained almost unchanged until the 1970s, when the wooden frames were replaced by aluminum. The width and angle of the shafts are adjusted to each horse. A racing sulky weighs about 26 pounds. Training sulkies are heavier: about 55 pounds.

DRIVER AND HORSE PROFILE

- Some drivers are also trainers. Although the average age of drivers is between 30 and 40, some will keep driving in important races up to the age of 60.

- Trotting requires the horse to have discipline and self-control. It must learn to lengthen its strides to the maximum without giving into the instinct to break to the gallop. Before it pulls a sulky, it is gradually accustomed to the gait and the harness. Then, a specific plan of timed exercises increases its speed step by step.

- Horses are prepared with specific objectives in mind: speed over short distances with very young horses is favored in the United States, while in Europe (mainly France, Russia, and Scandinavia) endurance is preferred and horses have longer racing careers. On both sides of the Atlantic, horses must be retired from racing when they turn 14.

- Blinkers are used on timid horses to limit their field of vision so that they will have less opportunity to be scared.

polo

The oldest known illustration of polo, inspired by Ferdowsi's Shah-Nama, a work on the history of Persian royalty (end of the 10th century).

Polo is played on a flat playing field, with two teams mounted on horseback using mallets to hit a ball into each other's goal. The principle of the game was probably invented in Persia around 600 B.C. The English discovered polo in the 1850s in the Himalayas, where they learned to play from the Indian nobility. They founded the first polo (from the Tibetan word pu-lu) club in Silchar in 1859, then imported the game to England. Introduced to Argentina by settlers and to the United States in 1876 by billionaire James Gordon Bennett, polo gained in popularity. The Hurlingham club, in London, established the first rules. England, which joined the world circuit in 1886, won the first Olympic gold medal in 1920. Argentina won not only the gold in 1924 and 1936, but the first Cup of the Americas, in 1928. England joined the world circuit in 1956 with the Gold Cup, founded by Lord Cowdray. The Federation of International Polo (FIP), founded in 1983 and based in Beverly Hills, California, organizes the World Cup every year, which attracts thousands of spectators.

THE GAME

A polo game involves two 4-player teams. It begins when the umpire throws the ball between the teams, which are lined up on either side of the center T. There are 6 chukkers (periods) lasting 7 minutes each, separated by stoppages of 3 to 5 min so that riders can change mounts (they may also do so as play goes on). A goal is scored when the ball goes through the goalposts of the opposing team; the teams change ends, but the game continues without stopping. In fact, a chukker is stopped only when a rider is on the ground and unable to move. Handicaps have been devised to equalize the teams' chances of winning. They are assigned on a scale of −2 to +10 to players by national commissions. A player with a 4 handicap can play in international matches. A team's handicap is the sum of the handicaps of its members. A team with a handicap of 30 playing against a team with a handicap of 40 starts the match with a 10-goal advantage.

Clock
It times 7 minutes, the duration of a chukker.

Team name
Most teams are sponsored. Today, some teams are funded by major commercial brands.

Player handicaps

ELLERSTINA

ADOLFO CAMBIASOH	10
MARIANO AGUERRE	9
GONZALO PIERES	10
CARLOS GRACIDA	10
	39

Team handicap

Player 3
The pivot between attack and defence. Usually, the captain or the player with the highest handicap plays in this position.

Tower
It holds the scorer, the announcer, and a referee who settles all disputes by watching a video replay of the game.

Side lines
On some fields, the side lines have boards. Players may cross them to hit the ball into play.

PLAYING FIELD

274 m

146 m

Player 2
He takes the ball into the opposing team's territory. Polo ponies in this position are the boldest.

Mounted umpires (2)
They are assisted by a referee on the sidelines.

27 m line

Player 1
His main mission is to score goals. His mount must be quick.

36 m line

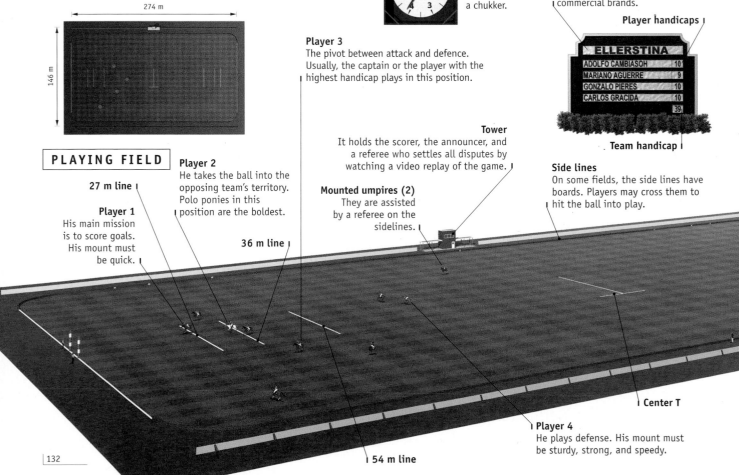

54 m line

Player 4
He plays defense. His mount must be sturdy, strong, and speedy.

Center T

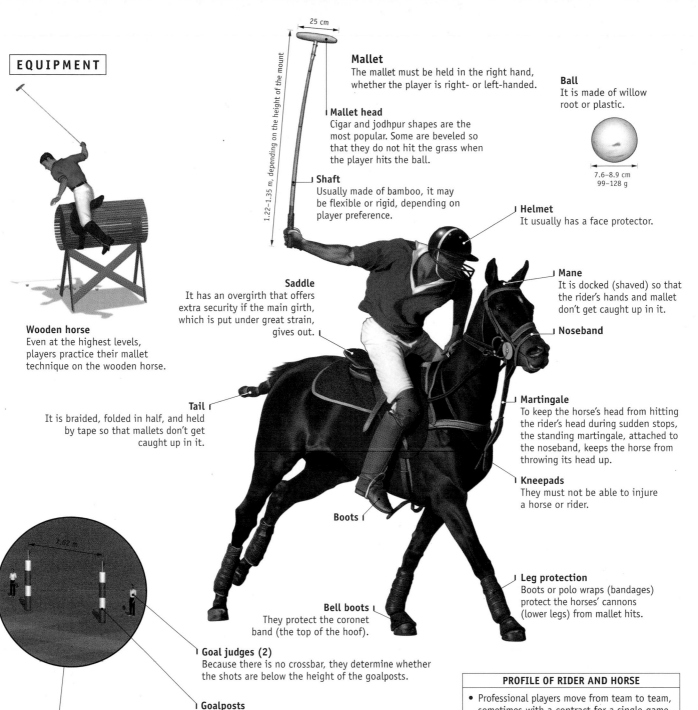

EQUIPMENT

25 cm

1.22–1.35 m, depending on the height of the mount

Mallet
The mallet must be held in the right hand, whether the player is right- or left-handed.

Mallet head
Cigar and jodhpur shapes are the most popular. Some are beveled so that they do not hit the grass when the player hits the ball.

Shaft
Usually made of bamboo, it may be flexible or rigid, depending on player preference.

Ball
It is made of willow root or plastic.

7.6–8.9 cm
99–128 g

Helmet
It usually has a face protector.

Mane
It is docked (shaved) so that the rider's hands and mallet don't get caught up in it.

Noseband

Martingale
To keep the horse's head from hitting the rider's head during sudden stops, the standing martingale, attached to the noseband, keeps the horse from throwing its head up.

Kneepads
They must not be able to injure a horse or rider.

Leg protection
Boots or polo wraps (bandages) protect the horses' cannons (lower legs) from mallet hits.

Saddle
It has an overgirth that offers extra security if the main girth, which is put under great strain, gives out.

Wooden horse
Even at the highest levels, players practice their mallet technique on the wooden horse.

Tail
It is braided, folded in half, and held by tape so that mallets don't get caught up in it.

Boots

Bell boots
They protect the coronet band (the top of the hoof).

7.62 m

Goal judges (2)
Because there is no crossbar, they determine whether the shots are below the height of the goalposts.

Goalposts
They are flexible and covered with wooden laths to avoid injuries. Players may pass between them.

PROFILE OF RIDER AND HORSE

- Professional players move from team to team, sometimes with a contract for a single game. To maintain their level of play, they are constantly looking for and purchasing high-quality polo ponies.

- According to riders, their mounts are responsible for 75% of playing success. Polo ponies must not be afraid of contact, sometimes rough, with other horses, and must calmly accept the acrobatic movements of their riders. Ability to stop, start, and turn suddenly is more important than pure speed.

- Horses are introduced to the game at age 4. Over two years, they learn immediate obedience to the rider's commands, how to place the rider in a good position to hit the ball, not to shy when the rider hits with the mallet, and that the objective of a race is to be the first to get to the ball.

Memo Gracida (USA)
This native of Mexico is one of an elite group (15 in the world) with a 10 handicap. He has won the prestigious US Open 14 times; in 1998, with the Isla Carroll team, he won the Gold Cup and the Sterling Cup.

CALENDAR OF INTERNATIONAL EVENTS

Argentine Open	Palermo, Buenos Aires	November
World Cup	Palm Beach, Florida	April
Gold Cup	Cowdray Park, England	July
Windsor Park International	England	July
Polo World Championship	Deauville, France	August

TACTICS AND TECHNIQUES

Polo is too fast and unpredictable a game for tactics to be devised in advance. Knowing the skills of the opposing riders and horses is essential. Players try to use their best polo ponies for the 4th or 6th chukkers, which are usually the most crucial to the outcome of the game. A basic principle of polo is the "line of the ball," which is intended to prevent accidents: the player following the path of a ball that he has just hit and the player closest to the ball after it is hit have right of way over the other players. No other player can ride them off.

Forehand and backhand hits

The ball may be hit forward, backward, or diagonally. It is a forehand shot if the ball is on the right-hand side of the polo pony, and a backhand if it is on the left-hand side. A good hitter can hit the ball the length of the field (274 m) in 2 shots. Standing in the stirrups increases the power of the shot.

Perpendicular hits

They are hit under the horse's neck or behind its tail. The most difficult hit, called the "millionaire's hit," is made under the horse's belly.

Hooking mallets

This is allowed when an opposing player is about to hit the ball. Hooking above shoulder level or in front of the horse's legs is a foul that is penalized by a free hit.

Riding off

Pushing against the opposing player to get him out of the line of the ball must be done from an angle of less than 45°.

Free hits and penalty hits

Free hits may be taken from the 27, 36, or 54 m lines, depending on how serious the umpires consider the foul to be. The team at fault may move on a free hit only if it is made from the 60 m line. When a defensive fault keeps an attacker from scoring a goal, the umpire may call a penalty hit: the player approaches the ball at a gallop and hits it at the goal from the 27 m line, without intervention by the opposing team.

Starting play

At the beginning of a game, the two teams line up on either side of the center T and a referee throws the ball on the line between them. When the ball goes out of play at a side line, the teams line up 4.6 m from where it went out of play. When it goes out of play beyond the end line, a defending player puts it back in play from the spot where it went out. Attackers must stay 27 m away, while defending players may position themselves where they want.

Precision and
Accuracy Sports

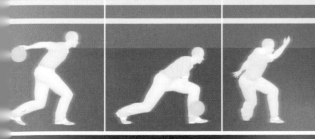

shooting

The Swedish team on the firing line; they won the gold medal at the Stockholm Olympics in 1912.

The first firearms were made in the late 15th century, but it was only in the 19th century that shooting became a sport. For all events, the principle is the same: to hit a still or moving target using a firearm. In the early 19th century, in England, the Old Hats Club developed a system of shooting at a running target. Colt invented the revolver cylinder in 1836, and this technological advance made shooting popular. Soon, the first rules for shooting competitions were written, and the first shooting associations were founded in Switzerland. Around 1860, live pigeons, used up to then as targets, were replaced by clay pigeons propelled by mechanical pullers. Shooting for men was included in the first modern Olympics in Athens in 1896. It was not until 1984 that women's shooting became an Olympic event. In 1907, the Union internationale de tir (International Shooting Union) was founded; in 1988, this organization became the International Shooting Sport Federation (ISSF). World championships take place every four years, alternating with the Olympics. Shooting competitions are divided into three main categories: shotgun, rifle, and pistol.

SHOTGUN

In this event, the shooter uses a shotgun to destroy saucer shaped clay pigeons in flight. The number of pullers and targets, how the targets are released, and the number of shots per target vary in the trap, skeet, and double trap events. In competition, shooters go to each shooting station one after the other. When the shooter gives the order to release the target ("Pull!"), a microphone placed at her feet electronically transmits the order to automatic or manual pullers.

SHOOTING RANGE

OLYMPIC TRENCH (TRAP)

Fifteen pullers are placed in groups of 3. Nine different release grids control the angle and speed of the clay pigeons. The competition involves 125 pigeons for men (5 rounds of 25 over 2 days) and 75 for women (3 rounds of 25). The 6 best shooters go to a final round of 25 clay pigeons. The 5 shooters on the firing line move to the next shooting station after each round. The points are calculated by counting destroyed clay pigeons (1 point per pigeon).

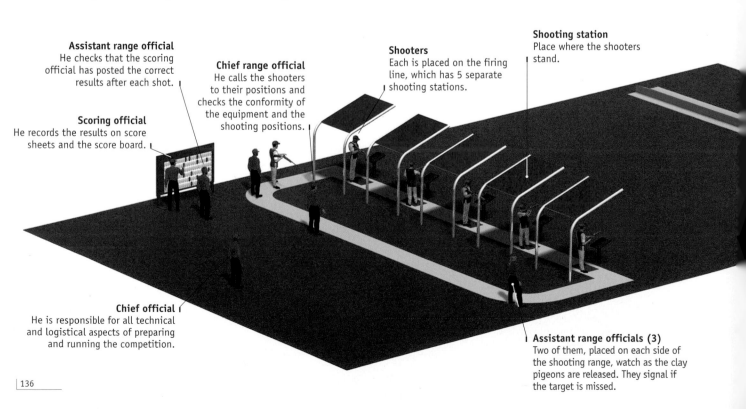

Assistant range official
He checks that the scoring official has posted the correct results after each shot.

Scoring official
He records the results on score sheets and the score board.

Chief range official
He calls the shooters to their positions and checks the conformity of the equipment and the shooting positions.

Shooters
Each is placed on the firing line, which has 5 separate shooting stations.

Shooting station
Place where the shooters stand.

Chief official
He is responsible for all technical and logistical aspects of preparing and running the competition.

Assistant range officials (3)
Two of them, placed on each side of the shooting range, watch as the clay pigeons are released. They signal if the target is missed.

SKEET

The firing line is a semi-circle with 7 shooting stations. The clay pigeons are released from 2 pullers at the ends of the semi-circle, and their flights may vary. Shooters have 2 cartridges to try to hit the 2 pigeons. They cannot shoot twice at the same pigeon. The number of pigeons and rounds is the same as for trap.

DOUBLE TRAP

Three pullers release 2 clay pigeons at angles and heights that the shooters know in advance. The competition involves 150 clay pigeons for men (3 rounds of 50 pigeons launched 2 by 2) or 120 for women (3 rounds of 40 pigeons). The 6 best shooters go to a final round with 50 clay pigeons for men and 40 for women.

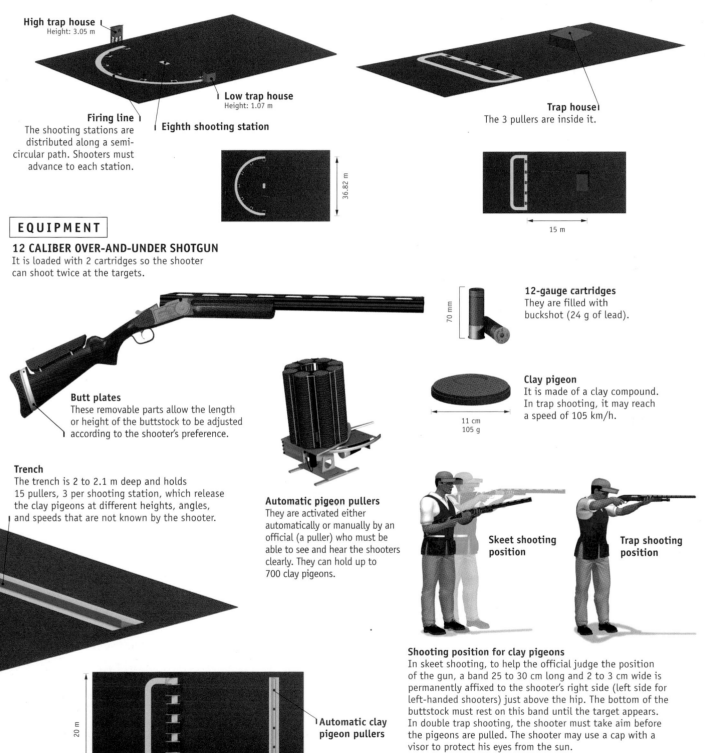

High trap house
Height: 3.05 m

Low trap house
Height: 1.07 m

Firing line
The shooting stations are distributed along a semi-circular path. Shooters must advance to each station.

Eighth shooting station

36.82 m

Trap house
The 3 pullers are inside it.

15 m

EQUIPMENT

12 CALIBER OVER-AND-UNDER SHOTGUN
It is loaded with 2 cartridges so the shooter can shoot twice at the targets.

Butt plates
These removable parts allow the length or height of the buttstock to be adjusted according to the shooter's preference.

12-gauge cartridges
They are filled with buckshot (24 g of lead).

70 mm

Clay pigeon
It is made of a clay compound. In trap shooting, it may reach a speed of 105 km/h.

11 cm
105 g

Trench
The trench is 2 to 2.1 m deep and holds 15 pullers, 3 per shooting station, which release the clay pigeons at different heights, angles, and speeds that are not known by the shooter.

Automatic pigeon pullers
They are activated either automatically or manually by an official (a puller) who must be able to see and hear the shooters clearly. They can hold up to 700 clay pigeons.

Skeet shooting position

Trap shooting position

20 m

Automatic clay pigeon pullers

15 m

Shooting position for clay pigeons
In skeet shooting, to help the official judge the position of the gun, a band 25 to 30 cm long and 2 to 3 cm wide is permanently affixed to the shooter's right side (left side for left-handed shooters) just above the hip. The bottom of the buttstock must rest on this band until the target appears. In double trap shooting, the shooter must take aim before the pigeons are pulled. The shooter may use a cap with a visor to protect his eyes from the sun.

RIFLE

The aim of the competition is to place as many bullets as possible as close as possible to the center of the target. Rifle shooting is divided into categories according to the caliber used. In all events, the shooters must respect rules for distance, time, position, and bore.

For 5.6 mm caliber rifles (.22 long rifle) and for 4.5 mm caliber air rifles, the events vary according to distance (10 and 50 m), number of shots (40, 60, or 120), and position (standing, kneeling, or prone).

- Sport rifle (women) 3 x 20: shooters make 60 shots from 50 m in a maximum time of 2:30 hours: 20 shots prone, 20 standing, and 20 kneeling.

- Free rifle (men) 3 x 40: shooters make 120 shots from 50 m: 40 prone in 1 hour, 40 standing in 1:30 hours, and 40 kneeling in 1:15 hours.

- Free rifle prone: shooters must make 60 shots from 50 m in 1:30 hours in the prone position.

- Air rifle (10 m) standing: shooters use a CO_2 or compressed-air rifle with a 4.5 mm bore. They shoot 60 times in 1:45 hours (40 times in 1:15 hours for women).

- Air rifle (10 m) on running target (men): shooters make 60 shots, 30 for precision and 30 rapid fire. In precision, the target is visible for 5 seconds; in rapid fire, it is visible for 2.5 seconds. Shooters use a regulation telescope.

POSITIONS

Prone

The shooter lies on the ground or on a regulation shooting mat supplied by the competition organizers. He must support the gun only with both hands and one shoulder, and he can place his cheek against the buttstock for aiming. He can use a strap linking the upper supporting arm to the rifle. The rifle must not touch any other surface. The forearms must not be in contact with the ground and must be held at an angle of at least 30° in relation to the ground.

Kneeling

Three points of contact with the ground are allowed: left foot, toes of right foot, and right knee (for a right-handed shooter). The rifle must be held in both hands and supported on the right shoulder. The shooter can use a strap as in the prone position. The left elbow cannot be more than 10 cm in front of the knee. The shooter can use a cushion under the right instep, but this foot cannot be at an angle of more than 45° underneath him.

Standing

The shooter stands with straight legs, both feet on the ground, and with no other support. The rifle is held in the hands and supported on the aiming shoulder; the aiming cheek may touch the rifle. The supporting arm (the left arm for a right-handed shooter) rests along the torso and the elbow is solidly supported on the hip. The other arm is unsupported.

EQUIPMENT

Depending on the event, the rifle is small bore (5.6 mm, .22 long rifle) or large bore (max. 8 mm). The total weight of the rifle must be 8 kg or less. Aiming sights are allowed as long as they are not magnifying lenses. In free rifle, the shooter may customize the gun by changing the length or height of the buttstock or increasing the length of the barrel using extension tubes within an authorized limit. Clothing is strictly regulated in terms of vest, leather gloves, pants, shoes, and even belt, which must have no component that can be used for support.

.22 (5.6 MM) RIFLE

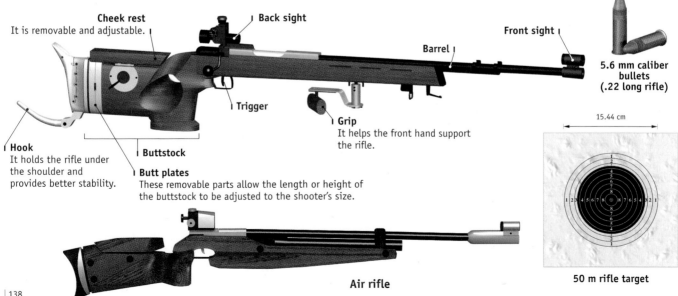

Cheek rest
It is removable and adjustable.

Back sight

Front sight

Barrel

5.6 mm caliber bullets (.22 long rifle)

Trigger

Grip
It helps the front hand support the rifle.

Hook
It holds the rifle under the shoulder and provides better stability.

Buttstock

Butt plates
These removable parts allow the length or height of the buttstock to be adjusted to the shooter's size.

15.44 cm

Air rifle

50 m rifle target

PISTOL

Like rifle shooting, the aim of this event is to place the largest number of bullets as close as possible to the center of the target. Most competitions use 5.6 mm caliber pistols (except for the center-fire pistol for men and 10 m air pistol). Standing is the only position used, and competitions vary according to number of shots and distance. The gun is held in one hand with a straight arm.

- Standard pistol (men only) 3 x 20: at a distance of 25 m from the target, shooters make 60 shots, divided into 3 rounds of 20. In the first round, they shoot 5 shots 4 times in 150 seconds; in the second round, 5 shots 4 times in 20 seconds; in the third round, 5 shots 4 times in 10 seconds.

- Free pistol (men only) 6 x 10: at a distance of 50 m from the target, the shooter makes 60 shots (6 rounds of 10) in 2 hours. Each round must be completed within 15 min.

- Rapid-fire pistol (men only) 2 x 30: at a distance of 25 m, the shooter shoots at 5 pivoting targets. He must make 60 shots in 2 rounds of 30 within a time limit. The rounds are: 5 shots 2 times in 8 sec; 5 shots 2 times in 6 sec; 5 shots 2 times in 4 sec. Each shot in the 5-shot group must be aimed at a different one of the 5 targets.

- Air pistol 10 m (men and women): women must make 40 shots in 1:15 hours; men, 60 shots in 1:45 hours.

- Sport pistol for women or center-fire pistol for men 2 x 30: shooters use a large-bore pistol (8 mm or 9.65 mm for men and 5.66 mm for women). They first make 30 "precision" shots: 6 rounds of 5 shots in 6 min, then 30 "rapid-fire" shots: 6 rounds of 5 shots in 3 seconds. The target disappears for 7 seconds after each shot.

POSITIONS

Competitor's table
The competitor must place her ammunition and gun on the table until the event starts.

Starting position

This position is required before each shot in the rapid fire pistol events. The gun is held at a 45° angle in front of the body.

Shooting technique

The legs are spread and the shoulders are square to the target. The free hand must not hang down, but is hooked into the belt or in a pocket.

Goggles
Protective goggles are mandatory.

Ear protectors
They are mandatory for shooters and shooting range officials.

TARGETS

Target sizes vary depending on the type of gun, bore, and shooting distance. Targets are made of numbered concentric circles.

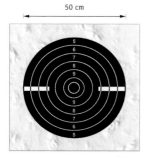

Rapid fire pistol 25 m

Precision pistol 25 and 50 m

EQUIPMENT

For all events, the gun must be held in one hand, the buttstock cannot be extended to provide support beyond the hand, and the wrist must be completely unsupported when the shot is made. The pistols are loaded with one bullet or lead shot at a time. Sighting lenses, optical sights, and mirrors are forbidden.

8 MM PISTOL

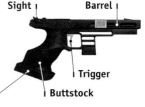

Sight | Barrel

Hypothenar eminence rest
This extension, which holds the outside edge of the hand to keep it from sliding, is placed on the front or side of the pistol grip.

Trigger

Buttstock

AIR PISTOL

PISTOL .22

Telescopic sight
They are allowed, but the telescope must not be attached to the gun or used while shooting.

Dress for pistol shooting
No equipment that supports or immobilizes any part of the body is allowed, not even shoes that support the ankles.

SHOOTER PROFILE

- In all shooting events, an exceptional ability to concentrate is essential. Shooters repeatedly practice precisely the same movements a great number of times and must be able to control all body motions. Instinctively, shooters pull the trigger between two heartbeats, as heartbeats can reduce the accuracy of the shot.

- Shooters must be in good physical shape. They do warm up and flexibility exercises for the wrists, arms, shoulders, and back, which bear the effort of carrying the weight of the gun. Shooters must also perform relaxation exercises to help to control their breathing and heart rate and get rid of nervous tension.

archery

"Archery at Hatfield," by Gorborild (1792)

Whether it is for hunting, war, or sport, the goal of archery is the same: to shoot arrows at a distant target. At first a hunting weapon, the bow and arrow became a weapon of war around 3000 B.C. This use continued until the Renaissance, when it was made obsolete by the first firearms. In the 19th century, the medieval Companies of Archers returned to fashion—no longer to do battle, but to parade and demonstrate their skill at target shooting. Archery slowly became a true sport, practiced mainly in northern France, where the Fédération française de tir à l'arc was founded in 1928, followed, three years later, by the International Archery Federation (FITA) in Poland. In spite of a brief appearance at the Olympics (1900 for men, 1904 for women, then 1908 and 1920 for both of them), archery became popular only after 1960, and it returned to the Games in 1972 for both men and women. Only target archery is an Olympic event, in four competitions: for men and women, either individual or in teams of three. The target archery world championships, created in 1931, have been held every two years since 1975.

THE COMPETITION

Archers must shoot their arrows as close as possible to the center of a target located at a set distance. Several disciplines are recognized by the FITA, each with its own rules concerning the distance, number of arrows, type of target, and equipment. In the Olympics and world championships, archers shoot a total of 144 arrows at 4 distances, starting with the longest, for a maximum of 1440 points.

The 64 best archers then shoot with 3 ends of 6 arrows. The best 8 go to the finals, where they compete one on one with 4 ends of 3 arrows. The competition for the gold medal involves 2 archers alternately shooting 4 ends of 3 arrows. All ends are shot at a distance of 70 m. Time limits are indicated by colored lights and sound signals.

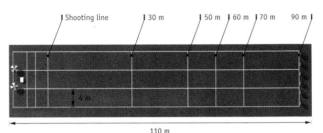

Safety zone
To avoid accidents, spectators must stay at least 10 m behind the shooting line and 20 m from the sidelines.

SHOOTING RANGE

Judge
He verifies the shooting distances, sizes of the targets, and legality of the equipment. He controls how shots are taken (shooter's position, time limits, equipment used). There must be at least one judge per 10 targets.

60 m line
In the first round, women shoot 36 arrows at a 122 cm target.

Signal lights

70 m line
In the first round, men and women shoot 36 arrows at a 122 cm target. This distance is used for all final rounds.

90 m line
In the first round, men shoot 36 arrows at a 122 cm target.

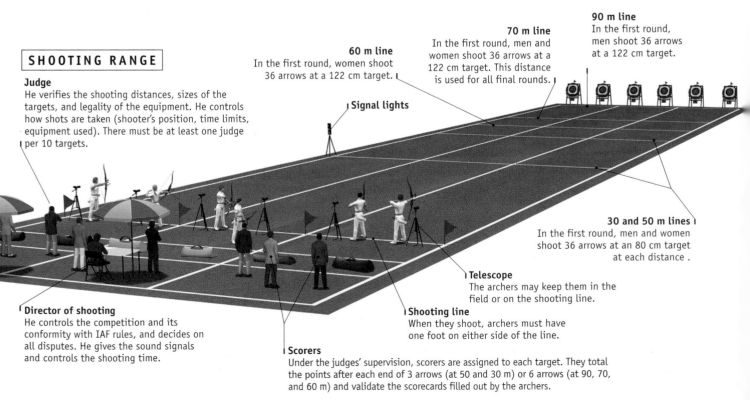

30 and 50 m lines
In the first round, men and women shoot 36 arrows at an 80 cm target at each distance .

Telescope
The archers may keep them in the field or on the shooting line.

Shooting line
When they shoot, archers must have one foot on either side of the line.

Director of shooting
He controls the competition and its conformity with IAF rules, and decides on all disputes. He gives the sound signals and controls the shooting time.

Scorers
Under the judges' supervision, scorers are assigned to each target. They total the points after each end of 3 arrows (at 50 and 30 m) or 6 arrows (at 90, 70, and 60 m) and validate the scorecards filled out by the archers.

TECHNIQUE

The archer has perfect control of his movements to the point that he automatically repeats each of the gestures in the shooting sequence. From taking the bow in hand to the follow-through takes between 15 and 20 seconds, during which the archer is oblivious to everything around him and concentrates on his sequence.

1. Preparation before the shot

2. Placing the arrow on the bow

3. Taking aim

4. Release

5. Follow-through

TARGETS

A target is composed of concentric circles numbered from 1 (outside) to 10 (center). A central mark is used to break ties.

Center of the target

1.3 m

22

Backward incline: 15° from vertical

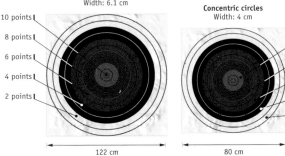

Concentric circles
Width: 6.1 cm

10 points
8 points
6 points
4 points
2 points

122 cm

Concentric circles
Width: 4 cm

9 points
7 points
5 points
3 points
1 point

80 cm

LIGHTS AND SIGNALS

Red
Accompanied by 2 sound signals: archers must take their place on the shooting line.

Accompanied by 3 sound signals: time has run out and the shot is terminated.

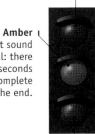

Amber
Without sound signal: there are 30 seconds to complete the end.

Green
Accompanied by a sound signal: the shot may begin.

OTHER DISCIPLINES

Field archery

All types of bows are allowed and sighting apparatuses are forbidden. Archers follow a course with 24 targets, 12 of which are at a distance known in advance and 12 of which are at an unknown distance. Archers may use 3 arrows for each target. The targets are marked with zones of 1, 2, 3, 4, 5, and 5+ points (5+ is used to break ties) and measure between 20 and 80 cm. Archers may shoot only when they arrive at a shooting zone located between 5 and 60 m from the target. The competition has an elimination round and a final, both for individuals and for teams.

Animal archery (on animal shaped targets)

The archer is placed in a hunting situation on a course of rough natural terrain. The targets (21 or 42, depending on the course) are shaped like animals, usually 3-dimensional, and are marked with two zones (killed and injured). For each target, the archer must shoot 2 arrows from different shooting zones within 30 seconds. The points are attributed first for the first arrow (killed, 20 points; injured, 10 points), then the second arrow (killed, 15 points; injured, 10 points).

Injured

Killed

Beursault archery

Beursault is similar to traditional archery as practiced in the Middle Ages. The event takes place on an archery "jeu": a lane 50 m long with a target at each end. The targets are 45 cm in diameter and divided into 5 zones. Archers shoot one arrow per target, alternating between the 2 targets, until they have shot 40 arrows. Each arrow that hits the target is called an "honneur." Rankings are determined according to the number of "honneurs" and, in the case of a tie, by number of points.

EQUIPMENT

ARROW

There is no limit on the length of arrows as long as they are within the required weight—a maximum of 28 g. Archers choose the length that suits them best. In general, the fletching is 2.5 cm from the arrow nock.

Tip
It is used as an adjustable weight on the front of the arrow according to the draw weight of the bow.

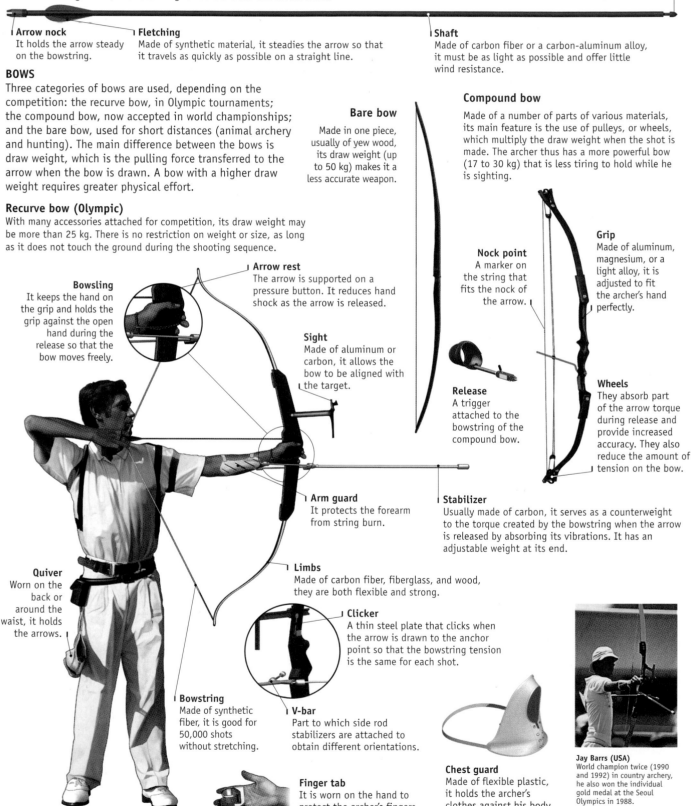

Arrow nock
It holds the arrow steady on the bowstring.

Fletching
Made of synthetic material, it steadies the arrow so that it travels as quickly as possible on a straight line.

Shaft
Made of carbon fiber or a carbon-aluminum alloy, it must be as light as possible and offer little wind resistance.

BOWS

Three categories of bows are used, depending on the competition: the recurve bow, in Olympic tournaments; the compound bow, now accepted in world championships; and the bare bow, used for short distances (animal archery and hunting). The main difference between the bows is draw weight, which is the pulling force transferred to the arrow when the bow is drawn. A bow with a higher draw weight requires greater physical effort.

Bare bow
Made in one piece, usually of yew wood, its draw weight (up to 50 kg) makes it a less accurate weapon.

Compound bow
Made of a number of parts of various materials, its main feature is the use of pulleys, or wheels, which multiply the draw weight when the shot is made. The archer thus has a more powerful bow (17 to 30 kg) that is less tiring to hold while he is sighting.

Recurve bow (Olympic)

With many accessories attached for competition, its draw weight may be more than 25 kg. There is no restriction on weight or size, as long as it does not touch the ground during the shooting sequence.

Arrow rest
The arrow is supported on a pressure button. It reduces hand shock as the arrow is released.

Grip
Made of aluminum, magnesium, or a light alloy, it is adjusted to fit the archer's hand perfectly.

Nock point
A marker on the string that fits the nock of the arrow.

Bowsling
It keeps the hand on the grip and holds the grip against the open hand during the release so that the bow moves freely.

Sight
Made of aluminum or carbon, it allows the bow to be aligned with the target.

Release
A trigger attached to the bowstring of the compound bow.

Wheels
They absorb part of the arrow torque during release and provide increased accuracy. They also reduce the amount of tension on the bow.

Arm guard
It protects the forearm from string burn.

Stabilizer
Usually made of carbon, it serves as a counterweight to the torque created by the bowstring when the arrow is released by absorbing its vibrations. It has an adjustable weight at its end.

Quiver
Worn on the back or around the waist, it holds the arrows.

Limbs
Made of carbon fiber, fiberglass, and wood, they are both flexible and strong.

Clicker
A thin steel plate that clicks when the arrow is drawn to the anchor point so that the bowstring tension is the same for each shot.

Bowstring
Made of synthetic fiber, it is good for 50,000 shots without stretching.

V-bar
Part to which side rod stabilizers are attached to obtain different orientations.

Jay Barrs (USA)
World champion twice (1990 and 1992) in country archery, he also won the individual gold medal at the Seoul Olympics in 1988.

Finger tab
It is worn on the hand to protect the archer's fingers.

Chest guard
Made of flexible plastic, it holds the archer's clothes against his body and protects his chest from string burn.

billiards

The origins of billiards remain unclear. According to some, billiards originated in China, while others contend that it was called "pall-mall," and was brought to Europe by the Crusaders returning from the Near East. Still others credit the invention of billiards in one form or another to either France, Italy, England, or Spain. The first billiard table would have been built in France in 1469 for King Louis XI. The game was previously played on the ground, and resembled bowling, although the Spanish "villorta" used a stick (known as "bilorta," later "billarda," and eventually "billiards") to move a ball in between two posts. Toward the mid 19th century, depending on whether the game was played in France, England or the United States, billards came in different forms: with or without pockets, and with three, four, or fifteen balls. The first world championships took place in 1873. Several variations of the game developed, including snooker, American billiards, and English billiards. Billiards (classic, American, and snooker) will be included in the 2004 Olympic Games as a demonstration sport. World championships are held every year for snooker, classic and American billiards.

Louis XIV and his court playing billiards in 1694 at Versailles (France)

HOW A MATCH IS ORGANIZED

Using a stick called a cue, the player must strike a ball so that it makes contact with other balls on the table. Depending on the specific game, struck balls must be sunk into the pockets located around the table, or moved to another area of the table to be hit in a subsequent shot. Matches are decided by the points scored by players when they "pocket," or sink, a ball or, in classic (carom) billiards, when they score a carom. A player continues to play for as long as he or she continues to score points. Once a shot is missed, the other player's turn begins. Matches can be played individually or in teams of 2, with the players alternating.

CLASSIC (CAROM) BILLIARDS

The playing surface is smooth, with no pockets. The game is played with three balls of the same diameter, one red and two white. To differentiate between the white balls, one has two black spots. Each player is assigned one of the two white balls, and hits only his ball. The object of the game is for each player to strike his ball so that it hits the other two balls. When the player's ball hits the other two, a point is scored, and the player continues his turn. With each shot, the player must hit the balls where they came to rest following the previous shot. When a player misses, it is his opponent's turn to shoot. A game is played up to a predetermined number of points (between 50 and 500, depending on the event) or innings. A new inning begins once both players have taken their turns.

There are several variations of classic billiards: straight rail, where caroms can be scored on any part of the table; balkline, which is played on an identical table on which lines drawn in chalk divide the table into six or nine zones; three-cushion, where a carom is scored only if the cue ball rebounds three times against the table's cushioned sides. Similar to classic billiards, English billiards is played with three marked balls. The table has six pockets (one at each corner and one at the center of each of the two long sides). Players score points by hitting object balls or by pocketing the balls.

Red ball
This is the object ball the player must hit for a successful carom. Players must not touch the red ball with their cue.

Classic billiard table

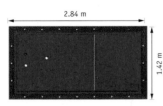

2.84 m

1.42 m

75–80 cm

White cue ball
This is the active player's ball. When it is his turn, a player can only touch his cue ball with the cue. When it is the opponent's turn, the role of the 2 white balls is reversed (1 player's cue ball is the other player's object ball).

White object ball
When it is his turn, the player uses his opponent's ball as an object ball to execute a carom.

Head string
The white object ball is placed at the center of this line for the opening break. The white cue ball must be at least 15 cm from this line.

SNOOKER

A game of snooker is played with 22 balls, and the object of the game is to alternately sink red balls and colored balls using the cue ball. Colored balls are immediately replaced on the table in their original spots when they are sunk. Once all the red balls have been sunk, the colored balls must be sunk in order of value. In addition to the points they score whenever they sink a ball, players also receive penalty points according to the fouls that they commit. Penalty points are then deducted from the player's total score. Penalties range from 4 to 7 points for fouls that include sinking the cue ball, missing all balls, or hitting the wrong ball (e.g. hitting a colored ball instead of a red one).

A player is "snookered" when he cannot hit an object ball because of obstructing balls between the cue ball and the object ball. The player must attempt the shot anyway, and is penalized if the object ball is missed or the other ball is touched. To win the game, a player tries to "snooker" his opponent as often as possible, causing his opponent to receive penalty points. The winner is the player with the highest score when the black ball is sunk according to the rules.

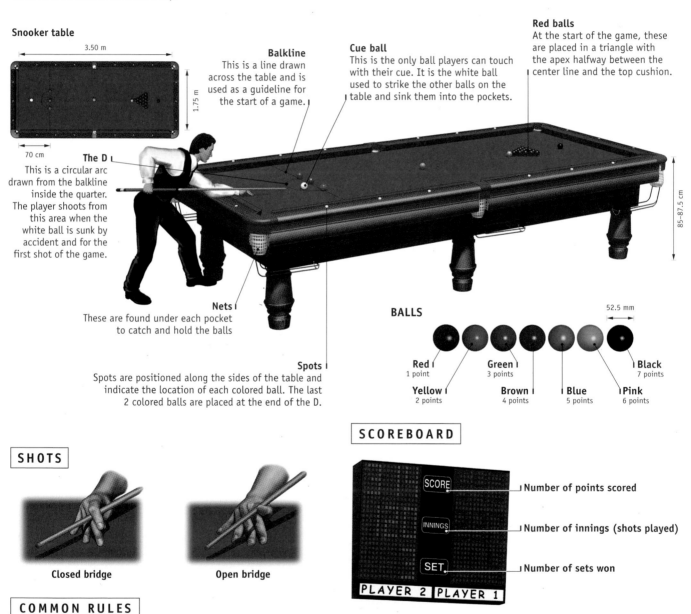

Snooker table

3.50 m

1.75 m

70 cm

85–87.5 cm

Balkline
This is a line drawn across the table and is used as a guideline for the start of a game.

Cue ball
This is the only ball players can touch with their cue. It is the white ball used to strike the other balls on the table and sink them into the pockets.

Red balls
At the start of the game, these are placed in a triangle with the apex halfway between the center line and the top cushion.

The D
This is a circular arc drawn from the balkline inside the quarter. The player shoots from this area when the white ball is sunk by accident and for the first shot of the game.

Nets
These are found under each pocket to catch and hold the balls

Spots
Spots are positioned along the sides of the table and indicate the location of each colored ball. The last 2 colored balls are placed at the end of the D.

BALLS

52.5 mm

Red
1 point

Yellow
2 points

Green
3 points

Brown
4 points

Blue
5 points

Pink
6 points

Black
7 points

SHOTS

Closed bridge

Open bridge

SCOREBOARD

SCORE — Number of points scored

INNINGS — Number of innings (shots played)

SET — Number of sets won

PLAYER 2   PLAYER 1

COMMON RULES

Some rules are common to all forms of billiards, and pertain to the possible fouls that players may commit during a game. In every case, a foul terminates the turn of the player at fault. The most common foul is a double hit, which occurs when the tip of the cue is in contact with the white ball when it touches another ball; a false hit, which

occurs when the white ball is touched by a part of the cue other then the tip; a jumped ball, which is a ball that jumps from the table; and playing a ball before the balls are completely stopped. Players must keep one foot in contact with the ground at all times.

AMERICAN (POCKET) BILLIARDS

There are several variations of American billiards, but all are played on an identical table, using the same number of balls (1 cue ball and 15 numbered balls). Depending on the game, the objective may be to sink the 15 balls in numerical order, or in a given sequence.

The most common version of American billiards is called "8 ball." The balls are split into 2 distinct groups of 7 (red and yellow, solid and striped, or numbered from 1 to 7 and 9 to 15). The 8 ball (black) does not fall into either group.

The starting player strikes the cue ball in the direction of the other balls. If the player sinks a ball, he chooses which group of balls he wishes to play, and then continues to play.

If the first player does not sink a ball, the table is considered "open," and the opponent is given the choice of which group to play. After the break, a player must indicate which ball he intends to sink,

and in which pocket. A player is allowed to sink his opponent's ball, as long as the white ball hits one of his balls first. He is not required to announce ricochet shots or the number of cushions. The player's turn continues as long as he sinks one of his balls with every shot.

Once a player sinks all of his balls, he must sink the black ball (8 ball), to win the game. A match can consist of several games (between 3 and 17, depending on the event).

A game is lost in the following situations: if the black ball is sunk during the game (before all the balls of one group are sunk); if the black ball jumps off the table; if the black ball is sunk following a foul; if the black ball is sunk in a pocket other than the one indicated; if the cue ball is sunk or jumped off the table when trying to sink the black ball.

American billiard table

2.54 m

1.27 m

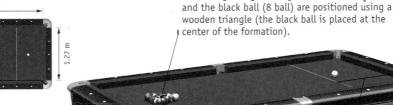

Triangle
At the beginning of the game, the 14 colored balls and the black ball (8 ball) are positioned using a wooden triangle (the black ball is placed at the center of the formation).

74–79 cm

Starting area
This is where the cue ball must be placed to start the game.

Nobuaki Kobayashi (JPN)
Eleven-time world vice-champion, two time world champion, and two time teams world champion in classic billiards.

EQUIPMENT

Triangle
The triangle is used to place the balls on a specific part of the table before the break.

Balls
Formerly made of ivory, billiard balls are now made of a blend of materials (plastic, fiberglass, resin), which makes them more shock resistant. Balls weight between 156 and 170 g and measure 57 mm in diameter.

Chalk
This is a small cube of chalk that players rub on the tip of their cue to prevent the cue from slipping when in contact with the ball.

CUE

This instrument is used by the shooter to strike and propel the ball. It consists of a piece of wood tapered at one end and divided into 6 sections. Players can select the diameter, length and weight of their cue (normally between 500 and 600 g).

Rest
A cue equipped with a metal fixture on which a shooter can rest his cue when the ball is far away.

Raymond Ceulemans (BEL)
Greatest champion in classic billiards, he won the world champion title 23 times in classic billiards, three-stripe specialty.

Shaft
The fingers on the hand not holding the butt are positioned around the shaft and guide the movement of the cue.

1.30–1.45m

Ferrule
Hard plastic piece located at the end of the cue between the shaft and the tip.

Tip
Round piece of leather fitted against the ferrule covering the smaller end of the cue. This is the only part of the cue that is permitted to touch the ball.

Joint
On 2 piece cues, the joint is located between the butt and the shaft.

Butt
This is the thick part of the cue. Shooters can select the diameter of the butt, because it must be perfectly adapted to the shooter's hand.

Bumper
A rubber piece affixed to the end of the cue that serves as a shock absorber.

Steve Davis (GBR)
First international snooker champion with 6 world titles.

lawn bowling

Lawn bowling, a game of British origins, is a close relative of Italian bocce and French petanque. The greatest concentration of skilled players is in Scotland and England. The oldest known lawn bowling green is in Southampton, England, and has been in operation since 1299. Lawn bowling was introduced to the United States in the early 17th century, to Canada in 1730, and to Australia in 1844. Today, the game has been standardized by the World Bowling Board, and it is an event in the Commonwealth Games; women's lawn bowling has been included since 1982.

Game of bowls in the 14th century

THE COMPETITION

The objective is similar to that for bocce, petanque, and curling: to deliver an object as close as possible to a target. The jack is thrown between 21 m from the mat and 2 m from the front ditch. The players, wearing their team's colors, throw their bowls toward the jack in turn. The player who throws her bowl closest to the jack wins the point. When all of the players have thrown their bowls, the end is over.

There are 4 categories of lawn bowling. In singles, the winner must score 25 shots; in pairs, the winning team is the one with the most points after 21 ends in European countries and 18 ends in the Americas. In both of these categories, each player throws 4 bowls. In triples, each player has 3 bowls and the game ends after the 18th end. In fours, each player has 2 bowls and there are 21 or 18 ends. In all categories, games last an average of 3.5 hours.

BOWLING TECHNIQUE

EQUIPMENT

Shoes
In a single color (white, brown, or black) with a smooth sole and no heel.

6.4 cm

Jack
Made of wood or lignite.

11.4–13.4 cm

Maximum 1.6 kg

Bowl
The new models are made of lignite; the traditional bowl is made of wood, rubber, or a combination of the two. It is not completely spherical; its degree of bias and the manufacturer's brand must appear on the two flatter sides.

THE GREEN

Outdoor greens, with a grass or artificial surface, measure 37 to 40 m in length and are divided into a number of rinks, or lanes, with a width of 5.5 to 5.8 m. Indoor greens are usually smaller; their dimensions are set by competition organizers.

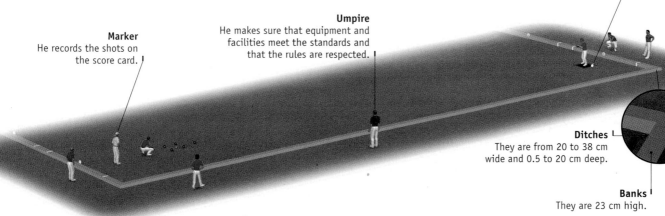

Mat
It is made of black rubber with a white border and measures 61 x 35.6 cm.

Marker
He records the shots on the score card.

Umpire
He makes sure that equipment and facilities meet the standards and that the rules are respected.

Ditches
They are from 20 to 38 cm wide and 0.5 to 20 cm deep.

Banks
They are 23 cm high.

petanque

Petanque was invented in La Ciotat, a small town near Marseilles, France, by Jules Le Noir, a veteran jeu provençal player confined to a wheelchair as a result of an accident. The game owes its name to the throwing position: the feet, or pieds, are tanqués, or together; piedtanque became petanque. Until the end of the Second World War, petanque was played only in southern France, from Marseilles to the French Riviera. Then, vacationers from other parts of the country took the sport back home and expatriate French nationals exported it to other countries. Today, petanque is popular in Europe, French-speaking Africa, North America, and Asia, particularly in Thailand. Both men and women play petanque recreationally and in international competition.

Legend has it that long ago, losing players had the consolation of kissing the derrière of a certain waitress of doubtful morals, Fanny, from a nearby petanque club. Tradition still has it that losers that have not scored a single point kiss a representation of Fanny's derrière (painting, sculpture, mold, or other).

THE GAME

There are 3 categories of petanque competition: singles (one on one); doubles (teams of 2), in which each player has 3 boules; and triples (teams of 3), in which each player has just 2 boules.

The game is played the same way for singles and teams. The side that throws the cochonnet is determined by random draw. A member of this side draws a circle 35 to 50 cm in diameter for the thrower to stand in and throws the cochonnet a distance of 6 to 10 m, then shoots a boule as close as possible to it. A player from the other team then enters the circle and shoots in his turn. The next boule is shot by the team that does not have the boule closest to the cochonnet, and the shots continue until one team has thrown all of its boules. The

other team then shoots its remaining boules. Points are calculated after all the boules have been shot. Each boule that a player has placed closer to the cochonnet than the opposing team's best boule wins a point. The end is over and the boules are picked up. The player who won the points makes a circle where the cochonnet was, throws it again, and another end begins. The game ends when a player or team has won 13 points.

There are 2 types of shots: point and tir. A player who shoots a point rolls his boule to place it as close as possible to the cochonnet; a player who shoots a tir tries to displace a boule belonging to the opposing team.

EQUIPMENT

Boule
It is made entirely of steel, and the manufacturer's brand and its weight must be engraved on it.

7.1–8.0 cm
650–800 g

Cochonnet
It is made entirely of wood.

2.5–3.5 cm

Measuring instrument
Telescoping "pullcord."

THE TRACK

Games are played on grass, earth, or sand, but competition tracks are standardized.

BASIC POSITIONS

There are 3 basic positions for throwing the cochonnet and the boule: squatting, knees bent, and standing. The position used depends on how far the player wants the boule to travel and with what characteristics.

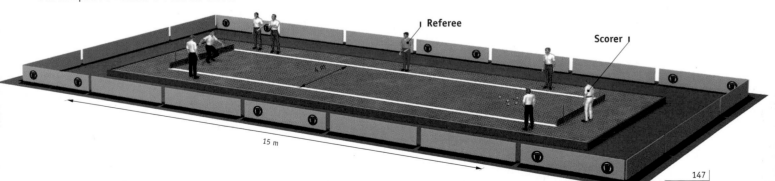

Referee

Scorer

4 m

15 m

ᴋ. bowling

Site of the American Bowling Congress tournament played in 1905

The principle of a game in which participants must knock down pins by rolling a ball at them goes back to ancient Egypt and Rome. In the Middle Ages, the sport spread throughout Europe. In Germany and the Netherlands, bowling was played at religious festivals. In fact, Dutch immigrants introduced the game to the United States in the 17th century. In the early 19th, the number of pins was raised from 9 to 10 and the rules began to be codified with the creation of the American Bowling Congress (ABC) in 1895. The first championships were held in 1901 for men and 1916 for women. Bowling developed mainly in the United States and was reintroduced to Europe after the Second World War. The Fédération internationale des quilleurs (FIQ), formed in 1952, organized its first world championships for men in 1954; they have taken place every four years since 1963 and women have participated since that date.

THE COMPETITION

Players must knock down 10 pins by rolling a ball at them. If they do not succeed on the first try, they must knock down the remaining pins with a second ball. A game is played in 10 10-pin frames. Points are scored from the total number of pins knocked down in each frame. In the first 9 frames, players bowl 2 balls in a row unless they knock over all of the balls with the first ball; this is called a strike. In the 10th frame, a player who bowls a strike gets to bowl 2 extra balls. A player who bowls a spare (all pins knocked down in 2 tries) gets to bowl 1 extra ball.

CUPS AND CHAMPIONSHIPS

Aside from the world championships (singles, teams of 3, teams of 5), professional bowling has a number of major tournaments. The most important are the US Open, played every year since 1941 (1949 for women); the Master's for men, since 1951; and the Queens for women, since 1961.

3 ft.

The pins are set up in an equilateral triangle.

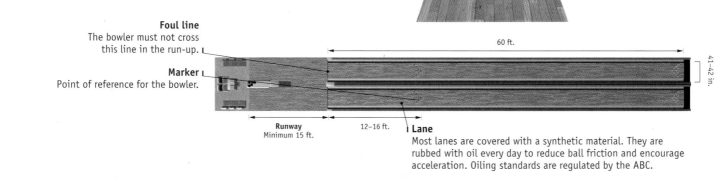

Foul line
The bowler must not cross this line in the run-up.

Marker
Point of reference for the bowler.

60 ft.

41–42 in.

Runway
Minimum 15 ft.

12–16 ft.

Lane
Most lanes are covered with a synthetic material. They are rubbed with oil every day to reduce ball friction and encourage acceleration. Oiling standards are regulated by the ABC.

RELEASING THE BALL

The approach is the most important part of bowling. The player takes 4 or 5 steps, starting slowly and accelerating until he lets the ball go. Each step is accompanied by an arm movement that prepares the ball and maintains the bowler's balance.

First step
The right foot (for a right handed player) moves forward slightly. The ball is held in both hands in front of the body.

Second step
The left foot moves forward, while the left hand releases the ball and helps the player balance.

Third step
The player bends his knees to accelerate the ball's motion. His left arm is held out to help him keep his balance.

Fourth step
The player swings his right arm forward to let go of the ball. The fingers provide final impetus as the left foot ends its slide.

EQUIPMENT

Pins
Made of wood, usually maple, with a plastic coating. Their center of gravity is calculated so that they fall when they lean more than 8 degrees.

15 in.

4½ in.

Minimum 2¼ in.
3 lbs.

Balls
Made of plastic and fiberglass, they must meet precise criteria for balance, hardness, and weight. A special scale is used to calculate the balance of the ball, and the hardness of the material is checked with a durometer.

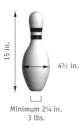

There are 3 finger holes (thumb, middle finger, and ring finger). The depth of the holes may be conventional (2 phalanges in the holes for the index and ring fingers) or "finger-tip" (one phalange).

8½ in.
Maximum 16 lbs.

Shoes
Professional players use 2 different soles: a right handed player uses a leather sole on the left shoe (to facilitate sliding) and a rubber sole on the right shoe (for traction).

Dick Weber (USA)
A bowling legend, he is the only player to win titles in 5 decades, from the 1950s to the 1990s. He holds the record for victories at the US Open in the 60s, as did Don Carter in the 50s. He was Bowler of the Year in 1961, 1963, and 1965.

SCORING POINTS

Each overturned pin counts for 1 point. When a player knocks down all of the pins in a frame in 1 or 2 tries, there are bonus points.

Strike
The player knocks over all pins in 1 try. A strike is indicated by an X, but the points are not calculated until the following frame; the score bowled in that frame will be added to the 10 points for the strike in the previous frame.

Triple
The 10 points are added to the total of the first frame (10 + 10 + 10 = 30). Points from frame 2 will be carried over to the following frame.

Spare
The 10 pins in frame 5 are knocked over in 2 tries (8 then 2). The player scores 10 points, but the total is carried over to the first ball of the following frame.

Strike
As in frame 1, points are not added until the 2 balls are bowled in the following frame.

Open frame
Not all the pins were knocked over in 2 tries. The player knocked over 9 pins with his first try. The total is added to the spare in frame 8 (10 + 9 = 19). Frame 9 is left open and the player scores only 9 points.

Frame number

1	2	3	4	5	6	7	8	9	10
X	X	X	7 2	8 /	F 9	X	7 /	9 -	X X 8
30	57	76	85	95	104	124	143	152	180

Total
A perfect total for a game (10 frames plus 2 extra balls, or 12 possible strikes) is 300 points.

Double
The player has made 2 consecutive strikes. The points are carried over to the first ball of the following frame.

7 pins knocked over in the first roll
The total is added to the score of frame 2 (10 + 10 + 7 = 27). In the second roll the player knocks over only 2 pins. The total for this frame (9) is therefore added to the strike in frame 3 (10 + 9 = 19). As frame 4 was left open, the player scores only 9 points.

Foul on first roll
The player scores 10 points for the spare in frame 5 and no bonus points for this first roll. In the second roll, he knocks over 9 pins. This score will be carried over to frame 6.

Spare
The 10 points for the spare are added to the strike in frame 7 (10 + 10 = 20). The total of frame 8 will be calculated after the first ball is bowled in frame 9.

Strike in frame 10
Allows 2 extra balls. The player bowls a strike then knocks down 8 pins. The total (10 + 10 + 8 = 28) is added to frame 10.

curling

Players from north and south of the Forth River play a game at the Grand Caledonian Curling Club in Linlithgow, Scotland (1853).

Curling is a game between two teams who slide stones (or "rocks") on a sheet of ice, the rink, toward a target, the tee. The game originated on the frozen ponds of Scotland, where it was probably introduced by Flemish immigrants in the 16th or 17th century. The first rules were written in Perth, Scotland, (where the Curling Museum is located) in 1716, but the game was not codified until more than a century later, in 1838, when the Grand Caledonian Curling Club was founded. Curling was exported to Canada in the 18th century, and the first major tournament took place in Edinburgh in 1847. It was a demonstration sport at the Olympics in Chamonix in 1924, but it did not become an official event at the time. The International Curling Federation was formed in 1966; it changed its name to the World Curling Federation (WCF) in 1991. The first world championships took place in 1959 for men and 1979 for women; they are held every year. Again a demonstration sport in 1988 and 1992, curling finally became an Olympic event in 1998.

THE COMPETITION

The objective is to place one or several stones as close as possible to the tee, while keeping the opposing team from doing so. The teams draw lots to see who will curl first. The skip (captain) of the team stands in the house and tells the player who is shooting where to deliver the first stone. The player must release the stone before it crosses the nearer hog line. The other two teammates help to control the stone's trajectory by sweeping the ice with brushes or brooms. Then the second team plays; the two teams alternate until the "end" is finished. A game has 10 ends. In each end, each player delivers 2 stones. The points are added up after the end and the team that scored begins the following end, in which stones are thrown in the opposite direction; the house alternates every end. A team is composed of the skip, the vice-skip, the lead, and the second.

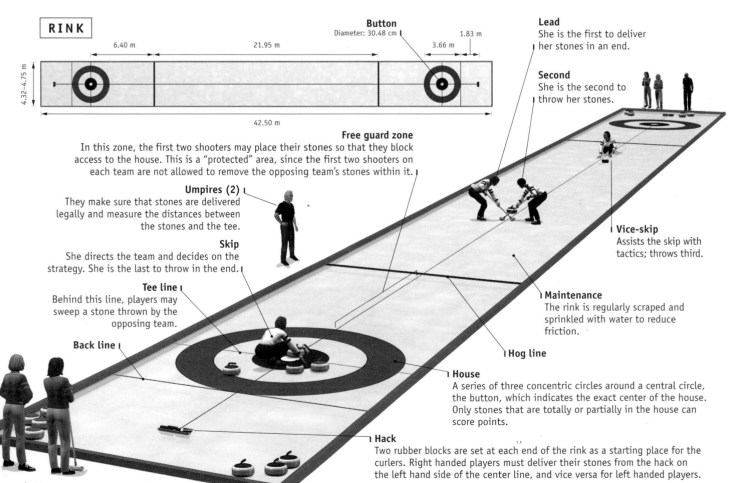

RINK

4.32–4.75 m

6.40 m   21.95 m   **Button** Diameter: 30.48 cm   1.83 m   3.66 m

42.50 m

Lead
She is the first to deliver her stones in an end.

Second
She is the second to throw her stones.

Free guard zone
In this zone, the first two shooters may place their stones so that they block access to the house. This is a "protected" area, since the first two shooters on each team are not allowed to remove the opposing team's stones within it.

Umpires (2)
They make sure that stones are delivered legally and measure the distances between the stones and the tee.

Skip
She directs the team and decides on the strategy. She is the last to throw in the end.

Tee line
Behind this line, players may sweep a stone thrown by the opposing team.

Back line

Vice-skip
Assists the skip with tactics; throws third.

Maintenance
The rink is regularly scraped and sprinkled with water to reduce friction.

Hog line

House
A series of three concentric circles around a central circle, the button, which indicates the exact center of the house. Only stones that are totally or partially in the house can score points.

Hack
Two rubber blocks are set at each end of the rink as a starting place for the curlers. Right handed players must deliver their stones from the hack on the left hand side of the center line, and vice versa for left handed players.

SCORING POINTS

The team with the stone closest to the button wins the end.

For each of its stones that is closer to the button than the opposing team's stones, this team scores a point. If there is a tie after 10 ends, one or several extra ends are played until one team wins.

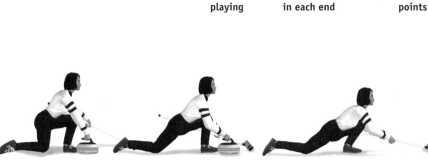

End number

Color of stones for each team

Team name

Team playing

Points in each end

Total points

TECHNIQUE

Delivering the stone

The player slides the stone forward to get it moving. Then she slides it backward so that it will move faster when she transfers her weight in the forward push. She slides with the stone, giving it a slight rotation with the wrist as she releases it, so that the stone follows the chosen trajectory.

Sweeping

The two sweepers affect the speed of the stone by correcting or quickening its movement toward the target. The sweepers are told what to do by the skip (or vice-skip), who checks whether the stone is following the planned trajectory.

EQUIPMENT

Minimum 11.43 cm

Maximum 29.09 cm
Maximum 20 kg

Stone

Made of granite, it is hewn to a circular shape, polished, and balanced. A plastic handle is then attached to the top to allow control at the release.

Shoes

They must be low cut so that they do not impede the thrower's ankle movement. The shoe for the supporting foot (left for a right handed thrower, right for a left handed thrower) has a slippery sole; the other has a nonslip gum sole.

Broom

As the broom sweeps, it melts the ice, reducing the friction between the stone and the ice. The stone will therefore slide farther on the sheet. Sweeping also reduces the draw (curl) of the stone. Therefore, a swept stone will have a straighter and longer trajectory. With less sweeping, the stone will not go as far but will draw more. Synthetic brooms are the most popular, since they do not leave wisps on the ice.

Sandra Schmirler (CAN)
Skip of the Canadian team, Olympic champion in 1998, and world champion in 1993, 1994, and 1997.

Universal joint

Allows the head of the broom to turn.

Competition measure

When two stones seem to be an equal distance from the tee, it is used to determine which stone is closer.

golf

The old St. Andrews (Scotland) course originally had 22 holes. In 1764, the Society of St. Andrews Golfers, which became later the Royal and Ancient Golf Club in 1834, reduced the number to 18. This innovation then spread to the rest of the world. When the 12th edition of the Open Championship took place there in 1873, the St. Andrews course was 500 years old.

Golf would be derived from a game played by Scottish shepherds in the 14th century, in which a wooden stick was used to hit small stones toward a specific destination. In the early 15th century, students at St. Andrews, near Dundee, in Scotland, became interested in the game, which they played with canes and real balls. With the foundation of the Royal and Ancient Golf Club of St. Andrews and the publication of the first rules for the game in 1754, more people began to play golf. The game spread throughout England and was taken to British colonies around the world; the Royal and Ancient became its main authority, with some 1,800 members who ensured that the rules were respected and changed when necessary. The British Open Championship of 1860 was the first major tournament; the United States quickly followed with the US Open in 1895 and the creation of the Professional Golfers' Association (PGA) in 1916, which gave rise to professional golf. Although the first women's tournaments apparently date from 1893, the Women's US Open was first played in 1946, and the Ladies' PGA championship in 1955.

THE TOURNAMENT

Golf is a game of precision, in which players hit a ball with a club on a course composed of 18 holes, each with a start point and a hole at the other end, into which the ball must drop. The objective is to play all 18 holes with a minimum of strokes. The major golf tournaments are played over a total of 4 rounds (72 holes), with one round played per day. This formula requires players to have remarkable consistency throughout the competition and rewards the player best able to overcome the technical difficulties of the course.

There are two generally recognized forms of competition:

• Match play, in which two players or two teams play a determined number of holes (18, 36, 54, or 72). A hole is won by the player or team that completes it with the least number of strokes.

• Stroke play, in which individuals or teams play a determined number of holes (18, 36, 54, or 72). The winner is the player or team with the lowest total number of strokes.

Within these two types of competition are several variations:

• In singles, each golfer plays against several opponents (in stroke play) or a single opponent (in match play).

• In doubles, a team composed of two golfers plays against an opposing team. There are three types of team competition. In "foursomes," each team puts a single ball in play, and players on a team hit it in turn. In "greensome," each player on each team puts a ball in play. At the second stroke, each team keeps only its better-placed ball, which they then play in turn. In "four balls, best ball," each player plays his own ball. After each hole the best score from each team is kept.

THE COURSE

A golf course has 18 holes set in a natural environment. Each course, laid out by a course designer, has its own characteristics. In addition to areas landscaped for the purposes of the game, the course has natural obstacles, which present challenges that are different for each hole. Holes may be from 100 to 600 yds. long.

Water hazards

These are ponds, streams, or artificial bodies of water. They can be situated alongside or across the fairway. If a player hits the ball into the water, he must play it where it lies. If the ball is not playable, he must drop a new ball at a place that is no closer to the flag than the point of entry of the old ball. Putting a new ball in play costs a one-stroke penalty.

Hole

It must have a diameter of 4¼ in. and a minimum depth of 4 in. A removable flag pole, serving as a visual reference point, stands in the center of the hole. A golfer has finished playing a hole when the ball is stopped inside the hole.

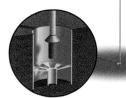

PAR

Depending on the distance and the difficulties on a course, a specific number of strokes for completing each hole is determined to serve as a reference: the par. During a stroke-play tournament, the total of each player is compared to the par for the course—the number normally needed to play all of the holes, usually 70 to 72. The holes on a course are either par 3, par 4, or par 5. When a player plays a hole one under par, it is called a birdie. An eagle is a hole played two under par, and a double eagle is a hole played three under par.

PAR 3

On a par 3 hole, the player must try to hit the ball as close to the hole as possible with his first stroke. Par 3 holes are usually the most difficult.

Putting green
Within this area of perfectly maintained, closely mowed grass is the hole at which the players are aiming the ball.

Bunkers
They are on the edges of the green. If a player hits a ball into a bunker, he must play it where it lies, without changing the surface of the bunker (flattening the sand or erasing marks) or touching the sand with his club before hitting the ball.

100–280 yds.

Fairway
This is the biggest part of a hole. It is 25 to 60 yds. wide and leads toward the putting green. The fairway must be completely recognizable and be distinguished by the natural environment by the height at which the grass is mowed.

PAR 4

On a par 4 hole, the player tries to place the ball so that he can reach the green with the second stroke and try for a birdie.

280–480 yds.

Teeing ground
This is a flat area, free of any nearby obstacles, where players tee off to start playing the hole. The player's ball must be placed within an area defined by tee markers; however, the player himself may stand up to two club lengths outside this area. There are several tees for every hole, one each for professional men, professional women, and amateurs.

PAR 5

Competition is generally strong on a par 5 hole: the best players try to make an excellent tee-off stroke, followed by a long approach stroke, and finish the hole with an eagle or a birdie.

480–600 yds.

Natural environment
It surrounds the course and is part of it. A golfer who hits his ball there must, in principle, play it where it lies. If he cannot find it, he must return to where he hit the ball and hit a new ball, taking a one-stroke penalty in the process. If the ball is blocked by a natural obstacle such as a tree, he may either try to hit it or declare it unplayable, in which case, he must drop a new ball into play near where the old ball stopped and add a one-stroke penalty to his scorecard.

Rough

CUPS AND CHAMPIONSHIPS

The world rankings of players are established over a two-year cycle under the aegis of the International Federation of PGA Tours. Each player accumulates points over a minimum of 40 tournaments, during four major championships, and on the men's professional circuit—Professional Golfers' Association (PGA)—all over the world (Europe, United States, South Africa, Asia, and Southern Hemisphere). The four major tournaments that make up the Grand Slam are the Masters (in Augusta, Georgia, since 1934), the US Open (since 1895, played on a different course every year), the British Open (since 1860, played in Scotland or England—some 10 courses may host this event), and the USPGA (since 1916, in the United States, on different courses).

The prestigious Ryder Cup tournament involves an American team and a European team. The competition has taken place every two years since 1927, on courses alternating between the United States and Europe. Finally, a World Cup for teams of three, the Dunhill Cup, has been played every year since 1953. The women's professional circuit is composed of some 40 tournaments per year. There are 4 major tournaments: the US Open (since 1946), the Ladies' PGA Championship (since 1955), the Nabisco Championship (since 1972), and the Du Maurier Classic (since 1984). Since 1990, a professional American team has played against a European team every two years in the Solheim Cup.

TECHNIQUES

Golfers must always adapt their technique to the terrain on which they are playing and take account of the climatic conditions—wind, rain, and wet ground—which have an important effect on the ball's trajectory.

Woods, long and medium irons
The first and second strokes of a hole, usually long, are very important to the score for the hole.
The player seeks a fluid movement, a sharp contact, and a good follow-through.

Short irons and wedges
When they are close to the green, players must estimate the distance to the hole and use the appropriate iron.
The golfer hits the ball toward the target with a lobbed or rolling approach stroke.

Hitting out of the bunker

The bunker is not always considered an obstacle. Some golfers prefer bunkers over high grass, since the ball's reaction on a sand surface is much more predictable. Using a sand wedge, the player hits behind the ball into the sand, without touching the ball.

Baseball grip

Overlapping grip

Interlocking grip

Putting

All putting greens on a course have a similar surface, but this does not mean that the balls will go at exactly the same speed. To help golfers predict their trajectories, the ball speed for each green is rated on a scale called the stemp meter. For the final putt, it is essential that the golfer "read" the green from various angles: he analyzes the ball's trajectory to the hole, then the trajectory from the hole to the ball. The stroke itself must be made with a pendulum motion, without tension.

GRIPS

Golfers must find the most comfortable grip for them. A good grip creates a minimum of tension in the hands and increases flexibility and accuracy.

EQUIPMENT

CLUBS

Several types of clubs are needed to play a course. Depending on the distance to cover and the particular situation, players choose a club with the appropriate characteristics.

The evolution in materials—the first clubs were made entirely of wood—and development of equipment to increase the accuracy of strokes and the distance the ball flies have clearly contributed to improvements in performance. As the balls were being made harder, stronger types of wood were needed for clubs, and synthetic materials gradually took over. Today, steel, graphite, titanium, and alloys have replaced wood for both the head and the shaft of the club.

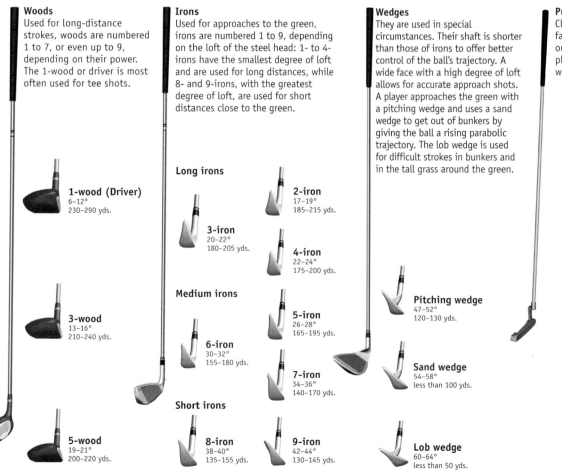

Woods
Used for long-distance strokes, woods are numbered 1 to 7, or even up to 9, depending on their power. The 1-wood or driver is most often used for tee shots.

1-wood (Driver)
6–12°
230–290 yds.

3-wood
13–16°
210–240 yds.

5-wood
19–21°
200–220 yds.

Irons
Used for approaches to the green, irons are numbered 1 to 9, depending on the loft of the steel head: 1- to 4-irons have the smallest degree of loft and are used for long distances, while 8- and 9-irons, with the greatest degree of loft, are used for short distances close to the green.

Long irons

2-iron
17–19°
185–215 yds.

3-iron
20–22°
180–205 yds.

4-iron
22–24°
175–200 yds.

Medium irons

5-iron
26–28°
165–195 yds.

6-iron
30–32°
155–180 yds.

7-iron
34–36°
140–170 yds.

Short irons

8-iron
38–40°
135–155 yds.

9-iron
42–44°
130–145 yds.

Wedges
They are used in special circumstances. Their shaft is shorter than those of irons to offer better control of the ball's trajectory. A wide face with a high degree of loft allows for accurate approach shots. A player approaches the green with a pitching wedge and uses a sand wedge to get out of bunkers by giving the ball a rising parabolic trajectory. The lob wedge is used for difficult strokes in bunkers and in the tall grass around the green.

Pitching wedge
47–52°
120–130 yds.

Sand wedge
54–58°
less than 100 yds.

Lob wedge
60–64°
less than 50 yds.

Putter
Club with a straight, full face used for rolled strokes on the green, when the player must aim the ball with maximum accuracy.

Putter
3–4°
on the green

Tiger Woods (USA)
Winner of the US Junior Amateur in 1991, 1992, and 1993, he also won the US Amateurs in 1994, 1995, and 1996, matching the legendary Bobby Jones. Winner of more than 15 professional tournaments, including the 1997 Masters, he became No. 1 in the world rankings in 1998. He equaled Ben Hogan with 6 consecutive victories on the professional circuit in late 1999 and early 2000.

155

BALL

Initially made of feathers covered with leather, then of gutta-percha (a substance extracted from latex), the ball is now made of a solid or liquid core covered with a plastic casing. Its dimpled surface makes it more stable in flight and more controllable when hit.

1.7 in.
max. 1.6 oz.

Early 17th century
Feather ball

1848
Gutta-percha ball

1898
Gutta-percha ball with rubber core

Tee
Made of wood or plastic, this small peg is used to raise the ball for the tee stroke.

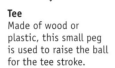

Glove
It is optional and is worn on one hand only to ensure a better grip on the club.

Shoes
Made of leather, they have soft or metal cleats attached to the sole.

Golf bag
At the professional level, it is carried by a caddie, who gives the player the different clubs as he needs them. A player can use no more than 14 different clubs during a tournament: he selects them from a wide range, depending on the course. Sometimes, the caddie advises the golfer about certain strokes.

GOLFER PROFILE

- For a golfer, psychology is all-important. Good golfers must control their emotions and remain calm and confident at all times. An ability to concentrate is essential. Coordination of movements and limbs, steadiness, accuracy, aim, and calculation are indispensable skills.

- Extremely talented players can play up to 7 or 8 under par. Among the many factors that make them champions are the quality and strength of their swing. Tiger Woods hits the ball an average distance of 289 yards and at a speed of up to 125 mph.

Gene Sarazen (USA)
Inventor of the sand wedge, he was one of the most influential players in the history of golf. Winner of the Masters in 1935, the US Open in 1922 and 1932, the British Open in 1932, the USPGA in 1922, 1923, and 1933. He is one of four golfers who has won all 4 Grand Slam tournaments.

Jack Nicklaus (USA)
Captain of the winning Ryder Cup team in 1983, with more than 70 victories on the professional circuit between 1962 and 1986, the "Golden Bear" was the best-known golf champion of his time. Among his major titles are the US Open in 1962, 1967, 1972, and 1980, the British Open in 1966, 1970, and 1978, the USPGA in 1963, 1971, 1973, 1975, and 1980, and the Masters in 1963, 1965, 1966, 1972, 1975, and 1986.

Nancy Lopez (USA)
World champion as an amateur in 1977 and as a professional the following year. She won 48 tournaments on the professional circuit, including the LPGA in 1978, 1985, and 1989. She also was named player of the year in 1978, 1979, 1985, and 1988.

Severiano Ballesteros (ESP)
One of the great golfers of the 1980s, in 1979 he was the youngest player to win the British Open, which he won again in 1984 and 1988. Among his 72 career victories were the Masters in 1980 and 1983, the World Cup in 1976 and 1977, and the Ryder Cup in 1985, 1987, and 1989.

Greg Norman (AUS)
Nicknamed the "Great White Shark," he won the British Open in 1986 and 1993, his only Grand Slam titles. With more than 75 victories on the professional circuit, he was one of the great stars of golf in the 1990s.

Multidisciplinary
Sports

43

triathlon

First phase (swimming) start at the Hawaii Ironman in 1993

The triathlon is three endurance events in one competition: swimming, cycling, and running. Inspired by survival tests performed by lifeguards in the United States around 1974, the triathlon was born from a challenge between American soldiers based in Hawaii to do each of the longest races held on the islands one after the other. The Hawaii Ironman, run since 1978, is a major international event. The Nice triathlon is another one. Since 1982, when American athlete Julie Moss collapsed, exhausted, in front of the television cameras, better training has considerably reduced the risk of incidents and has led to a clear improvement in performances. Today the triathlon is very popular, and the various competitions organized by the International Triathlon Union, formed in 1989, and national federations throughout the world draw about 1 million participants every year. The success of the triathlon has given rise to variants, including the snow triathlon (cross country skiing, cycling, and running), the snow duathlon (running and cross country skiing), and the aquathlon (swimming and running). The triathlon was included as an Olympic sport for the first time in Sydney in 2000.

THE COMPETITION

The principle of the triathlon is very simple: the timer starts when the first phase (swimming) starts and stops as the competitors cross the finish line of the last phase (running). Feeding stations as well as assistance to athletes during the cycling phase are allowed in Ironman competitions but are strictly forbidden in the classic events.

Transitions between the phases must be fast, and they are carefully prepared and rehearsed. In classic races, for the best triathletes, the transition between phases takes 8 to 10 seconds.

TYPES OF RACE

Race	Swimming	Cycling	Running	Average duration
Classic	1.5 km	40 km	10 km	under 2 h
Sprint	750 m	20 km	5 km	approx. 1:15 h
Half-triathlon	1.9 km	90 km	21 km	4.5–5 h
Triathlon (Ironman)	3.8 km	180 km	42.2 km	approx. 9 h

HAWAII IRONMAN

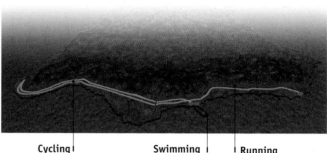

Cycling   Swimming   Running

Qualification

The Olympic races are the "classic" distance. Athletes qualify for the Games by accumulating points in qualifying races over a 2 year period.

1. SWIMMING

This phase usually takes place in the open water. No stroke is compulsory but most competitors use the crawl. If the water is cold, a neoprene suit may be needed; it must be tight enough not to increase the athlete's resistance in the water. Swimmers breathe once every 2 or 3 strokes. They are allowed to stop and grasp a buoy or an unmoving boat for support, but they may not use these for forward movement.

Swimming cap
Worn mainly for identification purposes, it is supplied by the organizers. In very cold water, swimmers use a neoprene cap to help prevent heat loss through the head.

Training

The way the hands enter the water, head and body position, and impulsion are improved in separate exercises. To get a better feel for their form breaks and to exercise their muscles more efficiently, triathletes attach pads to their hands or hobble their legs.

2. CYCLING

This phase is usually a road race. Athletes must keep a strong pedaling rhythm and a good aerodynamic position. Tactics play an important role: knowing how to draft behind other competitors can provide a decisive advantage. Athletes can reach an average speed of 45 km/h in classic races. They must carry the necessary tools to make repairs if needed. Fluid intake is very important; feeding stations are provided along the route for this purpose.

Training

To maintain steady speed throughout the pedal stroke, triathletes train with a rigid wheel hub (no gears) or pedal with one leg over flat terrain.

3. RUNNING

The run draws on the athlete's ultimate reserves of energy and endurance. Runners know how to alternate muscle tension and relaxation for maximum economy of movement. They run in an upright position, their eyes focused ahead; their shoulders are relaxed and their arms move parallel to the body to make breathing and leg motion easier. Stride length directly influences the runner's center of gravity, and the resulting fatigue.

Training

Contrasting exercises—jumping while running, running uphill and downhill, hopping on the ball of the foot, raising the knees—are done over 50 to 100 m along with normal running, so that faults in technique can be better perceived and corrected.

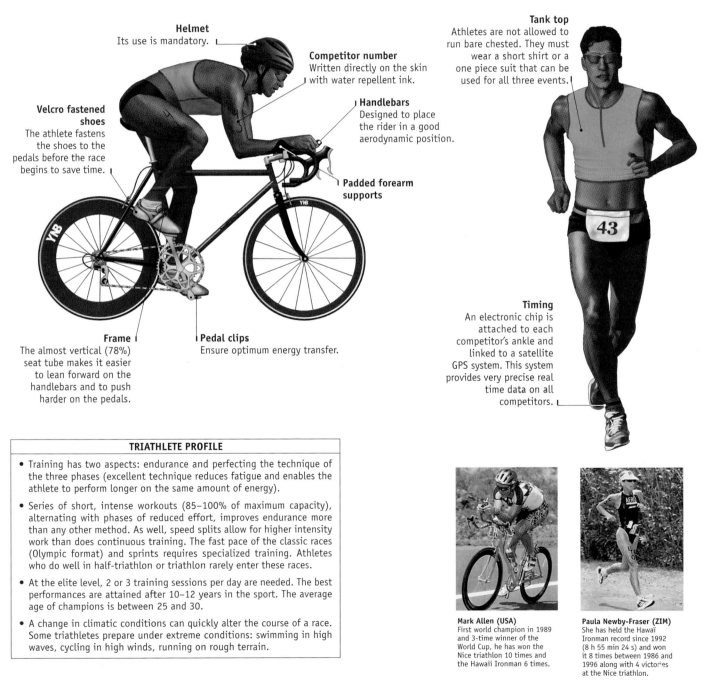

Helmet
Its use is mandatory.

Competitor number
Written directly on the skin with water repellent ink.

Velcro fastened shoes
The athlete fastens the shoes to the pedals before the race begins to save time.

Handlebars
Designed to place the rider in a good aerodynamic position.

Padded forearm supports

Frame
The almost vertical (78%) seat tube makes it easier to lean forward on the handlebars and to push harder on the pedals.

Pedal clips
Ensure optimum energy transfer.

Tank top
Athletes are not allowed to run bare chested. They must wear a short shirt or a one piece suit that can be used for all three events.

Timing
An electronic chip is attached to each competitor's ankle and linked to a satellite GPS system. This system provides very precise real time data on all competitors.

TRIATHLETE PROFILE

- Training has two aspects: endurance and perfecting the technique of the three phases (excellent technique reduces fatigue and enables the athlete to perform longer on the same amount of energy).

- Series of short, intense workouts (85–100% of maximum capacity), alternating with phases of reduced effort, improves endurance more than any other method. As well, speed splits allow for higher intensity work than does continuous training. The fast pace of the classic races (Olympic format) and sprints requires specialized training. Athletes who do well in half-triathlon or triathlon rarely enter these races.

- At the elite level, 2 or 3 training sessions per day are needed. The best performances are attained after 10–12 years in the sport. The average age of champions is between 25 and 30.

- A change in climatic conditions can quickly alter the course of a race. Some triathletes prepare under extreme conditions: swimming in high waves, cycling in high winds, running on rough terrain.

Mark Allen (USA)
First world champion in 1989 and 3-time winner of the World Cup, he has won the Nice triathlon 10 times and the Hawaii Ironman 6 times.

Paula Newby-Fraser (ZIM)
She has held the Hawaï Ironman record since 1992 (8 h 55 min 24 s) and won it 8 times between 1986 and 1996 along with 4 victories at the Nice triathlon.

modern pentathlon

An event combining completely different sports, the modern pentathlon was inspired by the adventure of one Napoleonic officer, who had to cross enemy lines with a message for his troops. True to the spirit of the ancient pentathlon, the modern competition was born at the Olympic Games in Stockholm in 1912, under Pierre de Coubertin's direct influence. The five phases—shooting, fencing, swimming, riding, and running—call upon a range of talents that corresponded to his vision of the "complete man." Although the Swedes, Russians, and Hungarians dominated the sport until the 1980s, athletes from Italy and France are now regularly on the podium. Women have been competing in the world championships since 1981 and was in the Olympics for the first time in Sydney in 2000.

Johan Oxenstierna (SWE) takes gold at the Los Angeles Games in 1932

THE COMPETITION

In international competition, the 5 phases take place in one day. A standard result, worth 1,000 pentathlon points, is pre-established for each phase. The competitors are ranked according to this standard: a lower result is penalized and a higher result is rewarded. At the end of the riding phase, the pentathlon points are converted into handicap seconds, so that the winner of the run wins the competition.

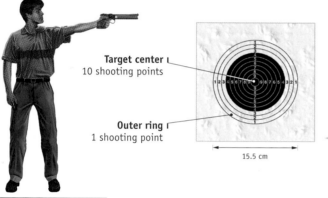

Target center
10 shooting points

Outer ring
1 shooting point

15.5 cm

2. FENCING

The weapon used is the épée, and each competitor fences against all others. Bouts last a maximum of 1 minute and end at the first touch. A bout with no touch is considered a defeat for both athletes. The standard result (1,000 pentathlon points) corresponds to 70% victories out of all bouts. The point value of a victory is determined by a calculation based on the number of competitors. The short duration of the bout reduces the attack phase to its simplest expression: foot or épée feints and false attacks that force the opponent to expose himself are favored. Any part of the opponent's body is valid for a touch, but most are made on the wrists, feet, or chest.

1. SHOOTING

The athlete makes 20 shots at a fixed target 10 m away. A maximum of 40 seconds is allowed for each shot. The weapon is a compressed-air or gas cartridge pistol. The standard result (1,000 pentathlon points) is set at 172 shooting points obtained in 20 shots. Each shooting point—above or below 172—is worth 12 pentathlon points: a total of 173 thus represents 1,012 pentathlon points; a total of 171, 988 points. Shooting requires concentration and relaxation, and control of respiration is essential to accuracy. Any system that helps to stabilize the arm or wrist is forbidden.

3. SWIMMING

The 200 m freestyle (usually the crawl) is run against the clock. Competitors are divided into heats according to the number of competitors and past performances. The standard result (1,000 pentathlon points) is 2:30 minutes for men and 2:40 minutes for women. One pentathlon point is earned for each tenth of a second below the standard; each tenth of a second over the standard costs 1 pentathlon point. The fastest athlete in each heat swims in the center lane. No bonus points are given to heat winners; only the time of each competitor is taken into account.

4. RIDING

The course is between 350 and 400 m and has 12 obstacles, including at least one double and one triple combination. A clear round is worth 1,100 pentathlon points. Knocking down a pole costs 30 points; a refusal or run-out before an obstacle costs 40 points; a fall by horse or rider costs 60 points. Each second over the time allowed deducts 3 points from the rider's score. If there is a tie between competitors, the fastest rider is the winner. The pentathlon riding phase can cause major changes in the standings: each athlete must ride a horse that he has never ridden before, drawn by lot. Riders can warm up for 20 minutes and take 5 jumps to get to know the horse.

5. RUNNING

This phase consists of a 3,000 m cross country race. The best placed athlete after the first 4 events starts first. The other athletes start at intervals corresponding to their points ranking: 4 pentathlon points correspond to 1 second. This way, the competitor who crosses the finish line first wins the competition.

Runner number
Corresponds to start position.

Pavel Lednev (URSS)
World champion from 1973 to 1975 and 1978, and Olympic medalist from 1968 to 1980.

CUPS AND CHAMPIONSHIPS

Until 1948, the modern pentathlon was administered by the Olympic committee. In that year, the Union internationale de pentathlon moderne (UIPM) was created and international competitions sprang up:

- The world championships, annual since 1949 except in Olympic years, bring together the 32 best athletes from 4 groups of semifinals.
- The team relay world championships involve 16 teams of 3 athletes selected through elimination rounds. Each member of a team shoots 10 times, swims 100 m, has 15 fencing bouts (against one competitor from each other team), runs 1,500 m, and jumps 8 obstacles in the riding phase.
- The World Cup, annual since 1990, involves 32 athletes selected based on their best 3 results in elimination rounds.
- Since 1998, the Pentathlon World Tour has presented a format based on the ancient pentathlon: athletes go head-to-head in 5 phases adapted for the purpose, with no pause, over 20 to 25 minutes. The winners of the head-to-head competitions go on to the following round, up to the finals.

PENTATHLETE PROFILE

- The pentathlon requires a variety of talents and capacities. Winners include athletes with very different builds. The psychological aspect of the sport (concentration and positive attitude) makes all the difference.
- The best performances are achieved by athletes over 28 years of age. Experience acquired in competition helps to compensate for a reduction in physical capacity—in swimming and running—by greater mastery of the technical phases.

orienteering

Orienteering, a race against the clock in a forest on a course marked with control sites, was originally a military exercise, introduced in 1895 by the Swedish army. In the 1910s, it became a recreational sport for people who enjoyed athletics and nature, and it rapidly spread to the rest of Europe, reaching North America and then Asia. The nations where the sport is most popular formed the International Orienteering Federation (IOF) in 1961, and the first world championships took place in Finland in 1966. Since then, more than 30 countries have taken part in the event every two years, alternating with the World Cup series. Today, there are more than 800,000 dedicated orienteers, men and women, in some 50 countries, but the Scandinavians remain the uncontested masters of the sport, having taken 162 championship medals out of 220 awarded between 1966 and 1995.

An instructor and a student from the Aberdovy Outward Bound School (GBR) on an orienteering exercise in 1949

THE COMPETITION

Whatever the scale of the competition, no participant knows where it will take place or has the map. From a selected gathering place, the competitors are taken to the starting point, where they pick up a topographic map of the region and leave one by one at regular intervals. They must reach the control sites in the order set by the organizers, using the map and a compass, by any route they choose. Each control site has equipment that enables the participants to prove that they have passed that point. The winner is the one who finishes the course in the shortest time. The number of officials varies according to the chosen terrain, the size of the competition, and the type of control system used; a judge and a timekeeper are present at the start and finish points. Other officials are sometimes hidden at strategic points where there is a risk of cheating. Orienteering has several variations and is also done in relays, on mountain bikes, on cross country skis, and in races over several days (long distance orienteering). In professional competitions, the distances and durations are variable: 10 to 20 km in 90 minutes for men, and 7 to 15 km in 75 minutes for women.

MATERIALS AND EQUIPMENT

Control site

There are two types of controls at the control sites. The older, and still more common, is a control card, which is perforated or stamped with the code of the control site. Technology has led to a more effective method: racers are equipped with a map with an electronic chip, which they validate at checkpoints linked to a computer. The organizers can thus make sure that the competition runs smoothly and know when each competitor has passed each checkpoint.

Topographic map

A basic part of the competition, it allows competitors to orient themselves on the terrain and to identify its features. It can be at a scale of 1:5,000 (introductory and training), 1:10,000, or 1:15,000 (competition). The symbols, in different colors, are standardized throughout the world.

30 cm

30 cm

Control flags
They mark the control sites.

■ **Water**

■ **Contours**

■ **Rocky features and built structures**

Vegetation with difficulty levels

Clothing

Orienteers wear clothing made of tough fabric that evacuates heat and sweat. Special shoes are required: light, waterproof, and resistant, they have metal and rubber cleats.

Shoes

Compass

A complement to the map, the thumb compass is the most popular, followed by the baseplate compass, filled with liquid to slow the needle's rotation; the needle always points to the north.

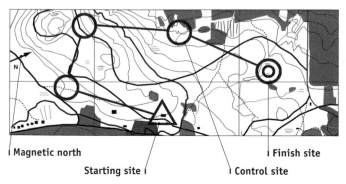

| Magnetic north

Starting site |

| Finish site

| Control site

ATHLETE PROFILE

- Elite competitors do rigorous muscle building and cardiovascular training so that they can complete difficult races. It is also important to be able to read the race map correctly and quickly without slowing down, a technique that demands much skill and is acquired only with experience.

Jergen Maartensen (SWE)
Winner of the world championships in 1991 and 1995 and the master's championship in 2000.

Ice Sports

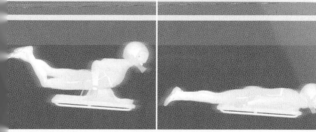

ice hockey

The 1958–59 Montreal Canadiens. Winners of the Stanley Cup 24 times and the only team to win it five seasons in a row from 1955–56 to 1959–60.

Ice hockey was invented in Canada in the mid 19th century. The principle of the game is simple: on a skating rink, two teams try to score goals by shooting a puck into the opposing team's goal with sticks. The first recorded game took place in Kingston in 1855. Twenty-four years later, students at McGill University in Montreal codified the rules, and a number of clubs and leagues sprang up all over Canada. The game developed rapidly, and the National Hockey League (NHL) was formed in 1917. In its first year of existence, five teams played a 22 game schedule. Today, the NHL is composed of 30 Canadian and American teams and is continually expanding. Men's hockey became an Olympic event in 1920; women's hockey, in 1998. World championships for amateur hockey have taken place annually since 1930. Hockey is played in some 30 countries and is most popular in North America, Scandinavia, and Russia.

THE GAME

Each team is composed of at least 20 players. During a game, 6 players from each team are on the ice at any one time, and the players change almost every minute. A hockey game is played in 3 20-minute periods of actual playing time, with 2 15-minute intermissions. With the many stoppages in play—offsides, penalties, injured players, etc.—a game usually lasts 2 to 3 hours. The teams change ends each period. When a team is playing short handed, it must have at least 4 players, including the goaltender, on the ice. If there is a tie at the end of a game, there may be an overtime period lasting 5 to 20 minutes. In international hockey, if there is a tie, a shoot-out ensues: 5 designated players from each team start at center ice and try to score a goal, with the teams alternating. In professional hockey, a 5 minute sudden death overtime period is played. In the NHL playoffs, overtime periods last 20 minutes.

THE RINK

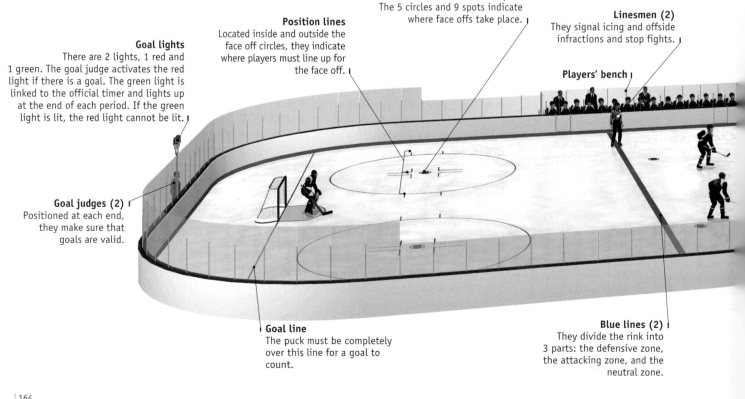

Goal lights
There are 2 lights, 1 red and 1 green. The goal judge activates the red light if there is a goal. The green light is linked to the official timer and lights up at the end of each period. If the green light is lit, the red light cannot be lit.

Position lines
Located inside and outside the face off circles, they indicate where players must line up for the face off.

Face off circles and spots
The 5 circles and 9 spots indicate where face offs take place.

Linesmen (2)
They signal icing and offside infractions and stop fights.

Players' bench

Goal judges (2)
Positioned at each end, they make sure that goals are valid.

Goal line
The puck must be completely over this line for a goal to count.

Blue lines (2)
They divide the rink into 3 parts: the defensive zone, the attacking zone, and the neutral zone.

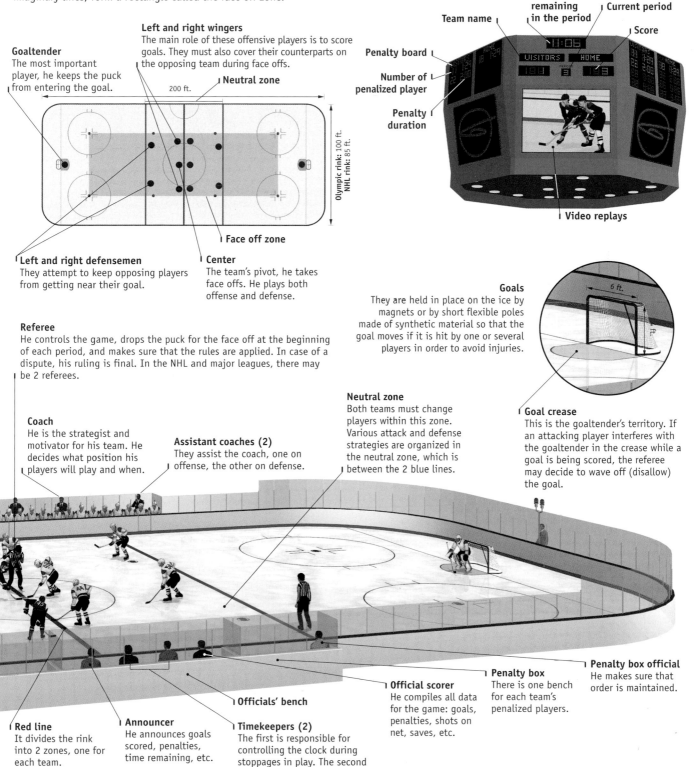

THE FACE OFF

At the beginning of a game or period or after a goal is scored, the face off takes place at the center spot in the center circle. During the game, face offs take place at one of the 8 other points that is closest to where an official called an infraction. These 8 points, linked by 4 imaginary lines, form a rectangle called the face off zone.

THE SCOREBOARD

It hangs over the center of the rink and displays information about the game: score, penalties, replays, etc.

Time remaining in the period

Current period

Team name

Score

Penalty board

Number of penalized player

Penalty duration

VISITORS   HOME

Video replays

Goaltender
The most important player, he keeps the puck from entering the goal.

Left and right wingers
The main role of these offensive players is to score goals. They must also cover their counterparts on the opposing team during face offs.

Neutral zone

200 ft.

Olympic rink: 100 ft.
NHL rink: 85 ft.

Face off zone

Left and right defensemen
They attempt to keep opposing players from getting near their goal.

Center
The team's pivot, he takes face offs. He plays both offense and defense.

Referee
He controls the game, drops the puck for the face off at the beginning of each period, and makes sure that the rules are applied. In case of a dispute, his ruling is final. In the NHL and major leagues, there may be 2 referees.

Coach
He is the strategist and motivator for his team. He decides what position his players will play and when.

Assistant coaches (2)
They assist the coach, one on offense, the other on defense.

Neutral zone
Both teams must change players within this zone. Various attack and defense strategies are organized in the neutral zone, which is between the 2 blue lines.

Goals
They are held in place on the ice by magnets or by short flexible poles made of synthetic material so that the goal moves if it is hit by one or several players in order to avoid injuries.

6 ft.

Goal crease
This is the goaltender's territory. If an attacking player interferes with the goaltender in the crease while a goal is being scored, the referee may decide to wave off (disallow) the goal.

Red line
It divides the rink into 2 zones, one for each team.

Announcer
He announces goals scored, penalties, time remaining, etc.

Timekeepers (2)
The first is responsible for controlling the clock during stoppages in play. The second times the penalties.

Officials' bench

Official scorer
He compiles all data for the game: goals, penalties, shots on net, saves, etc.

Penalty box
There is one bench for each team's penalized players.

Penalty box official
He makes sure that order is maintained.

TECHNIQUES AND TACTICS

Hockey is a game of both attack and defense strategies, with frequent exchanges of the puck among all players. Several different shots and passes are used.

THE SHOTS

The main types of shots in hockey are, in order of power, the slapshot, the snap shot, the wrist shot, and the backhand shot. These shots are made while skating or standing still.

Slapshot

The player's stick is not in contact with the puck. He swings his stick back to give the shot power. The slapshot is less accurate than the other shots.

Snap shot

The player pushes the puck forward and, at the right moment—the stick still in contact with the ice—he increases the pressure on the puck. This shot is also used for passes.

Wrist shot

Particularly accurate, quick, and effective in front of the goal, it is also used for long passes.

Backhand shot

More difficult to execute because of the curve of the stick blade, the backhand is generally feared by goalies, because it is difficult to see what trajectory the puck will take.

THE PASSES

They enable a team to control the puck for attack or defense purposes.

Passing the puck off the boards

This is a way to pass the puck to a player who cannot receive a direct pass.

Deflecting the puck

An attacking player scores a goal by deflecting a puck passed to him by a teammate.

Poke checking the puck

The goalie keeps another player from getting the puck by kneeling on the ice and quickly thrusting his stick forward. The poke check can be used by all players in any position.

THE POWER PLAY

The objective of a power play is to score a goal while the opposing team is playing short handed after being assessed a penalty. The coach uses his best scorers. From the face off, they try to gain control of the puck and enter the opposing team's zone. The players then pass the puck back and forth until an opening is created and the player in possession of the puck tries to score a goal. A power play lasts the length of a penalty (2, 4, or 5 minutes) or, in some cases, ends when a goal is scored.

OFFSIDE

The 5 lines that go across the width of the rink regulate the play. When an offside is called, the linesman stops the play and determines where the face off will take place: in the neutral zone at the face off spot closest to where the puck crossed the line.

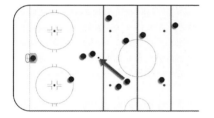

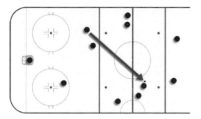

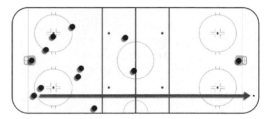

No player on an attacking team may cross the blue line into the other team's zone before the puck. Both of the player's skates must be completely in the other team's zone for him to be offside. A linesman who signals an offside can wave it off and let play continue if all players on the offside team leave the other team's zone before one of them touches the puck.

An offside is also called when a player passes the puck to a teammate across 2 lines.

Icing the puck occurs when a player on his own side of the center line shoots the puck across the opposing team's goal line (it is legal, however, when a team is short handed). There is no icing if a player from the same team touches the puck first or if the puck goes into the goal crease before crossing the goal line.

OFFICIALS' SIGNALS

These signals, used by the referees and linesmen, indicate a penalty or infraction of the rules. The game continues until the penalized team touches the puck. There are many penalties in hockey, most of which result in the player or players involved being taken out from the game for between 2 and 10 minutes. Some serious infractions lead to game misconduct penalties or suspensions lasting several games. The penalty time is counted in real playing time. Infractions of the rules are usually offsides and icing the puck.

Delayed penalty

The referee signals a penalty and stops the play when a player from the penalized team touches the puck.

Hooking

Hooking another player with the stick, with the intention of making him fall.

Cross checking

A check made on an opposing player with the stick held in both hands.

Slashing

Hitting a player with the stick.

Goal scored

Goal disallowed

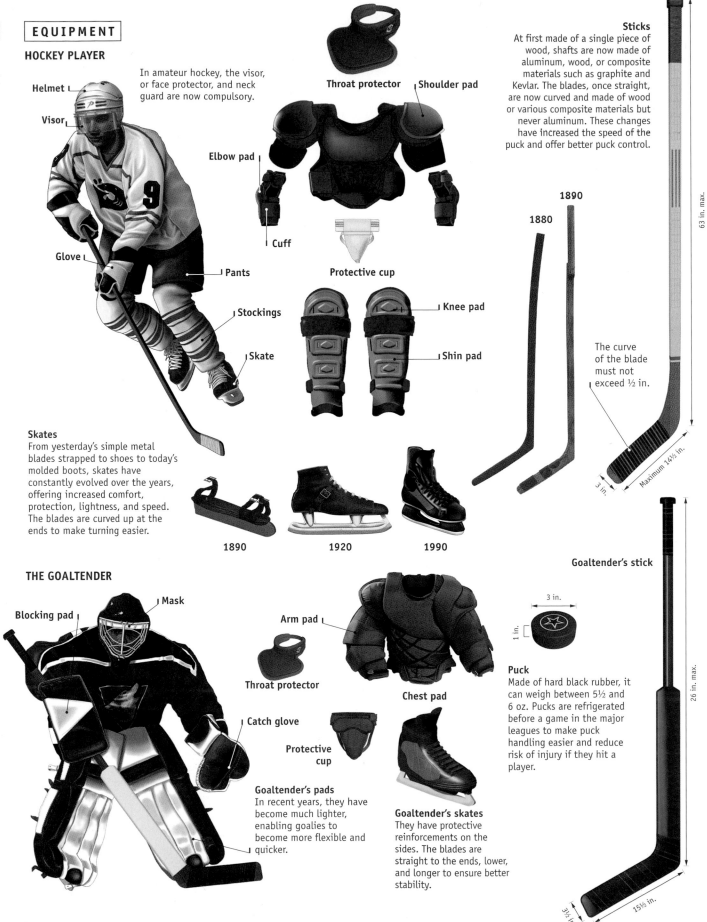

EQUIPMENT

HOCKEY PLAYER

In amateur hockey, the visor, or face protector, and neck guard are now compulsory.

Helmet

Visor

Elbow pad

Cuff

Glove

Pants

Stockings

Skate

Throat protector

Shoulder pad

Protective cup

Knee pad

Shin pad

Sticks
At first made of a single piece of wood, shafts are now made of aluminum, wood, or composite materials such as graphite and Kevlar. The blades, once straight, are now curved and made of wood or various composite materials but never aluminum. These changes have increased the speed of the puck and offer better puck control.

63 in. max.

1890

1880

The curve of the blade must not exceed ½ in.

Maximum 14½ in.

3 in.

Skates
From yesterday's simple metal blades strapped to shoes to today's molded boots, skates have constantly evolved over the years, offering increased comfort, protection, lightness, and speed. The blades are curved up at the ends to make turning easier.

1890

1920

1990

THE GOALTENDER

Blocking pad

Mask

Arm pad

Throat protector

Catch glove

Protective cup

Chest pad

Goaltender's pads
In recent years, they have become much lighter, enabling goalies to become more flexible and quicker.

Goaltender's skates
They have protective reinforcements on the sides. The blades are straight to the ends, lower, and longer to ensure better stability.

Goaltender's stick

3 in.

1 in.

Puck
Made of hard black rubber, it can weigh between 5½ and 6 oz. Pucks are refrigerated before a game in the major leagues to make puck handling easier and reduce risk of injury if they hit a player.

26 in. max.

3½ in.

15½ in.

HOCKEY PLAYER PROFILE

- Hockey is a rough game, requiring much strategy and excellent physical condition. It is also the fastest of the team sports: at full speed, a player may skate 37 mph and pucks may be shot at 120 mph. Players tire quickly and are replaced after playing for 45 seconds to 2 minutes.

- Qualities essential to the hockey player are physical endurance, aerobic capacity, muscular strength and resistance, and excellent perception, decision making, and body control.

- Hockey players run to improve their speed and endurance, bicycle to increase leg strength, skate on ice or on in-line skates to maintain their reflexes, work out on the treadmill, do muscle building exercises on resistance machines, and practice their shots.

- Before a game, players do stretching exercises in order to avoid injuries such as muscle pulls and tears. They rehearse their game techniques and the tasks they are assigned.

PROFESSIONAL CHAMPIONSHIPS

Stanley Cup	Winners	Finalists
1999	Dallas Stars	Buffalo Sabers
1998	Detroit Red Wings	Washington Capitals
1997	Detroit Red Wings	Philadelphia Flyers
1996	Colorado Avalanche	Florida Panthers

CUPS AND CHAMPIONSHIPS

The Stanley Cup was donated by Lord Stanley of Preston, the sixth Governor General of Canada. The original cup was much smaller than today's; a pedestal has been added to make room for inscription of the annual NHL champions. It is the oldest trophy awarded to a professional sports team in North America.

Original cup

Stanley Cup
As we know it today.

Original Stanley Cup

Wayne Gretzky (CAN)
"The Great One" equaled or broke more than 60 NHL records and was considered the greatest player of all time when he retired in April 1999.

Gordie Howe (CAN)
Nicknamed "Mr. Hockey," he played for 34 years with the Detroit Red Wings and the Hartford Whalers, and he retired at age 52. He was named best player in the NHL 6 times and for many years held the record for most points scored, 1,850.

Bobby Orr (CAN)
He was the only defenseman in the history of the NHL to score the most points in a season, in 1970 and 1975. He scored 915 points in 657 games and was elected to the Hall of Fame in 1979.

Maurice "Rocket" Richard (CAN)
He was the first player in the NHL to score 50 goals in 50 games. He played for the Montreal Canadiens for 18 years, and the trophy for the best scorer in the NHL was named after him in 1999.

Vladislav Tretiak (USSR)
First Soviet player to be elected to the Hall of Fame, he is considered one of the best goaltenders of all time and popularized, among other things, the "butterfly" style.

Jaromir Jagr (CZE)
First European to score the most goals in a season in the NHL, in 1995, 1998 and 1999, he is one of the stars of the Pittsburgh Penguins and was on that team's Stanley Cup winning teams in 1991 and 1992.

AMATEUR CHAMPIONSHIPS

World championship (men)

	GOLD	SILVER	BRONZE
1999	CZE	FIN	SWE
1998	SWE	FIN	CZE
1997	CAN	SWE	CZE
1996	CZE	CAN	USA

World championship (women)

	GOLD	SILVER	BRONZE
1999	CAN	USA	FIN
1997	CAN	USA	FIN
1994	CAN	USA	FIN
1992	CAN	USA	FIN
1990	CAN	USA	FIN

OLYMPICS

Olympic Games (men)

	GOLD	SILVER	BRONZE
Sapporo, 1972	USSR	USA	CZE
Innsbruck, 1976	USSR	CZE	FRG
Lake Placid, 1980	USA	USSR	SWE
Sarajevo, 1984	USSR	CZE	SWE
Calgary, 1988	USSR	FIN	SWE
Albertville, 1992	CIS	CAN	CZE
Lillehammer, 1994	SWE	CAN	FIN
Nagano, 1998	CZE	RUS	FIN

*Community of Independant States (Former USSR)

Olympic Games (women)

	GOLD	SILVER	BRONZE
Nagano, 1998	USA	CAN	FIN

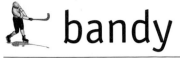

bandy

The Bury Fen Bandy Club (Great Britain), shown here in 1891, was the dominant team in the early years of the game.

Although evidence of games played with a stick and a ball date back to ancient times, "modern" bandy emerged in the 18th century in Bury Fen, England, with the creation of the Bury Fen Bandy Club. This sport involves 2 teams facing off on a skating rink and attempting to score goals in the opposing team's net using sticks with a curved blade to hit a small ball. The first match was played between 2 London clubs in 1875, and the rules were established in 1891 when the National Bandy Association in England was founded. At that time, bandy was normally associated with soccer clubs because it was played on a field with the same dimensions as a football field and the rules contained many similarities. The first Swedish club was founded in 1895, and the sport later expanded to Holland and Ireland before appearing in Germany, Switzerland, Russia, and in other Scandinavian countries. Bandy adopted its present form in 1955 when the International Bandy Federation (IBF) was formed. Today, bandy is also played in Canada, the United States, the Baltic States, Hungary, Belarus, and Kazakhstan. World Championships have been held every 2 years (in odd numbered years) since 1957.

COMPETITION

Each team has 15 players, including 2 goalkeepers. Eleven players from each team, including a goalkeeper, play on the rink at one time. Just like in soccer, a game of bandy is played in two 45-minute halves with a 10-minute interval at halftime, after which the teams switch sides. During championships, a tie game can result in up to two 15-minute overtime periods. There is very little physical contact in bandy, unlike in to hockey. This game of speed and strategy, with free strokes and corner strokes, bears a resemblance to soccer. At the beginning of the game, a coin is tossed to decide which team will stroke off. A stroke-off takes place at the center of the rink for each new period: the designated player pushes the ball into the opposing team's half and cannot touch it again until it has been touched by another player. The players on each team must stay in their half and cannot go within 5 m of the ball before the game starts. The winning team is the one that has scored the most goals by the end of the game.

THE RINK

Due to its size, the rink is usually outdoors. There are, however, some indoor rinks.

Referees (3)
In all international matches there are 3 referees – one head referee and 2 assistants. They control the match and keep track of the official time.

Penalty area
This is the goalkeeper's territory. Inside this area, he can use any part of his body to play the ball. If he catches the ball, he must return it to the game as quickly as possible. He cannot hold it in his hands for more than 5 seconds.

Low barriers
Removable barriers ranging in height from 12 to 15 cm are placed alongside the rink to stop the ball from rolling out of play.

Players' bench

Penalty point
Area in which the penalty stroke is taken.

Free-stroke spots (4)
The team taking a free stroke puts the ball into play at the spot where the foul was committed. However, if the foul was committed inside the penalty circle, the free stroke is taken from the nearest free stroke spot. Players on the opposing team must remain at least 5 m away from the ball.

Corner
If a defending player sends the ball behind his own team's goal line, a corner is given to the opponent. This provides an advantage to the offense because of the proximity to the opponent's net.

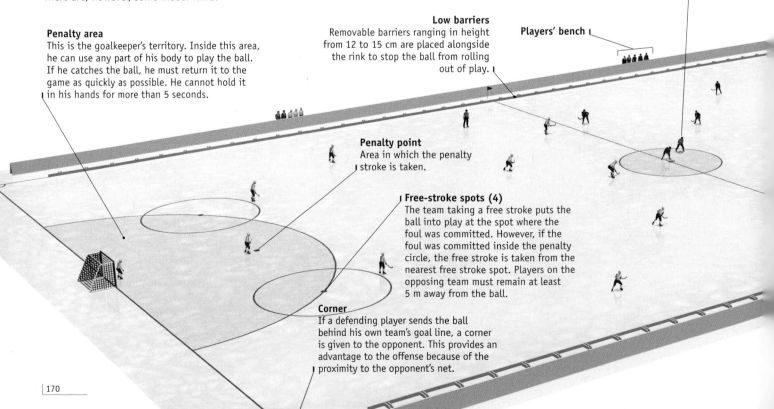

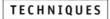

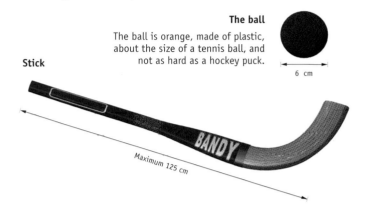

TECHNIQUES

STROKES

Because of the size of the rink and the hardness of the ball, strokes and passes are often spectacular. There are many types of strokes, such as the slap shot.

Slap shot

Without touching the ball, the player lifts the stick behind him in order to give force to the stroke. He hits the ball firmly while turning his body in a half-rotation. This stroke is powerful and fast.

EQUIPMENT

Much of the equipment resembles that used in hockey. However, it is lighter because there is no severe physical contact. The ball, the helmet, the stick and the gloves are different. The goalkeeper wears larger leg pads and padded gloves. For many players, the blades on the skates are longer than in hockey, similar to speed skates.

The ball
The ball is orange, made of plastic, about the size of a tennis ball, and not as hard as a hockey puck.

6 cm

Stick

Maximum 125 cm

BANDY

PLAYING SURFACE

Touchline
Mid-line
Center circle
Goal line
Goal
height: 2.10 m
width: 3.50 m
depth: 2 m

45–65 m

90–110 m

PLAYER PROFILE

- A vigorous game, bandy requires a lot of strategy and demands excellent physical condition.

- The player has excellent aerobic ability, powerful legs, and good muscular resistance.

- He is able to react quickly, to follow the game, and to make quick decisions.

Middle fullback
Placed at the farthest point in the defensive zone, he is the leader of the defending players and ensures the coherence of their moves with those of the other teammates.

Goalkeeper
His job on defense is of the utmost importance. He also plays an important offensive role in returning the ball to his teammates. He can represent 50% of the team's success. He plays without a stick, stopping or throwing the ball with his hands.

Corner flag
Located at each of the 4 corners of the rink to mark where corner shots are taken.

Fullbacks (2)
Their main task is to block their opponents before they enter the penalty area. They must be on top of the game and be aware of each player's position.

Halfbacks (2)
As the link between defending players and wingers, their main task is to be the first among the defending players to ward off the attackers of the opposing team.

Quarterbacks (2)
Along with the halfbacks, they are the catalysts of their team's offensive efforts. Their task is to receive their teammates' passes and, with the assistance of the wingers and the halfbacks, create an attack.

Wingers (3)
The task of these players is to score goals. They are constantly in motion, either with or without the ball, and must be ready at all times to receive passes from their teammates.

bobsledding

The British bobsled team at the 1936 Olympics in Berlin

Even though sliding on snow or ice with toboggans, sleds, or skis has long been popular in northern countries, bobsledding itself is a relatively modern sport. It originated at the end of the 19th century, when two crestas (old time competition sleds) were attached together with a board, and a steering mechanism was attached to the front sled. The popularity of bobsledding grew quickly, and the first competitions were organized in the streets of St-Moritz, Switzerland, in 1898. The first bobsled track was built at St-Moritz in 1902, by the local Bobsleigh Club. Over the years, bobsled tracks evolved, going from straight runs to twisting and turning. Meanwhile, the original wooden sleds gave way to aerodynamically streamlined fiberglass and metal sleds. In the early 1950s, weighting was introduced to compensate for the natural advantage of having a heavier team. The International Bobsleigh and Tobogganing Federation (FIBT) was founded in Paris in 1923, and the sport made its Olympic debut the following year at Chamonix, France. Women bobsledders will be competing in the Olympics for the first time at the 2002 Games. World championships are held each year, except during Olympic years, when participating in the Games is seen as equivalent to participating in the world championships. Bobsleds are also raced on ice covered roads, and this sport, which is very popular in Europe, has its own world championships and World Cup.

HOW A RACE IS ORGANIZED

A bobsled team consists of either 2 or 4 people. The driver gives the orders at the start, and steers the sled. Once the finish line has been crossed, the brakeman at the back of the sled brings it to a stop by applying first light and then firm pressure on the brake, a metal claw that digs into the ice. Speeds range from 120 to 135 km/h, with peaks of up to 150 km/h. The starting order for competitors is determined by random draw. The first few competitors have an advantage because of the condition of the ice. When the starter gives the signal, the red light goes out and the green light goes on, and timekeeping commences the instant the front of the bobsled passes the starting cells. The sled has 60 seconds to reach the starting cells.

TRACK

Modern bobsled tracks are made from concrete covered in a layer of artificial ice. A track must have a starting gate, straight sections, curves, Omegas, at least one labyrinth, and a deceleration area.

Start

The characteristics of the track, the roles of the officials, and the rules governing the allowable temperature of the runners are identical to those for skeleton.

Finish

FOUR MAN BOBSLED TECHNIQUES

1. Start

After getting into position around the sled, the team (driver, pushers, and brakeman) pushes off.

2. Push

All 4 bobsledders push the sled, while running, for about 50 m to give it the momentum needed for the descent.

3. Loading

While running and pushing, the team members jump into the sled before the first curve. The driver gets in first, followed by the pushers, and then the brakeman. Each team member retracts the handle he used while pushing.

EQUIPMENT

A bobsled is made from 2 separate sections, mounted on runners and connected by a semi-flexible platform on which the crew sits. The sled is steered by handles attached to a pulley system, and a handle near the back operates the brake. The streamlined pod is made of fiberglass, to which weight bars are attached by screws, if necessary. Bobsledders wear one piece or two piece lycra suits, similar to those used by cross county skiers.

Pushers (2)
They provide weight, and they shift their bodies in the curves to pick up speed.

Driver
He gives the orders, steers the sled, and is the only one who keeps his head up during the run.

Retractable handles
The handles are attached to the side of the sled, and make the push off easier. The rear handle is not retractable.

Brakeman
He operates the brake after the sled crosses the finish line.

Pod
The pod is made of fiberglass.

Runners

Helmet
The helmets are the same as those worn by Formula 1 race car drivers.

Shoes
The shoes have spikes along the edge of the sole to give better traction on the ice during the push off.

TWO MAN BOBSLED

67 cm

approximately 1.10 m

2.70 m
Maximum weight including crew, sled, and weight bars: 390 kg

FOUR MAN BOBSLED

67 cm

approximately 1.60 m

3.80 m
Maximum weight including crew, sled, and weight bars: 630 kg

1924

1952

4. Descent position

With the exception of the driver, the bobsledders sit with their heads down to reduce wind resistance, and remain in that position until the finish. Holding on to their grips, they sit still during straight runs and shift to the left or the right in the curves to gain speed. The brakeman pulls the brake handle to stop the sled.

PROFILE OF A BOBSLEDDER

- In addition to muscular strength, a cool head, stamina, good balance, and swift reflexes, bobsledders must also be daring and have nerves of steel.

- Training includes muscle building, particularly for the legs, and exercises such as skipping and jumping over hurdles, and sprinting over distances of 30, 50 and 100 m. Bobsledders also practice with the shot put, which increases the muscular volume of the torso and limbs.

- In some curves, the gravitational force exerted on bobsledders traveling at top speed can be as high as 4 times their body weight or more.

Jamaican Bobsled Team
Formed in a country where it never snows, this legendary team entered the 1988, 1992, 1994, and 1998 Olympic Games. Their perseverance helped to promote bobsledding around the world, and to interest sprinters in the sport. Their story was made into a movie.

Christoph Langen (GER)
He is one of the best bobsledders in the history of the sport. In 1996, he was the World and European Champion in both the four man and two man bobsled.

skeleton

Cresta (predecessor to skeleton) event in St-Moritz, Switzerland in 1908

Skeleton is an adaptation of cresta, a sliding sport that first appeared in Switzerland in 1892. The sport involves sliding at high speeds while lying flat on a sled. The first time cresta appeared outside of Switzerland was in 1905, in Austria, where the first championship event was held one year later. The International Bobsleigh and Tobogganing Federation (FIBT) was created in 1923, and the sport was then recognized as an Olympic event. The first gold medal was awarded to American Jennison Heaton in 1928. After a 20 year absence from the Olympic Games, cresta reappeared in 1948 in St-Moritz. Skeleton only became popular in the 1950s and 1960s. Originally, the sled's chassis resembled a skeleton, hence the name of the sport. Today, some 20 countries participate in world championships, and competitive events have been open to women since 1996. Skeleton is slated to make its Olympic debut at the 2002 Winter Games in Salt Lake City, in the United States.

HOW A RACE IS ORGANIZED

The starting order for competitors is determined by random draw. When the starter gives the signal, the red light goes out and the green light goes on, and timekeeping commences the instant the front section of the skeleton passes the starting cells. The sled has 30 seconds to reach the cells. The first few competitors have an advantage because of the condition of the ice. Speeds can reach up to 135 km/h.

TECHNIQUE

1. Start

Pushing off from the starting blocks, the sledder grips the handles of the skeleton and runs as fast as he can, without allowing his heels to touch the ground, over a distance of approximately 50 m. The start is crucial, because it determines sled acceleration.

2. Loading

To position himself on the skeleton, the sledder raises his legs into the air for a fraction of a second, then lets himself fall. This movement must be precise, or the sledder risks being thrown off balance and losing control of the skeleton.

EQUIPMENT

Participants are only required to wear elbow protectors. However, some athletes protect the parts of their bodies that are most frequently exposed by inserting padding under their suits. The sled is designed to be very shock absorbent.

SKELETON

The sled is made of steel or fiberglass. The combined weight of the sledder and the skeleton may not exceed 115 kg for men, and 92 kg for women. If the combined weight is higher, the sled must not exceed its minimum weight.

Temperature of the runners

Because of the advantage of having hot runners, the temperature is verified just before the run, and may not exceed the temperature of the reference runner by more than 4 °C (for bobsled and skeleton), or 5 °C (for luge). The temperature of the reference runner is first taken 1 hour before the race, and then every 30 minutes after the competition begins. The temperature of the air, the reference runner, and the ice is displayed on a board.

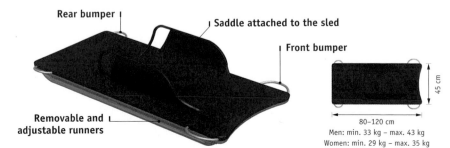

Rear bumper

Saddle attached to the sled

Front bumper

Removable and adjustable runners

45 cm

80–120 cm

Men: min. 33 kg – max. 43 kg

Women: min. 29 kg – max. 35 kg

TRACK

Skeleton is an individual sport performed on bobsled and luge tracks, a fact that has most certainly contributed to the sport's renewed popularity. The tracks, which are made from concrete covered in a layer of artificial ice, consist of many turns. On average, the tracks are 1,500 m long and 1.4 m wide. The slope grade ranges from 8% to 15%, depending on the location.

OFFICIALS

Race director

The race director ensures that the competition runs smoothly, and acts as a liaison between the track, which he inspects regularly, and the jury.

Technical delegate

He inspects the equipment, facilities, and skeletons at the start line. If necessary, the technical delegate supports the members of the jury in their decision.

Jury

Reporting to a chairperson, the jury is composed of 4 to 6 members, who oversee the smooth operation of the start and finish zones. They monitor the temperature of the runners at the start, and the weight of the skeletons and participants at the finish line. The chairperson ensures that the rules are applied, supervises the random draw, makes decisions concerning the weather (along with the jury members), and handles all protests.

Timekeeper

Based at the control tower, the timekeeper times the competitors with the help of a computer, which records the information transmitted by the photoelectric cells. Cells are installed at the starting zone, along the track, and at the finish zone. The times are displayed for the public on a giant screen. Video cameras positioned along the track make it possible to follow the progress of the race.

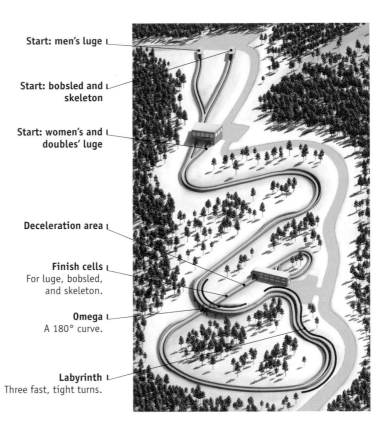

Start: men's luge

Start: bobsled and skeleton

Start: women's and doubles' luge

Deceleration area

Finish cells
For luge, bobsled, and skeleton.

Omega
A 180° curve.

Labyrinth
Three fast, tight turns.

3. Descent position

The sledder must position himself properly in order to perform the maneuvers that will be necessary during the run.

4. Control of the skeleton

The sledder shifts his weight slightly by moving his body from left to right in order to steer or to accelerate in the descent. At the finish, sledders sometimes use their feet to brake.

Helmet
The helmet is identical to that worn for downhill skiing, although it may be equipped with additional protection, such as a visor made and added by the participant, and a chin guard.

Shoes
Equipped with eight 7 mm cleats along the edge of the sole to facilitate the start, the shoes are the same as those worn by 100 m sprinters.

Alain Wicki (SUI)
National Champion in 1988 and World Champion in 1989, he ranked first overall in the general standings in the 1989 World Cup.

ATHLETE PROFILE
• The athlete has powerful legs, and is able to exert a maximum push in a very short period of time.
• Relaxation is essential in order to be able to visualize the track and the descent before the event.
• In a sharp curve, the athlete may be subjected to a centrifugal force of 4G (the equivalent of 4 times his body weight or more), or higher, for a fraction of a second.

luge

Luge racing is a relatively new sport that involves sliding down an icy track at high speeds. A luge is a type of sled, similar to the ones used by children, that was invented in 19th century Norway. The first official race, in 1893, attracted 21 competitors from six countries, and was run from the village of Davos to Klosters, Switzerland. In 1913, the International Luge Club was founded in Dresden, Germany, and a track was built there. The first European Luge Championships were held in 1914. In 1935, luge joined the International Bobsleigh and Tobogganing Federation (FIBT) and since 1945, thanks to Germany's influence, luge has become a major sport. In 1957, the International Luge Federation (FIL) was founded, and the following year saw the first World Championships, which are held each year, except during Olympic years. The first Olympic luge competition was held at the 1964 Games in Innsbruck, Austria. Both men and women compete in the sport.

Darasz and Zukowski, the Polish team in the 1964 Winter Olympics at Innsbruck, Austria

HOW A RACE IS ORGANIZED

Races are held in both singles and doubles (men and women), either on artificial or natural tracks. Competitors race against the clock, and the sledder with the best time wins. Each racer is allowed 2 to 4 runs, and the one with the lowest total time is the winner. The starting order for competitors is determined by random draw. When the starter gives the signal, the green light goes on, and timekeeping commences the instant the front of the luge passes the starting cells. The sledder has 30 seconds to reach the cells in singles, and 45 seconds in doubles. Races are held over distances of minimum 1,000 m and maximum 1,300 m (men's singles) or between 800 and 1,050 m (doubles and women's singles). Luge is a Winter Olympic sport in which time is measured in milliseconds.

TRACK

Whether natural or artificial, the average luge track is 1.5 km long, with several turns (right, left, S-curves and hairpin curves), and is coated with a thin layer of ice. Artificial tracks are designed around a carefully calculated, theoretical, but unseen ideal path of descent. Natural tracks are made on ice covered winding roads, and have no sidewalls. Luge racing on natural tracks is especially popular in Central Europe, where national and international meets are held.

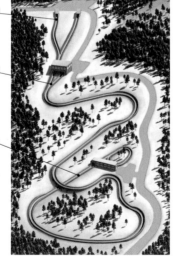

Start: men

Start: women and doubles

Finish cells

The characteristics of the track, the roles of the officials, and the rules governing the allowable temperature of the runners are identical to those for skeleton.

TECHNIQUE

1. Start

This is the critical moment, when the sledder has a decisive influence on the outcome of the race. Seated on the luge, the racer swings back and forth while holding on to the starting handles on each side of the track.

2. Push off

When ready, the racer starts off with a powerful push.

3. Acceleration

Once in motion, and after letting go of the starting handles, the sledder gains speed by paddling, or pushing against the ice with spiked gloves. The racer then grabs the luge handles and holds on to them for the remainder of the race.

4. Descent and steering

The sledder lies back to reduce wind resistance and to descend as fast as possible, and steers by shifting his weight slightly with a motion of the head and/or shoulders, or by exerting a bit of pressure on the runners. These body movements, combined with the gravitational force exerted in curves, increase speed.

EQUIPMENT

LUGE

A luge weighs 23 kg for singles and 27 kg for doubles. The maximum weight allowed, including the racer, clothing, and ballast, is 90.5 kg. An athlete weighing more than 90 kg cannot add ballast. Luges vary in length, depending on the athlete and the category of competition. The maximum and minimum distances between the bridges, which connect the seat to the runners, are regulated. The pod can measure up to 170 mm high and 550 mm wide.

Late 1950s

Singles luge

An average of 1.45 m

Doubles luge

Pod

Blades

Runners
Runners are fitted with steel blades that curve upward at the tip.

An average of 1.75 m

Visor

Helmet
The helmet is streamlined, and is specially designed for luge racing.

Ballast
Lighter racers can add ballast (lead discs or belt) under their suit.

Strap
The strap supports the top racer in doubles events.

Suit
The suit must be skin tight and aerodynamic, and meet FIL standards.

Luge shoes
They are aerodynamically shaped, and have smooth soles.

Spikes

Gloves
The gloves are fitted with spikes on 3 fingers or on the knuckles. The spikes measure up to 4 mm in length, and are used for gripping the ice when paddling at the start of a run.

PROFILE OF A LUGE RACER

- Luge racers are very sturdy athletes, both physically and psychologically, and they must have above average reflexes. During a race, most of the stress is on the upper part of their body (abdomen, chest, and neck), and on the feet, which control the runners.

- Sledders must be willing to attain speeds of up to 145 km/h in an open vehicle, with no protection or emergency brake.

Susi Erdmann (GER)
Three-time World Champion (1989, 1991, and 1997), she won the 1991 World Cup and the 1994 Winter Olympic silver medal.

Georg Hackl (GER)
The winner of the most medals in the history of luge, including the 1992, 1994, and 1998 Olympic gold medals, he won the 1989, 1990, and 1997 World Championships.

5. Braking and stopping

After crossing the finish line, the racer sits up, puts his feet on the ice, and pushes to raise the front of the sled. This forces the tail end of the runners to dig into the ice, and gradually brings the luge to a stop.

figure skating

Peggy Fleming (USA) gold medalist at the Olympics in Grenoble, France, in 1968, and world champion from 1966 to 1968

Figure skating, with its excitement and risk, is one of the most elegant sports in existence. Figures, spins, and difficult jumps, skating with harmony and flexibility, dancing as a couple to chosen music—this is the essence of figure skating and ice dancing. In the mid 19th century, skating became very popular as a leisure activity and organized sport. Skating rinks and clubs flourished all over the world. The Skating Club of London was formed in England in 1842, while the New York Skating Club was formed in the United States in 1860. In the 1860s, the sport was revolutionized by an American, who integrated dance movements. Twenty-four years later, the International Skating Union (ISU) was created; the first world championship took place in 1896 for men, and in 1906 for women. Figure skating became an Olympic sport in London in 1908. Figure skating as we know it today took shape in the 1950s. With TV broadcasts of skating competitions and exhibitions, it reaches a huge audience and has become very popular.

THE COMPETITION

There are 3 events in figure skating: singles, pairs, and ice dancing. Singles skating includes 2 phases: the short, or technical, program, and the long, or free, program. The short program lasts 2:40 minutes and is composed of 8 required technical elements with linking steps. The skaters choose the music. The long program lasts 4 minutes for women and 4:30 minutes for men. Competitors are judged on technique, choreography, interpretation of the music, originality of musical choice, and quality of execution. Pairs skating includes a short program with required elements and a long program. In both singles and pairs, the skaters must perform a certain number of technical elements—spins, compulsory and free jumps, and spirals.

THE RINK

26–30 m
Olympic: 30 m

56–60 m
Olympic: 60 m

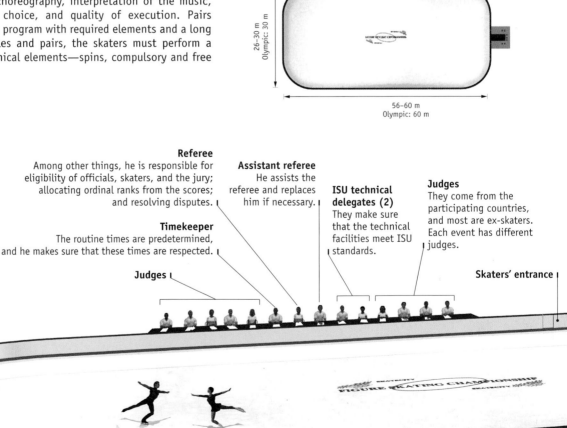

Referee
Among other things, he is responsible for eligibility of officials, skaters, and the jury; allocating ordinal ranks from the scores; and resolving disputes.

Assistant referee
He assists the referee and replaces him if necessary.

ISU technical delegates (2)
They make sure that the technical facilities meet ISU standards.

Judges
They come from the participating countries, and most are ex-skaters. Each event has different judges.

Timekeeper
The routine times are predetermined, and he makes sure that these times are respected.

Judges

Skaters' entrance

TECHNIQUES

All techniques—steps, jumps, step sequences, spirals, and spins—require great accuracy and are difficult to learn. The figures must be memorized, and concentration is needed at all times.

Required technical elements

In the short program, skaters execute required elements. For men, there are 8: 2 step sequences, 3 spins in 2 different positions, a double Axel, a triple jump preceded by footwork, and a triple combination including a double or triple Axel. For women, the elements are: 1 step sequence; 3 types of spins; a spiral sequence; a double Axel; a double or triple jump preceded by footwork; and a combination of triple, double, triple-double, or double-double jumps. For couples, the 8 elements include: a twist lift, solo jumps, solo spins with change of foot, a pairs spin, a death spiral, and a spiral step sequence.

SPIRALS

The best known are the front and back spiral, holding the skate, and the death spiral. The last is a required technical element for pairs. Death spirals can be skated in 2 positions, inside and outside, and the woman skater's position determines the direction of the spiral. The man energetically spins his partner by the arm. The woman leans back until her head is just a few centimeters from the ice. The goal of the death spiral is to have the woman as low as possible, with her back parallel to the ice.

Outside back death spiral

CALCULATION OF MARKS

Since 1988, the judges for international competitions have been drawn by lot from among the represented nations. This system is in force in the European and world championships. Two sets of marks on a scale of 0 to 6, the first for technical execution and the second for artistic presentation, are awarded by 9 judges. A list of deductions is given to the judges before each event. In addition to the basic marking scale, this list provides the judges with more accurate evaluation standards. Thus, for example, a poorly performed step sequence is penalized by 0.1 to 0.3 of a mark; poorly performed combinations, spins, or jumps cost 0.1 to 0.4 of a point, and an element not skated costs 0.5 of a point.

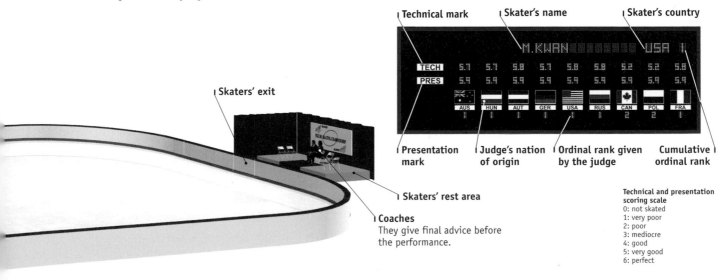

Technical mark

Skater's name

Skater's country

M.KWAN   USA

| TECH | 5.7 | 5.7 | 5.8 | 5.7 | 5.8 | 5.8 | 5.8 | 5.8 | 5.8 |
| PRES | 5.9 | 5.9 | 5.9 | 5.9 | 5.9 | 5.9 | 5.9 | 5.9 | 5.9 |

AUS HUN AUT GER USA RUS CAN POL FRA

Presentation mark

Judge's nation of origin

Ordinal rank given by the judge

Cumulative ordinal rank

Skaters' exit

Skaters' rest area

Coaches
They give final advice before the performance.

Technical and presentation scoring scale
0: not skated
1: very poor
2: poor
3: mediocre
4: good
5: very good
6: perfect

SPINS

A good spin meets 4 criteria: speed, aesthetic line, balance, and centering. These qualities must be present in the various basic positions: standing spin, sit spin, layback spin, and camel spin. There are 3 types of spin: scratch spins, flying spins, and combination spins.

The death-drop spin

Probably the most spectacular, this is a flying camel spin landing in a back sit spin. The skater jumps off the outside front foot and lands in a sitting position on the right foot.

JUMPS

Six main jumps, often executed as doubles or triples, are an integral part of figure skating. The Axel is considered the most difficult.

The Axel

Invented by Norwegian skater Axel Paulsen in 1882, this jump requires great accuracy and can be executed as a single, double or triple. The skater takes off facing forward.

The Salchow

Developed in 1909 by Ulrich Salchow, 10 time world champion. A complex jump, it requires accuracy and balance. It can be executed as a single, double, or triple. The skater takes off facing backward.

The flip

This jump is a Salchow performed off the toe pick in a straight line. The skater takes off facing backward.

The Lutz

Unique, spectacular, and very demanding physically, the Lutz was invented by Austrian skater Alois Lutz in 1913. The skater takes off facing backward.

The toe loop

The toe loop is the simplest of the toe pick jumps. The skater takes off facing backward.

EQUIPMENT DEVELOPMENTS

SKATE

1800

1940

Men's

1990

Women's

Boot

It must be comfortable and tight to support the ankle, which is under high stress.

BLADE

In steel for all levels and disciplines. There are 2 types of blade: one for the long program and one for ice dancing.

Blade for ice dancing

The heel is shorter and the toe picks smaller.

Blade for the long program

More curved than the blade for ice dancing, with toe picks that make it easier to execute jumps, spirals, and spins. It is forbidden to use the toe picks to start; this must be done with the flat of the blade.

Katarina Witt (GDR)
Gold medalist at the 1984 and 1988 Olympics, she was also world champion 4 times. With Sonja Henie, she is the only woman to win the Grand Slam twice, in 1984 and 1988.

Elvis Stojko (CAN)
Silver medalist at the 1994 and 1998 Olympics, world champion in 1994, 1995, and 1997. First skater to land a quadruple-triple toe loop jump combination (7 turns in total) successfully in competition.

COSTUME

Chosen by the competitors to be comfortable and attractive. It must retain body heat, dry rapidly, and be stretchy. For women, a skirt must cover the hips and upper thighs.

Ekaterina Gordeyeva and Sergei Grinkov (USSR)
World champions in 1986, 1987, 1989, and 1990. They were also Olympic champions in 1988 and 1994.

SKATER PROFILE

- The essential characteristics of skaters are great flexibility, excellent sense of balance, physical strength, accuracy, and creativity.

- Training has 4 aspects: technical (steps, jumps, spirals, and spins), physical (endurance, flexibility, and strength), artistic (choreography, movement), and psychological (motivation, concentration, visualization).

- The female partner must be smaller than her male partner for both aesthetic and physical reasons (partner's strength).

Kurt Browning (CAN)
In 1988, first skater to land a quadruple jump successfully in competition. He was world champion in 1989, 1990, 1991 and 1993.

ice dancing

Technical and choreographic changes to ice dancing in recent years earned it inclusion in official competitions, including the Olympics, starting in 1976. Although it is integrated with figure skating, it is an Olympic discipline in its own right. Acrobatic moves are not allowed, it is performed by couples only, and it is distinct for its choreographic aspect. The skaters must move without apparent effort and execute their movements in harmony and in time to the chosen music. They must also give the impression of being a true couple and not two individuals skating together. This discipline is both an athletic and an artistic challenge. In parallel with ice dance, precision skating, the newest skating discipline, created in 1957, became popular in the 1970s: teams of 12 to 20 skaters execute choreographed routines with prescribed figures. The figures must be geometric and the music is chosen by the athletes.

Jane Torvill and Christopher Dean (GBR)
In 1984, they revolutionized ice dance with a masterful performance of Ravel's *Bolero*.

THE COMPETITION

The ice dance competition involves 2 compulsory dances, an original dance with a set musical theme, and a 4 minute free dance with music chosen by the skaters.

THE PHASES

Compulsory dances

These 2 dances are chosen from among the 18 dances recognized by the International Skating Union (ISU). Made of steps and series of steps in a precise pattern, they are executed to music that determines the rhythm and speed.

It is essential to show timing with the music, musical expression, and step placement. The compulsory dances are the basis of all ice dancing, and their execution in competition makes up 20% of the final mark.

Original dance

In this phase, the type of dance, its rhythm, and its tempo are chosen by the ISU, which publishes the information 2 years in advance. However, the skaters choose the music and the choreography. The dance lasts 2 minutes. In international competition, the original dance makes up 30% of the final mark.

Free dance

This is a series of steps performed to music chosen by the couple. The dance lasts 4:30 minutes and represents 50% of the final mark in international competition.

Dances recognized by the ISU

Foxtrot

Rocker foxtrot

Kilian

Yankee polka

Quickstep

Paso doble

Rumba

14 steps

Harris tango

Argentine tango

Tango romantica

Blues

European waltz

American waltz

Westminster waltz

Viennese waltz

Starlight waltz

Ravensburger waltz

Isabelle and Paul Duchesnay (FRA)
World champions in 1991, they were known for their original and bold choreography.

SKATER PROFILE

- Both partners must have similar and complementary skills. It is essential that their styles match, that they have a sense of rhythm and synchronization, and that they have the same basic techniques. Power, flexibility, balance, and coordination are essential.

speed skating

Speed-skating race at the Chamonix, France, Winter Olympics in 1924.

There are two types of speed-skating events, long track and short track; competitions are for individuals and teams. Skating started as a means of transportation in Northern countries, and speed skating was later developed in Holland, although the first race was organized in Fens, England, in 1763. The International Skating Federation (ISU) was created in 1892, and the first world championships, held in 1889 in the Netherlands, featured 500 meter, 1,500 meter, 5,000 meter, and 10,000 meter races. Short track speed skating, spectacular because of the smaller rink, started races in Canada and the United States in 1905, and the first North American short track races took place in 1909. In the 1920s and 1930s, short track fans flocked to Madison Square Garden in New York. It was not until 1992, however, that short track speed skating became an Olympic event, while long track had been in the Olympics since 1924 for men and 1960 for women.

LONG-TRACK COMPETITIONS

There are two main competition categories: sprints of 500 m and 1,000 m, skated by both men and women, and the all-round, in which men race over 500 m, 1,500 m, 5,000 m, and 10,000 m, and women race over 500 m, 1,500 m, 3,000 m, and 5,000 m. Two skaters start together, and they race against the clock. The athletes' times are calculated on a scale equivalent to 500 m and then converted into points. The winner of the competition is the skater with the lowest total number of points. Skaters are not allowed to skate inside the blocks on the turns. Long track skaters may reach speeds of up to 60 km/h.

Crossing straight
It is where skaters change lanes.

111.98 m

Olympic oval
400 m

RINKS

LONG TRACK

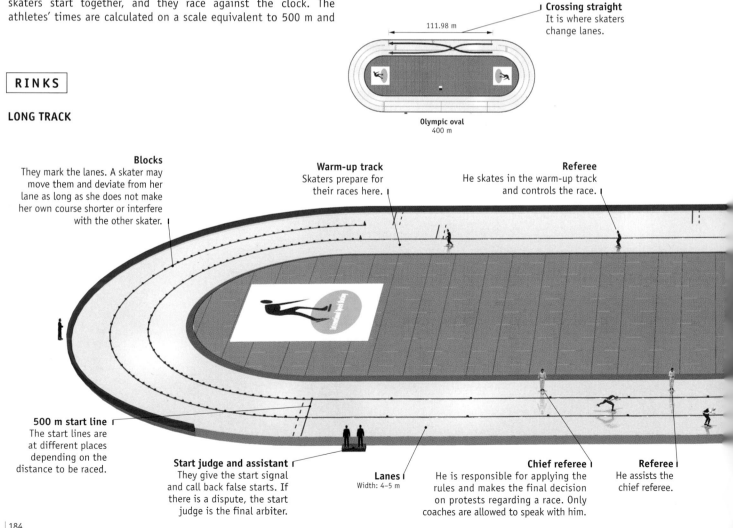

Blocks
They mark the lanes. A skater may move them and deviate from her lane as long as she does not make her own course shorter or interfere with the other skater.

Warm-up track
Skaters prepare for their races here.

Referee
He skates in the warm-up track and controls the race.

500 m start line
The start lines are at different places depending on the distance to be raced.

Start judge and assistant
They give the start signal and call back false starts. If there is a dispute, the start judge is the final arbiter.

Lanes
Width: 4–5 m

Chief referee
He is responsible for applying the rules and makes the final decision on protests regarding a race. Only coaches are allowed to speak with him.

Referee
He assists the chief referee.

SHORT TRACK COMPETITIONS

There are two types of races: individual and the relay, involving teams of 4 skaters. In individual races, 4 to 6 skaters start at the same time—the athletes race against each other—and the winner is the one with the best time in the final. Skaters must pass each other cleanly, without forcing the passed skater to slow down, and are penalized if they skate inside the blocks, but not if they move them. The skater in the lead must not interfere with the other skaters by using his arms or body to keep them from passing. Short track skaters can reach speeds of up to 50 km/h. Men and women skate the same distances: 500 m, 1,000 m, 1,500 m, and 3,000 m; in relays, however, women race over 3,000 m and men over 5,000 m.

Olympic rink

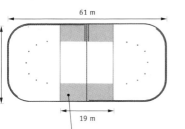

61 m

30 m

19 m

Relay zones (4)
During the race, relays may take place in any of the 4 zones between the blue lines. However, starting 3 laps before the end of the race, the relay must be completed before the red line.

SHORT TRACK

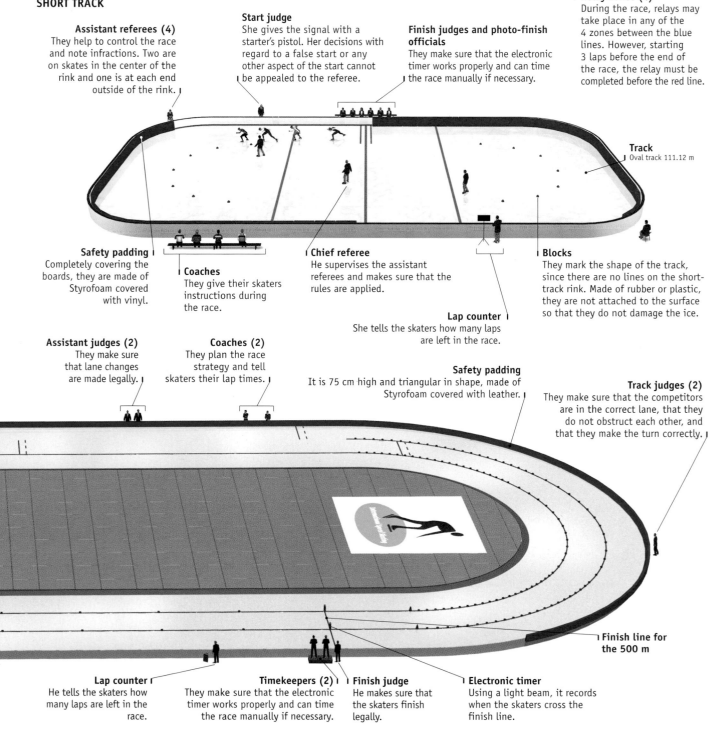

Assistant referees (4)
They help to control the race and note infractions. Two are on skates in the center of the rink and one is at each end outside of the rink.

Start judge
She gives the signal with a starter's pistol. Her decisions with regard to a false start or any other aspect of the start cannot be appealed to the referee.

Finish judges and photo-finish officials
They make sure that the electronic timer works properly and can time the race manually if necessary.

Track
Oval track 111.12 m

Safety padding
Completely covering the boards, they are made of Styrofoam covered with vinyl.

Coaches
They give their skaters instructions during the race.

Chief referee
He supervises the assistant referees and makes sure that the rules are applied.

Blocks
They mark the shape of the track, since there are no lines on the short-track rink. Made of rubber or plastic, they are not attached to the surface so that they do not damage the ice.

Lap counter
She tells the skaters how many laps are left in the race.

Assistant judges (2)
They make sure that lane changes are made legally.

Coaches (2)
They plan the race strategy and tell skaters their lap times.

Safety padding
It is 75 cm high and triangular in shape, made of Styrofoam covered with leather.

Track judges (2)
They make sure that the competitors are in the correct lane, that they do not obstruct each other, and that they make the turn correctly.

Finish line for the 500 m

Lap counter
He tells the skaters how many laps are left in the race.

Timekeepers (2)
They make sure that the electronic timer works properly and can time the race manually if necessary.

Finish judge
He makes sure that the skaters finish legally.

Electronic timer
Using a light beam, it records when the skaters cross the finish line.

185

LONG TRACK TECHNIQUES

START

The skaters try to have as powerful a push-off as possible.
The stroke of the skate, gliding, and concentration are important technical aspects. In sprints, it is an advantage to start on the inside lane and finish on the outside. Over all distances, the skaters must keep energy in reserve and know how many seconds they should take to complete each lap.

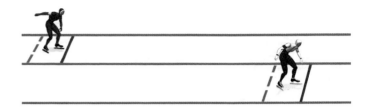

BASIC POSITIONS

Skaters propel themselves off each skate alternately.
In straightaways over distances of more than 3,000 m, they keep one arm behind their back to reduce wind resistance.
In sprints, they swing both arms at the start and finish.

Hand on the ice

In curves, the skater swings the arm on the outside of the curve to conserve speed and keep from drifting to the outside.

Straightaway

Strides with long, powerful strokes are used on straightaways.

Curve

Crossover steps make skating curves easier and help skaters to counter centrifugal force. This technique is difficult to master.

Long stride

Force of the thrust, arm swing, hip angle, and shoulder orientation are factors the skater must control efficiently.

SHORT TRACK TECHNIQUES

Different types of strides must be mastered: the start stride, the race stride, and the crossover.

START

Start strides are running steps that the skater uses to gain speed.

BASIC POSITION

Mastery of techniques related to the basic position enables the skater to make high speed curves. The skater's body leans forward and her knees are slightly bent. This position encourages better weight distribution, complete extension during the push-off, and a lower center of gravity.

Hand on the ice

The skaters are allowed to touch the ice with their hands to help them maintain their balance in curves. However, they should not keep their hand on the ice for long, as it slows them down.

Straightaway

The skater tries to maintain her basic position.

Curve

In short-track races, skaters crouch so low that their knees almost touch their midsection, and they lean toward the ice at a pronounced angle.

RELAYS

Relay races are run over distances of 3,000 m (27 laps) for women and 5,000 m (45 laps) for men. The race involves 4 4-skater teams.

To make a relay, a skater must touch a teammate; relays can be made anywhere on the track. The contact is usually in the form of a push.

EQUIPMENT

In long track, skaters wear a one-piece suit with a hood. In short-track, where there is a higher risk of falling, athletes protect the most exposed parts of their bodies.

LONG TRACK

One piece suit
It has a hood and minimizes wind resistance as much as possible.

SHORT TRACK

Safety helmet

Neck guard with bib

Gloves
They are made of leather to reduce the risk of cuts.

Shin guards

Knee guards

CLAP SKATE

42–46 cm

Blade
Width: 1 mm

The blade is straight, centered on the sole, and detaches from the heel of the boot, permitting the blade to remain in contact with the ice longer and helping the skater make a better push-off. The clap skate increases speed and helps skaters at the end of the race when fatigue sets in and they have a tendency to catch the front of their blade in the ice at the end of the stride.

SHORT-TRACK SKATES

Up to 46 cm

Blade
Width: 1.2–1.4 mm

The blade, curved in the direction of the turns, is attached to the sole diagonally and off-center.

SKATER PROFILE

- Most skaters choose to specialize in long-track or short-track between the ages of 15 and 20. Some athletes continue their careers in both events, which is very demanding. Athletes can race at the elite level until around age 30.

- In short track, skaters are agile and must be able to perform explosive starts.

- In long track, skaters have great physical strength, powerful legs, aerobic power, and high anaerobic capacity.

- The main muscles used are the quadriceps and gluteus maximus.

Johann Olav Koss (NOR)
Four times Olympic champion in 1992 and in 1994 (he beat the world record that latter year), he was also three times world champion: in 1990, 1991, and 1994.

Marc Gagnon (CAN)
Short track world champion several times, he was a gold medalist in the Olympic relay in 1998.

Eric Heiden (USA)
World champion in 1977, 1978, and 1979, he also won five gold medals at the 1980 Olympics (500, 1,000, 1,500, 5,000 and 10,000 m).

Karin Enke-Kania (RDA)
She won a total of 8 medals at the Winter Olympics in 1980, 1984, and 1988. Sprint world champion in 1980, 1981, 1983, 1984, 1986, and 1987, she was also world champion over all distances in 1982, 1984, 1986, 1987, and 1988.

Snow Sports

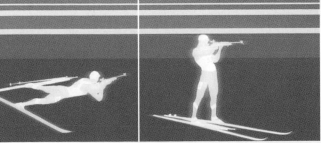

alpine skiing

The origins of skiing have been attributed to the Scandinavians, and date back around 4,500 years. Before becoming a popular pastime, skiing was an economical and effective means of transportation that was perfectly suited to the climates and mountainous terrain of the Nordic countries. Skiing was apparently developed as a sport in the first half of the 18th century in Norway. In 1888, Norwegian explorer Fridtjof Nansen's journey on nordic skis to Greenland inspired French, Swiss, German, and Austrian mountaineers, who imported skis from Scandinavia and expanded the sport's popularity in their respective countries. However, nordic skiing techniques did not work on mountainous terrain, so, by the end of the 19th century, they were adapted to the Alps, giving birth to alpine skiing. The International Ski Federation (FIS) was founded in 1924 and in 1931 it started organizing alpine skiing competitions. In 1936, combined (downhill and slalom) was introduced at the Olympic Winter Games for men and women, and in 1948, in Chamonix, downhill and slalom were admitted to the Games as separated events. Giant slalom appeared for the first time in the Oslo Games in 1952 (men and women), and Super Giant slalom for men and women was included in the Olympics for the first time in Calgary, in 1988. The annual World Cup, created in 1967, includes approximately 20 events. Every second year, the top skiers in the world compete in the world championships.

World Champion in 1956, the Austrian Anton Sailer was the first man to win three Olympic titles in the same year (downhill, slalom, and giant slalom, in 1956).

HOW A MEET IS ORGANIZED

All events involve timed races with staggered starts, where competitors ski down the hill one at a time, following the pre-established course and attempting to cross the finish line in the fastest time possible. Leaving the course results in disqualification. The four events are classified into three categories:

• Speed events, which involving a single run, include the downhill—a test of pure speed—and the Super-G (super giant slalom)—a speed event run on a shorter course and involving more gates.

• Technical events, which include the giant slalom (or giant) and the slalom (or special slalom). These are skied in two runs, and the final ranking is determined by adding the times.

• Combined events, which involve obtaining an overall result for several events (usually a downhill and a slalom).

COURSES FOR THE DIFFERENT EVENTS

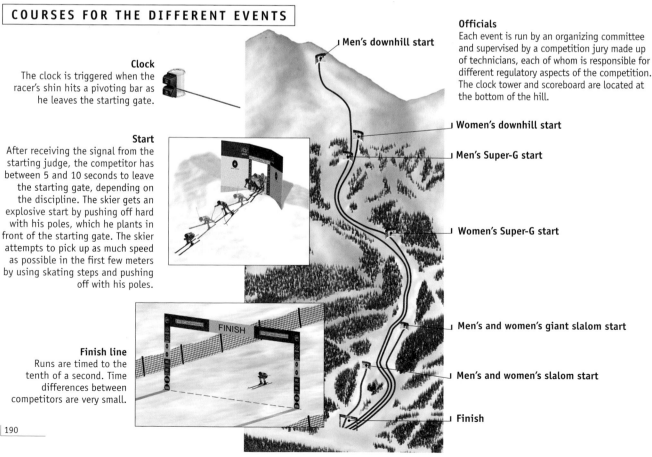

Clock
The clock is triggered when the racer's shin hits a pivoting bar as he leaves the starting gate.

Start
After receiving the signal from the starting judge, the competitor has between 5 and 10 seconds to leave the starting gate, depending on the discipline. The skier gets an explosive start by pushing off hard with his poles, which he plants in front of the starting gate. The skier attempts to pick up as much speed as possible in the first few meters by using skating steps and pushing off with his poles.

Finish line
Runs are timed to the tenth of a second. Time differences between competitors are very small.

Officials
Each event is run by an organizing committee and supervised by a competition jury made up of technicians, each of whom is responsible for different regulatory aspects of the competition. The clock tower and scoreboard are located at the bottom of the hill.

Men's downhill start

Women's downhill start

Men's Super-G start

Women's Super-G start

Men's and women's giant slalom start

Men's and women's slalom start

Finish

SPEED EVENTS

DOWNHILL

This spectacular event is the crown jewel of alpine skiing. The race is run on a steep slope, and involves long, straight lines and fast, sweeping turns. The skiers, who participate in three days of trials to study and experience the course, reach speeds of more than 120 km/h. The vertical descent is between 500 and 1,000 m for men, and between 500 and 700 m for women. The gates must be at least 8 m wide.

Jumps

The ability to negotiate jumps is a determining factor in all speed events. To maintain high speeds, the skier adopts the tuck position—knees bent into the chest and hands well out in front (a position similar to that used for accelerating)—in order to maintain balance and minimize wind resistance. The skier straightens his legs only when he makes contact with the course.

SUPER GIANT SLALOM OR SUPER-G

This recently developed discipline combines downhill speed with giant slalom technique. The event usually takes place on a downhill course. The course is shortened by several hundred meters, and gates are added to obtain a minimum of 35 changes of direction (30 for women), not counting the start and finish gates. The gates are between 6 and 8 m wide, and located at intervals of at least 25 m for open gates and 15 m for closed gates. Skiers prepare themselves for the course on the day of the race.

Schuss position

This is also called the "egg position." The skier adopts an aerodynamic position (knees bent, hands well out in front, shoulders curled inward to the body, and back rounded) in order to ensure minimum wind resistance. It is used mainly in speed events (downhill and Super-G) and in the straight segments of the giant slalom.

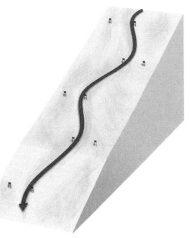

TECHNICAL EVENTS

SLALOM OR SPECIAL SLALOM

The slalom gates mark a tight course that is adapted to the terrain and which requires skiers to execute rapid turns and make contact with the gate poles in order to stay on course. The course is composed of red and blue horizontal (open) gates and vertical (closed) gates, 2 or 3 chicanes (a combination of 3 to 5 closed gates in quick succession), and at least 4 vertical double gates. Skiers must pass all the gates while respecting the alternating colors (red and blue). A course includes between 55 and 75 gates for men and between 45 and 65 gates for women. The minimum spacing between gates is 0.75 m.

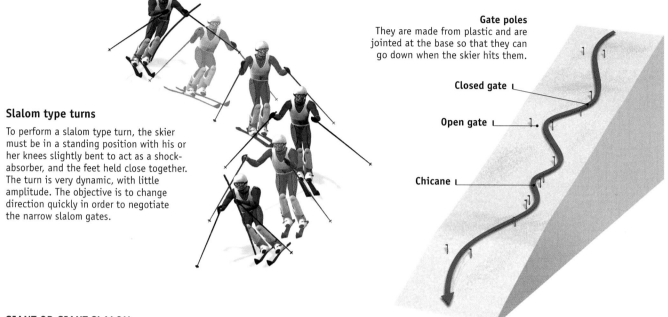

Slalom type turns

To perform a slalom type turn, the skier must be in a standing position with his or her knees slightly bent to act as a shock-absorber, and the feet held close together. The turn is very dynamic, with little amplitude. The objective is to change direction quickly in order to negotiate the narrow slalom gates.

Gate poles
They are made from plastic and are jointed at the base so that they can go down when the skier hits them.

Closed gate

Open gate

Chicane

GIANT OR GIANT SLALOM

The giant slalom event features fewer gates than the slalom, and is run on a slope that is not as steep. The course, which features longer curves, creates a rapid sequence of movements that call on the skier's technical ability—especially finesse of the ski-snow contact and a feeling for the proper trajectory. The number of gates, which are between 4 and 8 m wide and spaced at least 10 m apart, is established according to the elevation of the course. The gates are positioned where they can be seen quickly and easily, even at high speeds.

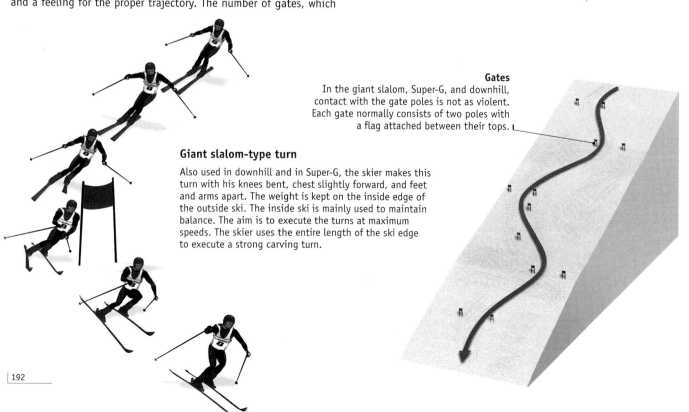

Giant slalom-type turn

Also used in downhill and in Super-G, the skier makes this turn with his knees bent, chest slightly forward, and feet and arms apart. The weight is kept on the inside edge of the outside ski. The inside ski is mainly used to maintain balance. The aim is to execute the turns at maximum speeds. The skier uses the entire length of the ski edge to execute a strong carving turn.

Gates
In the giant slalom, Super-G, and downhill, contact with the gate poles is not as violent. Each gate normally consists of two poles with a flag attached between their tops.

EQUIPMENT

SLALOM

Goggles
The use of goggles with filtering lenses can be critical when the weather makes it very difficult to make out the course—especially in overcast conditions.

Helmet with chin guard
This is used to protect the skier's head from contact with the gate poles.

Suit
Some slalom skiers still ski in tapered pants and a wool sweater, although most now wear a suit.

Poles
The poles are straight, light, and sturdy, and are made from aluminum alloy or composite fibers. The grip is in the form of a shell, and is used to push the gate poles as the gate is passed.

Shinguards
Like the grips on the poles, they are used to push the gate poles.

Boots
Made from a blend of plastics and composites, the boots keep the ankle steady and the foot solidly in line with the tibia. This allows the skier to use the full strength of his leg to transmit his "instructions" to the ski (lean, direction, etc.). Competition models are very sturdy in terms of lateral torsion and frontal flex, giving better control over the edges and greater accuracy of reaction to impulses from the foot. The degree of forward lean, which determines the skier's position, is adjustable. The sole has a tab at the heel and the toe to secure the boot in the bindings.

DOWNHILL, GIANT SLALOM, OR SUPER GIANT SLALOM

Helmet
The helmet is mandatory for speed events, and is worn by most skiers for all disciplines.

Poles
These are used mainly to guide the turn and help the skier maintain his or her balance. They are curved, and offer minimal wind resistance when the skier assumes the tuck position. They are light and rigid, and are made from aluminum or composite fibers.

Alberto Tomba (ITA)
Nicknamed "La Bomba" because of his flamboyant style, which is accented by strength and aggression, he was the Olympic slalom champion in 1988, the Olympic giant slalom champion in 1988 and 1992, and the world championship slalom and giant slalom champion in 1996. He won the World Cup 8 times between 1988 and 1998, and was the overall top ranked skier in 1995.

Ingemar Stenmark (SWE)
Winner of three World Cups overall, he was twice gold medalist (slalom and giant slalom) at the Lake Placid Winter Games in 1980. He also holds the most victories in World Cup (86).

Suit
The suit is form-fitted, and made from synthetic fibers. It offers a good air penetration coefficient while giving the skier complete freedom of movement.

EQUIPMENT

Skis

Skis are made up of three sections: the tail, the waist, and the spatula. A ski's performance on the snow depends on its length, width, and cut (differences in width between the spatula, waist, and tail). A longer ski (Super-G, downhill) is more stable, but less maneuverable than a slalom ski, which has a narrow waist that allows the skier to change direction faster. In the early 90s, parabolic skis with a more pronounced shape were introduced. The spatula and tail section of the ski, both much wider than the midsection (waist), increase the contact surface with the snow, and make it possible to use shorter skis to improve maneuverability, without losing stability. The larger spatula width allows for the easier initiation of turns, while the larger tail width allows the skier to pull out of turns much faster.

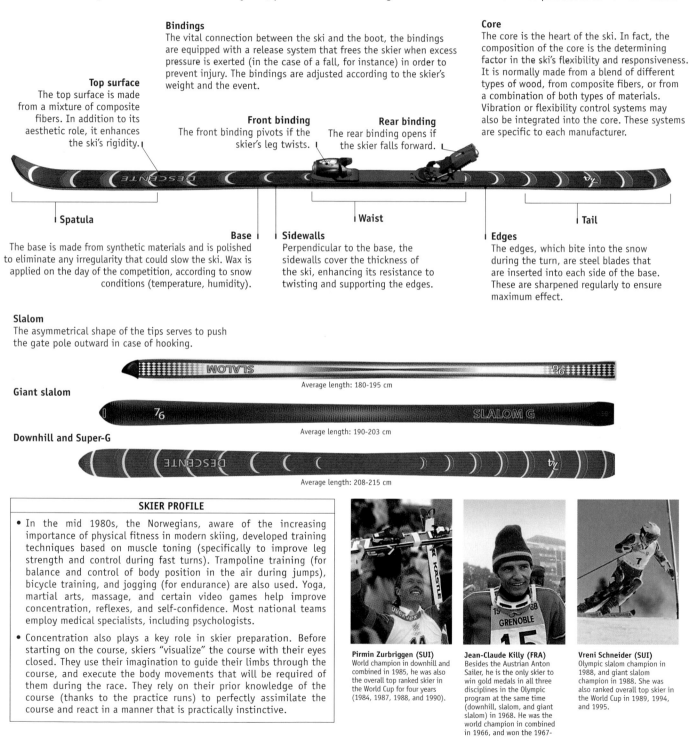

Bindings
The vital connection between the ski and the boot, the bindings are equipped with a release system that frees the skier when excess pressure is exerted (in the case of a fall, for instance) in order to prevent injury. The bindings are adjusted according to the skier's weight and the event.

Core
The core is the heart of the ski. In fact, the composition of the core is the determining factor in the ski's flexibility and responsiveness. It is normally made from a blend of different types of wood, from composite fibers, or from a combination of both types of materials. Vibration or flexibility control systems may also be integrated into the core. These systems are specific to each manufacturer.

Top surface
The top surface is made from a mixture of composite fibers. In addition to its aesthetic role, it enhances the ski's rigidity.

Front binding
The front binding pivots if the skier's leg twists.

Rear binding
The rear binding opens if the skier falls forward.

Spatula

Base
The base is made from synthetic materials and is polished to eliminate any irregularity that could slow the ski. Wax is applied on the day of the competition, according to snow conditions (temperature, humidity).

Sidewalls
Perpendicular to the base, the sidewalls cover the thickness of the ski, enhancing its resistance to twisting and supporting the edges.

Waist

Edges
The edges, which bite into the snow during the turn, are steel blades that are inserted into each side of the base. These are sharpened regularly to ensure maximum effect.

Tail

Slalom
The asymmetrical shape of the tips serves to push the gate pole outward in case of hooking.

SLALOM 96

Average length: 180-195 cm

Giant slalom

76 SLALOM G

Average length: 190-203 cm

Downhill and Super-G

DESCENTE 74

Average length: 208-215 cm

SKIER PROFILE

- In the mid 1980s, the Norwegians, aware of the increasing importance of physical fitness in modern skiing, developed training techniques based on muscle toning (specifically to improve leg strength and control during fast turns). Trampoline training (for balance and control of body position in the air during jumps), bicycle training, and jogging (for endurance) are also used. Yoga, martial arts, massage, and certain video games help improve concentration, reflexes, and self-confidence. Most national teams employ medical specialists, including psychologists.

- Concentration also plays a key role in skier preparation. Before starting on the course, skiers "visualize" the course with their eyes closed. They use their imagination to guide their limbs through the course, and execute the body movements that will be required of them during the race. They rely on their prior knowledge of the course (thanks to the practice runs) to perfectly assimilate the course and react in a manner that is practically instinctive.

Pirmin Zurbriggen (SUI)
World champion in downhill and combined in 1985, he was also the overall top ranked skier in the World Cup for four years (1984, 1987, 1988, and 1990).

Jean-Claude Killy (FRA)
Besides the Austrian Anton Sailer, he is the only skier to win gold medals in all three disciplines in the Olympic program at the same time (downhill, slalom, and giant slalom) in 1968. He was the world champion in combined in 1966, and won the 1967-1968 overall World Cup title.

Vreni Schneider (SUI)
Olympic slalom champion in 1988, and giant slalom champion in 1988. She was also ranked overall top skier in the World Cup in 1989, 1994, and 1995.

freestyle skiing

The three freestyle skiing events (moguls, aerials, and acro) closely combine artistry and athletic prowess to produce spectacular results. In 1905, in Austria, a gymnast named Mathias Zdarsky tried some ballet steps while on skis. Stein Eriksen of Norway began performing aerial stunts at ski shows around 1952. However, it was only in 1970 that "Hot-Dog" skiing, which combined moguls, jumps, and ballet, was born in the ski hills of California. Darryl Bowie, John Johnston, and Michel Daigle are credited with having invented the style. Following the first European Cup in 1973, 12 countries organized an international circuit, and the International Ski Federation (FIS) recognized it as a sport in 1979. The first World Cup competition was held in 1981, and an FIS sanctioned World Championship was held at Tignes, France, in 1985. The moguls competition made its Olympic debut at the 1992 Albertville Games, and aerials followed at the 1994 Games in Lillehammer, Norway.

Introduction to aerials at the Lillehammer Olympics in 1994

HOW A MOGULS COMPETITION IS ORGANIZED

The moguls event is held on a straight, steep slope covered with moguls, which the skiers must negotiate while descending as fast as possible. The course also contains two ramps, known as kickers. The skiers perform jumps from these kickers as part of the event. The two jumps must be taken from different categories. Singles competitions consist of one qualifying round and the finals. In dual moguls (a World Championship and World Cup event), two skiers descend at the same time. The winner, determined according to the same rules used in the singles event, qualifies for the next round. Subsequent elimination rounds determine the winner.

TECHNIQUE

Turns and jumps must be smoothly linked. Maneuvers are categorized by two criteria:

• Position of the skis (skis together or spread, forward or sideways);

• Horizontal rotation (360° to 720°).

Some maneuvers combine position and rotation. Most male competitors perform three or four different maneuvers during each jump (women perform two).

SCORING

Seven judges award points based on three criteria: the quality of the turns (line of descent, use of moguls, pliancy, body position) is rated out of 5 points; jumps, or air (difficulty, distance, performance), is rated out of 2.5 points; and speed (compared to a standard time that is set for the course) is rated out of 2.5 points. In dual moguls, the second skier's time difference is converted into points to be deducted from his score.

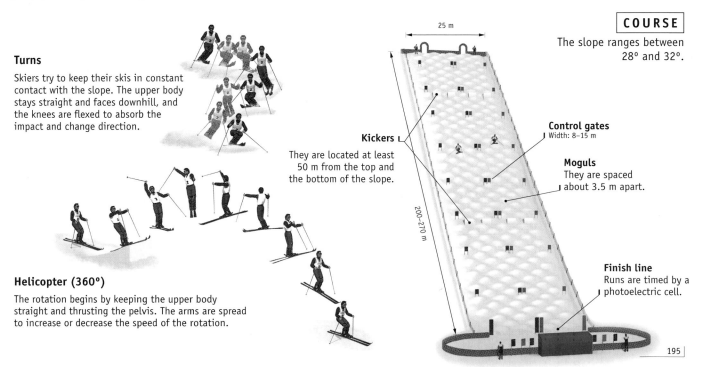

Turns

Skiers try to keep their skis in constant contact with the slope. The upper body stays straight and faces downhill, and the knees are flexed to absorb the impact and change direction.

Helicopter (360°)

The rotation begins by keeping the upper body straight and thrusting the pelvis. The arms are spread to increase or decrease the speed of the rotation.

25 m

200–270 m

Kickers
They are located at least 50 m from the top and the bottom of the slope.

COURSE

The slope ranges between 28° and 32°.

Control gates
Width: 8–15 m

Moguls
They are spaced about 3.5 m apart.

Finish line
Runs are timed by a photoelectric cell.

HOW AN AERIALS COMPETITION IS ORGANIZED

Skiers launch themselves into the air off a kicker to perform aerial acrobatics. Competitions consist of a qualifying round and finals. Two different jumps must be performed in each round. The skiers must submit a "flight plan" indicating which jumps they will perform and which kicker they will use. A maximum of three somersaults and five positions are allowed for straight jumps. Original maneuvers (new jumps) must first be submitted in writing to the official committee so that the difficulty can be rated.

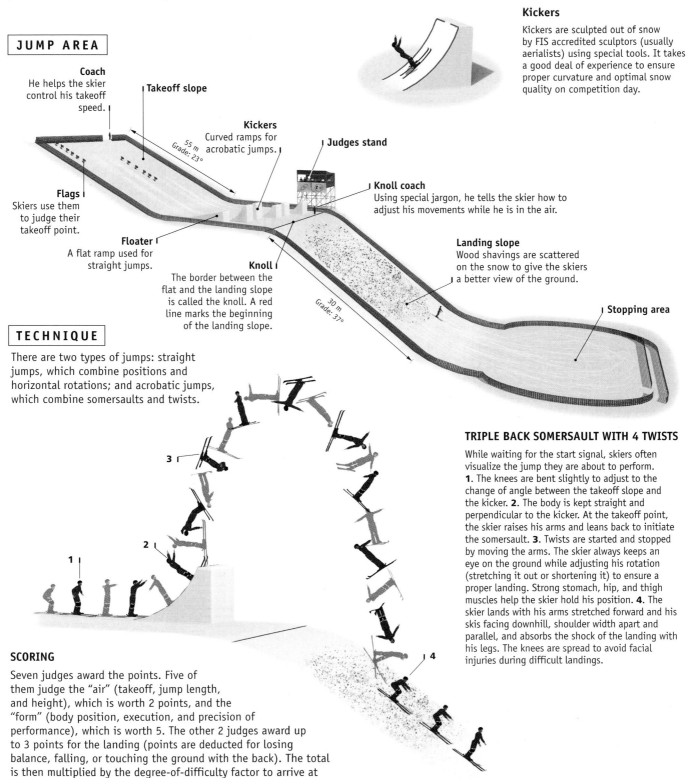

Kickers

Kickers are sculpted out of snow by FIS accredited sculptors (usually aerialists) using special tools. It takes a good deal of experience to ensure proper curvature and optimal snow quality on competition day.

JUMP AREA

Coach
He helps the skier control his takeoff speed.

Takeoff slope

Kickers
Curved ramps for acrobatic jumps.

55 m
Grade: 23°

Judges stand

Knoll coach
Using special jargon, he tells the skier how to adjust his movements while he is in the air.

Flags
Skiers use them to judge their takeoff point.

Floater
A flat ramp used for straight jumps.

Knoll
The border between the flat and the landing slope is called the knoll. A red line marks the beginning of the landing slope.

30 m
Grade: 37°

Landing slope
Wood shavings are scattered on the snow to give the skiers a better view of the ground.

Stopping area

TECHNIQUE

There are two types of jumps: straight jumps, which combine positions and horizontal rotations; and acrobatic jumps, which combine somersaults and twists.

TRIPLE BACK SOMERSAULT WITH 4 TWISTS

While waiting for the start signal, skiers often visualize the jump they are about to perform. **1.** The knees are bent slightly to adjust to the change of angle between the takeoff slope and the kicker. **2.** The body is kept straight and perpendicular to the kicker. At the takeoff point, the skier raises his arms and leans back to initiate the somersault. **3.** Twists are started and stopped by moving the arms. The skier always keeps an eye on the ground while adjusting his rotation (stretching it out or shortening it) to ensure a proper landing. Strong stomach, hip, and thigh muscles help the skier hold his position. **4.** The skier lands with his arms stretched forward and his skis facing downhill, shoulder width apart and parallel, and absorbs the shock of the landing with his legs. The knees are spread to avoid facial injuries during difficult landings.

SCORING

Seven judges award the points. Five of them judge the "air" (takeoff, jump length, and height), which is worth 2 points, and the "form" (body position, execution, and precision of performance), which is worth 5. The other 2 judges award up to 3 points for the landing (points are deducted for losing balance, falling, or touching the ground with the back). The total is then multiplied by the degree-of-difficulty factor to arrive at the final score.

HOW AN ACRO COMPETITION IS ORGANIZED

Acro consists of linked acrobatic maneuvers and steps, performed to music, with skis and poles, on a smooth, even slope. Competitors select their own music and choreography. Linked maneuvers are divided into three categories: spins, leverage moves, and somersaults. The various maneuvers are linked together by steps, performed according to the original choreography.

SCORING

Seven judges award points based on 2 criteria: technical merit (5 points) and artistic impression (5 points), with points being deducted for flaws in the performance. Harmony with the music, the variety of jumps, the choreography, and the fluidity of movements are the deciding factors.

Judges stand

ACRO SLOPE

The slope must be smooth and well groomed, with no bumps. Skiers usually start their performance at the top and finish at the bottom, near the gate, to make full use of the available surface.

35 m

150 m

Grade: approx. 24°

TECHNIQUE

A spin is a rotation made around the body's vertical axis while keeping the skis in contact with the ground. Leverage moves may or may not include a rotation around the body's vertical axis, with the skis not touching the ground. Somersaults are done with or without poles, with the skier's feet passing over his head.

Forward somersault

When done with poles, somersaults may include balancing on the poles before the skier's feet return to the ground.

EQUIPMENT

Aerial and mogul skis

Aerial and mogul skis are similar. The minimum length is 190 cm for men and 180 cm for women. The tips are flexible, and the tails are springy. The bottoms have no grooves, and the skis are cut straight to make it easier to start turns. Aerial skiers move their bindings forward about 4 cm to increase tail spring.

Acro skis

The minimum length is set at 81% of the skier's height (approx. 140 to 160 cm). Designed for easy pivoting, the bottoms are convex, with no grooves. The tails curve up to allow for backward steps and backsliding.

PROFILE OF A FREESTYLE SKIER

• The average height of a freestyle skier is approximately 1.72 m. Descents and jumps require pliancy, relaxation, flexibility, and endurance, along with solid technical mastery. Training is designed to get the skier into top shape by November, when the competitive season begins.

• Skiers can train on trampolines while wearing skis. To develop a sense of ease and spatial orientation while in the air, they practice jumping off kickers into water from May to October.

• High altitude workouts (in a thinner atmosphere) during summer ski camps are very effective for improving cardiovascular capacity, which is essential for moguls. It also helps skiers adjust to jet lag and the constant changes in altitude during the competitive season.

Helmet
A helmet is mandatory for aerial events.

Poles
In acro, poles must not exceed the skier's height. Poles used in moguls are shorter than normal (approximately 60 cm less than the skier's height). Aerial skiers do not use poles.

Tip

Ski suit
The suit allows the skier full freedom of movement.

Bindings
To protect the skiers, straps attaching the ski to the boot are not allowed. The bindings must have a brake to stops the ski from sliding if it comes off in a fall.

Tail

Jean-Luc Brassard (CAN)
A moguls expert, he entered the professional freestyle ski circuit in 1991, and went on to win the World Cup Grand Prix (1993, 1996, and 1997), the World Championships (1993 and 1997), and the Canadian Championships (1993 and 1995). He also won a Gold Medal at the Olympic Games in Lillehammer.

Nicolas Fontaine (CAN)
Co-champion at the 1992 Albertville Olympics, where aerials was a demonstration event, he won the freestyle World Championship and the World Cup in his category in 1997.

197

speed skiing

Michaël Prufer (FRA), gold medalist at the Albertville Olympics in 1992, where speed skiing was a demonstration sport

S peed skiing is a sliding sport whose origins, in relation to more conventional skiing, can be traced back to 1898, when a Californian named Tommy Todd shot down a hill at more than 130 km/h. The first official record registered with the International Ski Federation (FIS) dates back to 1931, when Italian skier Léo Gasperi was clocked at 136.6 km/h in St-Moritz, Switzerland. Speed skiing has been a professional sport, sanctioned by the FIS, since the 1960s. As much a spectacle as it is a sport, speed skiing is very popular in France, Italy, and Austria, and has attracted a growing number of enthusiasts in North America.

HOW A RACE IS ORGANIZED

Competition is open to men and women over 16 years of age. To qualify for a World Cup Pro event, competitors must have previously posted speeds of at least 180 km/h (170 km/h for women) at a previous official event. There are 3 categories of speed skiing: men, women, and production (using downhill ski equipment). The first day is dedicated to a mandatory training run, followed by 2 elimination rounds. In the first round, the racers start in order of their bib numbers. The starting order in the subsequent round is determined by the previously recorded times, with the slowest skier starting first. Before a race, the jury decides how many competitors will be eliminated after each round (those with the slowest times). The finals involve a single run, which takes place once the list of skiers has been reduced to 25 (5 for women). Setting a new world record automatically ends the competition in the category involved, regardless of how far the event has progressed.

TRACKS

The fastest tracks are in Europe, mainly in France. Races are usually held in March, so that surface preparation is not hampered by heavy snowfall. A winch is used to pull a grooming machine to the top of the track (because of the steep gradient) to even out the snow. The grooves created as a result of the grooming are erased by skiers who smooth out the snow on the track with the edges of their skis until the surface is completely flat. The track consists of 3 main areas: the acceleration area, the timing area, and the braking area. The drop is approximately 450 m over a total distance of 1,200 m. In the event of poor visibility or track conditions, or if winds exceed 15 km/h, the competition is postponed.

Run-up zone
A good run-up is a key factor in determining the skier's speed. Accelerating from 0 to 200 km/h in approximately 6 seconds, skiers anchor themselves to the ground and use their skis to control their trajectory. They reduce all possible sources of deceleration by keeping their skis flat on the ground and their bodies properly positioned. They "feel" the course more than they "see" it.

Timing area
As they approach the timing area, 11 or 12 seconds into their run, skiers reach or exceed 220 km/h. They are barely anchored to the ground—an air cushion is created between the skis and the snow—and they steer by playing on the air pressure and slight variations in position. They stiffen their muscles and momentarily hold their breath.

SCALE FOR AWARDING POINTS	
1st place	40 points
2nd place	34 points
3rd place	29 points
4th place	25 points
5th place	22 points

Acceleration area
At between 200 and 220 km/h, air pressure increases and the skis float. At these speeds, the skiers are skiing on air as much as on snow, correcting their position according to how the air streams off their bodies.

Slope
35–45°

450 m

100 m

30 m 20 m

Safety zone

Braking area
Once they cross the red line at the end of the timing area, speed skiers straighten out by shifting their weight forward and stretching their arms out for maximum air resistance. They ski 2 very wide turns to slow to a complete stop. The entire run lasts approximately 20 seconds.

Slope: maximum 2.7°

450 m

Clock
Two photoelectric cells, placed 100 m apart (measured to the nearest cm), ensure that the skiers' speeds are accurately recorded to the nearest 1/1000th of a second.

LIST OF EVENTS

In addition to national and European championships, record-breaking attempts, and demonstration events, each year top speed skiers participate in the World Pro Cup, which consists of 4 to 6 meets on different tracks. Participants accumulate points at each meet, and the skier with the most points at the end of the season is declared world champion. The season gets underway in February in the United States, and normally ends in April in Sweden.

EQUIPMENT

The heavier the skier, the faster he or she will ski. Some speed skiers weigh down their helmets or poles with small lead beads. However, in order to ensure that the competition is fair, the equipment is subject to a weight limit.

Regulation tracks

In addition to the tracks where World Cup events are held, there are others in France (La Plagne), Italy (Cervini), Finland, Sweden (Irde), Switzerland, the United States (Timberline, Mount Hood, Snowmass), and Canada (Blackcomb, Whistler, Sun Peaks).

SPEED SKIER PROFILE
• Off season: skiers must train daily. Muscle building and running (for speed and endurance) are the main components of the regimen. During the season, skiers focus on practicing the sport.
• Some skiers rely on specialized motivators who help them start the competition season in the best possible psychological condition.
• Performance in speed skiing is closely linked to technological developments in equipment: materials that allow better air flow, enhanced aerodynamic profile of helmets and poles, and working on skiing position in a wind tunnel.

Helmet
The helmet considerably enhances the skier's aerodynamics. Made from fiberglass or composite materials, it is perfectly adapted to the skier's morphology. The front of the helmet is often pierced, providing ventilation so that the visor does not fog up. The back of the helmet is equipped with a detachable profile, designed to break off if the skier falls. In accordance with regulations, the entire helmet must be able to fit through a 40 cm ring from any angle.

Maximum weight: 2 kg

Suits
They are often brightly colored, making them less sensitive to the sun's rays, thus preventing the fabric from heating up and expanding. Made from plasticized synthetic fibers to ensure optimal air penetration, the suit molds snugly to the skier's body. Underneath the suit, skiers wear 3/4 length underwear, and a high density foam dorsal protection pad, which is between 0.5 cm and 3 cm thick.

Fairings
Made from compressed foam, fairings are slipped under the suit to improve airflow without causing air turbulence around the legs. The distance from the front of the leg to the trailing edge of the fairing may not exceed 30 cm.

Profiled handles
They provide better air penetration.

Boots
Recent model, normally rear entry boots, they are made more aerodynamic when attached to the bottom of the suit with fabric or adhesive tape.
Maximum weight: 6 kg per pair

Bindings
Production model bindings are used. They cannot be modified or covered with aerodynamic profiles.

Skis
Skis must be between 2.20 and 2.40 m long. The tip is practically nonexistent, the bases are very thick, and the edges are not sharp so as to avoid abrupt turns, which are extremely dangerous at 200 km/h.

Maximum weight: 15 kg per pair with bindings.

Poles
Use of poles is mandatory. Their shape is not regulated, although it is carefully studied to avoid creating turbulence. Two designs are used: a curved design that follows the contour of the hips and is used only to help the skier keep his or her balance; and the Z shape, which allows the skier to lock his or her position by leaning into the curve of the pole.

Maximum weight: 2 kg per pair

Philippe Billy (FRA)
First man to ski at 230 km/h at top speed, he established a world record in 1997: 243.902 km/h.

Harry Egger (AUT)
World record holder with a speed of 248.105 km/h, set May 2, 1999, at Les Arcs in the French Alps.

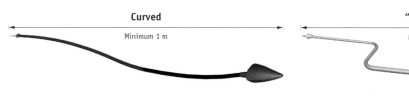
Curved
Minimum 1 m

"Z" shaped
Minimum 1 m

ski jumping

Championship ski jump ramp in Falun, Sweden, in 1954

Ski jumping involves skiing down a ramp and then flying as far as possible through the air, with a certain style and under the scrutiny of judges. The sport was born in 19th century Norway as one of the events at winter carnivals. It gained official recognition as a sport in 1892, with the creation of the King's Cup, which was awarded by the Norwegian royal family to the winner of the annual meet at Holmenkollen. It spread to North America, where its acceptance helped the sport expand worldwide. Recognized by the International Ski Federation (FIS), ski jumping was on the program at the first Winter Olympics in 1924 at Chamonix, France, and today remains one of the most prestigious events for northern Europeans. Although there is no women's ski jumping at the Olympic level, women do compete in World Cup meets.

HOW A MEET IS ORGANIZED

Ski jumpers compete in 3 events: individual jumps on a large (120 m) and normal (90 m) hill, and a team competition on the large hill (120 m). In the individual events, each skier is allowed 2 jumps, and receives a score based on distance and style. For the first jump, the order of the skiers is determined by drawing names. For the second jump, the skier with the lowest score jumps first. The winner of the event is the skier with the highest score after 2 jumps.

The score is calculated by adding the points obtained for style and for distance.

Five judges award a maximum of 20 points for style, based on precision, control during takeoff, and the skier's position while in flight, on the landing, and while decelerating. Style points are deducted if a jumper falls. The skier's highest and lowest scores are not included in the final total.

The distance of a jump is measured from the takeoff point to the midpoint between the jumper's feet upon landing. A skier who reaches the hill's K point receives 60 points. Points are deducted for landing short of the K point, and added on for landing past it. Each meter is worth 2 points on the 90 m hill, and 1.8 points on the 120 m hill.

THE K POINT

The K point marks the length of an ideal, theoretical jump. It represents the recommended landing point, which is used as a reference and is located where the slope begins to flatten out. The distance between the K point and the end of the ramp is 90 m on a normal hill, and 120 m on a large hill. In the 2002 Winter Olympics, a ski flying event, with a K point somewhere between 170 and 185 m, will replace the normal hill event.

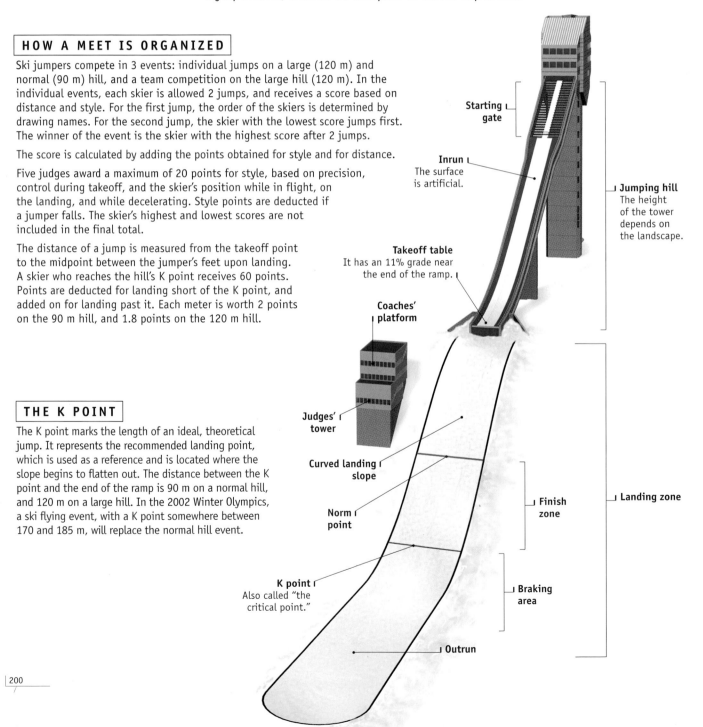

Starting gate

Inrun
The surface is artificial.

Jumping hill
The height of the tower depends on the landscape.

Takeoff table
It has an 11% grade near the end of the ramp.

Coaches' platform

Judges' tower

Curved landing slope

Norm point

K point
Also called "the critical point."

Finish zone

Landing zone

Braking area

Outrun

TECHNIQUE

From starting gate to landing, a ski jump lasts between 5 and 8 seconds. During that brief period, jumpers are expected to maintain both stance and balance: arms close to the body, skis horizontal and spread in a V shape during flight, then the telemark position, and a controlled outrun until they come to a stop at the safety fence. The judges deduct style points for uneven skis, flapping arms during flight to retain balance, and premature preparation for landing.

1. Inrun

The jumper drops into an aerodynamic crouch, and maintains that position until the takeoff point. Skiers attain speeds of over 80 km/h on K90 hills, and over 90 km/h on K120 hills.

2. Takeoff

This is the critical point of the jump: taking off too early or too late can substantially reduce distance. The jumper has to stretch out immediately upon reaching the takeoff point. The skier's body straightens out very quickly and leans forward.

3. Flight

The skier leans forward toward the tip of the skis to reduce drag. The tips are spread, creating a V shape to provide greater lift and distance for the flight. Between takeoff and landing, the skier is in the air for 2 or 3 seconds.

4. Landing

The force of the landing is the equivalent of 3 times the skier's weight. The telemark position (one leg slightly in front of the other) allows the shock to be absorbed by the forward leg and flow through the entire body before the skier is steady enough to start braking.

Espen Bredesen (NOR)
Large hill world champion in 1993. Normal hill Olympic champion at the 1994 Lillehammer Games in his native country. He also won the World Cup that year. Holder of the all-time record for the longest jump: 209 m in Planica, Slovenia.

Matti Nykänen (FIN)
Winner of the gold medal in the 1982 World Championship, and large hill champion at the 1984 Winter Olympics. Four years later, he accomplished an incredible Olympic feat by winning three golds: large hill, small hill, and team competition. He was also World Cup champion in 1986 and 1988.

SKI JUMPER PROFILE

- Ski jumpers who compete in international meets start jumping at about the age of 5: the best way to train is to gradually jump off higher and higher hills.

- Powerful leg muscles provide greater thrust at takeoff: to build them up, most skiers walk back up the hill after every training jump.

- Exercises to improve technique—perfecting the inrun and timing of the takeoff, position during flight, landings—are usually done on smaller hills to make concentration easier.

- During the summer, ski jumpers train on the same hills as in the winter. Covered with nylon and constantly sprayed, they are at least as slippery and as safe as when they are covered by snow.

EQUIPMENT

Jump suit
Made of a foam lined synthetic fabric, its thickness has shrunk from 12 to 8 mm to reduce wind resistance by about 30% and increase the length of jumps. Officials carefully inspect the suits before every jump.

Protective helmet

Gloves

Ski boots
Although more flexible than the boots used for downhill skiing, they nonetheless keep the ankle stiff; sprains caused by poor landings are the most common injury among ski jumpers.

Skis
Longer and wider than downhill skis, their maximum length is 80 cm more than the skier's height, and their maximum weight is 7.27 kg. They are usually made of wood and fiberglass. The skis have no edges and there are 5 lengthwise grooves along the bottom that increase stability during the run. Depending on snow conditions, the jumpers may use ski wax to increase their speed during the inrun.

Bindings
Their distance from the tip cannot be more than 57% of the ski's total length. The heel has free play, so that the skier can lean forward and attain the ideal angle during flight.

cross country skiing

The objective of cross country skiing competitions is to ski a set distance in the minimum time. The origin of cross country skiing goes back at least to the third millennium B.C., and the oldest skis discovered were found in Scandinavia. Born of the need to travel over icy and snowy surfaces before it became a sport, cross country skiing is probably the most popular form of skiing in the world. Competitions took place in Norway in the late 17th century, and many races were held in the 19th century. It was not until 1900, however, that cross country skiing was recognized as a sports event. The International Ski Federation (FIS) regulates the sport since 1924, and that same year, it was included on the Olympic program in 1924 in Chamonix, France, but races for women were not included until 1952.

Winner (GER) crossing the finish line for the cross country race at the Berlin Olympics in 1936

THE COMPETITION

There are 2 styles of cross country skiing, classical and freestyle, and both are on the Olympic program. The sport is evolving, however, and every 4 years the styles alternate at the Winter Olympics for the various races: classical, freestyle, pursuit, and relay. A new event, the sprint, was added to the World Cup in 1995 and to the Olympic program in 2002. A cross country course must include equal portions of ascents, descents, and flat areas. The easiest part must be at the beginning of the course, and the most difficult part must be in the middle. For courses of less than 30 km, the total climb must be between 600 and 900 m for women, and between 900 and 1,200 m for men. For most races, the start order is drawn by lot and the competitors leave at 30 second intervals. Skiers must follow a set course that has a series of checkpoints. For individual races, the skis are marked before the start so that they cannot be changed during the race. Races are against the clock, except for relays, the second part of the pursuit, and the sprint, in which the winner is the first to cross the finish line.

TECHNIQUES FOR CLASSICAL STYLE

Skiers use the traditional diagonal stride and double poling on trails that have a track. Average speed among the best skiers can be more than 25 km/h.

DIAGONAL STRIDES
The skis must always be parallel and stay in the tracks, except in turns. Herringbone strides are used for climbing when the incline is steep.

1. Pushing phase

The movement starts with a quick extension of the leg to push off, followed by the hip. The body leans forward and the ankle of the supporting leg is bent. The opposite arm and leg are then fully extended.

2. Gliding phase

The shoulder and arm are stretched forward to plant the pole on the opposite side from the propelling leg. The body forms a straight line at the end of the push and the weight is transferred to the supporting ski as the other foot moves forward.

3. End of movement

The arms and poles return to the starting position.

DOUBLE POLING

Used for slight hills and on the flat. Both legs slide forward together, as the arms propel the skier. The movement begins with the body extending up and forward before the poles are planted. The push on the poles is started by bending the body and then the arms, forearms, and wrists. The skier lets himself fall forward. The body remains bent until the push with the poles is completed; then the arms are quickly brought forward.

TECHNIQUES FOR FREESTYLE

Freestyle uses all movements, including diagonal striding. It has, however, become synonymous with "skating." Freestyle was included in the Olympics for the first time in Calgary in 1988. Average speed among the best skiers can reach 30 km/h.

SKATING STRIDE

The skier propels himself with both legs in a skating style. Sliding one leg forward, he pushes off on the other leg, which is placed at an angle to obtain a better push-off. He pushes sideways, off the inside edge of the ski. The slower the skier is going, the more propulsion is gained from the upper body.

PURSUIT

The pursuit combines a classical race (10 km for men and 5 km for women) and a freestyle race (15 km for men and 10 km for women). The finish order in the classical race is used to determine the start order for the second race. The first competitor across the finish line wins.

RELAY

Teams of 4 skiers race over a course of 4 x 10 km for men and 4 x 5 km for women. The first skiers in each team have a group start. The first 2 stages are skied in classical style, and the last 2 in freestyle. The exchange between team members must take place in a rectangular area 30 m long, and the arriving skier must touch the teammate's hand. The first team to cross the finish line wins.

OFFICIATING

At the winter Olympics, there is a 5 member jury: the technical delegate who is the president of the jury, the chief of competition, the chief of course, and 2 other members are designated by the FIS. The jury makes sure that the competition complies with the FIS rules; its decisions are based on a majority vote. Five minutes before the competition starts, the officials must have taken off their skis and taken their assigned places on the course.

RACES AT THE OLYMPICS
Styles alternate every 4 years

	Men	Women
Classical	10 km	5 km
	30 km	15 km
Freestyle	50 km	30 km
Pursuit	25 km	15 km
Relay	4 x 10 km	4 x 5 km
Sprint	1,500 m	1,500 m

EQUIPMENT

Poles
Made of graphite and Kevlar, they are designed to be rigid and light. They are thinner at the ends to make the recovery movement easier and quicker; they are slightly longer for freestyle skiing.

Bindings
They must be placed so that the skier's weight is at the point on the ski that ensures best contact with the snow.

Ski hat

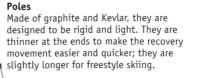

Yelena Valbe (RUS)
She won 14 world championships gold medals, 41 victories in World Cup races, and 5 gold medals at the world championships in Trondheim, Norway, in 1997.

Bjorn Daehlie (NOR)
The skier with the most Winter Olympics medals—a total of 12, including 8 gold. He has won 36 World Cup races. He was also winner of the World Cup in 1993, 1994, 1996, 1997 and 1999 and came in second in 1992, and 1995.

Waxing
Special kinds of wax are applied to the running surface of the skis. In classical style, a gliding wax is applied to the shovel and heel of the ski, and a grip wax is applied to the center of the ski, underneath the binding. In freestyle, a gliding wax is applied on the entire running surface of the ski. Different waxes are used to match different snow conditions.

One piece suit
Made of Lycra, it must be form fitting and light, since a skier in constant motion generates a great deal heat.

SKIS

Light and solid, they are often made of woven carbon fibers with a honeycomb structure. Although skis are no longer made entirely of wood, it is always used to some extent because of its mechanical qualities. Skis are always taller than the skier; the heavier the skier, the stronger the instep must be.

Freestyle
They sometimes have a wider shovel to facilitate the skating movement, and the tips are less curved upward than are those for classical style. The harder the snow, the shorter the skis used.

1.75–2 m

Classical style
It is very important that the skis be rigid. They are longer than those used in freestyle to distribute the skier's weight more evenly.

Running surface
Identical in freestyle and classical skis, it is made of plastic and graphite with anti-static qualities for better gliding.

Up to 2.30 m

BOOTS
Only the front of the boot is attached to the ski.

Freestyle
They provide good lateral control and ankle support. The sole is fairly rigid and a movable shell encloses the ankle.

Classical style
They are flexible and provide good ankle mobility.

PROFILE OF THE SKIER

- Cross country skiing is a sport that requires endurance and muscular power, since skiers may have to race long distances in competitions.

- A cross country skier's summer training consists of developing endurance by running, cycling, roller skiing, and glacier skiing.

- Cross country skiing requires strong and well developed technical skills. Psychological preparation also plays a major role. Elite athletes are able to undertake extreme exertion.

snowboarding

The increasingly popular sport of snowboarding involves sliding down snow covered surfaces on a board equipped with bindings, which is steered by flexing the knees. This sport first emerged in the 1960s, when Sherwin Popper, an American, had the idea of attaching two skis together. The first official competition was held in Leadville, Colorado, in 1981, and the International Snowboard Association (ISA) was created in 1989, before becoming the International Snowboard Federation in 1991. In 1995, the IOC decided to make snowboarding an Olympic sport and, despite the existence of the ISF, the responsibility for regulating this new sport was entrusted the International Ski Federation (FIS). Snowboarding made its Olympic Games debut in 1998, in Nagano, Japan. The ISF organized the first World Championship in 1992 and the first World Cup Series in 1994. Competitions are open to both men and women.

In 1998, at the Nagano Games, Ross Rebagliati (CAN) became the first Olympic giant slalom gold medal winner

LIST OF EVENTS

There are 4 types of events: freestyle, alpine, freeride, and boardercross. The men's and women's half pipe competition and the men's and women's giant slalom events were featured at the Nagano Games. The parallel giant slalom and half pipe will be featured in the 2002 Olympic Games in Salt Lake City. In freestyle, or acrobatic snowboarding, riders perform spectacular acrobatic maneuvers inside special snow ramps called half pipes. Alpine snowboarding, which resembles downhill skiing, includes slalom, giant slalom, and parallel, or duel, slalom events. Boarders race against the clock, which requires extensive physical and mental preparation. Freeride is practiced off course, and involves adapting one's style to the environment. In boardercross, boarders start in groups of 4 or 6 on a course that includes moguls, raised turns, and jumps.

HOW A HALF PIPE COMPETITION IS ORGANIZED

The half pipe event is accompanied by music, and the boarder must execute acrobatic maneuvers (jumps, twists, and aerial maneuvers) while going down the half pipe, alternating from one side to the other. Four to six judges, along with one head judge, award each boarder a score out of 10, taking into consideration the following criteria: non-rotation maneuvers, rotation maneuvers, height, and overall performance.

COMPETITION SITE

The half pipe resembles a pipe that has been cut in half lengthwise.

Start

3–4 m

13–17 m

Judges' stand

Finish area

100–120 m
incline: 18°

TECHNIQUES

There are many aerial maneuvers in snowboarding, which are often inspired by skateboarding maneuvers, including the Backside air (jumping while holding the edge of the board), the Corkscrew (twisting), and the McTwist.

McTWIST

This movement, invented by Mike McGill in the early 1980s, involves rotations of 540° (around the vertical axis) and 360° (around the lateral axis). **1.** The move starts with a strong rotation of the head and torso in the direction of the feet, combined with a swift body motion toward the edge of the board, followed by flipping the legs upward. **2.** While in flight, the rider assumes a tuck position, the head and torso continue to rotate toward the edge of the board, and the hand grips the inside edge of the board. **3.** Once the rotation is complete, the boarder releases the board and assumes a standing position. He is then in the proper position to slide to the other side of the half pipe. The shock of the landing is absorbed by flexing the knees.

HOW A GIANT SLALOM COMPETITION IS ORGANIZED

The race is timed in 2 segments, during which the boarder must negotiate a course containing a series of triangular gates, without missing any. If the boarder falls, he or she is not automatically disqualified unless a gate is missed. The course is designed symmetrically to ensure a fair start for both goofies and regulars (in snowboarding, a regular boarder is one who rides with the left foot forward, while a rider whose right foot is forward is called a goofy). Before the race, boarders study the course during the inspection period. The distance between the gates allows the rider to execute long curves, where efficiency is the key to keeping unnecessary movements and lost time to a minimum.

TECHNIQUES

Backside turn

With her back perpendicular to the ground, her hips facing the obstacle, and her upper body turned outward, the boarder tucks her body into a low, leaning position to guide herself through the turn. She spreads her arms for optimal balance.

Frontside turn

The boarder leans toward the ground, flexes her knees, and hugs the inside pole to turn at a very high speed. Her eyes focus on the next gate to anticipate the edge change and the upcoming curve.

PARALLEL GIANT SLALOM COURSE

This event, which will be included in the 2002 Winter Olympic Games, takes place on a course with a vertical drop of between 120 and 250 m. After the timed qualification rounds, the 16 boarders (8 in women's events) with the best times meet in the final elimination round.

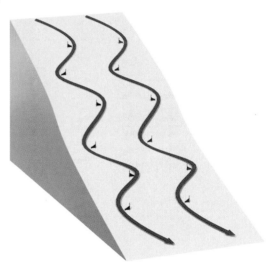

Gate

There must be at least 7 to 15 m between gates.

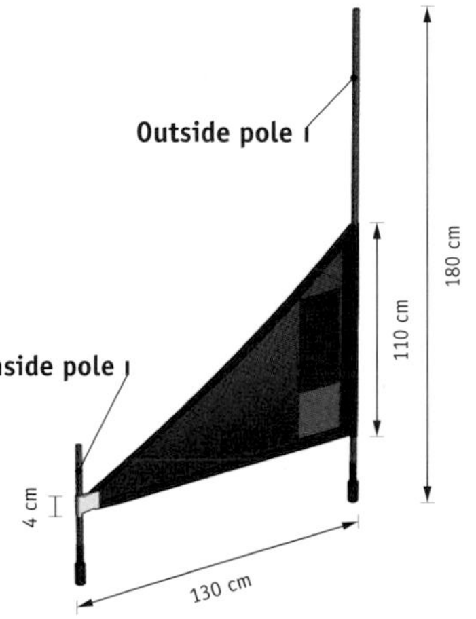

Outside pole

180 cm

110 cm

Inside pole

4 cm

130 cm

EQUIPMENT

Snowboards have greatly evolved since the 1980s. Snowboarding has benefited from the technological advances that have taken place in skiing, specifically in the use of better performing materials. Today, snowboards stand out for their versatility and their ability to perform off or on trails, and on packed or powdered snow. The narrower the board, the faster it goes, and the more sensitive it is to turns.

1977

1980

Freestyle board

Used for half pipe events, it is ideal for smooth jumps and landings. It has an effective edge of 120 cm, and the nose and tail are identical to allow for takeoffs and landings in either direction.

Alpine board

Designed for high speeds, it is narrow and rigid, and it widens slightly at the nose. The effective edge can measure as much as 140 cm. It is used with plate bindings and hard boots for maximum stability.

24 cm

134–158 cm

Plate (hard boot) binding
Used with hard boots for alpine boarding.

Tail

Nose

18–20 cm

145–175 cm

Soft binding
Used with flexible boots for acrobatic and all-terrain boarding.

Aluminum alloy to protect the tips of the board.

Edge
Steel edge along the sole of the board—not to be confused with the "effective edge," which is the part of the board that is in contact with the snow. The longer the board, the more stable it is at high speeds, and the better it performs in turns.

Karine Ruby (FRA)
She won the FIS World Cup in 1996, 1997 and 1998 in the overall placing and in slalom and giant slalom. She also won the first Olympic medal in alpine snowboarding.

Flexible boot
Flexible and comfortable, this boot slows the transmission of body movement to the board. It is intended for freestyle and freeride boarding.

Hard boot
Ideal for precision and performance, it allows for immediate transmission of body movements to the board. It is used in alpine competitions.

Ross Powers (USA)
Currently ranked first by the ISF in halfpipe, he won the World Cup in 1996, when he was 17, and again in 1999. He was also a bronze medalist at the 1998 Olympics.

Helmet
The helmet is mandatory for speed events.

Suit
The suit is made from synthetic fibers, and molds to the shape of the body.

Ski goggles

Glove

Shin guards

PROFILE OF A SNOWBOARDER

- Training involves trampoline exercises, inline skating, skateboarding, and "Swiss ball." Alpine snowboarding champions follow regular training similar to that followed by skiers. Training includes muscle building, stretching, and appropriate diet. Training begins in the summer, on glaciers, to give boarders power and toning.

- Snowboarding is a state of mind that fosters freedom of spirit and movement, and has become a constant on the landscape of winter sports.

biathlon

Magnar Solberg (3) (NOR), gold medalist at the Grenoble Olympics (France) in 1968, completing the 20 km course in 1 h 13 m 45.9 sec.

Biathlon combines cross country skiing and small bore rifle shooting. Cave paintings from more than 3,000 years ago portray hunters on skis with bows and arrows. In 1767, on the border between Norway and Sweden, border patrols organized the first races. A demonstration sport at the Winter Olympics in Chamonix in 1924, biathlon was officially integrated into the Union internationale de pentathlon moderne in 1956. The first world championships took place at Saalfelden, Austria, in 1958, and biathlon was an official event at the Squaw Valley Olympics in 1960. It was reserved for military competitors until 1978, when .22 caliber rifles were adopted and the target distance was reduced to 50 m, making it easier for civilians to train and compete. More types of races were added (individual and relay), and women competed for the first time at the world championships in 1984 and at the Olympics in 1992. The International Biathlon Union (IBU) was founded in 1993. A new event, the Pursuit, was included in the world championships and the World Cup in 1997 and will be part of the Olympics in 2002.

THE COMPETITION

Athletes ski a cross country course against the clock, during which they stop to shoot at targets. In the shooting phases, athletes alternate between prone and standing positions and must use a limited number of bullets. Each missed target adds time penalties to the running time of the ski phase, which competitors must make up in different ways, depending on the race. The winner is the biathlete (or team) with the lowest total time. Individual races and sprints have staggered starts: the competitors succeed each other by an interval of 30 seconds or 1 minute in an order drawn by lot. In the relay, the teams are composed of 4 biathletes: all first team members start together, finish their leg, and make a relay to the next teammate by touching him on the body or the rifle. In a pursuit race, the winner of the preceding sprint starts first and is followed by the other competitors at intervals equivalent to how far behind each was to the sprint winner.

FACILITIES

There is a shooting range with a penalty loop (150 m oval track) and a number of ski trail loops between the ranges. The total elevation on a 10 km course (men's sprint) must be 300 to 450 m; on a 20 km course (men's individual), 600 to 750 m.

RACE	DISTANCE AND NO. OF SHOOTING PHASES	PENALTY
Individual	20 km (15 km women) 4 shooting phases	1 minute per missed target
Sprint	10 km (7.5 km women) 2 shooting phases	1 extra loop (150 m) per missed target
Relay	7.5 km and 2 shooting phases per teammate	1 extra loop (150 m) per missed target
Pursuit	12.5 km (10 km women) 4 shooting phases	1 extra loop (150 m) per missed target
Group start	15 km (12.5 km women) 4 shooting phases	1 extra loop (150 m) per missed target

Shooting lanes

In races with a staggered start, skiers can choose whichever lane they want. During group starts and in relays, the target number must correspond to the competitor's bib number. For safety reasons, no competitor may handle his weapon until he has completely stopped and put his ski poles down; failure to do so will cause disqualification. In the standing position, both skis must be on the shooting mat before the first shot is taken.

width: 2.5–3.0 m

When they are skiing, the athletes carry their rifle on their back.

Lane numbers

Nonslip shooting mat

Shooting range referees
They make sure that the shooting phases are conducted legally. There may be up to 50 referees in the competition area, depending on the size of the event.

TECHNIQUE

Whatever the shooting position, the biathlete must keep both skis on and can use no support. The main difficulty for the athlete is to slow his heart rate so that he can aim accurately. Each shot is made between 2 breaths to ensure maximum stability. Athletes try to gain time by limiting the number of breaths taken between each shot.

SHOOTING IN PRONE POSITION

The rifle may touch the hands, shoulder, and cheek. The wrist of the supporting arm must be noticeably above the ground. The other arm may touch the ground for a maximum of 10 cm between the elbow and the wrist. It takes 25–35 seconds to complete the shooting phase.

EQUIPMENT

The skis and poles are the same as those used for cross country skiing. The .22 caliber rifle may be loaded with a magazine (5 bullets) or manually (extra bullets).

SHOOTING IN STANDING POSITION

As he approaches the shooting range, the athlete must slow down to rest his legs and arms before standing still to shoot. The rifle may touch the hands, cheek, shoulder, and chest. It takes 30–35 seconds to complete the shooting phase.

Gloves
The right index finger (for a right handed shot) is often perforated. Athletes may take a glove off to feel the trigger when they shoot and put it back on without losing skiing time.

Skis
They must be at least as long as the athlete's heigh less 4 cm. There is no maximum length.

Poles
Their total length, including tip, must not be greater than the athlete's height.

BIATHLETE PROFILE

- On average 25 to 30 years old, biathletes are in exceptional physical condition: sprints (10 km) are run in 23 min and 20 km races in about 55 min. Because accuracy of shooting is linked to heart rate, they increase their speed of recovery by developing their endurance and respiratory capacity.

- Because disappointment on the shooting range is a very important psychological aspect of the sport, many athletes work on their concentration with specialized psychologists.

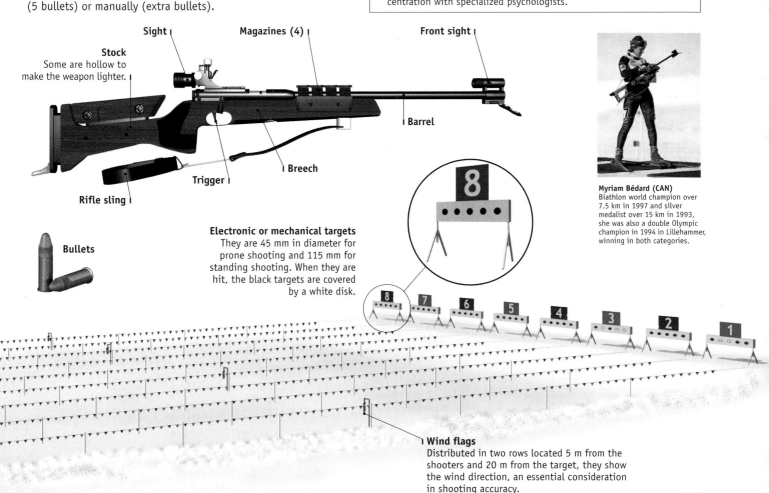

Stock
Some are hollow to make the weapon lighter.

Sight

Magazines (4)

Front sight

Barrel

Breech

Trigger

Rifle sling

Bullets

Electronic or mechanical targets
They are 45 mm in diameter for prone shooting and 115 mm for standing shooting. When they are hit, the black targets are covered by a white disk.

Myriam Bédard (CAN)
Biathlon world champion over 7.5 km in 1997 and silver medalist over 15 km in 1993, she was also a double Olympic champion in 1994 in Lillehammer, winning in both categories.

Wind flags
Distributed in two rows located 5 m from the shooters and 20 m from the target, they show the wind direction, an essential consideration in shooting accuracy.

Nordic combined

A discipline reserved for male athletes, Nordic Combined is a sport that includes ski jumping and cross country skiing. It was introduced in Norway in the mid 19th century. Ski jumping and long cross country treks were part of the daily routine for military officers patrolling the borders of this vast land. In response to the age old dispute between ski jumpers and cross country skiers, each claiming that their sport was more demanding, a competition called "Nordic Combined" was introduced. This event boasts many practitioners, and it was one of the original events at the first Winter Olympics, held in Chamonix in 1924. World championships are held every year, and a team event was added at the 1988 Winter Olympics in Calgary.

Martin Crawford, captain of the American team, in flight at the Olympics in Cortina (Italy) in 1956

HOW A COMPETITION IS ORGANIZED

The event is held over two days, with the jumping taking place on the first day. Each skier performs three jumps, and the two best results are counted. The cross country ski race is held on the second day. The individual race is 15 km long, and the team race consists of 4 legs of 5 km each. The winner of the Nordic combined event is the athlete with the best combined results for both events.

INDIVIDUAL JUMPING

The competition is held on a 90 m jumping hill. Points are awarded for distance and technique, with the distance calculated according to the K Point, which is located 90 m from the end of the jump where the slope ends. A jumper who reaches the K Point earns 60 points, along with an additional 1.6 points for each extra meter. A jumper who does not reach this point is penalized 1.6 points for every meter that he falls short. Athletes normally jump with their skis in a "V" position, rather than parallel. A jumper can reach speeds of 80 km/h during the two second jump. The jumper bends his knees when he lands, in order to absorb an impact equivalent to three times his weight. The distance is measured from the start line to the center point—between the skier's feet—at the time of landing. Five judges in the tower, 20 judges on the track, a distance supervisor, a starting judge, and a technical representative ensure that the event runs smoothly.

V jump

INDIVIDUAL CROSS COUNTRY SKIING

The starting order for the 15 km individual cross country skiing event is determined by the results of the jumping competition using the Gundersen formula, which converts points earned during the event into seconds. This table has been used during major competitions since 1985, and allows spectators to easily follow the progress of the competition, since the front-runner in the cross country ski race is also the leader of the entire competition. For example, if skier B is 1.5 points behind skier A after the jumping phase, he starts 10 seconds after skier A. All styles are permitted, although the majority of skiers use the "freestyle," or "skating step" style, instead of the classic "skiing in the grooves" style. Skiers are timed to the tenth of a second. A starting judge, who is assisted by 2 officials, a head timekeeper, and a team of between 2 and 10 timekeepers ensure that the race runs smoothly.

Skating step style

TEAM RACE

The team race takes place on a 20 km course, and each member of the team (2 or 4 skiers) skis either 5 or 10 km. Starting positions are determined by the points accumulated by each team during the jumping event, and team members change at a specific point. Physical contact is not necessary for the changeover.

Kenji Ogiwara (JPN)
Winner of the Nordic combined World Cup in 1993, 1994, and 1995, he won the individual event at the world championships in 1993 and 1997, and the team event in 1993 and 1995. He was also the team Olympic champion in 1992 and 1994.

PROFILE OF A SKIER

- All Nordic Combined athletes have the characteristics required to practice both disciplines. Jumps require courage, concentration, coordination, and an excellent mastery of movement.

- Cross country skiing requires stamina and strength, particularly in the legs.

- Jumpers must have the ability to "feel" the wind, and to adjust according to its direction and strength.

Mountain Sports

rock climbing

Media coverage of climbing owes much to the Frenchman Patrick Edlinger, who popularized the sport in the early 1980s. He won the first professional competition, the International Sport-Climbing, which took place at Snowbird, United States, in 1988.

A variant of mountain climbing—climbing on rocks, snow, or ice, usually at high altitude—rock climbing consists of climbing small boulders, rocky cliffs, rock walls several hundred meters high, or artificial walls with bare hands and light equipment. The sport was created in the late 19th century and was first practiced with limited, handmade equipment around the great mountain-climbing centers in Germany, England, Austria, France, and Italy. Two styles quickly developed: aid climbing, in which equipment was used for both upward progress and climber safety, and free climbing, in which equipment is for safety only. Free climbing, the more popular form, has several specialties, including bouldering, indoor climbing, solo climbing, and sport climbing. Improved safety and climbing equipment and training techniques have made the activity more accessible and popular. From the cliffs of Yosemite Park in the United States, to Verdon Gorge in France, to sites in Australia and Spain, rock climbing is now a worldwide activity. Competitions are open to both men and women. Associations and national federations are members of The International Mountaineering and Climbing Federation (UIAA), which governs the sport.

THE COMPETITION

The objective is to climb the highest and the fastest in the shortest amount of time. There are 2 categories of competition: classical and speed.

- In classical competitions, the routes are designed to be difficult. The order of start is drawn by lot, and climbers have between 30 seconds and 1 minute to choose a route. The time limit is 2 minutes so that climbers are encouraged not to waste time. Points are awarded for style, and routes are designed with variable and progressive difficulty.

- In speed competitions, climbers are timed in a first climb then matched in pairs—the fastest with the slowest. They climb identical walls at the same time, and the one who reaches the top first wins. As soon as a competitor reaches the top, a light on her wall turns on and a light on the second wall is disabled, so that there is no confusion about who has won. Generally, competitions take place with a pulley attached to a belaying beam or ring at the top, on artificial climbing walls.

THE GOALS

Freestyle climbing, the more popular style, is divided into 3 categories:

- Bouldering: climbing on blocks or boulders about 5 m high, generally without a rope.

- Top roping, in which the climber is attached to a pulley with a rope, on walls about 25 m high.

- Lead climbing, which has 2 forms: sport climbing or aid climbing with equipment on walls about 100 m high (with pre-installed fixed protections), and traditional free climbing on surfaces of unlimited length, using holds.

Competitions take place on outdoor and indoor artificial structures. Increasingly popular with spectators, they are held at all levels, including an annual World Cup and world championships every 2 years.

FREESTYLE CLIMBING TECHNIQUES

Lead climbing

Two or more climbers are linked together to climb. The most experienced climber ascends first.

Lead climbing on rock faces more than 25 m high

1. The lead climber, belayed by the follower, climbs and installs the protections required to avoid a fall to the ground.

2. The lead climber installs clips, belays himself, and takes up the slack in the rope as the follower ascends.

3. The follower, belayed from above by the lead climber, collects the clips and protections as he climbs.

Descent by rappelling

This technique allows the climber to descend safely from one wall to another using a double rope attached to a rock face or an anchor. The rope slides through a figure 8 descender.

KNOTS

There are a great variety of knots, essential for safety, as they permit braking, belaying, attaching a rope, etc.

Figure 8
The most-used knot, it is simple to make and solid.

Prusik knot
Belayer for rappelling

Clove hitch
Enables the climber to belay himself directly with the rope.

Belaying beam and anchor
They support belaying ropes at the belay point.

PULLEY CLIMBING TECHNIQUE

This technique is used on rocks or artificial climbing walls about 25 m in length. The climbers take turns climbing. Energy and balance are the basis for climbing movements. Mastery of techniques and holds is essential for effective, safe climbs.

HANDHOLDS AND FOOTHOLDS

There are many handholds and footholds. Among the most popular handholds are open hands, crimps, finger crimps, underclings, pockets, jams, and pinches. Footholds include smears, crimps, ledges, inside and outside edges, heel hooks, and jams.

Pinch

Crimp

Open hand

Belaying anchor

Timekeepers
They make sure that the allowed time is respected. Climbing on a path lasts 6 to 8 minutes, and climbers may not exceed this time.

President of the jury
He supervises all activities at the competition and settles disputes. He is assisted by a category judge who is responsible for the competition and application of the rules. Finally, route setters prepare holds and replace broken ones.

Route judge
Placed at the foot of the wall, he sees to safety and observes the athletes' maneuvers. Competitions are recorded by a video camera.

Belayers
They belay the climbers and make sure that they do not have visual contact with those who have already climbed to exchange information on the event underway.

EQUIPMENT

Ropes, carabiners, harnesses, straps, belaying equipment, and various other equipment is safe and light.

Helmet
It protects against falling stones and knocks against rock walls.

Crack pitons

Expansion pitons

Pitons
These protections are attached to the wall that are used for belaying and climbing. There are 2 types of pitons: crack pitons, of various shapes, placed with a hammer, and expansion pitons, which require a drill.

Clothes
Light, resistant, and simple, they do not impede the climber's movements.

Chalk bag
It holds chalk, which dries perspiration on the fingers and increases hand adherence.

Climbing harness
It supports the climber's thighs and hips and is attached to the rope.

Runner
Nylon strap, with a width between 10 and 25 mm. Carabiners are attached to the ends to make a quick-draw.

Quick-draw
A short strap with carabiners at each end. When it is attached to a protection (piton or chock), the climber runs the rope through it to limit possible falls.

Climbing boots
There are a wide variety of models. They must be adherent and close fitting so that the climber can feel holds. Depending on the use and the climber's experience, they are rigid, flexible, or very flexible. They fit tightly for greater effectiveness and precision.

Descenders
Their shape slows and brakes the rope while protecting it during descents.

D   Locking

Carabiners
These are devices that attach, for example, a nut to a rope. They are light and strong, made of aluminum or steel, and are D-shaped or oval.

Isabelle Patissier (FRA)
Winner of the World Cup and the World Masters Invitational in 1990 and 1991. In the latter year, she also won the Climbing Masters International.

Ropes
They vary in diameter (from 8 to 11 mm) and are as long as 60 m. Made of nylon, they have a braided core that provides strength, and a woven sheath that protects the core. Ropes must be solid and flexible; they must not twist easily, must have a good capacity to absorb energy, and resist rubbing.

Passive nut

Nut
There is a wide variety of passive nuts with a steel cable at one end. Mechanical cams, called "friends," are spring-loaded so that they can be squeezed into cracks.

PROFILE OF THE CLIMBER

- Climbers must have flexibility, quick perception, coordination, and the ability to improvise so they can make the right movement at the right time. Rock climbers must be able to resist fatigue and stress. Endurance, physical strength, and self-control are also required.

Aerial
Sports

parachuting

Members of the U.S. Army infantry doing parachute training in 1940. They climbed to the top of a 38-m tower and parachuted along a cable.

Parachuting now encompasses a wide variety of sports and techniques, from free fall to paragliding. Although Leonardo da Vinci is generally recognized as having invented the principle of the parachute, it was only in 1797 that Frenchman André Jacques Garnerin applied it by letting himself fall from a balloon with an open parachute equipped with a basket. The first jump from an airplane took place in the United States in 1912. Parachuting was initially used for military purposes: as a rescue method during the First World War and a tool for invasion during the Second World War. In the late 1940s, as techniques and equipment improved, civilians began to parachute in the United States and Europe. When it was recognized as an aeronautic sport by the Fédération aéronautique internationale (FAI), the International Parachuting Commission (IPC) was founded. The first world championships, involving accuracy landing, took place in 1951. The world championship of formation skydiving was held for the first time in 1975, followed in 1986 by the world championship of canopy formation. The World Air Games, first held in 1997, had competitions in freestyle and skysurfing. Paragliding, also an event in the World Air Games, launched its own championship, the Paragliding World Cup, that same year.

ACCURACY-LANDING COMPETITION

This event is open to men and women, in their respective categories, and has individual and team competitions. The jumps are made from 1,000 m. The competitors must land with their toe or heel on a yellow dead-center disk 3 cm in diameter, or as near to it as possible. The disk is placed in the center of a square. The order of jump is determined by random draw. In the team event, the 4 teammates jump together and open their parachutes at different altitudes so that they succeed each other in landing on the target at regular intervals (20 to 30 seconds).

Jump judges with electronic measuring instruments establish each competitor's exact landing point. Distances between the landing point and the disk are measured in centimeters, up to 16 cm. After a set number of jumps in the competition, the winner is the parachutist or team with the fewest points. A variant of this type of competition, practiced on mountains, paraski, combines 6 accuracy-landing jumps and 2 runs of giant slalom (downhill skiing). The winner is the competitor with the best combined results in both events.

DROP ZONE

An international jury composed of IPC members determines the number of judges to be on the ground and their nationality. A jump master is on board the plane. Ground-to-air radio communications from the base inform the parachutists about the atmospheric conditions on the ground.

Parachutist
He uses a very stable square parachute controlled with brake loops. After a series of turns, he places himself in the ideal position for landing: facing into the wind and slightly behind the target.

Meet director
He is responsible for setting up the site and making sure that the competition runs smoothly, especially the technical aspects.

Wind sock
It is placed 50 m from the target and must be sensitive enough to indicate a wind of 2 meters per second.

Drop-zone controller
He makes sure that the drop zone is safe and that jumps go smoothly. If weather conditions deteriorate, he may decide to interrupt the competition.

Target
Made of a light color and 10 m in diameter, it helps the competitors spot their objective in the first part of the jump.

Jump judges (3)
They determine the landing point.

Observers
Under a judge's supervision, they observe each jump (opening of the parachute and descent).

Jump judges

COMPETITIONS

Although accuracy-landing is the oldest event, many other parachute techniques are now used in competition at the international level. All are open to both men and women.

Free fall style

Jumping from 2,200 m, the parachutist must perform a series of 6 required figures in free fall in a minimum time. The figures, oriented very precisely with regard to 3 reference axes (vertical, horizontal, and lateral), are turns to the right and left and somersaults. Execution faults are penalized by the addition of seconds or fractions of seconds to the total time.

Formation skydiving

Teams of 4, 8, or 16 parachutists in free fall perform a series of required figures, drawn by lot before the event begins. They repeat the series as many times as possible in the time allowed (35 seconds for teams of 4, 50 seconds for teams of 8). Jumps start at 3,000 m and 3,800 m, respectively.

Canopy formation

Created after square parachutes were invented in the 1970s, the event involves teams of 4 or 8 parachutists who jump from 2,000 m and perform groupings by joining hands or touching their feet to the parachutes of their teammates. There are 3 different events:

• The 4-way sequence is performed within a time limit of 2.30 min, during which the teammates make and repeat as many times as possible a series of 4 or 5 required figures drawn by lot.

• The 4-way rotation takes place within a time limit of 1.30 min, during which the teammates make a stack and then make as many rotations as possible. During a rotation, the teammate on top moves away from the formation and places himself under the lowest teammate. A point is given for each completed stack.

• The 8-way formation consists of making a formation, drawn by lot, of all 8 teammates as quickly as possible. The timer is started when the first teammate leaves the plane and stopped when the last teammate joins the formation.

Freestyle and freeflying

Freestyle competitors present a choreography in free fall composed of required and free figures, similar to those in gymnastics and trampoline. They are filmed by a partner whose role is essential: the jump is judged from the film. Aside from difficulty and execution, the aesthetic quality of the presentation and the quality of the images are taken into account. Freeflying is a choreography for 2, generally including nontraditional figures such as head-down rotation and fall in vertical or sitting position.

Skysurfing

This spectacular event is based on the same principle as freestyle; it consists of figures performed in free fall with a skysurf board. The lift created by the board requires a different technique and allows for rapid and larger movements.

Protection
Attached to the rim of the board, it reduces the risk of injury if the board comes into contact with another jumper.

Skysurf board
Its area (length and width) is carefully adapted to the jumper's build. The harness system includes a device attached to the jumper's hips, enabling him to release the board in an emergency (for example, an uncontrollable spin).

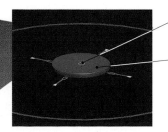

Dead-center disk
diameter: 3 cm

Square
Electronic target
diameter: 16 cm

PARAGLIDING

The paraglider is a parachute shaped like a glider wing that allows the jumper to take off from a mountain, or from flat terrain using a winch, and gain altitude by finding rising air currents. Competitions usually consist of paragliding a course as quickly as possible while photographing existing reference points or markers from a precise angle to prove that they passed the spot. There are races against the clock, races to a finish line with group start, and distance competitions.

FREE FALL TECHNIQUE

In both acrobatics and formation skydiving, parachutists control their speed and position in all 3 dimensions with very specific movements.

BACK SOMERSAULT

1. The parachutist adopts the basic free fall position, called "box" or "square."

2. He then moves his hands and arms forward and lifts his legs toward his body.

3. This movement starts a rotation on the lateral axis and positions the parachutist on his back.

4. He continues the rotation on the lateral axis by hollowing his lower back.

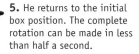

5. He returns to the initial box position. The complete rotation can be made in less than half a second.

EQUIPMENT

PARACHUTE

Its 3 essential components are the main chute, the reserve chute, and the harness.

Main chute
It is rectangular in shape and usually has 7 to 9 cells but can have up to 21. The cells are divided in half by an internal membrane. As air fills the cells, the chute acquires the properties of an airplane wing.

Stabilizers
These are triangular pieces of fabric on either side of the chute.

Pilot chute
Miniature parachute that deploys the main chute.

Goggles
They are recommended mainly for free fall.

Automatic release
Mechanical or electronic, it deploys the reserve chute when the safety altitude is passed.

Suspension lines
Ropes that attach the parachutist to the chute.

Slider
It slows the opening of the chute.

Audio altimeter
It can be preset to make a sound alerting the parachutist that he has reached the altitude of his choice.

Brakes
The group of suspension lines and control loops that allows the chute to be steered.

Harness container
The harness attaches the parachutist to the main chute and reserve chute (generally similar to the main chute). The container is the group of bags that contains the chutes and enables them to deploy properly.

Straps
There are 2 types: those that hold the thighs and those that hold the harness at shoulder level.

Altimeter
It is essential in free fall so that the parachutist knows his altitude at all times.

Suit
Usually a one-piece coverall, it is designed to reduce the risk of getting caught up in the equipment.

Camescope
It is required for freestyle and skysurfing competitions.

Helmet
It may be made of leather or plastic. Although the plastic helmet provides better protection, the leather helmet is very popular because it is comfortable.

PARACHUTIST PROFILE

- Although each discipline requires different and very specific skills and techniques, all competition parachuting requires perfect knowledge of air currents and turbulence, total mastery of spatial orientation, and rigorous and complete training for dealing with emergencies.

- Free fall—especially free fall style and freestyle—requires physical qualities and abilities similar to those of international-level gymnasts or divers.

Cheryl Stearns (USA)
Gold medalist at the national championships 17 times in accuracy landing, she was also 3-time champion in the general rankings, men and women. She has held 29 world records, including 4 at the same time. In 1974, she was the first woman to join the Golden Knights, the U.S. Army's elite parachuting team. In addition, she won the prestigious Leonardo da Vinci Award for her incomparable performance.

Ball Sports
(Small Ball)

baseball

The legendary Babe Ruth (USA) won the World Series seven times: three times for the Boston Red Sox (1915, 1916 and 1918) and four times for the New York Yankees (1923, 1927, 1928 and 1932). He is one of the first players to be inducted into the Hall of Fame in 1936.

The concept of a sport involving the hitting of a ball with a bat and running a certain distance before the ball is caught probably dates back 4,000 years to a game played by Egyptian shepherds. Over the centuries, the sport took various forms in Europe and the Near East, and eventually led to the development of baseball, as we know it, in the United States. In 1839, as a form of relaxation, General Abner Doubleday invited his soldiers, who were posted in Cooperstown, New York, to play a game that entailed hitting a ball with a bat and running a circuit made up of several bases. In 1845, Alexander Cartwright founded the first club, the New York Knickerbockers. Professional clubs first appeared in 1871, and the National League, the first professional league, was founded in 1876. Its first rival, the American League, was formed in 1901. Two years later, the top teams from both leagues met head-to-head in the World Series, a media event created by the New York *World* newspaper. Certain changes were introduced in 1904, including the distance between pitcher and batter, and modern baseball was born. The sport is primarily played by men, and was officially included in the Olympic Games in 1992. The World Cup, featuring national teams, has been held since 1938 (every two years since 1974).

HOW A GAME IS PLAYED

A baseball game is played between 2 teams of 9 players each, and lasts 9 innings. Each inning has 2 halves, with the teams alternating from offence to defence. The goal of the offensive team is to hit the ball with a bat and score runs. The defensive team throws the ball, and tries to prevent the offensive team from reaching the bases. A run is scored when an offensive player returns to the starting point, or home plate, after having touched the other 3 bases.

FIELD

Covered in grass or an artificial surface, the field is delineated by 2 perpendicular lines that join at home plate.

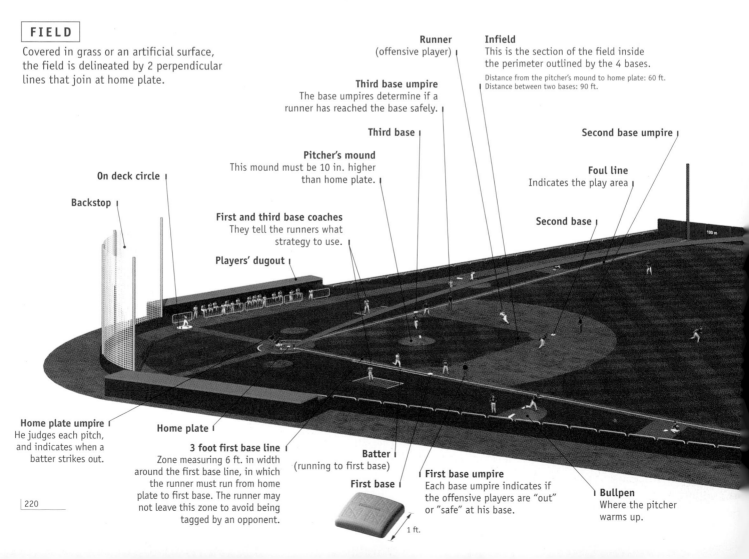

Runner
(offensive player)

Infield
This is the section of the field inside the perimeter outlined by the 4 bases.
Distance from the pitcher's mound to home plate: 60 ft.
Distance between two bases: 90 ft.

Third base umpire
The base umpires determine if a runner has reached the base safely.

Third base

Second base umpire

Pitcher's mound
This mound must be 10 in. higher than home plate.

Foul line
Indicates the play area

On deck circle

Second base

Backstop

First and third base coaches
They tell the runners what strategy to use.

Players' dugout

Home plate umpire
He judges each pitch, and indicates when a batter strikes out.

Home plate

3 foot first base line
Zone measuring 6 ft. in width around the first base line, in which the runner must run from home plate to first base. The runner may not leave this zone to avoid being tagged by an opponent.

Batter
(running to first base)

First base

First base umpire
Each base umpire indicates if the offensive players are "out" or "safe" at his base.

Bullpen
Where the pitcher warms up.

1 ft.

DEFENSIVE PLAYER POSITIONS

The manager of each team selects 9 players from the group of 25 to appear on the score sheet. He must indicate the players' names and the batting order to the umpire in chief and to the manager of the opposing team. These 9 players start the game. When playing offence, they bat in the order in which they are listed (batting order). The defensive players take their positions on the field. When playing defence, each team must designate a pitcher, who puts the ball into play by pitching it to the batter on the other team. The offensive role of a team ends once 3 offensive players are "out" during the same inning. When playing offence, the players must use all their skill, precision, and strength when up at bat, and all their speed and strategic expertise when running bases. When playing defence, players must have outstanding coordination, positioning, and speed of execution in order to prevent their opponents from scoring runs.

Left fielder
This player covers the section of the field located behind third base.

Third baseman
A powerful player, capable of making throws directly to first base.

Shortstop
The shortstop is the key player when the ball is in the infield. He covers a large area of the field, and throws to first or second base.

Pitcher
The pitcher puts the ball in play by pitching it to opposing batters.

Center fielder
This player covers the largest area. He can see the catcher's signals, and must anticipate the hit. He controls the movements of the outfielders.

Catcher
The catcher signals to the pitcher the type of pitch to throw. The catcher watches the runners on base and defends home plate.

Second baseman
He has the same priorities as the shortstop, although he is less powerful. He is involved in many defensive plays.

First baseman
This player is involved in most of the defensive plays, because most "outs" are made at first base. The first baseman must be very agile, in order to catch balls thrown or hit in his direction.

Right fielder
Located behind first base, the right fielder usually has an excellent arm for throwing to third base.

SCOREBOARD

Number of the player at bat

Number of balls thrown by the pitcher

Strikes against the batter

Number of offensive players "out" during the inning

Extra innings
If the teams are tied after 9 innings, one or more extra innings are played until one of the teams wins the game.

Home run
When a player hits the ball past the perimeter of the playing field between the foul lines, the batter is credited with a "home run." Because none of the defensive players can reach the ball, the batter is allowed to run around the bases to home plate and score a run. If there are runners on base when the home run is hit, they also run around all the bases and each score a run.

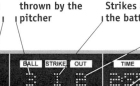

Number of errors committed

Total number of base hits

Total runs

Inning number

Runs scored per inning

Team names
The home team always bats second. If the home team has the lead in the ninth inning before going to bat, it wins the game.

Warning track
This indicates to outfielders the proximity of the fence.

Fence

Outfield
This is the playing area between the 2 foul lines and beyond the infield. The point farthest from home plate is located at least 400 ft. away.

Foul pole
Indicates the end of the foul lines.

BALLS AND STRIKES

The batter assesses the pitch, and decides whether to try to hit the ball or not. If he decides not to hit the ball, two situations can arise:

• If the batter allows a bad pitch to go by, a "ball" is counted against the pitcher. After 4 "balls," the batter proceeds to first base.

• If the batter allows a good pitch to go by, a "strike" is counted against the batter. After 3 strikes, the batter is "struck out."

If the batter tries to hit the ball, 3 situations can arise:

• If the batter swings at the ball but misses, a strike is called, whether the pitch is good or bad.

• If the batter swings and hits the ball into foul territory, a strike is called against him, regardless of the kind of pitch, unless the batter already has 2 strikes, in which case the swing is not counted. However, if the batter attempts to bunt when he already has two strikes against him and hits the ball into foul territory, he is out.

• If the batter swings and hits the ball into the field, the ball in considered to be in play, and the batter must run to first base.

Strike zone
The area above the plate between the batter's knees and chest.

17 in.

OUTS

There are four ways a player can be called "out":

• after three strikes have been called against a batter;

• when a batter hits the ball and it is caught by a defensive player before it touches the ground;

• when a defensive player who is in possession of the ball tags an offensive player who is not on a base;

• when a defensive player has the ball in his hand and touches the base that a runner is running to (in the case of a "force play," where the offensive player is forced to run to the next base).

Infield out

The batter hits a ground ball—a low ball hit toward the ground—to the shortstop, who fields the ball and throws it to the first baseman before the batter reaches the base.

BASE HITS

A batter who hits the ball into the field must run to first base. Once he touches it, he is considered "safe" if the ball is not caught in flight by a defensive player, or if the ball does not reach first base before the batter. An offensive player who reaches a base after hitting the ball is credited with a "base hit." Depending on the number of bases the hitter reaches safely, the base hit is called a single, double, triple, or home run.

Once a batter reaches base, he becomes a "runner." He then makes his way to home plate, depending on his teammates' hits. He may also attempt to "steal" a base by running to the next base while the pitcher throws to the plate or if the catcher drops the ball.

DEFENSIVE PLAY IN THE INFIELD

The defensive player positions himself in front of the ball, with his shoulders and his torso squared to cover more space. He positions his glove on the ground, and uses his free hand to help control the ball. He then moves his free hand into the glove and grabs the ball. The fielder rotates his body to prepare to throw to his teammate: a movement that must be executed from the feet up.

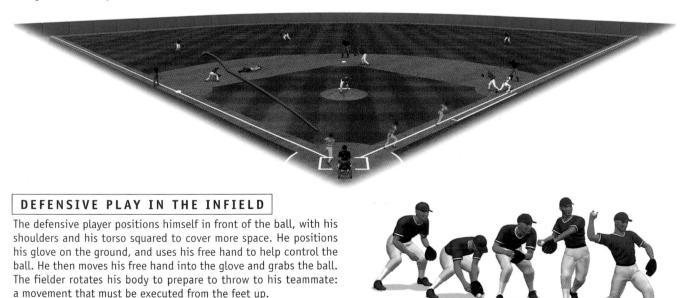

PITCHING TECHNIQUE

To throw a pitch, the pitcher positions himself on the pitcher's mound, then throws the ball toward the batter. The catcher from the defensive team is positioned behind the batter. He must catch the ball to complete the pitching sequence.

1. Set position

The left foot is back, and the right foot is on the pitching rubber. The pitcher's weight is on his rear foot, so that his sudden shift forward is as powerful as possible.

2. Wind up position

The pitcher starts his wind up on his right leg. His left leg is raised to a 90° angle, and the pitcher attempts to maintain this position until he finds his balance.

3. Stride

The pitcher brings his left foot forward, plants it on the ground, and transfers his body weight onto this foot. This is the most powerful pitching position. The pitcher swings the hand holding the ball over his head.

4. Pitch

The pitcher projects the arm holding the ball in the direction of the batter, and throws the pitch. He follows through on this movement until his torso is parallel to the ground, at which point he takes a quick step forward in order to re-establish a defensive position.

TYPES OF PITCHES

Pitchers use a variety of pitches to get batters out. The trajectory of the ball changes according to the position of the pitcher's fingers, and the motion with which he releases the ball. There are many different pitches, each enhanced by the pitcher's personal touch.

Curve ball

Two fingers are placed over the seams on the ball to maximize the effect of the ball's rotation. As soon as it is released, with a twisting wrist motion, it curves sideways and drops.

Knuckle ball

The position of the fingers prevents the ball from rotating. Air resistance, which is the most important factor for this pitch, makes its movement unpredictable.

Fork ball

This fast ball drops suddenly before it reaches the batter.

Fastball

Two fingers are placed on the top of the ball to give it a straight trajectory. The main characteristic of this powerful pitch is its speed.

Change up

This pitch is thrown with the same arm motion as the fastball, but because of the grip it travels more slowly and is designed to upset the batter's timing.

BATTING TECHNIQUE

When gripping the bat, the hands must be placed together on the handle. The bat is held with the base of the fingers, and not with the palm. The fingers are aligned at the knuckles.

1. Wind up

Before hitting the ball, the batter starts his wind-up with his shoulders and elbows spread apart. The batter moves the bat backwards, below his shoulders, with a slight rotation of his torso.

2. Swing

The batter must lift his left foot, move it forward, and put it back down at the moment of contact. His body weight is transferred onto this support leg as his arms propel the bat toward the ball.

3. Follow through

Once he hits the ball, the batter follows through with his arm movement until he is facing the pitcher.

BUNT

In order to surprise the defensive team, or to help a teammate advance to another base, a batter may decide to bunt the ball. To do so, he pivots while moving one hand toward the end of the bat. The ball should bounce in front of him while remaining in play.

EQUIPMENT

BATTER

Helmet
The helmet is made from extra-hard plastic, and protects the batter's ears and temple while he is facing the pitcher.

Cap
Caps are worn by defensive players to avoid being blinded by the sun or stadium lights.

Shoes
Baseball shoes are made from leather, and have metal or plastic cleats to ensure that players do not slip while running or standing on dirt or grass. On a synthetic surface, some players wear leather shoes with smaller plastic cleats.

Batting glove

Bat
The bat must be smooth and rounded at the end. There are two types of bats: wooden and aluminum. Aluminum bats cause the ball to travel farther, but only wooden bats are allowed at the professional level.

2¾ in.

42 in.

Ankle guards
Made from hard plastic, ankle guards absorb the shock of a foul ball.

CATCHER

The catcher must be protected from the impact of a pitched or batted ball. His equipment is made from hard plastic, with the exception of the chest protector, which is padded to protect the torso. The traditional mask (with a removable grill) is increasingly being replaced by a one piece version similar to that worn by hockey goalies.

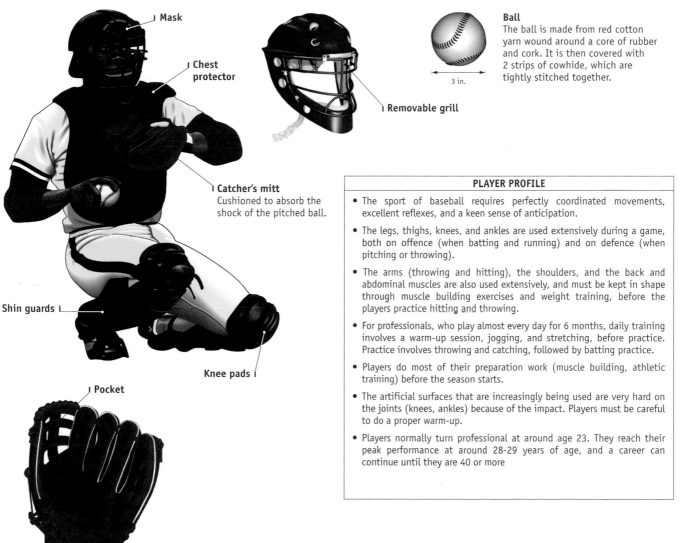

Mask

Chest protector

Removable grill

Ball
The ball is made from red cotton yarn wound around a core of rubber and cork. It is then covered with 2 strips of cowhide, which are tightly stitched together.

3 in.

Catcher's mitt
Cushioned to absorb the shock of the pitched ball.

Shin guards

Knee pads

Pocket

Glove
The glove, which is made from leather, allows the player to catch the ball. The size of a player's glove varies, depending on his position on the field. The first baseman's glove has a longer pocket than infielder gloves, which have a maximum width of 8½ in. Infielders must be able to remove the ball from their glove quickly in order to throw it. Outfielders' gloves have a longer pocket than those worn by infielders, making it easier to catch the ball.

PLAYER PROFILE

- The sport of baseball requires perfectly coordinated movements, excellent reflexes, and a keen sense of anticipation.

- The legs, thighs, knees, and ankles are used extensively during a game, both on offence (when batting and running) and on defence (when pitching or throwing).

- The arms (throwing and hitting), the shoulders, and the back and abdominal muscles are also used extensively, and must be kept in shape through muscle building exercises and weight training, before the players practice hitting and throwing.

- For professionals, who play almost every day for 6 months, daily training involves a warm-up session, jogging, and stretching, before practice. Practice involves throwing and catching, followed by batting practice.

- Players do most of their preparation work (muscle building, athletic training) before the season starts.

- The artificial surfaces that are increasingly being used are very hard on the joints (knees, ankles) because of the impact. Players must be careful to do a proper warm-up.

- Players normally turn professional at around age 23. They reach their peak performance at around 28-29 years of age, and a career can continue until they are 40 or more

Cy Young (USA)
With 511 victories in 23 years, he remains the greatest pitcher ever, and the award for best pitcher bears his name. In 1904, he pitched three remarkable games: one perfect game (he retired 27 batters in a row), and 3 no-hitters.

Hank Aaron (USA)
He hit 755 home runs during his 23 year career (1954–1976), a record that has never been broken. He also had 3,771 hits, and scored 2,174 runs.

Sadaharu Oh (JPN)
During his 22 year career with the Tokyo Giants, the best player in the history of Japanese baseball hit 868 home runs, and was named Most Valuable Player 9 times. He was on the Intercontinental Cup winning team in 1973.

Cal Ripken Jr (USA)
From 1982 to 1998, he set the record for the most consecutive games played (2,632). He was named Most Valuable Player twice (in 1983 and 1991), and had close to 400 home runs and about 3,000 hits. In 1983, he won the World Series with Baltimore.

softball

Women's softball league players wearing their new uniforms in 1944. The uniform was designed to allow players more freedom of movement while looking "feminine" as they played a "men's" sport.

Softball was invented by the end of the 19th century, when baseball players decided to play their game outside of the regular season, both outdoors and indoors. Changes were made to the baseball rules concerning the size of the field, the ball, and the throwing technique. Since then, softball has become, in one or another of its forms (fast-pitch, slow-pitch, or 16-inch slow-pitch), one of the most widely played games. It is one of the few sports in which men and women play on the same team, outside of major national and international competitions. Women's softball (fast-pitch) was a demonstration sport at the 1996 Olympics in Atlanta and has become an official Olympic event. Fast-pitch world championships are played every four years. Softball has been regulated by the International Softball Federation (ISF) since 1952.

THE GAME

Softball uses most of baseball's techniques and objectives. Two 9 player teams alternate at batting (offense) and fielding (defense). The fielding team's pitcher delivers the ball in a way that makes it difficult for the batter to hit it. If the batter hits the ball, the fielding team tries to keep him from scoring a point. The players on the team at bat must touch the 3 bases in turn and return to home plate to score a point. A game is played in 7 innings.

Third base

Infield

Home plate

First base

Distance between bases:
Fast-pitch: 60 ft.
Slow-pitch: 65 ft.

Second base

Fast-pitch: 200–225 ft.
Slow-pitch: 265–275 ft.

Distance between home base and the pitcher's plate
Fast-pitch: Men: 46½ ft.
Women: 40 ft.
Slow-pitch: Men: 50 ft.
Women: 46 ft.

THE FIELD

Backstop screen

Batter's box

On-deck circle

Base umpires (3)
They signal whether runners are out or safe at each base.

Third-base coach
He signals runners whether to run or stay on base.

Foul pole
Two poles stand at the end of the foul lines along the fence. A ball that directly goes behind that line is foul.

Foul line
Two lines extending from home plate demarcate fair territory.

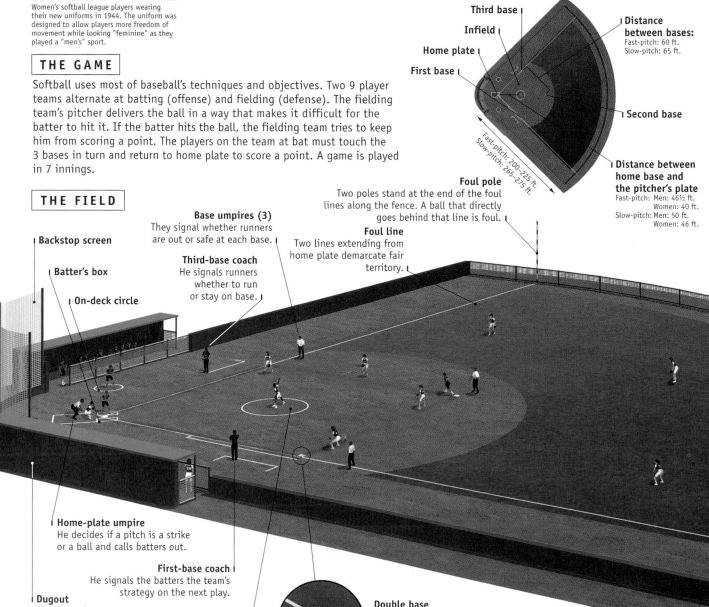

Home-plate umpire
He decides if a pitch is a strike or a ball and calls batters out.

First-base coach
He signals the batters the team's strategy on the next play.

Dugout
Members of the team at bat wait here.

Pitcher's circle
When the ball is in play and enters the pitcher's circle, play stops and runners may not advance.

Double base
A double base is used at first base. The hitter-runner can touch the orange part to avoid contact with the first baseman.

TECHNIQUES

Softball has 3 variations, according to the type of pitch: fast-pitch, slow-pitch, and 16-inch slow-pitch. The pitcher must always stay on the pitcher's plate in the middle of the circle.

Fast-pitch

The pitcher gets a signal from the catcher. Both of her feet must be touching the pitcher's plate. She then pauses before starting her pitching sequence. Her arm makes a windmill rotation from front to back, then she throws the ball underhand, releasing it at hip level. The ball's trajectory must be straight toward the batter's strike zone.

Slow-pitch

The pitcher may have one or both feet on the pitcher's plate. She pauses before starting her pitching sequence. The ball must be thrown underhand. The pitcher may throw in any way as long as the ball moves at a moderate speed toward the batter and its trajectory forms an arc with a minimum height of 6 ft. and a maximum height of 12 ft. The home-plate umpire judges whether the ball's speed and trajectory are acceptable. The pitcher must pitch the ball directly at the batter in a continuous movement, without changing her arm motion.

16-inch slow-pitch

The pitcher gets a signal from the catcher before beginning her pitching sequence. She must have at least one foot touching the pitcher's plate. The ball must be in one hand, and the hands must be separated. When she releases the ball, she must not take more than one step forward in the batter's direction. She releases the ball in one swing of her arm past the hips toward the front, without bending her elbow.

Warning track
It tells the defending player that he is near the wall.
Width: 6 ft.

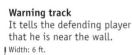

Outfield

EQUIPMENT

3¾ in.
6¼ oz

Ball
It is larger than a baseball, but made identically: a nylon thread wound around a rubber and cork core, covered with a layer of latex onto which two pieces of leather are sewn together.

Gloves
They are longer and wider than baseball gloves, because they are used to catch a bigger ball. Catchers and first basemen may use longer, padded gloves.

Bat

2¼ in.

34 in.

lacrosse

Sioux warrior holding a baggataway stick in 1830, 10 years before lacrosse was popularized in Canada.

Lacrosse is one of the oldest ball sports. The players use a stick (crosse) with a net (pocket) on the end to catch, carry, and throw a ball into the opposing team's goal. The game was adapted from baggataway, played by indigenous peoples of North America in the 15th century, by early French settlers who named it la crosse—a reference to bishops' crooks (or hooked staffs). A game of technique and agility, lacrosse as it is played today first appeared in Quebec, Canada, around 1840. Canadians created a national lacrosse association in 1867, followed by England in 1892. The International Lacrosse Federation (ILF) has organized men's world championships every four years since 1967; women's lacrosse has been governed by the International Federation of Women's Lacrosse Associations since 1969. An Olympic event at the St. Louis Games in 1904 and the London Games in 1908, lacrosse was a demonstration sport at the Games in 1928, 1932, and 1948. In spite of numerous efforts to have lacrosse return to the Olympics, it was last featured in Los Angeles in 1984. There are currently four forms of lacrosse: men's, or international, lacrosse; women's lacrosse; intercrosse; and indoor lacrosse.

MEN'S LACROSSE

In men's lacrosse, each team has 10 players and up to 13 substitutes. The game is divided into 25 minute quarters with a 10 minute halftime. The captains choose their side of the field with a coin toss. At the start of each quarter and after goals, the umpire calls 2 opposing players to center field for a face off. When the whistle blows, the players in the wing areas can run after the ball. The other players must wait until a player is in possession of the ball, until it is out of bounds, or until it is in the goal area before starting to move

on the field. Players must use their crosses to catch, carry, and pass the ball; they can also roll and kick the ball. Body checks are permitted if the opposing player has the ball or if it is loose within 5 m of that player. Physical contact must be limited to the front and side of the body, between the hips and the shoulders, and both hands must stay on the crosse. If the score is tied at the end of regulation time, 2 4-min overtime periods may be played.

THE FIELD

International lacrosse is played outdoors on a field of grass or synthetic turf.

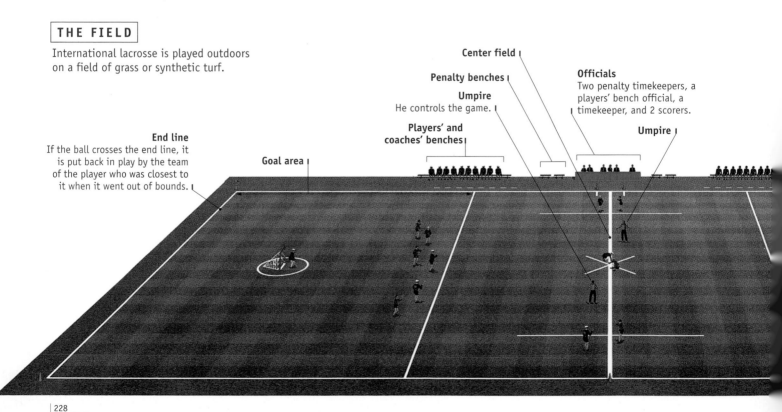

Center field

Penalty benches

Umpire
He controls the game.

Officials
Two penalty timekeepers, a players' bench official, a timekeeper, and 2 scorers.

Players' and coaches' benches

Umpire

End line
If the ball crosses the end line, it is put back in play by the team of the player who was closest to it when it went out of bounds.

Goal area

WOMEN'S LACROSSE AND VARIANTS

Women's lacrosse is also played outdoors, with the same basic rules as the men's version. However, the field measures 72 x 120 yds. and does not have boundary lines. Teams are composed of 12 players. The ball is put in play by 2 players facing each other, their crosses parallel to the ground. Physical contact is forbidden, but crosschecks to dislodge the ball with the crosse are permitted if they are not done violently. Women are not allowed to push the ball with their feet. The game has 2 25-min periods and a 10 min halftime, after which the teams change sides.

Indoor lacrosse (called "box lacrosse" in Canada) is usually played in hockey rinks in the off-season. It is the roughest variant of lacrosse, and the players wear protective gear. Games are usually divided into 3 20-min periods. In the early 1980s, in reaction to the violence of this game, a new version was created. Intercrosse stresses 4 values: respect (no contact), movement (the players keep running all the time), autonomy, and communication (players must not keep the ball more than 5 seconds). Teams are co-ed, there are no time outs, and the umpire's role is reduced to a minimum.

PLAYER POSITIONS

During face offs, in addition to the player taking the face off at center field, the goalkeeper and three players must be in the goal area, three players in the opposing goal area, and one player in each wing area.

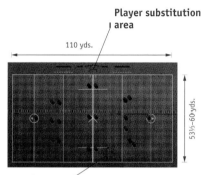

Player substitution area

110 yds.

53⅓–60 yds.

Wing area

Side lines and back lines
If a player with the ball touches or passes a side line or the end line or if his crosse touches or passes it, the ball is out of bounds. It is put back in play with a free throw by the player of the opposing team who was closest to the ball when it went out of bounds.

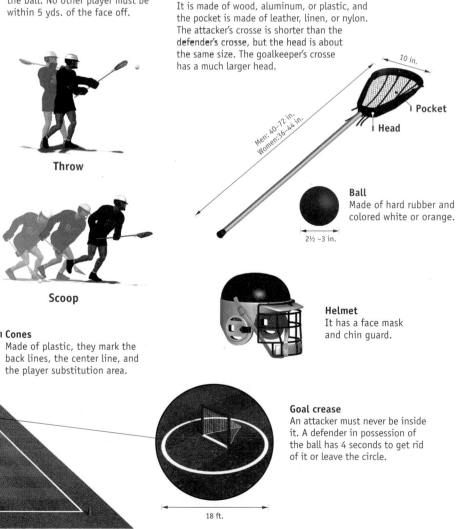

TECHNIQUES

Face off

When the referee blows his whistle, both players try to get control of the ball. No other player must be within 5 yds. of the face off.

Throw

Scoop

Cones
Made of plastic, they mark the back lines, the center line, and the player substitution area.

EQUIPMENT

Players' uniforms
Players wear shorts and a shirt in the team colors. Men must wear padded gloves and a helmet. Use of a chin guard and elbow guards is optional. The goalkeeper may wear kneepads and a chest protector. Except for mouth guards and sometimes gloves and shin guards, women do not wear protective gear.

Crosse
It is made of wood, aluminum, or plastic, and the pocket is made of leather, linen, or nylon. The attacker's crosse is shorter than the defender's crosse, but the head is about the same size. The goalkeeper's crosse has a much larger head.

10 in.

Men: 40–72 in.
Women:36–44 in.

Pocket

Head

Ball
Made of hard rubber and colored white or orange.

2½ –3 in.

Helmet
It has a face mask and chin guard.

Goal crease
An attacker must never be inside it. A defender in possession of the ball has 4 seconds to get rid of it or leave the circle.

18 ft.

cricket

W.G. (William Gilbert) Grace (GBR) is the most famous player in the history of cricket. Playing for the Gloucestershire Club in Britain, he dominated the cricket scene from 1865 to 1895. A member of the London County Club starting in 1899, his career came to an end in 1908, when he was 60 years old.

Cricket is a sport played by both men and women using a ball and a wooden bat. Rounders, the predecessor to cricket, was already a popular sport in 13th century England, during the reign of King Edward I. The first major official match was held between the counties of Kent and Middlesex in 1719, and the first rules were written in 1744. The Marylebone Cricket Club, founded in 1787, became the club of reference for the code of ethics employed in cricket, and remains so to this day. The foundation of this club marked the adoption of the sport by the rich and the nobility. Throughout the first half of the 20th century, the game spread to other Commonwealth countries, including the British West Indies in 1920, and New Zealand and India in 1932. Cricket is administered worldwide by the International Cricket Council (ICC), which organizes the ICC Trophy every 4 years. There are 9 test-playing countries and more than 20 associated or non-test-playing countries who are members of the ICC. The 3 top teams of the ICC Trophy are included in the World Cup that follows, along with the 9 test-playing countries. The first World Cup was held in 1975; it is normally held every 4 years. Although women play cricket, the sport is essentially male-dominated at the professional level.

HOW A MATCH IS ORGANIZED

Two teams of 11 players and a spare play alternately on a field with a rectangular strip (the pitch) located between 2 wickets in the center. The choice of the team batting or fielding is determined by a toss of a coin between the 2 captains, who have previously selected which positions on the field each team member will play. The bowlers and batsmen are positioned at each end of the wickets. At the umpire's signal, the fielding team takes its place on the field around the pitch, while the first 2 batsmen for the opposing team take their positions in front of their wickets. The remaining 9 team members wait in the clubhouse for their turn to bat. This marks the beginning of an inning (or time at bat), which ends once 10 batsmen on one team are out. The bowler bowls the ball toward the wicket in order to make the bails fall off the wicket (called breaking the wicket). If he succeeds, the batsman is out. Batsmen have to defend their wickets and attempt to hit the ball out of reach of their opponents in order to have enough time to run from one wicket to the other, while passing each other (called a run). The batsmen attempt to score as many runs as possible before the ball is returned. The other members of the fielding team try to stop the batsmen from scoring runs by recovering the ball as quickly as possible and throwing it at one of the 2 wickets in an attempt to break it before the batsmen complete the run. A run is completed when the 2 batsmen cross each other and reach their opposite ends. A series of bowls (minimum of 6) is called an over. The bowler switches position with one of the players on his team once his over is completed. After an over, the fielding team changes ends. The winning team is the one who has the most runs.

PLAYING AREA

Field

The field is the section of the playing area surrounding the pitch. It may be covered with closely cropped grass or a synthetic material. The field is divided by an imaginary line that separates the Onside (or Legside) from the Offside. For a right-handed batsman, the Onside is on the right and the Offside is on the left. This division is used to position the players on the field.

Clubhouse

The clubhouse contains the players' locker rooms and benches. It is also the place where the batting team members await their turn. The scorekeeper, timekeeper, and video camera operator are stationed at the top.

Umpires

Two umpires supervise the match. One stands at the bowler's wicket, the other perpendicular to the batsman's wicket. The umpires determine if the bowl is good and if the batsmen should be dismissed, and ensure that the bat meets regulations. They change positions after each over.

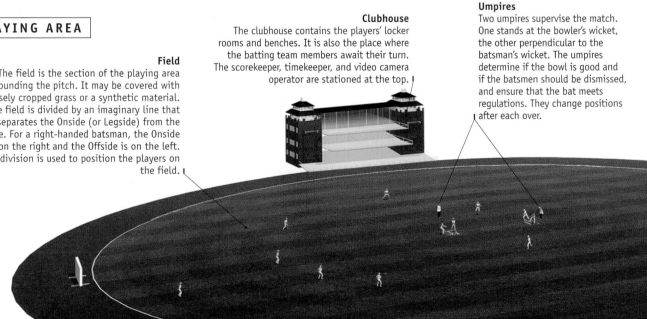

DURATION OF A MATCH

The duration of a match varies according to the level. Two pre-determined factors are usually taken into consideration: game time and the number of overs. A test match consists of 2 innings and lasts no more than 5 days (8-10 hours per day). It is quite common for each team to score more than 500 runs during a test match. The match ends if the result is reached within the stipulated time frame or finishes in a drawn match. Test matches cannot be postponed, regardless of the weather conditions. In response to an audience interested in having matches start and end on the same day, one-day matches have been played for the past 30 years. Although purists frown upon this form of cricket, it is becoming increasingly popular and lucrative. Major amendments have been made to the rules for one-day matches: there is only one inning per team, and the number of overs is limited. Each bowler is permitted to bowl limited overs.

PLAYER POSITIONS

There are more than 30 possible positions on the field. The captain assigns each player a position and decides on the strategy for effectively covering the field, according to the strengths and weaknesses of each opposing batsman. The role of the fielders is to use any part of their body to catch or stop the ball hit by the batsmen. Spares (one per team) cannot be batsmen or bowlers, their role is limited to playing in the field. In case of injury or illness, a spare is allowed to play if the captain of the opposing team agrees. The key positions are lined up as follows:

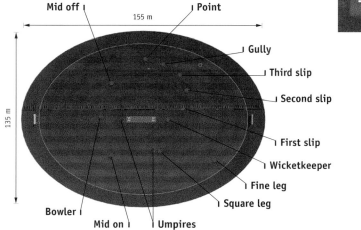

Mid off | Point
155 m
Gully
Third slip
Second slip
First slip
Wicketkeeper
Fine leg
Square leg
135 m
Bowler
Mid on | Umpires

PITCH
The pitch is the rectangular area on which the bowler and batsman face off. Most of the action of the game takes place on the pitch.

Pitch ends | Wicket | 1.22 m
Between the wickets: 20.12 m | 1.22 m
2.64 m | 3.66 m

Popping crease | **Pitch area**
The bowler must bowl the ball before he passes the popping crease. The ball must be bowled inside the pitch ends. The bowl is called wide if it is too high or if it is bowled too far to the left or right of the pitch ends.

WICKET
22.8 cm
Bails
The bails are balanced on the stumps and fall if the wicket is touched by the ball.
11.1 cm
Stumps
6 cm
71.1 cm
7.5 cm

Batsman
The batsman is not considered out until a player on the fielding team appeals to the umpire, saying "How's that?" The umpire then raises his finger, thereby authorizing the out or dismissal of the batsman.

Wicketkeeper
Only the wicketkeeper is allowed to wear gloves. Fielders try to recover the ball hit by the batsman and then throw it to the wicketkeeper to break the wicket. The wicketkeeper will not go in front of the wicket until the batsman hits or is touched by the ball.

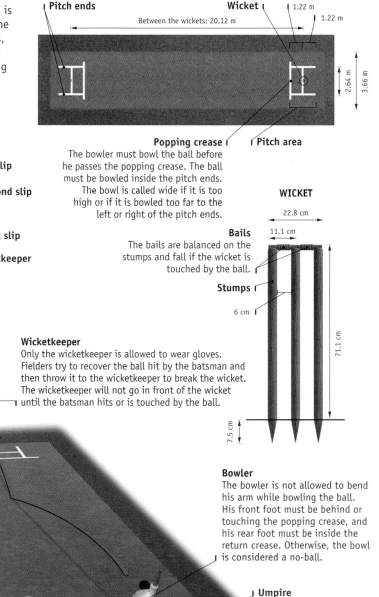

Screens
These allow the batsmen to closely follow ball movement.

Bowler
The bowler is not allowed to bend his arm while bowling the ball. His front foot must be behind or touching the popping crease, and his rear foot must be inside the return crease. Otherwise, the bowl is considered a no-ball.

Umpire

Batsman

231

TECHNIQUES

BOWLER

The fast bowler runs an average of 20 feet before pitching the ball and uses speed or a curved trajectory to try to make the batsman miss. The bowler can also use special techniques on the bowl. He normally tries to outsmart the batsman by changing the direction and trajectory of the ball. A slower bowler may give the bowl a spin to the right or the left to encourage the batsman to hit the ball hard and give the fielders a chance to catch it before it touches the ground, thereby putting the batsman out. Cricket balls can travel at speeds of 165 km/h or more.

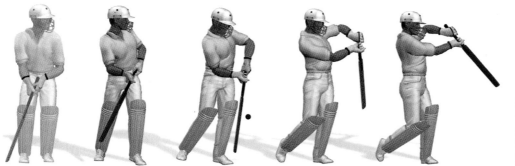

BATSMAN

The batsman can hit the ball in any direction. The flat surface of the bat allows him to hit the ball wherever he chooses. The batsman runs with his bat and must touch the ground within the popping crease with the bat or with any part of his body in order to score a run. 100 runs scored by the same batsman in a single inning is called a century, and 50 runs is called a half-century.

BALL IN PLAY

The ball remains in play even if it hits an umpire, if a wicket is broken (unless a batsman is dismissed), if a decision is fruitlessly contested, and even when the bowler begins his run-up. The ball is considered dead when it is in the hands of the bowler or wicketkeeper, if it goes out of bounds, if it becomes caught in the batsman's or the umpire's equipment, when the batsman is dismissed, in the case of a serious injury, if the batsman is not ready, or if the bowler inadvertently drops it.

UMPIRING

The umpire uses different hand signals to ensure that the scorekeepers instantly understand his decisions.

No-ball

This is normally the result of an infraction during the bowl, for instance, if one of the bowler's feet is outside the zone delineated by the popping crease and the pitch ends.

Boundary

If the ball hit by the batsman crosses the boundary line after bouncing inside the perimeter, the batsman is awarded 4 runs.

Over boundary

If the ball hit by the batsman crosses the boundary line without touching the ground, the batsman is awarded 6 runs.

AWARDING OF RUNS

In addition to the batsmen running, runs can be scored in several ways:

- when a run is made without the ball touching the bat or any other part of the batsman's body. This is called a bye;
- when the ball is unintentionally touched by any part of the batsman's body except his hands. This is called a leg bye;
- when a bowl is a no-ball, meaning that it is bowled with a bent arm, or if the bowler crosses over the line. The batting team is awarded one run;
- if the batted ball touches or crosses the boundary line after touching the ground, 4 runs are awarded;
- if the batted ball lands outside the boundary line without touching the ground, the batsman is awarded 6 runs.

In addition to scoring runs, the batter must also defend his wicket. He is not required to run, even if he hits the ball. This benefits a batsman who might not hit the ball very far.

There are several ways to dismiss a batsman:

- if the ball partially or completely destroys the wicket, even if it touches the bat;
- when a batted ball is caught by a fielder before it touches the ground;
- when the batsman's leg or any part of his body prevents the ball from touching the wicket;
- if the batsman breaks the wicket by hitting it;
- if the batsman touches the ball with his hand;
- if the batsman gets in the way of an opponent trying to catch the ball;
- if he runs toward a wicket but does not get there in time to place his bat between the edge of the popping crease and the wicket before an opponent breaks the wicket;
- if he is near his wicket but outside the pitch area, and the wicketkeeper breaks the wicket.

WORLD CUP

Played as a one-day match, the World Cup involves the following test-playing countries: Australia, the British West Indies, England, India, New Zealand, Pakistan, South Africa, Sri Lanka, Zimbabwe, and the 3 top countries in the ICC Trophy. The ICC Trophy is played one year before the World Cup by associates or non-test-playing countries.

WORLD CUP WINNERS

Year	Winner	Year	Winner
1975	British West Indies	1992	Pakistan
1979	British West Indies	1996	Sri Lanka
1983	India	1999	Australia
1987	Australia		

PLAYER PROFILE

- Players are expected to behave like gentlemen. They train in a pitch-like area that is surrounded by nets. Training camps are organized for teams competing at the international level.

- One-day cricket matches have greatly improved the health of players. Today, cricketers are high-caliber athletes.

BATSMAN'S EQUIPMENT

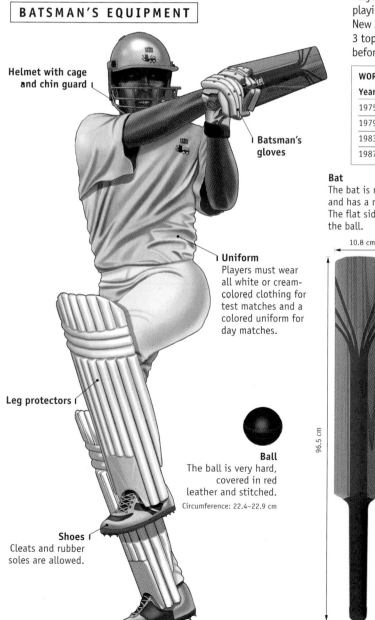

Helmet with cage and chin guard

Batsman's gloves

Uniform
Players must wear all white or cream-colored clothing for test matches and a colored uniform for day matches.

Leg protectors

Shoes
Cleats and rubber soles are allowed.

Ball
The ball is very hard, covered in red leather and stitched.
Circumference: 22.4–22.9 cm

Bat
The bat is made of willow and has a rubber handle. The flat side is used to hit the ball.

10.8 cm

96.5 cm

Sachin Tendulkar (IND)
In 1989, at the age of 16, he became the youngest test player in Indian history. At age 19, he was the youngest player to complete 1,000 runs, and he passed the 2,000-run milestone one month before his 21st birthday. At the age of 23, he was made captain of the Indian team.

D.G. Bradman (AUS)
Over the course of his career (1927-1949), he accumulated 6,996 runs and 29 centuries, and ended his career with an average of 99.94 runs per match. He remains the best test-match batsman ever. A cricket legend in Australia and around the world, his prowess has led to his being known as Sir Don Bradman.

field hockey

Young women playing field hockey in England in the late 19th century

Games resembling hockey have been played since 2000 B.C. The Persians, Egyptians, Greeks, and Romans all left evidence of an activity consistent with playing a game with a ball and sticks. The game evolved in different ways in various European and Asian countries: in some places, it was played on horseback and became polo; in other places, it was played on ice. The rules for modern field hockey were first codified in England and Scotland, where shinty (a Gaelic sport played by two 12-player teams on a field more than 150 m long) was very popular in the late 18th century. The Blackheath club in London was the first to be founded, in 1861, and the first official matches were played several years later. Men's field hockey was an event in the 1908 Olympics; women's field hockey became an Olympic event only in 1980. The International Hockey Federation (FIH) was founded in 1924 by seven European countries. Today, it has 119 members nations. Aside from the Olympics, the World Cup is the main tournament. Started in 1971 (1974 for women), it takes place every four years.

THE GAME

Field hockey rules and play are similar to those for soccer. Two 11-player teams play for 2 35-min periods, with a 5 or 10 min halftime. Using sticks, they try to get the ball into the opposing team's goal; each goal is worth 1 point. Each team has 1 goalkeeper and 5 substitutes that can enter play at any time, except during penalty corners. The umpire blows his whistle to signal the start of play. Players contact the ball with the face of the stick or with the part of the handle that is an extension of the face. A player can take part in the game only if he has his own stick in his hands, and he must not use his stick to play the ball when it is above his shoulders. The ball is put in play with a center pass at center field, during which all players must be on their own half of the field. At the umpire's signal, the team in possession of the ball puts it in play with a pass in any direction. No opposing player may be within 4.55 m of the ball until it is played.

FIELD

Shooting circle
A goal is scored only if an attacker in the defending team's shooting circle touches the ball before it enters the goal.

Sideline
When the ball crosses this line, it is put in play at the point where it went out by the team that was not the last to touch it. The player who puts the ball in play with a pass may not touch it twice in a row.

Officials' table
The 3 officials at the table are responsible for checking player equipment, their conduct on the bench, and substitutes. They also fill out the score sheet.

PLAYER POSITIONS

Tactics involve a balance between attack and defense. The teams use various game plans based on the players' individual skills and the opposing team's weaknesses. The most common tactical system is 5-3-2-1 (5 forwards, including inside forwards, 3 halfbacks, 2 fullbacks, and a goalkeeper).

Right and left inside forwards
They make offensive plays. They take passes from their fullbacks or halfbacks and pass the ball on to the wingers or center forward to start an attack.

Center halfback
He is the team's pivot, receiving the ball and passing it in any direction. In defense, he covers the opposing center forward.

Goalkeeper
He stops shots at the goal. He is the only player allowed to touch the ball with his body, but he cannot immobilize it or pick it up.

Right and left fullbacks
Their main responsibility is to cover the opposing inside forwards and keep them from creating attack situations. When they recover the ball, they must be able to pass it quickly to a teammate to start an attack.

Right and left halfbacks
They must control the midfield with the inside forwards. They try to take the ball from opposing players before they have an opportunity to shoot on goal and pass it to the inside forwards or forwards. In defense, they cover the opposing wingers.

55 m

91.4 m

Center forward
He stays close to the shooting circle and tries to score goals. In defense, he impedes the progress of the opposing fullbacks.

Right and left wingers
They stay in the opposing half of the field, often near the sidelines. They must often get by an opposing player before passing the ball to the center forward.

22 m line
If the ball goes out of bounds between the 22 m lines, the teammates of the player putting the ball back in play can be within 1 m of that player. If the ball is put in play between the 22 m line and the goal line, both teammates and opposing players must be at least 4.55 m from the ball.

Back line
When the ball is shot by an attacker beyond this line but not into the goal, a free hit is awarded: a defender puts the ball back in play at a spot up to 14.63 m from the point where it went out and on a line parallel to the sideline.

Goal backboard
It is made of wood and placed on the inside of the goal below the net. It is 45 cm high.

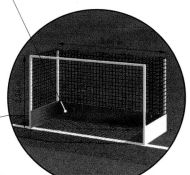

Penalty spot
It is located 6.4 m from the goal line.

Corner flag

5 m line
When a defending player puts the ball out of bounds behind his own goal line, the attacking team puts the ball in play at the 5 m line.

Referees (2)
Each controls one half of the field and the sideline near which he is placed. They make sure that the rules are observed and can sanction players with a warning (green card), a 5 min temporary suspension (yellow card), or expulsion (red card).

Center line
The ball is put in play at the center of this line at the beginning of each period and after each goal.

TECHNIQUES

Controlling the ball with the stick is the most important aspect of the game. Players must be able to pass the ball to a teammate, take it away from an opposing player, or shoot on goal.

Push

This stroke is used when the player wants to send the ball a short distance or get rid of it quickly. The right hand is placed low on the stick and pushes the face forward, while the left hand brings the handle toward the body.

Hit

This is a powerful stroke used for long passes or shots on goal. The player winds up by raising the stick then hits the ball hard, following through with his body.

Flick

This technique is used to shoot on goal and for penalty strokes. The movement is similar to that for a push, except that the player straightens up and plays the ball upward rather than forward. The ball must be lifted from as low as possible to create an upward motion.

PENALTY CORNER

A penalty corner is awarded in 3 cases: when a defending player intentionally hits the ball out of bounds over his back line, commits an intentional foul in the 22 m zone but outside of the shooting circle, or commits an unintentional foul inside the shooting circle. A penalty corner is played by the attacking team from a point located at least 9.14 m from the closest corner pole.

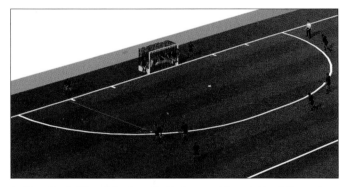

1. When the ball is put in play, all attackers must be outside of the shooting circle. Five defenders (generally 4 field players and the goalkeeper) must remain behind the goal line until the ball is in play. All other defenders stay beyond the center line. No player may come within 4.55 m of the ball.

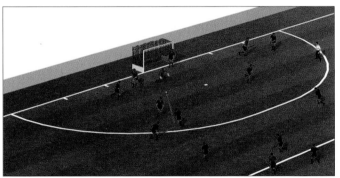

2. The player who is putting the ball in play sends it to a teammate outside the circle, who must stop the ball before sending it back into the circle. When the ball is inside the circle again, an attacking player may flick the ball toward the goal, pass to another player, or shoot on goal. In the last case, the ball's trajectory must be such that it hits the goal backboard. If it goes into the goal above the backboard, the defending team puts the ball back in play in its shooting circle.

PENALTY STROKE

A penalty stroke is awarded in 2 cases: when a defender commits an intentional foul inside his shooting circle or an unintentional foul that keeps a goal from being scored. The player shooting the penalty stroke places the ball on the penalty spot; the goalkeeper must be on his goal line.

All other players must be behind the 22 m line. The penalty shooter can push or flick the ball toward the net, but not hit it. He may touch the ball only once, after which he must not approach the ball or the goalkeeper. If the ball goes completely inside the goal, a goal is scored. In any other case, the penalty stroke has missed and play resumes with a free hit by the defending team: the ball is put in play with a push or a hit, facing the goal, 14.63 m away from the back line. The penalized team must stay 4.55 m away from the ball.

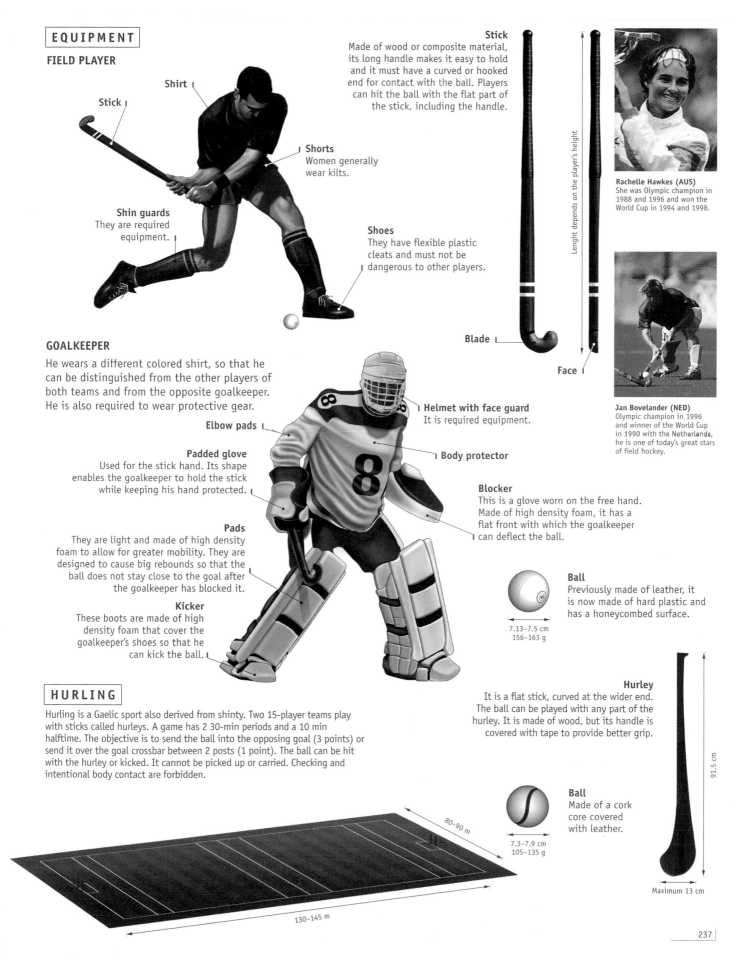

EQUIPMENT

FIELD PLAYER

Shirt

Stick

Shin guards
They are required equipment.

Stick
Made of wood or composite material, its long handle makes it easy to hold and it must have a curved or hooked end for contact with the ball. Players can hit the ball with the flat part of the stick, including the handle.

Shorts
Women generally wear kilts.

Shoes
They have flexible plastic cleats and must not be dangerous to other players.

Lenght depends on the player's height

Blade

Face

Rachelle Hawkes (AUS)
She was Olympic champion in 1988 and 1996 and won the World Cup in 1994 and 1998.

Jan Bovelander (NED)
Olympic champion in 1996 and winner of the World Cup in 1990 with the Netherlands, he is one of today's great stars of field hockey.

GOALKEEPER

He wears a different colored shirt, so that he can be distinguished from the other players of both teams and from the opposite goalkeeper. He is also required to wear protective gear.

Elbow pads

Padded glove
Used for the stick hand. Its shape enables the goalkeeper to hold the stick while keeping his hand protected.

Pads
They are light and made of high density foam to allow for greater mobility. They are designed to cause big rebounds so that the ball does not stay close to the goal after the goalkeeper has blocked it.

Kicker
These boots are made of high density foam that cover the goalkeeper's shoes so that he can kick the ball.

Helmet with face guard
It is required equipment.

Body protector

Blocker
This is a glove worn on the free hand. Made of high density foam, it has a flat front with which the goalkeeper can deflect the ball.

Ball
Previously made of leather, it is now made of hard plastic and has a honeycombed surface.

7.13–7.5 cm
156–163 g

HURLING

Hurling is a Gaelic sport also derived from shinty. Two 15-player teams play with sticks called hurleys. A game has 2 30-min periods and a 10 min halftime. The objective is to send the ball into the opposing goal (3 points) or send it over the goal crossbar between 2 posts (1 point). The ball can be hit with the hurley or kicked. It cannot be picked up or carried. Checking and intentional body contact are forbidden.

Hurley
It is a flat stick, curved at the wider end. The ball can be played with any part of the hurley. It is made of wood, but its handle is covered with tape to provide better grip.

91.5 cm

Ball
Made of a cork core covered with leather.

7.3–7.9 cm
105–135 g

Maximum 13 cm

80–90 m

130–145 m

pelota vasca (Basque ball)

The great pelotari Joseph Apesteguy (ESP), known as Chiquito de Cambo, began playing in 1899. He developed a passion for the large cesta, and his long carreer ended in 1946.

Games involving a ball being sent back and forth between two players or teams were played in most ancient civilizations. The most direct ancestor of pelota vasca is the handball game that was invented by the Romans and played for centuries in France, Spain, Italy, and the Netherlands. Court tennis (short and long), in which two players face each other from across a net, was played in the Basque provinces of southwestern France and northwestern Spain. The introduction of rubber in the mid 19th century transformed the sport. Balls could be bounced and propelled against a wall. The reduced playing area and solid wall led to the evolution of different forms of the sport. The equipment also evolved: the introduction of rubber-cored balls along with rackets and cestas led to development of new games. Today, the various games are collectively known as pelota vasca, or Basque ball. The world championship disciplines of the sport were included as demonstration sports at the Olympic Games in Paris in 1924, Mexico City in 1968, and Barcelona in 1992. The frontenis and pelota de goma disciplines are now open to women competitors. World championships have been held since 1952.

HOW A GAME IS PLAYED

Two players, or 2 teams of 2 players each, must alternately return a ball by propelling it against a wall. The ball may not bounce on the ground more than once before a player returns it. A player or team scores a point when the opponent is either unable to return the ball after a rebound or sends it out of play. Depending on the particular form of pelota vasca, each game is played to between 25 and 50 points.

Service lines
These lines mark the service area. In jai alai, a serve must be made from behind line no. 10. The ball is propelled against the front wall, and must then bounce between line no. 4 and line no. 7. Each game has its own service rules. Any ball that touches a line is dead. When a ball goes beyond the pasa line, the server, or scorer, gets a second try.

PLAYING AREA

The playing area varies depending on the game. The 4 types of courts on which the world championships are contested are the 36 m polished cement fronton, the 54 m polished cement grand fronton, the 30 m synthetic surface fronton, and the polished cement trinquet.

FRONTON
A covered area formed by a frontis (front wall) measuring 9.25 m to 10 m in height, a rebote (back wall), and a lateral (side wall) measuring between 30 m and 54 m, and covering the entire left hand side of the playing area. Games played on this type of court are bare handed, pelota de goma, leather paleta, pala corta, frontenis and cesta punta.

Front court player
He covers the area closest to the front wall, attempts to intercept the ball and return it so that the opposing back court player will have difficulty, and handles the returns off the back wall.

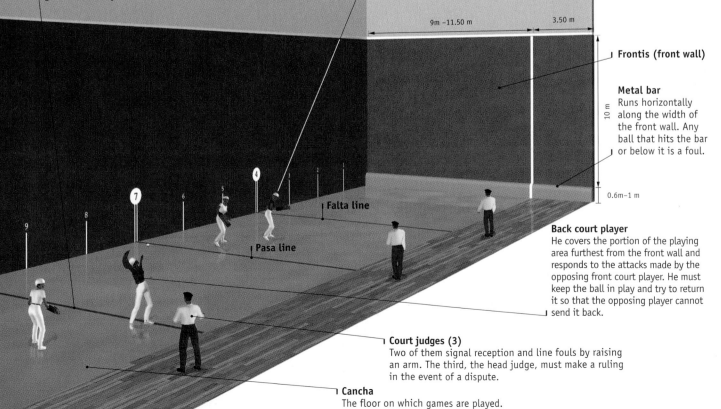

9m –11.50 m 3.50 m

Frontis (front wall)

Metal bar
Runs horizontally along the width of the front wall. Any ball that hits the bar or below it is a foul.

10 m

0.6m–1 m

Falta line

Pasa line

Back court player
He covers the portion of the playing area furthest from the front wall and responds to the attacks made by the opposing front court player. He must keep the ball in play and try to return it so that the opposing player cannot send it back.

Court judges (3)
Two of them signal reception and line fouls by raising an arm. The third, the head judge, must make a ruling in the event of a dispute.

Cancha
The floor on which games are played.

TYPES OF GAMES

Seven forms of pelota vasca are officially recognized and played at the world championships, which consist of one-on-one events and contests between national teams.

- **Bare handed** is played on a cancha measuring 28.5 m (trinquet) or 36 m (fronton). It is played one-on-one or two-on-two. The players alternate returning the ball by hitting it with their palm or the base of their fingers.

- **Frontenis** and **pelota de goma** are played on a 30 m fronton by teams of two. Pelota de goma is also played on a trinquet. In frontenis, a tennis racket with reinforced strings is used.

- **Leather paleta** is played on a trinquet or on a 36 m fronton by teams of two. Pala corta is only played on a 36 m fronton. The balls are propelled using solid wood rackets.

- **Xare** is played with a small leather ball on a 28.5 m trinquet by teams of 2. It is played using a loosely strung racket with a wooden frame. A player must catch the ball in the racket and, in the same movement, propel it back to the wall with a powerful whip of the wrist.

- **Cesta punta** (or **jai alai**) is played with a large cesta on a 54 m fronton. Games are played by teams of two (professional matches are contested by teams of two or one-on-one). When it leaves the cesta, the ball can reach speeds of 300 km/h.

Players are allowed to move back 2 steps after receiving the ball in the basket of the cesta. They are then allowed to take 2 run-up steps before propelling the ball back against the wall, all in the span of 2 seconds. The ball must not bounce above the cesta basket when it is caught.

TRINQUET

This is the direct descendant of court tennis. The trinquet measures 28.5 m long and 9.3 m wide. The metal bar is positioned 80 cm from the floor on the front wall.

Scorekeeper
This person, positioned in one of the galleries, keeps track of the points scored and displays them either manually or on an illuminated screen.

Tambour
The inclined roof of the gallery: the ball can bounce off it or roll on top of it and remain in play.

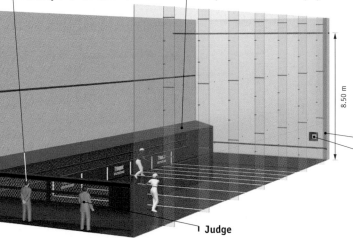

8.50 m

Judge

PELOTARI PROFILE

- Whether played bare handed, with a racket, or with a cesta, pelota vasca requires exceptional speed, power, endurance, and reflexes.

- The leg muscles (starting and stopping) and the joints are worked the hardest. The arms, back, and abdominal muscles are also used.

- The principal enemy of bare handed players is the "Nail," a piercing pain in the hand caused by repeatedly striking the ball with the palm. Serious nerve, tendon, ligament, and bone trauma can result. A cesta punta player risks developing "Basque pain," an arthrosis of the hip caused by sudden rotation when making shots.

Pampi Laduche (FRA)
Son of the legendary Joseph Laduche, he has become the greatest player of the modern era. Laduche has been the World Bare Handed Champion many times, and is the first man from northern Basque to win two Spanish professional championships.

EQUIPMENT

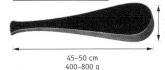

10–20 cm

45–50 cm
400–800 g

5 cm

Pala
Pala and paleta are the names given to the solid wood rackets used in several forms of pelota vasca (pelota de goma, leather paleta, and pala corta). These rackets are made from beech or chestnut.

Balls (pelotas)
The size, weight, and composition of the ball vary according to the game for which it is made. In most cases, the ball consists of a latex core wrapped in a layer of wool covered with two leather strips sewn together. A more resistant vellum covering is used for cesta punta balls. The ball used in frontenis and pelota de goma is made with a latex core that contains a pressurized gas, which makes the ball extremely lively.

Cesta
Created in 1857 by a young man who came up with the idea of using a small curved basket designed for harvesting, the cesta quickly replaced the old leather glove, which was too heavy and expensive.

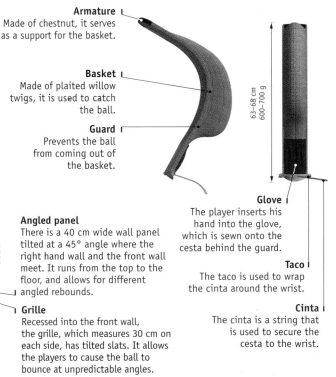

Armature
Made of chestnut, it serves as a support for the basket.

Basket
Made of plaited willow twigs, it is used to catch the ball.

Guard
Prevents the ball from coming out of the basket.

63–68 cm
600–700 g

Glove
The player inserts his hand into the glove, which is sewn onto the cesta behind the guard.

Taco
The taco is used to wrap the cinta around the wrist.

Cinta
The cinta is a string that is used to secure the cesta to the wrist.

Angled panel
There is a 40 cm wide wall panel tilted at a 45° angle where the right hand wall and the front wall meet. It runs from the top to the floor, and allows for different angled rebounds.

Grille
Recessed into the front wall, the grille, which measures 30 cm on each side, has tilted slats. It allows the players to cause the ball to bounce at unpredictable angles.

handball

A game of tactical skill, handball is played by bouncing a rubber ball in an enclosed space, using either hand. The first depictions of men striking a handball date back to 2000 B.C. in Egypt, and 1500 B.C. in Central America. The pastime spread to Europe with the Romans. In the 1840s, Ireland exported the game to North America and Australia. Between the 1920s and 1950s, national tournaments proliferated in Anglo-Saxon countries. The Court Handball Commission was founded in 1924 to give the sport an international structure. Since 1964, the World Championship has been held every three years, bringing together some 10 countries. Today, Mexico and Australia in particular are challenging the traditional supremacy of the United States, Canada, and Ireland.

Students at a Bronx high school play a game in a YMCA in New York (USA) in 1954.

HOW THE GAME IS PLAYED

Handball can be played by 2 players (singles), or by teams of 2 (doubles), on a one, three, or four wall court. The hands are the only part of the body that may be used to strike the ball. Play ends when one of the 2 opponents is unable to return the ball. A correct return takes place before the ball hits the ground twice, and it must touch the front wall before hitting the ground. The first player (or duo) to win 2 21-point games wins the match. In the event of a tie, a third 11-point game is played as a tiebreaker. Only the serving player may score a point. The receiver who wins a serve becomes the server.

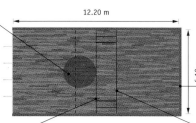

Play zone
Handball is a game of motion. A rally is won by forcing the opponent to leave the center of the court, by making the opponent lose balance, or by picking up speed.

12.20 m

6.10 m

Front wall

Short line
After rebounding off the front wall, the service ball must pass the short line before it hits the ground.

Service line
The server must not step beyond this line when serving the ball.

TECHNIQUE

The ball is usually struck between knee and hip height, using the palm of the hand (sometimes the fist). The wrist remains loose, and the forearm moves parallel to the ground. Rotating the wrist gives the ball a spin after the rebound. Mastering all of the moves with both hands is critical.

Warm up

To avoid being bruised by the ball, players increase their blood circulation by clapping or warming their hands. Service is the most powerful weapon, followed by the kill shot, which is struck close to the ground, in the corners.

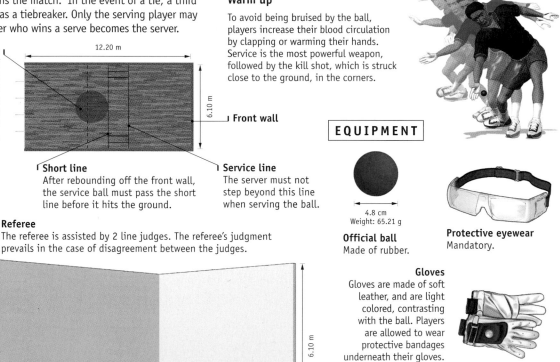

EQUIPMENT

4.8 cm
Weight: 65.21 g

Official ball
Made of rubber.

Protective eyewear
Mandatory.

Gloves
Gloves are made of soft leather, and are light colored, contrasting with the ball. Players are allowed to wear protective bandages underneath their gloves.

PLAYER PROFILE

- Powerful, quick legs, good cardiovascular endurance, and solid shoulders and arms are essential. Bodybuilding in the gym and long distance running are useful, but the most essential physical and technical training takes place on the court.

- It is not uncommon for players to maintain peak performance for 10 to 15 years, until about age 35.

THE COURT

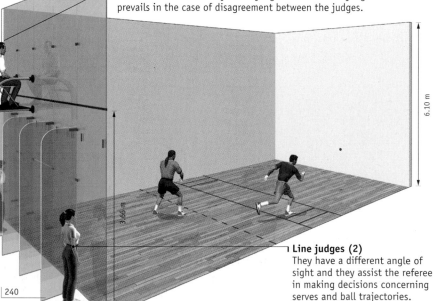

Referee
The referee is assisted by 2 line judges. The referee's judgment prevails in the case of disagreement between the judges.

6.10 m

3.66 m

Line judges (2)
They have a different angle of sight and they assist the referee in making decisions concerning serves and ball trajectories.

Ball Sports (Large Ball)

soccer

Edson Arantes do Nascimento, nicknamed Pele (BRA), first superstar of televised soccer. He won World Cups in 1958, 1962, and 1970, and scored 1,280 goals in his career.

Soccer is a ball sport played between two teams. Its roots go back to antiquity (called *sphaira* by the Greeks and *ollis* by the Romans); in Renaissance Italy, a more elaborate version, *calcio*, was played. Soccer as we know it today was invented in England in the mid 19th century (1848). The first club, Sheffield Football Club, was formed in 1863, and the first competition, the Football Association (FA) Challenge Cup, was organized in 1872. The Fédération internationale de football association (FIFA) was founded in 1904. A demonstration sport in the Olympics of 1900 and 1904, soccer became an official Olympic event in 1908. Soccer is universal because its equipment and rules are simple and because of global coverage of the World Cup. No other international event is followed so closely, due mainly to television broadcasting of matches since 1958 (1.7 billion viewers watched the France–Brazil final in 1998). Today, 203 countries are FIFA members.

THE MATCH

The objective of soccer is for one team to send the ball into the opposing team's goal by propelling it with the feet or any other part of the body but the arms or hands. Two teams with a maximum of 11 players (1 goalkeeper and 10 field players) play two 45-min periods with a halftime of not more than 15 min. The referee keeps track of stoppages in play and may extend the periods beyond the regulation 45 min if he deems it necessary (injuries, player changes, etc.). During a World Cup game, if there is a tie at the end of regulation time, the teams play two 15-min overtime periods. If there is still a tie after the overtime periods, a penalty shoot-out takes place. The referee decides which goal will be used for the penalty kicks; the team to kick first is determined by a coin toss. Each team chooses 5 players to take the kicks; the teams take turns, and the team that has the most goals after 5 kicks wins the game. If the teams are still tied after 5 kicks each, the teams keep taking penalty kicks until one team wins.

THE SOCCER FIELD

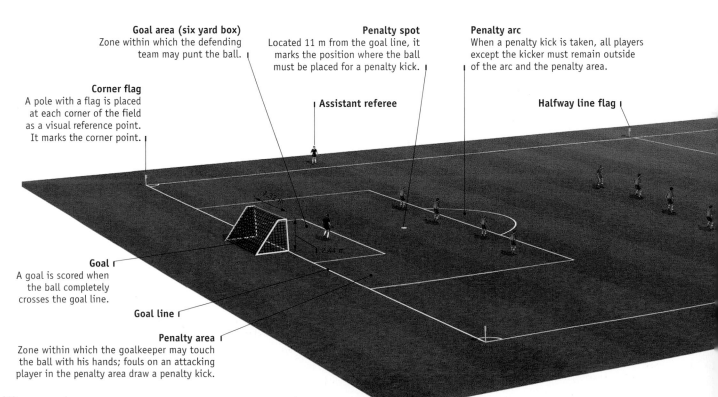

Goal area (six yard box)
Zone within which the defending team may punt the ball.

Penalty spot
Located 11 m from the goal line, it marks the position where the ball must be placed for a penalty kick.

Penalty arc
When a penalty kick is taken, all players except the kicker must remain outside of the arc and the penalty area.

Corner flag
A pole with a flag is placed at each corner of the field as a visual reference point. It marks the corner point.

Assistant referee

Halfway line flag

Goal
A goal is scored when the ball completely crosses the goal line.

Goal line

Penalty area
Zone within which the goalkeeper may touch the ball with his hands; fouls on an attacking player in the penalty area draw a penalty kick.

BASIC FORMATIONS

A number of tactical formations are used in soccer, from the WM (3–2–2–3) popular in the 1950s to today's 4–4–2 (4 defenders, 4 midfielders, and 2 strikers). Other variations are used as needed (3–5–2, 4–5–1, etc.) by professional teams to respond to the tactics of the opposing team. Today, the key to success resides in controlling the game in midfield.

Backs (right and left)
They must stop the progress of an opposing attacker in their zone or slow him down to enable their teammates to get into defensive formation. In offense, they use their speed to start play quickly on their side of the field.

Strikers
They convert passes that come to them and create goal-scoring situations by trying to escape the opposing defenders and passing the ball to their teammates. Their defensive work consists of keeping the opposing team from forming an attack.

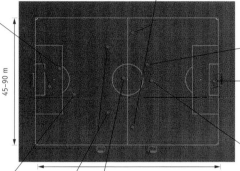

45–90 m

90–120 m

Stopper
He covers an opposing forward to keep him from getting into a scoring position.

Goalkeeper
The only player allowed to use his hands, he must stop shots from the opposing team. He is his team's last line of defense and directs his teammates when the other team is attacking.

Sweeper
Placed behind his teammates, he directs the defense. He is not concerned with covering an opposing player, but anticipates and fills defensive gaps. He is thus free to launch an attack.

Attacking midfield
He directs offensive play and organizes attacks. He dictates the pace of play for his teammates and must be capable of scoring goals.

Midfielders (right and left)
They play both defense and attack. In defense, they must take the ball away from an opposing player before he can organize an attack. In offense, they relay the ball to the attacking midfielder or strikers and provide support. They are the transition between defense and attack.

Defensive midfield
He must try to get the ball away from the opposing team as quickly as possible. he thus helps his fellow defenders and tries to get an attack going as quickly as possible.

Corner arc
This indicates the zone within which the ball must be placed for a corner kick. The opposing players must stay at least 9.15 m away from the corner point until the ball is in play.

Referee
The referee controls the match and the clock and is the absolute authority on the soccer field. The referee's decisions cannot be appealed.

Center circle
During a kickoff, each team must stay in its own half of the field. The team that is kicking can have any number of players inside the circle, while opposing players may not come closer than 9.15 m (the radius of the circle) to the ball until it is in play.

Technical areas (benches)
There is one for each team. They are for the technical personnel (coach and assistant coaches, trainers, physiotherapists, etc.) and 5 substitute players. Each team may make a maximum of 3 substitutions during the game.

Halfway line
Defines each team's side.

Center spot
Spot where the ball is positioned for a kickoff. Kickoffs occur at the beginning of each period (to start play) and after a goal is scored.

Assistant referees (3)
They signal out-of-play balls, goalkeeper runouts, corners, offsides, and fouls that the referee did not see. They also supervise player substitutions.

Touch line
When the ball crosses this line, it is out of play. It is thrown back into play by a player from the opposing team.

ATTACK

Corner kick

A corner kick is awarded when a defender puts the ball out of play behind his team's goal line. An attacking player must then try to send the ball in front of the goal for another attacker to head, or make a short pass to a teammate.

Run

In a run, a player rushes up the side of the field to destabilize the opponent's defense. The player may penetrate deep into opposing territory. The run usually ends with a cross to an attacker who deflects the ball into the net.

Wall
This line of players protects the goal area during a free kick.

Dribbling

Dribbling is a feint made with the feet that allows the player to keep control of the ball and get by an opposing player.

Heading the ball

An attacker heads the ball to redirect it toward the net. A defender heads the ball to deflect it away from the goal.

Free kick

A free kick is awarded when a player has been fouled. In the direct free kick, the ball can be kicked directly at the goal, without a teammate touching it. In the indirect free kick, the ball must be passed to a teammate before being directed at the goal. A free kick taken near the opposing team's goal provides an excellent scoring opportunity. Several players on each team specialize in this play, which requires great accuracy. Free kicks often make the difference in the score.

Penalty kick

A penalty kick is awarded when a foul is committed by a defender in the penalty area. The ball is placed on the penalty spot and the attacking player tries to kick it directly into the goal. The goalkeeper must stand still on the goal line before moving to stop the ball. He can move forward only after the ball has been kicked.

DEFENSE

Zone defense

In zone defense, the defensive zone is divided into a grid, and each player covers part of the field. This type of defense is a tactical choice influenced by the strength of the opposing team.

Sliding tackle

The tackle is a defensive play, in which a player tries to get the ball away from an attacker by sliding, without touching the attacking player.

1–2 relay (give and go)

The 1-2 relay is a quick series of passes between two players that takes an opposing player out of the play. The defender tries to follow the ball, but finds himself with his back to it and cannot follow it effectively. The player passes to his teammate, who immediately passes it back to him behind the defender's back and he continues his run. Relays are usually made with a single kick, directly and without controlling the ball.

2-on-1 coverage

In 2-on-1 coverage, a player assists a teammate who is trying to take the ball from an opposing player. The covering player will intervene if the attacker gets by the first defender. Coverage play is very effective for recapturing the ball "safely," without taking extra risk.

1-on-1 defense

In 1-on-1 defense, each player on the defending team "covers" a player on the attacking team, following his every move, trying to keep him from receiving the ball, kicking or passing it.

OFFSIDE

Players are offside when they are closer to the opposing goal line than the ball, unless two defenders are between the attacker and the goal. The offside, considered a defensive tactic (the entire defensive line moves rapidly in a wave to put the attackers offside), is a double-edged sword that requires synchronization and discipline on the part of the defenders. An offside is very difficult to judge, because it must be called when the ball is kicked, and at this moment the linesmen must be watching both the player passing the ball and the position of his teammate on the receiving end.

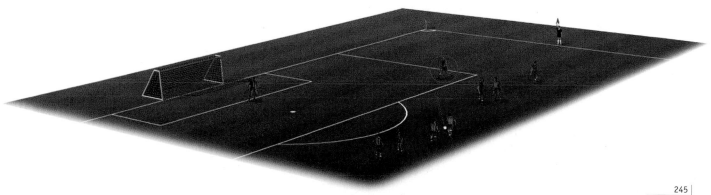

GOALKEEPING TECHNIQUES AND TACTICS

Throwing the ball

After a stop, the goalkeeper often starts play again by passing the ball to a nearby defender. The goalkeeper is the only player allowed to touch the ball with the hands. If the attack preceding the stop came from the left, the goalkeeper will try to start play to the right, since there are fewer opposing players on that side, and vice versa. Throwing is more accurate than punting and enables the defending team to keep possession of the ball and prepare an attack.

Fist block

When the ball is kicked powerfully, often from a distance, goalkeepers cannot always catch it safely. Hitting it with the fist enables them to deflect the shot over the goal or to the side. If it is a high cross and a number of attackers are blocking the zone trying to head the ball into the goal, the goalkeeper has no choice but to hit the ball with one or both fists (punching the ball). Since he cannot catch the ball without the risk of dropping it, it is better to deflect it away.

Lateral dive

This move requires perfect coordination of the dive as the ball is shot. It allows the goalkeeper to stop or deflect a shot when he is not directly in the ball's path. As well, he must avoid a ball bouncing back in front of the goal.

Punting the ball

To send the ball deep into the offensive zone, the goalkeeper punts the ball and his teammates rush to where the ball will fall to try to take possession. However, kicking is not always accurate.

REFEREEING AND DISCIPLINARY SANCTIONS

Warning (yellow card)

Players receive a warning if they regularly break the rules, do not respect the referee's decision, delay the start of play, are argumentative, or show unsportsmanlike conduct.

Expulsion (red card)

Players are expelled if they commit a serious foul, are violent, use abusive, offensive, or insulting language, or receive a second yellow card during the game.

CUPS AND CHAMPIONSHIPS

Competitions are ranked according to importance (world, continental, national) and to whether they involve national or club teams. FIFA organizes the World Cup (national teams) and, since January 2000, the World Club Cup. The six continental confederations organize international tournaments (Euro, African and Asian Nations Cups, Copa America, etc.), and interclub tournaments, which involve the best clubs in a country (Champions League in Europe and Africa, Copa Libertadores in South America, etc.). The national federations organize competitions within their own countries (championships and cups). Every year, the Intercontinental Cup is played between the winners of the Champions League (Europe) and the Copa Libertadores.

WORLD CUPS			
Year	Host country	Champion/Finalist	Score
1930	Uruguay	Uruguay/Argentina	4–2
1934	Italy	Italy/Czechoslovakia	2–1
1938	France	Italy/Hungary	4–2
1950	Brazil	Uruguay/Brazil	2–1
1954	Switzerland	West Germany/Hungary	3–2
1958	Sweden	Brazil/Sweden	5–2
1962	Chile	Brazil/Czechoslovakia	3–1
1966	England	England/West Germany	4–2
1970	Mexico	Brazil/Italy	4–1
1974	West Germany	West Germany/Netherlands	2–1
1978	Argentina	Argentina/Netherlands	3–1
1982	Spain	Italy/West Germany	3–1
1986	Mexico	Argentina/West Germany	3–2
1990	Italy	West Germany/Argentina	1–0
1994	United States	Brazil/Italy	0–0 (3–2 on penalty kicks)
1998	France	France/Brazil	3–0

EQUIPMENT

Goalkeeper's gloves

Goalkeeper's shirt
The goalkeeper's shirt has long sleeves with padded elbows.

Shorts

Shin guard

Knee socks

Shirt
Each team has at least two different uniforms: one in traditional colors for home play, and one for playing away games. Each player has a short-sleeved shirt for summer games and a long-sleeved jersey for winter games. The player's number must appear on the back of the shirt.

Shoes
They are made of leather, soft rubber, and/or plastic.

Ball
Made of leather covered with synthetic material.

Circumference: 68–70 cm
Weight: 410–450 g
Inflation pressure: 600–1,100 g/cm²

Cleats
They are of different sizes and are screwed in so that they can be changed depending on field conditions. Molded cleats may be used on dry fields.

Maximum diameter: 12.7 mm
Maximum length: 18 mm

Diego Maradona (ARG)
This midfielder, nicknamed El Pibe de Oro (the golden boy), is known for his unique sense of game strategy and his quickness, dribbling, and ability to control the ball. World champion in 1986.

PLAYER PROFILE

- There is not really a typical profile of a soccer player, although superior athletic ability is essential at the highest level.

- Daily training involves exercising (stretching), practicing basic techniques, and planning and practicing key plays or team tactics. Training lasts one or two hours, except on game day, when it is replaced by a warm-up session.

- In addition to natural talent, a high-level player should be in good physical condition, be quick and agile, and have excellent technique, a good vision of the game, and strong team spirit.

Michel Platini (FRA)
A midfielder, he was famous for his perfect free kicks and unprecedented sense of the game. He led the French team to fourth and third places in the 1982 and 1986 World Cups, and was national coach for the French team from 1988 to 1992.

Franz Beckenbauer (GER)
Nicknamed the Kaiser (the emperor). A defender then sweeper on Munich's famous Bayern team and the West German national team, he was known for his faultless technique and his spectacularly powerful and direct runs. European champion in 1972 and world champion in 1974 as captain; also world champion in 1990 as coach.

Mia Hamm (USA)
The major female star in soccer, she has played in more than 150 international matches and scored 108 goals. She was Olympic champion in 1996 and world champion in 1999.

rugby

Frantz Reichel of the French national team at the 1900 Paris Olympics, the first time rugby was an Olympic event

Rugby is a sport played by 2 teams of 15 players each, in which a ball is moved with the hands and feet. First played at Rugby School in England in 1823, the game flouted the rules of the day governing soccer by allowing players to take the ball in their hands. Rugby was initially played with a round ball. The oval ball was adopted in 1851. The first club, Guy's Hospital, was formed in 1843, and it was only in 1871 that the first rules were codified, under the name of Rugby Football. In 1877, the number of players went from 20 to 15, and in 1886, Ireland, Scotland, and Wales founded the International Rugby Football Board (IRFB), which established the rules of play. England became a member four years later. In 1895, a split led to the creation of the Northern Rugby Football Union and 13-a-side teams. The game became an Olympic sport in 1900, at the Paris Games, and remained so until 1924. In 1910, The first Tournament of Five Nations brought together the four IRFB member teams and France, which only joined the federation in 1978. The first World Cup was organized jointly by Australia and New Zealand in 1987 and women had their first own World Cup in 1991. In 1995, high level rugby players acquired professional status.

HOW A MATCH IS PLAYED

A team is made up of 15 players on the field and 7 substitutes. The ball may be moved with either the feet or the hands. Each team attempts to score points by placing the ball in the opposition's in-goal area by hand, or by kicking the ball between the uprights of the goal posts above the crossbar. A match consists of 2 40-min halves, with an intermission lasting not longer than 10 min. At the kickoff, the team that gained possession of the ball by winning the toss kicks the ball into the opponent's zone from the center spot. The ball must cross the opposition's 10 m line to be considered in play. When the ball is played with the hand, it must not be passed forward. However, it may be kicked forward. When the attacking team places the ball in the other team's in-goal area, it scores a try, which is worth 5 points, and which can then be converted. A convert is a kick at the goal made by an attacking player, from the distance of his choice, directly in line with the spot where the try was scored. All the opposition players must remain in their in-goal area. If the ball passes between the uprights and above the crossbar, the convert is good and is worth 2 points. If not, only the 5 points scored for the try are counted. The team that has given up points puts the ball back into play at the halfway line. A goal scored from a penalty kick (a kick made from where a foul was committed, with the penalized team not being allowed to interfere) is worth 3 points. Any player may attempt a drop goal at any time. This is worth 3 points if the ball goes between the uprights and above the crossbar. The team having scored more points at the end of the match is declared the winner.

THE PLAYING AREA

The playing area is grass covered, and includes the two in-goal areas, which are delimited by the goal line and the dead ball line.

Flag posts (14)
Flag posts are located along the touchlines at the 2 ends of the dead ball lines, the goal lines, the 22 m lines, and the halfway line; they indicate the boundaries of the playing field.

Dead ball line
It marks the end of the in-goal area.

Goal line
It marks the edge of the in-goal area.

Touchline
When the ball crosses this line, it is no longer in play, and must be put back into play by means of a line-out.

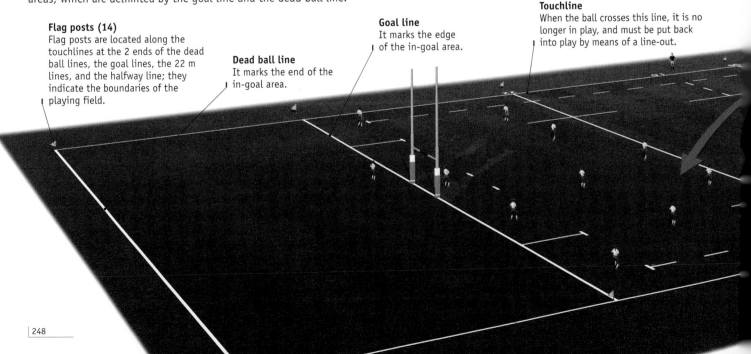

PLAYER POSITIONS

The number of a player's jersey generally corresponds to a specific position on the field.

Fullback
The fullback is the last line of defense when an opponent is attempting to score a try. He must also gather clearing kicks from the opposing team and relaunch his team's attack, either moving the ball by hand or with a clearing kick.

Three-quarters (centers and wingers)
On defense, they must be good tacklers in order to prevent the opponents from moving across the field. On offense, they move the ball around quickly by hand to beat the opposing defenders. Centers are excellent passers, and are able to go forward to challenge the opposing centers in order to create imbalances in their defense. The wingers, thanks to their speed, elude defenders to score.

Centers | **Winger**

Winger

Fly half
The fly half acts as a link between the scrum half and the three-quarters. He initiates his team's attacks.

Scrum half
He serves as the link between the forwards and the back lines. During scrums, it is up to him to recover the ball and put his three-quarters into an attacking position.

Third row
They form the last line of players in a scrum. They must keep the ball between their feet until the scrum half can recover it. During play, they must relay the ball from the front row to the halves.

Second row (locks)
Solid players who bind, or support, the front row during a scrum. Their role is to win or recover the ball during throw-ins or scrums.

Tight head prop | **Loose head prop**

Hooker

Front row
They are in contact with the opposition during a scrum. The hooker is responsible for winning the ball and heeling it to his teammates behind him. The prop forwards bind the hooker and attempt to move the scrum forward by pushing their opponents in order to gain ground. During play, they attempt to stop the opposing team from advancing and winning the ball during scrums.

10 m | 22 m | 22 m | 10 m

66–70 m

95–100 m

CUPS AND CHAMPIONSHIPS

Rugby World Cup (RWC)
Alternating between the Northern and Southern Hemispheres, it has been staged every 4 years since 1987. Twenty countries take part in the finals.

Six Nations Tournament
Formerly the Five Nations Tournament, it includes England, Scotland, Wales, Ireland, France, and Italy (since 2000). Each country plays every other country once, alternating home and away games.

Rugby Super Twelve
This tournament, which began in 1996 and involves clubs from the Southern Hemisphere, involves 12 club teams (three from Australia, five from New Zealand, and four from South Africa), each representing a province or city. They play each other once at home and once away between February and May. The top 4 meet in the semi-finals, and the 2 semi-final winners meet in the final.

Tri-Series
In this annual tournament, Australia, New Zealand, and South Africa play each other twice.

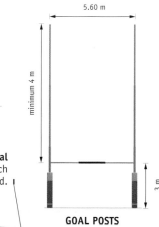

5.60 m

minimum 4 m

3 m

GOAL POSTS

Halfway line
The halfway line marks the division between the two teams' territories.

10 meter line
During a kick-off, the team not in possession of the ball must not cross this line. The team putting the ball into play must send the ball beyond this line.

In-goal
The area within which a try can be scored.

Lock line
Situated 15 m from the touchline, it indicates the furthest position that may be occupied by the lock, the last player in line, during a line-out.

Throw-in line
Situated 5 m from the touch-line, it indicates the position to be occupied by the first player in line during a line-out.

22 meter line
This line marks the spot where the ball is put back into play with a drop-out kick.

TECHNIQUES AND TACTICS

The team in possession of the ball can move it forward using either the hands (passes) or the feet. A player carrying the ball may run toward the opposition's in-goal with no restrictions on his movement. Playing the ball with the foot can be a defensive tactic. When a player gathers the ball in defense and cannot pass it to a teammate, he propels it away from his in-goal with a clearing kick. It can also be an offensive tactic that serves to get the ball over the opponent's first line of defense or to push the other team back in its own territory.

Passing

Enables a team to maintain possession of the ball by moving it around among several teammates. A pass must always be made backward. A rapid succession of passes creates openings in the other team's defense that are used to move toward the in-goal area. Mastery of passing is fundamental.

Mark (fair catch)

A player makes a direct catch of a forward kick or pass by the opposing team between his own in-goal and 22 m line and shouts "Mark!" A mark can be made even by a player who has both feet off the ground. The player having made the mark is then entitled to a free kick.

Place kick (penalty kick)

The ball is on the ground, standing vertically, and the kicker attempts to kick it between the 2 posts, and over the crossbar. His non-kicking foot remains slightly behind the ball so that his kicking foot strikes as close to the base of the ball as possible, giving it an upward trajectory.

Drop kick

The kicker lets the ball fall and kicks it the moment it hits the ground. The kicking foot must strike it at exactly the moment it bounces to give it an upward trajectory. This type of kick also allows for better ball control.

Hold

A hold takes place when the ball carrier is tackled by one or more opponents and, while he is being held, his feet and another part of his body are touching the ground. When on the ground, the held player must immediately release the ball, without attempting to play it in any way, and get up and move away.

Tackle

A defensive tactic where an opponent carrying the ball can be blocked and prevented from continuing to move forward. A defender is allowed to grab an opponent in the area between the knees and the torso. Only the player in possession of the ball can be tackled. A tackled player who falls to the ground must release the ball.

Ruck

When a player is tackled to the ground, he must immediately release the ball, which is then free. A player close by can recover it and continue the play sequence. Otherwise, the 2 teams form a ruck to attempt to gain possession of the ball. When the ruck is formed, it is forbidden to propel the ball forward on the ground by pushing it with the hand. A player cannot move it in his territory except by heeling it, i.e. pushing it with his foot behind him to the scrum half. Players joining a ruck must bind with at least one arm around a teammate, having come up from behind (not from a sideways position, since this constitutes an offside).

Set scrum

Takes place after a foul (knock forward, forward pass, improper line-out, or improper throw-in). The scrum is formed by 8 players from each team (3 front row players, 2 second row players, and 3 back row players) grouped in such a way as to allow the ball to be thrown on the ground between them. The non-offending team puts the ball back into play. The hooker (front row center) is responsible for "heeling" the ball, i.e. pushing it with the foot towards the back of the scrum. Players must not leave the scrum before the ball comes out. Those not in the scrum must remain behind the hindmost player of his scrum.

Maul

Occurs when the ball carrier has been stopped by a defender without being taken to the ground, and several players come and struggle for possession of the ball. The maul is formed by a number of players from the 2 teams who are on their feet when they contact the ball carrier and encircle him. A maul ends when the ball is on the ground, when the ball becomes loose, when the player carrying it frees himself, or when a scrum has been called.

Line out

When the ball or the player in possession of it touches or crosses the touchline, the ball is in touch. The ball is put back into play by the team that did not have possession prior to the ball or player going into touch. The line-out is formed by at least 2 players from each team, standing in two straight lines at right angles to the touch line. The team putting the ball into play decides how many players will line up. A space of 1 m between the 2 rows of players, called the tunnel, must be respected. The line-out extends from the throw-in line to the lock line. The player putting the ball into play must throw it, using one or both hands, directly between the two lines of players. Players not in the line-out must remain 10 m from the ball. During the throw-in, it is permitted to support a teammate who has jumped to grab the ball. If a team benefiting from a penalty kicks the ball into touch, it takes the throw-in.

Throw-in

The player taking the throw-in positions himself outside the playing field equidistant from the 2 lines of players. He throws the ball into the tunnel, and the 2 sides attempt to recover it.

PENALTY

A penalty is awarded to the non-offending team when the opposing team has broken the rules (offside, knock forward, unsportsmanlike conduct). The team benefiting from the penalty can decide what form it will take. It can choose a goal kick, in which case the referee must be advised so that his assistants position themselves at the foot of the goal posts in order to judge the attempt. It is permitted to play a penalty with the hand in order to keep possession of the ball. In this case, the player making the throw-in must touch the ball with his foot before taking hold of it and passing it to a teammate. Opposing players must remain at least 10 m from the ball.

Offside

A player is considered to be offside if he is ahead of the ball when it is being played by one of his teammates, unless he is not interfering with play. During a scrum, a ruck, a maul, or a line-out, a player is offside if he remains ahead of or moves ahead of the hindmost player of his team in the scrum. When a player kicks the ball, any teammates in front of him are automatically offside. They must move back behind him or wait until he passes them to be onside again.

Offside position
The players are positioned in front of the hindmost player of their team in the scrum.

Knock forward and forward pass

A knock forward occurs when the ball goes forward toward the opposition's dead ball line after a player has lost possession of it or propelled it with his arm or hand.

A forward pass occurs when the ball carrier passes the ball by hand or otherwise throws it, and the ball moves towards the opponent's dead ball line. A knock forward or forward pass results in the calling of a scrum that benefits the non-offending team.

Advantage

In the case where a foul leads to a scrum or a penalty, the advantage rule allows the non-offending team to continue playing if the foul gives it an advantage such as a ground gain or ball possession. The referee decides whether the advantage rule is to be applied or whether a penalty or scrum should be called.

Penalty try

When a defender commits a foul that deprives the attacking team of a certain try, or forces the attacker to score a try in a less favorable position than he otherwise would have had, the referee awards the attacking team a penalty try, which is worth 5 points, between the goal posts. A convert may be attempted after a penalty try.

Free kick

A free kick is awarded to the non-offending team if a technical foul is committed. The kicker has the choice of kicking the ball or playing it with his hand. Attempting a shot on goal is not permitted. Opposing players must remain at least 10 m from the ball.

VARIATIONS OF RUGBY

13-a-side rugby (Rugby League): This variation grew out of a split in the English Rugby Football Union. A dissident league, the Northern Rugby Union, was created, and organized 13 man professional rugby. Along with the number of players, certain rules were modified to make the game more spectacular. The ruck was done away with, the hold was introduced, and the charge became all the more important since ball movement increased. The two third-row flanks, who impede ball movement, were eliminated. The throw-in was replaced by the scrum. Rugby League conferred professional status upon its elite players well before Rugby Union did. It is the most popular form of rugby in the Southern Hemisphere.

7-a-side rugby: Created in 1880 in the small town of Melrose in southern Scotland for economic reasons (the need to reduce the costs of lodging and organizing tournaments), it quickly spread across the world. The first tournament was held in 1883. The awarding of points differs from classic rugby. A try is worth 2 points, a convert is worth 3, and a drop goal is worth 4. 7-a-side rugby is played in 2 halves of 7 or 10 minutes on the same size field as 15-a-side rugby, and is governed by the same rules. A 7 man rugby team is made up of 3 forwards and 4 backs (or three-quarters). The RWC Sevens World Cup is an international tournament played every 4 years since 1993. Since 1996, an annual international circuit has comprised 12 tournaments grouping 12 to 16 national teams.

Gaelic football: Most popular in Ireland, it features 2 teams of 15 players (plus 3 substitutes). A match lasts 70 min. Goals can be scored 2 ways: under the crossbar (which explains the goalkeeper), or over the crossbar, as in rugby. However, goals scored under the crossbar are awarded only if the ball has been directed with the feet or hit with the hand. Goals scored in the goal are worth 3 points, those scored above the crossbar are worth 1.

Gaelic football is played with a round ball, which can be passed forward to a teammate. There is no play behind the goal area, and play with the hand is very limited, which explains why the charge is not as important. The ball must not be thrown, but can be carried for 4 steps. It can be bounced only once before being hit with the fist or kicked.

GAELIC FOOTBALL

137 m

82 m

EQUIPMENT

Dress

Thick shoulder pads are not permitted. However, the referee may authorize the wearing of soft protective equipment (padding, foam rubber, or a similar soft material) that complies with strict technical specifications.

Jersey
The number worn on the back of the jersey corresponds to the player's position on the field.

Shorts

Socks

Rugby shoes
The cleats may be of leather, plastic, rubber, or aluminum. They must not exceed 18 mm in length.

Ball
The ball is made of treated leather or polyvinyl chloride (PVC) so that it is water and mud resistant. It must be constructed of four sections, and conform to regulation dimensions. Originally round, it took its oval form when an egg shaped pig's bladder was first used.

circumferences:
760–790 mm/580–620 mm
400–440 g

1851

1923

OFFICIATING AND SANCTIONS

A referee and 2 assistants ensure that the rules of play are respected on the field. They penalize all rough play or dangerous behavior by a series of sanctions: free kicks, penalties, and yellow and red cards. They also penalize any unsportsmanlike conduct that goes against the rules and does not constitute fair play, such as insults or obstruction. All unsportsmanlike conduct results in a penalty.

Yellow card

A yellow card is handed out in the case of rough play or dangerous behavior. It constitutes a warning, and results in a 10 min expulsion. A player who receives a second yellow card is expelled for the rest of the match.

Red card

A red card is handed out in the case of especially rough play or dangerous behavior, or if a player has repeatedly contravened the rules. It results in the player's immediate expulsion.

RUGBY PLAYER PROFILE

The current style of play favors players with a fully developed physique, but skills and body size may vary according to the particular position:

- A back is often tall and slender. He must have the qualities of a sprinter and a kicker.
- The three-quarters are also chosen for their speed and stamina, and must be able to make long runs.
- The halfs are generally stocky, have a low center of gravity, and are quick and mobile.
- The forwards are big and sturdy (6'2" m and over 220 lbs). The forward is the archetypal rugby player.

Preparation begins with basic training (running, endurance, bodybuilding) and physical exercises (stretching). Players then move on to technical training (passing games) and tactical maneuvers (positioning during throw-ins and scrums). A player reaches the peak of his career around the age of 26 or 27.

Rory Underwood (GBR)
A winger who scored 51 tries in 85 matches (an English record), he was a member of the winning team in the Five Nations Tournament in 1991, 1992, and 1995, and a member of a finalist team at the 1991 World Cup and 1997 European Cup, with Leicester.

Jean-Pierre Rives (FRA)
A third row flank, nicknamed "Casque d'or" because of his blond hair, he captained the French national team 34 times in 59 matches. A member of the winning team in the Five Nations Tournament in 1977 and 1981, and the best French player in 1977, 1979, and 1981, he was the symbol of the French national squad during the 1970s and 1980s.

Michael Lynagh (AUS)
A fly half and the World record holder for points scored (914), including 17 tries in 72 matches with the Australian national team between 1984 and 1995, he is considered one of the world's top players. He was a member of the 1991 World Cup winning team.

Australian rules football

Phillip Read, of the West Coast, and Shane Crawford (right), captain of the Hawthorn Hawks, play in an Ansett Cup game in 2000. In 1999, Crawford won the Brownlow Cup for best player in the league.

A team contact sport played with an oval ball, Australian rules football borrows as much from rugby as from Gaelic football. Considered as off season training for cricket players, Australian football is played on cricket fields. An initial version of the game and official rules were developed in 1858, and in the same year, the first official game took place between Melbourne Grammar School and Scotch College. The foundation of the Victorian Football League in 1896 marked the beginning of a major expansion. Interprovincial matches began to be held at the same time, and, by 1914, most of the other Australian states were participating. The annual championship ends in September with the Grand Final, the match between the two finalist teams, that today attracts more than 5 million television viewers. In the early 1990s, the Victorian Football League was renamed the Australian Football League (AFC), and the creation of the Ansett Cup, a summer championship event, keeps football in the Australian limelight all year.

HOW A MATCH IS PLAYED

At the start of each quarter and after each goal, the field umpire puts the ball into play by bouncing it on the ground in the center circle. The only players allowed into the center square are the center, the rover, and the two followers for each team. A match consists of four 20 minute quarters, which are usually extended to compensate for interruptions in play (because of injuries, replacements, etc.). Two teams of 18 players each attempt to place or kick the ball between the opposing team's goal posts to score points. The team with the most points at the end of the game wins. Players are not allowed to throw the ball to a teammate; they must hit it with their foot or fist. A player can move freely with the ball, but must ensure that the ball touches the ground every 15 m. When a foul is committed against a player, he is entitled to a free kick from the site of the foul. A player who is in possession of the ball can be held or checked on any part of the body between the shoulders and knees. The player must be allowed to pass the ball at all times. A player located within a 5 m radius of the ball may be pushed or checked, but not held. The player holding the ball is allowed to defend himself against an attacker by pushing back with his free hand.

Wings (2)
The wings ensure the ball's progression in the offensive zone, provide back up for the half-forwards and forwards on offence, and score goals. They are the center's linemates.

Field umpires
Since 1994, in response to the increasingly fast pace of the game, three field umpires preside over the game. Each umpire supervises a different section of the oval, and rules on illegal moves.

Halfback
Halfbacks recover the ball behind their line and return it to the center and the wings. They ensure the transition between defence and offence.

Boundary umpires (2)
They notify the field umpires when the ball leaves the field, and return it to play.

Center
The center is the link between the offensive and defensive players. This key position is filled by players who are able to anticipate the play.

OVAL

Back pockets (2)
These are the fullback's linemates.

50 m line
Located at a 50 m radius from each goal line, it is used as reference point.

Fullback
The fullback is the player in the farthest back position. His role is to recover the ball and relaunch the attack.

Interchange players (4)

SCORING

A goal (6 points) is scored only if the ball passes directly between the goal posts following a kick, without being touched by another player. A "behind" (1 point) is awarded when the ball passes directly between the goal post and a behind post, when it hits a goal post, or when it is carried or pushed beyond the goal line or the behind line.

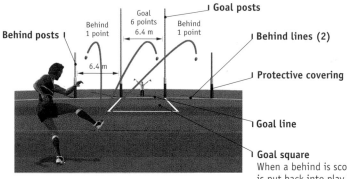

Behind posts

Behind 1 point

Goal 6 points 6.4 m

Behind 1 point

6.4 m

Goal posts

Behind lines (2)

Protective covering

Goal line

Goal square
When a behind is scored, the ball is put back into play by one of the defenders, who must kick off from within the goal square.

PLAYER POSITIONS

A team is made up of 18 players, who are positioned in 5 lines across the field, and 4 interchange players. Each player is assigned a specific strategic position, but may move freely around the entire oval. The rover and the two followers stay near the ball during every phase of the game.

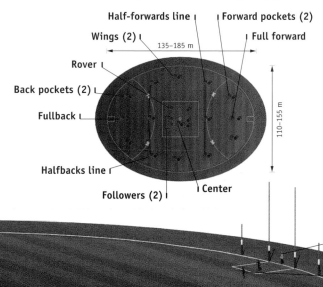

Half-forwards line

Forward pockets (2)

Wings (2)

Full forward

135–185 m

Rover

Back pockets (2)

110–155 m

Fullback

Halfbacks line

Followers (2)

Center

TECHNIQUES

MARK

A mark is awarded when a player catches the ball kicked by his teammate positioned at least 10 m away, before the ball touches the ground or another player. The player who marked is given the option of putting the ball in play by passing it, or using an unopposed free kick, which makes it an important strategic element.

HANDBALLING

The speed of handballing makes it an excellent offensive football maneuver. The ball, which rests on the palm on the open hand pointed in the desired direction, is hit with the thumb and index finger of the clenched fist of the other hand.

EQUIPMENT

The uniform consists of shorts, a sleeveless jersey (numbered according to the player's position), and socks in the team colors. Only mouthguards, shin pads, and a light head protector are allowed.

Ball
The ball is made from four pieces of leather sewn together, covering a synthetic bladder-shaped bag.

circumferences:
720–730 mm/545–555 mm
450–500 g

Goal umpires (2)
They determine if a score is a goal or a "behind."

Full-forward
His role is to recover the ball in the offensive zone and score goals or behinds.

Forward pockets (2)
These are the full-forward's linemates. They help him to recover the ball in the offensive zone and support him in his attempts to score.

Half-forwards
They attack the ball, attempt to score, and keep the ball in the offensive zone.

Boundary line
When the ball crosses this line, a boundary umpire puts it back into play. If it crosses this line directly after a kick and without touching the ground or another player, a free kick is granted to the nearest player on the opposing team.

Interchange players (4)

Center square

Interchange zone

american and canadian football

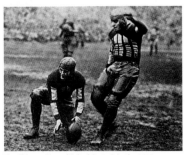

The Chicago Bears (United States) in the 1920s

Football was invented at Princeton University in 1867 as a variant of soccer. Called Princeton Rules, it was exclusively a college sport, played at the most prestigious universities (Princeton, Yale, Harvard, etc.). In 1876, the Intercollegiate Football Association was founded and the first rules were written. Walter Camp, a Harvard player, developed the game after 1880 by introducing the quarterback, the number of downs allowed to advance 10 yards, and a points system. In Canada, the Canadian Rugby Football Union, founded in 1882, became the Canadian Rugby Union (CRU) and organized a championship in 1892. In the United States, the codification of the rules was almost completed by 1912. In 1920, the first professional league, the American Professional Football Association, was born; it was renamed the National Football League (NFL) two years later. A rival league, the American Football League, provided competition for the NFL starting in 1960, and the champions of the two leagues met in a championship game that became the Super Bowl. The leagues then merged as the NFL. The Canadian Football League (CFL), the successor to the CRU, has been in existence since 1958.

THE GAME

Two teams of 11 players (12 in Canadian football) play for 4 15-minute quarters. There is a 12 minute halftime (14 minutes in Canadian football) between the second and third quarters. Each team has a maximum of 45 players, divided into three formations: offense, defense, and special teams.

The game begins with a coin toss that determines which team will kick off. The ball is placed on a kicking tee on the 30 yard line of the team that is kicking off (35 yards in United States college football and Canadian football). Following reception of the ball, the offensive unit of the team that has received the kick off comes onto the field, as does the defensive unit of the team that kicked off. Each team's objective is to score more points than the other team. The offense has 4 downs (3 downs in Canadian football) to advance 10 yards. If it does so on the 1st, 2nd, 3rd, or 4th down, it starts a new series of downs. The ball is moved forward by running or passing.

A touchdown (6 points) is awarded to the team that places the ball on or over the goalline. The touchdown can be converted (1 extra point) by a kick between the uprights, or by a pass or run into the end zone (2 points). The team that has made the touchdown places the ball at least 2 yards from the goal line (5 yards in Canadian football). A safety (2 points) is scored by the defense when a member of the offensive unit is tackled in his own end zone, or when the offensive unit loses control of the ball in its end zone and the ball goes out of bounds.

If the offense cannot advance 10 yards in 4 downs, the other team takes possession of the ball. However, if the offense is in a 4th down situation it has three options: to push the other team as far back as possible with a punt; if it is close enough, to kick the ball between the uprights for a field goal (3 points); or, if it is late in the game and the other team is ahead, to attempt to gain a first down by running with the ball or passing it.

AMERICAN FOOTBALL FIELD

Pylons
Plastic or foam rubber pylons are placed at the four corners of each end zone.

Lines
They are spaced at 5 yard intervals. Between the lines, hash marks indicate each yard. The ball is placed on or between the hash marks before each play.

Safety zone
Photographers and technicians for the electronic media must stay outside of this clear zone.

End zone
A touchdown is awarded when a team reaches the opposing end zone in possession of the ball. The goal line is part of the end zone.

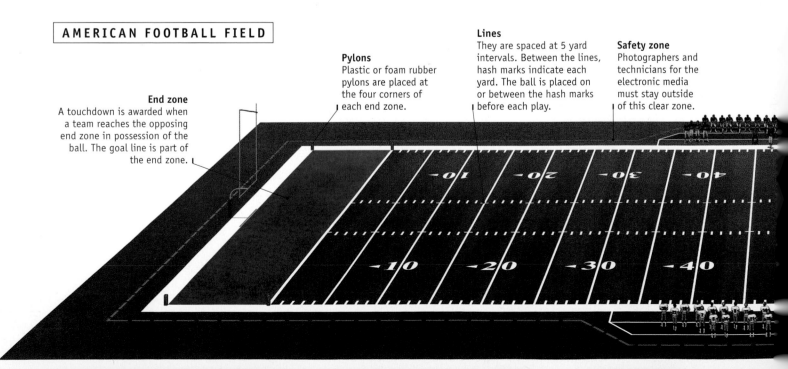

FIELDS

The size of the field is different for American and Canadian football. The surface is grass or synthetic turf. Synthetic surfaces are stickier and favor sudden changes of direction, thus encouraging a faster-paced game and more violent contact. Currently, there is a trend to return to natural grass, on which weather (rain, snow, etc.) has a greater effect. Natural surfaces help to prolong players' careers because they are much easier on the joints, especially the ankles and knees.

AMERICAN FOOTBALL

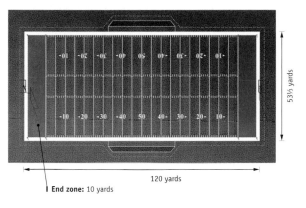

53⅓ yards

120 yards

End zone: 10 yards

CANADIAN FOOTBALL

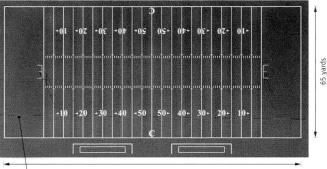

65 yards

150 yards

End zone: 20 yds.

Yardage chain
The chain is 10 yards long and attached to sticks at either end. One stick is placed where the ball was played in the last down of a series. The other stick indicates the point that must be reached to start a new series of downs. A down marker between the sticks indicates the number of downs played.

Back judge
He counts the number of defensive players and watches pass receivers. He also times the intervals between plays.

Field judge
He checks the legality of blocks and defensive infractions. He also whistles down players who go out of bounds in possession of the ball.

Side judge
His main responsibility is to mark where players in possession of the ball go out of bounds.

Line of scrimmage
An imaginary line across the width of the field where the ball is put in play. The offense and defense line up to face each other across the line of scrimmage. Between them is a neutral zone the length of the ball (one yard in Canadian football) that cannot be crossed until play starts.

Players' bench

Line judge
He covers the kicks and, with the head linesman, offsides. He also times the game.

Referee
The senior official on the field, he controls the game and supervises the work of the other officials.

Umpire
He watches for equipment violations and the line of scrimmage.

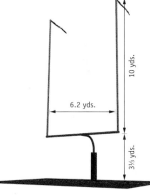

10 yds.

6.2 yds.

3⅓ yds.

Goalposts
The ball must pass between the uprights for a field goal or a conversion after a touchdown. The goalposts are placed at the back of the end zone. (In Canadian football, they are on the goal lines.)

Head linesman
He calls offsides and indicates the exact spot where the ball must be put in play when it has gone out of bounds.

OFFENSE

The quarterback huddles with his teammates and gives them directions for the next play. He gives the offensive formation, the play to be executed, the player designated for the play, and the snap count after which the ball will be put in play by the center. The offense may also go to the line of scrimmage without a huddle; in this case, the quarterback calls the play with a spoken code and hand signals. The offense must have 7 players on the line of scrimmage. The other players can reposition themselves on the field before the ball is snapped; a one second pause is required following these changes. After that, only one player may be in movement, and he must move parallel to the line of scrimmage. The offense has 40 seconds between the end of one play and the beginning of the next.

Quarterback
He is the team leader and has an excellent arm. Although he receives instructions from the offensive coordinator, he may decide to change the strategy depending on the situation on the field.

Tailback
Speed is his main asset when he attacks any opening that he can find. His ability to catch short and long passes makes him a more dangerous player.

Fullback
He is an excellent blocker who protects the quarterback in a passing situation. He also makes key blocks for the tailback when he runs with the ball.

Tight end
Player who helps the offense dominate the line of scrimmage. He can catch short passes, and sometimes long passes.

Offensive tackles (2)
They are placed at the ends of the line of scrimmage and protect the quarterback when he passes.

Center
He snaps the ball. He tells his teammates what positions the defense is taking so that they can adjust their blocking schemes.

Guards (2)
They are the key blockers during running plays. They are able to pull quickly to the right and left to get the best blocking angles on the defense.

Wide receivers (2)
They use their speed to force the opposing defense to cover them over long distances. They are always trying to transform a short gain into a long play; with their great speed and ability to adjust to the ball, they are exceptional athletes.

Exchange

The offense usually begins with the center snapping the ball to the quarterback, who is placed either directly behind the center or 5 yards away (shotgun formation) to receive the ball. Tactically, the center may snap the ball to another player of the offense.

Quarterback's drop back

After receiving the ball from the center, the quarterback takes 3, 5, or 7 steps back. The receiver's pattern is proportional to how far the quarterback backs up: short drop back/short pattern, long drop back/long pattern. The farther back the quarterback goes, the more difficult it is to protect him. He may also roll out to left or right before passing to break the rhythm of the defense.

Quarterback pass

The quarterback makes the pass after moving into the pocket and locating the receiver. The pass must be quick and accurate. When he throws, the quarterback grips the ball with his fingers on the laces and a slight gap between the palm of his hand and the ball so that he can give it a spiral rotation. Passes can be short (5 or 6 yards) or very long (up to 60 yards, or more).

Pass reception

The receiver must create a separation between himself and the defensive player assigned to cover him so that he provides his quarterback with a target. The receiver stretches his arms to catch the ball and keep the defensive halfback from knocking it to the ground. He must never take his eyes off the ball until he has it securely between his hand and inside of his forearm. When he catches the ball, the receiver must have both feet in bounds (one foot only in Canadian football).

Running game

A balanced running game can run through the center or to the outside. It is effective because it allows the team to control the ball and the pace of the game. While the defense must concentrate on breaking up the run, play action becomes an extra attack asset. Running is the favorite strategy for a team that is ahead and wants to let the clock run down as much as possible before turning over the ball to the other team.

DEFENSE

The defense must identify the offense strategy (running, play action, or pass) as quickly as possible and react appropriately. Often, the middle linebacker forms a huddle to give directions. Once the offensive team takes its position, he assigns defense positions, identifies changes in responsibilities if necessary, and designates the players responsible for pass coverage. During a running play, the defense is responsible for plugging any gaps that might be attacked. In a passing situation, the defense must put pressure on the quarterback and contain him in the pocket. Both short and deep zones must be protected; the ultimate goal of the defense is to cause turnovers (fumbles, interceptions), keep big plays from being made, and prevent touchdowns.

Defensive tackles (2)
They must not be moved from the line of scrimmage. They have to force the offensive line to double team them. In passing situations, they must collapse the pocket.

Middle linebacker
The core of the defense, he moves sideways quickly to attack the ball carrier. He is one of the most physical and consistent tacklers on his team.

Defensive ends (2)
They must force any running attempt to the inside and keep the quarterback from getting to the outside. Their ability to get to the quarterback in passing situation is crucial.

Outside linebackers (2)
They are mobile enough to put pressure on the quarterback or perform man-to-man coverage on a ball carrier or tight end. They line up in front of the tight end or back from the line of scrimmage.

Weak side safety
He is used mainly for his skill in covering passes, although he also needs to be involved in running plays.

Strong side safety
He is placed on the side where the offensive is more likely to attack. He is known for physical tackles on ball carriers and can perform man-to-man coverage in passing plays.

Cornerbacks (2)
They must be as fast as the wide receivers. They are isolated and often the last line of defense against a touchdown.

The tackle

The tackler must keep his feet moving to follow the ball carrier's dekes. At the moment of contact, he must be able to change his trajectory suddenly by keeping his knees bent and controlling his speed. The ball is always the main target. On impact, the tackler accelerates and generates power through his legs, then rolls his hips to transfer the power to his upper body. He finishes the tackle by wrapping around the ball carrier.

Pass coverage

In zone defense, the defender always keeps the quarterback in his peripheral vision, so that he can track the intended receiver and react more effectively. In man-to-man defense, he follows the pass receiver step for step, watching his eyes and hands, which indicate that the pass is about to arrive. At this moment, he decides either to knock down the ball, to intercept it, or to make a sure tackle on the receiver. The defender can disturb the receiver, from the line of scrimmage to a distance of 5 yards, using his hands to force the receiver to change directions or regain his speed.

Blitz

This tactic is applied against both passing and running plays. It consists of overloading the offense with defensive players, either inside or outside. The blitz may be run by a linebacker, a cornerback, or a safety. The quarterback must be pressured quickly, because the pass receivers will get opened too easily.

Cornerback blitz

In this type of blitz, the cornerback (**1**), rather than covering the pass receiver (**2**), rushes the quarterback (**3**) while the safety (**4**) covers the receiver (**2**).

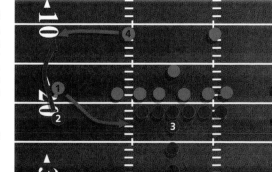

Dick Butkus (USA)
Linebacker for the Chicago Bears from 1965 to 1973, his intensity was legendary. The trophy awarded to the best linebacker in American college football is named after him. He played in 8 All-Star Games in 9 seasons.

SPECIAL TEAMS

They are used in situations that require specific preparation. Each team has specialists: punter, kicker, holder, long and short snappers, and punt/kick returners. They are supported by regular offense or defense players, depending on the circumstances. When the offense and defense are on the sidelines, the special teams are on the field.

Punt

The punter starts 15 yards away from the center. A good hang time on his punt will give his teammates the time to force the returner to ask for a fair catch, in which the play ends when he catches the ball. There is no fair catch in Canadian football.

Field goal and extra point

A field goal can be attempted from anywhere on the field. The player holding the ball stands 7 yards from the center; the coordination between the holder, the center, and the kicker is essential. Most place kickers do not want the ball placed with laces facing them. A field goal is worth 3 points.

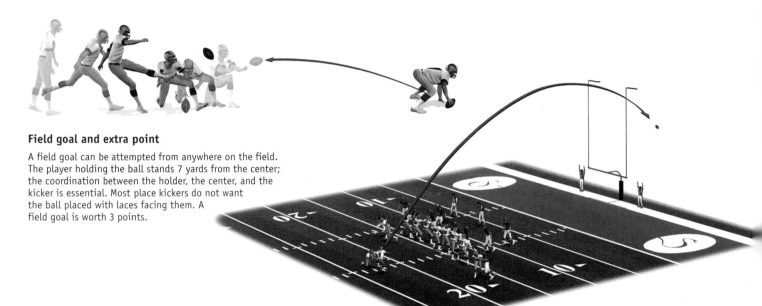

OFFICIAL SIGNALS

The speed and precision of plays make refereeing football very difficult. There are 7 referees calling the game, each with a specific function on the field. Their signals are transmitted to the head referee (who wears a white cap), who makes the final decision. He uses 36 different signals to announce and explain his decision. Moreover, he has a microphone. Because the objective is to gain yards, penalties often involve the loss of yards or downs.

Holding
A player has illegally held an opposing player. His team is penalized 10 yards.

Points scored
A touchdown, conversion, or field goal has been scored.

First down
The offensive team has covered at least 10 yards in 4 downs or less. It can continue its advance with a new series of downs.

Offside
A defending player has advanced into the neutral zone of the line of scrimmage before the ball is played. His team is penalized 5 yards.

Interference
A player has interfered with an opposing player during a pass. If the defense is at fault, the ball is placed at the site of the infraction and the attacking team gets a first down. If the offense is at fault, the team is penalized 15 yards.

EQUIPMENT

Some pieces of equipment are worn by all players at all levels of play and positions: shirt, pants, helmet, face mask, tooth guard, athletic cup, and shoes with cleats. Professional players may add thigh pads, knee pads, hip pads, rigid rib pads that absorb blows, and lumbar pads. Some linesmen wear additional protection on their forearms, upper arms, and hands, and wear a helmet support to prevent neck injuries. All players use tape bandages to support and protect their ankles.

QUARTERBACK

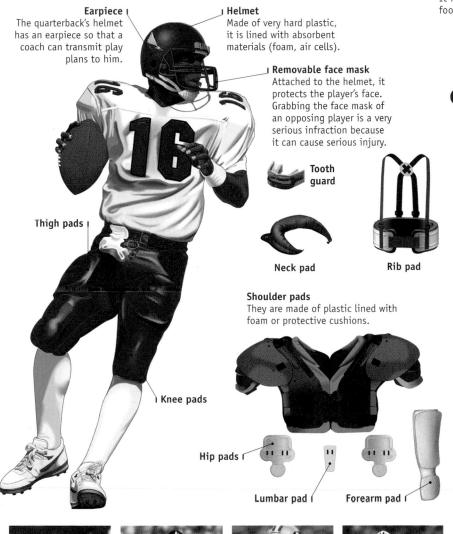

Earpiece
The quarterback's helmet has an earpiece so that a coach can transmit play plans to him.

Helmet
Made of very hard plastic, it is lined with absorbent materials (foam, air cells).

Removable face mask
Attached to the helmet, it protects the player's face. Grabbing the face mask of an opposing player is a very serious infraction because it can cause serious injury.

Tooth guard

Neck pad

Rib pad

Thigh pads

Shoulder pads
They are made of plastic lined with foam or protective cushions.

Knee pads

Hip pads

Lumbar pad

Forearm pad

Ball
It is made of leather and has laces. In Canadian football, two white stripes make it more visible.

Canadian football

circumferences:
27.75–28.25 in.
14 oz.

American football

circumferences:
28–28.5 in.
14 oz.

PLAYER PROFILE

- Given the diversity and specificity of roles, each player has a physique corresponding to his position: professional players range in height and in weight. This being said, a player who does not have the typical physique for his position may still play it consistently well.

OFFENSE

- The quarterback (6'3", 220 lbs.) must be mobile and quick. He works on arm strength and accuracy of passes.

- The ball carrier (6', 220 lbs.) is quick and has exceptional acceleration. He must be strong enough to block opposing players.

- The tight end (6'4", 225 lbs.) is a powerful and multi-talented player who must often block the best opposing players at the point of attack.

- The wide receiver (5'11", 190 lbs.) is very mobile and relies on speed and excellent traction with the ground to change direction suddenly; size is an asset.

- Offensive line players (6'5", 300 lbs.) are the most physically imposing. They are extremely solid so that they can block opposing players or protect the quarterback.

DEFENSE

- The defensive tackles (6'4", 285 lbs.) are strong and powerful, while defensive ends are very mobile and can pressure the quarterback.

- Linebackers (6'3", 245 lbs.) must have athletic skills to be effective in running or passing play. The middle linebackers must work from tackle to tackle to stop the run.

- The cornerback (5'11", 190 lbs.) is the most outstanding athlete of the defense, with as much speed as the wide receivers.

- The strong safety (5'11", 200 lbs.) and the weak safety (6'3", 200 lbs.) must be able to play the run and the pass, the strong safety being mostly involved in the running plays.

Mike Pringle (USA)
Ball carrier for the Montreal Alouettes of the CFL, he is the first player in the history of professional football to accumulate more than 2,000 yards running (2,065) in a single season.

Walter Payton (USA)
He won Super Bowl XX with the Chicago Bears, his team from 1975 to 1987. He ran with the ball 3,838 times, for a total of 16,726 yards (all-time leader in this category). He accumulated a total of more than 21,803 yards (passing and running). Selected nine times for the All-Star Game and member of the Hall of Fame, he died in 1999.

Jerry Rice (USA)
Many consider him the best all-time pass receiver. He played in 10 All-Star Games and has many records, including most touchdowns scored (175), most receptions (1,139), and most yards passing (17,612).

Joe Montana (USA)
He helped the San Francisco 49ers win Super Bowls XVI, XIX, XXIII, and XXIV. He completed 3,409 passes for 40,551 yards and 273 touchdowns. He was selected for eight All-Star Games (Pro Bowls) during his career (from 1979 to 1994), and is considered by many the best quarterback ever.

basketball

Students at Western School in Washington State playing a game in 1899.

The rules of basketball are designed to produce a very fast-paced, offensive game, making it one of the most technically demanding ball sports. Invented in 1891 by a Canadian, James A. Naismith, at what is now Springfield College in Massachusetts, the game was exported to Europe in 1893 where it has been played ever since. In 1936, one year after the first European championship was organized by the International Basketball Federation (FIBA), the sport made its Olympic debut at the Berlin Games. However, basketball became truly popular in Europe only after the Second World War, due to the presence of American troops. The first official National Basketball Association (NBA) match pitted Minneapolis against Syracuse, in 1950. The rise of women's basketball had been thwarted by more restrictive rules until the early 1970s, and it became an Olympic sport only in 1976. At the 1992 Barcelona Games, the overwhelming dominance of the American men's team—nicknamed "The Dream Team"—made NBA basketball popular around the world.

HOW A GAME IS PLAYED

Two teams of 5 players each try to score points by tossing the ball into the opposing team's basket. They may use only their hands to control the ball, and are not allowed to run while holding it. A field goal counts for 2 points, or 3 points if it is thrown from outside the 3-point line. A free throw is worth 1 point. The team with possession of the ball must launch an attack within the following time limits:

- After taking possession of the ball, they have 10 seconds to move the ball forward across the mid-court line, and 30 seconds to take a shot at the basket;
- A player who is hemmed in by an opponent must move the ball by dribbling, throwing, or passing it within 5 seconds.

THE COURT

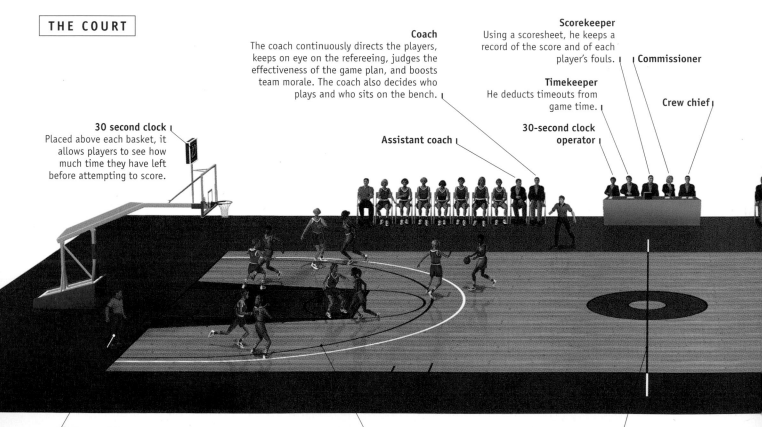

Coach
The coach continuously directs the players, keeps an eye on the refereeing, judges the effectiveness of the game plan, and boosts team morale. The coach also decides who plays and who sits on the bench.

Scorekeeper
Using a scoresheet, he keeps a record of the score and of each player's fouls.

Commissioner

Timekeeper
He deducts timeouts from game time.

Crew chief

Assistant coach

30-second clock operator

30 second clock
Placed above each basket, it allows players to see how much time they have left before attempting to score.

Referees (2)
They generally remain on the sidelines to keep out of the players' way.

3-point line (FIBA)

Mid-court line

CUPS AND CHAMPIONSHIPS

In the United States, NBA championship games have been an annual event since 1949. Following playoff elimination rounds, 2 teams meet in a 7-game final series. The first team to win 4 games wins the championship.

Teams have competed for the FIBA World Championship every 4 years since 1950.

The European Championship has been held every 2 years since 1935.

The top teams in Europe vie for the Liliana Rochetti (women's) and Korach (men's) Cups.

SCOREBOARD

Time remaining

Team's score

30-second clock

Fouls
Total number of fouls committed by each team.

PLAYER POSITIONS

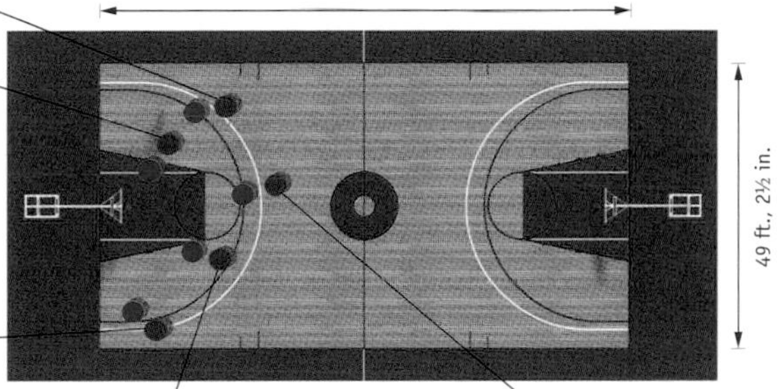

Forward

91 ft., 10 in.

49 ft., 2½ in.

Center
(inside player)
The tallest player on the team, he protects the basket from close-in throws and takes the ball on rebounds.

Forwards
They act as a link between the rear guard and the center, and play either defensively or offensively, depending on which team has the ball.

Rear guard
He covers the most dangerous opponent, helps the point guard, and shoots for the basket whenever possible.

Point guard
This player sets the pace of the game and leads the offense.

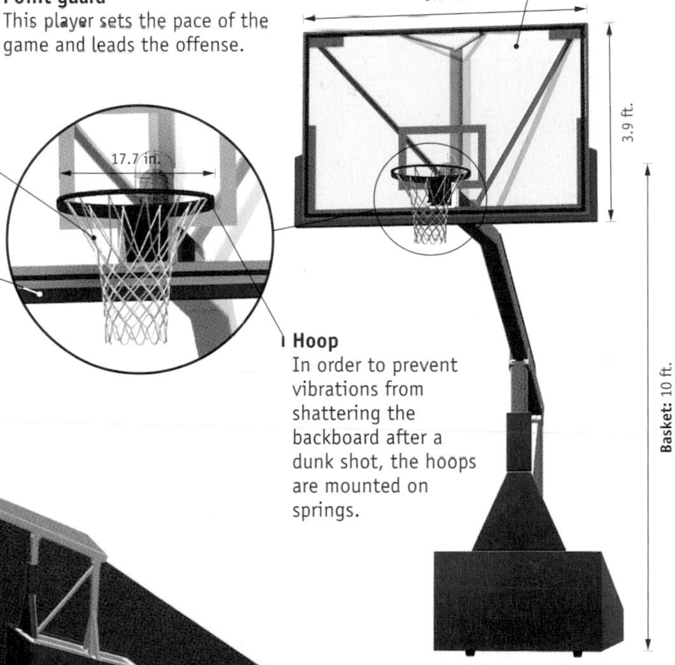

Backboard
The backboard is made of Plexiglas, to avoid obstructing the view of spectators seated behind it.

5.9 ft.

3.9 ft.

Net
The net slows the ball down so that it can be observed passing through the hoop.

17.7 in.

Protective padding
Attached to the bottom of the backboard to protect players from injury.

Players on the bench
A team consists of 10 to 12 players. There is no limit on the number of substitutions during a game.

Hoop
In order to prevent vibrations from shattering the backboard after a dunk shot, the hoops are mounted on springs.

Basket: 10 ft.

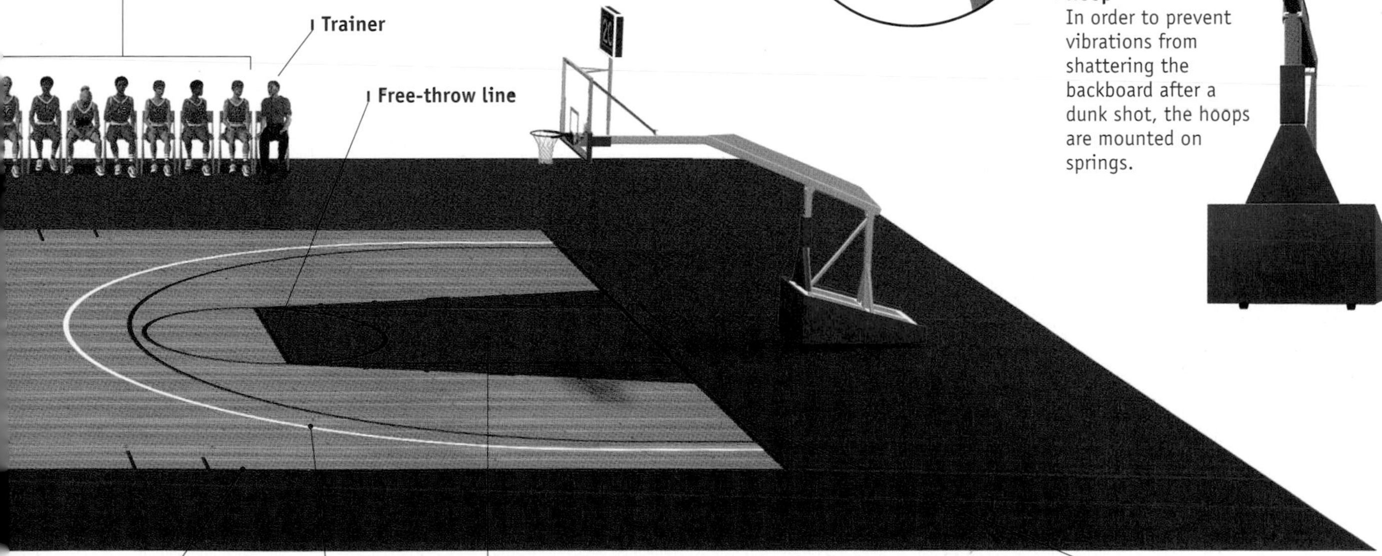

Trainer

Free-throw line

Sideline

3-point line
(NBA)

The key
Players on the team with possession of the ball may remain in this area for no more than 3 seconds at a time.

Endline

263

TECHNIQUES

OPENING JUMP BALL

A basketball game begins with the referee tossing the ball straight up into the air between the opposing centers, who try to tap it toward a teammate. They are allowed to push or hit the ball, but not to grasp it.

MOVING ON THE COURT

Players are allowed anywhere on the court, but are not allowed to run while holding the ball. Pivoting and dribbling are two techniques used to move around without passing.

THE PIVOT FOOT

Pivoting is a restricted motion. The player's position upon getting the ball determines which foot becomes the pivot foot:

- If the player catches the ball in the air, the first foot that touches the ground becomes the pivot foot.

- If the player catches the ball with both feet on the ground, he can choose his pivot foot; if the ball is caught while one foot is on the ground, that foot becomes the pivot foot.

The only way to free the pivot foot while retaining possession of the ball is to start dribbling.

PASSES

To catch opponents off guard, and to reduce the chances of an interception, most passes are short and direct, and almost always made without looking at the receiver.

Chest pass

This pass is used when there is nothing between the thrower and receiver. The ball is gripped in front of the chest with both hands and thrust forward by the arms and a flick of the wrists.

Bounce pass

Used to get past an opposing player who creates a screen between the thrower and the receiver, since the area over which he has the least control is the area close to the floor.

Baseball pass

This often gives a hard-pressed player a better angle for a pass. The player's free hand follows and protects the ball during the windup.

DRIBBLING

The player with the ball can move freely while bouncing the ball on the floor. The hand doesn't strike the ball, but taps it with flicks of the wrist. A dribbling player doesn't watch the ball, but signals his teammates and keeps an eye on opponents. Stopping and restarting a dribble is against the rules.

Low dribble

The low dribble is used against a looming opponent, or when trying to penetrate the opposing team's defense, because the player can switch hands or direction more quickly. The ball is bounced knee-high, and shielded by the player's free hand and body.

High dribble

A high dribble is usually used during a counter-offensive. A player in the clear can move faster while bouncing the ball at waist or shoulder height.

SHOTS

The ultimate purpose of every move in the game is to get a player into a good scoring position. The accuracy of a shot at the basket depends on balance and speed of execution. Jumping and throwing are two separate movements that must be properly coordinated.

Jump shot

This is the most common shot, because of the tremendous opportunities it provides—particularly for 3-point shots. One hand is used to hold the ball in place, and the other to shoot it toward the basket. The ball is released at the top of the jump.

Lay-up

After charging past opponents, the player jumps close to the basket and lays the ball in. The player's wrist remains stiff while the hand pushes the ball in from underneath.

Dunk

The player dunks or jams the ball into the basket with one or both hands, thus preventing any opponent from stopping it. This is the most spectacular shot.

OFFENSIVE AND DEFENSIVE REBOUNDS

Most points are scored from inside the restricted area, or key. Missed shots rebound off the hoop or backboard, and may lead to both teams fighting for possession of the ball. Control of the ball under the basket is a prime advantage. Shots at the basket may be deflected only before the ball begins its descent. If the ball is blocked illegally, the opposing team is awarded 2 points.

OUT OF BOUNDS

A ball that touches or goes outside the court boundaries is considered out of bounds. It is put back into play by the team that did not have possession of the ball when it went out of bounds. Once the referee blows the whistle, the player with the ball has 5 sec to put it back into play.

An offensive rebound gives the team on offense another chance to score a basket.

Before jumping, the players jostle for the best position beneath the ball's downward trajectory.

A missed shot gives the defensive team a chance to launch a swift counter-attack by moving the ball toward the sidelines.

VIOLATIONS AND FOULS

The referees call violations when the rules of motion (pivot foot, dribbling, traveling) or the time limits (3 seconds, 5 seconds, 10 seconds, or 30 seconds) are broken. The opposing team is then given possession of the ball.

- Technical fouls stem from the conduct of coaches or players on the court: not respecting the officials or delaying the game. The opposing team is awarded 2 free throws. The ball can be recovered after the second rebound, or put back into play after the second shot, depending on the result.

- A personal foul is called against a player who interferes with an opponent's progress, whether or not he has the ball. A tally is kept of each player's fouls, and they are added to the team's total. After the eighth foul, the victim of the personal foul is given 2 free throws, providing an opportunity to score without interference.

FREE THROWS

On average, each team commits about 25 fouls per game. Free throws provide an opportunity for 35 points. This makes them an integral part of the game.

No player may interfere with the ball's flight, nor touch it before it lands in or on the basket.

No one may step into the key, or interfere with the thrower in any way.

The thrower stands behind the free throw line, and her feet are not allowed to touch or overstep the line.

REFEREES

The speed of the game and the complexity of the rules make basketball one of the most difficult games to referee. The referees on the court must often make split-second decisions as to whether to call a foul or let the game continue. They use hand signals to communicate with the scorer and other officials.

RULE DIFFERENCES	NBA	FIBA
Length of game	48 min. (4 12-min. periods)	2 x 20 min. or 4 x 12 min.
Number of referees	3	2
Second clock	24 seconds	30 seconds
Court dimensions	94 ft. x 50 ft.	91.9 ft. x 49.2 ft.
Three-point line	23.75 ft.	20.5 ft.
Maximum fouls permitted per player	6	5 (6 in 4 x 12 min. games)
Timeouts allowed	7 per game	2 in first half, 3 in second
Person who can call a timeout	Coach or player	Coach

Foul

Timeout

Charging

Traveling

Double dribble

THE EVOLUTION OF BASKETBALL GEAR

1891

1895

1891

Sheryl Swoops (USA)
The number-two national player in 1993, she was named Most Valuable Player at the NCAA Finals that year, after scoring 47 points in one game. She was an Olympic champion at the 1996 Atlanta Games, and a WNBA champion in 1997 and 1998, with the Houston Comets.

Kareem Abdul-Jabbar (USA)
During a 20-year career that began in the 1960s, he won six NBA championships and six Most Valuable Player awards. He holds the NBA all-time scoring record, with 38,387 points.

EQUIPMENT

Ball
The ball is made from 8 pieces of leather stitched together and filled with air.
Circumference: 29.5 in.–30.7 in.
Weight: 21–23 oz.

Uniform
Each team wears a light-colored uniform for home games.

Player number
NBA players pick their own numbers; in FIBA games, they must be between 4 and 15.

Shoes
They must provide solid ankle support, as sprained ankles are the most common injury.

Toni Kukoc (CRO)
Winner of the European Cup of champion clubs from 1989 to 1991, world champion in 1990, and European champion, he then crossed the Atlantic to win three NBA championships (1996, 1997, and 1998).

Michael Jordan (USA)
Considered the greatest player of all time, he was the NBA's leading scorer from 1987 to 1993, and from 1996 to 1998. He played more than 1,000 consecutive games in which he scored at least 10 points. An NBA champion from 1991 to 1993, and from 1996 to 1998, he was also an Olympic champion in 1984 and 1992.

The Harlem Globetrotters played their first game in 1927. The first all-African-American team, they enjoyed a long stretch in the top ranks and even defeated the Minneapolis Lakers in two straight games in response to a challenge. The NBA's first two African-American players came from the Harlem Globetrotters.

BASKETBALL PLAYER PROFILE

- Ability to think and move fast, good peripheral vision, and an understanding of the game are three fundamental skills. The corresponding athletic abilities—explosive power, acceleration, and coordination—are developed through training that is adapted to the height of the players (average height: 6'1" to 7'1").

- Top players must be capable of peak performance under extreme fatigue, stress, or psychological pressure. Studies have shown that a move must be practiced some 200,000 times before it becomes an automatic reflex in any situation.

- Daily workouts last several hours. The best players are virtually self-coached and know how to adjust their play as the game progresses, but it is the coach's job to keep the team functioning as a unit.

netball

Game between students at Cambridge University and the London civil services team in Cambridge, England, in 1935

Netball is traditionally played by women. Invented by James Naismith in the United States in 1891, the game involves two teams trying to shoot the ball into the opposing team's goal, or "ring," to score points. The division of the court into three separate zones, or "thirds," arises from an error of interpretation of Naismith's text regarding the role of players. After being exported to England, netball reached the Southern Hemisphere in 1906. The All England Netball Association was formed in 1926, and Australia and New Zealand have been meeting in tournaments regularly since 1938. Depending on the country, netball was played in teams of 7 or 9 players—even 12 in a Dutch variant called Korfball. In 1957, the United States and 6 of the Commonwealth nations standardized the teams at 7 players, and this rule was adopted by the International Federation (IFNA), established in 1960. The first world championships, involving 11 countries, took place in 1963. Netball is very popular in Oceania and was recognized by the IOC in 1995; it has been part of the Commonwealth Games since the 1998 games in Kuala Lumpur, Malaysia.

(ball sports — side tab)

THE GAME

The game starts with a center pass: when the referee's whistle blows, the center passes the ball to a teammate. No other player can enter the center third before the referee's whistle blows. The game is divided into 4 15 min periods separated by 3 min breaks (10 min at half-time). Each player has a very precise role, corresponding to her position on the court, and wears a bib bearing the initials for that position. Only the goal attack (GA) and goal shooter (GS) may shoot at the goal, and only if they are inside the goal circle. No player may keep the ball for more than 3 seconds.

Movements

Dribbling is not allowed, but players may take one step after receiving the ball:

• If a player lands on one foot when she receives the ball, she may pivot in any direction on that foot, moving her other foot. If her landing foot leaves the floor, she must pass the ball before she puts that foot down.

• If a player receives the ball with both feet on the floor, she can make one step with either foot. If she jumps, she must pass or shoot the ball before either of her feet touches the floor.

Infractions

A personal foul (contact or obstruction) committed outside of the goal circle gives the opposing team a penalty pass: the player who committed the foul must stand still until the ball is put in play by a pass. If a foul is committed in the goal circle, it may result in a penalty throw (throw directly at the ring without intervention by the opposing team) or a penalty pass, depending on the player's choice. An infraction of the zone or movement rules leads to a free pass for the opposing team: play is stopped and the ball is thrown in at the place of the infraction.

COURT

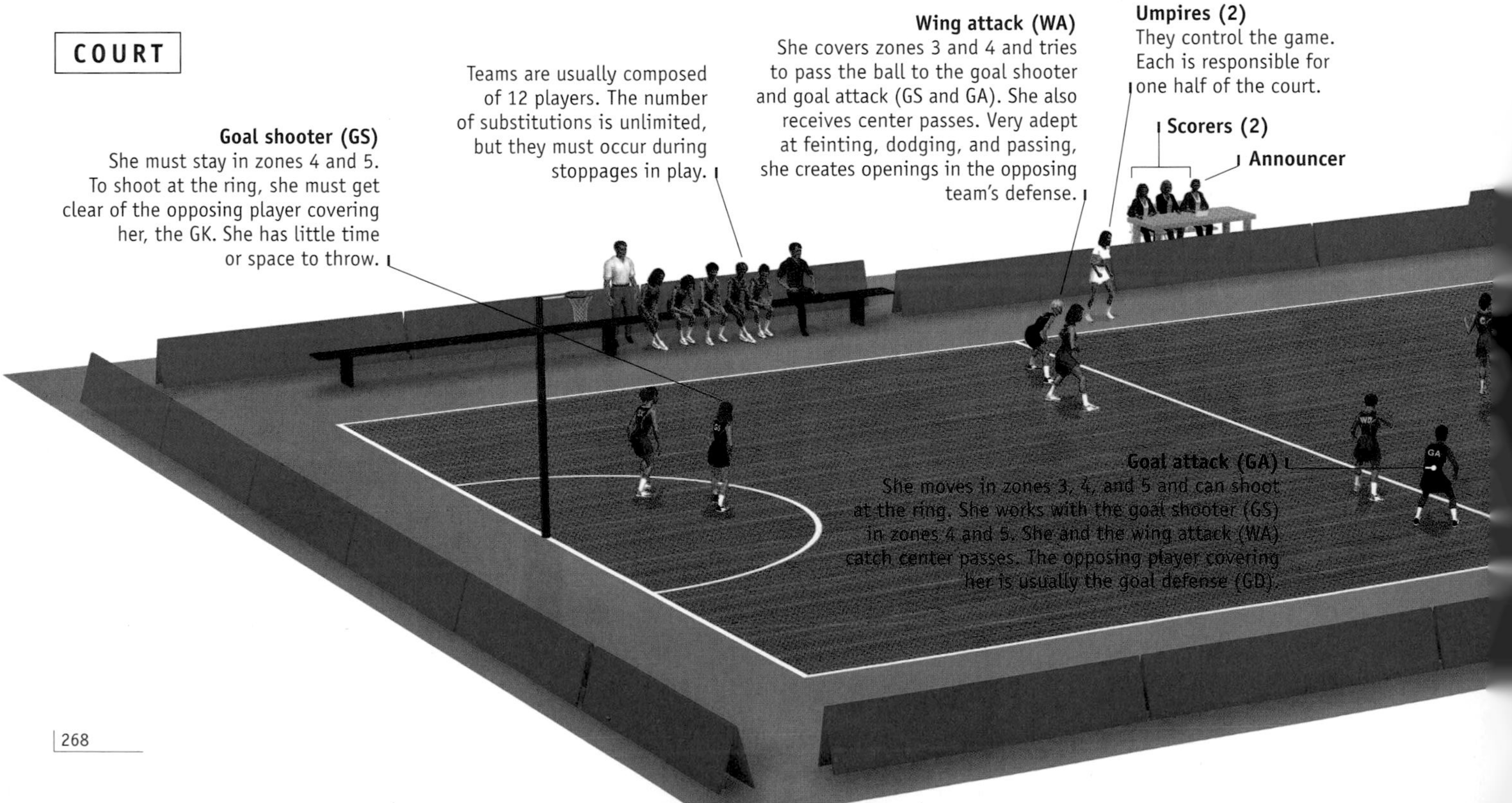

Goal shooter (GS)
She must stay in zones 4 and 5. To shoot at the ring, she must get clear of the opposing player covering her, the GK. She has little time or space to throw.

Teams are usually composed of 12 players. The number of substitutions is unlimited, but they must occur during stoppages in play.

Wing attack (WA)
She covers zones 3 and 4 and tries to pass the ball to the goal shooter and goal attack (GS and GA). She also receives center passes. Very adept at feinting, dodging, and passing, she creates openings in the opposing team's defense.

Umpires (2)
They control the game. Each is responsible for one half of the court.

Scorers (2)

Announcer

Goal attack (GA)
She moves in zones 3, 4, and 5 and can shoot at the ring. She works with the goal shooter (GS) in zones 4 and 5. She and the wing attack (WA) catch center passes. The opposing player covering her is usually the goal defense (GD).

TECHNIQUES

Passes

They can be thrown or bounced but not rolled. The ball can be tipped or hit with one or two hands (but not with a closed fist). Involuntary contact with the ball by another part of the body is not an infraction.

Defense

Defending players must stay at least 92 cm away from attackers. No intimidating gestures are allowed. Any contact (deliberate or involuntary) that impedes the ball carrier is an infraction.

Shooting at the ring

Players aim for the ring on the opposing team's side. The ball is held over the head in open hands and thrown with an extension of the knees. The ideal trajectory is high, with the ball falling vertically into the ring.

Thirds

The ball may not go through any third without being touched by a player in that third. Any player who leaves her playing zone is offside.

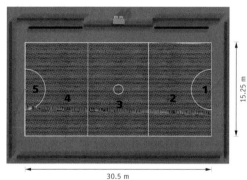

15.25 m

30.5 m

PLAYER PROFILE

- Average height is about 5'7". The tallest athletes are generally goal shooters. Center and defense players are often specialists in these positions. Netball is a rapid game that requires relaxation and speed, with a well-developed overall perspective and the ability to resist pressure.

- In training, emphasis is placed on quick reactions and positioning. Aiming of passes and shots is improved through simulated games.

Goal defense (GD)

Her direct opponent is the goal attack (GA) in zones 1, 2, and 3. She and the goalkeeper (GK) defend the goal zone and can provide support for attacks. She has several roles: anticipation, interception of thrown or bounced passes, and defense.

38 cm

Goalkeeper (GK)

She defends zones 1 and 2 and her team's goal against attackers, especially the goal shooter (GS). Anticipation, interception of balls, and one-on-one defense are part of her role.

Ball
Circumference: 69–71 cm
400–450 g

3.05 m

Court boundaries

When the ball crosses them, it is thrown in at the same spot by a player from the team that was not in possession of the ball when it went out of bounds.

Center (C)

She plays in every zone but the goal circles. As the link between her team's attack and defense zones, she passes the ball and establishes the pace. Her position requires an overall view of the game and sure, accurate passes and movements.

Wing defense (WD)

She plays in zones 2 and 3. To defend against the wing attack (WA), she must be an expert in one-on-one defense. She takes part in attacks starting in zone 3.

volleyball

In 1895, American William G. Morgan invented a new indoor game, "Mintonette," which became volleyball. It was a working class sport and inexpensive—a compromise between two other new games, basketball, and tennis, which were played by the wealthy. Exported to Europe by Americans during the First World War, the game took root in Eastern Europe, where the cold climate favored the development of indoor activities. Volleyball was a demonstration sport at the 1924 Olympics in Paris, and became an official sport in 1947, when the Fédération internationale de volley-ball (FIVB) was founded. Two years later, in 1949, the first men's world championship was played in Prague, Czechoslovakia, and volleyball was part of the Olympic Games in Tokyo in 1964. The first World Cup was played the following year, in Poland. The Men's World League, the first worldwide professional structure, was set up in 1990 and has been supported by major grants and extensive international television coverage.

Volleyball's 1952 world championships in Moscow. The USSR won over Bulgaria 3–0.

THE GAME

Volleyball involves 2 teams of 6 players who try to send the ball over the net to touch the ground on the opposing team's side. The team that wins a rally wins a point or, if it was not serving, wins the right to serve. A set is won by a score of 25 points (15 points in the fifth and deciding set) with a lead of at least 2 points. If there is a tie at 24–24, the game continues until one team has a 2 point lead. A match is won in 3 sets out of 5. The ball is put in play by the back-row player on the right, who can serve anywhere along the 9 meter width of the service zone. She has 8 seconds after the referee blows his whistle to make her single attempt to get the ball over the net. The rally ends when the ball touches the ground, when it is hit out of bounds, or when one of the teams does not return it legally.

When a team wins service, the players rotate one position clockwise. This rule was instituted so that players would have to play in both the front and back zones. Each team can touch the ball a maximum of 3 times, in addition to the block, before sending it into the other team's court. Once a player has touched the ball, he cannot touch it again until it has been touched by another player on either team. The ball can touch any part of the body, and it must be hit, not held or thrown. It is illegal for a player or players to form a screen to keep the other team from seeing the server, and for a player to hit the ball from inside the opposing team's zone. A team can make a maximum of 6 substitutions per set.

THE COURT

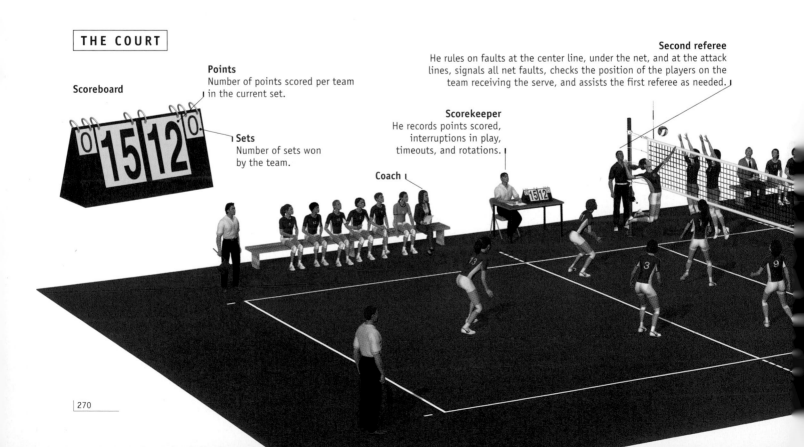

Scoreboard

Points Number of points scored per team in the current set.

Sets Number of sets won by the team.

Coach

Scorekeeper He records points scored, interruptions in play, timeouts, and rotations.

Second referee He rules on faults at the center line, under the net, and at the attack lines, signals all net faults, checks the position of the players on the team receiving the serve, and assists the first referee as needed.

PLAYER POSITIONS

After a serve or attack, the back row players try to dig the ball and get it to the passer. The passer then usually tips it to the front row players or the spiker, who tries to score a point with a spike or tip into the other team's zone.

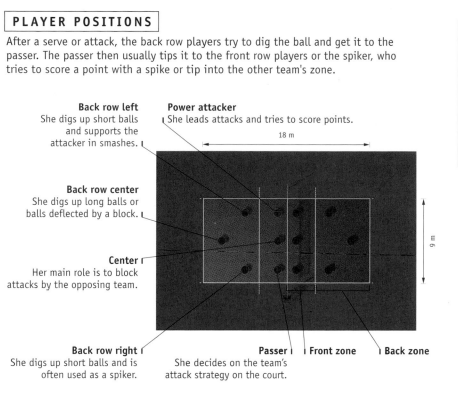

Back row left
She digs up short balls and supports the attacker in smashes.

Power attacker
She leads attacks and tries to score points.

18 m

Back row center
She digs up long balls or balls deflected by a block.

Center
Her main role is to block attacks by the opposing team.

9 m

Back row right
She digs up short balls and is often used as a spiker.

Passer
She decides on the team's attack strategy on the court.

Front zone

Back zone

Karch Kiraly (USA)
Gold medallist at the 1984 and 1988 Olympics, he also won the World Cup in 1985 and the world championships the following year. He also won the gold medal, with Kent Steffes, at the 1996 Olympics, in beach volleyball.

Mireya Luis (CUB)
Gold medalist at 2 consecutive Olympics (1992 and 1996) and at the volleyball world championships in 1994.

EQUIPMENT

Ball
Made of an outer layer of soft leather covering a rubber bladder. Pressure is 294 to 319 mbar.

Net
Contact with the net is a fault unless it is accidental and made by a player who is not intending to play the ball.

9.50 m

1 m

Men: 2.43 m
Women: 2.24 m

Circumference 65-67 cm

Kneepad

Antenna
Marks the zone within which the ball is in bounds.

Libero
A specialist in digging and receiving serves, she is designated for the entire match or tournament and cannot change position on the team. She must wear a different color than her teammates so that she can be identified.

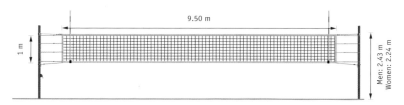

Line judges (4)
They use a red flag to signal service faults, contact with the antennas, whether the ball passes outside the antennas, and ball outs.

Free zone
International matches: 5 m
National matches: 3 m

First referee
He directs the game and looks down on the net by about 50 cm. His decisions are final.

Attack line
The back row players must attack the ball from behind this line, without touching or crossing it.

Center line
This line separates the 2 sides. If a player crosses it, her side loses the point.

TECHNIQUE

The serve (tennis)

The server can stand anywhere behind the 9 m line. Although an underhand serve is legal, international level players use an overhand serve, mainly the tennis or jump serve. The latter is executed as a spike behind the service line. If it is well hit, the jump serve is a powerful offensive weapon.

The tip

A rally technique used only during the match, the tip is a transitory move between reception and attack. It is made with an upward movement of the arms and legs. Contact with the ball is with the fingertips.

The floor dig

This is performed to retrieve a ball that otherwise would be impossible to play, using a one or two hand bump. The player may then roll to absorb the violent contact with the floor and regain his feet more quickly to rejoin the play. It is important to keep moving after playing the ball to focus attention on the game and avoid making an error in hitting the bump.

The bump

The bump is both defensive (keeping the ball from falling to the floor, receiving serve, digging an easy ball) and offensive (restarting the attack by bumping toward the passer, who, in turn, tips the ball to the spiker). It is the first contact with the ball (service reception), thus an important technical movement. The bump provides the transition between defense and attack.

The spike

A pure attack hit. The first spike was recorded in 1920 in the Philippines (the "Philippine bomb"). Players who execute the spike have an excellent sense of balance in the air and can perceive and anticipate the actions and positions of the opposing team members. Contact with the ball may take place above the net when it is in the front zone.

The block

It may be executed by one, two, or three players and is the first line of defense against the spike. Blockers are not expected to block all spikes but to serve as a screen, reducing the floor space that must be covered by the players behind them. To block, a player has to have good anticipation of the play and be tall (the tallest player is usually a team's main blocker).

beach volleyball

Originally a family leisure activity, beach volleyball had its first official 2-against-2 tournament in 1943 in State Beach, California. The California Beach Volleyball Association (CBVA) was founded in 1965, and rules were written and tournaments organized. In the 1970s and 1980s, the sport underwent unprecedented growth; in 1983 the Association of Volleyball Professionals (AVP) was formed, and many Olympic volleyball stars joined. The first professional championship took place the following year. The Women's Professional Volleyball Association (WPVA) was formed in 1986. The following year, the FIVB organized the first men's beach volleyball world championship in Ipanema, Brazil. Six years later, in 1993, the FIVB presented a women's world championships. Beach volleyball became an Olympic sport in 1996 at the Atlanta games. The countries with the most titles are the United States and Brazil.

Liz Masakayan and Karolyn Kirby, the American pair who dominated women's beach volleyball from 1993 to 1995

THE COMPETITION

Beach volleyball is played by 2 teams of 2 or 4 players on a sand court. The players play barefoot (shoes are allowed upon authorization of the referee) and are dressed in bathing suits or shorts and T-shirts and a cap. One handed tips (pushing the ball gently over the net to fool the opposing players) are forbidden in attacks; the ball must be hit. A block is counted as a hit. There are 2 match formats: a single set, in which a team wins the set and match by scoring 15 points with a 1 point lead (in the case of a 16–16 tie, the team that scores the 17th point wins the match with a 1 point lead), and 2 12-point sets out of 3 with a tie breaker similar to that in tennis. In the case of an 11–11 tie, the team that scores the 12th point wins the set. If both teams have won a set, a third set, the "deciding set," is played. To win the match, the deciding set must be won by scoring 12 points with a 2 point lead. The deciding set is played as a tie breaker: a point is scored when a team wins a rally.

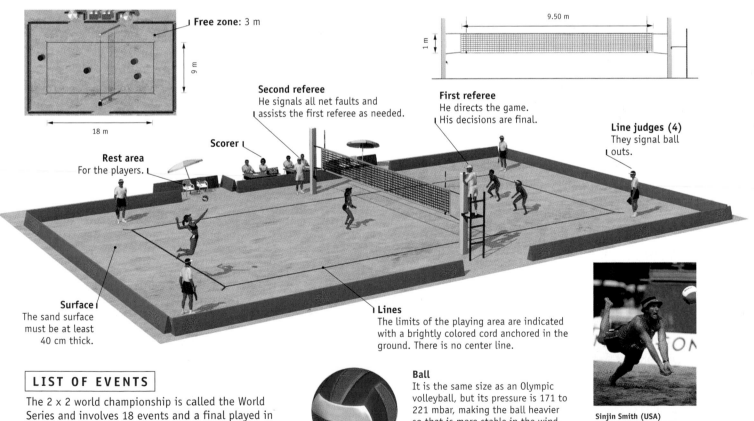

Free zone: 3 m

9 m

18 m

9.50 m

1 m

Second referee
He signals all net faults and assists the first referee as needed.

First referee
He directs the game. His decisions are final.

Line judges (4)
They signal ball outs.

Scorer

Rest area
For the players.

Surface
The sand surface must be at least 40 cm thick.

Lines
The limits of the playing area are indicated with a brightly colored cord anchored in the ground. There is no center line.

LIST OF EVENTS

The 2 x 2 world championship is called the World Series and involves 18 events and a final played in Rio de Janeiro, Brazil. It has been played since 1997 with an elimination tournament. Matches are played in 2 out of 3 21-point sets.

Ball
It is the same size as an Olympic volleyball, but its pressure is 171 to 221 mbar, making the ball heavier so that is more stable in the wind.

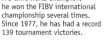

Sinjin Smith (USA)
A 5 time world champion, he won the FIBV international championship several times. Since 1977, he has had a record 139 tournament victories.

♟ handball (team)

Handball was developed in Germany at the end of the 19th century by Konrad Koch, a gymnastic instructor. Frederik Knudsen codified the game in 1911, in Denmark. The Danish version had 7 player teams; in the German version, teams were composed of 11 players. The International Amateur Handball Federation was formed in 1928 during the Amsterdam Olympics. Handball for 11 player teams was a demonstration sport at the Berlin Olympics in 1936, and the first world championships for 11 and 7 player teams were organized in 1938 in Germany which won both titles. Both forms of the game coexisted for several decades, but the 11 player version gradually disappeared, as the 7 player version became more popular. Handball, now governed by the International Handball Federation (IHF), has been an Olympic event for men since the Munich Games in 1972, and for women since the Montreal Games in 1976.

German women's teams play a game in Berlin (Germany) in 1935

THE GAME

A handball game is played between two teams of 12 players (7 players and 5 substitutes). The object of the game is to score more goals than the opposing team; a goal is scored when the ball goes entirely inside the goal. The game is played in two 30 min periods, with a 10 min halftime. Players may throw, push, hit, stop, and catch the ball with their hands, arms, head, body, thighs, and knees but never with their feet. They must not hold on to the ball for more than 3 seconds. Only the goalkeeper is allowed inside the goal area (6 m line). The game starts with a throw-off at center court by the team that won a coin toss: while the player with the ball passes it to a teammate; each team must stay on its half of the court. The player throwing off must keep one foot in contact with the center line until the ball leaves his hand. A player in possession of the ball may pass it, dribble it (bounce it off the ground), or hold it; he may not hold the ball for more than 3 seconds or take more than 3 steps while holding it. When a goal is scored, the team that was scored against puts the ball in play with a throw-off at center court.

THE COURT

Timekeeper

Scorekeeper
He keeps track of playing time, entry and exit of substitutes, and penalty suspension times.

Secretary
He assists the referees, controls the player list, and keeps the scorecard.

7 m throw
This is a throw made directly on goal from the penalty mark. A player gets a 7 m throw (or penalty throw) when an opposing player has kept him from throwing at the goal or creating an opportunity to score, or when a defender is within the 6 m area and blocks an attacker. The thrower must not touch or cross the 7 m line until the ball has left his hands. All other players, except the goalkeeper, must stay outside the 9 m zone.

Goal referee

PLAYER POSITIONS

There are two tactics for zone defense: 0–6 or flat defense (all defenders lined up on the 6 m line) and stepped defense (1–5, 2–4, 3–3, 1–2–3), in which one or more defenders, depending on the formation, play 1 or 2 m in front of their teammates to keep the ball from moving freely and prevent long shots from the backcourt.

CUPS AND CHAMPIONSHIPS

The IHF organizes world championships for national teams. First played in 1938 for men and in 1957 for women, they have taken place every two years since 1993. Continental confederations organize their own continental championships (European Cup, Asian Cup, etc.) every two years.

Each country also organizes its own championships for club teams. The winners of these championships enter continental tournaments (such as the League of European Champions) played every year.

Circle runner
In attack, he slides between the opposing team's defenders, creating openings that let his teammates shoot or pass him the ball when he is in scoring position.

Right winger

Right backcourt player

Goalkeeper
He must stop or deflect shots from the opposing team. He is the only one allowed to touch the ball with his feet.

EQUIPMENT

Players' uniforms
Players must wear appropriate shoes, shorts, and shirts numbered 1 to 20. The numbers must be at least 20 cm high on the back and 10 cm high on the front. It is forbidden to wear face and/or head protection, jewelry, or glasses without an elastic strap or with hard frames, as well as any other object that might be dangerous for the players.

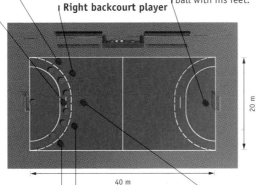

40 m

20 m

Left winger
When attacking, the wingers run up each side of the field to draw the defense or create scoring opportunities for themselves. On defense, they try to keep the opposing wingers from passing them.

Left backcourt player
In defense, the backcourt players cover the circle runner and opposing defenders and try to block shots. In attack, they remain far from the opposing defenders so that they have room to make running throws.

Center
In defense, he directs his team's backcourt tactics. In attack, he directs his team's offense.

Ball
It is generally covered with leather or a synthetic material that must not be shiny or slippery.

Circumferences
Men: 58–60 cm
Women: 54–56 cm

Goal area
This area is defined by a semi-circle 6 m away from the goal. Only the goalkeeper may enter this area. A player in possession of the ball may jump above the line when shooting at the goal.

Team coach
He is the only one allowed to speak to the secretary, the timekeeper, or referees.

Side line
When the ball crosses this line, it is thrown in by the team that did not have possession when it went out.

9 m line (free throw line)
When a free throw is awarded to a team, no attacking player may enter the 9 m area until the ball is in play.

6-m line

Goal
Located at the center of the goal line, it must be solidly attached to the ground.

3 m

2 m

Goal line

Referees (2)
They control the match, taking turns being center referee and goal referee. When a team attacks, the referee on that team's side controls the court, while the other places himself near the defending goal. When the defending team begins an attack, they switch roles.

Fallaway throw

The fallaway throw is a spectacular variation on the jump throw. It is used for throws from the wing, at the edge of the goal area. The shooter jumps up, and just before he throws, he twists laterally so that he is almost horizontal in the air. The hand holding the ball is above his body. This movement enables the shooter to get closer to the center of the 6 m area and open his shooting angle on the goal. To be legal, the throw must be made before the thrower falls into the goal area.

Jump throw

The shooter jumps up to throw at the goal. To be effective, the jump throw should be preceded by a run up of a maximum of three steps. Although it is less powerful than the standing throw, it is more accurate and allows the player a direct shot at the net as he jumps above a defender who might otherwise block the ball. The throw can be made in the rising phase of the jump (quick and hard) or be delayed and made in the falling stage of the jump, to confuse defenders and the goalkeeper. It is possible to make a jump throw within the 6 m area as long as the shooter does not touch the line or the ground inside the area while he is holding the ball.

Jackson Richardson (FRA)
As circle runner for the French team, he was world champion in 1995, and a bronze medalist at the 1992 Olympics. Named best player in the world in 1995, he has a spectacular style that helped to increase the popularity of handball.

Goalkeeper technique

During the game, the goalkeeper must face a series of powerful shots from close in. Rather than trying to stop the ball, he deflects it from the goal. To give opposing players less to shoot at, he advances a step in front of his goal line (which cuts down the angle for the thrower) and uses his entire body to block the shot: arms raised to the side, legs apart. The goalkeeper must always be on his toes so that he can react quickly and kick out his leg to deflect the ball.

Pass

A basic element of play, the pass is an essential move in handball. The ball may be passed to a teammate in a variety of ways. The speed and accuracy of passes are often the gauge of a team's skill level.

PLAYER PROFILE

- Handball is a fast and physically demanding sport in which speed, energy, and endurance are essential. Training focuses specifically on these attributes. Power, especially in the arms, is another crucial asset for handball players. The combination of speed and strength determines power. Strength can be increased through specific muscle building exercises. Individual techniques and the moves specific to handball are constantly being developed through practice.

- The joints (ankles, knees, elbows, and wrists) are always being used, so pre-game preparation must include various stretching exercises.

- The size of elite players is an important aspect. Average height is more than 6'2" for men and more than 5'7" for women.

Dribbling

This is a way to advance the ball by bouncing it off the ground, while respecting the 3 second and 3 step rules. A player can take 3 steps holding the ball, then dribble it. If, after dribbling, he picks up the ball and takes another step before passing it, he will be penalized by a free throw. Similarly, a player may not dribble the ball, pick it up, and then dribble it again before passing.

Standing throw

This is the most powerful type of throw. In a standing throw, one or both of the player's feet are in contact with the ground when he throws. Often used for long throws by backcourt players who are trying to break through the defensive wall and surprise the goalkeeper, it can be made while running, or from a standstill, the thrower choosing to make the allowed three steps or not, before shooting.

Racket
Sports

tennis

Tennis is a racket sport in which two players, or teams of two players, send a ball over a net in such a way that it is difficult to return legally. Modern tennis has its roots in the old French game of paume, for which the rules were written in Paris in 1592. English major Walter Clopton Wingfield drew on these rules when he patented the game of tennis on February 23, 1874; 25 rules for play were defined in May 1875. The first championship took place at Wimbledon, a suburb of London, in July 1877, and the first international championships were held in the United States in 1881, in Australia in 1905 and in France in 1925. Tennis was part of the first Olympic Games of the modern era, in Athens in 1896; it was withdrawn from the Olympics after 1924 and reinstated in 1988. Since 1913, the sport's governing body has been the International Lawn Tennis Federation, which became the International Tennis Federation (ITF) in 1977. Tennis is played in most countries, and players range from 5 or 6 years old to veterans of over 80. The game is played in men's singles, women's singles, men's doubles, women's doubles, and mixed doubles.

THE MATCH

The side of the court that each player will occupy first and who will serve first are both chosen by draw; the player who wins the draw may choose to have the opponent serve first. The server has 2 chances to serve, and usually puts the most effort into the first serve, trying to unsettle the opponent with its power or placement. The player scores a point if the serve is an ace—if the opponent cannot touch the ball or if the opponent returns it out of bounds or into the net. A served ball must always be returned after it has bounced once. During the rest of the rally, players may return the ball before or after it bounces.

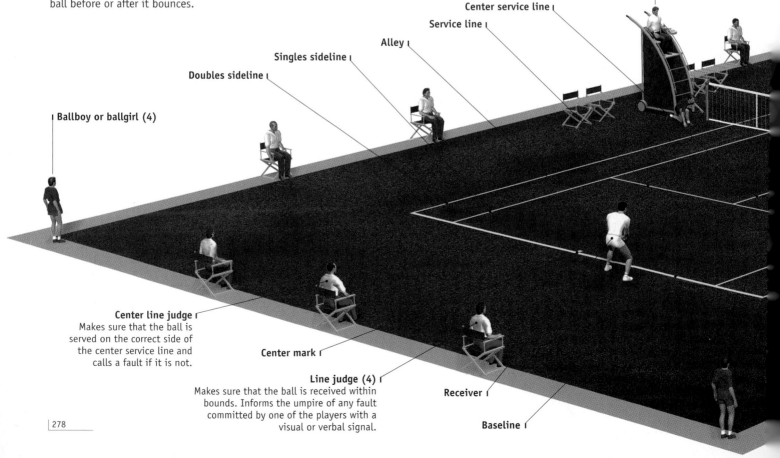

Chair umpire
Oversees the match, makes sure the rules of the game are respected, and checks player equipment. Announces the score after each point, game, and set. Can reverse judges' decisions in case of error. The chair umpire applies a three-stage set of penalties: warning, loss of point, suspension of the match.

Center service line

Service line

Alley

Singles sideline

Doubles sideline

Ballboy or ballgirl (4)

Center line judge
Makes sure that the ball is served on the correct side of the center service line and calls a fault if it is not.

Center mark

Line judge (4)
Makes sure that the ball is received within bounds. Informs the umpire of any fault committed by one of the players with a visual or verbal signal.

Receiver

Baseline

SCORING

A match is divided into sets, games, and points and may be played in 2 out of 3 sets or 3 out of 5 sets, at the organizers' discretion.

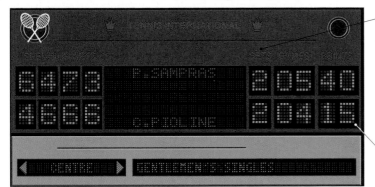

Player identification
The server's score is always given first. The players change ends at each odd-numbered game.

Set
A series of games. The winner of 6 games wins the set, as long as the margin is 2 games. If the score is tied at 6–6, a tiebreaker is played. The first player serves once, then each player serves twice. The player who reaches 7 points by a margin of 2 points wins the game and the set.

Game
A series of points, scored as follows: 0 ("love"), 15, 30, 40, and game. If the players are tied at 40 ("deuce"), one of them must score 2 consecutive points to win the game. The first of these points is called "advantage."

Steffi Graf (GER)
The only female player in history to have won all Grand Slam events and an Olympic gold medal in the same year (1988).

Rod Laver (AUS)
Only player in tennis history to win the Grand Slam twice, in 1962 and 1969.

Service judge

Right service court

Net

Net tape
The ends of the net (3½ ft.) are higher than the center (3 ft.).

Server

Left service court

Referee
He assigns courts, suspends or interrupts matches if weather or lighting is poor, and has the power to disqualify a player for misconduct, tardiness, or refusal to comply. The referee's decisions are final on all questions dealing with rules.

A ball that falls on a line is considered to be in play.

Net judge
Makes sure that the ball does not touch the net when served and that it does not go through the net mesh. Also, checks the height of the net before and during the match.

Fore court

Aft court

27 ft.

18 ft.

21 ft.

78 ft.

4½ ft.

TECHNIQUES

Aside from the serve, all strokes are identified as forehand or backhand. For a right handed player, all strokes on the right side of the body are forehand and all strokes on the left side of the body are backhand. The word "backhand" comes from the fact that a right handed player makes strokes on his left with the back of his hand facing forward. For left handed players, the reverse is true.

Serve

This is the stroke that starts play. The server stands behind the baseline and has 2 tries to send the ball into the diagonally opposite service court. In the first serve, the player tries to unbalance the opponent with the speed or placement of the ball. If the first serve misses, the server uses the second serve to put the ball in play. The first serve in the match is made from the right side of the court, and the players then change sides after each point. A draw determines the server of the first game.

Return of serve

The receiver is placed diagonally opposite the server near the baseline. Depending on the difficulty of the serve, the receiver may use a defensive or attacking return.

STROKES AFTER A BOUNCE

Ground strokes

They are usually played from near the baseline. Used for rallies, they provide a powerful, accurate attack.

Approach strokes

They are used when the opposing player's ball lands short. The receiver hits the ball from midcourt then advances to the net.

Half-volleys

The player hits the ball immediately after it bounces, at a height not above the knees. It is a stroke made mainly when the player is advancing to the net and uses a compact technique similar to that for the volley. A half-volley may also be played from the baseline.

STROKES BEFORE A BOUNCE

Volleys

These strokes are made before the ball touches the ground. Volleys are usually made close to the net. When they are made from midcourt, they are called approach volleys, as they allow the player to go to the net.

SPECIAL STROKES

Lob

The ball is sent high and far so that it bounces as close as possible to the baseline. The lob is used either to outmaneuver an opposing player who has come to the net or to force him to make a smash. In doubles, it may be played as a volley.

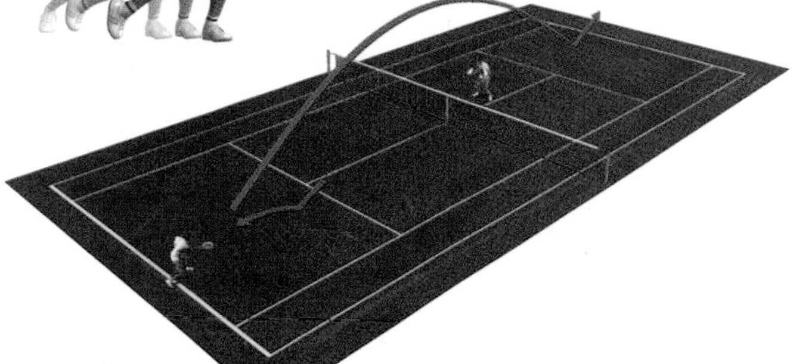

Drop shot

With this short stroke, the ball drops short so that it is difficult for the opposing player to reach it before it bounces twice. It is made both as a ground stroke and as a volley.

Smash

This powerful overhead stroke is generally made in response to a lob and leaves the opponent little opportunity to respond. It is hit before or after the ball bounces.

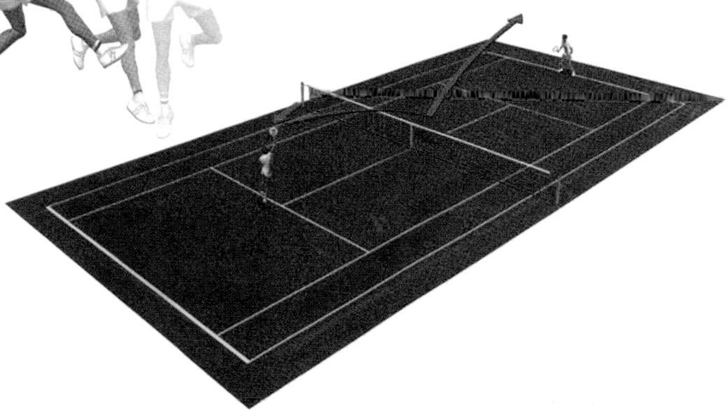

RACKET GRIPS

The grip used is generally related to the stroke the player is making.

Two-handed grip
There are many variations of this type of grip, used mainly for backhand strokes.

Eastern grip
It tends to produce a flat ball trajectory with a slight topspin, and is used for high volleys and ground strokes.

Continental grip
It is used mainly for volleys and serves, with a backspin effect.

Western and semi-western grips
They are used for topspin and ground strokes.

EFFECTS

These describe the way that different strokes and angles of hitting affect the ball's rotation. At the same hitting speed and traveling the same distance, effects make the ball follow different trajectories. A topspin effect causes the ball to rotate forward and travel a shorter distance; a backspin effect causes the ball to rotate backwards and travel a greater distance; a slice creates a curve in the ball's trajectory.

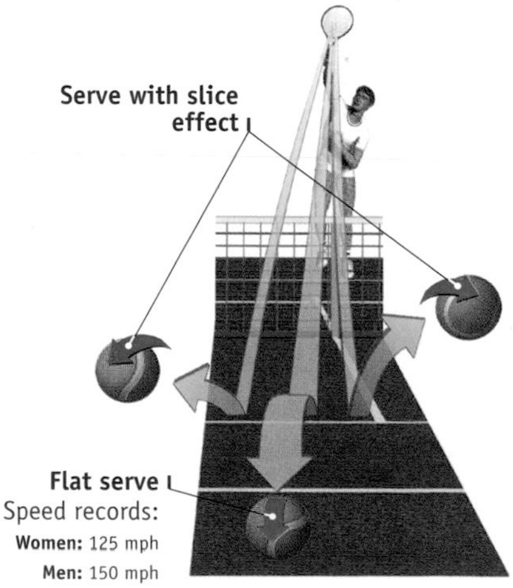

BALL TRAJECTORIES

The ball's trajectory results from the combination of the type of stroke and the rotation put on the ball. The various trajectories of a tennis ball cause the ball to bounce in different ways, and these effects increase or decrease depending on the playing surface.

Distance a ball travels for a stroke at the same speed and height

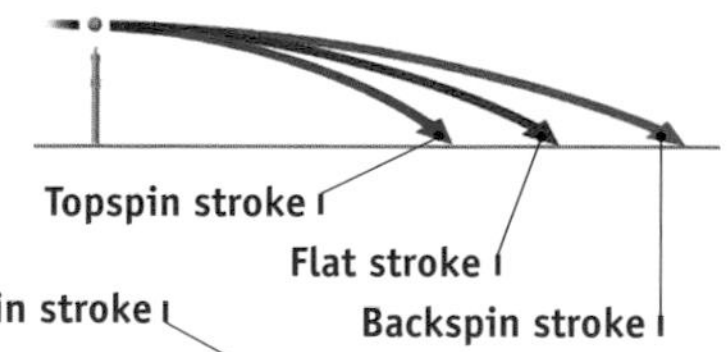

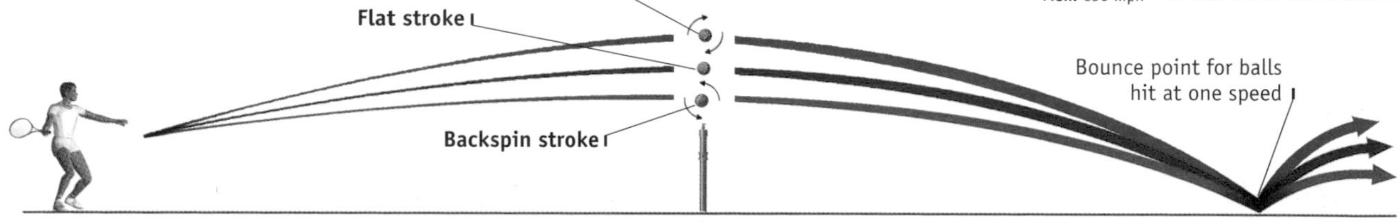

Topspin stroke

Flat stroke

Topspin stroke

Backspin stroke

Flat stroke

Backspin stroke

Bounce point for balls hit at one speed

Serve with slice effect

Flat serve
Speed records:
Women: 125 mph
Men: 150 mph

PLAYING SURFACES

In 1877, tennis was always played on rolled grass, which is why it is sometimes called lawn tennis. As the sport's popularity grew, other surfaces began to be used. There are now a variety of outdoor and indoor surfaces. Each surface has its own characteristics, which have an impact on tactics and stroke techniques. In indoor tennis, the surfaces are made of a hard synthetic material or rubber mats, and play is faster.

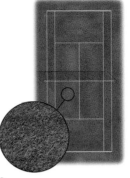

1. Grass

Favors serve-and-volley and limits the length of rallies from the baseline, since the ball slides and the bounce is low.

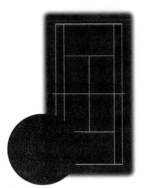

2. Clay

Allows a wider arsenal of shots to be used, and players can slide as they move. Balls bounce very slowly, so rallies tend to be long.

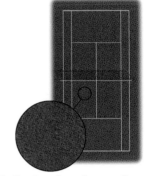

3. Hard surface (cement)

Favors bounce because of the uniformity of the surface, unlike grass (variable weather) and clay (uneven surface). However, can increase risk of knee and tibia injury.

4. Synthetic surface

Very popular among players. Flexible and springy, it offers excellent bounce and reduces risk of injury.

TOURNAMENTS

The ATP (Association of Tennis Professionals) which has had amateur and professional members since 1972, has published world player rankings since 1973, and presents a series of tournaments in which players' cumulative performances determines their annual ranking. The WTA (Women's Tennis Association) is for women tennis players throughout the world, and it follows the ATP's formula.

The Davis Cup is a men's tournament that takes place throughout the year among a number of countries, with a final in December. The Federation Cup, founded in 1963, is a tournament for women's national teams.

TOURNAMENT	DATE	PLACE	SURFACE
The Grand Slam (3 sets out of 5)			
Australian Open	late January	Melbourne	Synthetic surface
French Open	early June	Paris (Roland-Garros)	Clay
Wimbledon	early July	Wimbledon	Grass
US Open	early September	Flushing Meadows	Cement
Davis Cup (3 sets out of 5)	early December	Host country's choice	Host country's choice
Federation Cup (3 sets out of 5)	mid-September	Host country's choice	Host country's choice

DOUBLES MATCH

Special techniques and tactics are used by doubles players, because the partners must work as a team. Each player has a particular role to play as the point begins: server, server's partner, receiver, and receiver's partner. One player may hit several strokes in a row, without the partner intervening. Once a point is started, team members position themselves to cover the court effectively depending on the opponents' shots, rather than simply covering their half of the court. Servers alternate after each point, and the partners can switch the order of serve after each set. Receivers always return from the same side in a set, and they can switch positions after each set. Aside from serves, which must be made into the diagonally opposite service court, all strokes may be made anywhere in the opposing court within the doubles lines.

Receiver

Server's partner

Server

Receiver's partner

EVOLUTION OF THE TENNIS RACKET

Changes in the game have been directly linked to changes in the tennis racket itself, which have made strokes more powerful and accurate with more pronounced spin effects. The interaction of the racket's components and the size of the frame, the strings, and the grip influence the accuracy of the stroke, absorption of vibration, and speed of stroke execution.

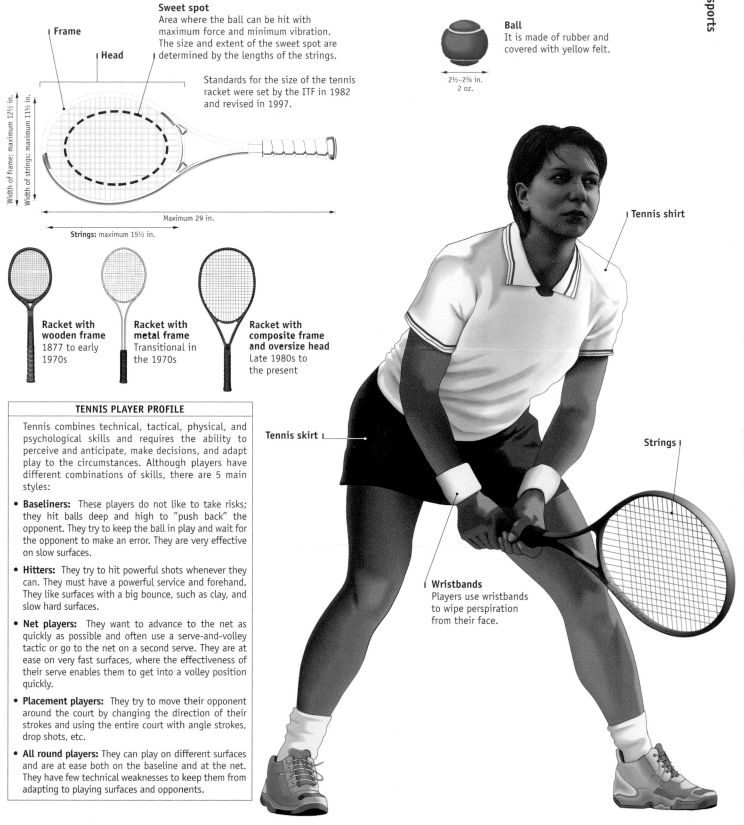

Frame

Head

Sweet spot
Area where the ball can be hit with maximum force and minimum vibration. The size and extent of the sweet spot are determined by the lengths of the strings.

Standards for the size of the tennis racket were set by the ITF in 1982 and revised in 1997.

Width of frame: maximum 12½ in.

Width of strings: maximum 11½ in.

Maximum 29 in.

Strings: maximum 15½ in.

Ball
It is made of rubber and covered with yellow felt.

2½–2⅝ in.
2 oz.

Racket with wooden frame
1877 to early 1970s

Racket with metal frame
Transitional in the 1970s

Racket with composite frame and oversize head
Late 1980s to the present

Tennis shirt

Tennis skirt

Strings

Wristbands
Players use wristbands to wipe perspiration from their face.

TENNIS PLAYER PROFILE

Tennis combines technical, tactical, physical, and psychological skills and requires the ability to perceive and anticipate, make decisions, and adapt play to the circumstances. Although players have different combinations of skills, there are 5 main styles:

• **Baseliners:** These players do not like to take risks; they hit balls deep and high to "push back" the opponent. They try to keep the ball in play and wait for the opponent to make an error. They are very effective on slow surfaces.

• **Hitters:** They try to hit powerful shots whenever they can. They must have a powerful service and forehand. They like surfaces with a big bounce, such as clay, and slow hard surfaces.

• **Net players:** They want to advance to the net as quickly as possible and often use a serve-and-volley tactic or go to the net on a second serve. They are at ease on very fast surfaces, where the effectiveness of their serve enables them to get into a volley position quickly.

• **Placement players:** They try to move their opponent around the court by changing the direction of their strokes and using the entire court with angle strokes, drop shots, etc.

• **All round players:** They can play on different surfaces and are at ease both on the baseline and at the net. They have few technical weaknesses to keep them from adapting to playing surfaces and opponents.

racquetball

An offensive racket sport, racquetball is played in a rectangular closed court. It was invented in 1949 in the United States by Joe Sobek, who wanted to create a sport similar to tennis that was easy to learn. Manufacturing and distributing the equipment himself in the 1950s, Sobek contributed greatly to the popularization and development of the sport. The International Racquetball Federation (IRF) was founded in 1979. The first world championships, in 1981, drew the attention of the International Olympic Committee, which officially recognized racquetball as a developing sport. Racquetball was included in the Pan-American Games in 1995, and there are now 17 million players in more than 70 countries.

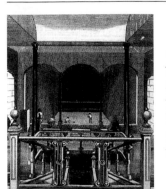

The Prince's Racquet Club Courts in Belgrave Square (Great Britain) in 1857, an ancestor of today's racquetball courts

THE GAME

Racquetball can be played singles (2 opponents) or doubles (2 teams of 2 players). Each side hits the ball in turn. It must be hit before the second bounce on the floor and can touch all walls, but must touch the front wall before touching the floor. The objective is to serve or return the ball in such a way that the opponent cannot keep it in play. The game begins with the announcement "Zero serves zero." It is played in 2 sets of 15 points. If there is a tie, a third set of 11 points determines the winner. Only the server can score a point. If the receiver wins a rally, he becomes the server.

Receiving line
To limit risk of collision with the server, the receiver must not enter the service zone until the ball has passed the receiving line after bouncing off the front wall.

Service zone
The ball must bounce once in the service zone before being hit. It must first touch the front wall, then bounce off the floor — after having bounced off the side walls or not — behind the service line.

Tactical area
This zone provides the best playing conditions. Keeping control of it is an important tactic.

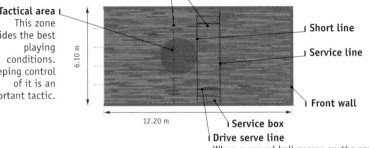

Short line

Service line

Front wall

Service box

Drive serve line
When a served ball passes on the same side of the court as the server, he must make sure that neither his body nor his racket passes this line. He must not block the receiver's view of the ball, which would keep him from returning serve under the best conditions.

6.10 m

12.20 m

COURT

Referee
He may be assisted by 2 line judges during tournaments. If they do not agree, final decisions are made by majority vote.

Back wall
Any ball hitting the wall above this line (3.66 m) is out of bounds.

Line judges (2)
If a player appeals, they may declare themselves in agreement or disagreement with the referee's decision.

6.10 m

Kill shot
This offensive stroke is impossible for the opponent to hit, as it hits the front wall about 15 cm from the floor.

TACTICS

Forcing the opponent to move as far as possible, forcing him to return with a weak or defensive shot, and keeping control of the tactical area are the 3 main objectives.

OFFENSIVE SHOTS

They are played on the bounce toward the bottom of the front wall.

DEFENSIVE SHOTS

They are played on the bounce toward the ceiling or the corners at hip level.

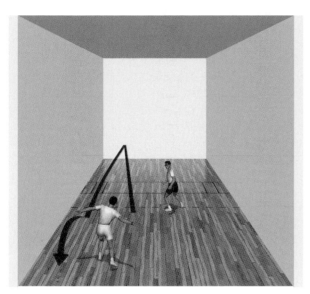

Pass shot

When this shot is powerful and accurate, the opponent is forced to leave the tactical area.

Ceiling shot

Forces the opponent to retreat to the back of the court and hit the ball high, for a less offensive shot.

RACKET GRIP

The power and accuracy of shots depends on the position of the racket when it contacts the ball. The ideal angle — perpendicular to the floor — is obtained by changing the grip following backhand or forehand shots.

Example of grip: Forehand
The "v" formed by the thumb and index finger is on top of the racket handle.

EQUIPMENT

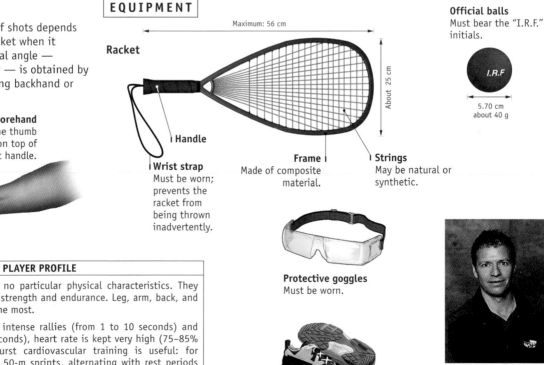

Maximum: 56 cm

Racket

About 25 cm

Handle

Wrist strap
Must be worn; prevents the racket from being thrown inadvertently.

Frame
Made of composite material.

Strings
May be natural or synthetic.

Official balls
Must bear the "I.R.F." initials.

I.R.F

5.70 cm
about 40 g

Protective goggles
Must be worn.

Shoes
As for squash, they must have a white or clear sole that does not mark the floor.

Sherman Greenfeld (CAN)
Team world champion in 1988 and 1996, and 10 time national champion in singles.

PLAYER PROFILE

- High level players have no particular physical characteristics. They have explosive muscular strength and endurance. Leg, arm, back, and thigh muscles are used the most.

- With the alternation of intense rallies (from 1 to 10 seconds) and short rests (about 10 seconds), heart rate is kept very high (75–85% of maximum). Short burst cardiovascular training is useful: for example, 5 series of 10 50-m sprints, alternating with rest periods equal to 3 times the duration of exertion.

- Some technical and tactical training can be done alone (serving, regularity and accuracy of basic shots), but practice sessions with other players are also essential.

table tennis

Viktor Barna (GBR), a Hungarian by birth (1911–1972), won 15 world titles, including 5 in singles, in the 1930s.

This fast moving offensive racket sport is played with light balls on the smallest game surface known. Invented in Great Britain around 1880, it took its current form in 1900 with the advent of celluloid balls, imported from the United States by Englishman James Gibb. The sound the balls make when they bounce inspired the name "ping pong"; this name was patented in the United States, so Europeans called the sport table tennis. The International Table Tennis Federation (ITTF) was formed in Berlin in 1926, and the first world championship took place the same year. The Hungarians, Czechs, and English dominated the sport until the 1950s, and then the Japanese and Chinese took over, bringing most of the technical and tactical innovations to the game up to 1979. Although the Swedish men have regularly been on the podium since the 1980s, women's table tennis has been dominated exclusively by Asians since 1971. Table tennis became an Olympic sport in Seoul in 1988.

THE MATCH

Players must hit the ball, after it bounces once on their side, onto the opponent's side of the table. A point is won if the opponent cannot return the ball or if it is played before the first bounce or after a second bounce. Tournaments feature singles (2 players), doubles (2 teams of 2 players), and mixed doubles (1 man and 1 woman per team) matches. Matches are played in 2 out of 3 or 3 out of 5 21-point sets, and a lead of at least 2 points is needed to win a set. Each player serves 5 times in a row. If there is a 20–20 tie, service changes at each point. In doubles, service rotates so that each player serves and receives from each other player in turn. In rallies, team members must hit the ball alternately, no matter where it lands on the table.

TABLE

2.74 m

1.525 m

Table height: 76 cm

The lines are part of the playing surface.

The center line is used only in doubles, when the serve must be made in a diagonal direction.

1.83 m

15.25 cm

Assistant umpire
He posts the points announced by the umpire, signals out of bounds balls (hitting the side of the table facing him), and can declare a serve illegal.

SCOREBOARD

Number of sets won by the player.

Number of points won by the player during the current set.

If a service ball touches the net before touching the table on the opponent's side, the ball is served again.

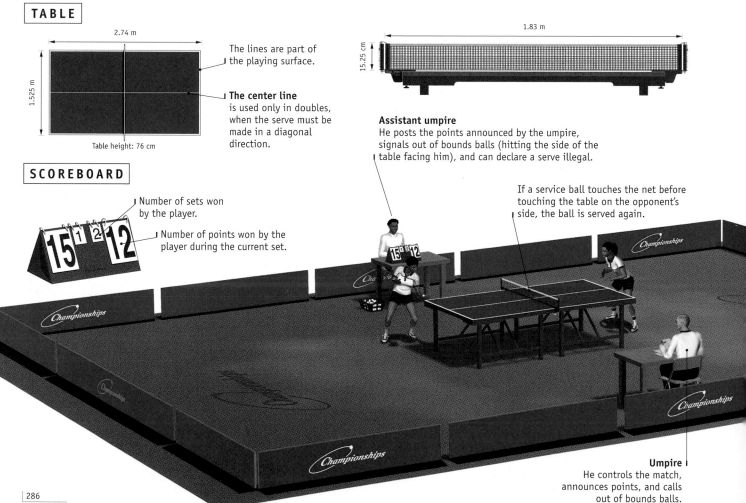

Umpire
He controls the match, announces points, and calls out of bounds balls.

RACKET GRIPS

Orthodox grip

The most widespread. It allows the player both to attack and to defend, but the transition from forehand to backhand is slow.

Penholder grip

Invented by the Japanese in the 1950s, it is perfect for an offensive game but the disadvantage when playing backhand must be compensated by very quick movement.

EQUIPMENT

Changes to the racket have caused a tactical evolution in the sport by directly influencing the style of play. The racket's surface is made of a piece of pimpled rubber or a rubber and foam "sandwich." Players can use different surface materials on each side of their rackets, but one side must be black and the other side red.

1870
1900

Ball
Made of celluloid, weighs 2.5 g.

38 mm

Racket
It can be any shape, size, and weight.

Covering
Maximum thickness must be 4 mm on each side of the blade.

Blade
Must be made of at least 85% wood.

TYPES OF COVERINGS

Thanks to rapid drying glues, coverings are applied to the blade a few minutes before the match, so that they keep their elasticity.

Inside pimples
The "backside" covering is very sticky and good for both attack and defence. The "anti-spin" covering, less sticky, is used mainly in defence.

Outside pimples
Short pimples are perfect for attacks close to the table.

Long pimples
They are preferred by defensive players who vary their shots.

Jan Ove Waldner (SWE)
Only player to hold the titles of world, European, and Olympic champion, between 1989 and 1997.

Deng Yaping (CHN)
Doubles and singles Olympic champion in 1992 and 1996, she was world champion in singles in 1991, 1995, and 1997 and in doubles in 1989, 1995, and 1997.

PLAYER PROFILE

- Concentration, coordination, and rapidity are essential. Cardiopulmonary capacity is improved with endurance runs, while quick movement is acquired by developing the leg muscles with jumping sessions and short sprints.

- Technical and tactical exercises at the table represent 70% of total training time. Players return the ball an average of 3 times before losing or winning a point. They must know how to direct play to place their best shots rapidly and keep opponents from using their best shots.

Floor
Must be made of wood or nonreflective synthetic material.

Panels
They are 75 cm high. They define a play area measuring 14 x 7 m and prevent errant balls from interfering with other games.

Playing surface
The top edges of the table are part of the playing surface.

In bounds ball

Out of bounds ball

THE SHOTS

Players can hit the ball in a wide variety of ways, changing its trajectory to put the opponent off balance.

Sidespin

In the serve, the ball must bounce on the server's side of the table, go over or around the net, then bounce on the receiver's side. Sidespins change the trajectory a great deal. Combinations of sidespin shots, forehand and backhand, are used to put the opponent off balance.

Backspin

The ball travels far, does not bounce high, and loses speed after the bounce. On the opponent's racket, it tends to drop toward the net. It is generally a defensive stroke.

Topspin (backhand)

The ball descends more quickly and accelerates forward after the bounce. It tends to rise on the opponent's racket.

Topspin (forehand)

The perfect attack shot, it is used during rallies or as a service return to hit long balls.

Counterattack

Powerful stroke that is flat and near the table, it does not change the ball's trajectory but relies on speed for its effect.

End shot

Its objective is to win the point immediately. The racket speed is maximum when it hits the ball. The player grips the racket handle hard to make the impact sharp. The ball is hit at or just before the top of the bounce.

badminton

A very popular racket sport in royal courts in the 18th century, badminton was not officially born until 1873, in Badminton, England. Inspired by an Indian game, poona, it spread rapidly with publication of the rules by Colonel Selby in 1867. The English federation was founded in 1893, and the All England Championship, one of the most prestigious tournaments in the international circuit, was first held in 1899. The Thomas Cup (for men) and Uber Cup (for women), two other famous tournaments, were founded in 1948 and 1956, respectively. The International Badminton Federation was founded in 1934. Badminton is very popular in Southeast Asia and Indonesia, which have produced many top players. The world championships have been held every two years since 1977. Badminton became an Olympic sport in 1992, after being a demonstration sport in 1972 and 1988.

Miss Larminie, gold medalist, and Miss Gowenlock, finalist, at the 1911 badminton championships

THE MATCH

Players hit a shuttlecock back and forth over a net with a racket. There are two ways to win a rally: getting the shuttlecock to hit the ground on the opponent's side of the net or forcing a fault. A fault occurs when the shuttlecock is hit out of bounds, touches the ground, does not go over the net, or touches a player or his clothing. The server wins points on service or by winning a rally. If the receiver wins the rally, he wins the serve. The match is played in 3 15-points games (for women's singles, 11 points).

The winner of 2 games wins the match. Badminton is played singles (2 players), doubles (2 teams of 2 players), and mixed doubles (one man and one woman per team). Mixed doubles is considered a specialty on its own: even at the top level, many players enter this discipline only.

Service judge
Checks execution of the serve: player position, illegal moves, reception of shuttlecock in the appropriate zone.

Umpire
Assisted by the line judges and service judge, he makes sure that the match is played properly. His decisions cannot be appealed.

Line judges (10)
They make sure that the shuttlecock is within bounds and inform the umpire of any faults committed by the players.

COURT

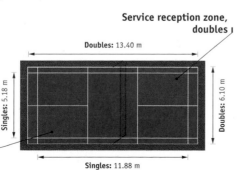

Posts
They are part of the playing surface.

Singles side line

Doubles side line

Short service line

Safety zone
Minimum width of 1.22 m around the court.

Long service line

SERVICE COURTS

Serves always travel diagonally across the court. If the server's score is even, the server uses the right service court; if his score is odd, he uses the left service court.

Service reception zone, doubles

Service reception zone, singles

Doubles: 13.40 m

Singles: 5.18 m

Doubles: 6.10 m

Singles: 11.88 m

Net

The shuttlecock moves so fast that it is not easy to see. The size of the net mesh is fine enough that the shuttlecock cannot pass through it. For the same reason, the net is attached snugly to the posts.

1.55 m

TECHNIQUES AND TACTICS

In singles, the current trend is toward a "flying game." By jumping, moving quickly, and hitting the shuttlecock harder, players try to generate an element of surprise. In doubles, the rallies are even quicker than in singles. Play becomes strategic, with the goal of gradually putting the other team in a difficult position. Hitting and deception techniques are studied in detail: being able to conceal one's shots till the last moment keeps the opponent from being able to predict the shuttlecock's trajectory.

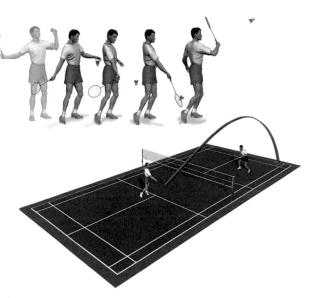

Service

Serves must be hit below the waist. The very popular long serve falls near the long service line; it forces the opponent to the back of the court, leaving the server more time to prepare for the return.

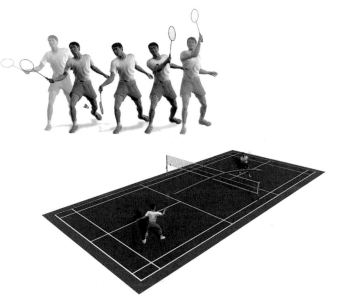

Drive

A quick offensive stroke with a horizontal trajectory, it forces the opponent to return the shuttlecock high and makes it possible to end the rally with a smash. A drive can be forehand or backhand.

Backhand

This defensive stroke is used mainly when the player is in difficulty. Hit below the waist or over the head, it can be a drop shot or go cross-court to catch the opponent flatfooted.

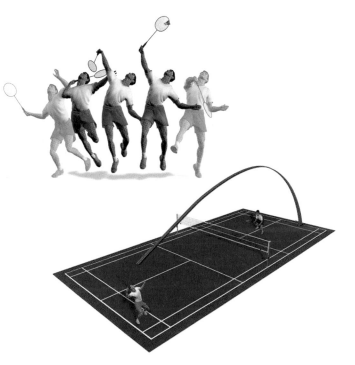

Clear

Usually a forehand stroke, it lands deep in the opponent's court. As a defensive shot, it slows play and gives the player a chance to get back into a good position. Hit hard, it becomes an offensive shot, making the opponent reach up.

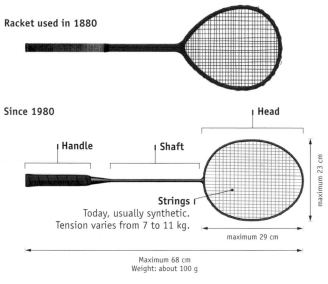

Net play

Shots made near the net in such a way as to put the shuttlecock close to the net on the other side are mainly attack techniques: their short trajectory reduces the opponent's reaction time and forces him to move a long distance.

Smash

In a smash, the shuttlecock may initially travel at up to 200 km/h. It is the most powerful attack shot, generally used to end a rally. It is hit on high shots and is aimed to land short.

EQUIPMENT

Racket

It is light and rigid thanks to the use of composite materials (graphite-carbon or carbon-boron) and titanium based alloys, which are very strong.

Racket used in 1880

Since 1980

Handle | Shaft | Head

maximum 23 cm

maximum 29 cm

Strings
Today, usually synthetic.
Tension varies from 7 to 11 kg.

Maximum 68 cm
Weight: about 100 g

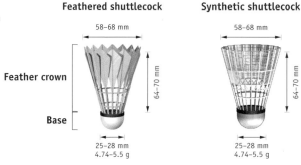

Feathered shuttlecock

58–68 mm

Feather crown

64–70 mm

Base

25–28 mm
4.74–5.5 g

Synthetic shuttlecock

58–68 mm

64–70 mm

25–28 mm
4.74–5.5 g

Shuttlecock

A competition shuttlecock is made of 14 to 16 goose feathers, inserted and glued into a cork base. A piece of lead or a screw is sometimes added to stabilize the trajectory and correct variations in weight. Shuttlecocks are very fragile: around 10 are usually destroyed in a high-level match. Because the shuttlecock is so light, badminton can be played only on indoor courts.

PLAYER PROFILE

- Because matches feature many sudden stops and starts, the exertion level is very high: a badminton player must be both quick and strong. Physical training is centered on "explosive energy" and endurance of the thigh and calf muscles.

- Athletes practice their footwork to increase the speed and accuracy of their positioning in relation to the shuttlecock. On court, they do movement exercises and learn a range of steps corresponding to situations found in competition.

Rudy Hartono (INA)
World champion in 1980, he held 8 singles titles at the All Englands.

Judy Hashman (USA)
She won 10 victories at the All Englands and held 12 titles in the U.S. between 1954 and 1967.

squash

Jonah Barrington, all-time best British player and first squash professional. World champion a number of times between 1966 and 1972

Text content:

A sport of endurance and strategy, squash is played with a stringed racket and a soft rubber ball on a rectangular court closed on all four sides. The name comes from the fact that the ball can be "squashed." Squash was invented around 1830 in England, and was exported to North America in 1885. For many years, the winners of the British Open, a prestigious tournament played every year since 1930 (1950 for women), were Australian and Pakistani. Countries with an Anglo-Saxon influence have dominated at the team world championships, inaugurated in 1967, and the individual world championships, inaugurated in 1975. Today, Canada, Scotland, and England are well placed in the world professional rankings. The World Squash Federation (WSF) regulates the sport.

THE COMPETITION

In both singles and doubles, the ball is hit so that the opponent cannot return it legally. A return is valid if the ball touches the front wall before bouncing on the floor twice; the ball can bounce any number of times on the side and back walls. A match is played in five 9 point games. Only the server can score a point. If the receiver wins a rally, he wins the serve. Professional tournaments are played in 15 point games in which the player who wins a rally wins the point, whether he is server or receiver.

THE "LET" RULE

Because opponents "share" the court, they sometimes block each other accidentally. If one of the players feels that his view or freedom of movement has been impeded, he can ask for the point to be replayed. If obstruction has obviously caused him to lose a point, he is awarded the point directly. The referee makes the decisions regarding lets and "let and points."

COURT

Scorer
He calls the play, signals faults, and announces the score.

Referee
He intervenes when the scorer appeals to him for a decision. Players address their requests for lets to him.

Service

A serve may be made forehand or backhand. The ball is thrown up and hit before it touches the floor or walls. After bouncing off the front wall, it must cross the service line and bounce off the back court opposite to the server's side. It is served onto the front wall. Serves very rarely win points: they are made to force the opponent to make a defensive return.

racket sports

Front wall
Singles court: 6.4 m
Doubles court: 7.62 m

9.75 m

5.50 m

1.6 m

Half court line

Short line

Ideal bounce zones

Service box
At the beginning of each rally, the server chooses which service box he will use. He then alternates between boxes until he loses serve. Until he hits the ball, one of his feet must remain in contact with the floor inside the box without touching the lines.

The "T" strategy
Players try to dominate the "T" in order to control the game. This is the best position for returning all types of shots. To force the opponent to leave the "T," a player hits long balls off the side walls that bounce near the back corners.

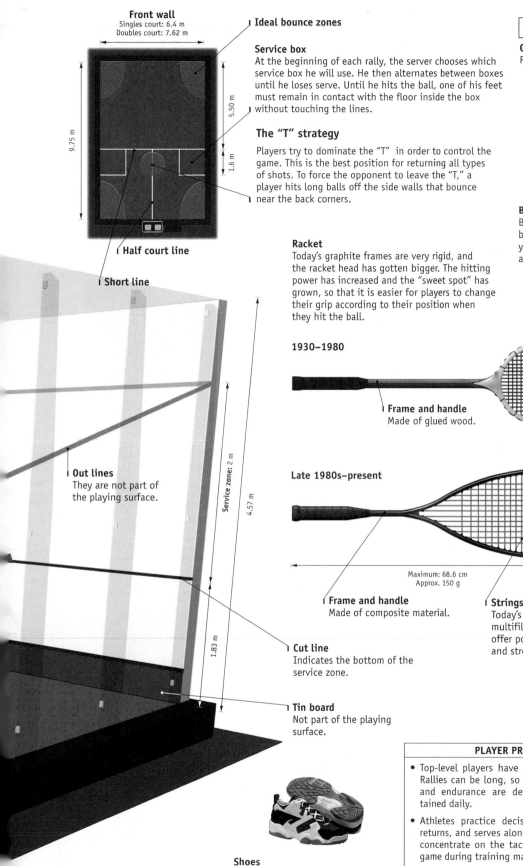

Out lines
They are not part of the playing surface.

Service zone: 2 m

4.57 m

1.83 m

Racket
Today's graphite frames are very rigid, and the racket head has gotten bigger. The hitting power has increased and the "sweet spot" has grown, so that it is easier for players to change their grip according to their position when they hit the ball.

1930–1980

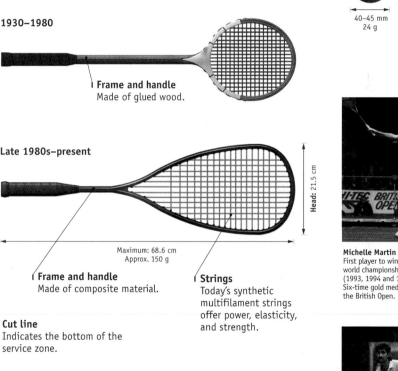

Frame and handle
Made of glued wood.

Late 1980s–present

Head: 21.5 cm

Maximum: 68.6 cm
Approx. 150 g

Frame and handle
Made of composite material.

Strings
Today's synthetic multifilament strings offer power, elasticity, and strength.

Cut line
Indicates the bottom of the service zone.

Tin board
Not part of the playing surface.

Shoes
They have a white or clear sole so that they do not mark the floor.

EQUIPMENT

Goggles
Players may wear protective goggles.

Balls
Balls are hollow and made of rubber. Low-bounce balls (used in competition) are marked with a yellow dot; high-bounce balls (used in training) are marked with a blue dot.

40–45 mm
24 g

Michelle Martin (AUS)
First player to win 3 consecutive world championships in singles (1993, 1994 and 1995). Six-time gold medalist at the British Open.

PLAYER PROFILE

- Top-level players have powerful, fast legs. Rallies can be long, so respiratory capacity and endurance are developed and maintained daily.

- Athletes practice decisive shots, difficult returns, and serves alone on the court. They concentrate on the tactical aspects of the game during training matches.

Jahangir Khan (PAK)
World champion from 1982 to 1988, he was unbeaten for 5 years, in more than 500 matches in a row, and became world champion without losing a single game.

TECHNIQUES

The ricochet

This defensive shot is used when the opponent has returned the ball very close to a back corner. There is not enough room to place the racket properly between the ball and the back wall and make a direct return on the front wall.

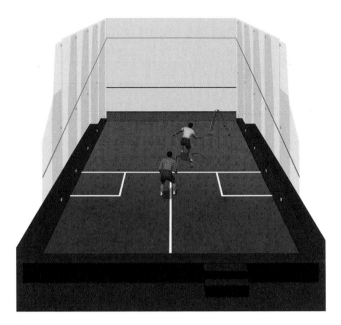

The drop shot

With the drop shot, the ball bounces very little and the opponent is forced to run toward it. He thus loses his strategic position in the "T" and puts himself in danger of being passed. A well played drop shot is a very effective attack shot.

The volley

The volley is an attack shot that breaks the rhythm of a rally and gives the opponent less time to prepare. It is more difficult to make a drop volley, with a short bounce, than a hard hit volley.

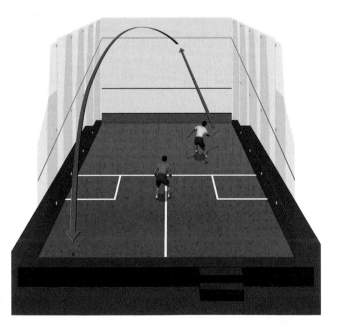

The lob

The lob goes over the opponent's head out of his reach. It falls almost vertically in a back corner and does not bounce much. It is a very difficult shot to return, but if it is not perfectly placed it offers the opponent an excellent attack opportunity.

Combat Sports

karate

Funakoshi Gichin (JPN), the founder of modern karate

Karate is a Japanese martial art that combines combat, self-defence, physical fitness, and spiritual development with techniques involving the human body's natural weapons (hands, elbows, arms, feet, knees, and head). Modern karate is derived from Chinese combat techniques and from Te, a bare handed combat art practiced on Okinawa Island. Two main schools, the Shorin-Ryu and the Shorei-Ryu, evolved from the combination of these two methods; today, there are over 70 styles of karate. Funakoshi Gichin, the founder of modern karate, was one of the first to bring to Japan the knowledge and skills that he acquired on Okinawa Island. In the early 20th century, he created the Shotokan style, based primarily on the Shorin-Ryu. Other masters developed styles that are widely practiced today. For example, Hinori Ohtsuka, a disciple of Funakoshi and a jujitsu expert, introduced Wado-Ryu; Chojun Miyagi was inspired by the Shorei-Ryu and developed Goju-Ryu, and Masutatsu Oyama created Kyokushinkai based on Shotokan and Goju-Ryu. Karate meets started in the 1950s, although women only began to participate in competitions in the 1980s. Today, the sport is governed by several international federations.

HOW A COMPETITION IS ORGANIZED

Although regulations vary from one organization to another, there are basically three types of competitions: breaking demonstrations (tameshi wari), simulated combat against one or more imaginary aggressors (kata), and sparring (shiai or kumite).

In certain styles of karate, such as Kyokushinkai, breaking demonstrations are very popular; however others do not involve any breaking. In the demonstrations the athletes use planks of wood, cement slabs, ice, etc. These are individual events.

In a kata demonstration, the competitor executes a series of choreographed combat techniques. In evaluating the level of expertise of the karateka, officials consider technical precision, comprehension of the movement, breathing, strength, coordination, rhythm, balance, and concentration. Competitions are individual or team events. In team events, participants simultaneously execute their movements in as synchronized a manner as possible.

Combat events normally last 1 to 3 min. Opponents bow to each other, and the match begins. As a general rule, hits must stop before they touch the opponent's body, although in some forms of combat, contact is permitted (semi-contact, full contact, fighting karate, kenka-karate, etc.). However, attacks to the groin, throat, joints, spine, temples, and back of the head are always prohibited. In some competitions, the aim of the karateka is to apply a perfectly controlled technique that combines accuracy of position, precision, vigor, rhythm, and proper attitude. If the participant is successful, he scores a point, known as an ippon. The first karateka to score 2 ippons is declared the winner, or, if the allotted time has elapsed, the opponent with the most points wins. A match may be stopped before 2 ippons are scored or before the time expires if one of the opponents leaves the mat or can no longer compete owing to a blow received.

Table of honor
High ranking practitioners of the art attend the match. They have the authority to overrule any decision made by the officials.

Umpire in chief
This official supervises the combat. He awards points, and hands out warnings and penalties. He announces any decisions as well as the start and end of a match.

COMPETITION AREA

Matches are held on the ground or on a mat.

Officials
During matches, there are between 3 and 7 officials, who oversee the application of the rules.

WEIGHT CATEGORIES

Not all organizations classify athletes according to weight category. In reference to the martial dimension of the discipline, some are of the view that a karateka must be able to save his life with a mortal blow to any opponent, regardless of size.

GRADES

Several elements are evaluated in progressing from one grade to the next: knowledge and mastery of techniques, kata demonstration, and combat. At the advanced levels, athletes are sometimes required to pass written tests and breaking tests. The higher the grade, the more extensive the requirements. Although it may only take a matter of months to obtain some of the beginner belts, it can take several years to move to the advanced grades.

SHOTOKAN STYLE GRADING SYSTEM			
Grades	Colors	Grades	Colors
9th to 6th kyu (beginner)	white	2nd kyu	blue
5th kyu	yellow	1st kyu	brown
4th kyu	orange	1st to 8th dan	black
3rd kyu	green	9th and 10th dan	red

PROFILE OF A KARATEKA

- Karate is practiced in a classroom called a dojo (seat of wisdom). Children start training as young as 6 or 7.

- Depending on the style practiced, the age and size of the athletes vary from one federation to another. While excellent performances have been executed by karatekas who are 20 years old, there are also champions 35 years of age. Women normally reach their peak a few years before men.

- At higher levels, the karateka masters technique, speed, and power. His hips are solid and supple, and his thighs are strong. He is extremely flexible.

- As this martial art requires great flexibility, training always begins with stretching exercises involving neck, arm, and ankle rotations, and specific hip and leg exercises. Schools dedicate approximately one third of their teaching time to exercises such as these.

- Breaking techniques (shiwari) allow the karateka to demonstrate his precision and, more especially, the strength of his attack, which cannot be demonstrated during combat, since blows may not be given at full strength. These demonstrations nonetheless put considerable strain on the joints, and over the long term can cause malformations and arthritis.

- Karate is practiced bare-handed, although the handling of weapons (tonfa, nunchaka) may be considered as a complement to training.

Bow

Maintaining eye contact, the opponents bow to each other. After the referee's signal marking the start of the combat, and up to the moment of the first attack, the opponents remain approximately 1 m apart. This is known as the critical distance.

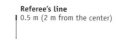

Referee's line
0.5 m (2 m from the center)

8 m

3 m

Opponents' positions
The opponents stand here at the start of the match, and whenever combat is stopped.

Corner judges (4)

These judges assist the referee. Using flags representing the participants' colors (red or white), the judges give their opinions when the referee makes a decision or when they request his attention.

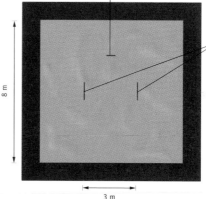

Scorekeeper

Time-keeper

TECHNIQUES

Regardless of the karate style, katas always begin with a defensive move followed by a counterattack. This is followed by several sequences that alternate between defences and attacks in different directions.

HEIAN GODAN

This basic kata in the Shotokan style consists of a sequence of 23 movements. It takes approximately 50 seconds to execute.

1. Start of the kata

With intense concentration and steadiness owing to a low stance, the karateka executes a block with his left wrist. The rotation of the hips that accompanies the movement of his upper body increases his speed. He never takes his eyes off his imaginary opponent.

2. Intermediate phases

Every block is followed by a counterattack. Preparation is made for each movement by inhaling, and the movement is executed upon exhalation, most of the strength being concentrated at the end of the exhalation. The shoulders always remain relaxed. The abdominal muscles are contracted, allowing the athlete to keep his balance.

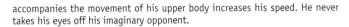

3. End of the kata

After meeting the imaginary attacks coming from the four cardinal points, the karateka resumes his starting position. There should be no hesitation during the demonstration.

TRAINING RANDORI OR KUMITE

Although they vary greatly from one style to another, these sequences (one to five attacking and defensive techniques) all form part of training since they constitute a bridge between the study of the technique and sparring.

1. Direct punch

The attacker throws his fist forward. The punch lands the moment the foot on his corresponding leg is set down and his rear leg extends strongly. The shoulders remain low during the entire movement.

2. Forward kick

The attacker holds his chest straight and his shoulders relaxed. His rear fist protects his plexus. The hips shift along with the movement of his leg, which extends only at the moment of impact so as to ensure maximum power. Any previous tension will slow down the kick.

EQUIPMENT

PROTECTION

It is at the discretion of the organizers to decide what protective gear is optional, mandatory, or prohibited. Some require hand guards, foot guards, a helmet, and a mouthguard. Shin guards are normally optional, as is the use of a protective cup for men and a protective cup and chest guard for women. Opponents are always barefoot during competitions.

Alain Le Hétet (FRA)
National champion in the heavyweight category in 1991, 1992, and 1994, European Champion in 1993 (team champion in 1993 and 1995 to 1997), and World Champion in 1994 (team champion in 1994 and 1996), he has also been serving as Captain of the French team since 1995.

Obi (belt)
The color of the obi indicates the level of the karateka. The color system and number of belts used varies depending on the karate style and the particular school. In order to distinguish between opponents in sparring competitions, one competitor wears a red belt and the other wears a white one, regardless of their level.

Karate-gi
Normally white in color, the jacket and pants are made of cotton. Women wear a T-shirt under the jacket.

3. Dodging

In an agile manner, the competitor quickly removes the threat by trying to avoid touching the attacking part of the opponent's body. Hip movements are very important, although to be effective, they should be as subtle as possible. The absence of contact with the opponent's body makes it possible for the competitor to conserve his energy for the counterattack.

4. Counterattack with the outside of the hand

The instantaneous retaliation blow is used when an opponent is off balance. An energetic rotation of the hips accompanies the arched trajectory of the arm. The palm of the hand turns upward only on contact, hitting, in a whipping motion, the temple, the carotid artery, or nape of the neck. The forearm, wrist, and hand form a solid block, while the arm and elbow remain relaxed.

jujitsu

T he forerunner of judo and aikido, jujitsu, the Japanese term for "science of combat" or "art of flexibility," is a martial art based on Indian and Chinese fighting techniques more than 2,000 years old. This self-defense method became popular in the 12th century, when it began to be used by samurai and ninja, who developed a number of battlefield combat techniques. The basis of jujitsu is the desire to kill or disable the opponent by any means, using a minimum of strength. Over the centuries, jujitsu was influenced by Chinese combat arts and techniques used on the island of Okinawa. In the 17th century, in Japan, the military techniques of jujitsu became a martial art, which was codified during the Meiji Period (1868–1912). It has since been transformed further to become a self-defense technique and a competition event stripped of its fatal techniques and practiced in various forms.

Portrait (1890s) of a Japanese samurai wearing armor and carrying a katana. When they were disarmed, these warriors used jujitsu.

THE BOUT

There are four types of competition: pairs, grappling, sport jujitsu, and extreme combat. Rules for fights vary from one organization to another. There are weight and age categories for bouts.

Pairs

In a pairs competition, pairs of athletes take turns presenting a series of simulated attacks, the level and content of which are determined before the competition by the chief referee. The quality of the presentation is evaluated in terms of attitude, effectiveness, speed of execution, control, and power.

Grappling and sport jujitsu

In these bouts between two fighters, the goal is to grab the opponent, throw him to the ground, and immobilize him for a predetermined time or cause him to give up through a submission hold. These fights, which last 2–5 min, are characterized by body-to-body wrestling. Between 1 and 4 points are awarded when a fighter executes a recognized technique or makes his opponent submit. In grappling, hitting is forbidden, while in sport jujitsu it is allowed, but not to the face, throat, spine, groin, or joints. The winner is the competitor who has scored the most points during the fight.

Extreme combat

In these very violent fights, which take place in a fenced-in combat area with padded posts, all blows are permitted. The longest fights last 3 20-min periods. The athletes' goal is to knock out their opponents or force them to give up. If both fighters survive to the end of the time designated by the organizers, the referees choose a winner based on superior combativeness.

JUJITSU COMPETITION AREA

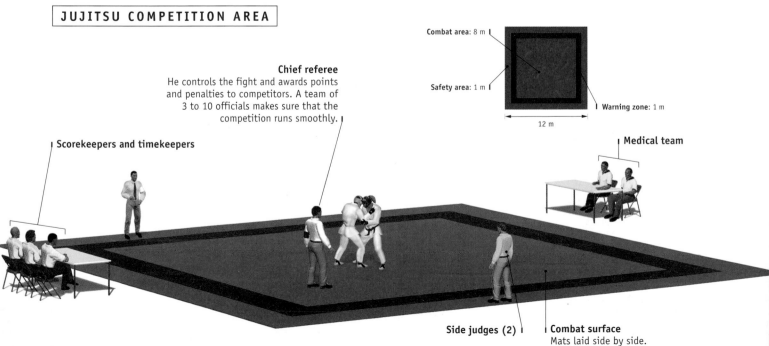

Chief referee
He controls the fight and awards points and penalties to competitors. A team of 3 to 10 officials makes sure that the competition runs smoothly.

Scorekeepers and timekeepers

Combat area: 8 m
Safety area: 1 m
Warning zone: 1 m
12 m

Medical team

Side judges (2)

Combat surface
Mats laid side by side.

BASIC TECHNIQUES

Jujitsu is characterized by a quest for maximum efficiency in flexibility and by a wide variety of techniques: throws, holds, punches to vital organs, kicks, strangling, dislocation of joints or limbs by blocking, leverage, armed techniques, and more. The fighter must be able to gauge the strength of the opponent and use it against him. He must be capable of dodging attacks and know how to unbalance the opponent, use leverage to throw him to the ground, and immobilize him by twisting or dislocating his limbs or by strangling. He must also be able to perform controlled blows on vital points.

1. Kick to the legs

The combatants are concentrating very hard. They keep their bodies straight, with shoulders low and relaxed. Their knees are bent so that their bodies are as stable as possible. The attacker breathes out and kicks the opponent's leg to unbalance him.

2. Grab

In an explosive motion, the attacker charges at her opponent. She grabs him and tries to get his body as close as possible in order to avoid being hit.

3. Throw

The attacker throws her opponent to the ground and falls on top of him. The goal is to be in the upper position, with 4 solid points of support, over the opponent lying on his back.

4. Submission

The attacker makes her opponent give up by strangling him. To accomplish this submission hold, the attacker must keep control over the opponent by staying very close to him and maintaining the 4 points of support at all times.

EQUIPMENT

Protection

In grappling, the competitors wear a mouth guard and an athletic support; in extreme combat, hand guards are added. In sport jujitsu, athletes wear hand guards, shin guards, foot guards, and mouth guard. Men wear an athletic cup and women a breast guard. Use of a helmet is recommended. Competitors must have short fingernails.

Weight categories in sport jujitsu	
Women	Men
Up to 55 kg	Up to 62 kg
Over 55 up to 62 kg	Over 62 up to 69 kg
Over 62 up to 70 kg	Over 69 up to 77 kg
Over 70 kg	Over 77 up to 85 kg
	Over 85 up to 94 kg
	Over 94 kg

Belt ranking system in extreme combat	
6th kyu	white
5th kyu	yellow
4th kyu	orange
3rd kyu	green
2nd kyu	blue
1st kyu	brown
1st to 4th dan	black
5th to 7th dan	red and white
8th and 9th dan	red
10th dan	white

HEAD HOLD

Gi
Usually consists of a white cotton jacket and pants. Black and blue gi are also worn. Women wear a T-shirt under the jacket.

Obi
Colored belts indicate the different ranks. Different schools use different color systems.

Royce Gracie (BRA)
A 4th dan black belt, he has won the world championships in extreme combat 3 times: once in 1993 and twice in 1994.

PROFILE OF THE FIGHTER

- The most successful fighters on the international level are generally between 20 and 30 years old. Of medium height, they have a small waist and powerful legs and abdominal muscles. Their necks are often massive and their trapezius muscles are well developed.

- Many blows target the joints. Stretching of the shoulders, forearms, hips, and knees is therefore essential.

- Training includes exercises to strengthen different parts of the feet, which are placed under great stress during kicks.

- Muscle strengthening, while keeping the muscles supple, is combined with endurance and cardiovascular training.

judo

Jigoro Kano (JPN) founder of judo and the only holder of a 12th dan.

Judo means "gentle way" in Japanese. This unarmed style of fighting is distinguished from other martial arts by its hand-to-hand fighting throws to the ground. Based on jujitsu, a martial art from the feudal period, and developed at the end of the 19th century by Japan's Jigoro Kano, the main focus of judo is the physical and moral betterment of its practitioners. The underlying principle of Judo is that the judoka never resists his opponent's force, but rather turns it back on his attacker. Simultaneously a defensive art, a spectator sport, and a competitive sport, judo first appeared in the Olympic Games at Tokyo in 1964, but was only permanently admitted as a men's sport at the Munich Games in 1972. While the men participated in their first World Championship in Tokyo in 1956, the first women's World Championship was held in 1980 in New York. Women's judo was a demonstration sport at the Seoul Olympic Games in 1988, and became an Olympic event in 1992 in Barcelona.

HOW A COMPETITION IS ORGANIZED

Random draws from the same ranking determine the contestants for each fight. The judokas who lose a fight are eliminated, except those who lose in the semi-final round—they fight each other for the bronze medal. The two finalists fight for the gold and silver medals. Combatants may fight 5 to 6 matches in the same day before they reach the final. The first judoka called to fight wears a blue judogi, while the second wears a white judogi. They bow to each other before moving onto the tatami, position themselves on the marks corresponding to the color of their judogi, and bow again.

The referee starts the fight with the word "Hajime!" The competitors bow to each other again before they leave the tatami, a sign of respect and discipline, two features of the practice of judo. A fight ends when a competitor scores an ippon (10 points), or when the time limit expires (5 min for men and 4 min for women in international competition). If an ippon is not scored, the judoka with the highest point total wins the match.

COMPETITION AREA

Referee
The referee stays in the fight area. If a dispute arises, the final outcome must be decided unanimously by the two judges and the referee. When a judge indicates his disagreement with a call, a decision is made by a majority vote of the three officials.

Corner judges (2)
Using an appropriate gesture, they must clearly indicate whether the action falls inside or outside the contest area.

Scorers and timers

Mat judge

Scoreboard
There are two scoreboards for each competition area: one manual and one electronic. They are used to display points and penalties. Two blue crosses and two white crosses indicate medical intervention.

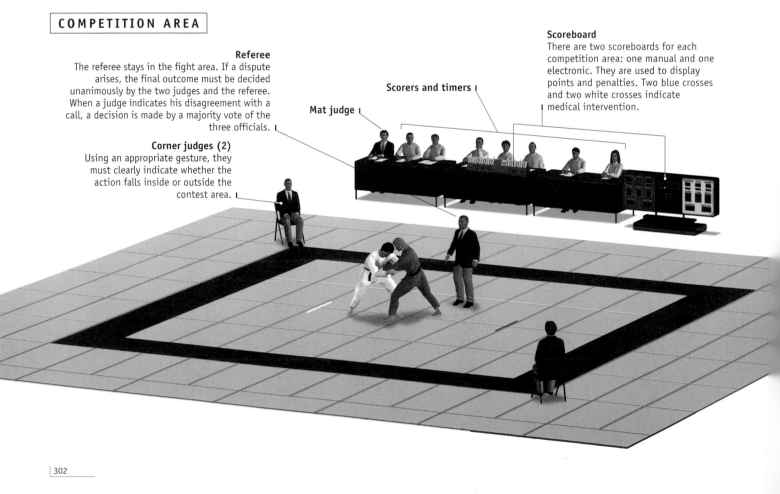

JUDGING

In recent years, a certain change has been noted in the rules: defensive judo is being increasingly penalized, with a more dynamic style being favored.

If no ippon is scored before regulation time for the match runs out, the koka, yuko, and waza-ari are added to determine the winner. During a bout, kokas and yukos cannot be combined for the required 10 points. The accumulation of two waza-aris is equivalent to one ippon (10 points), and ends the contest.

Ippon

There are three ways to score an ippon: by throwing the opponent onto his back with control, force, and speed; by forcing the opponent to submit using an arm-lock or choking technique; by pinning the opponent to the ground (osaekomi), for 25 seconds.

Waza-ari

A controlled throw of the opponent using a technique missing 1 of the 4 elements necessary to score an ippon (landing the opponent on his back, control, force, or speed), or achieving an osaekomi of 20 to 24 seconds.

Yuko

A controlled throw using a technique missing 2 of the 3 other elements necessary to obtain an ippon, or achieving an osaekomi of 15 to 19 seconds.

Koka

A controlled throw of the opponent onto his shoulder, leg, or buttock with force and speed, or an osaekomi of 10 to 14 seconds.

VIOLATIONS

When a competitor is penalized, his opponent receives the corresponding number of points. If a judoka commits more than one violation of the same level of seriousness, he receives a higher penalty. By issuing a higher penalty, the prior penalty and the equivalent points that were awarded to the opponent are cancelled. Penalty points are not deducted from points scored.

Some of the violations penalized by the officials include: intentionally leaving the tatami area; overly defensive conduct; faking attacks; striking the opponent; intentionally falling to the ground; and disobeying a judge. Any dangerous gestures or actions intended to injure the opponent, or that are contrary to the spirit of judo, are prohibited.

Matte

To interrupt the fight, the referee calls for "Matte!" The contestants must separate and return to their respective marks.

Penalty		Opponent gains
Shido (observation)	3 points	**Koka**
Chui (comment)	5 points	**Yuko**
Keikoku (warning)	7 points	**Waza-ari**
Hansokumake (disqualification)	10 points	**Ippon**

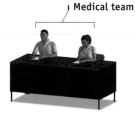

Medical team

Tatami
Small mats placed side by side, measuring 1 m x 2 m, designed to cushion falls.

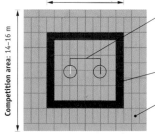

Contest area: 8–10 m

Competition area: 14–16 m

Marks for start and end of contest
Combatants return to their marks if the fight has been stopped or has ended. They bow to each other and wait for the announcement of the winner.

Danger area
Width: 1 m

Safety area
Width: 3 m

TECHNIQUES AND TACTICS

Competitors seek to gain the advantage at the start of the contest and to continue the attack, controlling the pace and progress of the fight. They try to take advantage of the smallest error committed by the opponent, throw him off balance and counter him with carefully chosen and rapidly deployed techniques. With their trainers' assistance, judokas prepare two to five special movements, designed for maximum effectiveness according to their size, body shape, and skills. During a fight, the judoka tries to use these techniques as often as possible. Combatants can benefit from studying their opponent's style prior to a match in order to anticipate his offensive strategy.

THROWING AND GRAPPLING: STANDING ON THE MAT

1. Ready position

The combatant tries to grab his opponent quickly and throw him off balance by moving or feinting before attacking, while at the same time trying to avoid giving his opponent a favorable angle.

2. Gripping

The judoka who successfully grabs his opponent (kumi kata) has the advantage. Arm movements are short and vigorous, and the wrists are solidly locked.

3. Positioning

The seized combatant tries to escape from the kumi kata, while his attacker prepares the next throw. He checks his grip, repositions his feet, and corrects his position to ensure maximum stability, in order to maintain control.

4. Throwing

After throwing his opponent off balance, thereby depriving him of his powers of self defense, the attacker throws him onto his back with force and control. The thrown athlete tries to turn onto his stomach, roll himself into a ball, or get up on his hands and knees.

5. Pinning

The attacker increases the pressure on his opponent's body as quickly as possible, especially on the shoulders. When pinning an opponent, no part of the judoka's body may be controlled by his opponent's legs.

CHOKING

Using his hand and forearm, along with the back of his opponent's jacket, the attacker cuts off his opponent's breathing by compressing his trachea, or compresses the two carotid arteries in order to reduce the flow of blood (and thus oxygen) to the brain. To prevent his opponent from breaking free from this hold, he uses his entire bodyweight.

ARM LOCK

The attacker holds onto his opponent's arm while pulling it as straight as possible. He then locks it by applying pressure to the elbow joint, and maintains pressure until his opponent gives up.

EQUIPMENT

Judogi

In international competitions, the judogi consists of a white or blue cotton jacket and pants, which are neither too thick nor too stiff to allow the opponent to get a proper grip. Women wear a white T-shirt or leotard under their jacket. Competitors must be barefoot.

Jacket

Belt

Pants

Anton Geesink (NED)
The first judoka (10th dan black belt) to beat the Japanese on their home turf, at the 1964 Olympic Games in Tokyo. World Champion in 1961 (Open) and 1965 (Heavyweight), he was European Champion 13 times.

Ingrid Berghmans (BEL)
The most accomplished judoka in the history of women's judo, she won 6 World Championships in the 1980s.

Belt

The 3 m long belt is wrapped twice around the waist, and indicates the judoka's rank. Although the black belt is a goal for many, it is merely the first stage in the search for the "gentle way." Each national federation has its own criteria for awarding belts. In Japan, there are no intermediate ranks between the white and black belt, whereas western countries have introduced colored belts.

RANKS

In order for a judoka to move up a rank, he must know and master a new set of techniques. Once the rank of 1st dan black belt is reached, the practitioner must execute techniques, imposed and drawn at random, before a jury of high-ranking dans.

Rank	Color	Rank	Color
6th kyu (beginner)	white	3rd dan	black
5th kyu	yellow	4th dan	black
4th kyu	orange	5th dan	black
3rd kyu	green	6th dan	white and red
2nd kyu	blue	7th dan	white and red
1st kyu	brown	8th dan	white and red
1st dan	black	9th dan	red
2nd dan	black	10th dan	red

PROFILE OF A JUDOKA

- Men generally start their international careers at the age of 20, whereas women start earlier, some as young as 15. Maximum performance is usually achieved between the ages of 24 and 28, for both men and women.

- Size varies greatly, given the different weight classes, but a judoka always has solid back muscles and strong legs. As the male torso is more highly developed, women have a lower center of gravity than their male counterparts.

- For athletes in the extra lightweight to middleweight classes, training is very technical, and focuses on speed. In the higher classes, muscle building is more important.

- Flexibility and stretching exercises are essential to correct certain negative effects of judo: shortening of the most often used muscles; loss of range in certain movements; and stiffening of the lumbar and cervical spine.

- Athletes must keep the nails of their fingers and toes short.

Weight categories	Men	Women
Extra lightweight	up to and including 60 kg	up to and including 48 kg
Half lightweight	over 60 up to and including 66 kg	over 48 up to and including 52 kg
Lightweight	over 66 up to and including 73 kg	over 52 up to and including 57 kg
Half middleweight	over 73 up to and including 81 kg	over 57 up to and including 63 kg
Middleweight	over 81 up to and including 90 kg	over 63 up to and including 70 kg
Half heavyweight	over 90 up to and including 100 kg	over 70 up to and including 78 kg
Heavyweight	more than 100 kg	more than 78 kg
Open category	all categories	all categories

In theory, the open category includes judokas of any weight. However, in practice, primarily athletes weighing more than 100 kg fight in this class.

aikido

A ikido, "the path of harmony and unification," is a Japanese martial art that uses rapid dodging movements and counter holds to turn the opponent's strength against him during an armed or bare handed attack. Aikido practitioners master a technique that enables them to be in harmony with the world around them. In principle, aikido is not a competitive sport, but certain schools have incorporated freestyle competitions. Aikido was created in the 1930s by Morihei Ueshiba. After studying the martial arts traditionally practiced by samurai (jujitsu, kenjutsu, combat with sticks in the Daito-ryu tradition, using the naginata, a weapon almost 2 m long with a blade on the end), Morihei melded the techniques to create a method combining the spirit of decision making (kime), knowledge of anatomy, quick reflexes, and a spiritual component. Since the 1950s, aikido has spread beyond Japan to the rest of the world.

Master Morihei Ueshiba (1883-1969), who created aikido in the first half of the 20th century

TECHNIQUE

The aikidoka seeks, through effective and powerful movements, to unbalance and neutralize the opponent, making him understand that it is useless to fight. Aikidoka must be able to respond to all types of attacks by harmonizing their reaction to redirect the assault. Aikido includes many movements that allow practitioners to escape a hand hold, throw the opponent to the ground, and immobilize him with joint twisting and pinning techniques. Atemi, blows to the vital points of the opponent's body, and strangling are also used. Many aikido techniques include circular or spiraling movements. To be effective, the techniques must be applied with strength, speed, fluidity, and coordination, with gliding movements and low body positions. Aikidoka train in a dojo (training room) on tatami (mats). Partners repeat series of techniques until they master them, regularly changing roles from attacker to the one attacked.

GYAKUHAMNI KATATETORI SHIHONAGE

1. Grab

The aikidoka's wrist is grabbed by the opponent, who intends to hit him in the face.

2. Loss of balance

The aikidoka rotates his hips and moves to the side, deflecting the opponent from his line of attack.

3. Twist

He firmly grasps the opponent's wrist and, in a circular movement, slides under his arm.

4. Throw

By moving in a semi circle, he regains a position of strength and increases the pressure on his opponent's arm, throwing him to the ground.

KATATORI NIKKYO

1. Loss of balance

The aikidoka moves sideways. The attacker is overextended and cannot maintain his hold.

2. Hit

He replies with a blow to the face in order to overcome the opponent's desire to attack.

3. Twist

He twists the attacker's wrist. At the same time, a rotation of his hips gives his movement more power.

4. Pin

By increasing pressure on the joint, he puts the attacker on the ground and pins him.

5. Submission

In this position, he can cause great pain in the opponent's shoulder and elbow.

SUWARI WAZA SHOMENUCHI IKKYO

1. Loss of balance

The aikidoka blocks a vertical attack with his arm; with a thrust of his hips, he unbalances the opponent.

2. Descent

With a circular movement, he pushes the attacking arm to the ground and increases pressure on the opponent's elbow.

3. Pin

The aikidoka may use his body weight to increase the pressure on the opponent's arm. Any twisting produces sharp pain in the shoulder.

KUMITACHI

1. Block

Staying as balanced as possible, the counterattacker blocks the opponent's attack by moving slightly to the side and parrying with his saber (bokken).

2. Riposte

By moving his body weight forward, the counterattacker unbalances the opponent and, with a circular movement, brings his bokken up to head level and hits him in the neck.

RANKS

To rise from one rank to the next, aikidoka must accumulate days of practice: a few months for the lower ranks (5th to 1st kyu), many years for the higher ranks (1st to 10th dan). They must also pass examinations that evaluate their mastery of the required techniques and, at higher levels, their mastery of freestyle combat and ability to defend themselves against several attackers, both armed and unarmed.

EQUIPMENT

Jo Bokken

1 m

1.55 m

Stick

Training usually includes the art of handling the long stick (jo) and the wooden saber (bokken).

PROFILE OF THE AIKIDOKA

- Aikido requires rapid reflexes, balance, and quick decision making in a spirit of profound concentration.

- Aikidoka should harmoniously develop their muscles by increasing their flexibility. Extra work on the legs improves stability and enable practitioners to move more quickly and accurately.

- Aikido can be started at age 7 or 8 and practiced throughout life.

Aikidogi
White shirt made of thick cloth.

Obi
The belt goes around the hips twice to hold the shirt on. It also shows the aikidoka's rank: white from 5th to 1st kyu, black from 1st to 10th dan.

Hakama
Until she gains her black belt, the aikidoka wears white pants made of a light fabric. In the higher ranks, she also wears a hakama, long, very wide pants inspired by the dress of samurai in the Tukogawa period. The white hakama is reserved for the great masters. Tactically, the hakama hides the position of the feet.

Yamada Yoshimitsu (JAP)
After studying for more than 10 years with Morihei Ueshiba, this great master with a rank of 8th dan founded the Aiki-kai in New York, helping to spread aikido in North America.

kendo

combat sports

In the early 20th century, masters Sasaburo Takano and Miromichi Najayama using sabers in a Japanese fencing match.

Kendo is a method of combat in which participants use a bamboo sword known as the shinai, which represents the traditional Japanese sword. The sport is an offshoot of kenjutsu (sword technique), the Japanese martial art of handling the sword (ken). We do not know exactly when the art of the sword originated, although it was apparently adopted and perfected by the samurai in the Middle Ages. During the Tokugawa period (1603-1867), this Japanese form of fencing changed considerably. The number of schools multiplied and techniques were refined. Kenjutsu evolved into kendo: "the way of the sword." In the 18th century, protective equipment was introduced and the blade was replaced with the shinai, which allowed for realistic combat without putting the lives of the participants at risk. In 1945, following the defeat of the Japanese in the Second World War, kendo, like all martial arts, was prohibited in Japan, but was reintroduced in 1950 as a sport. The world championships, which take place every three years, were first held in Tokyo in 1970. Women competed officially for the first time in 2000, in Santa Clara, California.

HOW A MATCH IS ORGANIZED

A match, or shiaï, lasts 3 or 5 minutes. It officially starts when the referee gives the signal to begin (hajime). The first kendoka to earn two points, or ippon, is declared the winner. To score an ippon, an athlete must attack with his body, his sword, and his voice, all at the same time. The attacker may strike the head, the forearm, the sides of the chest, or the throat, and contact must be made with the upper third of the blade of the shinai. If only one ippon is scored during a match, the scoring kendoka is declared the winner. In the case of a tie, the match is either declared nil or extended by 1 or 2 minutes, and the first combatant to score an ippon is declared the winner. If the match is still tied after the allotted extra time, there are three possibilities: the match remains a tie; it is extended again; or the referees award the match to the kendoka who exhibited the superior performance. The referees give warnings to a combatant who commits a mistake, such as an illegal strike with the body or shinai, leaving the ring, tripping, dropping the shinai, etc. If a participant commits two mistakes, his opponent is awarded one ippon. Actions or words that are disrespectful of the opponent or the referees result in disqualification. At the world championships, nitoryu, or the use of two shinai—one long and one short—is permitted.

MATCH AREA

Matches take place on a smooth wooden floor so that the kendoka's bare feet can slide easily.

Combatants' starting positions

2.8 m

9–11 m

9–11 m

Danger zone: 1.5 m

Center
A visual symbol indicating the center of the court.

Before attacking, the kendoka assumes the defensive posture (diudon). With his body straight and his chin down, he leans his body forward slightly, as if ready to leap. The shinai is held with a firm but relaxed grip. The left hand is held one fist length away from the body. The sword points to the opponent's throat.

Scorekeepers

Timekeeper

Referees (3)
Positioned in a triangle on the court, the referees ensure that the match runs smoothly. They use a red or a white flag to indicate that a combatant has scored a point. The referees also give warnings, and their decisions are final.

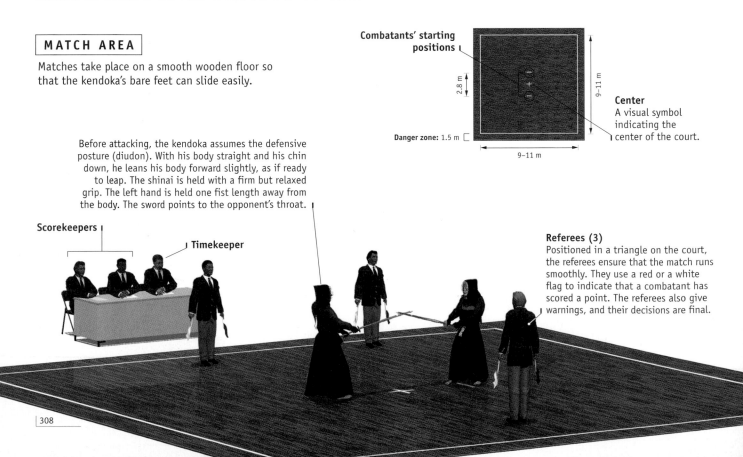

BASIC TECHNIQUES

During an attack, kendokas use their bodies, their swords, and their voices (ki-aï) all at the same time. The ki-aï is the vocalization ending a forceful exhalation of breath, and is meant to channel energy and focus determination in an effort to intimidate or distract the opponent. In striking, the attacker must simultaneously yell out the name of the targeted body part. Posture must be correct during and after the attack.

Men-uchi
Vertical blow to the forehead

Men-uchi is a powerful thrusting movement that starts at the left heel and projects the attacker's body forward. The moment the right leg hits the ground, the shinai hits the target.

Kote-uchi
Strike on the right wrist

Similar to the men-uchi, the hit involves a vertical movement that follows the central line of the body. Only the targeted area differs.

Do-uchi
Descending blow on the right side

The do-uchi consists of a blow to the side at a 45° angle. The symbolic objective of this attack is to cut the adversary in half.

Tsuki-uchi
Strike to the throat

With the whole body moving forward, the most direct strike possible is made with the tip of the shinai. The hit must be very accurate.

LEVELS OF EXPERTISE

Unlike other martial arts, there are no outward signs or belts indicating the 16 possible grades of a kendoka, which are: 6th to 1st kyu (lower levels), 1st and 2nd dan, 3rd to 9th dan (higher grades). During competitions, matches generally take place between kendoka of the same level. Earning a new kyu normally takes a minimum of 2 years. The requirements for earning these grades are at the discretion of the master. However, starting with the 1st dan, the kendoka must pass an examination, consisting of combat and kata, performed before a committee of judges mandated by the federation. At the higher grades, it takes several years to progress from one level to the next.

KENDOKA PROFILE

- In Japan, children can start kendo at the age of 4. Participants in international championship events are generally between the ages of 25 and 35.

- A kendoka must be able to use several parts of the body and channel the maximum amount of energy into movements that must be perfectly synchronized.

- The kendoka must demonstrate a high degree of self-mastery in a spirit of peace and well-being, and balance between body and spirit. Discipline, etiquette, and courtesy are integral components of training and competition.

- To maintain and improve technical skill, kendoka perform kata, a series of combat movements. These are executed without body armor, using a wooden sword (bokotu) or a practice sword with a metal blade (iaito).

EQUIPMENT

Men
A thick cotton helmet equipped with a metal alloy mask.

Tenugui
Piece of cotton worn under the men (helmet) to absorb sweat.

Shinai
Sword made from four pieces of split bamboo.

Kote
Thick cotton protective gloves.

Do
Chest protector made from fiberglass or bamboo covered in leather.

Tare
Protective apron consisting of five layers of thick cotton.

Hakama
Long divided skirt that allows for free movement.

Women's equipment is generally white, although blue is allowed.

sumo wrestling

The ultimate goal of a sumo wrestler, or sumotori, is to push his opponent out of the ring or throw him off balance so that some part of his body other than his feet touches the ground. The origins of sumo wrestling (from sumai, or "fight" in Japanese) are shrouded in the mists of Japan's early history, but the oldest chronicle containing a reference to it mentions a tournament held in 23 B.C. Sumo matches were part of a ritual to appease the Shinto gods. They were also used to settle political disputes. Matches were free-for-alls in which the winner either forced his opponent to concede or kill him. It is only during the Heian period (794-1185) that rules were adopted and techniques refined. From the early 17th century until the 1990s, sumo wrestling was a professional sport for men only. Although sumo is essentially practiced by men, the International Sumo Federation (IFS) strongly encourages women to become involved so that sumo can become part of the Olympic Games.

Wrestler Umekagawa Fujitaro wearing a tortoise, signifying longevity, in a painting by Hirasawa Kuniaki (1869)

HOW A MATCH IS ORGANIZED

Following the announcer's introduction, the gyoji (referee) sings the names of the sumotori, who then enter the dohyo (ring) and go to their respective corners, where they stomp the ground. They are then given water by another sumotori (either the winner of the last match or one waiting to fight). After rinsing out their mouths, they wipe their lips with white paper (some also wipe their armpits), sprinkle salt on the dohyo, and clap their hands to call for spiritual protection. They open their hands, palms up, to show that they are not concealing anything, and head for the center of the ring, where they stomp the ground and stare each other down. During the fight, they may return to their corners four or five times to rinse out their mouths and sprinkle more salt on the dohyo. The lower ranking practitioners of the sport have less elaborate ceremonies, or none at all. Fights often last no more than a few seconds. Punching, kicking, and choking are prohibited, as are attacking the stomach or eyes, pulling hair, and hitting below the belt. Slapping is allowed. A bout can never result in a tie; the gyoji must decide a winner. If the judges disagree with his decision, they can call for a rematch.

DOHYO

The raised canopy is reminiscent of the roof of a Shinto shrine.

Flat clay surface, covered with a thin layer of sand.

The ring is outlined in strands of braided rice straw.

Mage
Sumo wrestlers have long hair. The highest ranked sumotori tie their hair into an o-icho-mage, or complex knot; lower-ranking wrestlers wear the simpler chonmage knot. When a famous sumo wrestler retires, fans will pay to cut off this symbol of dignity with golden scissors as part of an elaborate ceremony.

Mawashi
A thick belt made from a band of silk around 10 m long, folded in 6 and wound 5 to 7 times. It is fundamental to the technique of the sport, because it is necessary to grip the mawashi in many maneuvers.

Gyoji
The referee who controls the match wears a samurai kimono and a hat similar to the one worn by Shinto priests in the Middle Ages, and carries the battle fan of Japanese generals. If the outcome of a match is in doubt, or if the officials disagree, the four other judges mount the dohyo to resolve the issue. Their decision is final.

Sagari
Decorative tassels made from the same cloth as the mawashi.

Judges
Four former sumo wrestlers officiate, one on each side of the ring.

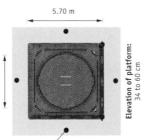

5.70 m

4.55 m

Elevation of platform: 34 to 60 cm

Water

Salt

Step

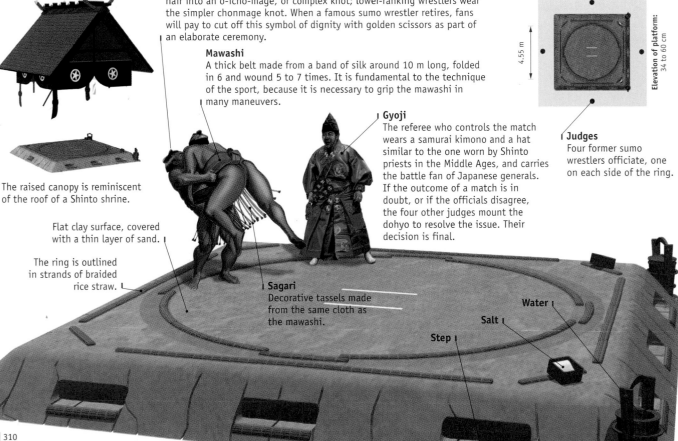

TECHNIQUES

There were originally 48 officially recognized techniques for winning a match. That number rose to 70 in 1960.

Ketaguri

Attacking from the side, the sumotori forces one of his opponent's legs off the ground with a quick push of the foot against his inside ankle. At the same time, he applies strong pressure to his opponent's shoulder, back, or neck, or pulls an arm, to throw his opponent off balance.

Tsukidashi

The attacker uses a rhythmic series of flat-handed blows to the chest to push his opponent out of the dohyo.

Uwate-nage

With a firm grip on the mawashi, the attacker pulls his opponent forward and down while turning. The arm motion is almost perfectly horizontal, while keeping his body centered and steady.

Koshi-nage

Grabbing his opponent, the attacker lifts him up and, using his hip for leverage, throws him to the ground on his back.

TOURNAMENTS

Every year, Japan's Sumo Wrestling Association televises six major tournaments for its approximately 800 wrestlers. A committee decides which wrestlers of the same rank will fight each other. During the 15-day event, sumotori in the top juryo and maku-uchi ranks meet an average of 15 opponents, while those in the lower ranks fight only seven times. The champion receives the Emperor's Cup, numerous gifts, and a hefty winner's purse.

RANKINGS

Ranks in sumo wrestling are not based on weight, but on six grades of skill—achieved by winning a series of fights. A wrestler can be downgraded after a series of losses, except for those who have achieved the highest rank (yokozuna), who retire if they start to lose too often. The top category, maku-uchi, has five levels. Only one of out every 60 sumo wrestlers ever attains the rank of juryo, and only 67 have attained the highest rank of yokozuna since the 17th century when the title was created.

```
        yokozuna
        ozeki
        sekiwake
        komusubi
        maegashira
   maku-uchi •
     juryo
   makushita
   sandamme
    jonidan
   jonokuchi
```

Akebono (USA)

A 234 kg, 2.04 m tall giant of a man, Hawaiian-born Chad Rowan, who fights under the name of Akebono, was the first non-Japanese sumotori to attain the rank of yokozuna. He has won nine tournaments in the maku-uchi category since 1990.

Takanohana (JAP)

Descended from a family of wrestlers, he attained the rank of yokozuna in 1994, when he was only 22 years old. The 65th yokozuna in history, his real name is Koji Hanada.

Kesho-mawashi

Sumo wrestlers holding the rank of juryo or higher wear ceremonial aprons made from silk embroidered with gold and silver, and sometimes studded with diamonds, which normally bear the name of their sponsors.

SUMOTORI PROFILE

- Beginners, who are usually about 15 years old, must weigh at least 165 lbs and be at least 5'7". While serving more experienced sumotori in their heya (training camp and home), they learn to silently endure the physical and psychological humiliation that constitutes an integral part of their education. During this period, the young wrestler chooses a shikona, or ring name.

- The average sumo wrestler is very strong and muscular, standing 5'7" and weighing 350 lbs. Some sumotori, however, are over 6'2", and weigh more than 440 lbs. Sumotori train seven days a week.

- Heavier wrestlers generally have a lower center of gravity, which makes it harder to throw them off balance. At a certain point, however, further weight gains decrease stability. In order to put on weight, sumo wrestlers eat thousands of calories each day; they eat two meals a day invariably consisting of chanko-nabe (a protein-rich stew), rice, beer, and saké, and go to sleep immediately afterwards.

- A yokozuna usually retires at the age of 30.

kung fu

Lam Sai Wing (CHN), student and disciple of Wong Fei Hung, father of Fu Hok Sheong Yin Kuen, inspired by the tiger and crane movements. After many years of study, Lam Sai Wing opened his own kung fu school, where he perpetuated the Hung Gar style, which is very close to the original Shaolin style.

Philosophically influenced by Buddhism, Taoism, and Confucianism, kung fu is the name used to encompass Chinese combat techniques involving the use of weaponry or bare hands. In China, the terms more commonly used are kuoshu or wushu. More than just a means of preparing human beings for combat, "kung fu," which means "skill from effort," is essentially a method aimed at maximizing overall human potential. The earliest forms of Chinese martial arts were developed approximately 4,000 years ago. Around A.D. 525, an Indian monk named Bodhidharma taught the monks at the Shaolin Temple in China a series of movements intended to strengthen their bodies and souls, which helped them to forge a reputation as invincible warriors. His teachings, which brought together Indian and Chinese techniques, are the basis of several major schools of kung fu. In the 1970s, Chinese instructors began teaching their art in the Western world. Today, even though many styles remain secret, several hundred are known to exist. Women have practiced kung fu since the Middle Ages, and meets have been held throughout the world, although their forms and regulations vary.

LIST OF EVENTS

There are many types of meets, with very different rules, including traditional non-contact combat, semi-contact, full contact, long fist, barehanded combat, combat using traditional Chinese weaponry, and exhibitions of style (combat against imaginary opponents, known as tao or chuan).

HOW A MEET IS ORGANIZED

During a match, opponents mainly use open-hand techniques, punches, kicks, body turns, holds, jumps, flips, and throwing off balance. In some combat styles, where full contact to the entire body is permitted, with the exception of the genitals, eyes, and back, the attack may continue until a KO results. In semi-contact matches, certain moves are prohibited, and the amount of force is regulated. Before each chuan style match, either with or without weapons, the judges decide on the points to be awarded according to the caliber of the competitors. In semi-contact matches, points are awarded when specific areas of the body are hit using authorized techniques. Semi-contact matches last between 2 and 6 min, while full contact matches comprise 2 to 10 rounds lasting 2 or 3 min each. Each match is preceded and followed by a salute. In semi-contact competition, opponents may be classified according to their weight and skill level.

SEMI-CONTACT AND FULL-CONTACT RING

Raised ring

Combatants' starting positions

8 m

COMPETITION AREA

The area differs from one type of competition to the next. Style exhibitions are held on a wooden floor or a mat, while semi-contact matches take place in a raised ring or traditional boxing ring.

Protective gear
Authorized protective gear varies, depending on the type of contact permitted during the match. This gear includes mouth guards, head shells, protective cups, chest protectors, helmets, chest guards, gloves, foot protectors, and shin guards.

Officials
A minimum of 4 judges ensure that matches run smoothly.

Physicians

Scoreboard
The scores for the 2 participants, the time, and the combatants' category are displayed.

Corner judges
They are consulted in the case of ambiguity.

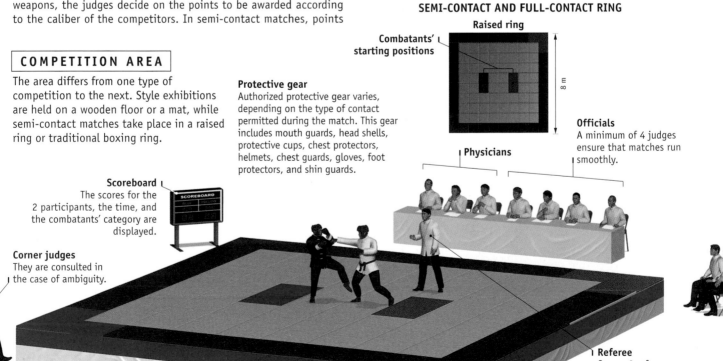

Referee
One or 2 referees ensure that the rules are followed during the match.

BASIC TECHNIQUES

1. Wrist block

The attacker attempts to connect with a direct punch. The defender counters with a wrist block. A steady leg position allows for rapid movement and ripostes. Competitors seek both balance and relaxation, which is more conducive to swift action than a rigid stance.

2. Tiger claw to the neck

The defender counterattacks with a tiger claw to the neck. Blows are generally directed at specific body parts: the eyes, nose, throat, larynx, sternum, heart, solar plexus, or groin.

3. Forearm block and escape

The attacker blocks the tiger claw to the neck with his forearm, simultaneously moving his body out of the defender's line of attack. His legs are bent, allowing him to keep his balance.

4. Palming

Before the attacker has time to attempt a second attack, the defender rotates his body and retaliates, striking his opponent's face with his open palm, a move that is intended to push his adversary back.

STYLES

There are several hundred styles of kung fu, many of which are inspired by animal movements, and which rely on specific skills: the tiger (resistance), the crane (agility), the leopard (strength), the snake (internal strength and the ability to strike the vital points of the body), and the dragon (energy and fluidity of movement).

CHI

According to the Chinese, chi is internal energy, or a universal force, which is essential to health, and which, when channeled through special exercises, allows the athlete to increase his strength and resistance. Some masters claim that their chi is so powerful that it makes them nearly invincible, allowing them to break objects around them or to make their bodies impenetrable.

Hung-gar-Kuen

This style is characterized by low positions that are solidly anchored on the ground, alternating techniques displaying strength and flexibility, wrist attacks, blocks, and defensive moves. Strikes with the feet are never higher than the opponent's waist.

Tong-long

Hand movements imitate the hooked forelegs of an attacking praying mantis, and fast footwork is reminiscent of the insect's jumping actions as it fights.

Wing-chun

A steady position is conducive to the application of simple, brutal techniques, flexible defensive moves, and staggering counter-attacks complete with vocalization. This style is aimed at maximum effectiveness while keeping movement to a minimum.

EQUIPMENT

Traditional costume

Normally fastened with buttons and bearing an officer's collar, the costume is often black, although combatants may choose to wear red, yellow, or white—traditional Chinese colours.

Sash

The sash is a colored belt, which normally indicates the different skill levels. The colors vary from one style to the next, depending on the school or the level.

Bruce Lee (CHN)
As a big-screen martial arts celebrity, he heightened awareness of kung fu around the world. He created his own style of kung fu known as jeet kune do.

PROFILE OF A PARTICIPANT

- Combatants boast speed, coordination, and well-channeled inner strength (chi). They are flexible and energetic, and have sharp reflexes. Size is rarely an indication of ability.

- Participants compete from about the age of 15. International champions are normally in their 20s. Becoming an accomplished kung fu master requires many years of training, during which combat often plays only a very small role.

- Stretching the muscles and tendons increases flexibility and allows for better development, specifically for kicking and punching.

- According to tradition, novices must demonstrate patience, perseverance, and sincerity before being admitted to a school, and they must maintain this attitude throughout their training.

tae kwon do

Korean Kyung-Keun Lee and Egyptian Arm Hussein in the finals at the Seoul Olympics in 1988. Korea won the gold medal.

Tae kwon do is a Korean art of self-defense and combat featuring rapid and spectacular action, with most blows made by the feet. According to some researchers, it is descended from tae kyon or subak, a martial art born in Korea some 2,000 years ago. Others say that it was first taught by the monk Bodhidharma at the Chinese temple of Shaolin (around A.D. 520). A third hypothesis has it that tae kwon do was inspired by Okinawan karate in the 16th century. The Japanese forbade its practice during the occupation of Korea (1910-45), but it was revived after the liberation, enriched with Chinese and Japanese techniques. In the 1950s, it was dubbed tae kwon do, "the art of punching and kicking," a form of martial art that seeks a synthesis of body and mind through technique and harmony between humans and nature. The first world championship for men took place in Seoul, South Korea, in 1973; for women, in Barcelona, Spain, in 1987. A demonstration sport at the Olympics since 1988 in Seoul, tae kwon do became an official Olympic sport in Sydney in 2000.

THE CONTEST

There are 2 types of competition: the demonstration of forms, or poom-se, which is a series of techniques executed facing 1 or several imaginary opponents, and combat, or kyoruki, between 2 competitors in a weight class, who score points by targeting specific areas. Only kyoruki is part of international competitions. A random draw determines the pairing of competitors, individually or in team competition. In the latter case, the total of victories won by the members of a team in individual contests determines the winning team. A kyoruki comprises 3 3-min periods. A legal technique—a foot or fist technique to the solar plexus or the stomach and ribs, or a foot technique to the face—earns 1 point. Infractions, leading to warnings and point deductions, include hand or foot attacks below the waist, striking the back or back of the head, hits with the knee, immobilization, butting, and punches to the face. The result of a contest cannot be appealed if one of the opponents is knocked down with a permitted technique. Points are added throughout the 3 periods, and the winner is the one who has scored more points at the end of the contest. If there is a tie, the referee decides in favor of the fighter whose quality of performance he judges to be superior.

COMPETITION AREA

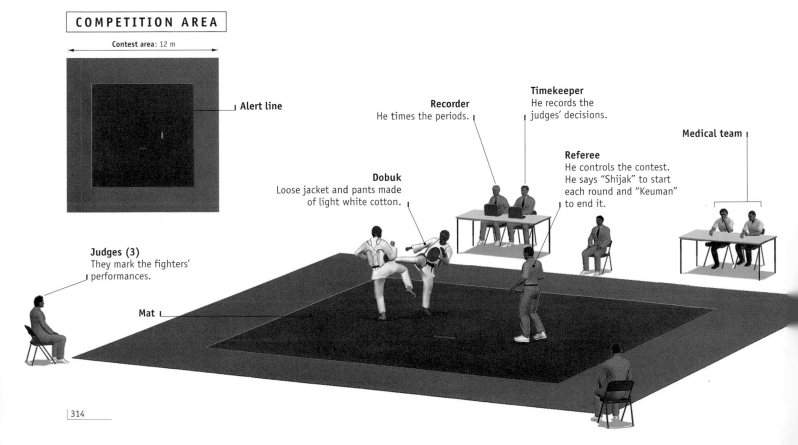

Contest area: 12 m

Alert line

Judges (3)
They mark the fighters' performances.

Mat

Dobuk
Loose jacket and pants made of light white cotton.

Recorder
He times the periods.

Timekeeper
He records the judges' decisions.

Referee
He controls the contest. He says "Shijak" to start each round and "Keuman" to end it.

Medical team

FIGHTING TECHNIQUE

Ninety percent of blows are landed by the feet. The fighter must be able to attack and defend himself as well in the air as on the ground and in all possible positions.

SERIES OF PERMITTED TECHNIQUES

1. Crouch

Positions are crouched and mobile. The fighter moves quickly to present as small an impact area as possible and tries to find a chink in the opponent's defense by making him lose his concentration.

2. Foot technique

The attacker prepares to deliver a foot technique to the ribs. A relaxed movement with rotation of the hips allows for maximum power. The defender begins to jump.

3. Extension

Through a complete extension, the defender jumps out of range.

4. Roundhouse kick

The defender attempts a roundhouse kick to the head. The power of this movement comes from the hips and becomes explosive when the leg is completely extended.

5. Block

The block is used to deflect a kick. An effective block can reduce the strength of an attack by almost 75%.

WEIGHT CATEGORIES AT THE OLYMPICS	
Men	**Women**
Up to 58 kg	Up to 49 kg
Over 58 up to 68 kg	Over 49 up to 57 kg
Over 68 up to 80 kg	Over 57 up to 67 kg
Over 80 kg	Over 67 kg

THE RANKS

Demonstration of increased skill in techniques allows athletes to rise through the ranks, symbolized by different colored belts. There is also a black band on the collar of black belt athletes' dobuk.

Fighter level	Belt color
10th keup (beginner)	white
9th keup	white with yellow stripes
8th keup	yellow
7th keup	yellow with green stripes
6th keup	green
5th keup	green with blue stripes
4th keup	blue
3rd keup	blue with red stripes
2nd keup	red
1st keup	red with black stripes
1st to 10th dan	black with gold stripes

EQUIPMENT

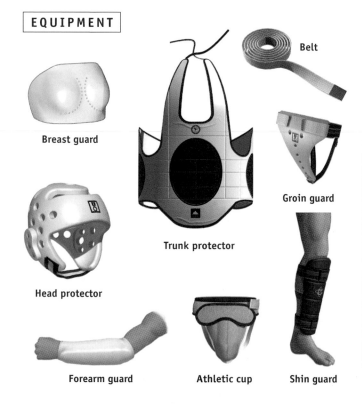

Breast guard

Belt

Groin guard

Trunk protector

Head protector

Forearm guard

Athletic cup

Shin guard

FIGHTER PROFILE

- Strong, rapid, and accurate, generally at the peak of skill from 20 to 28 years of age.

- Breaking objects is an essential part of training. Athletes test the effectiveness of their techniques by striking and breaking objects. Those under 18 years of age should avoid this exercise because of the risk of permanent deformation of the joints of the fingers and toes.

- Endurance exercises aimed at raising the heart rate and improving physical condition (swimming, jogging, jumping rope) may complement the training program.

- Warming up and stretching are concentrated on the legs, hips, and back. If tendons and ligaments lack elasticity, proper execution of leg techniques may be impeded and risks of sprains and tears increased.

- In Korea, tae kwon do is practiced in elementary and high schools and in colleges.

 boxing

B oxing is a combat sport in which two opponents hit each other with only their fists while remaining within the confines of a square area bounded by ropes, called "the ring." Pugilism, an early form of boxing, first appeared as an Olympic sport at the 23rd Games, in 668 B.C. The pugilists, the forefathers of modern day boxers, limited their movements to throwing and blocking punches. To prevent fractures, their hands were firmly wrapped with a leather thong, two centimeters wide and two meters long, known as a cestus. Later it became common to reinforce the cestus with lead balls or studs, and fights became increasingly fierce and violent. Boxing first appeared in England in the 18th century and, beginning in 1857, was governed by a set of rules formulated by the Marquis of Queensberry. These rules form the basis of English boxing as we know it. In North America, boxing gained official recognition in 1888, and became an Olympic sport at the St. Louis Games in 1904. In 1994, women's boxing, which had formerly been prohibited, was recognized by the International Amateur Boxing Association (IABA), an organization founded in 1946 and made up of over 180 national federations. Since the early 1990s, women's boxing, amateur and professional, has enjoyed a steadily growing popularity.

George Carpentier (FRA) (1894–1975), the first European boxing champion. He was world champion in the middleweight category in 1920 and fought in 113 matches, in various categories, over his career.

HOW A FIGHT IS ORGANIZED

Before every fight, the fighters must weigh in and undergo a medical examination. A boxing match is divided into rounds, separated by 1 min rest periods. Professional matches consist of anywhere from 4 to 12 3-min rounds. In Olympic boxing, there are only 3 or 4 2-min rounds. After each round, the boxers are awarded points on the basis of punches landed, on technique, and on adherence to the rules. Unless a match ends before the time is up, the winner is determined on points. This is known as winning by a decision. A fight can also be won before the end by a knockout (which occurs when a fighter is knocked down and cannot get up within 10 seconds), by the referee stopping the fight, by disqualification, or by either opponent conceding the fight. Only punches "above the belt" are allowed, excluding the back, the nape of the neck, and the back of the head. The belt is an imaginary line just above the hips. Punches must be delivered with the part of the glove covering the metacarpus. In Olympic boxing, this area of the glove is colored white.

Referee
He ensures that fight rules are followed, and the boxers are required to obey his instructions.

Timekeeper
Rings the bell to mark the beginning and end of each round.

THE RING

Judge

Trainer

Second

Fight doctor
His attendance at all matches is mandatory.

Federation representative
The person responsible for supervising the fight.

Judge

THE FACILITIES

THE RING

The ring area is circumscribed by three or four rows of rope attached to the posts in each corner.

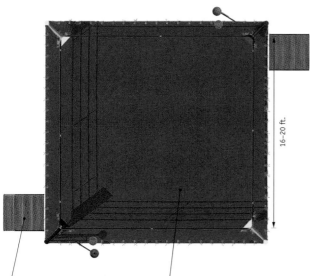

16–20 ft.

Steps (2 sets)
Installed at opposite corners, used for entering the ring.

Floor
Covered in shock-absorbing padding, installed on a platform between 3 ft. and 4 ft. high.

Trainer
Always present at a fight, gives the boxer strategic advice.

Ropes

Second
Every boxer has one to attend to him between rounds.

Judge
Three or five judges score a boxing match. At the end of each round, the judges award a score to each boxer based on points for punches landed successfully.

BELTS AND CHAMPIONSHIPS

Four different international organizations hold professional world championship fights, and accordingly, there can be four world champions in each weight division. The title of champion is symbolized by the belt awarded to the winner.

Professional Boxing Organizations

WBC: World Boxing Council

WBA: World Boxing Association

IBF: International Boxing Federation

WBO: World Boxing Organization

Belt

PROFESSIONAL AND AMATEUR BOXING WEIGHT DIVISIONS		
Division	Amateur (Olympic)	Professional
Strawweight	not recognized	105 lbs.
Junior Flyweight	106 lbs.	108 lbs.
Flyweight	112 lbs.	112 lbs.
Junior Bantamweight	not recognized	115 lbs.
Bantamweight	119 lbs.	118 lbs.
Junior Featherweight	not recognized	120 lbs.
Featherweight	125 lbs.	126 lbs.
Junior Lightweight	not recognized	130 lbs.
Lightweight	132 lbs.	135 lbs.
Junior Welterweight	139 lbs.	140 lbs.
Welterweight	147 lbs.	147 lbs.
Junior Middleweight	156 lbs.	154 lbs.
Middleweight	165 lbs.	160 lbs.
Super Middleweight	not recognized	168 lbs.
Light Heavyweight	178 lbs.	175 lbs.
Cruiserweight	not recognized	190 lbs.
Heavyweight	201 lbs.	over 190 lbs.
Super Heavyweight	over 201 lbs.	not recognized

AMATEUR AND PROFESSIONAL BOXING

There are major differences between the rules governing amateur (or Olympic) boxing and those that apply to professional boxing. Apart from the fact that professional boxers fight bare-chested and do not wear protective helmets, their sport is basically money-driven. Some matches are even auctioned off by promoters, with the right to hold the fight going to the highest bidder.

Marquis of Queensberry Rules

• Boxers must wear gloves and be weighed.

• Boxers are classified by weight.

• The size of the ring is stipulated.

• Fights are divided into 3 min rounds, separated by 1 min rest periods.

• A 10 second count is mandatory if a boxer is knocked down. If he does not get back up within the 10 seconds, the opponent is declared the winner.

With a few minor changes, these rules still apply today. In Olympic boxing, judges have been using an electronic scoring system since 1992.

TECHNIQUE

Boxing is an aggressive sport, and the referee reprimands boxers who refrain from fighting or who adopt a passive attitude. There are both offensive and defensive techniques in boxing.

OFFENSIVE MOVES
The three basic punches are straights, hooks, and uppercuts.

1. Straight
A swift, direct punch, delivered with the arm extended almost horizontally, is called a straight right or a straight left. Jabs are short straights thrown with the leading hand, and are used to keep the opponent at a distance.

2. Hook
A hook is a short, powerful blow, delivered from the shoulder with the elbow bent.

3. Uppercut
An uppercut is a swinging upward blow delivered under the opponent's guard.

DEFENSIVE MOVES
The three basic defensive moves are weaving, parrying, and blocking.

1. Weaving
The boxer eludes an opponent's blow by slipping, turning movements. He twists his hips and lowers his center of gravity in preparation for a counterattack.

2. Parrying
The boxer wards off an opponent's blow with the hand on the same side, thus throwing his opponent off balance and allowing the boxer to counterattack.

3. Blocking
The boxer uses both gloves or forearms to stop an opponent's blow from hitting its target.

BOXER PROFILE

- Since boxers are only classified by weight, two opponents in the same category may nevertheless have vastly different physiques. A boxer's training routine, which is designed to increase stamina, resistance, and flexibility, takes a variety of forms.

- Boxers work out regularly to strengthen their hands, forearms, upper arms, and abdominal region. Various training techniques are used in the gym: skipping rope to improve footwork, shadow boxing in front of a mirror, or punching a heavybag or a speedbag. Jogging is another important part of a boxer's training routine.

- Diet also plays a key role. Because of the large number of weight categories, a boxer may try to lose a few pounds to qualify for a lower category and fight a lighter opponent. Accordingly, in the days leading up to a match, boxers intensify their training and reduce their intake of food.

Cassius Clay, a.k.a. Muhammad Ali (USA)
Olympic Light Heavyweight Champion in 1960. World Heavyweight Champion from 1964 to 1967, then again in 1974 and 1978.

Rocky Marciano (USA)
World Heavyweight Champion from 1952 to 1956.

Sugar Ray Robinson (USA)
World Welterweight Champion from 1946 to 1951, and World Middleweight Champion in 1951 and from 1955 to 1958.

EQUIPMENT

Professional and amateur boxers use different equipment.

OLYMPIC BOXING

Boxers wear a protective helmet, a blue or red sleeveless jersey, trunks, an abdominal protector, and a mouthpiece.

PROFESSIONAL BOXING

Boxers wear neither helmet nor jersey.

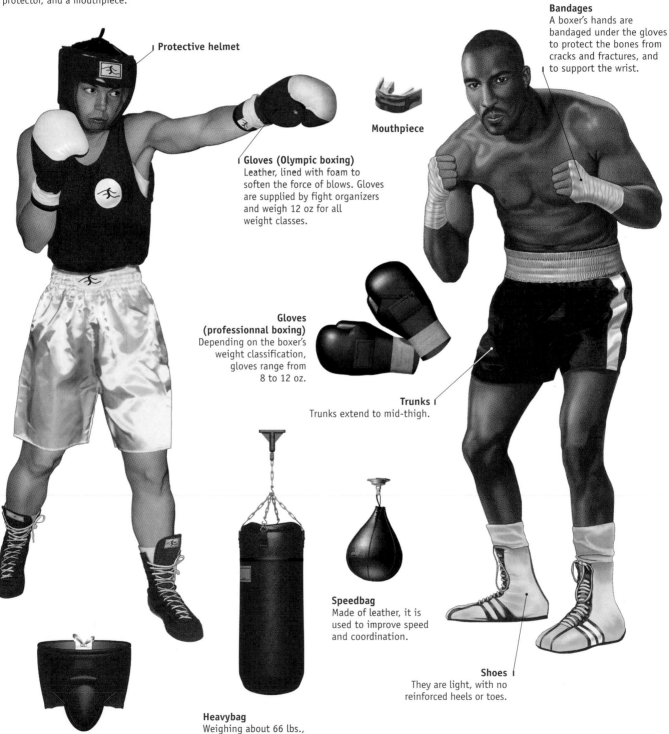

Protective helmet

Bandages
A boxer's hands are bandaged under the gloves to protect the bones from cracks and fractures, and to support the wrist.

Mouthpiece

Gloves (Olympic boxing)
Leather, lined with foam to soften the force of blows. Gloves are supplied by fight organizers and weigh 12 oz for all weight classes.

Gloves (professionnal boxing)
Depending on the boxer's weight classification, gloves range from 8 to 12 oz.

Trunks
Trunks extend to mid-thigh.

Speedbag
Made of leather, it is used to improve speed and coordination.

Shoes
They are light, with no reinforced heels or toes.

Abdominal protector

Heavybag
Weighing about 66 lbs., and covered in leather or canvas, it is used to develop power.

kickboxing and full contact

Kickboxing is a combat sport that combines boxing style punches with kicks derived from the martial arts (such as karate, Thai boxing, and tae kwon do). In the early 1970s, the practice of martial arts became popular in the United States and karate experts, inspired by the European sport of "full contact", developed kickboxing, a combination of boxing and karate. Unlike other fist and foot combat sports, kickboxing prohibits blows delivered with the elbows or knees, and direct blows below the belt. Kickboxing is both an amateur and professional sport and, for the most part, is open to women.

Kickboxing match in Bangkok, Thailand, in 1968

HOW A FIGHT IS ORGANIZED

Two fighters meet in a ring and try to put each other out of the fight by punching and kicking the face and chest. Biting and head-butting are prohibited, as are elbow blows, which are considered too dangerous. The fight is supervised by a member of the organization responsible for arranging it. Fights range in length from 3 to 12 2 min rounds, depending on the type of competition, with a 1 min rest period between rounds. After each round, the boxers are awarded points based on punches successfully landed and on technique. Each fighter must land at least 8 kicks per round, or he

loses the fight. Unless a match ends before the final bell, the point totals determine the winner. This is known as winning by a decision. A fight can also be won by a knockout (which occurs when a fighter is knocked down and cannot get up within 10 seconds), by the referee or doctor stopping the fight, by a fighter conceding the fight, or by the trainer throwing in the towel.

THE RING

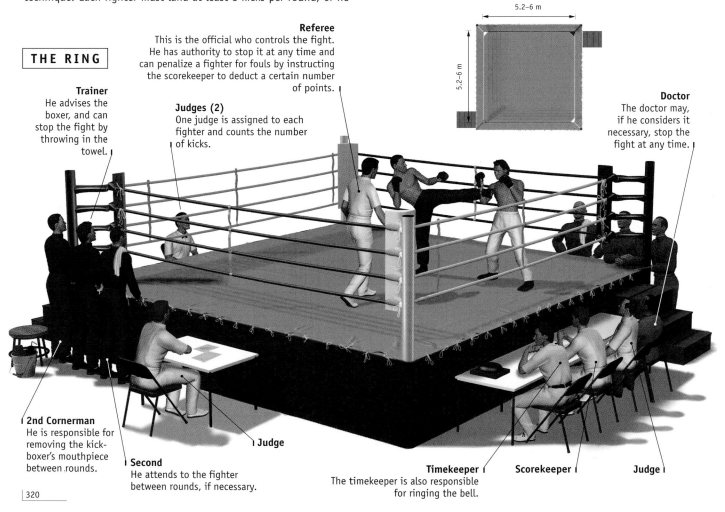

Referee
This is the official who controls the fight. He has authority to stop it at any time and can penalize a fighter for fouls by instructing the scorekeeper to deduct a certain number of points.

Trainer
He advises the boxer, and can stop the fight by throwing in the towel.

Judges (2)
One judge is assigned to each fighter and counts the number of kicks.

Doctor
The doctor may, if he considers it necessary, stop the fight at any time.

5.2–6 m
5.2–6 m

2nd Cornerman
He is responsible for removing the kick-boxer's mouthpiece between rounds.

Judge

Second
He attends to the fighter between rounds, if necessary.

Timekeeper
The timekeeper is also responsible for ringing the bell.

Scorekeeper

Judge

TECHNIQUE

The punches used in kickboxing are the same as those used in boxing, and have the same names: straight right or straight left, right or left hook, and uppercut. The kicks are derived from karate and tae kwon do. Approximately 80% of the kicks delivered in kickboxing are front, side, or spin kicks. Front hook and drop kicks are also used, as are overhead straight kicks and hook kicks. As in judo and karate, sweeping is used to throw an opponent off balance. Defensive moves include dodging with the head and the chest, blocking, and deflecting blows.

Front kick

Spin kick

Side kick

WEIGHT DIVISIONS – MEN	
(according to the World Kickboxing Association)	
Flyweight	Up to 50.5 kg
Super Flyweight	Over 50.5 and up to 52 kg
Bantamweight	Over 52 and up to 53.5 kg
Super Bantamweight	Over 53.5 and up to 55.5 kg
Featherweight	Over 55.5 and up to 57 kg
Super Featherweight	Over 57 and up to 59 kg
Lightweight	Over 59 and up to 61 kg
Super Lightweight	Over 61 and up to 63.5 kg
Welterweight	Over 63.5 and up to 67 kg
Super Welterweight	Over 67 and up to 70 kg
Middleweight	Over 70 and up to 72.5 kg
Super Middleweight	Over 72.5 and up to 76 kg
Light Heavyweight	Over 76 and up to 79 kg
Super Light Heavyweight	Over 79 and up to 83 kg
Cruiserweight	Over 83 and up to 86 kg
Super Cruiserweight	Over 86 and up to 90 kg
Heavyweight	Over 90 and up to 95 kg
Super Heavyweight	Over 95 kg

WEIGHT DIVISIONS – WOMEN
Women's weight divisions range from 48 kg to over 64 kg, with the weight class changing every 2 kg (i.e. 48 kg, 50 kg, 52 kg, etc.).

EQUIPMENT

Mouthpiece

Groin protector

Headgear
Headgear is mandatory for amateurs, and prohibited for professionals.

Chest protector for women
Optional.

Gloves
Gloves' weight may be either 227 or 286 g for the men, depending on the competition, but are always 286 g for women.

Pants

Footpad

Shinpad

KICKBOXER PROFILE

- A kickboxer's training focuses on developing flexibility, muscular strength, and resistance.

- Skipping rope, jumping in place, pulling exercises for the arms, exercises for the abdominal muscles, and floor exercises are all an integral part of training. Fighters also use punching bags, shadow boxing, and engage in practice fights in the gym.

fencing

Engraving from the École des Armes (1763)

Fencing is a combat sport in which two opponents fight with a foil, épée, or saber. Whether for war, training, show, honor, pleasure, or sport, fencing has been performed with a wide variety of weapons: Roman sword, Japanese saber, Turkish scimitar, Carolingian épée, Spanish rapier, or modern electrical foil. An Egyptian bas-relief from the time of Ramses III portrays fencers wearing masks and using buttoned weapons. In the Middle Ages, rules for tournaments were written down. Fencing became popular in Spain in the 15th century, and in 1567, Charles IX, King of France, created the Academy of Masters at Arms. The foil, used with elegance, courtesy and skill, first appeared in the 17th century. In the 19th century, although duels were banned and firearms were becoming widespread, novels recalling the cape-and-rapier era by Féval, Dumas, and Scott fascinated the public and fencing became popular once again. In France, the École de Joinville, founded in 1852, trained students and made fencing a real sport. Fencing—foil and saber—was included in the first modern Olympic Games, and épée was added in 1900. Aside from the addition of electrical signals, the rules and techniques of fencing have changed very little since its beginnings.

THE COMPETITION

Once the signal to start is given, a bout continues until a touch (or hit) is recorded, an illegal move is signaled, the fencers' bodies touch, or a fencer's foot goes out of bounds. A bout is composed of 3 3-minute segments with 1 minute of rest between each segment. The winner is the first fencer to score 15 hits, or the leader if neither reaches 15 before time expires. If the score is tied after 9 minutes, 1 minute of sudden-death time is added. The advantage—the winning point—is first given to one of the fencers by draw. The extra time then starts, and if neither fencer scores a touch, the bout is awarded to the one who had the advantage. All three fencing events have individual and team competitions. The épée is also one of the 5 events in the pentathlon. The International Fencing Federation sanctions international competitions, and world championships take place every year, except on Olympic years.

PISTE

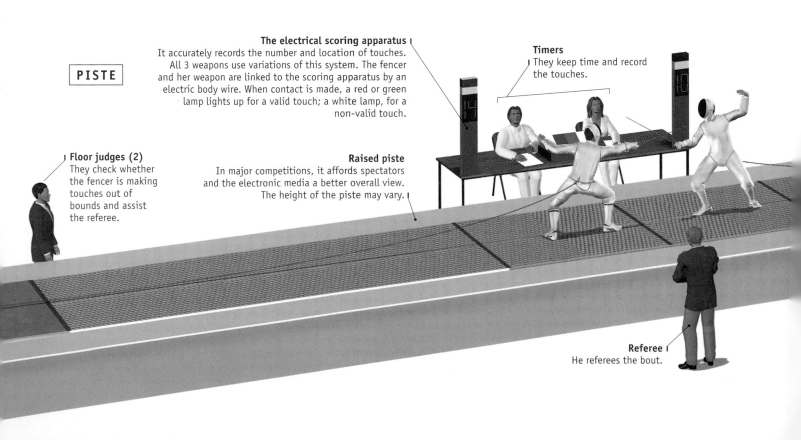

The electrical scoring apparatus
It accurately records the number and location of touches. All 3 weapons use variations of this system. The fencer and her weapon are linked to the scoring apparatus by an electric body wire. When contact is made, a red or green lamp lights up for a valid touch; a white lamp, for a non-valid touch.

Timers
They keep time and record the touches.

Floor judges (2)
They check whether the fencer is making touches out of bounds and assist the referee.

Raised piste
In major competitions, it affords spectators and the electronic media a better overall view. The height of the piste may vary.

Referee
He referees the bout.

BASIC POSITIONS AND LINES

The 8 basic positions—prime, seconde, tierce, quarte, quinte, sixte, septime, and octave—combine to make up the basic parries. There are 4 lines: 2 high and 2 low. Each line has 2 positions that are determined both by the placement of the blade in relation to the hand—tip higher or lower than the hand—and by the way the hand is placed—in supination, with the nails up, or pronation, with the nails down. The fingers control the weapon: the wrist acts as a hinge and extension of the hand. This control enables a fencer to "sentir le fer" ("feel the iron")— a heightened perception of the opponent's reactions.

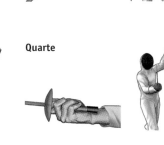

Prime

Seconde

Tierce

Quarte

Quinte

Sixte

Septime

Octave

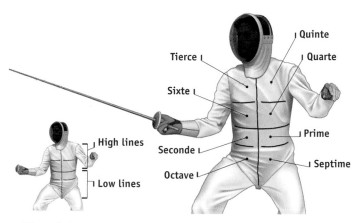

Quinte

Tierce

Quarte

Sixte

Prime

High lines

Seconde

Septime

Low lines

Octave

The salute

This traditional gesture of courtesy is made with the face uncovered before and after each bout. It is addressed to the opponent, the referee, the jury, and the public. After a bout, the fencers shake hands with each other and the referee.

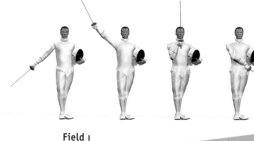

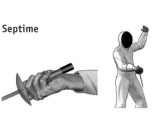

Scoreboards
They are located at each end of the piste so that the audience can follow the competition.

Out of bounds zone
When a fencer leaves the piste with both feet, a touch is awarded to the opponent.

Reel
It keeps the wire taut, reeling it in and letting it out as necessary.

Field

Floor judge

Safety zone
It prevents falls from raised pistes.

Surface
It is covered with an anti-slip metallic mesh. The mesh is grounded so that floor hits do not register as off target touches.

Colored zone
It tells the fencer that he is near the end of the piste.

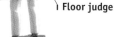

14 m

1.5-2 m

2 m

TECHNIQUES

ATTACK AND DEFENSE

These fundamental fencing techniques are used with all 3 weapons. The 2 basic techniques are based on the on guard position: knees bent, back arm bent upward, and armed hand held out toward the opponent. The mise-en-garde is the starting position for offense, defense, and counterattack.

The attack

This movement is a continuous offensive motion toward the opponent. Attacks can be direct or compound. The arm is extended, and the movement is often accompanied by a lunge or flèche.

The parry

This essentially defensive movement consists of deflecting the opponent's weapon with one's own. Parries include warding off the opponent's weapon, blocking a thrust, and retreating. Parries bear the names of the positions in which they are taken and correspond to the 4 lines that form the targets.

The unarmed arm raised

This is a characteristic position for the foil: the arm is placed this way with the hand hanging so that it cannot protect the fencer's torso, which is a target area. In addition, the positions of the free arm provide balance in some movements.

The riposte

This is the counterattack after a parry. It is immediate or delayed, simple or compound, executed from a standing or moving position.

THE MOVEMENTS

These are the basic fencing movements. In both cases, the body stays upright and the legs bent.

Step forward

Step back

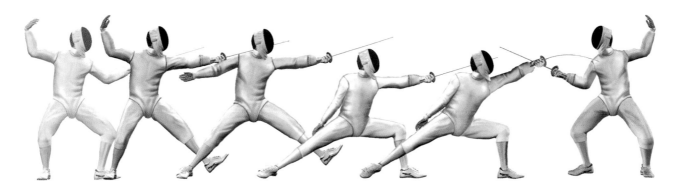

The lunge

In this attack technique, the armed hand is rapidly thrust forward, as the fencer pushes off the back leg and moves his other foot forward. The weapon is pointed at the opponent.

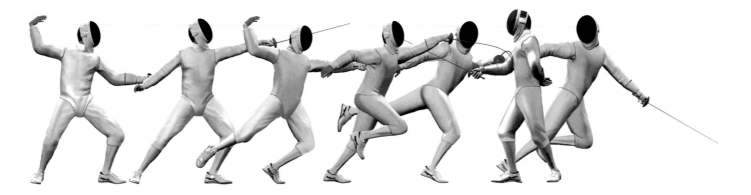

The flèche

This is a rapid and spectacular running attack technique. The armed hand is extended as the attacker makes an explosive forward movement with his front leg, and the tip of the weapon must touch the opponent before the attacker's other foot touches the ground. A flèche usually takes less space than a lunge.

THE FOIL

It is a thrusting weapon, which means the touches are made with the tip only. It began as a training and study weapon. Bouts with a foil require excellent technique and can be very animated, like bouts with the saber, or cautious, like bouts with the épée. The foil is an Olympic event for men and women.

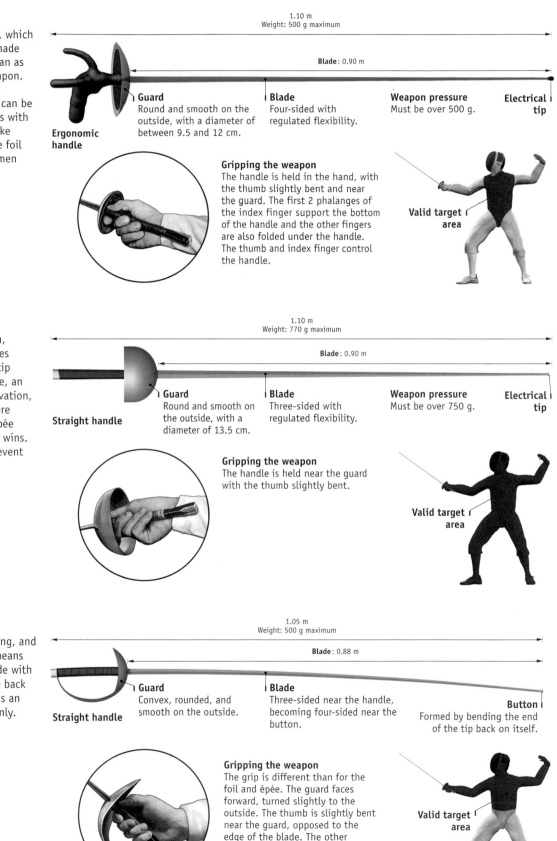

1.10 m
Weight: 500 g maximum

Blade: 0.90 m

Ergonomic handle

Guard
Round and smooth on the outside, with a diameter of between 9.5 and 12 cm.

Blade
Four-sided with regulated flexibility.

Weapon pressure
Must be over 500 g.

Electrical tip

Gripping the weapon
The handle is held in the hand, with the thumb slightly bent and near the guard. The first 2 phalanges of the index finger support the bottom of the handle and the other fingers are also folded under the handle. The thumb and index finger control the handle.

Valid target area

THE ÉPÉE

It is a thrusting weapon, which means that touches are performed with the tip only. It requires patience, an excellent sense of observation, and nerves of steel. There are no conventions in épée bouts: the first to touch wins. The épée is an Olympic event for men and women.

1.10 m
Weight: 770 g maximum

Blade: 0.90 m

Straight handle

Guard
Round and smooth on the outside, with a diameter of 13.5 cm.

Blade
Three-sided with regulated flexibility.

Weapon pressure
Must be over 750 g.

Electrical tip

Gripping the weapon
The handle is held near the guard with the thumb slightly bent.

Valid target area

THE SABER

This is a thrusting, cutting, and slicing weapon, which means that touches can be made with the tip, the edge, or the back of the blade. The saber is an Olympic sport for men only.

1.05 m
Weight: 500 g maximum

Blade: 0.88 m

Straight handle

Guard
Convex, rounded, and smooth on the outside.

Blade
Three-sided near the handle, becoming four-sided near the button.

Button
Formed by bending the end of the tip back on itself.

Gripping the weapon
The grip is different than for the foil and épée. The guard faces forward, turned slightly to the outside. The thumb is slightly bent near the guard, opposed to the edge of the blade. The other fingers are held together and hold the handle against the palm of the hand. The weapon is held lightly and steadily.

Valid target area

EQUIPMENT

The outfits used in fencing are designed mainly for safety. They must not impede freedom of movement. White is the most common color.

Mask
Made of a metallic mesh and a bib that protects the neck. The mesh is 2.1 mm and the wires are 1 mm in diameter. Transparent masks are the latest innovation; they are being used increasingly in competition.

Bib

Gloves
They are lightly padded, and the cuffs cover half of the forearm. The body wire passes through them.

Fencing outfit
It must conform to the standards in effect. The lower part extends at least 10 cm below the top of the knickers. The jacket, plastron, and knickers are made of Kevlar to avoid perforation. Foil and saber fencers wear metallic scoring jackets over their outfits so that valid touches can be recorded. Men may wear an athletic cup; women, breast protectors.

Body wire
It connects the fencer to the electric touch signaling system. One end of the wire is attached to the reel, the other runs through the back of the fencer's overjacket, down the sleeve and across the glove, and is connected to a plug inside the weapon's guard. Models vary according to the weapon.

Jacket

Breast protectors

Knickers
They are fastened below the knees and held up with suspenders. They are waist high.

Stockings
They are obligatory and knee high.

FENCER PROFILE

- Fencing is a sport of speed, flexibility, coordination, reflexes, and tactics. Strength, concentration, a sense of observation, perseverance, and self control are skills essential to fencers.

- Footwork in fencing is compared to that in boxing. The sport of fencing is sometimes referred to as a "chess game with muscles."

- Athletes must have good respiratory and cardiovascular systems and be able to recover easily, as fencing involves a series of intense exertions lasting 5 seconds to 3 minutes. To maintain or improve their physical condition, fencers do muscle building and flexibility exercises to reinforce the most used joints and muscles in the arms and legs. Jogging is excellent for warming up and priming the cardiovascular system. As a general rule, high ranking fencers specialize in a single weapon. Reaching a high rank requires years of training and much discipline. An international level career may last 15 to 20 years.

Jean-François Lamour (FRA)
Individual Olympic champion in saber in 1984 and 1988, he was also a team silver medalist in 1984 and a bronze medalist in individual and team competition in 1992. He was also French champion more than 10 times.

Éric Srecki (FRA)
Individual Olympic champion in épée in 1992 and team gold medalist in 1988, he was individual world champion in 1995 and 1997 and a member of the championship team in 1994.

Ilona Elek (HUN)
Olympic champion in foil in 1936 and 1948, she was a silver medalist in 1952. The longevity of her career was remarkable.

Greco-Roman and freestyle wrestling

W restling is a barehanded combat sport in which two opponents try to throw each other down and pin their shoulders to the ground using holds and techniques. One of the oldest forms of combat sport, wrestling was an integral part of military training in ancient Greece and was in the ancient Olympics for the first time in 708 B.C. A high point of the games, wrestling was a brutal sport that had little in common with the modern form. In 186 B.C., the sport was introduced into the Roman circus in a less violent form, and it was practiced until the 4th century before falling into obscurity. In the Middle Ages, wrestling reappeared in England, France, and Japan. It was on the program of the first modern Olympics in 1896, and today there are two forms: freestyle, included in the Games in 1904, and Greco-Roman, included in 1908. The International Federation of Associated Wrestling Styles (FILA) was formed in 1912. Women's freestyle wrestling is gaining in popularity; the world championships were created in 1987.

Sculpture by Antonio Canova, 1775 (Gallerie dell'Accademia, Venice, Italy)

THE COMPETITION

A bout is composed of 2 3-min periods with a 30-second pause between periods. The goal of the fight is to put the opponent on the ground and pin his shoulders for long enough for the referee to signal complete control (a fall). A fall is an automatic victory. When their names are called, the adversaries must go to the corner of the mat that is the same color as the singlet they have been assigned. The referee, standing in the middle of the mat, calls the wrestlers, checks their singlets and fingernails, makes sure that they are not covered with any greasy or sticky substance, and that they are not perspiring. The wrestlers must be barehanded and have a handkerchief. The adversaries salute each other and shake hands before the referee signals the start of the bout. In Greco-

Roman wrestling, unlike freestyle, only holds above the hips are allowed, and it is absolutely forbidden to use the legs actively in any action. As in other sports, the athletes are considered to be obliged to take risks. An ineffective wrestler, standing or on the ground, is said to be passive and acting in a manner contrary to the spirit and aims of wrestling.

Wrestling area
At the beginning of the bout, the wrestlers must stand on each side of the white circle at the center of the wrestling area.

Protection area
The bout is stopped when a wrestler who is standing puts one foot on the protection area, a wrestler on his knees has both hands in the area, or a wrestler flat on his stomach touches it with his head.
Width: 1.2–1.5 m

7 m

12 m

Passivity zone
It borders the wrestling area.
Width: 1 m

COMPETITION AREA

Bout number

Time

MATCH

Period

Wrestlers' points

Referee
He works in close collaboration with the judge. The referee wears a blue cuff on one arm and a red cuff on the other and raises the appropriate arm and fingers to indicate the wrestler and the points earned. The judge then verifies the points.

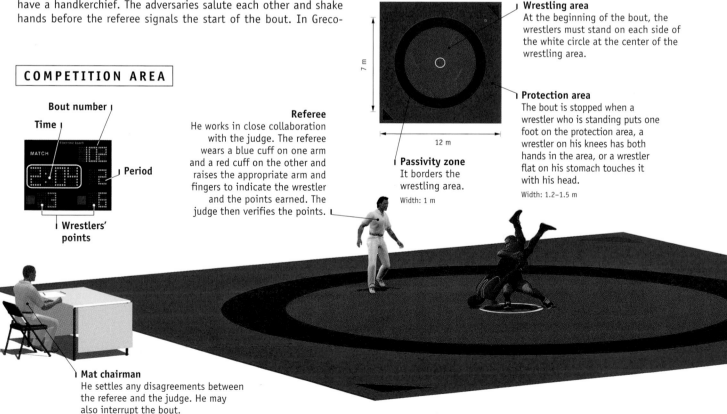

Mat chairman
He settles any disagreements between the referee and the judge. He may also interrupt the bout.

TECHNIQUES

- There are 2 types of holds in Greco-Roman wrestling: standing holds and mat holds. Among the main standing holds are the front, side, and back locks, the flying mare, the shoulder throw, the hip toss, and the head toss. Freestyle wrestling uses the same holds and adds leg holds.

- In wrestling on the ground, there are head holds, arm grappling, and reversals.

- In freestyle wrestling, the holds include the leg trip, the leglock, the leg hook, the leg scissors, and the crotch hold. All of the technical rules applicable to men are applicable to women.

STARTING POSITION

Standing position

In Greco-Roman wrestling, the bout starts in the standing position.

Crouching position

In freestyle wrestling, the crouching position protects the legs.

From the starting position, the bout starts with a scrimmage in which the wrestler tries to control his opponent in order to upset his balance and throw him to the mat.

GUT WRENCH

1. The attacker places himself behind his opponent.

2. He puts his arms around his opponent from behind and places his knee on the side to which he will turn him.

3. He pulls his opponent toward him and puts his knee under his body.

4. The attacker then arches strongly, pushing his hips forward and up.

5. He then makes the bridge by pivoting on his left side with the opponent in order to pin his shoulders to the mat.

DOUBLE LEG TACKLE

  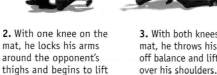 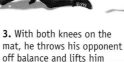

1. The attacker crouches slightly to grab the opponent's legs.

2. With one knee on the mat, he locks his arms around the opponent's thighs and begins to lift him up.

3. With both knees on the mat, he throws his opponent off balance and lifts him over his shoulders.

4. The attacker pivots, puts one foot on the mat, and turns his opponent toward the mat, falling on top of him.

5. The attacker then immobilizes his opponent by pinning his shoulders to the mat.

Judge

The judge follows the bout carefully and awards points for each action that he records on his score sheet in agreement with the mat chairman. The judge and the mat chairman are responsible for verifying points awarded.

FRONT BRIDGE

A wrestler is in the danger position when the line of his back (or shoulders) is facing the mat and forms an angle of less than 90°. The wrestler resists with his upper body so that he is not put in a fall position. He can resist with his head, elbows, and shoulders, placing himself in a bridge or half-bridge position.

HIP TOSS

1. In this move, the attacker takes the opponent's right arm under his left armpit and grabs the opponent's head firmly with his right arm.

2. Pivoting, the attacker unbalances his opponent with a hip block and throws him forward.

3. Then, following the curve of the opponent's trajectory, he falls to the ground with him, putting him in a danger or fall position.

REVERSE HIP TOSS

1. The wrestler on top firmly seizes his opponent's hips by taking hold of the thigh on the far side.

2. He then raises the opponent's body toward him, placing his bent right leg under the opponent to carry the weight.

3. From this position, the attacker energetically throws himself backward, flipping the opponent.

EQUIPMENT

Singlet
One-piece and stretchy, in either red or blue.

Boots
They are made of soft leather, have no heel, and must not have any metal parts.

WRESTLER PROFILE

- Wrestling uses all muscles in the body and requires strength, flexibility, coordination, and a sense of balance.

- Psychological preparation is part of the wrestler's training; wrestling is truly a way of life.

Alexander Karelin (URSS)
Holder of three Olympic titles, winner of 11 world championships and 12 European championships, he was named Greco-Roman wrestler of the year in 1989, 1990, 1992, and 1995.

John Smith (USA)
Gold medalist at the 1988 and 1992 Olympics in freestyle, and world champion from 1987 to 1991. When he retired, he became a coach for the American wrestling teams.

Sports
on Wheels

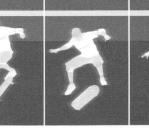

skateboarding

Creativity and defying gravity are two essential aspects of skateboarding, an acrobatic sport that combines technique and determination. Invented in California in the early 1960s, skateboarding is dominated by male athletes. The first official competition took place in Anaheim Stadium, in California, in 1965. It was not until the invention of urethane wheels and moving trucks that acrobatic techniques developed and international competition began. The first European championship took place in Frankfurt, Germany, in 1977. Most subsequent events were organized through private sponsorship. Today, the Munster World Cup takes place every year in Munster, Germany. Since 1995, the X (extreme sports) Games in the United States have featured the best skateboarders in this increasingly popular event.

Tim Levis training at Skate City in London for the world championships on September 21, 1977.

THE EVENTS

The half pipe

This term designates both the competition area and the event. The competitors have 45 seconds to perform a series of aerial acrobatics on a tube shaped ramp with vertical sides (verts). The tricks are executed on the verts or in the air above the half pipe. If a competitor falls, he may continue his run if he wishes.

Street

In a specified time of between 45 seconds and 2 minutes, depending on the competition, the skateboarder executes a series of tricks using obstacles set around a course of about 1,200 square yards. The main types of obstacles are inspired by those found on city streets: the springboard, the sidewalk, and the fun-box, a group of surfaces with various inclines and of various sizes; stairs with a hand-rail may also be included. The jury consists of 3 to 5 judges; each gives an overall score out of 100, evaluating the competitor's technique and style.

HALF PIPE TRICKS

There are three types of tricks: lip tricks, executed on the coping of the half pipe; aerials, in the air above the half pipe; and plants, executed with hand or foot on the edge. All tricks can be performed front side (back toward the inside of the half pipe) or back side (facing the inside of the half pipe). There is no rule about foot position: skateboarders may roll with the left foot front (regular foot) or right foot front (goofy foot).

Grab 540 backside

1. The skateboarder rolls up the vert at high speed. **2**. With his back foot, he gives extra impetus to the skateboard as he passes the edge so that it rises with him as he goes into tuck position. **3**. Holding the skateboard with his right hand, he begins a 360° rotation with a vigorous motion of his left arm. **4**. He looks in the direction of movement. In the airborne phase, he controls his trajectory and balance using his left arm. **5**. He turns the last 180° at the beginning of the descent, when he can see the half pipe. **6**. To decide when to let go of the skateboard, he must anticipate when he will come into contact with the half pipe. The fluidity of the entire movement is due mainly to the flexibility of the legs, which are bent at takeoff and during the flight, and extended for the landing.

Skateboarding surface
It is usually made of very dense, smooth woven cardboard fiber (masonite), about 0.4 in. thick.

STREET TRICKS

Ollie kick flip

A variation of the ollie, the ollie kick flip adds one or several rotations of the skateboard. The skateboarder hits the skateboard with the tip of his shoe to make it rotate. Contact with the skateboard just before the landing is the most difficult part of the trick.

Ollie

This basic trick is used to jump over an obstacle. In the approach, the legs are bent. The skateboarder's weight is on his toes and his feet move back on the board. As the jump starts, pressure is applied to the tail of the skateboard. To keep the skateboard touching his feet, the skateboarder creates friction between the board and his feet with the help of grip tape on the top of the board. He bends his knees and ankles to make a stable landing.

5/0 grind

The 5/0 grind starts with an ollie; the athlete then slides along a metal bar on the trucks of the skateboard. The athlete's body and the skateboard must be parallel to the bar. He balances by bending his legs and moving his arms. He must always visualize his trajectory and anticipate his landing.

SKATEBOARDER PROFILE

- Average weight and height of 6 ft. or under allows for best control of aerial tricks. Particularly on the half pipe, an athlete with a lighter frame needs to make less effort. These physical characteristics are less important than perfect coordination between speed and the pace of execution.

- Technical execution of acrobatic tricks requires great explosive power, a sense of balance, and strong, flexible muscles, acquired through muscle building and stretching.

- Professional skateboarders train mainly by rehearsing their tricks, increasing the rhythm of execution and the number of repetitions constantly, to achieve muscle memory of the movements.

- The average age of elite skateboarders is 20. Some champions, however, stay at the top until age 30.

Tony Hawk (USA)
Winner of the Munster World Cup in 1991 and the X Games in 1995, 1997, 1998 and 1999, he is the only skateboarder currently performing a 900° (2½ rotations in the air).

EQUIPMENT

Skateboard
Made of wood, usually concave in shape.

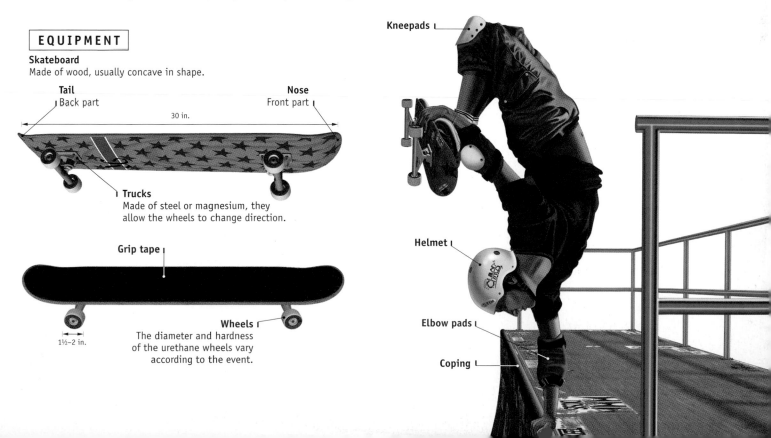

Tail
Back part

Nose
Front part

30 in.

Trucks
Made of steel or magnesium, they allow the wheels to change direction.

Grip tape

1½–2 in.

Wheels
The diameter and hardness of the urethane wheels vary according to the event.

Kneepads

Helmet

Elbow pads

Coping

roller hockey

Hockey on roller skates is a relatively old sport. It can be traced back to around 1875, and the first rules, written by the Men's Hockey Association of London, date from the same period. Initially dominated by England, hockey on traditional four wheeled roller skates (rink hockey) is very popular in Latin countries, including Portugal, Italy, Spain, and Argentina, where it is not uncommon for more than 10,000 people to attend a game. It is played with a ball and a stick similar to that used in field hockey. The first World Championships were held in Stuttgart, Germany in 1936, and featured teams from seven countries. World Championships are now held every two years. Roller hockey was included as a demonstration sport in the 1992 Olympic Games in Barcelona. The introduction of in-line roller skates in the early 1980s paved the way for in-line roller hockey in the early 1990s, and it quickly became a sport on its own. In-line roller hockey was developed in the United States to allow ice hockey players to train during the off season and the first national championships were played in 1995.

A rink hockey match in London's Victoria Park in 1948

HOW A GAME IS PLAYED

Two teams face each other, in an indoor or outdoor arena, and try to score as many goals as possible against the opposing team, using sticks and a ball in rink hockey, or a puck in in-line roller hockey. A team consists of one goaltender and four players (one winger, one center, and two defensemen). Each team has a captain, who is the only team member permitted to discuss the interpretation of the rules with the referee. A goal is scored when the ball or puck completely enters the goal. Line changes are made without interruption of play, although they may also be made while the game is stopped.

In-line roller hockey

Except for a few minor differences, the rules for in-line roller hockey are identical to those for ice hockey. However, because there is no offside, the game has fewer interruptions. Body checking and intentional physical contact are prohibited. Teams are made up of between 14 and 18 players, including two goaltenders. The game is divided into two periods of 22 minutes of continual play (including stoppages), with a 5 minute halftime, after which the teams change ends. In the case of a tie, an overtime period is only permitted during tournaments and championships. If a goal is not scored during the overtime period, it is followed by a shoot out, which entails shooting on goal.

Any violation of the rules results in a penalty to the offending player. The referee blows his whistle to signal the infraction and to stop the game, and the player who committed the foul is sent to the penalty bench. This gives the opposing team a 1 man advantage for the duration of the penalty. The most common penalties last 2 minutes, although certain infractions, such as insubordination toward an official, may lead to more serious penalties and even result in ejection from the game.

Rink hockey

As is the case in in-line roller hockey, intentional physical contact is prohibited. However, the rules concerning fouls draw their inspiration from soccer—free hits and penalty shots are awarded. The referee uses three disciplinary cards: a yellow card for a first violation; a blue card for a temporary expulsion of 2 to 5 minutes; and a red card for expulsion from the game. Teams can consist of up to 10 players, and must include two goaltenders. The game is divided into two periods of 25 minutes each (20 minutes during tournaments), with a 10 minute break, after which the teams change ends. If there is a tie, two 5 minute overtime periods are played. If the game is still tied at the end of these periods, there may be a series of shots on goal.

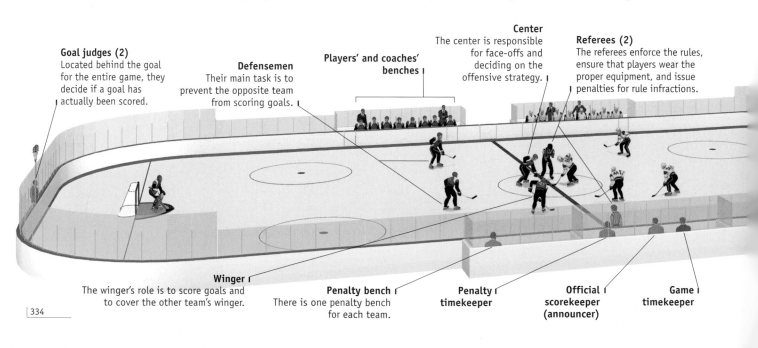

Goal judges (2)
Located behind the goal for the entire game, they decide if a goal has actually been scored.

Defensemen
Their main task is to prevent the opposite team from scoring goals.

Players' and coaches' benches

Center
The center is responsible for face-offs and deciding on the offensive strategy.

Referees (2)
The referees enforce the rules, ensure that players wear the proper equipment, and issue penalties for rule infractions.

Winger
The winger's role is to score goals and to cover the other team's winger.

Penalty bench
There is one penalty bench for each team.

Penalty timekeeper

Official scorekeeper (announcer)

Game timekeeper

EQUIPMENT

Ball (rink hockey)
Hollow and light
(155 grams), the ball
is made from plastic with
or without cork inside.
It must be of one color
only and in contrast to the
color of the rink surface.

7–8 cm

90–115 cm

**Stick
(rink hockey)**

Puck (in-line roller hockey)
Made from hard rubber, the
puck is equipped with bumps
to limit surface friction, or
ball-bearings to facilitate
movement.

7.62 cm

Maximum: 1.52 m

**Stick (in-line roller
hockey)**

Goal

1.70 m

1.05 m

Goaltender
The goaltender is responsible for stopping the
puck. His position gives him a full view of the
playing surface, which allows him to coordinate
the movements of his defensemen when the
opposing team is attacking.

**Rink hockey skates
(quads)**
These are slower than in-
line hockey skates, although
they allow for faster starts
and stops.

Wheels
Made from polyurethane,
the wheels must measure
at least 3 cm in diameter.

Toe stop
The toe stop is used for stopping, and
for getting off to a fast start.

In-line roller hockey skates
The center of gravity is lower and
the boot is slightly canted to the front
to facilitate movement.

Boot
The boot is made from leather or nylon.

Chassis
The chassis is usually made
from reinforced nylon,
aluminum, or titanium.

Wheels
The wheels are made from
polyurethane, and contain
ball bearings.

72–76 mm

Players' equipment
In rink hockey, gloves, knee pads,
shin guards, and elbow pads are
recommended. The goaltender must
wear a helmet with a face mask,
padded gloves, and leg pads.

For in-line roller hockey, a helmet
with face mask, protective cup, and
gloves are mandatory. Depending
on the organization, shin guards,
protective pants, and elbow pads are
either mandatory or recommended.

PLAYING SURFACE

The surface must be smooth and seamless, and made of wood, cement, asphalt, or plastic.
Slippery surfaces are prohibited. At the center of the playing area, a circle drawn on the
center line is used for face-offs at the start of each period and after each goal. In in-line
roller hockey, the playing surface is surrounded by boards measuring between 91 cm and
1.22 m high, and topped with panes of glass. The nets are the same size for both games,
although rink hockey is played on a smaller playing surface. The latter is surrounded by a
barrier of minimum 1 m high, of which at least the bottom 20 cm must be made of wood.

In-line roller hockey

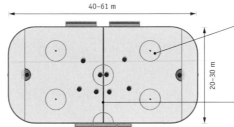

40–61 m

20–30 m

Face-off circles
Used after the play stops
during the game.

Center line
This line divides the rink
into two equal sides, one
for each team.

Rink hockey

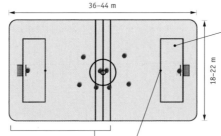

36–44 m

18–22 m

Penalty zone
If a foul is committed in this zone,
a free hit is taken from the nearest
corner. If the goaltender or a
defending player commits the foul,
the opposing team is awarded a
penalty shot from the penalty point.

Defensive zone
Players in possession of the
ball have 10 seconds to move
it into the offensive zone.

Penalty point

⛸ in-line skating

European championship at the Empire Pool and Sports Arena, Wembley (England), 1938

Both a recreational and performance activity, in-line skating takes various forms: acrobatic ("aggressive") skating, speed skating, and hockey. The concept of footwear with wheels attached is more than 200 years old; in 1760, the Belgian Joseph Merlin tried to invent a form of locomotion with clogs on wheels. In 1823, Englishman Robert John Tyres developed rolitos, the ancestors of today's in-line skates, and they were used at the Berlin Opera to replace ice skates. The first traditional roller skates—with two front and two back wheels—were produced in 1863 by American James Plimpton. In 1884, ball bearings were invented, and roller skating began to develop. In-line skates first appeared in the 1980s in the United States, following the invention of polyurethane wheels. Within a decade, the sport grew in popularity; now, world championships in speed and aggressive skating are held each year.

AGGRESSIVE SKATING COMPETITION

There are 2 types of competition: half pipe and street. The half pipe is a wooden semi-tubular structure. Competitors perform aerial acrobatics in 2 rounds of 60 or 90 seconds. The winner is the one who achieves the best height, technical difficulty, and fluidity of figures.

In street competitions, the skater (or "streeter") performs figures on various modules and obstacles in 2 rounds of 60 to 90 seconds. The judges give marks for technique and style. Competition zones, in an area of about 1,000 m², are spaced 8 m apart, and competitors must return to them more than once.

HALF PIPE

540 flat spin

1. The competitor starts up the side of the half pipe with maximum speed. **2.** After leaving the coping of the half pipe, he begins a diagonal rotation. **3.** Once in the air, he controls his balance and rotation with his free arm. **4.** During the first 360°, he holds one of his skates. **5.** When the 360° is completed, he lets go of the skate. **6.** He performs another half turn before landing. Throughout the airborne phase, the skater anticipates return to contact with the half pipe; as he lands, he stretches his legs to absorb the impact.

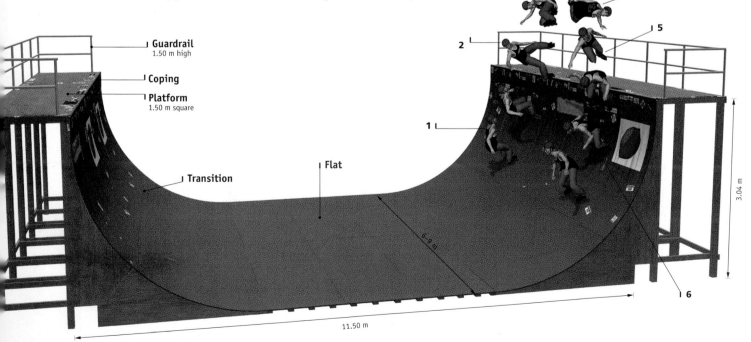

Guardrail
1.50 m high

Coping

Platform
1.50 m square

Transition

Flat

6-9 m

3.04 m

11.50 m

MISTY FLIP

This difficult maneuver has a total rotation of 540°.

1. The athlete skates up the ramp at maximum speed, extends his arms, spreads his legs, and turns his upper body to begin the rotations. **2.** He begins a two-way rotation—180° vertical, 360° horizontal. **3.** To perform the movement, he tucks his chin toward his chest, holds his thighs, and bends his legs. **4.** He continues the sequence by releasing his legs and relaxing his arms. **5.** He lands facing the ramp, legs slightly bent and the skates parallel to maintain balance.

STREET
Soul grind

1. Before starting the jump, the competitor visualizes her momentum and trajectory and approaches at a speed that will enable her to jump onto the rail at a comfortable angle. **2.** With her shoulders perpendicular and at a slight angle to the bar, she uses her arms and hands to balance. The front skate sits on the slider and the back skate sits on the back outside edge of the plate; the feet thus form a T. **3.** During the slide, she bends her back leg and balances on it. The front leg is stretched and provides direction. To avoid falls and prepare for landing, the skater always looks straight ahead.

Pyramid
This module can have different shapes and is used for all sorts of figures.

SPEED SKATING COMPETITION

There are various types of competition: individuals and teams against the clock, elimination, group starts, endurance, in-line, relays, stages, pursuit, and elimination combined with in-line.

These competitions are open to both men and women, and world championships are held every year.

TRACK

May be indoors or outdoors; in either case, it must be between 125 and 400 m long. Some tracks, with banked curves, are between 125 and 250 m long.

Surface
Usually cement or asphalt; sometimes wood or synthetic materials. It must be smooth, with no holes or cracks.

Start and finish line
It is white and 5 cm wide.

Relay zone
Located between the start and finish line and the beginning of the turn.

EQUIPMENT

Acrobatic skate
The boot of the acrobatic skate is made of hard plastic and has a lace-and-buckle closure system. The boot is lined to absorb shock.

Speed skate
Made of leather and carbon, the boot is light, flexible, and has a lace closure system. The boots are usually molded to the athlete's feet.

Boot
Holds the foot comfortably.

Shell
It absorbs shocks.

Wheels
Diameter of 40 to 70 mm; hardness varies depending on discipline.

Slider
Small curved plate that makes sliding easier and protects the plate.

Plate
It is made of polyurethane with lateral reinforcments that hold 4 wheels.

Bearing
Speed and precision are assisted by the quality of the bearing components.

Plate
Made of aluminum and carbon, it holds 5 wheels with a diameter of 80 to 84 mm.

1863

Helmet
Required in competition, it is similar to a cyclist's helmet and must have a chin strap.

PROTECTION
The most exposed parts of the body are the knees, elbows, wrists, hands, and head.

Wrist guards
Their reinforcements, made of hard plastic, can be removed.

Elbow pads
They are made of light material. They must stay still without being attached too tightly.

Knee pads
They must bend with the knee and are made of material that evacuates perspiration. The shell is made of plastic; the lining is foam.

Fabiola da Silva (BRA)
Three-time gold medalist (1996 to 1998) in half pipe (vert) at the X-Games, she was also first in street and second in vert at the 1997 ASA Pro World Tour Championship.

SKATER PROFILE

- The skater must have coordination, balance, and excellent reflexes.
- Warm up exercises are essential for avoiding injuries.
- In aggressive skating, the muscles in the legs, back, shoulders, and neck supply the main effort.
- In speed skating, endurance and quick reflexes are essential. The legs (thighs and ankles) must be exercised before the skates are put on.

Motor
Sports

 motor sports

T he invention of the four-stroke engine by German engineer Nikolaus Otto in the early 1870s marked the beginning of motor sports. In 1885, Otto's former assistant, Gottlieb Daimler, completed his work on the Einspur, regarded by historians as the first motorcycle. That same year, Karl Benz of Germany built the first production line car. Manufacturers soon began competing against each other in informal races, with everyone attempting to break speed or distance records. In 1904, the Fédération internationale de l'automobile (FIA) was founded and the same year saw the founding of the Fédération internationale des motocycles clubs (FIMC), which later became the Fédération internationale de motocyclisme (FIM). Since then, automobile and motorcycle competitions of all kinds (closed circuit, open road, and off road races) have been held regularly.

In 1947, Italian driver Enzo Ferrari (1898–1988) left racing for race car construction. The Ferrari stable, the only one present since the F1 world championships were started in 1950, has won more than 113 Grand Prix, 9 Formula 1 world championships for drivers, and 9 manufacturers' world championships—an unequaled record.

MECHANICAL PRINCIPLES

A vehicle's performance is determined by 3 main factors: power, which is expressed in horsepower (hp); rev band, which is the engine revolution range within which the power is delivered; and weight of the vehicle. Two vehicles equipped with 100 hp engines will not necessarily be equal in terms of performance. A car weighing 1 metric ton will not perform nearly as well as one weighing only 700 kg equipped with the same type of engine. Similarly, 2 identical cars, both propelled by 100 hp engines, will perform differently, depending on the engine speed at which maximum power is produced.

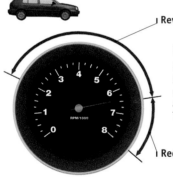

Rev band

Passenger vehicle tachometer

Power is available over a wide band, so that the driver can make use of it at all engine speeds and in all driving situations. The emphasis is on versatility.

Red zone

Rev band

Racing car tachometer

Given that performance is all important, power is delivered at very high engine speeds within a narrow power range. Racing cars have 6 or 7 very short gears, thus allowing the driver to quickly reach the critical power range.

Red zone

MAIN SIGNALS AND FLAGS

Black and white flag
This flag is displayed as a warning to a driver who has acted in an unsportsmanlike manner and is accompanied by the number of the car involved.

Black flag
Accompanied by the number of the car that has contravened a particular rule, it obliges the driver to return to the pits to serve a penalty.

White flag
It signals the presence of an ambulance, an emergency vehicle, or a slow moving vehicle on the track. In American racing series (such as CART and NASCAR), it indicates that the race is into its final lap.

Blue flag
This flag is displayed to let a driver know that a faster car is preparing to pass, so that the driver of the slower car will not impede the other car.

Yellow flag
When shown, this flag signals a dangerous situation. Drivers must reduce speed, and are not permitted to pass in the area where the yellow flag is being displayed.

EQUIPMENT

During automobile races, drivers must wear the following clothing and accessories:

Undergarment
The two piece undergarment must cover the neck, and preferably have a turtleneck.

Balaclava
It must be made of at least 2 layers of fire retardant fabric. The bottom must fit inside the driving suit or under the undershirt all around the neck, and must remain tucked in even when the head is turned.

Driving suit
All drivers must wear a driving suit made of fire retardant fabric, which must protect a driver from third degree burns for a period of at least 12 seconds. The driver's ankles, neck, and wrists must be covered at all times by at least 2 pieces of protective clothing. When advertising patches are put on the protective clothing, thermofusing is not permitted, and the suit must not be cut. It is recommended that the backing of the advertising patches be made of fire retardant fabric.

Gloves
The backs of the gloves must be made of at least 2 layers of fire retardant fabric. Gloves must close at the wrist, and cover the ends of the sleeves of the driver's suit.

Ear plugs
They must reduce ambient noise but allow for radio contact between the driver and the pit crew.

Helmet
It must be a full face type, and must conform to FIA-recognized standards. Helmets must be made of composite materials (such as Kevlar or carbon fiber), and must weigh at least 1.2 kg.

Knee socks
Must be made of fire retardant fabric, be at least one layer thick, and weigh at least 180g/sq. m.

Shoes
Must cover the entire foot and ankle. All materials used on the inside, and all fasteners or laces, must be of non-fusible manufacture. The manufacturer must certify that the soles are hydrocarbon and flame resistant.

CAMERAS

In most televised motor sport events, the vehicles carry one or more cameras for the duration of the race. Cameras are installed at up to 5 positions on the vehicle to provide viewers with different viewing angles. Since the early 1990s, cars and motorcycles that race on closed circuits have been equipped with telemetry systems that enable team engineers in the pits to continuously monitor the critical components in the vehicle during the event.

OFFICIALS

Automobile and motorcycle races held on closed circuits are supervised by a team of officials who are responsible for ensuring that the event runs smoothly. The race director is the most senior authority. He starts the race, shows the checkered flag to the winner, and oversees the event. The race director stops or interrupts the race if necessary, and imposes sanctions on drivers who have committed an infraction. Technical stewards ensure that all technical regulations are complied with (i.e., that vehicles conform to regulatory requirements). Race stewards are responsible for applying the sporting rules (with regard to the running of the event). Timers record each driver's lap times, and are responsible for monitoring the prescribed running time of the event. Marshals give pertinent information to the drivers by displaying various flags, and they help the competitors when necessary (for example, when a driver loses control, or in the event of mechanical failure). They are positioned at all turns (at least 3 per turn) and along the pit lane. A medical team (ambulance personnel and doctors) must also be on duty at every race.

Checkered flag
It is shown first to the winner of the race, and signals the end of the race or practice session.

Black flag with orange disk in the center
Accompanied by the number of the car in question, this flag is shown to a driver when, unknown to him, a part on his car constitutes a danger to him or to other competitors. The driver must return to the pits.

Yellow flag with red stripes
It signals a deterioration of surface adhesion, the presence of oil or other liquids, or debris on the track.

Red flag
Displayed at the start and finish line, and simultaneously by the track marshals, the red flag signals that the race or practice session is being stopped.

Green flag
It signals that a warning flag no longer applies, and is displayed after a yellow flag, indicating that drivers can now pass.

341

formula 1

Juan Manuel Fangio (ARG), F1 record holder with five world-championship titles (1951 and 1954–57). A legend of the automobile-sports world, he is considered by many experts to have been the best driver ever.

The pinnacle of automobile sports, Formula 1 features races between single seat cars on circuit racecourses (permanently built or on city streets). The first Formula car was built in 1885 by the German carmaker Karl Benz, and the first official race took place on a 126 km course between Paris and Rouen, in France, on July 22, 1894. Until 1906, a series of "City to City" races, linking European capitals, formed an international championship. The Fédération internationale de l'automobile was founded in 1904 and became the world governing body for automobile sports. The first Grand Prix was held in Le Mans, France, in 1906, while the first Formula 1 world championship was held in 1950; the champion was the Italian Giuseppe Farina, driving an Alfa Romeo. Over the decades, F1 has come to be heavily covered by the media, and high technology and money reign supreme in the sport.

THE GRAND PRIX RACE

The event lasts 3 days. Friday and Saturday morning are devoted to testing, during which the drivers drive as many laps as they need to get their car properly adjusted. A one hour official qualifying period is held on Saturday afternoon. The drivers go on the course at any point during this hour and have a maximum of 12 laps to record a qualifying time that will determine their position on the starting grid. Their quickest lap is used as their qualifying time. To qualify, drivers must achieve a time that is no more than 7% (the "107% rule") slower than the pole position time (the quickest in the session). The race itself takes place on Sunday afternoon. Thirty minutes before the start, the cars leave the pits, take a courtesy lap, and line up on the grid.

Any car that has not left its pit 15 min before the start will have to start from the exit to pit row, after the last car has passed, without taking part in the warm-up lap. Engines are started 1 min before the warm-up lap, which is a lap of the course at reduced speed (no passing is allowed) to warm up the tires before the official start of the race. Tires reach optimal efficiency at 100 °C. After completing the warm-up lap, the cars take their places on the starting grid. Five red lights come on one by one at 1-sec intervals. The race starts when all 5 lights go out together.

RACE COURSE

Italy (Monza)

The number of laps varies depending on the length of the circuit. A race on the Monza circuit, 5.77 km long, must be 53 complete laps to reach the regulation distance of 305 km.

Chicane
A twisting part of the circuit that breaks up a straightaway and forces drivers to slow down.

Gravel pits
They help a skidding car decelerate and are most effective in spins.

Curbs
They are placed at the entrances and exits of turns to serve as visual reference points and indicate the edge of the track.

Tire barriers
They offer the most effective shock absorption in a collision.

GRAND PRIX COURSES

They are between 3 and 7 km long. A Grand Prix must be a total of 305 km.

THE POINTS SYSTEM

The Formula 1 world championship involves 16 or 17 races; 12 teams, each with 2 drivers, compete. The driver with the most points at the end of the season is the champion.

There is also a manufacturers' championship. The carmaker that has the most points, according to a set scale and the performances of its drivers, wins this championship at the end of the season.

Points are awarded to the top six drivers on the following scale:

Position	1st	2nd	3rd	4th	5th	6th
Points	10	6	4	3	2	1

The driver with the most points at the end of the season is the world champion.

Driver	No. of titles	Victories	Pole positions
Juan Manuel Fangio	5	24	28
Alain Prost	4	51	33
Ayrton Senna	3	41	65
Jackie Stewart	3	27	17
Niki Lauda	3	25	24
Nelson Piquet	3	23	24

Spain (Barcelona)
A very fast course that is hard on the brakes. It offers a wide variety of turns and highlights the quality of the car's chassis.

Germany (Hockenheim)
This course taxes engines to the maximum, and speeds reach up to 340 km/h on the very long straightaways.

Monaco (Monte Carlo)
The slowest F1 course, Monaco is a city street circuit that requires absolute precision by the drivers.

Japan (Suzuka)
A long course, in which engine power is decisive, due to the long straightaways; races involve many passes.

Belgium (Spa Francorchamps)
The drivers' favorite circuit. It is also the most spectacular and difficult because of its extremely fast curves.

Pit row
Located between the track and the pits, it is used by the cars needing to refuel or change tires.

High speed turn
Turn negotiated at high speed (more than 160 km/h) that tests the car's stability and the driver's courage.

The pits
Each team has its own pit, where it does everything from mechanical work to telemetry during a Grand Prix.

STARTING GRID
The cars are arranged in a staggered formation in positions determined by their qualifying times. Each line is separated by 8 m.

Pole position
Top position on the grid, occupied by the driver who recorded the fastest time in qualifying.

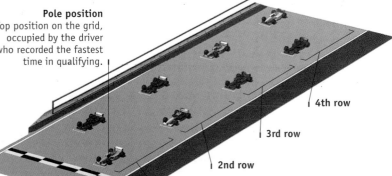

4th row

3rd row

2nd row

1st row

F1 SINGLE-SEAT CARS

The cars develop phenomenal power (more than 800 hp) and reach speeds of over 320 km/h. They have four-stroke engines with a displacement not exceeding 3,000 cm³ (3 liters). In F1, turbocharging is forbidden. The gearbox has 4 to 7 speeds and a reverse gear. Four-wheel drive is forbidden.

REQUIRED SIZE OF F1 CARS

maximum 180 cm

365–380 mm   305–355 mm

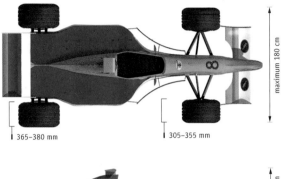

maximum 95 cm

Average: 4.4 m
Minimum weight: 600 kg (with driver)

TIRES

Depending on weather conditions during the race, different types of tires are used. Slick tires are used in dry weather. Rain tires have deep treads that evacuate large quantities of water (26 liters per second at 300 km/h). A variant of the rain tire, called "intermediate," has shallower treads for use on damp tracks.

A wide variety of rubber types—of varying adherence and durability—are also available. The choice of rubber (from soft to hard) is crucial in a race; this decision must be made before the qualifying session, and the team must use these tires for the rest of the event.

Rain tire

Slick tire

Grooves
Since the beginning of the 1999 season, front and back tires are required to have 4 grooves, which increase safety by slowing the cars.

Steering wheel
Due to a number of technical improvements, instruments once distributed around the cockpit and instrument panel are now on the steering wheel. Clutch engagement and gear selection are performed with fingertip controls.

Telemetry
All cars are equipped with a telemetry system that has a transmitter on one of the rearview mirrors. This system lets the crew in the pits keep track of the car's main functions during the race.

Radio aerial
Allows for communication between the driver and the team during the race.

Pitot tube
An aerodynamic air intake that calculates the car's real speed taking wind speed into account.

Camera
Cars have 2 cameras that run throughout the event. There are 5 places on the car where they can be attached.

Roll bars
These noncrumple structures protect the driver if the car flips. The back roll bar must be at least 70 mm higher than the driver's helmet.

Wings
They create air pressure to increase the load on the back and front axles, and therefore tire adherence to the track. The wings are adjusted to change the aerodynamics of the car depending on the circuit.

Black box
Like airplanes, F1 cars have data recorders that are used to analyze parameters if there is a breakdown or accident.

Side fairings
Structures that crumple to absorb the energy of a collision. They contain the radiators and electronic components and channel fresh air to the engine.

Safety harness
The driver is securely strapped in by the safety harness, which includes 2 shoulders straps, 2 belly straps, and 2 leg straps.

WIND RESISTANCE

Surprisingly, a sedan has a better wind resistance profile and consumes less fuel than an F1 car, which uses the wind resistance of its external components (wing, wheels) to stay glued to the track at very high speeds.

THE EVOLUTION OF F1 CARS

It has been not so much top speeds—cars were reaching 300 km/h by the 1950s—as average speeds that have risen dramatically with technical advances in design over the decades.

1950–1960
In the first Grand Prix, cars had engines in the front and the most competitive bodies were made of aluminum.

1960–1970
After the arrival of rear engine models and monohull chassis in the early 1960s, no front engine model ever again won a Grand Prix.

1975
The addition of wings in the mid 1970s was revolutionary: it improved car stability and handling.

1980–1990
The 1980s were fertile years for technical advances. The dominance of turbocharged engines—which produced up to 1,200 hp—led to their being banned in 1989.

1990–2000
The return of normally aspirated engines and a concern for safety led to the development of slightly longer cars with the best performances ever.

TECHNIQUES

DRAFTING

The wake of a race car creates an "air tunnel" that reduces the wind resistance of the car immediately behind it, which can temporarily increase speed, then move out of the draft and pass the competitor.

PASSING IN A SLOW TURN

The blue car brakes late in order to pass a competitor. Its position on the inside of the curve puts it in a better position to follow an ideal track out of the curve.

DRIVING THROUGH A CHICANE

Although a chicane is a twisting part of the course, drivers try to preserve their speed and drive through in a straight line to take the shortest possible route.

PIT STOP

During a race, cars make one or two refueling stops. In a highly choreographed series of moves, no fewer than 18 mechanics refuel the car and change all 4 tires in less than 8 seconds.

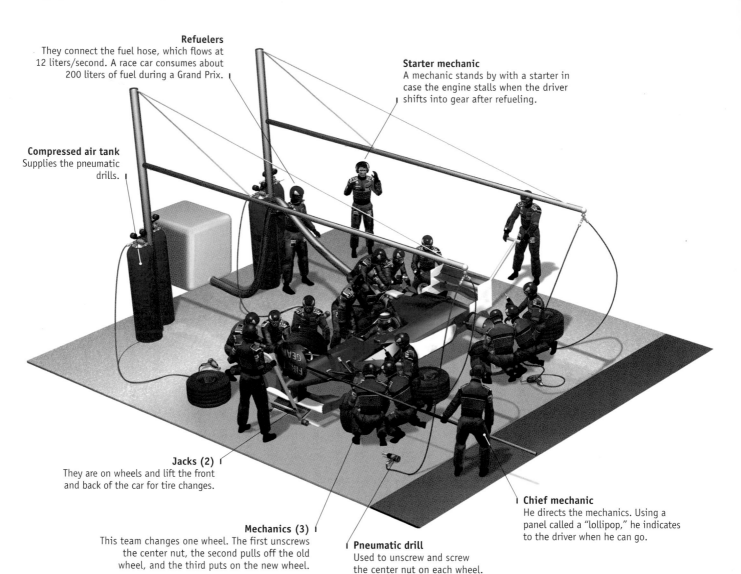

Refuelers
They connect the fuel hose, which flows at 12 liters/second. A race car consumes about 200 liters of fuel during a Grand Prix.

Starter mechanic
A mechanic stands by with a starter in case the engine stalls when the driver shifts into gear after refueling.

Compressed air tank
Supplies the pneumatic drills.

Jacks (2)
They are on wheels and lift the front and back of the car for tire changes.

Mechanics (3)
This team changes one wheel. The first unscrews the center nut, the second pulls off the old wheel, and the third puts on the new wheel.

Pneumatic drill
Used to unscrew and screw the center nut on each wheel.

Chief mechanic
He directs the mechanics. Using a panel called a "lollipop," he indicates to the driver when he can go.

DRIVER PROFILE

- Driving an F1 car requires more endurance than physical strength. Tolerance for heat is essential, since the temperature in the cockpit may reach 50°C. Drivers lose up to 4 kg during a race.

- Training consists of muscle strengthening with a focus on the neck, forearms, abdominals, and legs. Vision and coordination must be excellent.

- A healthy cardiovascular system is essential; in a race, a driver's heart rate is around 160 beats per minute, and up to 190 during an incident.

Michael Schumacher (GER)
He has 35 victories in 128 races, including 19 for the Benetton team, with which he won the world championship in 1994 and 1995. With the Ferrari team since 1996, he has 16 GP victories.

Ayrton Senna (BRA)
Three time F1 world champion (1988, 1990, 1991) with 41 victories and 65 pole positions (a record) in 161 Grand Prix. He died in Imola during the San Marino GP in 1994. No doubt one of the greatest talents in the sport.

Jim Clark (GBR)
One of the great F1 drivers. He won 25 out of the 72 GPs he entered and had 33 pole positions. World champion in 1963 and 1965, he died during a Formula 2 race in Hockenheim in 1968.

Alain Prost (FRA)
Four time world champion (1985, 1986, 1989, 1993), he became legendary when he surpassed the record number of victories held by Scotsman Jackie Stewart. He won 51 GPs out of 199 between 1980 and 1993. Since 1998, owner of the Prost/Peugeot F1 team.

formula indy (CART series)

The CART series for single seater racing cars is one of the most popular forms of auto racing in the United States. It traces its roots back to 1909, when automobile manufacturers approached the American Automobile Association (AAA) with the idea of creating a championship in an effort to promote their products. Between 1909 and 1930, many events were held as part of the AAA National Championship Racing series. Races were run on dirt and cinder tracks. The advent of one mile asphalt oval courses gave the championship new life. In 1955, after a terrible accident at the Le Mans 24 Hours in France, the AAA withdrew from racing, and the United States Auto Club (USAC) took its place. In 1978, Championship Auto Racing Teams (CART) was formed. CART took control of Formula Indy racing and staged its inaugural race in March 1979, at Phoenix, Arizona. Since that time, numerous changes have allowed the CART series to become hugely successful, both in the U.S. and abroad. In 1997, a dispute arose between CART and the owners of the Indianapolis Motor Speedway, the site of the Indianapolis 500, the crown jewel of Formula Indy racing, since 1911. This dispute led to the creation of the Indy Racing League, a competing series with races run strictly on oval courses.

Al Unser, Sr. (USA), one of the greatest drivers in the history of Formula Indy racing. A three-time Formula Indy champion (1970, 1983, and 1985), he won 39 championship races, including the Indianapolis 500 four times (1970, 1971, 1978, and 1987).

CARS

The single seater cars are heavier and sturdier than the F1s that they resemble. They are equipped with a 2.65-liter turbocharged engine that develops 850 hp. Five chassis manufacturers and four engine builders (Honda, Mercedes-Benz, Ford, and Toyota) supply all the teams. The cars reach phenomenal speeds: up to 370 km/h on the superovals. Formula Indy cars run on alcohol based methanol fuel.

Because methanol is highly volatile, and its flame is not visible in daylight, it constitutes a real danger in the event of an accident. Formula Indy cars are specifically configured to the circuits on which races are held. For example, the airfoils, or wings, will be set one way for an event being run on a superoval and another way for a race on an oval or a road course.

Ovals and road courses
Because top speed is not such a critical factor as on the superovals, the wings provide considerable downforce, pressing the car down onto the track.

Superovals
Smaller wings provide little downforce and allow for maximum top speed.

Pop off valve
This device releases the surplus pressure from the turbocharger to ensure that all teams respect the maximum turbo pressure limit.

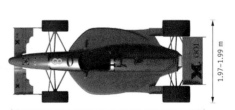

0.81 m

1.97–1.99 m

4.83–5.05 m
Ovals: 691.73 kg
Superovals: 703.07 kg

Brakes
Brake discs and pads are made of steel, which increases braking distance when compared with carbon brakes. A Formula Indy car moving at 300 km/h requires 85 m to come to a stop, as opposed to only 60 m for an F1. In Formula Indy, only carbon brakes are allowed on the superovals, for safety reasons.

HOW A RACE IS ORGANIZED

The Formula Indy championship is contested by 15 to 20 teams, with one or two drivers each, participating in the 20 races during the season.

QUALIFYING
Oval tracks and superovals
Each driver has either 2 or 3 timed laps in which to record his qualifying time. The order in which the drivers make their qualifying attempts is determined by a random draw.

Road courses
There are 2 group qualifying sessions for road-course events, each lasting 30 min. The two sessions are not usually held on the same day. For the first session, the drivers are divided into 2 groups, according to the qualifying times recorded at the last road-course event, with the faster drivers forming the first group and the slower drivers forming the second group. The times recorded during the first qualifying session determine the composition of the groups for the second session. The slower drivers now form the first group. The best lap time recorded by a driver during the 2 sessions is his qualifying time.

Starting grid
To qualify, a driver must record a lap time that is less than 110% of the average of the best times of the 2 fastest drivers in qualifying. There cannot be more cars on the starting grid than there are spaces in the refueling pit area.

CIRCUITS

Formula Indy races are run over distances of 200, 300, 400, or 500 miles, on 3 types of circuits: ovals, superovals, and road courses. The ovals, or speedways, are asphalt or cement tracks measuring between 1.6 and 2.5 miles around. Ovals longer than 1 mile with steeply banked turns are called superovals, or superspeedways. Road courses, which measure between 1.5 and 4 miles in length, may be either temporary tracks on city streets or specially designed permanent courses. Since the early 1990s, the CART series has become increasingly international in nature, with drivers from many different countries now taking part in the championship. Races are held in the United States, Australia, Brazil, Japan, and Canada.

Cars line up 2-by-2 on the grid. The driver who has earned the pole position by posting the fastest qualifying time starts in the front row, and chooses either the left or the right side starting spot. The other drivers line up on the row and in the spot corresponding to their qualifying position.

Starting procedure
On oval and superoval tracks, a rolling start is used: after getting a signal from the race director, the drivers head out onto the track to complete one or more warm-up laps, remaining in their respective grid positions. The pace car must maintain a constant speed, and no one can try to improve his position before the green flag is displayed.

At a road course event, the race director indicates beforehand whether the start will be a dry start, in which case drivers can choose the tires they are going to use, or a wet start, in which case all drivers must start on rain tires. Unlike Formula 1, pre-heating of tires is not permitted in Formula Indy.

In the CART series, drivers make many pit stops during a race to refuel and change tires.

The first driver to cross the finish line when the checkered flag is displayed is the winner of the race.

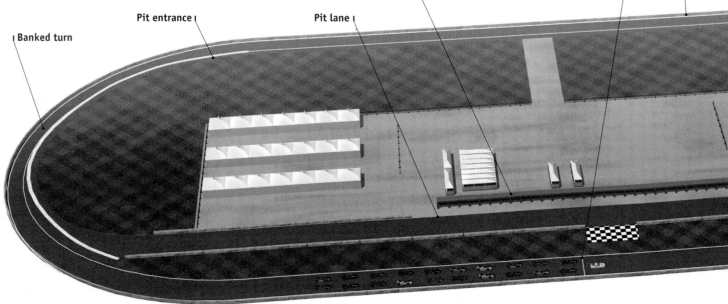

Cement retaining wall
Formula Indy tracks do not have safety run-off areas. The cement retaining walls are unforgiving.

Pits
Tires and fuel tanks are stored here. A maximum of 6 team members may work on a car.

Start/finish line
It is here that the cars are timed and that the green flag and the checkered flag are displayed.

Pit entrance

Pit lane

Banked turn

PENALTIES

When a driver breaks one of the rules governing a particular event, the race director may impose different penalties, depending upon the seriousness of the infraction.

- **Lap penalty** (e.g. illegally passing the pace car): one or more laps are deducted from the actual number completed by the penalized driver.

- **Loss of position** (e.g. passing under a yellow flag): the guilty driver may be moved down one or more positions in the finishing order. This penalty may be handed out during or after the race.

- **Penalty served in the pit lane ("stop and go")**: any driver who exceeds the speed limit in the pit lane (60 mph or 100 km/h), runs over a piece of equipment (tire, hose, etc.), or commits an infraction under a green flag or a yellow flag could be obliged to return to the pit lane, stop, and then go again when signaled by the appropriate race official, or he might be required to rejoin the race at the back of the field.

- **Suspension** (e.g. dangerous maneuver): officials may impose a suspension of one or more races on any driver who has committed a serious breach of regulations.

2000 SEASON EVENTS			
Ovals	Superovals	Road courses	
		Temporary	Permanent
Rio de Janeiro	Fontana	Cleveland	Portland
Chicago	Michigan	Long Beach	Laguna Seca
Milwaukee		Toronto	Mid-Ohio
Gateway		Vancouver	Road America
Motegi		Detroit	
Nazareth		Houston	
Homestead		Surfers Paradise	

FORMULA INDY VICTORIES BETWEEN 1909 AND 1998		
Position	Driver	Victories
1	A.J. Foyt	67
2	Mario Andretti	52
3	Al Unser	39
4	Michael Andretti	37
5	Bobby Unser	35
6	Al Unser Jr.	31
7	Rick Mears	29
8	Johnny Rutherford	27
9	Rodger Ward	26
10	Gordon Johncock	25
11	Bobby Rahal	24
12	Ralph DePalma	24
13	Tommy Milton	23
14	Tony Bettenhausen	22
15	Emerson Fittipaldi	22
16	Earl Cooper	20
17	Jimmy Bryan	19
18	Jimmy Murphy	19
19	Ralph Mulford	17
20	Danny Sullivan	17
21	Alex Zanardi	15
22	Tom Sneva	13
23	Paul Tracy	13

Mario Andretti (USA)
Second in all time Formula Indy victories with 52, including the Indianapolis 500 in 1969, four time Formula Indy Champion (1965, 1966, 1969, and 1984), and Formula 1 World Champion in 1978, he recorded 12 F1 wins in 128 races between 1968 and 1982. He also won the 1967 Daytona 500 (NASCAR series).

"Roadster" version (1936)
Home-made single seater with a very powerful front engine, rounded lines, and narrow tires.

F1 influence (1965)
Rear engine and very streamlined bodywork.

Since 1975
Aerodynamic revolution: appearance of wings and ground effects to keep the cars glued to the track. Turbocharged 8 cylinder engines.

Anthony Joseph Foyt (USA)
First in all-time Formula Indy victories with 67, including four wins at the Indianapolis 500 (1961, 1964, 1967, and 1977), he won the Daytona 24 Hours twice and the Le Mans 24 Hours in 1967. He retired from Formula Indy following an accident in 1992.

Pace car
Sets the pace for the field before the start and during caution periods when the cars must maintain their respective positions.

Pit exit

formula 3000

E stablished in 1985 at Silverstone in Great Britain as a replacement for Formula 2, the Formula 3000 championship is contested with single seater cars that run on closed circuits. Regarded as a training ground for Formula 1, the championship is designed to offer similar competition conditions at a much lower cost. Between 1985 and 1995, teams developed their own cars using chassis and engines supplied by different manufacturers. Since 1996, all participants have been required to use exactly the same equipment: the Fédération internationale de l'automobile (FIA) has designated official suppliers to all teams for a pre-determined number of years. While certain countries have created their own specific national championship, the international Formula 3000 championship is contested on circuits throughout Europe, in conjunction with Formula 1 Grand Prix events.

Jean Alesi of France. French F3 champion in 1987, and F3000 champion in 1989, he moved up to F1, where he finished fourth in the drivers' standings in 1996 and 1997.

HOW THE RACE RUNS

The starting grid is determined by the times recorded during qualifying sessions, with the fastest driver winning the pole position (the first starting spot). The greater the difference between a driver's time and the fastest time, the greater the distance between his starting position and the pole position. To qualify for the race, a driver must post a time that is less than 107% of the pole winner's time. A maximum of 26 cars may start the race. The race distance depends on the particular circuit: it equals the number of full laps required to pass the 205 km mark. At the end of a warm-up lap, the cars take their positions on the grid with their engines running. The race begins from a standing start.

DRIVERS' CHAMPIONSHIP						
Scale						
Position	1st	2nd	3rd	4th	5th	6th
Points	10	6	4	3	2	1

At the end of each race, points are awarded to the 6 highest finishing drivers. The season champion is the driver who has accumulated the most points during the 10 to 12 races that make up the championship.

THE CAR

Engine
A 500 hp. 3000 cc V8 engine equipped with a 9000 rpm rev limiter.

Cockpit
The cockpit is designed so that a driver wearing his full racing uniform and seat belts can get out in a maximum of 5 seconds.

Braking system
Steel disk brakes, on 2 separate circuits (front and rear), operated by the same pedal. ABS systems are banned.

Rear wing
It keeps the car "glued" to the ground, thanks to its air resistance. Its shape cannot be changed. Only the angle of the end plate can be adjusted.

Body
Constructed of Kevlar and carbon fiber, its aerodynamic shape is strictly regulated.

Tires
All competitors use the same model tire.

Chassis
Bodywork type supporting structure, molded from carbon-aluminum composite material. Its flat bottom reduces the ground effect (suction, created by the flow of air, which "glues" the car to the track).

Front wing
Like the rear wing, only its angle can be adjusted to aerodynamically adapt the car to the particular circuit layout.

TECHNIQUES AND TACTICS

With all drivers in technically identical cars, the difference between the fastest qualifying time and the 10th fastest time is rarely more than one second. Driving talent and the ability to precisely determine an efficient car set up are critical factors in how successful a driver will be.

DRIVER PROFILE

• A graduate of karting competitions, the average driver is about 20 years of age. His goal is usually to move up to F1, or to become a test driver for car manufacturers after 2 or 3 good seasons in F3000.

drag racing

A race of pure speed involving two vehicles, a drag race is to automobile racing what a sprint is to track and field. A typically American sport, drag racing began in southern California, where unofficial races were held, often illegally, on dry lakebeds or secondary roads. The founding of the National Hot Rod Association (NHRA) in 1951 allowed for the further development of the sport in the 1950s and 1960s. In 1975, the financial support of the R.J. Reynolds Tobacco Company led to the creation of the NHRA Winston Championship, which became a national event, attracting sponsors and network television coverage. In 1993, the NHRA and drag racing were officially recognized by the Fédération internationale de l'automobile (FIA), which created a drag racing commission. The NHRA now enjoys international status, and oversees the development of drag racing outside the United States.

Competition vehicles assembled prior to the 1959 Pre National Championship Drag Races at the air and naval base at Charleston, South Carolina.

HOW A RACE IS ORGANIZED

Drag racing consists of elimination heats, in which pairs of participants race against each other on a straight line track. Pairings are determined by a random draw. The winner of each race moves on to the next round, until only two competitors remain. These two racers meet in the final. To start each "run," the two drivers line up in their respective lanes, facing the electronic start signal lights. If a driver crosses the start line before the green light goes on, he is disqualified. The time the drivers take to react to the green light is called the reaction time, and is recorded by the timekeepers. It is added to the amount of time that the competitors take to cover the race distance to determine the winner of the race. Drivers have excellent reflexes and the ability to quickly assess track conditions, which enables them to make necessary adjustments to their start strategy and their engine before a race.

TRACK

The first 50 yds of the track is made of cement, which improves traction, and the rest of the track is paved with a mixture of asphalt and granite particles. A special seal is applied to the entire track to provide sufficient traction for the vehicles' tires. The course measures ¼ or ⅛ mile. Drivers can heat up their tires in a special area near the start line. At the end of the course, there must be a deceleration zone equal in length to one-and-a-half times the race distance. Races are not held in the rain because the track seal makes the surface too slippery.

Yellow lights (4)
They light up when the vehicles are in their starting positions.

Yellow lights (3)
They light up consecutively, and precede the green light.

Green light
Signals the start.

Red light
Signals false starts and defeats.

Christmas tree
The electronic start signal lights, which is called a Christmas tree because of the array of lights mounted on it.

Lanes
The lanes are perfectly straight, and are separated by a center divider. Any competitor who crosses into his opponent's lane, either voluntarily or involuntarily, is eliminated.

VEHICLES

There are more than 200 classes of drag racing vehicles, which are grouped into 12 categories, including 4 professional classes: Pro Stock, Moto Pro Stock, Funny Car, and Top Fuel.

Wheelie bars
It keeps the vehicle from overturning during acceleration.

Aerodynamic shell
Streamlined and extremely low to the ground, it measures more than 20 ft. in length.

Pro Stock
Resembling a production vehicle, it runs on gasoline. The exhaust pipe, chassis, and suspension are modified, and the vehicle can reach speeds in excess of 186 mph in 6 seconds.

Moto Pro Stock
With a 2- or 4-valve modified gas engine, it can cover the ¼ mile distance in 7.2 seconds, at more than 186 mph.

Funny Car
Developing more than 6,000 hp, it can cover the ¼ mile. distance in less than 5 seconds, at a speed of more than 186 mph.

Top Fuel
Equipped with a nitromethane fuel-injected engine, it develops more than 6,000 hp, and can cover the ¼ mile. distance in less than 4.5 seconds, at a speed of more than 330 mph.

rallying

Participants in the 1954 Monte Carlo Rally

A rally is a race run on roads (usually closed to traffic) consisting of point-to-point stages with fixed time schedules and special races against the clock during which drivers must respect the rules of the road. Many city-to-city races have been held since the beginning of the 20th century, but it was thanks to the president of the Automobile and Cycle Club of Monaco that the first true rally, the Monte Carlo Rally, was created in 1911. He proposed that the 23 participants in the event's inaugural edition make their way to Monte Carlo in seven days, starting from various points. England's Royal Automobile Club staged its first rally in 1932. The sport became extremely popular in the 1950s and 1960s, and events sprang up all over Europe: the Swedish Rally in 1950; the 1,000 Lakes Rally in Finland in 1951; the Acropolis Rally in Greece in 1953; and the Tour of Corsica and the San Remo Rally in Italy in 1956. In 1994, the Fédération internationale de l'automobile (FIA) created the World Rally Championship, consisting of a drivers' championship and a manufacturers' championship. Since 1997, it has included 14 events run in Europe, Africa, China, Argentina, New Zealand, and Australia.

HOW A RALLY IS ORGANIZED

The driving team (a driver and co-driver) shares the duties. While the driver is maneuvering the vehicle, the co-driver, or navigator, reads from the route card and calls out the different features along the course. The route card, which is provided by the event organizer, is the official summary of the route, with details concerning the dangers or characteristics of the course, including turns, dips, bumps, etc. Each team also receives a control book, in which the time allotted to complete the distance between two checkpoints is indicated. A route generally covers a distance of between a few dozen and several thousand kilometers (in the case of off-road rallies). A rally consists of two types of stages: most are point-to-point stages, in which drivers must complete the route in the time specified in the route card while

respecting the rules of the road. There are also special staggered-start timed stages, which are speed races, sometimes held at night, either on closed sections of roads or on permanent race circuits. Mechanical assistance (repairs made during the event) is permitted. Scores are awarded by the officials when the teams present their control book at the different checkpoints. If a team arrives at a checkpoint a minute (or even a fraction of a minute) late, it receives a 10-second penalty. If it arrives early, the penalty equals the amount of time the competitors are ahead of schedule. Points are distributed the same way as in Formula 1: the driver who has accumulated the most points at the end of the season is declared the World Champion. Extra points are awarded to the winners of the last special stage of events.

VEHICLES

Rallies are open to touring cars in Group N (production vehicles) and Group A (prototypes produced in quantities of at least 2,500). Since 1997, competitions have also been open to World Rally Cars (WRC), faster vehicles subject to fewer restrictions (a minimum production run of 20 is required for sanctioning purposes). Group B encompasses grand touring cars with a maximum engine capacity of 1600 cc. Today, most special stages are run on dirt courses, which explains the prevalence of four-wheel-drive cars.

TECHNIQUES

A car's gearbox is modified according to the particular route and, during reconnaissance runs, the driver and navigator agree on the gear changes, which are noted in the route card. Reconnaissance runs allow the teams to familiarize themselves with the route prior to the event. Rally driving requires a driver to be able to visually estimate the degree of traction a section of course offers. Speed can thus be adjusted so that the sliding of the car is controlled.

Night lamps
An essential piece of equipment for events that are run at night.

Juha Kankkunen (FIN)
The first four-time World Rally Champion (1986, 1987, 1991, and 1993), he won 24 World Championship events. He also won the 1988 Paris-Dakar Rally.

off-road rallying

O ff-road rallies are sporting events in which the accent is as much on adventure as on performance. The concept of off-road rallying is as old as the automobile itself. In 1907, a 12,000-km race was held between Paris and Peking. In 1931, the French automaker Citroën staged an expedition called "La Croisière Jaune," in which two teams, one starting from the Middle East and the other from Europe, had to traverse several deserts and mountain ranges, including the Himalayas, to reach Peking. In 1968, the London-Sydney Rally, with a route that crossed nearly 90 countries, proved a great success, and was followed by a London-Mexico Rally. In 1978, Frenchman Thierry Sabine organized the most important off-course rally to date, the Paris-Dakar, today called the Dakar. In this event (Grenada-Dakar in 1999 and Dakar-Cairo in 2000), cars, motorcycles, and trucks compete against each other across the Sahara Desert. The rally, which receives extensive media coverage, has spawned a number of other African rallies, including the Rally of the Pharaohs, the Atlas Rally, the Tunisian Rally, and the Rally of the Gazelles. The World Cup for Cross Country Rallies, sanctioned by the FIA, is won by the team with the most victories at the end of a season.

The Paris-Dakar Rally in 1984

HOW AN OFF-ROAD RALLY IS ORGANIZED

The route, which crosses desert regions, usually stretches several thousand kilometers. It comprises point-to-point stages and special timed sections. Technical assistance is authorized and provided by mechanical support crews who follow the competitors in trucks. Repairs are allowed during the stages and when the vehicles arrive at the finish of the section, before they are parked in an enclosed area until the start of the next stage the following morning. Prior to each stage of the rally, teams receive a route card, which describes in detail the route to follow, and indicates the places where they can receive assistance. Competitors must follow the route guide, and do not require maps. Vehicles are refueled at the refueling points indicated on the route card. Rally teams, which may drive for 8 to 24 hours without stopping, depending on the length of the stage, are allowed to use a Global Positioning System (GPS), with which they can determine their longitude and latitude by satellite link. However, this equipment must be supplied by the organizers.

TECHNIQUES

Run over several weeks, off-road rallies are true physical and psychological endurance tests. A team's technical skills and the reliability of the vehicle are severely tested. Many of the major manufacturers are represented. They hire professional car drivers to try to win top honors.

THE DAKAR 2000

Run entirely in Africa, it stretches 11,000 km, and includes 17 stages, including 3,040 km of point-to-point stages in which the time allotted for each section must be respected, and 7,444 km of special stages that are a race against the clock.

Egypt
Arrival in Cairo

Libya

Niger

Mali

Senegal
Start in Dakar

Burkina Faso

Stéphane Peterhansel (FRA)
The Paris-Dakar Rally motorcycle record holder for all categories combined (1991, 1992, 1993, 1995, 1997, and 1998), he was the World Enduro 250 champion in 1997, winner of the 1992 Paris-Peking Rally, French Enduro champion 11 times since 1984, and winner of the 1998 24 Heures de Chamonix (24 hour car race on ice).

VEHICLES

Cars
Most are four-wheel-drive vehicles adapted from production models. Vehicles must be produced in quantities of at least 1,000 in order to be sanctioned to race. A Prototype category groups two-wheel-drive and individually produced vehicles.

Motorcycles
Motorcycles must have a minimum engine capacity of 450 cc, and a range of 380 km. Most are production models, with the different manufacturers having developed a whole range of specialty bikes for this type of event.

Trucks
Event organizers have recently encouraged the participation of trucks with front axle-mounted engines and a loading platform of the type first used when this category of vehicles was created. The four-, six-, and eight-wheel-drive trucks are improved production models.

motorcycling

British rider B.G. Stonebridge in action during the famous Motocross des Nations event, held at Brands Hatch (Great Britain) in 1952.

Although two-wheeled vehicles powered by steam engines first appeared in the United States and Europe in 1868, the first patent was applied for only in 1871, in France. In 1894, the first motorcycle marketed in Europe used a gasoline engine. The use of gearboxes spread, and in 1903 a record of 120 km/h was set. In the same period, the sidecar (one-wheeled pod attached to the side of the motorcycle) was invented and sidecar motorcycle races began to be held. In 1904, following the first major road race (the Coupe du Motocycle-Club in France), England, France, Germany, Austria, Belgium, and Denmark founded the Fédération internationale des Motocycles-Clubs (FIMC). The first edition of the legendary Tourist Trophy, run on the roads of the Isle of Man (Great Britain), took place in 1907. In 1922, the first 24 hour endurance race, the Bol d'Or, was held in France. Motocross was invented by motorcyclists who found trial, an event run on natural terrain, too slow and monotonous. Motocross was recognized as an event on its own shortly after 1945. Races then began to be held all over the world, and in 1949 the FIMC became the Fédération internationale motocycliste (FIM). Today, 27 events, divided into road and off road races, are recognized by the FIM.

THE SPEED GRAND PRIX

It takes place on a closed circuit. During testing, riders can familiarize themselves with the track and make adjustments to their motorcycles. On the Saturday preceding the race, two official one hour qualification periods are held to determine the position of the riders on the starting grid; the fastest riders occupy the front positions. The race is held on Sunday. The drivers are placed on the starting grid according to their qualification times. They ride one or two warm up laps in formation and return to the grid with their motors running. The starting signal, a red light followed by a green light, is given by the course director. Speed races require riders to have great endurance, as they generally last 20 to 30 minutes. The first rider across the finish line at the end of the race is the winner.

CUPS AND CHAMPIONSHIPS

Considered the pinnacle of motorcycle road racing, the speed racing world championships take place over 16 Grand Prix in Europe and elsewhere in the world. The first 15 competitors across the finish line of each race are awarded points: 25 points for first place, 20 for second, 16 for third, and so on. The rider with the most championship points at the end of the season is declared world champion in his category. Speed races and endurance championships have a sidecar category.

DISPLACEMENT CATEGORIES			
Category	Power	Weight	Top speed
GP125	45 hp	70 kg	240 km/h
GP250	95 hp	95 kg	270 km/h
GP500	135–180 hp	101–130 kg	320 km/h
Superbike	145–180 hp	155–160 kg	300 km/h

COURSES

They may be permanent (built specifically for racing) or temporary (set on existing roads equipped for the purpose of the race). They are between 3.5 and 10 km long, and the start area must be a straightaway of at least 250 m. For safety reasons, race officials are positioned along the course to warn racers if there is a fall or if debris or oil slicks are on the track.

Track
It must never be less than 10 m wide.

Pits
Area where technical and mechanical teams adjust and repair the motorcycles.

Stands
They provide seating for officials and spectators.

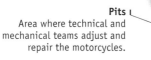

TECHNIQUES

Turning technique

This consists of taking advantage of the motorcycle's adhesion to the track when the rider reaches the inside point of the curve and using all of the available acceleration as early as possible when coming out of the turn. **1.** The rider starts braking before he enters the curve and gradually eases up on the brakes as he reaches the inside point of the curve. **2.** He moves his hips to the outside as he leans the motorcycle to the inside of the curve. **3.** He moves his inside knee outside of the fairing to gauge his degree of lean by contact with the ground. He keeps his hips to the outside of the motorcycle, shifting his weight so that the suspension does not have to work so hard. **4.** The acceleration phase starts gradually as soon as he passes the inside point of the curve. **5.** To stay on an ideal racing line, the rider lets the motorcycle drift outward the entire width of the track, if possible.

Inside point of the curve

This is the point where the trajectory is closest to the inside of the curve.

Start

The rider moves his weight to the front of the motorcycle to keep the front wheel from lifting during acceleration. He tries to use all the power of the engine without raising his front wheel too high, or he will have to slow down to regain control. He tucks his helmet behind the windshield to reduce wind resistance and gain speed. The front forks have shock absorbers designed to reduce front end wobble which is oscillations of the handlebars, caused by speed and the state of the track, that destabilize the motorcycle.

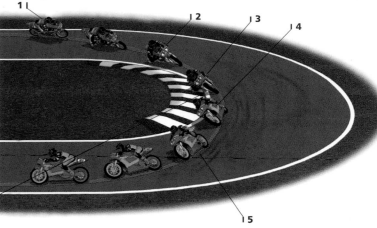

EQUIPMENT

To obtain better handling and a better weight-power ratio for acceleration, lightness of motorcycles is a constant concern: frames are usually made of aluminum or titanium alloys. Fiber-carbon fairings must allow for a lean of 50° without touching the ground. Grand Prix motorcycles in the 125, 250, and 500 cc categories are prototypes designed by manufacturers. Superbikes must be production motorcycles at least 500 units of which have been marketed in order to qualify. Improvements are allowed, but the competition motorcycles are very similar to models sold to the general public.

Neck support
It butts up against the helmet to keep the head from jerking backward during falls.

Racing suit
It is a one piece suit made of leather, with synthetic fibers in the places that are least exposed (such as the inside of the arms). Extra padding is incorporated in the hips, knees, and elbows. Back protection is worn under the suit.

Rub protection
Made of hard, slippery plastic, they are attached with Velcro to the places where the suit most frequently rubs against the track so that they can be easily changed.

Boots
They are made of leather, with Kevlar reinforcement mainly around the ankles.

Disk brakes
They are usually made of carbon.

Wheels
They may be made of carbon fiber for lightness: this reduces the gyroscopic effect and makes it easier to lean the motorcycle in turns.

Air outlet

Full face helmet
It meets FIM standards and must be changed after a crash.

Visor
It is covered with layers of plastic film that can be removed during the race when they get dirtied by sprayed oil and dust.

Gloves
They are made of leather with Kevlar and carbon-fiber reinforcements on the fingers.

Air intake for engine cooling

Tires
They are designed to ensure contact with the ground even when the motorcycle is in an extreme lean. Slick tires are used on dry tracks, and grooved tires on wet roads. The qualities of the rubber are constantly being developed, and it offers exceptional adhesion.

MIXED AND OFF ROAD RACES

Mixed events (road and off road) and off road races are as varied as the terrain on which they are run. Enduro is an endurance race in which the reliability of the motorcycles and skills of the riders are put to the test. Every year, the FIM supervises the Six-Day International Competition, which involves 6 1-day races. The total distance run is between 1,200 and 1,600 km.

Motoball, played on a football field, involves 2 6-rider teams who try to score goals into the opposing team's net.

Speedway (cinder track), grass track (run in fields), and ice races take place on oval tracks made of earth, grass, or ice. The motorcycles have no brakes and are fueled by methanol.

In the United States, supermotard races take place on a track made of 70% clay and 30% asphalt. In impossible climb competitions, 2 racers start at the bottom of a ski hill and have to make 3 jumps before climbing a steep hill at least 150 m long. The modified motorcycles are fueled by nitro-methanol.

MOTOCROSS – SUPERCROSS

A spectacular event featuring speed and jumps, motocross is raced on a closed circuit. The track, located on natural terrain, involves sharp drops and hills and many bumps, moguls, ruts, and various obstacles. Supercross is run on an artificial track, sometimes indoors, made of earth or a mixture of sand and clay with obstacles that lead to very high jumps. Starts are made by groups of 25 racers in a line, and the

winner is the first one across the finish line. World motocross and supercross championships involve 16 races each, with points accorded to the first 15 finishers. The world champion in each category is the rider (or team for sidecar racers) with the most points at the end of the 16 courses.

Group start

The competitors stand with their engines running. The official holds up a card indicating 30 seconds, then another indicating 5 seconds. If there is a false start, signaled by a red flag, racers must return to the waiting area and a new start is given as soon as possible.

Starting gate
Use of a starting gate is required. The gate has a transversal bar at least 50 cm high that folds down or lowers at the start.

Turns
Most passes are made in turns, especially at the beginning of the race, when the riders are jockeying for position in the pack and passing is easier.

SUPERCROSS TRACK

The track must be at least 300 m long and at least 5 m wide. The open vertical space between the track and any obstacle above it must be at least 3 m. The race involves about 15 laps, and

about 20 race officials are placed along the track to inform the racers of possible dangers with yellow flags.

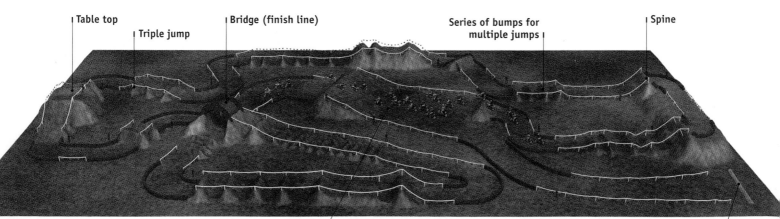

Table top

Triple jump

Bridge (finish line)

Series of bumps for multiple jumps

Spine

Rockers

Start area
The width of the track at the start line allows for a line of a minimum of 25 solo racers or 15 sidecar racers. Each solo motorcycle must have a space 1 m wide, and each sidecar motorcycle must have 2 m. The starting line must be placed in such a way that it allows a fair start with equal chances for all racers on the line.

Jump

On the ramp, the rider moves forward toward the handlebars before taking off. Once in the air, he moves backward, extending his arms. To align his motorcycle for a good landing angle, the rider accelerates to lower the back of the motorcycle or brakes to lower the front. On landing, the driver moves forward toward the handlebars to gain speed.

TRIAL

This is an event in which the emphasis is placed on the rider's skill, concentration, riding finesse, and sense of balance, rather than speed. The racers, or teams in the case of sidecars, must ride over a rough and very uneven course that can be all-terrain (small roads, country roads, underbrush, etc.) or inside a stadium (indoor). The course is divided into 15 sections, each of which is at most 60 m long, and the rider must cross them in numerical order; if he puts a foot on the ground, he loses points. If any part of the competitor's body or the motorcycle (except the tires, footpegs, engine block, and its protections) touches the ground or leans on an obstacle (tree, rock, etc.), it is considered the same as putting a foot on the ground. The start order is drawn by lot. The sections must be crossed by one competitor at a time. The winner is the competitor with the least points.

MOTORCYCLIST PROFILE

- Motorcycling is a sport that requires great endurance and concentration. Off-season training for riders includes muscle building and aerobics. Riders watch their food intake and go on special diets consisting of large amounts of liquids before races.

- Before competition, most riders isolate themselves so that they can concentrate and visualize the race.

EQUIPMENT

Trial motorcycle
It is light (about 70 kg) and maneuverable. The center of gravity is very low for better stability. During competitions, the riders let air out of the tires to obtain better adhesion on the obstacles.

Protective equipment
There is padding for the torso, arms, elbows, knees, and back. However, it is not required and its use is in decline.

Pants and shirt
They are light and made of synthetic fabric.

Motocross boots
They are made of leather and plastic.

Protective plate
It protects the engine from bumps and keeps it from sticking on obstacles by letting it slide over them.

Motocross helmet
It is mandatory and must meet FIM standards.

Protective goggles
They are covered with several layers of plastic film that the rider can take off if they get dirty.

Gloves
Made of synthetic material, they are padded inside and outside.

Nubby tires
There are 3 types of tires for different terrain: soft, hard, and mud. The back wheel has a diameter of 48 cm; the front wheel, 53 cm.

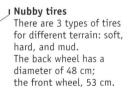

Giacomo Agostini (ITA)
Winner of 15 world champion titles (8 in 500 cc and 7 in 350 cc). He won a total of 122 races from 1965 to 1977, including 22 in a row, and is considered the greatest Grand Prix rider of all time.

Jeremy McGrath (USA)
With 77 victories in the motocross and supercross categories, he is ranked first by the American Motorcycling Association (AMA). He is the only motorcyclist to have won the AMA Supercross 6 times, the last time in 1999. He was also gold medalist at the Motocross des Nations in 1996.

snowmobiling

Joseph-Armand Bombardier (CAN), inventor of the snowmobile

Formerly a simple means of transport used in certain regions that were difficult to access in winter, snowmobiling has developed into a leisure activity and an international sport featuring increasingly hi-tech and spectacular forms of competition. In 1920, automobiles were modified for travel on snow, with the rear tires equipped with studs and the front wheels replaced with skis. In 1937, Canadian Joseph-Armand Bombardier took out a patent on a sprocket wheel endless-track traction system (a sprocket wheel drove the track). In 1959, the first motorized sled was produced and marketed under the name Ski-Doo. Since 1960, snowmobiling has continued to develop, and some four million people practice the sport today. Its growth is due in large part to activities staged by local clubs, and the creation of networks of trails, some of which stretch several hundred miles. International competitions, like the Kanada Challenge, are held each year.

HOW A RACE IS ORGANIZED

Once their race has been announced, drivers must be ready to start within 2 min. Depending on the type of event, there can be up to 25 competitors at the start, lined up in 3 rows. Starting positions are determined by a random draw, and if there are more than 25 racers, elimination heats are held. The start is signaled with a green flag (or a green light). In the case of an accident, the technical director will inspect the snowmobiles involved and decide whether they can rejoin the race.

TYPES OF RACES

Sno-cross: Sno-cross is run on a snow-covered track, which is between one half mile and 2 miles in length and made up of difficult left hand and right hand curves. Because of the obstacles that the racers have to deal with, sno-cross is spectacular to watch, and it is attracting more and more spectators. The race is timed, and usually lasts about 12 min.

Ice le Mans: This race is run on a sno-cross type of track, on which the snow has been replaced with ice. There are no obstacles, and the snowmobiles can reach speeds of 100 mph on the straightaways.

Cross-country: Comparable to sno-cross, but held in a natural setting, this type of event is run on a winding circuit that can stretch several hundred miles. There are checkpoints, the location of which are not known to the racers, and refueling spots spread out along the course.

Drag racing: With the advent of this event, snowmobiling has joined the domain of extreme sports. There are several types of snowmobile drag races, with events staged on asphalt, grass, snow, ice, and water.

The track is straight, measures 25 ft. wide and 500 to 660 ft. long, and includes a deceleration zone. The goal is to reach the finish line as quickly as possible.

Radar speed run: This event has more to do with pure performance than with racing. The goal is to determine the snowmobile's maximum speed (up to 130 mph). It is run on straight tracks covered with ice or snow.

Mountain climbing: This type of race involves racing up a steep hill (generally a ski hill) that is covered with snow or ice. One at a time, competitors go up the hill as fast as possible. The snowmobiles used are substantially modified and very elongated.

OVAL TRACK

A track 875 to 1,094 yds. long is laid out on snow or ice, and is covered with a layer of ice that is approximately 27½ in. thick. Snowmobiles can reach speeds of 100 mph, and the minimum distance to be covered is three laps.

Marshals (4)
Supervised by the chief marshal, they are responsible for warning drivers of danger by displaying flags. The yellow flag (or yellow light) tells racers to exercise caution. The red flag (or red light) signals an immediate stop in the event, regardless of the respective positions of the competitors.

Technical director
The technical director verifies the safety of the snowmobiles and the track prior to the race. After the race, he ensures that the vehicles of the top two or three finishers and the fuel they have been using conform to the regulations. During the event, the technical director remains outside the track, in a reserved and protected enclosed area.

Chief marshal
Positioned at the start-finish line, the chief marshal remains in radio contact with the other marshals stationed in the corners around the track.

Timers (2)
The timers are located inside the building.

Race director
The race director has complete authority over the race, and he is responsible for the flag.

EQUIPMENT

These powerful machines can accelerate from 0 to 60 mph in four seconds, and reach a speed of 130 mph. There are many different types of snowmobiles, which are built around a common chassis. The power of the engine (capacity), expressed in cubic centimeters (ccs), determines what class the vehicle falls into: the higher the level of the competition or the more extreme the event, the greater the engine capacity. There are approximately 40 classes, comprised of different specific models of snowmobiles. "Stock" models are the manufacturers' original models, which must not be modified in any way. Modified models can be altered in three ways: improvements made by the manufacturer, changes made by the driver, or changes made by the driver's team. The degree of modification determines the class in which the racer belongs. Only models made by certain manufacturers are approved for use in competitions.

EVOLUTION OF SNOWMOBILES

B-12
The ancestor of the snowmobile, this vehicle was first produced in 1946. It was made of wood, and could transport up to 12 people.

First model (1960)
It had wooden skis and a metal fairing.

SNO-CROSS SNOWMOBILE

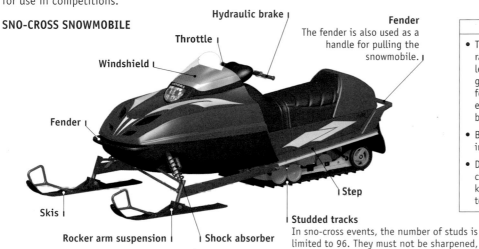

Hydraulic brake

Throttle

Windshield

Fender
The fender is also used as a handle for pulling the snowmobile.

Fender

Skis

Rocker arm suspension

Shock absorber

Step

Studded tracks
In sno-cross events, the number of studs is limited to 96. They must not be sharpened, machined, or modified in any way.

SNOWMOBILE RACER PROFILE

- These professional athletes, who often also race motocross motorcycles, must be in excellent physical condition. They train in the gym to strengthen their back, arms, and forearms, which are subject to considerable exertion during a race. Cycling is also a basic part of their training.

- Before each race, the drivers perform stretching exercises to warm up.

- During the off-season, snowmobile racers participate in stock car and motocross racing to keep their skills sharp and to work on their techniques.

Safety vest
Padded with compact foam, it protects the chest and the spinal column.

Helmet
Wearing of a helmet is mandatory. It must have a visor, and be colored orange over at least 75% of its surface.

Competition suit
A safety vest protects the upper part of the driver's body. Shin guards are mandatory. Gloves and boots, which must extend at least 5.9 in. above the ankle, are made of leather, and must conform to regulations. The portions of the driver's suit covering the torso and back must be colored orange for safety reasons. However, there must not be any orange on the snowmobile itself.

Jacques Villeneuve (CAN)
Brother of the late auto racer Gilles Villeneuve, Jacques Villeneuve is a remarkable snowmobile racer. He has won the world snowmobile championship at Eagle River, Wisconsin, USA, three times (1980, 1982, and 1986).

SNOWMOBILE FOR OVAL TRACK RACING

TECHNIQUE USED IN OVAL-TRACK RACING

The driver is seated in the center of the machine on the straightaways, but he leans to the inside when entering a corner. The front left ski lifts slightly, which allows the driver to turn easily and avoid continuing straight ahead. The driver reduces speed going into the corner and accelerates progressively, shifting his weight to offset the centrifugal force.

powerboat racing

Since 1938, the Valleyfield Regatta (CAN) has drawn competitors from all over the world for special events such as the World Regatta (1967 and 1976) and the world championships in 1992.

Powerboat racing refers to all races for motorboats on the ocean, on lakes, or on rivers. Motors were installed on boats in the middle of the 19th century, but it was not until 1902 that the sport was organized with the founding of the Marine Motoring Association in Great Britain. One year later, the New York's Columbia Yacht Club (now the American Power Boat Association [APBA]) was founded in the United States. In 1903, races took place on the Seine River, France, and a race across the English Channel was held: the boats, with straight stems and flat bottoms, were not very hydrodynamic and depended on pure power. In 1908, the Association internationale du yachting automobile, based in Paris, organized races in Europe, while there were some 10 annual races started in the United States in 1917. The Union internationale motonautique (UIM), founded in 1922, published its rules and a calendar of official races in 1927. Major technical improvements were made after the Second World War and powerboating diversified: the APBA supervised its development in the United States, while the UIM coordinated international races. Personal watercraft—designed for sea rescues—appeared in the United States around 1970. In 1980, the International Jet Sports Boating Association (IJSBA) was founded; it now has 39 member nations and a professional world championship. The UIM launched a Formula 1 powerboat world championship in 1981 and included personal watercraft in a Class Pro world championship in 1996. As of 1997, the UIM had 57 member nations.

BOAT RACES

There are speed and endurance races. Endurance races generally take place with private yachts on the ocean. The UIM's world speed championships are run on the open ocean (Offshore Classes 1 to 3) or on closed circuits marked with buoys on bodies of calm water (Formula 1 and Formula 3). The APBA coordinates the American championships in many other categories and classes—including hydroplane—not yet recognized by the UIM.

F1 GRAND PRIX RACE

The F1 World Championship includes 8 to 10 Grand Prix, during which drivers accumulate points depending on their finish in each race. Competitors have 2 timed qualifying sessions to determine their start positions. Starts are made in a line, engines dead, from a floating jetty or a pier, with racers positioned so that the fastest driver in the qualifications (holder of the pole position) has the advantage. The official responsible for lining up the 24 competitors gives the start signal, which is usually in the form of green and red lights illuminating in sequence. The number of laps is determined as a function of an ideal race duration of 45 minutes, and the winner of the race is the driver who finishes in the shortest time.

RACE COURSE

The circuit may be set on a river—as is the 6 Heures de Paris—a lake, or a well-protected bay. Depending on the configuration of the body of water, it may have left or right turns. Straightaways between 2 turns may not be longer than 850 m.

Safety team
The boat is equipped with a winch, and the team is composed of rescue divers supervised by a physician. Because of the danger of drowning, the team must be able to react in less than 30 seconds after an accident.

Start jetty
It has a minimum length of 75 m for safety reasons, and it must be located at least 300 m from the first turn.

Pit area
This is where cranes are used to put the boats in the water.

EQUIPMENT

Drivers must wear a protective helmet, a life jacket, and fireproof isothermal clothes. Emergency oxygen masks are recommended but not required. Boats have anti-crash safety cells—protective compartments in case of accident—similar to those in Formula 1 automobiles, and safety cockpits similar to those in fighter planes.

BOATS

Propellers
Most teams use a dozen types of propellers, generally with 6 blades; various propeller diameters and blade shapes are used for different sea conditions. They are made of stainless steel.

Approximately 14 m

Offshore Class 1

The crew consists of two racers: the driver and his teammate (throttleman), who alone controls boat acceleration. The boats are monohull or catamaran with a structure made of aluminum or reinforced polymer. They are powered by 2 (sometimes 3) V12 8-liter gas or 10-liter diesel engines. Their top speed is over 250 km/h, and average speed on course is near 200 km/h, with turns negotiated between 160 and 180 km/h. The teammates communicate with each other and officials by radio. They navigate using GPS (global positioning system).

Back wing
It increases directional stability of the boat. It is fixed.

Hot-air exhaust

Engine

Air intake

Cockpit

Pontoon

Kevlar cowling

8.50–9.75 m

Front wing
It is often equipped with movable flaps adjusted by the driver to stabilize the boat during the race.

"Unlimited" hydroplane

Developed mainly in the United States under the aegis of the APBA, the hydroplane draws its name from the wing-shaped profile of the central part of its hull. Because only the back of the boat is in the water, its draft is reduced and speed is increased. In the "Unlimited" category, hydroplanes reach an average of 270 km/h in races, and over 310 km/h on straightaways. The engine, based on aeronautical turbine or piston engines, is linked to a propeller with a maximum diameter of 40 cm and 2 or 3 blades.

5.80 m

Formula 1 outboard

Powered by a 2 to 3 liter 350-hp gas-powered engine, it reaches 100 km/h in 3.5 seconds, and its top speed is over 220 km/h. It is equipped with a self-inflating buoy balloon that keeps the safety cell afloat in case of collision. The design of the 2-float hull may be simple catamaran type or "tunnel" (which creates air turbulence between the 2 floats to lift the boat). The front ends of the floats and fuselage detach in case of collision. F1 outboards use propellers with 3 or 4 blades, depending on course conditions.

Buoys
Each turn is marked by 2 buoys: yellow for a right-hand turn and orange for a left-hand turn. If a racer destroys or damages the first buoy, he must take a penalty lap, while any damage to the second buoy causes disqualification.

PERSONAL WATERCRAFT (PWC) RACES

There are professional world championships in a number of categories corresponding to the type of PWC used: single-seat, double-seat, and triple-seat Runabout (driver seated) with engine displacements of 785 to 1,200 cc, and single-seat aquabike driven standing (Ski Division). All races are open to men and women:

• Slalom is a race against the clock (86-m straight-line course marked with 9 buoys). Each competitor has 2 runs, and the faster time is retained.

• Speed races take place in several heats on a course with turns marked with buoys.

• Freestyle is an event with 3-minute runs of acrobatic maneuvers. The choreography, number of maneuvers, and quality of execution are marked by 5 judges (2 drivers and 3 officials), who give points on a scale of 1 to 10. Each run must include required and free maneuvers.

• Endurance races take place in several stages over a total of about 150 km, or with 2-person crews taking turns driving the PWC. A good strategy for refueling and relays between teammates is essential.

SPEED COMPETITION

Depending on the number of competitors registered for the event, it may be necessary to have elimination rounds. The length of a speed circuit is between 2,000 and 3,000 m in the Runabout 785 to 1,200 cc categories (1,000 to 2,000 m for the Ski Division). The course must have 8 to 30 buoys. The start is generally made from a jetty or a beach: competitors line up behind a cable, engines running, and the PWC is held by 2 mechanics. At the official's signal (green flag), the competitors start and make 15 to 25 laps, depending on the length of the course. The competitor who completes the required number of laps the most quickly wins. The first 12 finishers in each race gain points that determine their world championship ranking at the end of the season.

Double track
On a certain part of the course (dotted line), competitors may take a second track; it is often used for passing attempts, to avoid the wake of other competitors, and to gain speed.

Buoys
On UIM courses, red buoys indicate a left-hand turn and white buoys a right-hand turn (yellow on IJSBA courses). Jumping a buoy results in a 20-second penalty.

Finish line
It is marked by 2 checkerboard buoys on UIM courses (white on IJSBA courses).

First buoy
It must be 100 m from the start.

Marshalls (4)
They are positioned in the center and at both ends of the course. They signal and provide protection if a driver falls into the water, and they assist competitors who must stop during the race.

EQUIPMENT

PWC are powered by turbines that draw water in at the front and propel it out the back. The water jet is directional and controlled by the handlebars, which means that no centerboard is necessary and maneuverability is exceptional.

Single-seat driven standing (Ski Division)

It is used in freestyle and in the speed Ski Division. It must weigh over 102.1 kg, and it must not be longer than 304.09 cm.

Safety vest
It is reinforced to absorb bumps, especially against the handlebars.

Wetsuit
It is made of neoprene. Protective padding is added to legs and hips, used mainly by Ski Division drivers who are in the water for starts and at higher risk for collisions with other watercraft.

Helmet
Required to protect drivers against bumping the hulls of other watercraft if they fall into the water.

Goggles
They protect the eyes from spraying water.

Throttle

Gloves
They give the driver a better grip on the handlebars.

Single-seat driven seated (Runabout)
It is used for speed races in the Runabout 785 to 1,200 cc categories and for endurance events. It must weigh over 113.4 kg and be no longer than 304.8 cm.

Handle pole
Because it is hinged for vertical mobility and allows the driver to transfer weight, it facilitates jumps and very rapid, tight changes of direction.

Sports of
Aestheticism

♀ bodybuilding

Ben Weider, co-founder of the International Federation of Body Building, in a training session in 1940

lthough bodybuilding and weight training have been around since Antiquity, it was not until the late 19th century that weights, barbells, and muscle building became popular. By the 1930s, bodybuilding competitions proliferated in the United States, and in 1939 the American Athletic Union created the title of Mr. America. After the Second World War, many federations dedicated to the sport sprang up in the United States and Europe; the International Federation of Body Building (IFBB), founded in 1946 by Ben and Joe Weider, is now an umbrella organization for more than 170 national federations. However, the discipline received provisional recognition from the IOC only in 1998. The goal of bodybuilding is harmonious development of the physique through a series of exercises, using free weights and resistance machines, that shape each muscle group. Each muscle is overworked in order to develop its volume. The development of muscle quality through weight training is part of the program of athletes in a number of sports that require power, strength, and body mass.

THE COMPETITION

The jury is usually composed of 9 accredited judges appointed by the IFBB's Judges Committee. They evaluate 4 basic qualities: muscle mass, balanced muscular development, muscle density, and muscle definition. If there are more than 15 competitors, there is an elimination round with 4 mandatory poses: the front double biceps, the side chest pose (competitor's choice of side), the back double biceps, and the abdominals and thighs. The 15 finalists must appear in a group in the hands-on-hips pose front and back. The competition takes place on a raised platform so that the judges have a complete view of the competitors.

There are 6 main muscle groups.

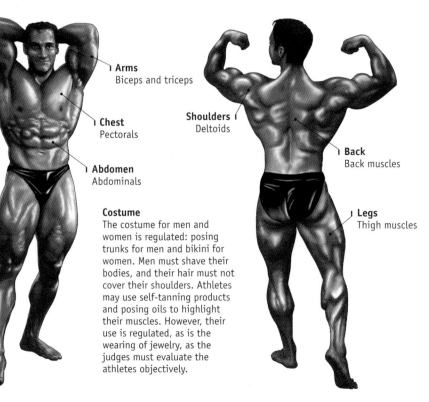

Arms
Biceps and triceps

Chest
Pectorals

Abdomen
Abdominals

Shoulders
Deltoids

Back
Back muscles

Legs
Thigh muscles

Costume
The costume for men and women is regulated: posing trunks for men and bikini for women. Men must shave their bodies, and their hair must not cover their shoulders. Athletes may use self-tanning products and posing oils to highlight their muscles. However, their use is regulated, as is the wearing of jewelry, as the judges must evaluate the athletes objectively.

EVOLUTION

Since the 1960s, both the discipline and the athletes' physiques have evolved considerably. Drug use has forced federations to institute drug testing and adopt an extremely strict anti-drug policy to make bodybuilding a "clean" sport. Random drug tests are conducted just before competitions and winners are systematically tested. Among women, muscular overdevelopment is no longer desirable, and a new branch of the sport, called fitness, combines moderate muscle building, gymnastics, and aerobic exercises.

COMPETITION LEVELS

Recognized by more than 120 national Olympic committees, bodybuilding is not yet an Olympic sport. Athletes, amateur or professional, prepare for competitions, which are more exhibition than athletic events, with intense training at the gym. There are many types of amateur and professional competitions on the local, national, and international levels. Amateur competitions generally have 4 men's categories based on the athlete's age and weight: Junior, Senior, Master 1, and Master 2. There are 2 women's categories, Master and Female (all ages), and a category for pairs.

MANDATORY POSES

There are 7 mandatory poses (5 for women and couples) marked by judges in international competitions.

Front double biceps

Front lat spread (men only)

Side chest pose (athlete's choice of side)

Side triceps pose (athlete's choice of side)

Back lat spread (men only)

Back double biceps

Abdominals and thighs

Arnold Schwarzenegger (USA)
Bodybuilding became popular when Schwarzenegger began to compete. He won most of the international titles between 1969 and 1980, including the most prestigious of all, Mr. Olympia, 7 times.

Lenda Murray (USA)
For 6 consecutive years, from 1990 to 1995, she won Joe Weider's prestigious Miss Olympia competitions.

Bench press bench

Pull down apparatus for back muscles

EQUIPMENT

There are hundreds of exercises performed with free weights and machines. The most popular apparatuses are pivot machines, which can be multifunctional or single function, and cam machines.

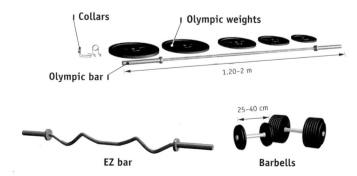

Collars

Olympic weights

Olympic bar

1.20–2 m

25–40 cm

EZ bar

Barbells

Smith apparatus

Leg press apparatus

acknowledgments

Preparation of Sports: The Complete Visual Reference would not have been possible without the invaluable assistance of the many sports federations, experts, coaches and athletes who helped us obtain up-to-date and precise information. We would like to express our gratitude to the following people and organizations:

Jean-Guy André, Catherine Damblant, Raymond Damblant, Jocelyn East, Richard Leduc, RDS Archives.

Aikido
Claude Berthiaume

Alpine Skiing
Christian Femy, Vincent Lévesque

American and Canadian Football
Jacques Dussault, Jacques Moreau

Apnea Freediving
Johan Valentin

Archery
Gabriela Cosovan, Gilbert Saint-Laurent

Artistic Gymnastics
Emmanuel Jacquinot

Australian Rules Football
Bruce Parker

Badminton
Gaëtan Jean

Bandy
Morris Glimcher, Arne Giving

Baseball
Marc Griffin, André Lachance

Basketball
Philippe Nasr

Biathlon
Jean-Guy Levesque

Billiards
Gaston Roy

BMX
Michel Lecourt, Pierre Thibault, Dylan Jagger Vanier

Bobsledding
Ermanno Gardella, Owen A. Neale, Pascal Richard, Jean Riendeau, Sarah Storey, Katja Waller

Bodybuilding
Benoit Brodeur, Marie-Anne Cherkesly, Ben Weider, Rémi Zuri

Bowling
Robert Langlois

Boxing
Kenneth Piché

Canoe-kayak: Flatwater Racing
Mark Granger

Canoe-kayak: Whitewater
Tim French, Jonathan Tremblay

Competitive Aerobics
Hélen Laliberté

Cricket
Ali Hassamie, Paul Kirpaul, Danish Petel

Cross country Skiing
Stephane Barrette

Curling
Benoit Cyr

Diving
Donald Dion, Donald Normand

Drag Racing
Jacques Lebel

Equestrian Sports
Marie-Josée Delisle, Daniel Dubé, Marcelle L'Heureux

Equestrian Racing: Turf, Trot and Pace
Jean Laroche

Fencing
Danek Nowosielski, Claudia Viereck

Field Hockey
Josette Babineau, Chantale Berridge, Suzanne Nicholson

Figure Skating
Diane Choquet, Deanne Graham, Professional Skating Association.

Formula 1, Formula Indy and Formula 3000
René Fagnan

Freestyle Skiing
Luc Belhumeur

Golf
Louis Lavoie, Sylvain Leblanc

Greco-Roman and Freestyle Wrestling
Dominique Choquette

Handball
Danny Bell

Handball (Team)
Denis Dubreuil

Ice Hockey
Chris Clow, Gaétan Ménard

Judo
Patrick Vesin

Jujitsu
Yoland Grégoire, Robert Kranstz, Jacques Lavoie

Karate
Ronald Auclair, Chanh Chau Tran

Kendo
Richard Goulet

Kickboxing and Full Contact
Patrick Giroux

Kung Fu
Lorne Bernard, Mario Hétu, Fernand Morneau, Jocelyn Toy

Lacrosse
Pierre Filion

Lawn Bowling
Claude Bouthillier, René Lecomte

acknowledgements

Luge
Sandy Caligiore, Birgit Valentin, Katja Waller

Marathon
Daniel Furlong, Mark Selig

Modern Pentathlon
Denise Fekete

Motorcycling
Buddy Ford, Bertrand Gahel

Mountain Biking
Michel Leblanc

Netball
Marina Leigertwood

Nordic Combined
Bruce Keith, Rob Keith

Ocean Surfing
Maurice Muise

Orienteering
Marie-Catherine Bruno

Parachuting
François Leblanc, Bernard R. Parker

Pelota Vasca (Basque Ball)
Gérard Venmans

Petanque
Bernard Aurouze

Polo
Regan Dellazizzo, Elizabeth Hallé

Powerboat Racing
Daniel Plouffe, Marc Rousse, Pierre Savoie

Powerlifting
Marcel Saint-Laurent

Race Walking
Roger Burrows, Octavio Castellini, François Pap

Racquetball
Josée Grand'Maitre

Rallying
Yves Barbe, Patrick Mannoury

Rhythmic Gymnastics
Daniela Arendasova

Rock Climbing
Michelle Hurni, Charles Laliberté

Roller Hockey
Dave Easter, Eric LaTerreur, Bernard Seguy, Carlos Graça

Rowing
Vincent Vandamme

Rugby
Jean-Michel Rabanel

Sailboarding
Stephane Ouellet

Sailing
Suzanne Cadieux, Simon Forbes, Meredith Gray, Jérôme Pels, Roch Pilon, Heinz Staudt, Marc Wilson

Shooting
Ralph Arnold, Jean Delisle, Serge McKenzie, Mario Methot, Jean-François Sénéchal

Skateboarding
Patrick Arsenault, Jean-François Brault

Skeleton
Ryan Davenport, Mark Kaye, Jean Riendeau

Ski Jumping
Andrew Rhéaume

Snowboarding
Jean-Louis Donaldson, Rémi Laliberté

Snowmobiling
Michel Brault, Musée Bombardier de Valcourt

Squash
Yvon Provençal

Soccer
André Gagnon

Softball
Gisèle Vezina

Speed Skating
Ginette Bourassa, Robert Bourassa, Susie Gibbon, Isabelle Laferrière, Serge Lemieux, Sean Maw, Stuart Pass, Pierre Sammut

Sumo Wrestling
Graham Clarke

Synchronized Swimming
Diane Lachapelle

Swimming
Claude Warren

Table Tennis
Rodrigue Bédard, Pierre Desjardins

Tae Kwon Do
Michel Jobin

Tennis
Louis Cayer, Eugene Lapierre, Frederic Ledoux

Track and Field
Louis Brault, Linda Coupal, Serge Jeudy, Daniel Mercier, Michel Portmann, Serge Thibodeau

Track Cycling and Road Racing
Louis Barbeau

Trampoline
Alain Duchesne

Triathlon
Roger Perreault

Volleyball
Alain D'Amboise

Waterpolo
Paul-David Bernard

Water Skiing
Francis Millaire, Philippe-André Tellier

Weightlifting
Augustin Brassard

index

index

photo credits

The number of photographs on each page is in parentheses.